A History of
Modern Psychology

For Yawen

Sara Miller McCune founded SAGE Publishing in 1965 to support the dissemination of usable knowledge and educate a global community. SAGE publishes more than 1000 journals and over 600 new books each year, spanning a wide range of subject areas. Our growing selection of library products includes archives, data, case studies and video. SAGE remains majority owned by our founder and after her lifetime will become owned by a charitable trust that secures the company's continued independence.

Los Angeles | London | New Delhi | Singapore | Washington DC | Melbourne

A History of Modern Psychology

The Quest for a Science of the Mind

David C. Ludden, Jr.

Georgia Gwinnett College

SAGE

Los Angeles | London | New Delhi
Singapore | Washington DC | Melbourne

OR INFORMATION:

SAGE Publications, Inc.
2455 Teller Road
Thousand Oaks, California 91320
E-mail: order@sagepub.com

SAGE Publications Ltd.
1 Oliver's Yard
55 City Road
London EC1Y 1SP
United Kingdom

SAGE Publications India Pvt. Ltd.
B 1/I 1 Mohan Cooperative Industrial Area
Mathura Road, New Delhi 110 044
India

SAGE Publications Asia-Pacific Pte. Ltd.
18 Cross Street #10-10/11/12
China Square Central
Singapore 048423

Printed in the United States of America

ISBN: 9781544323619

Acquisitions Editor: Abbie Rickard
Content Development Editor: Jennifer Thomas
Editorial Assistant: Elizabeth Cruz
Production Editor: Bennie Clark Allen
Copy Editor: Christina West
Typesetter: C&M Digitals (P) Ltd.
Proofreader: Dennis W. Webb
Indexer: Mary Mortensen
Cover Designer: Scott Van Atta
Marketing Manager: Katherine Hepburn

This book is printed on acid-free paper.

20 21 22 23 24 10 9 8 7 6 5 4 3 2 1

Brief Contents

Detailed Contents

PART II   EARLY SCHOOLS OF PSYCHOLOGY

PART III MODERN DISCIPLINES OF PSYCHOLOGY

Chapter 13 Developmental Psychology 299

Preface

Like many instructors who teach a history of psychology course, I have no formal training in the subject. The first time I was scheduled to teach History and Systems of Psychology—quite early in my career—I saw it as an opportunity to learn about the history of my discipline. Since then, I've come to teach the course nearly every semester, and each time it's been a learning experience for both me and my students. Over the years, I've used many of the standard history of psychology textbooks on the market, and while they're all well researched and engagingly written, I've also noticed two shortcomings that seem to be common to all of them. The first is too much emphasis on the history of philosophy, and the second is not enough coverage of developments in psychology from the middle of the twentieth century onward. These are the issues I've tried to address in *A History of Modern Psychology*.

Organization of the Book

Without doubt, a good foundation in philosophy is essential for an understanding of the history of psychology. However, when a third or more of the course is devoted to a survey of the major philosophers from Ancient Greece to the nineteenth century, students often wonder—and with good reason—whether they've enrolled in a course in philosophy or psychology. In *A History of Modern Psychology*, I've laid out the major trends in Western philosophy in a single chapter, touching only on those topics that are relevant to the development of psychology. This is then followed by a chapter on trends in nineteenth-century science that led to the emergence of an experimental approach to the study of the mind. These two chapters form Part I of the book.

Part II then consists of seven chapters, each devoted to one of the major schools of psychology that arose around the turn of the twentieth century. These chapters survey familiar content that can be found in any history of psychology textbook—structuralism, functionalism, and behaviorism in North America, as well as Gestalt psychology and psychoanalysis in Central Europe. However, in Part II we also consider two other important schools that operated outside the mainstream of psychology during the first half of the twentieth century even though they eventually had a major impact on the field. One of these was the clinically based psychology that was practiced in the French-speaking region of France and Switzerland, and the other was a unique approach to experimental psychology that developed in the Soviet Union. Today, the contributions of Jean Piaget, Lev Vygotsky, and their colleagues are universally recognized, but their work remained virtually unknown to English-speaking psychologists until the 1960s or 1970s.

Finally, Part III brings the reader up to date on developments in psychology since the middle of the twentieth century. World War II was a watershed event in human history, and it had a significant impact on our field as well. The prewar schools distinguished themselves by their unique approaches to pursuing scientific psychology as well as by their philosophical differences regarding the nature of mind and behavior. After the war, however, the old schools were gradually abandoned as a new generation of psychologists defined themselves according to the topics they studied. Thus, we see the rise of the modern disciplines of psychology—cognitive, social, developmental, personality, and so on. It's in Part III that *A History of Modern Psychology* differs from any other book on the market, in that it brings the story of our field well into the twenty-first century. Indeed, since most of what would be considered the canon of psychology has been developed since the end of World War II, we can rightly say that Part III is the heart of the book. Here's where students will encounter familiar names and ideas, and they'll also learn how these are interconnected.

Key Features

History is a form of storytelling, and the two words even come from the same etymological root. Thus, this book isn't *the* history of modern psychology, but rather *a* history. I have my interpretation of events, but others may differ in their opinions. And this includes our students. History isn't just the dry exercise of memorizing people, places, and dates. Rather, it's an attempt to understand who we are today by examining our past. To this end, I've endeavored to create a text that encourages critical thinking. Each chapter ends with a set of discussion questions that asks students to go beyond what's presented in the text in order to find additional connections and alternative interpretations. I also invite students to go onto the internet and search for additional information. Oftentimes, a five-minute video can elucidate a concept far better than 5,000 words of text.

There are two general approaches to writing a history. The first is known as the "great person" approach, and it sees history as unfolding through the actions of particular movers and shakers in society. Without Charles Darwin, according to this view, we wouldn't have a theory of natural selection, or at least its discovery would have been much delayed. The other approach focuses on what historians call the "Zeitgeist," using the German expression for "spirit of the times." According to this view, great persons are nothing more than accidents of history, the ones who got credit for supposedly coming up with ideas that were already current in their society. For instance, at the same time that Darwin was working out his thoughts on the origin of species, Alfred Wallace independently came up with a very similar theory of evolution by natural selection. If Darwin had drowned during the voyage of the *Beagle*, we'd recognize Wallace today as the one who showed us how evolution works.

I believe there are merits to both approaches. Without question, certain ideas are "in the air" at any given time in a particular society. Nevertheless, those ideas do crystalize within particular individuals who give them voice. The great persons in history are the ones who clearly articulate and enthusiastically promote the Zeitgeist. For me, the key to understanding the flow of history is to properly conceptualize where the spirit of the times resides, namely in the social interactions and intellectual exchanges of the key players in the field. The social nature of scientific discovery is a theme that runs throughout the book.

The image of the lone scientist working in an ivory tower has popular appeal, but it's absolutely false. Science is, above all, a social enterprise. And for this reason, I emphasize the interconnectedness of the psychologists we meet in *A History of Modern Psychology*. The narrative fleshes out the social networks in which these researchers worked, which are further illustrated in Academic Family Trees included throughout the book.

Digital Resources

ⓈSAGE edge™

Instructor Resource Site

Instructors, sign on at **edge.sagepub.com/ludden1e**

The instructor resource site supports your teaching by making it easy to integrate quality content and create a rich learning environment for students with many resources.

- A **password-protected site** provides complete and protected access to all text-specific instructor resources.

- **Test banks** provide a diverse range of ready-to-use options that save you time. You can also easily edit any question and/or insert your own personalized questions.

- **Multimedia resources** direct students to video and websites that help explain the history of psychology and how developments fit within the context of world events.

- **Sample course syllabi** for semester and quarter courses provide suggested models for structuring your courses.

- **Editable, chapter-specific PowerPoint® slides** offer complete flexibility for creating a multimedia presentation for your course.

- **Lecture notes** summarize key concepts by chapter to help you prepare for lectures and class discussions.

Acknowledgments

I too live within a complex social network, and many people have played a role in the shaping of this book. Here I acknowledge the debt of gratitude I owe them, naming as many as I can and hoping that any I forget will forgive me for the omission. I certainly know that I could never have written this book with the help of a great many people—many more than I can possibly know or name. Still, your assistance is greatly appreciated.

First, I'd like to recognize all the wonderful people at SAGE. I want to thank Reid Hester, the editor of my first book (*The Psychology of Language*), who suggested that I might have it in me to write a second book. He put the bug in my ear, as it were, and it's stayed with me ever since. I also need to offer my profound appreciation to Abbie Rickard, who took on the editorship of this project. She gave me impossible deadlines that I always somehow seemed to meet, she shoved me out of my rut whenever I was spinning my wheels, and she nudged me back in the right direction each time I wandered astray. Thanks, Abbie, for cracking the whip! Without your guidance and encouragement, I would have given up on this project a long time ago. I wish to express my sincere gratitude to my copy editor Christina West, who meticulously revised my jumbled text into readable form. My heartfelt thanks also go to the production team of Jennifer Thomas, Elizabeth Cruz, and Bennie Clark Allen, who through some sort of magic have transformed my plain manuscript into a beautiful book. I know there are others at SAGE who've played a role in bringing this project to fruition, and even though I don't know your names, I'm still grateful for all you've done for me.

Next, I'd like to express my appreciation to the remarkable people at Georgia Gwinnett College. To my colleagues, I want to let you know that your camaraderie makes GGC a fun place to work, greatly easing my mind for the travails of writing. In particular, I need to thank my dean, Laurel Holland, for her continued encouragement and support. Laurel, your can-do attitude is infectious, and it certainly kept me going on more than one occasion. I also wish to thank the students who read—and provided feedback on—the manuscript version of this textbook as part of the assigned readings for their History and Systems of Psychology course.

I'd also like to thank the instructors who reviewed this book in its draft form and provided feedback that helped to shape the content:

Suzanne C. Baker, James Madison University

Diane Byrd, Fort Valley State University

Jennifer R. Clark, Pacific University School of Graduate Psychology

Kevin M. Clark, Indiana University Kokomo

Brian Day, Butler University

Michael J. Disch, St. Edward's University

W. Jay Dowling, University of Texas at Dallas

Judith A. Easton, Texas State University

Cynthia A. Edwards, Meredith College

Charles R. Fox, Worcester State University

Joseph S. Freedman, Alabama State University

Jeffery K. Gray, Charleston Southern University

Michael Holdren, Cazenovia College

Matthew Hunsinger, School of Graduate Psychology at Pacific University

Janet Kottke, California State University, San Bernardino

Mark E. Mattson, Fordham University

Scott P. Merydith, Rochester Institute of Technology

Darrell Rudmann, Shawnee State University

Emily Stark, Minnesota State University, Mankato

Brian R. Uldall, University of Nevada at Las Vegas

Finally, there's my network of family and friends, each of whom gave me aid and comfort on various occasions. High on my list are my two dear friends, Jin Hui and Ye Guangsheng, who so generously hosted my wife and me for the two Decembers of 2018 and 2019 at their home in Shanghai, China. You provided me with a retreat from the "real world," where I could devote all of my time—all day every day—to writing. Those sojourns in your home were the most productive periods of this entire project. Thank you so much for your gracious hospitality and enthusiastic support! Your genuine human kindness has shaped my thinking more than any scholarly book or article ever could.

That leaves me with my immediate family. Heartfelt gratitude goes to my parents, David and Carol, who have in a sense been shaping this book for the last fifty-nine years. By showing me your continued interest in this project, you have sustained me through this long process. Thanks also to my grown children, Jenny and Jason, who ask how the book is coming along each time they call home. Your interest means a lot to me. Finally, I have to somehow find the words to express the boundless appreciation I have for my wife, Yawen, who has sustained me throughout this voyage. Yawen, you gave me time and space when I needed it, the courage to carry on when I felt like giving up, and valuable feedback on many of my ideas when they were still but mere phantasms in my mind. And on top of that, you fed me meals on a daily basis that rivaled any restaurant in Atlanta! Through it all, you provided sustenance—both physical and emotional—for this struggling author.

Whatever strengths there are in this book, I credit to all the people I've mentioned above. Any weaknesses, of course, are nobody's fault but my own. Like an adventurous journey through uncharted territory, I know that the writing of this book was often arduous. And yet in looking back, all my memories are happy and exciting ones. I genuinely hope that you enjoy reading this book even a fraction as much as I've enjoyed writing it.

About the Author

 **David C. Ludden Jr.** is professor of psychology at Georgia Gwinnett College near Atlanta. He earned his Ph.D. in cognitive psychology at the University of Iowa in 2002. Although he is a psycholinguist by training, he has also had a secondary interest in the history of psychology from early in his career. His first faculty position after graduation was at a small liberal arts college where he was responsible for teaching half of the psychology curriculum. This experience greatly expanded his appreciation for the enormous diversity of viewpoints within the field of psychology. In 2014, he moved to Georgia Gwinnett College, where his main teaching responsibility is the capstone History and Systems of Psychology course, which thus provided the impetus for writing this book. *A History of Modern Psychology* is his second book, and it was preceded by *The Psychology of Language* in 2016, also published by SAGE. David Ludden lives in the greater Atlanta area with his wife and intellectual companion of thirty years, Yawen Ludden, who is a musicologist. She fills his life with great music, wonderful food, and an inimitable *joie de vivre*.

Precursors to Modern Psychology

Psychology as an experimental science is a fairly recent phenomenon, arising only toward the end of the nineteenth century, hundreds of years after the natural sciences had become established. And yet the questions psychologists ask today are the same that people have pondered for millennia. People are insatiably curious about themselves, and it's easy to imagine even prehistoric hunters and gatherers sitting around the fire at night, speculating about human nature. Since we live within complex social networks, we need to understand why people behave the way they do, so we're all amateur psychologists.

The first recorded efforts to systematically understand human nature come from the philosophers of Ancient Greece around twenty-four centuries ago. The Greeks were a seafaring people, and as they encountered alien cultures with worldviews different from their own, they began to question the myths that had sustained their ancestors for millennia. Rejecting belief in mythology or religion as a way of knowing the world, the Ancient Greek philosophers adopted logic and careful observation as their guides. This new mode of inquiry, in which knowledge accrued through argument and evidence rather than through tradition and revelation, is a defining feature of Western civilization. Indeed, the Ancient Greeks created the model of philosophical and scientific exploration that continues to the present day, and so it's only fitting that our story begins with them.

Part I consists of two chapters that lay the groundwork for the construction of a scientific approach to psychology. Chapter 1 surveys Western philosophical thought from the Ancient Greeks to the nineteenth-century European thinkers, necessarily focusing only on those aspects that are relevant to the development of psychology. Chapter 2 then provides an overview of trends in nineteenth-century science that made the emergence of an experimental approach to psychology possible. From there, we'll continue on to Part II, where we'll learn about the various early schools of psychology that sprung forth from the intellectual excitement of the late nineteenth century.

iStock.com/Juan Carlos Hernández Hernández

Philosophical Roots of Psychology

Timeline

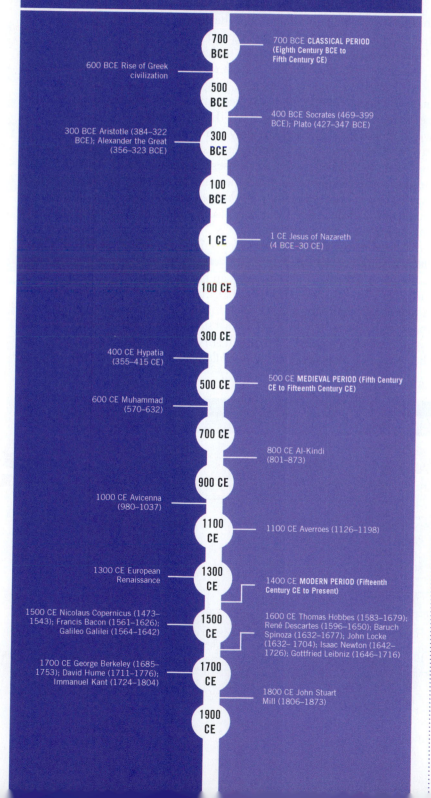

700 BCE	700 BCE **CLASSICAL PERIOD** (Eighth Century BCE to Fifth Century CE)
600 BCE Rise of Greek civilization	
500 BCE	
	400 BCE Socrates (469–399 BCE); Plato (427–347 BCE)
300 BCE Aristotle (384–322 BCE); Alexander the Great (356–323 BCE)	**300 BCE**
100 BCE	
1 CE	1 CE Jesus of Nazareth (4 BCE–30 CE)
100 CE	
300 CE	
400 CE Hypatia (355–415 CE)	
500 CE	500 CE **MEDIEVAL PERIOD** (Fifth Century CE to Fifteenth Century CE)
600 CE Muhammad (570–632)	
700 CE	
	800 CE Al-Kindi (801–873)
900 CE	
1000 CE Avicenna (980–1037)	
1100 CE	1100 CE Averroes (1126–1198)
1300 CE European Renaissance	**1300 CE**
	1400 CE **MODERN PERIOD** (Fifteenth Century CE to Present)
1500 CE Nicolaus Copernicus (1473–1543); Francis Bacon (1561–1626); Galileo Galilei (1564–1642)	**1500 CE**
	1600 CE Thomas Hobbes (1583–1679); René Descartes (1596–1650); Baruch Spinoza (1632–1677); John Locke (1632–1704); Isaac Newton (1642–1726); Gottfried Leibniz (1646–1716)
1700 CE George Berkeley (1685–1753); David Hume (1711–1776); Immanuel Kant (1724–1804)	**1700 CE**
	1800 CE John Stuart Mill (1806–1873)
1900 CE	

Learning Objectives

After reading this chapter, you should be able to:

- Outline the major philosophical trends of the Classical Period, particularly the ideas of Socrates, Plato, and Aristotle.

- Evaluate the psychological contributions of the Islamic philosophers Al-Kindi, Avicenna, and Averroes.

- Contrast the various positions taken by the Continental Rationalists on the mind-body problem.

- Survey the development of thinking on the nature of the mind by the British Empiricists.

Looking Back

For millennia, philosophers have pondered questions that laid the groundwork for modern psychology. We can group these philosophical ponderings into two sets:

- What does it mean to know something? Where does knowledge come from? What is the role of learning and experience? Are there things we just know without ever having learned them? Are there things we can never know?

- What is the nature of the mind? What is the relationship between mind and body? What is the relationship between our psychological experience and physical reality? Does the mind continue to exist after the death of the body?

Although philosophers ask all sorts of questions about the nature of the world, these two sets are the ones that are most relevant to psychology (Figure 1.1).

The first set of questions illustrates a branch of philosophy known as **epistemology**. This is *the study of knowledge, which asks questions such as what it means to know something and how knowledge can be acquired.* Philosophers have long considered such questions, and they've proposed many theories. However, it's only been in the last century and a half that psychologists have employed scientific methods to test these theories.

Philosophers working in the field of epistemology can be divided into two camps. One camp argues for **rationalism**, which is *the philosophical stance that knowledge can only be obtained through reason.* Rationalists believe that our senses can deceive us, so we need to look inside ourselves instead to find true knowledge. The other camp argues for **empiricism**, which is *the philosophical stance that knowledge can only be obtained through experience.* Empiricists acknowledge that our senses can deceive us, but they also maintain that we can learn about the true nature of the world if we observe it carefully.

The second set of questions comes from a branch of philosophy known as **metaphysics**. This is *the philosophical inquiry into the nature of the universe.* Although metaphysics considers questions about the natural world, it also includes an inquiry into what is known as the **mind-body problem**. This is *the question of how psychological experience is related to the physical world.* There are two ways of thinking about this problem. The first is **dualism**, which is *the philosophical stance that mind and body consist of distinct substances and are subject to different laws.* If you believe you have a conscious soul that will survive the death of your body, then you're a dualist. The second is **monism**. This is *the philosophical stance that mind and body*

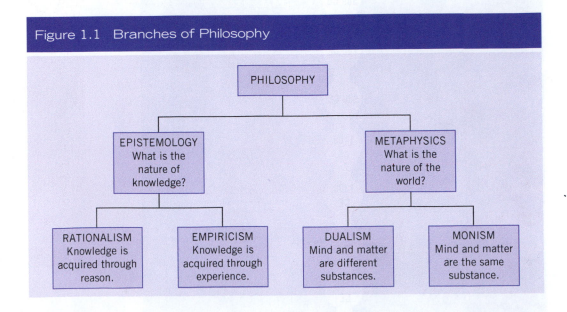

Figure 1.1 Branches of Philosophy

consist of the same substance and are subject to the same laws. If you believe your mental states arise from brain activity, then you're a monist.

Most people don't think deeply about epistemology or the mind-body problem. They'll credit a musician with born talent for the piano (nativism) while recognizing the years of dedicated practice that were needed (empiricism). Likewise, those same persons who put a finger to their skull and say they're pointing at their mind (monism) often also believe their mind will continue in their souls after death (dualism). Philosophers, in contrast, have struggled with these questions in all their intricacies for millennia. In this chapter, we begin in Ancient Greece twenty-five centuries ago, when these questions were first asked in a systematic way. And we end in nineteenth-century England, when the time had finally come for a science of the mind.

Classical Period

Western civilization has its roots in the various cultures that sprang up along the coasts of the Mediterranean Sea. The climate was mild, the land was fertile, and the great internal sea allowed for easy trade and the exchange of ideas. But there was also much political intrigue and warfare as various kingdoms and city-states vied for local and regional power. About six centuries before the beginning of the current era, a loose band of city-states rose to regional prominence in the northeastern Mediterranean. Although they weren't a political unit, they were united by a common Greek language and culture. Among these city-states, Athens was the most powerful. There, at the end of the fifth century before the Common Era (BCE) is where our story begins.

Socrates

Chaerephon thought his friend Socrates might be the wisest man in the world, so he went to the oracle of Delphi to find out for sure.

"Is there anyone wiser than Socrates?" he asked the oracle.

"No one is wiser than Socrates," the oracle replied.

So Chaerephon went back to Athens and told Socrates what the oracle had said.

Socrates laughed. "I only know one thing," he said. "And that is, I know nothing."

But Socrates wondered why the oracle had said such a thing, so he sought out the great men of Athens (Plato, *Apology* 20e–23a). He found they all said they knew things they in fact didn't know, so Socrates concluded that the oracle must be right. *The argument that true wisdom comes from knowing the limits of one's knowledge* is called **Socratic ignorance**. Socrates wasn't claiming that he was completely ignorant, only that he was aware of how little he knew and how worthless that knowledge was.

Socrates (469–399 BCE) was an *Ancient Greek philosopher who was one of the first to turn philosophy toward questions about the nature of the mind*. He spent his days in the marketplace of Athens debating philosophy with anyone who was willing to talk with him. When someone made a vague or unfounded statement, he challenged them by asking, "What is it?" For instance, if you said dying for your country was the greatest honor, his comeback would be: "What is honor?" He'd mastered *the instructional technique of asking questions to guide students in a self-exploration of their own thoughts*, now known as the **Socratic Method**. No doubt you've had teachers who taught in this way.

Young people enjoyed learning from Socrates and became loyal followers. But the wealthy rulers of Athens felt threatened and charged him with defiling the city's gods and corrupting its youth. They wanted to silence Socrates, but at his trial he proclaimed that he could never be silent, because "the unexamined life is not worth living" (Plato, *Apology* 38a). So instead they sentenced him to death. His followers offered to help him escape, but

Photo 1.1
Sculpture of Socrates

the aging Socrates refused. He'd lived his entire life in Athens, and there he would die, by drinking a cup of poison hemlock while surrounded by his friends.

Socrates's enemies may have killed him, but they didn't silence him. Instead, he marked a turning point in Greek philosophy. The pre-Socratic philosophers had mainly concerned themselves with questions about the natural world, and the Sophists had sought out skillful arguments for winning court cases. But Socrates turned philosophy to the study of human nature. Socratic ignorance and the Socratic Method became the hallmarks of intellectual inquiry in the West.

Socrates's impact on psychology has been significant. Traditionally, the Greek word for "soul," or *psyche*, was used to mean the "breath of life" or the "vital spirit" that animated a living being and departed when one died. But Socrates attributed a rich private experience to the *psyche*, and he maintained that the most important thing that people can do is care for and cultivate their *psyche*. In this sense, we can say that Socrates was the first psychologist.

Plato

To the best of our knowledge, Socrates never wrote down any of his ideas, and all we know about him comes the writings of his students. Most important of these was **Plato** (427–347 BCE), the son of an aristocratic family in Athens who came under the influence of Socrates as a young adult. Plato's writings take the form of dialogues with his master, in which he demonstrates the use of the Socratic Method as a teaching device. Since Plato only reports what Socrates said and not what he himself thinks, many scholars have come to the conclusion that Plato used Socrates as a mouthpiece to voice his own opinions. Nevertheless, we know Plato as the *Ancient Greek philosopher who argued that all knowledge comes from reason.*

In his philosophy, Plato builds on his teacher Socrates's concept of an active *psyche* or "soul" that drives our thoughts and actions (Katona, 2002). Thus, *psyche* is much more like "mind" in the modern sense than "life force" of the Greek tradition. Furthermore, Plato divides the soul into three parts:

- An *appetitive* part that consists of our drives for food, drink, and sex.

- An *emotional* part that contains our passions.

- A *rational* part that seeks truth and should rule over the other two parts.

**Photo 1.2
Sculpture of Plato**

For Plato, mental health was obtained through the proper balance of these three parts of the soul.

Plato viewed the soul as the repository of our knowledge. And because he believed the soul was immortal, our knowledge must survive in the soul after our death (Plato, *Apology* 40c). This also means that we inherit knowledge from our previous lives. Of course, we ordinarily aren't aware of this innate knowledge. However, it can be drawn out with the proper use of the Socratic Method. Take for example the **allegory of Meno's slave**, *a story in which Plato shows how Socrates draws out knowledge of geometry from an uneducated boy* (Plato, *Meno* 81a–86b). In the allegory, Socrates leads the boy to the discovery of a geometric proof through guided questions. He then declares that the boy knew this all along but only needed help in finding it within him. Knowledge, Plato concludes, is in our soul before we're born.

According to Plato, this innate knowledge reflects the true reality, and he doesn't trust the information gained through our senses. The **Theory of Forms** is *Plato's idea that the world as we experience it is but a poor reflection of the world as it truly is.* He expounds on this idea in many of his writings, but the most famous example is in the *Republic*, where he tells the **allegory of the cave**. This is *a story in which Plato argues that knowledge can only come from reason because the senses can deceive us* (Plato, *Republic* VII.514a–520a).

In the allegory, he asks us to imagine a cave with a large opening toward the sunlight, with a row of men in chains facing toward the back wall of the cave. As people pass by the entrance of the cave, their shadows are projected against the back wall, and for the men in the cave, these shadows constitute the only reality they know. Likewise, our senses only project to us the shadows of reality, not its true essence. If one of those men were to break free and dash to the entrance of the cave, he'd at first be blinded by the sun, but once his eyes accustomed to the light, he'd see reality as it truly is. And so it is with philosophers.

Plato's idea of intrapsychic conflict and a three-part soul were particularly influential to Sigmund Freud (Chapter 7) in the early 1900s. Furthermore, in emphasizing the rational functions of the mind, he set the foundation for cognitive psychology (Chapter 11) in the last half of the twentieth century.

Aristotle

Unlike his teacher Plato, **Aristotle** (384–322 BCE) was more than just a philosopher (Green, 1998). Instead, he was more like a modern scientist, making careful observations of the natural world, describing it as precisely as he could and using logical inference to come up with explanations. And unlike his teacher, who believed all knowledge is innate, Aristotle argued instead that all knowledge is acquired through the senses. However, he conceded, we need to use reason to organize and understand the information our senses provide us. Thus, we know Aristotle today as an *Ancient Greek philosopher who argued that all knowledge comes from experience.*

About a third of Aristotle's treatises discuss topics in biology. He was the first to create a system of categorizing and organizing life forms that is similar to what biologists use today. He accomplished this through a careful examination of over 500 different animal species. Many times, his descriptions and explanations went unsurpassed until the eighteenth or nineteenth century. But Aristotle also got some things spectacularly wrong. For example, he believed the heart was the organ of cognition, relegating the brain to the function of cooling the body.

We can name at least three important areas where Aristotle has had an impact on modern psychology. Specifically, these are his thoughts on the mind-body problem, the nature of causation, and the characteristics of happiness and a life well lived. Let's consider each in more detail.

Aristotle's first contribution to modern psychology was his challenge of the prevailing notion that the soul (or mind) had a spiritual existence separate from the body (Katona, 2002). Like his teacher Plato, Aristotle believed that all living things had a soul but its structure depended on the complexity of the animal. In Aristotle's scheme, the three-part soul comprises the following:

Jastrow (2006)

Photo 1.3
Bust of Aristotle

- The *nutritive soul* enables the organism to grow and reproduce.

- The *appetitive soul* gathers information from the senses and drives behavior.

- The *rational soul* is the seat of reason, used to make plans and decisions.

These three tiers underlie the traditional division of living things into plants (nutritive soul only), animals (nutritive and appetitive souls), and humans (all three). Aristotle's idea of a three-part soul greatly influenced the early twentieth-century psychoanalyst Sigmund Freud (Chapter 7), who proposed a three-part structure of the unconscious mind (namely, the id, ego, and superego) that had similar properties.

In his treatise *On the Soul*, Aristotle lays out his views on the relationship between body and soul (Aristotle, *De Anima* III.5). Unlike Plato who viewed the soul as separate from the body, Aristotle believed that body and soul were united. This position derives from his more fundamental belief that all things consist of both matter and form. Take for instance an object such as an iron ball, the name of which even indicates both its matter and its form. In other words, the matter of the object is iron and the form is roundness. Likewise with living objects, which are composed of matter such as flesh, bones, and blood. However, what gives the body its living form is the soul. That is to say, Aristotle viewed the soul as a sort of life force that animates the body. Thus, in life the body (matter) and the soul (form) are united, but in death they're separated. Aristotle rejected the notion that the soul with an intact mind could survive the death of the body, and in particular he dismissed the notion of reincarnation, which was a fairly common belief among earlier Greek philosophers. Aristotle's monistic stance on the mind-body problem was problematic for both Christian and Islamic philosophers of the Medieval Period as well as much of the Modern Period. However, it does reflect the thinking of most experimental psychologists in the twenty-first century.

Aristotle's second contribution to modern psychology is his thinking on the nature of causation, in particular his distinction between efficient and final causes (Howard, 1998). The *efficient cause* is the action that leads to an end result, whereas the *final cause* is the reason why the action took place. For instance, you stumbled because I pushed you out of my way (efficient cause) because you were blocking my view (final cause). *An emphasis on the final result in a process as opposed to its initial conditions* is known as **teleology**. During the Medieval Period, European philosophers preferred teleological explanations, but with the scientific revolution there was a backlash against teleology in favor of initial, mechanical causes. However, since psychology deals with the purposeful behaviors of living creatures, it can't always shun teleology.

Aristotle's third contribution to modern psychology is his work on ethics and happiness (Aristotle, 1999). In his *Nicomachean Ethics*, he considers the question of what it means to live a good life. He starts with the assertion that a happy life must also be one that is filled with pleasure, since a life of nothing but pain and misery can hardly be called a happy one. However, Aristotle also distinguishes three types of happy life. The first involves the slavish pursuit of sensual pleasures, such as good food, drink, and sex. Certainly these are all components of a happy life, but these alone can never lead to a completely fulfilling one. The second is the pursuit of a political or social life in which the goal is to attain honor. Certainly it's a great pleasure to be respected and esteemed by your peers, but again Aristotle insists it isn't enough to be truly happy. The third is a life devoted to philosophical contemplation, which was the only true path to a truly fulfilling life.

It's important to note that Aristotle isn't suggesting there are three separate pathways to a happy life with only the last being truly fulfilling. Indeed, Aristotle himself was known to indulge in sensual pleasures, and he played important public roles in both Athens and his native Macedonia. Rather, he's saying that engaging in philosophical contemplation is what led to the greatest happiness in his life. Thus, it's a combination of all three—each in good measure—that leads to what he called *eudaimonia* (pronounced *you-die-muh-NEE-uh*). Although the term is often translated as "happiness," it literally means "good spirits" but with the connotation of "well-being." The question of what constitutes the good life became of central concern to the humanistic psychologists after World War II, and positive psychologists at the turn of the twenty-first century have picked up Aristotle's concept of *eudaimonia* as one of their guiding principles (Chapter 15).

In sum, Aristotle's thinking diverged significantly from that of his teacher, Plato. The debate between Plato's nativism and Aristotle's empiricism has echoed through the centuries and still pops up in psychological discussions today. For instance, consider the question of whether intelligence is due mainly to innate or environmental factors. This is just one example of the nativism-empiricism debate that will run through many of the chapters in this book. But without question is the fact that Plato and Aristotle set Western philosophy on its course.

At the time of Socrates, Plato, and Aristotle, Greece was unified only in terms of a common language and culture. Politically, it was broken up into a large number of small city-states that were often at war with each other. Both Socrates and Plato were citizens of Athens, but Aristotle was from the northern Greek province of Macedonia. He traveled to Athens as a young adult to study with Plato, and he stayed there twenty years. But after Plato's death, Aristotle returned to Macedonia to become the private tutor to Alexander, heir to the Macedonian throne. Alexander become king of Macedonia at the age of twenty, and he cleverly united the Greek city-states against a common enemy—the Persian Empire. After subduing Persia, Alexander then marched his troops into Syria, Palestine, and Egypt. At the time of his death at the age of 32, Alexander the Great (356–323 BCE) remained undefeated in battle and had created one of the largest empires ever known. Although that empire soon split into separate political units, Alexander's conquests spread Greek culture around the eastern Mediterranean all the way to India. He also established a number of cities, the most important of which for our story is Alexandria in Egypt, which became the center of Greek learning and culture for many centuries afterward.

Hypatia

Around this same time that Alexander was building his empire in the east, another power was rising in the west. This was Rome, which spread its military power first throughout the Italian peninsula and then into modern France and Spain. By the beginning of the current era, the Roman Empire had completely encircled the Mediterranean, absorbing remnants of Alexander's empire along the way. However, the Romans had great admiration for Greek culture and modeled their own culture after it; hence, we often describe the Classical Period as one of Greco-Roman civilization. Many religions were practiced in the Mediterranean region, but in the early fourth century, the emperor Constantine converted to Christianity, thus giving it important political clout within the empire.

Photo 1.4
Portrait of Hypatia

Alexandria was still the most important cultural and intellectual center of the Greco-Roman world, and it was home to the largest library in the world (Booth, 2013). There worked **Hypatia** (355–415 CE; pronounced *hip-PAY-shuh*), one of the most famous woman philosophers of the Classical Period. None of her writings have survived, and all we know about her comes from comments by other writers. Instead, what she's most famous for is the horrendous way she died. Thus, Hypatia is remembered today as the *woman Greco-Roman philosopher who has become a symbol for the struggle between science and religion.*

Hypatia was part of a philosophical movement known as Neo-Platonism, which favored the rationalism of Plato over the empiricism of Aristotle (Grant, 2009). They were mostly interested in mathematics and astronomy, but Hypatia seems to have been well read in other areas of philosophy as well. She gave frequent public lectures and was a popular figure in the city. She also got drawn into politics at a time when a ruthless power struggle was underway.

Two men were vying for control of the city (Grant, 2009). One was the Roman governor Orestes, who was a Christian but tolerant of other religions. The other was the archbishop Cyril, who sought to rid the city of non-Christians. As Orestes's confidant, Hypatia advised him to take a firm stance against Cyril. This in turn made Hypatia the target of Cyril's wrath. One day, a Christian mob surrounded her carriage, pulled her from it, and beat her to death. They then hacked her body to pieces and burned them. Those loyal to Hypatia blamed Cyril for instigating the mob, but those loyal to Cyril insisted he had nothing to do with it. At any rate, Cyril eventually took control of the city and was canonized as a saint after his death.

Over the centuries, the story of Hypatia has been used as a common plot in fiction (Doherty, 2015). In some accounts from the Medieval Period, she's portrayed as a sorceress who bewitched the poor people of Alexandria until they were rescued by Saint Cyril. Especially in the nineteenth century, the story of the hostility between Hypatia and Cyril became an allegory for the conflict between science and religion. And in more recent times, Hypatia has been adopted as a symbol for the feminist movement, representing the intelligent woman who dared to speak her own mind in a world dominated by men. Her name has also been taken for the title of a feminist philosophy journal. One of the most recent retellings of her story is the movie *Agora* (Bovaira, Augustin, & Amenábar, 2009). The movie got mixed reviews, but you can watch and decide for yourself whether the themes it presents are legitimate or not.

Medieval Period

The decline of the Roman Empire began around the turn of the fourth century. Barbarian invasions plagued the empire, especially in the west. By the fifth century, the empire had fractured in two, with Germanic kings occupying Rome. Around this same time is when Constantine, still emperor in the east, established his capital at Constantinople, or modern-day Istanbul in Turkey. Christianity had been widely adopted in both the eastern and western portions of the empire, and the political influence of the Catholic Church was growing ever stronger. While a greatly reduced Eastern Roman Empire survived another thousand years, the western portion disintegrated into a number of small political entities.

The time spanning the fifth through fifteenth centuries is often referred to as the Dark Ages. In Europe, there was a drop in population due to disease, warring factions, and foreign invasions. The Catholic Church also had a stranglehold on the intellectual life of the continent, as the Greco-Roman learning of the Classical Period was largely abandoned in favor of Christian theology. And so Europe remained for nearly a thousand years, until the Renaissance of the fourteenth century kindled a renewed interest in science and philosophy.

However, the term "Dark Ages" is something of a misnomer. On the Arabian Peninsula, the new religion of Islam arose in the seventh century. Unlike early Christianity, early Islam maintained a positive attitude toward nonreligious learning, and Muslim scholars of the Islamic Golden Age not only preserved the learning of the Classical Period but also expanded on it, especially in the area of medicine. Because all was not dark during the millennium between the Classical and the Modern Periods, it's better to refer to this time as the Medieval Period, or more colloquially as the "Middle Ages."

Islamic Golden Age

The religion of Islam was founded by Muhammad (570–632). According to Islamic doctrine, Muhammad was the final prophet in a series that included Abraham, Moses, and Jesus, among others, who taught belief in a single God in contrast to the polytheistic beliefs of most of the classical world. Thus, Islam is considered an Abrahamic religion together with Judaism and Christianity, and its holy book is the Quran. Muhammad used Islam to bring together the various tribes of Arabia into a single religious-political unity. During the following century, Islam spread rapidly across much of the classical world, extending as far east as India and as far west as North Africa and Spain.

Early Muslim rulers tended to be tolerant of non-Muslim peoples in their dominions (Simonton, 2018). The Islamic world comprised many different cultures whose people spoke a wide array of languages. However, Arabic served as the common language for religious and political purposes, much as Latin did in Europe. It was this open exchange of ideas that led to the Islamic Golden Age, which started around the eighth century. In Baghdad, for instance, the Caliph Harun al-Rashid established the House of Wisdom, where Jewish, Christian, and Muslim scholars were tasked with translating all surviving books from the Classical Period into Arabic. This practice of patronizing scholars regardless of their faith was adopted by a number of Muslim rulers during this time period. Within a century, Muslim scholars were completely versed in the learning of ancient Greece and Rome, and they also began to develop that knowledge further.

Al-Kindi

Known as Islam's first philosopher, **Al-Kindi** (801–873) was responsible for translating many of the works of Plato and Aristotle into Arabic (Cerami, 2012). Born to a politically influential family, Al-Kindi was educated at the House of Wisdom in Baghdad. There, he also led a group of scholars who translated and commented on Greek texts. But he was more than just a translator. Rather, he tried to demonstrate in his works that there was no contradiction between the learning of the Greeks and the teachings of the Quran. Thus, we recognize Al-Kindi as the *Islamic philosopher who tried to integrate Greek philosophy with Islamic theology*.

Al-Kindi produced over 300 works on a variety of subjects (Langermann, 2000). These manuscripts of course include standard texts of Greek learning, such as philosophy, mathematics, medicine, optics, and astronomy. However, he also translated and commented on works dealing with a wide range of topics, including astrology, meteorology, and zoology. He also wrote texts on the manufacture of valuable commodities such as glass and mirrors, jewelry and perfumes, as well as sword making. In addition to translations, he also produced a large number of original works. Thanks to the work of Al-Kindi and his students, subsequent generations of Islamic scholars had at their fingertips the bulk of classical learning in the familiar Arabic language instead of the unfamiliar Greek.

More than just introducing Greek learning to his fellow Muslims, Al-Kindi's goal was to show how classical philosophy could be integrated with Islamic doctrine (Staley, 1989). Much of his work was based on the neo-Platonic tradition, and this mathematical and rational approach to understanding the world was fairly consistent with the Islamic belief in knowledge through revelation. However, Al-Kindi's intellectual hero was Aristotle, whose empirical approach to science was more difficult to reconcile with Islamic faith. In his most important treatise, *On First Philosophy*, Al-Kindi argues that because both philosophy and religion seek truth, any contradiction between them is only apparent and can eventually be resolved. And even if we need revelation to gain knowledge of the Divine, the empirical approach is still the best way to understand the natural world.

Photo 1.5
Portrait of Al-Kindi

However, there was one point of Aristotelian philosophy that Al-Kindi took issue with (Staley, 1989). Because every event must have a cause, Aristotle reasoned that there could never have been a beginning to the universe. Instead, he saw an endless chain of causality extending for an eternity into the past. This point, of course, contradicted the Islamic doctrine that God created the universe. For Muslims, as well as for Jews and Christians, God is the "unmoved mover," the one entity that requires no cause but is the ultimate cause of all things. If Islam is true, then Aristotle must be wrong, at least on this point. But to err is human, Al-Kindi contended, and just because the great philosopher was mistaken on this point, it didn't mean that all the rest of his science was flawed.

Al-Kindi laid the groundwork for the Islamic Golden Age by making the great extent of classical learning available to Muslim scholars (Staley, 1989). Although he maintained that any contradiction between religion and science was only apparent, he ceded to theology whenever philosophy conflicted with it. This may have been necessary, since he was extending an invitation to the Islamic intellectual world to learn about the natural world, and he dared not offend religious sensibilities. Later Islamic scholars, however, would be more willing to challenge religion when it contradicted science.

Avicenna

Abu 'Ali al-Husayn ibn Sina was the most significant philosopher of the Islamic Golden Age, although he's better known in the West as **Avicenna** (980–1037; pronounced *av-uh-SENN-uh*; Rizvi, 2017). A physician by training, Avicenna can also count as Islam's first neuroscientist, as he proposed a theory of how the brain performs the tasks of perception and memory. Although the theory is spectacularly wrong by modern standards, it was nevertheless a great advance in that it attributed at least lower cognitive functions to physiology rather than supernatural forces. But most importantly, Avicenna is known today as the *Islamic philosopher who provided an influential thought experiment regarding the nature of self-awareness known as the "flying man" argument.*

Photo 1.6
Portrait of Avicenna

Avicenna is most famous for two books whose titles are somewhat misleading (Rizvi, 2017). The first book is the *Canon*, which was a medical textbook. Avicenna was a renowned physician and surgeon, and in the *Canon* he collected the extent of medical knowledge known in the Western world at the time. This book continued to be the standard text in medical schools well into the Modern Period, both in the Islamic world and in Europe. The second book is the *Cure*, in which Avicenna surveys the extent of Aristotelian science, including not only mathematics and logic but also his work in the natural sciences. It's in this book that Avicenna presents his ideas on human psychology, including his brain-based theory of cognition as well as his "flying man" argument. This book was controversial within the Islamic world, and when it was later translated into Latin, it created quite a stir in Europe as well, challenging scholars to question fundamentalist Christian theology and eventually sparking the Renaissance.

In the *Cure*, Avicenna also proposed the idea that humans are born as "blank slates" with no innate knowledge (Rizvi, 2017). Instead, he maintained, all knowledge was acquired through experience and education. On this point, Avicenna was even more of an empiricist than his model Aristotle. This idea also challenged common assumptions in both Europe and the Islamic world about the need to posit some innate knowledge, such as an awareness of God. As we'll see later in this chapter, Avicenna's radical empiricism would be taken up by the British Empiricists during the early Modern Period. Furthermore, this stance served as the cornerstone of the American behaviorist movement of the twentieth century, as we'll learn in Chapter 5.

Avicenna's neuroscience was based on the concept of *inner senses* (Kemp, 1998). The outer senses, such as vision and hearing, received images of the external world. These images then left impressions on the inner senses, thus accounting for processes such as perception, imagination, and memory. Aristotle, like many classical philosophers, believed that the heart was the organ of thinking. But no doubt because of his extensive medical knowledge, Avicenna understood that the brain played an important role in cognition. According to his theory, these low-level cognitive processes took place in the ventricles of the brain, which he believed to be filled with a fluid he called *animal spirits*. This fluid received images from the external world and made impressions on the interior walls of the ventricle. In the acts of imagination or memory, these animal spirits then "read" the impressions that have been left behind. While the theory is incorrect in its entirety, it's still important because it represents one of the first attempts to explain cognition in terms of physiology. However, Avicenna wasn't able to completely give up supernatural explanations. As a Muslim, he of course believed in the existence of the immortal soul, to which he attributed the human ability to use reason.

In Avicenna's thinking, the soul is also the seat of self-awareness (Rustom, 2018). Although he could simply accept this proposition as a tenet of Islam, Avicenna believed he could use the logic of philosophy to demonstrate it as fact. He attempted this by means of the **flying man argument**, which is *a thought experiment intended to demonstrate the existence of self-awareness outside of the body*. Avicenna asks us to imagine a man created fully formed and suspended in mid-air. Because his senses are muted, he will have no knowledge of the outside world. Furthermore, his limbs are fully extended so that no part touches another. As a result, Avicenna maintains, he will have no knowledge of his own body. What, if anything then, will the man be aware of? He will be aware of his own thoughts, Avicenna tells us. In other words, the flying man will only know one thing—that he has a self of which he is aware. Modern philosophers note the similarity between Avicenna's flying man argument and the method of doubt proposed by the seventeenth-century French philosopher René Descartes, who famously concluded, "I think, therefore I am." However, Avicenna's proof for the existence of the self as an independent "thinking thing" precedes that of Descartes by more than six centuries.

Avicenna's thinking was remarkably advanced for his time period. His work is an outstanding example of the intellectual advancement taking place with the cosmopolitan atmosphere of early Islam. As his books made their way into Europe, they awoke scholars on that continent from their intellectual slumbers. Slowly they turned their attention away from the otherworldly with a new curiosity about the nature of the physical world, including the psychology of the people who inhabited it.

Averroes

By the twelfth century, the Islamic Golden Age had begun its decline (Simonton, 2018). Fundamentalist theologians were attacking the philosophy of Avicenna and others contradictory to Islamic doctrine. Although there were still rulers who saw the advantages of keeping scholars in their courts, the general population had grown more conservative and less tolerant of foreign ideas. These were the times into which was born the last great Islamic philosopher, Abu al-Walid Muhammad ibn Ahmad ibn Rushd. Better known as **Averroes** (1126–1198; pronounced *uh-VERR-oh-izz*), ibn Rushd represents a transitional figure during a period when Islamic scholars were turning from philosophy to theology at the same time that European academics were gaining a renewed interest toward science. As a result, Averroes's influence was greater in the Christian West than in the Muslim East, and thus he's known as the *Islamic philosopher who reintroduced Aristotelian philosophy to Europe.*

**Photo 1.7
Statue of Averroes**

Averroes was born in Córdoba (in modern Spain) near the end of Muslim dominion over the Iberian Peninsula (Delgado, 2012). Thus, it was easier for his ideas to make their way into Europe, especially France, where a group of French scholars became dedicated to his teachings after his death. In his hometown, however, his daring philosophy was unwelcomed. There he saw his books burned, and he was banished from the city. He did, however, find a warmer reception with the caliph of Marrakesh (in modern Morocco), where he spent much of his career.

Because of his staunch support for Aristotle's empiricism over Plato's rationalism, Averroes was a controversial figure among both Muslims and Christians (Delgado, 2012). He insisted that observation was the only source of knowledge, for instance by performing autopsies to increase his medical knowledge. He even dared to challenge Aristotle himself when his own observations were counter to what the great master had claimed. Averroes agreed with Avicenna that there should be no conflict between religion and science, but he also denounced what he saw as his predecessor's willingness to forsake reason for dogma when convenient. Instead, he insisted, when scientific observations contradicted religious doctrine, then scripture must be read as allegory rather than as fact. In other words, empirical science was a more reliable source of knowledge than even divine revelation.

Averroes presented his ideas on psychology most fully in his *Aristotle on the Soul* (Hillier, 2017). In this book, he expanded Aristotle's three-part soul into one with five parts, but with the last part, the *rational soul*, being unique to humans. He also proposed a faculty of the mind he called *common sense*, which integrated the separate impressions of the senses into an experiential whole. For instance, when you hold an apple in your hand, you see its redness and roundness, you feel its heft, and you smell its fragrance. When you bite into it, you also hear its crunch and taste its tanginess. In Averroes's philosophy, it's the common sense that binds all these separate experiences together, and it's a remarkably insightful observation. The question of how such an integration takes place was a key concern of the structural psychologists (Chapter 3) working at the turn of the twentieth century, and modern cognitive psychologists (Chapter 11) refer to this process as multimodal perception.

Averroes's views on the soul were in line with those of Aristotle, and they contradicted both Islamic and Christian doctrine (Delgado, 2012). Rather than thinking of the soul as a spirit that survives the death of the body, he saw it instead as a force that animates it. He also agreed with Avicenna's theory of the ventricles in the brain as the seat of cognition, for the reason that this soul—as a physical entity—would need to occupy a hollow space within the body. He also developed a model of localization of brain function, with the frontal ventricles being responsible for imagination, the medial for thought, and the posterior for memory. Of course, this theory is contradicted by evidence from modern neuroscience. However, the significance of this proposal is that it's the first purely brain-based theory of cognition, with no recourse to supernatural explanations. In other words, Averroes was a materialist and a monist who saw the brain as the organ that produces the mind.

As part of this monistic worldview, Averroes held views about human psychology that are remarkably modern (Delgado, 2012). For example, he challenged the commonly held notion that dreams are of supernatural origin. Instead, he maintained that the content of dreams is nothing more than the random recollection of sensory impressions and thoughts from the previous day. This explanation of dreams is quite similar to theories proposed by the American psychologist Mary Calkins (Chapter 4) and the Austrian psychoanalyst Sigmund Freud (Chapter 7) in the late nineteenth century. Furthermore, he disputed the idea that humans were fundamentally rational creatures. Instead, he insisted that our reasoning is always guided by our emotions, a perspective shared by many psychologists in the twentieth and twenty-first centuries.

During the Medieval Period, European scholars largely forsook classical learning because of its perceived contradiction with Christian faith (Chavoushi et al., 2012). Yet during roughly this same time span, Islamic scholars and the rulers who supported them welcomed Greek philosophy as a complement to their new religion. Although many of the classical texts were lost in Europe at the beginning of this period, by the twelfth century the writings of Plato and Aristotle were reintroduced to the continent by way of great Islamic philosophers such as Avicenna and Averroes. However, these scholars weren't just preservers of ancient learning but rather they actively expanded that knowledge base. Avicenna's *Organ* was the standard medical textbook in Europe for centuries, and Averroes's return to Aristotle's empiricism helped spark the Renaissance that marked the transition to the Modern Period. Indeed, the Islamic Golden Age set the stage for the scientific era we live in today.

Modern Period: Continental Rationalism

As Europe awoke from its slumber during the Renaissance, copies of these preserved works returned to the Continent, and European philosophers endeavored to integrate Christian faith with Aristotle and Plato. By the seventeenth century, the scientific revolution was in full swing. Natural philosophers like Galileo Galilei (1564–1642) and Isaac Newton (1642–1726) proposed a mechanical, "clockwork" view of the world. Even the human body could be described as a biological machine. This was the intellectual climate into which the French philosopher René Descartes was born.

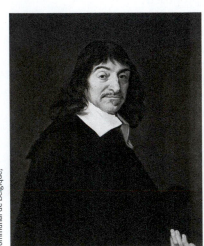

Photo 1.8
Portrait of René Descartes

René Descartes

The seventeenth-century philosopher **René Descartes** (1596–1650; pronounced *day-CART*) would lie in bed until noon, just thinking (Damjanovic, Milovanovic, & Trajanovic, 2015). According to legend, he came up with the idea of Cartesian geometry while watching a fly walk along the ceiling. From this late-morning lounging came one of the most important discoveries in mathematics. But he also gave considerable thought to the mind-body problem, so psychology knows René Descartes as the *French philosopher who was one of the first thinkers of the early Modern Period to provide a detailed model of how the mind and body interact.*

In the early 1630s, Descartes wrote his *Treatise on Man*, in which he argued that the human body is just a machine (Damjanovic et al., 2015). He based this premise on his studies of animal vision systems, in which he had traced the optic nerve from the back of the eyeball to a center in the brain known as the pineal gland, which he surmised to be the center of visual perception. We now know that he was wrong in this regard, but nevertheless his anatomical investigations led him to an appreciation for the complex network of nerves running between the brain and the body. In Descartes's view, the brain was clearly a control center for the body, and even though he was careful not to suggest that the brain was the seat of the mind, he still feared repercussions from religious authorities. After all, the famous Italian astronomer Galileo Galilei had just recently been sentenced by the Inquisition to house arrest for proposing the heretical notion that the Earth revolves around the sun. So he left this treatise with friends to be published after his death, which they did in 1664.

In the *Treatise on Man*, Descartes (1664/1972) presents various machines as analogies to the workings of the human body. For instance, all the rage at the time were moving statues that worked by hydraulics. As you walk through a garden, you step on a flagstone, which releases a flow of water through a pipe. A figure leaps from the bushes and dances about. When you step off of the stone, the figure retreats to the shrubbery. Maybe the nervous system works by hydraulics as well, Descartes thought. Imagine you touch a hot flame. Particles of heat press against your skin, causing a fluid he called "animal spirits" to flow up to the brain. As the sensory portion of the brain swelled with these animal spirits, it pressed against the motor portion, which in response squirted more animal spirits down to the muscles to move your hand away. If you replace "animal spirits" with "electro-chemical signals" and make a few other tweaks, you have a rough outline of our modern conception of the reflex arc (Figure 1.2). Of course, Descartes knew nothing of electricity, let alone chemistry.

It's in his *Meditations on First Philosophy* that Descartes lays out his vision of the relationship between body and soul (Descartes, 1641/1911). According to Christian theology, our

Figure 1.2 Descartes's Reflex Arc

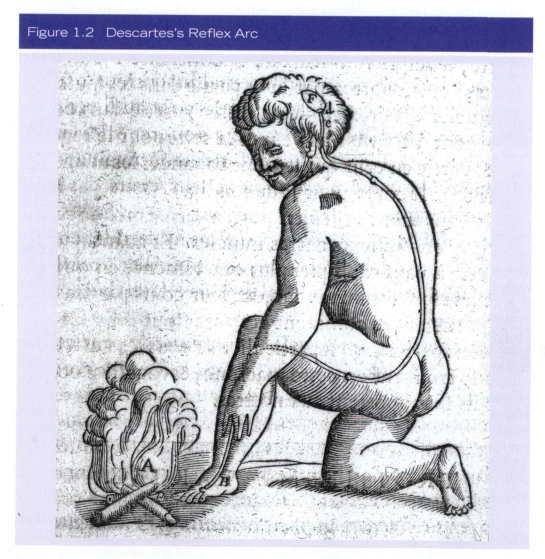

soul is immortal and survives the death of our body with our personal memories intact. Otherwise, how could we know why we were being rewarded with heaven or punished with hell? Thinking on this issue was murky before Descartes, but he was the one who gave us the modern concept of mind as a set of mental processes, which he equated with the soul of Christian theology.

Descartes (1641/1911) begins his *Meditations* by clearing his mind of all thoughts he doesn't absolutely know to be true. He does this with his **method of doubt**, which is *Descartes's way of avoiding unwarranted assumptions by questioning everything that cannot be logically verified.* Because the senses can deceive, how does he know for certain that he's lying in bed awake staring at the ceiling? Perhaps he's just dreaming. And if so, how does he know his entire life isn't a dream? Or worse, suppose some evil demon has seized control of his senses and is causing him to hallucinate. As far as he knows, all of the physical world around him, including his own body, could be an illusion created by this evil demon. Now, Descartes isn't arguing that the world is an illusion. He's just saying that if it were an illusion, he wouldn't know. He'd still think his experiences were real.

Once Descartes has rid himself of the physical world and even his own body, what's left? He's still aware of his own thought processes, hence his famous quote, "I think, therefore I am." But wait. Couldn't even his own thoughts be deceptions produced by this evil demon? If so, there must still be an "I" that's been deceived. So "I" must exist, Descartes concludes. However, "I" isn't a physical thing, it's a "thinking thing." And if "I" am my thoughts and not my body, then there must be two kinds of things in the world, physical stuff and thinking stuff.

By separating body and soul as distinct entities, Descartes can have his religion and his science too. Because he packs the mind inside a disembodied soul, Descartes explains how we could experience an afterlife with all of our mental functions intact. And by removing the soul from the physical world, he can now talk about the body as a machine without committing heresy. Note that this is essentially the same conclusion that the Islamic philosopher Avicenna arrived at with his flying man argument some six centuries earlier, with much the same motivation of preserving an immortal soul while giving a mechanical account of the body.

Cartesian dualism then is *the proposal that the mind and the body are separate but interact with each other.* Furthermore, Descartes proposed, the point where the body and soul connect is the pineal gland, which he'd supposed to be the seat of vision. However, by making a clear distinction between the physical body and the spiritual mind, Descartes has put himself in a difficult position. Clearly the mind can affect the body, but in the clockwork universe he subscribes to, all physical events must have physical causes. There can be no supernatural intervention in the natural world, yet Cartesian dualism demands it. Another troubling conclusion falls out from Cartesian dualism. According to Christian theology, only humans have souls. If the mind is in the soul and not the body, then nonhuman animals can't have minds or any sort of conscious experience. Descartes viewed animals as mindless machines, but most people today would probably have serious doubts about this conclusion.

René Descartes developed the modern conception of mind as a unified conscious experience and gave us the concept of the sensorimotor reflex. His solution to the mind-body problem is unsatisfactory, and in fact many of his contemporaries pointed this out. Cartesian dualism results from a conflict between the theological need to posit an immortal soul that encapsulates our sense of self with the scientific evidence that the body is a biological machine subject to the laws of physics. As we'll see, many other philosophers of the modern era have struggled with this same issue, each focusing on a particular set of problems. Nevertheless, it was Descartes who gave us the first clear articulation of the mind-body problem, and in that sense every other proposal since then has come as a response to Cartesian dualism.

Thomas Hobbes

When the English Civil War erupted in 1642, **Thomas Hobbes** (1583–1679) fled to Paris with other supporters of the monarch. Mostly known as a political philosopher, Hobbes argued in his best-known work, *Leviathan*, that without a strong central government, society would dissolve into chaos, just as had happened during the decade-long civil war. In his view, this was because humans were no different from other animals, both of which he saw simply as biological machines driven by their passions. Thus, we know Thomas Hobbes as the *British philosopher who argued that the mind is nothing more than the product of a mechanical brain.*

Unlike Descartes, Hobbes was an atheist, so he didn't need an explanation for the afterlife (Meehan, 2009). Instead, he held *the view that there is only matter and that no separate substance is needed to explain the mind.* This is known as **materialism**. Furthermore, he maintained, if mental processes are mechanical, then there can be no such thing as free will. Instead, we only believe we have free will because we're unaware of the external causes of our urges.

We can think of Cartesian interactionist dualism and Hobbesian materialist monism as two poles on the mind-body problem, with all other accounts as intermediate positions between them. Since the twentieth century, however, Hobbes's position has become far more influential among experimental psychologists, who as scientists necessarily take a materialist worldview. For example, many neuroscientists today believe that all mental processes will ultimately be explainable in terms of brain activity. Although Descartes's name is more frequently mentioned, it is Hobbes's viewpoint that is more widely accepted among psychologists today.

Photo 1.9
Portrait of Thomas Hobbes

John Michael Wright, National Portrait Gallery, via Wikimedia Commons

Baruch Spinoza

A generation younger than both Descartes and Hobbes, **Baruch Spinoza** (1632–1677) had the opportunity to consider the strengths and weaknesses of their opposing solutions to the mind-body problem (Meehan, 2009). At first glance, his philosophy appears to be a compromise position between his two predecessors. But on further inspection, we find a nuanced worldview that in fact may be more in line with twenty-first century sensibilities than either Cartesian dualism or Hobbesian monism. Today we know Baruch Spinoza as the *Dutch philosopher who argued that mind and matter are but two aspects of the same underlying nature.*

In his *Ethics*, Spinoza (1677/2009) responded to both Descartes's mind-body dualism and Hobbes's materialistic monism. Like Hobbes, Spinoza rejected Cartesian dualism in favor of monism, but he didn't agree that mind is product of the body. Instead, he proposed what is now known as **double-aspect monism**. This is *the view that mind and body are two facets of the same universal substance.* Mind and body are like two sides of the side coin, with no way to separate one from the other. Thus, it's meaningless to talk of an interaction between mind and body because they aren't separate entities. Furthermore, he agreed with Hobbes that free will was nothing more than an illusion, because all of nature is determined by the laws of physics.

Photo 1.10
Portrait of Baruch Spinoza

Via Wikimedia Commons

Spinoza's writings were often suppressed during the centuries following his death because of the way they challenged religious dogma (Meehan, 2009). During subsequent centuries, debate on the mind-body problem was largely polarized between the Cartesian and Hobbesian points of view. While Hobbes's materialism appealed to many experimental psychologists in the twentieth century, its inability to provide a satisfactory account of subjective conscious experience has troubled some psychologists in the twenty-first century. For this reason, Spinoza's dual-aspect monism has gained renewed interest in recent decades, especially among neuroscientists who view the brain and mind as correlated systems (Chapter 16).

Gottfried Leibniz

Like Descartes, **Gottfried Leibniz** (1646–1716) was a devout Christian who was also devoted to the idea of a mechanical universe. He understood that an immortal soul had to

Photo 1.11
Portrait of Gottfried Leibniz

be immaterial, so there must two different kinds of substance, physical and spiritual. But he also saw the logical inconsistency of Cartesian interactionism, and he proposed an alternative dualist approach to the mind-body problem. Thus, Gottfried Leibniz is best known as the *German philosopher who argued for psychophysical parallelism as an alternative to Cartesian dualism.*

Challenging Hobbes's materialistic monism, Leibniz offered the **mill argument** (Jorati, 2019). This is *Leibniz's thought experiment demonstrating that mental processes cannot be produced by mechanical means.* Even if we produced a machine that acted as if it were conscious, he said, we'd never find anything among its internal gears and springs that was actually producing consciousness. Instead, Leibniz argued, only souls can have consciousness, and the material world is mindless.

Leibniz sought a way to align the physical and spiritual worlds (Fancher, 2000). He asks us to imagine two pendulums hanging from a beam. To get them swinging in harmony, all we need to do is push them both at that same time. After that, they'll swing together even though there's no interaction between them. So it is with the physical and spiritual worlds, Leibniz claims. *The idea that mind and body act in harmony even though they do not interact* is known as **psychophysical parallelism**. If you cut your finger, your body will bleed in response. But your mind will also feel pain, because it was established at the beginning of the universe that the body and soul would always act in harmony.

Unlike Descartes, Leibniz believed animals perceive the world just as humans do, which he attributed to the workings of the physical body rather than the spiritual mind (Duarte, 2009). But what made humans different is that they can think about their experiences as opposed to merely acting on them. *The ability to reflect on one's own perceptions* is what Leibniz called **apperception**. This was a common concept in both philosophical and experimental psychology up to the early twentieth century, but it fell out of use as the functionalists and behaviorists focused on empirical observations of outward behavior.

In his own time, Leibniz was a provocative person, and many of his arguments don't mesh well with thinking in modern psychology. His psychophysical parallelism is difficult to justify with the materialist worldview of science. However, his mill argument has resurfaced in various guises with the rise of artificial intelligence and the question of machine consciousness. Even after four centuries, though, Leibniz still provides food for thought.

Immanuel Kant

During his lifetime, **Immanuel Kant** (1724–1804) was an international celebrity, even though he never traveled more than a few miles from his birthplace. He wrote major works that changed the course of Western philosophy, and he made early contributions to a number of the emerging natural and social sciences. Although he famously opined that psychology could never be a "real" science, he nonetheless proposed a theory of the human mind that is remarkably similar to the thinking of twenty-first-century cognitive scientists. And all this he accomplished from the university town where he spent his entire life. Today, we remember Immanuel Kant as a *German philosopher who sought to reconcile the rationalist and empiricist approaches by arguing that knowledge is acquired through experience but ordered by innate rational processes.*

Kant lived in a time commonly known as the **Age of Enlightenment**, which was *a period during the eighteenth century when religious dogma was questioned and reason was held as the ultimate authority.* Science was questioning cherished religious beliefs. However, Kant argued that there is in fact no contradiction between science and religion. This is because science deals with the universe as we perceive it through our senses, but there's also a part of the universe beyond the reach of our senses. This is where God, soul, free will, and the afterlife fit in. Although we can't perceive this realm, we can know through reason that it must exist.

Photo 1.12
Portrait of Immanuel Kant

In his most famous book *Critique of Pure Reason*, Kant (1781/2017) tries to bridge the gap between the rationalist and empiricist approaches to the acquisition of knowledge. While acknowledging that we can only learn about the world through our experiences, he also maintained that the human mind contains innate principles for organizing our perceptions. This assertion then leads to the concept of **transcendental idealism**, which is *Kant's contention that human experience consists solely of appearances and not of things in themselves.* The reason why we can't see things as they truly are is because our minds are preconditioned to experience the world in a particular way, and so there are aspects of the world we have no direct access to.

As examples of how our minds organize our perceptions, Kant argued that three-dimensional space and time are not attributes of the universe but rather of our minds (Mikkelsen, 2000). In other words, our minds impose a space-time structure on our experiences even though these aren't attributes of the universe as it truly is. For Kant, transcendental idealism represented a "Copernican shift" in human thinking. The sun appears to circle around the Earth, rising every morning in the east and setting each night in the west. But the Polish astronomer Nicolaus Copernicus (1473–1543) showed that this is just an appearance and not reality. Only through reason can we know that the Earth circles the sun as it spins on its axis. Kant's theory of human cognition was radical for its time, but it has had considerable influence on psychological thinking up to the present day. In particular, the Kantian concept of innate organizing principles was a cornerstone of Gestalt psychology (Chapter 6), which arose in Germany in the early twentieth century.

Kant also took exception to the general belief at the time that perception was a passive process of accumulating sensory impressions (Palmer, 2008). Instead, Kant viewed perception as an active process. For instance, we organize the sensory input according to our innate structures of time and space, we make judgments about what categories particular objects or events belong to, and we make inferences to fill in the gaps. In other words, perception constructs a conscious experience out of the bits and pieces that come in through our senses. Kant's view of perception as a constructive process had an important influence on the thinking of the great nineteenth-century scientist Hermann von Helmholtz (Chapter 2), who helped lay the foundation for a scientific psychology.

According to Kant, transcendental idealism allowed for free will within a mechanical universe, and therefore humans needed a code of morality to guide their actions (Soloviev, 2018). In Kant's view of morality, when my choices affect no one but myself, I can do as I please. But when my decisions affect others, I must follow what he called the **categorical imperative**. This is *Kant's fundamental moral law that we must always act in such a way as to respect the humanity of other people.* This imperative is "categorical" in the sense that it absolutely applies in all cases and to all persons. Once you unpack the Kantian language, you see that he's talking about the Golden Rule of treating other people the way you want to be treated. However, Kant changes it from a recommendation to an absolute principle of morality that has no exceptions.

Although Kant lived at the end of the Enlightenment, he is viewed today as one of its most important philosophers who changed the course of modern philosophy. And as we'll see in upcoming chapters, his ideas have had great influence on the study of perception and cognition from the nineteenth century up to the present day. Although Immanuel Kant never traveled more than a few miles from his home, his ideas about the human experience continue to influence psychologists from around the world.

Modern Period: British Empiricism

The British have always had an ambivalent relationship with the rest of Europe. On the one hand, they view themselves as "mostly" European, but on the other hand they've always insisted on their independence from the Continent. Enlightenment philosophers in Continental Europe followed the lead of René Descartes, but British philosophers of the Enlightenment rejected both nativism and rationalism. Instead, they argued that we're born as blank slates and only acquire knowledge through experience. Historians generally credit Francis Bacon as the father of British Empiricism.

Francis Bacon

One of the great inventions of the Ancient Greek philosophers was the method of **deduction**. This is *a method of reasoning that applies general rules to specific cases*. Deductions are often framed in terms of syllogisms, which present the general rule (or major premise), the special case (or the minor premise), and the conclusion on three lines. Aristotle demonstrated this with his famous syllogism about Socrates:

- All men are mortal. (Major premise)

- Socrates is a man. (Minor premise)

- Therefore, Socrates is mortal. (Conclusion)

Medieval European scholars were enamored with this sort of syllogistic reasoning, and early scientists such as Galileo and Descartes relied on the method. However, one of the first thinkers of the Modern Period to challenge the usefulness of deductive reasoning in the realm of science was **Francis Bacon** (1561–1626), the *English philosopher and the father of British empiricism who introduced the method of induction.*

In the method of deduction, Bacon argued, the premises are assumed to be true. But how do we know that Socrates is a man or that all men are mortal? You can only know these things to be true from careful observation of the world. That is to say, all knowledge ultimately comes from our experiences. Through deduction, we can come to understand the characteristics of specific cases, but it can never lead us to an understanding of the general laws of nature.

If we want to unlock the secrets of nature, Bacon argued, then we have to run the reasoning process in reverse. In other words, we have to use *a method of reasoning that examines specific cases in order to discover general rules*. Bacon called this the method of **induction**. The way Bacon envisioned it, the scientist collected lots of examples of the item under investigation and searched for patterns among them. Using the method of induction, Bacon (1620/2007, I, 19) wrote, our knowledge will increase through a "gradual and unbroken ascent" from specific instances to more general principles about the world. He disparaged philosophers who used the art of deductive logic to "prove" their pet theories, likening them to spiders who spin their webs out of themselves (I, 95). The true scientist, in contrast, was like a bee collecting nectar from many flowers to make honey.

As a keen psychologist, Bacon (1620/2007) knew that even smart people can fool themselves. The **doctrine of the idols** is *Bacon's assertion that the human mind is beset with biases that lead it to predictable errors* (I, 38–69). These idols keep us from understanding the world as it truly is. It's important to note that Bacon is using the term *idol* in its original Greek sense of "image" or "phantom." Bacon says that our perceptions don't reflect the world as it truly is. Rather, our mind is like a crooked mirror that distorts its reflections. However, if we're aware of these idols, we can find ways to overcome them.

Bacon's doctrine of the idols challenged the prevailing notion that the human mind was essentially rational even though it could be led astray by the passions (Smith, 2000a). Instead, he pointed out that merely taking an intentional stance to think in a rational manner wasn't enough, because the idols can deceive us into believing we are reasonable when in fact we're not. Bacon's doctrine of the idols presaged by more than four centuries the recognition of perceptual and cognitive biases that are the mainstay of any cognitive or social psychology course.

Francis Bacon had a great impact on philosophy and science in his own day, and his influence continues to the present (Smith, 2000a). Among his near contemporaries, both Descartes and Leibniz praised Bacon's insights, although Spinoza dismissed his method of induction. A few generations later, Kant praised Bacon as a founder of the modern era and dedicated his *Critique of Pure Reason*

Jacobus Houbraken (1698–1780), via Wikimedia Commons

Photo 1.13
Portrait of Francis Bacon

to him. British scientists in particular recognized the power of the inductive method and adopted it in their work. However, induction didn't replace deduction altogether, as Bacon had advocated. Instead, what developed was a scientific method that incorporated both inductive and deductive reasoning. The Baconian ideal of scientific progress was especially embraced by American psychologists in the twentieth century, who sought to develop an experimental psychology that would be useful for society.

Photo 1.14
Portrait of John Locke

John Locke

In his 1690 *Essay Concerning Human Understanding*, **John Locke** (1632–1704) challenges us to consider the source of our knowledge:

> Let us then suppose the mind to be, as we say, white paper, void of all characters, without any ideas: How comes it to be furnished? . . . To this I answer, in one word, from experience. (Locke, 1690/2004, II.i.2)

Our minds are void of knowledge at birth, according to Locke, but as we go through life, our experiences are written on this blank sheet, and our understanding of the world is built up as we associate new experiences with previous ones. Thus, we know John Locke as the *British empiricist philosopher who developed a mental philosophy known as associationism.* Because we experience the world through our senses, nothing can be in the mind that isn't first in the senses. Furthermore, each of us has only limited experience with the world, so our knowledge of it must be incomplete. But Locke did believe the scientific method was the most reliable way of gaining accurate knowledge about the world.

Although the mind is empty of content at birth, Locke (1690/2004) said, it does contain innate processes, or faculties, for organizing the information that is brought in. In Locke's view, we have two types of senses:

- *Outer senses* provide us with information about the outside world. You see the bacon frying in pan, and you hear it sizzle in the hot oil. You smell the bacon, you taste it, and you feel pain when it burns your tongue. Locke uses the term *sensation* to refer to experiences brought into the mind by the outer senses (II.i.3).

- *Inner senses* tell us what's happening inside our bodies and minds. You feel hunger. You experience a strong desire to eat something, and you imagine the taste of cooked bacon. Locke uses the term *reflection* to refer to experiences brought into the mind by the inner senses (II.i.4).

Perception and memory then were built up from the combination of simple sensations and reflections.

The natural philosopher Robert Boyle (1672–1691), a longtime friend, had introduced Locke to the new atomic theory, which claimed all matter was composed of tiny, indivisible particles. These simple atoms then combine to create all the complex material objects of the world. Locke applied this atomic theory of the material world to the mental world, and he viewed the basic unit of thought as an *idea* (Introduction.i.8). According to Locke, sensations and reflections make up *simple ideas* (II.iii.1). These simple ideas then combine to form *complex ideas*. When we pick up an apple and bite into it, we experience many sensations—redness, roundness, heaviness, crispness, sweetness, tartness. All of these simple ideas combine together to create the complex idea of "apple." *The theory that knowledge develops as simple ideas combine to form complex ideas* is known as **associationism**.

Locke (1690/2004) argued that we can have complex ideas of things we've never experienced as long as we've stored all of the simple ideas contained in it (II.xii.1). Think about all the fantastic beasts of cultures around the world—they're always made up of familiar parts. A unicorn is a horse with a horn. A centaur is half man, half horse. Angels have human bodies with wings on their backs. Dragons are giant lizards with wings that exhale fire. No one has ever experienced a unicorn, centaur, angel, or dragon in the real world, and yet they're easily imagined.

Conversely, Locke (1690/2004) maintained that we can't have a simple idea without first having a sensory experience of it. To demonstrate this assertion, he offers the following thought experiment (II.ix.8). Consider a man born blind who has learned to identify a cube by touch. That is, he has a complex idea of "cube" that is composed of all the tactile sensations he's had while holding it. Now if his vision were somehow restored, Locke says, he'd be unable to identify the cube by sight alone, even though he knows what a cube is. Only when he picks up this mysterious object and identifies it first by touch will he know what a cube looks like.

Locke (1690/2004) warns us that we need to view our knowledge of the world as tentative. This is because knowledge is built from sensory experiences, and the senses don't portray the world objectively. He demonstrates this with the following thought experiment (II.viii.21). Fill three buckets with water—one hot, one tepid, and one cold. Put your left hand in the hot water and your right hand in the cold water. After a while, put both hands in the tepid water. Your left hand will tell you the water is cool, while your right hand will tell you it's warm. So our senses don't always accord with reality. Rationalists would argue that this is exactly why you can't rely on experience to provide accurate knowledge of the world. But empiricists like Locke say sensory experience is all we've got, and so we need to understand its limitations and use it wisely.

Subsequent British empiricists strove to work out the mechanics of how ideas are associated in the mind, and psychologists picked up the problem in the twentieth century. In exploring the limits of human knowledge, Locke saw himself playing a supporting role in the newly developing science. He also reminds us that all knowledge—even that of science—is only tentative, and that we may need to change our minds about what we think we know as new information comes in.

George Berkeley

John Smybert (1688–1751), via Wikimedia Commons

Photo 1.15
Portrait of George Berkeley

George Berkeley (1685–1753; pronounced *BARK-lee*) was a man of science, but he was also a man of deep religious faith. So his conundrum was how to reconcile the mechanical universe with his Christian beliefs. While at Trinity College in Dublin, Ireland, he produced his two great philosophical works, his *New Theory of Vision* and his *Treatise*. After that, he gave up philosophy for religious and philanthropic work. Today, George Berkeley is known as an *Irish philosopher who did groundbreaking research on depth perception and promoted the philosophy of idealism.*

In his *New Theory of Vision*, Berkeley (1709/2002) calls to mind a sweeping view of a house, some fields, and a river. As you scan this panorama, you have no difficulty perceiving distance. However, the image on your retina is flat. Rationalist philosophers claimed that we used geometric patterns in the retinal image to make inferences about distances. But Berkeley disagreed, maintaining that we *learn* to make inferences about distance as we interact with the world.

Imagine baby Suzie playing on the floor. She sees a wooden block and crawls to it. Picking it up, she turns it about in her hand to examine its shape, and she squeezes it to find out that it's solid. Just holding it, she senses its weight. According to Berkeley, properties of an object like size, shape, and heaviness can only be known through the sense of touch. He also claimed that we learn to judge distance in a similar manner—the image of the object looms large when Suzie brings it close to her face, and it shrinks when she holds it at arm's length. Berkeley's theory of depth perception was revolutionary for its time and still has relevance to vision researchers today.

In his *Treatise*, Berkeley (1710/2002) presents a radical solution to the mind-body problem. He understood that the clockwork universe left no room for God or free will, and so it contradicted the teachings of Christian theology. His purpose wasn't to reject science, but rather to save it from the skeptics and atheists. In other words, he sought a way to reconcile science with religion. He believed the problem lay in materialism, which in his view included Cartesian dualism and its contention that the material and spiritual worlds interacted with each other. It was materialism in any form, he maintained, that gave skeptics and atheists fodder for their arguments. The solution, Berkeley thought, was **idealism**. This is *the philosophical stance that the world consists solely of minds and the ideas they produce.* Berkeley wasn't denying the existence of a physical universe, only that it was composed of matter. Rather, every object in the universe exists because it's an idea in the mind of God.

As perceivers, Berkeley (1710/2002) maintains, our knowledge begins at sensation, and we can't say with certainty what causes those sensations. In fact, there are good reasons *not* to assume sensations are representations of a material world. After all, when we dream or use our imagination, we have perceptions that are clearly not representations of material objects. Furthermore, he contends, even the scientists can't come up with a clear definition of matter, admitting that all we know of the material world is what we perceive through our senses.

In Berkeley's (1710/2002) philosophy, then, the world consists only of things that are perceived, which he calls *ideas*, and agents that perceive, which he calls *spirits*. Ideas are passive, simply the objects of perception. Spirits are active in that they not only perceive ideas but can also willfully create them. Humans are spirits in that their essence lies not in a material body—which doesn't exist anyway—but rather in an immaterial soul. Humans can create perceptions through memory or imagination. However, their senses also present them with perceptions originating from a higher spirit, namely God. Berkeley doesn't reject the existence of a physical universe, only one that's material. In his view, the laws of nature still hold in his idealist world. It's just that they don't describe the behavior of matter in motion but rather the regularities of our perceptual experience, which God has created for us. Thus, Berkeley believes he has made science consistent with religion and defeated the skeptics and atheists.

The general consensus among philosophers today is that Berkeley's arguments for an idealist solution to the mind-body problem are fundamentally flawed (Robinson, 2000). However, his theory of vision does still have relevance in psychology. The question of whether various aspects of perception are learned or innate is one that's still discussed by psychologists today. In particular, the topic of perceptual learning will come up again in Chapter 13 when we review the work of Eleanor Gibson. Although psychologists have rejected Berkeley's idealism, they've nonetheless found ample inspiration in the logic of his theory of vision.

David Hume

David Hume was one of those atheists Berkeley was so concerned about. Hume clearly understood there could be no God in a mechanical universe. He was inspired by Locke's associationism, but he felt Locke had succumbed to Cartesian dualism. Seeing himself as the Isaac Newton of mental philosophy, **David Hume** (1711–1776) was a *Scottish philosopher who developed laws of mental association.*

The **laws of association** are *Hume's description of how simple ideas adhere to each other to form complex ideas.* In his *Treatise of Human Nature*, Hume (1739/1896) maintained that we tend to associate ideas under the following circumstances:

- *Resemblance*: when two ideas resemble each other.

- *Contiguity*: when two ideas co-occur in time or space.

- *Causation*: when two ideas follow one after the other.

In physics, Newton's laws of gravitation and motion are basic, Hume maintained, so they need no explanation. Likewise in his theory of the mind, the three laws of association are basic, and he expects his readers to accept them as self-evident.

Photo 1.16
Portrait of David Hume

In his *Enquiry Concerning Human Understanding*, Hume (1748) further develops his thoughts on association by causation. Using the example of two billiard balls, he illustrates how causation is inferred and not perceived. We observe a white ball rolling toward a red ball, and just when the two come into contact, the white ball stops and the red ball moves. Even though we believe the white ball *caused* the red ball to move, all we really know is the contact of the two balls and the resemblance of their motion. So we don't actually observe causation—we infer it instead. To Hume, the perception of cause and effect is merely a custom of thinking and nothing more.

Hume contributed other important ideas to psychology as well. We tend to see reason and emotion as opponents battling for control of our minds, but Hume challenges this notion. Reason is just thought, and thinking alone cannot move us to act—only feeling can do that. As he famously stated, "Reason is . . . the slave of the passions, and can never pretend to any other office than to serve and obey them" (Hume, 1739/1896, II.III.III.4). This view of emotion as the driving force of behavior is remarkably modern. It accords with Freud's theory of motivation (Chapter 7), and since the late twentieth century, many psychologists have recognized the role of intuition and emotion in decision making.

Hume's laws of association laid the foundations for several early schools of psychology (Rychlak, 1998). Although his philosophical works were largely dismissed during his own lifetime because of their skeptical and atheistic stance, he nonetheless had considerable influence on following generations of philosophers and scientists. John Stuart Mill further developed Hume's laws of association. Immanuel Kant recognized Hume's influence as he struggled to reconcile rationalism with empiricism in his *Critique of Pure Reason*. Charles Darwin also reported finding inspiration in Hume as he was developing his theory of evolution by natural selection. Furthermore, Hume's philosophy still has considerable relevance to twenty-first-century psychology.

Photo 1.17
Portrait of John Stuart Mill

John Stuart Mill

In his *System of Logic* (1843/2009), **John Stuart Mill** (1806–1873) laid out his vision for a new psychology, challenging the prevailing view that a study of human behavior and thought processes was beyond the reach of the natural sciences. Instead, he maintained the materialist position that both mind and body were subject to the laws of nature, and hence amenable to study in a scientific fashion. Thus, John Stuart Mill is known as the *British empiricist philosopher who declared that psychology was ready to become a natural science that could be used to improve individual lives and society as a whole.*

In his *Autobiography*, Mill (1873/2003) takes on the question of how to reconcile free will with a materialist worldview. If there is nothing but a physical world, then all events have prior causes and so free will should be impossible. And even if we take a dualist worldview, we still have the question of how free will in the spiritual world can influence our behaviors in the materialist world. To Mill, this contradiction is only apparent, and he makes *the argument that human free will can still exist even in a fully deterministic world*. This position is now known as **compatibilism**. Unlike billiard balls transferring their motion or planets orbiting the sun, many factors play a role in determining human behavior, including our past experiences, our present emotional state, aspects of the current situation, and our expectations for the future.

According to the compatibilist position, we could in principle know all the antecedents of a behavior, but in practice it's simply not possible (Hart, 2017). We're faced with a multitude of decisions in our daily lives, and as long as there's the possibility that we could have chosen otherwise, we can say that we have free will. Which choice you make is ultimately determined by the complex interplay of many factors. And if any of them changed even in the slightest, your decision may be different. Even though all our decisions are determined, the fact that we might have chosen otherwise means that we have free will. It's up to you to decide (or maybe it's not) whether you can accept this definition of free will. Although many philosophers find this argument weak, there are also plenty who accept some form of the compatibilist position.

For Mill (1873/2003), compatibilism provides a way of thinking about psychology as a natural science. Astronomers can predict with great accuracy the movements of the planets because the laws that govern them are simple and few. Psychologists, though, will never be able to predict human behavior so precisely because the laws are complex and many in number. At best, we can only make tentative predictions about how someone will act, but the fact that we can do even this indicates that there are underlying regularities.

Mill (1873/2003) also contends that some of the laws that govern the operation of the mind are already known. He assumes the associationist principles of Locke and Hume, but he adds a new process based on analogy with chemistry, in which atoms combine to form molecules with entirely new properties, such as the gases hydrogen and oxygen combining to form water. *Mill's argument that complex ideas can have features not found in any of its components* is known as **mental chemistry**. This idea presages thinking in the Gestalt school of the early twentieth century.

According to Mill (1873/2003), these laws of the mind form the foundation for a natural science of human behavior. Furthermore, this science can have practical consequences. First, we can develop better ways of raising and educating children so that they'll grow up to be happy persons who are contributing members of society. Furthermore, as we come to understand the laws of human interactions, we can restructure society to ensure social harmony and moral behavior. In other words, we can use psychology to achieve the greatest good for the greatest number. In this sense, Mill's psychology underlies all of his political philosophy and social commentary.

Mill believed that people's lives can be improved through better education and the optimal organization of society. Furthermore, he maintained that a scientific psychology would lead the way forward. Very much ahead of his time, he argued for equal rights for all people, including women and the native populations of the British colonies. As we'll see in the chapters to come, psychology has often played an important role in building a more equitable society, just as John Stuart Mill had envisioned.

Looking Ahead

Like rebellious teenagers, modern psychologists often disown their philosophical heritage. But in fact, philosophers work in tandem with experimental psychologists in the quest for a science of the mind. By the nature of their work, psychologists tend to focus on narrow questions that can be tested with the tools of science. It's then the job of the philosophers to read broadly across the psychology literature, integrating findings and considering their implications. In a sense, the philosophers have the harder job, since they need to know both the philosophy and the science of the mind. However, as we'll see in the following chapters, many of the great psychologists of the twentieth century were both philosophers and scientists.

Today, philosophers of mind mostly work in a field known as **cognitive science**, which is *an interdisciplinary approach to studying the mind and how it works.* Cognitive scientists are drawn from six different fields:

- Philosophy
- Psychology
- Anthropology
- Linguistics
- Artificial intelligence
- Neuroscience

Each of these fields provides a different perspective on the nature of the mind, and the hope is that the combined effort of all six branches can provide us with an understanding that is both broader and deeper than can be obtained by any one approach alone.

Several modern philosophers of mind have made it into the public consciousness, as it were, by publishing popular books on the subject. Here are but a few examples:

- *Marvin Minsky* (1927–2016) was a philosopher who believed that someday machines will become just as intelligent as humans if not more so.

- *John Searle* (Born 1932) is a philosopher who believes that consciousness is a unique property of living things, and that nonbiological machines can never become sentient.

- *Daniel Dennett* (Born 1942) is a philosopher of mind who's a staunch defender of compatibilism in an era when most cognitive scientists reject the existence of free will.

- *Patricia Churchland* (Born 1943) is a philosopher who believes that once we fully understand the brain, concepts like "free will" and "mind" will become meaningless.

Many of these modern philosophers have a presence on the internet in the form of YouTube videos and TED Talks, so you can hear them present their ideas in their own words.

CHAPTER SUMMARY

In this chapter, we surveyed nearly twenty-five centuries of philosophy, starting with the Ancient Greeks in the fifth and fourth centuries before the Common Era (BCE). Socrates introduced a method of inquiry that involved questioning everything, and it became a mainstay in the Western philosophical tradition. His student Plato was a rationalist who believed that knowledge was innate and had to be discovered through logical reasoning. In contrast, Plato's student Aristotle was an empiricist who believed that all knowledge is gained through experience. The rationalist-empiricist debate continues to the current day. Late in the Classical Period, the murder of the woman philosopher Hypatia came to symbolize the struggle between religion and science that also extends to current times. During the Medieval Period, the Catholic Church severely circumscribed intellectual inquiry in Europe, but in the Islamic world, philosophy was valued by the ruling elite if not the religious leaders. During the centuries of the Islamic Golden Age, philosophers such as Al-Kindi, Avicenna, and Averroes not only maintained classical learning but also developed it further. As the works of the Islamic philosophers gradually made their way north, a Renaissance began in Europe that eventually led to the Modern Period. On the continent, philosophers tended to be rationalists, and their disputes centered on the mind-body problem (Table 1.1). René Descartes proposed an interactionist dualism, while Thomas Hobbes favored materialist monism. Taking middle positions, Baruch Spinoza proposed dual-aspect monism, whereas Gottfried Leibniz favored psychophysical parallelism. Finally, Immanuel Kant developed a philosophy that attempted to reconcile the rationalist and empiricist division. On the British Isles, philosophers were generally empiricists who sought to understand how the mind comes to be formed from its experiences. Francis Bacon introduced the inductive method, in which scientists build their understanding of nature through the inspection of many examples. John Locke argued that knowledge is built from the association of sensory impressions, while George Berkeley analyzed the ways that visual perception is learned through experience and David Hume investigated the types of associations that lead to new knowledge. Finally, the nineteenth-century British philosopher John Stuart Mill declared that psychology was ready to become a natural science that could be used to improve individual lives and society as a whole.

Table 1.1 Various Positions on the Mind-Body Problem

Dualism	The body belongs to the physical world, and the mind belongs to the spiritual world.
Interactionism	The physical body and the spiritual mind interact with each other.
Parallelism	The physical body and the spiritual mind run in parallel without interaction.
Monism	The body and the mind belong to the same world, either physical or spiritual.
Materialism	Only the physical world exists, so the mind is physical as well as the body.
Idealism	Only the spiritual world exists, and the physical world is nothing but a perception.
Double-aspect monism	The physical and spiritual are two facets of the same universal substance.

DISCUSSION QUESTIONS

1. What are the two main branches of philosophy? What sorts of questions does each ask?

2. Discuss the difference between rationalism and empiricism, clarifying the assumptions that usually go along with each position.

3. Discuss the similarities and differences among the Ancient Greek philosophers Socrates, Plato, and Aristotle.

4. Discuss the contributions to psychology made by the Islamic philosophers Al-Kindi, Avicenna, and Averroes.

5. Discuss the similarities and differences among the Continental Rationalists Descartes, Hobbes, Spinoza, Leibniz, and Kant.

6. Discuss the similarities and differences among the British Empiricists Bacon, Locke, Berkeley, Hume, and Mill.

7. Compare and contrast systems of thought between the Continental Rationalists and the British Empiricists.

8. Explain Descartes's method of doubt and how it led him to Cartesian dualism. What are the strengths and weaknesses of this approach?

9. Discuss the motivations behind the responses that Spinoza, Hobbes, Leibniz, and Berkeley made to Cartesian dualism.

10. Compare and contrast the various solutions to the mind-body problem offered in this chapter. What sorts of assumptions underlie each position?

11. Explain the concepts of free will, determinism, and compatibilism. For each of the philosophers discussed in this chapter, make an inference about which position he or she would support, providing evidence for each inference.

12. Among all the philosophers we met in this chapter, whose ideas resonated most with your worldview? Explain.

ON THE WEB

You can find plenty of video clips on YouTube that discuss the ideas of each of the philosophers we met in this chapter. These videos are of variable quality, so watch with a skeptical eye. The 2009 movie *Agora* about the life and death of Hypatia may be available on internet streaming services. Keep in mind that this is a fictionalized account, but you can judge for yourself whether the themes are relevant to modern society or not. If you'd like to get a taste of modern philosophy of the mind, watch videos by **Marvin Minsky**, **John Searle**, **Daniel Dennett**, and **Patricia Churchland** on YouTube and TED Talks.

Nineteenth-Century Foundations

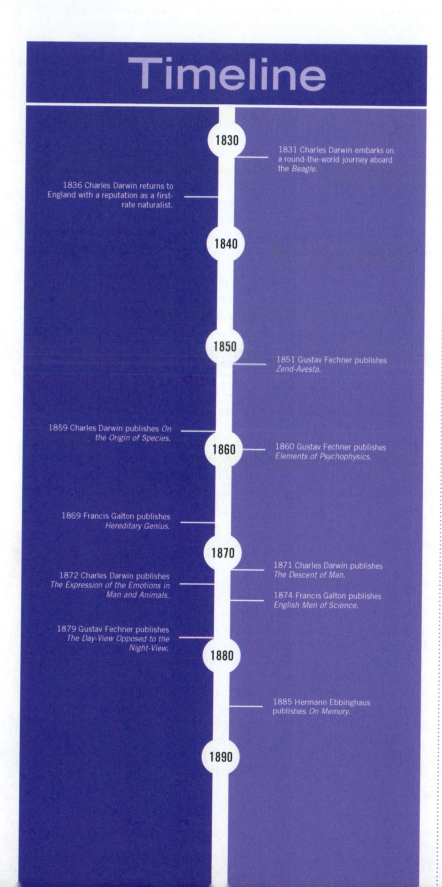

Timeline

1830

1831 Charles Darwin embarks on a round-the-world journey aboard the *Beagle*.

1836 Charles Darwin returns to England with a reputation as a first-rate naturalist.

1840

1850

1851 Gustav Fechner publishes *Zend-Avesta*.

1859 Charles Darwin publishes *On the Origin of Species*.

1860

1860 Gustav Fechner publishes *Elements of Psychophysics*.

1869 Francis Galton publishes *Hereditary Genius*.

1870

1871 Charles Darwin publishes *The Descent of Man*.

1872 Charles Darwin publishes *The Expression of the Emotions in Man and Animals*.

1874 Francis Galton publishes *English Men of Science*.

1879 Gustav Fechner publishes *The Day-View Opposed to the Night-View*.

1880

1885 Hermann Ebbinghaus publishes *On Memory*.

1890

Learning Objectives

After reading this chapter, you should be able to:

- Outline Darwin's theory of natural selection and the historical context in which he developed it.

- Identify and evaluate the contributions Francis Galton made to the development of psychology as an empirical science.

- Explain the importance of psychophysics as a foundation for experimental psychology.

- Discuss the work of the early experimental psychologists Hermann von Helmholtz, Christine Ladd-Franklin, and Hermann Ebbinghaus.

Looking Back

The 1800s could be called the "Century of Polymath." A **polymath** is *a scholar who makes important contributions to several different fields*. Sometimes the term "Renaissance man" is used, and certainly great men of the Renaissance, such as Leonardo da Vinci (1452–1519) and Galileo Galilei (1564–1642), come to mind.

But there was something about the nineteenth century that enabled scientists with talent and ambition to excel in multiple disciples. For one thing, travel and communication had become easier. Books and letters could be distributed around the world, and travel to other lands for meetings or study was now within the reach of many scholars. For another thing, the natural sciences were still young, and there was less material to master before you could make an original contribution.

In this chapter, our story focuses on two countries, England and Germany. These two nations drove the phenomenal growth of science and technology in the nineteenth century. Yet they each had a different model for doing science.

The German system is more familiar to modern readers. Germany had developed a network of research universities in which professors were paid to do research and train graduate students. In other words, the scientist was an employee of the university whose job was to do science. Moreover, "science" had a broader meaning in German than it did in English—German scientists were seekers of new knowledge, whatever that may be.

In England, the situation was quite different. There were only two major universities in the entire country—Oxford and Cambridge—and both were dominated by the Anglican Church. Although there was some research going on at "Oxbridge," the role of the professor was to provide a well-rounded education to the next generation of the British upper class.

Thus, there were few paid positions for scientists in England. Instead, science was a hobby for those with the financial means to support their interests. Those without independent means could join the clergy as one route to fund a research career. A parson's duties were light, and the job provided a comfortable living. Since his father didn't approve of his "beetle collecting" at first, Charles Darwin thought he might have to take this route.

Most British "men of science" were financially secure. They had the leisure to do research and the funds to pay for their expensive hobbies. As we'll see, both Darwin and his cousin Francis Galton were members of a wealthy extended family, and each pursued his career as a gentleman-scientist.

Despite the two different approaches to research, scientists in England and Germany laid the groundwork for an experimental approach to psychology. And generally speaking, they helped build a scientific psychology only after first making significant contributions in the natural sciences. The nineteenth century was indeed the century of the polymath.

Charles Darwin

Charles Darwin was the son and grandson of doctors, so it was assumed he'd follow in the family tradition (Dewsbury, 2009). But young Charles didn't like studying medicine at Cambridge. Instead, he passed the time playing cards and riding horses. He also picked up the hobby of collecting beetles, which was something of a fad among Cambridge students back then. Seeing his son's interest in specimen collecting, Charles's father suggested he study for the Anglican priesthood. That way, Charles could earn his keep and still have plenty of time for his hobby. And so that's what he did.

After graduation, however, one of Darwin's teachers recommended him for the position of naturalist on board the *Beagle*, which was embarking on a five-year exploratory mission around the world (Burghardt, 2009). His job entailed keeping the captain company and collecting specimens of plants and animals to send back to England from the places they visited. Against his father's wishes, Darwin accepted the unpaid position. The specimens Darwin sent back astounded scientists in England, and when he returned in 1836, he found that his reputation as a first-rate naturalist had preceded him. Darwin's father was also impressed by the accomplishments of his ne'er-do-well son, and he established an investment portfolio so his son could live as a gentleman-scientist.

Although we now know **Charles Darwin** (1809–1882) as a *nineteenth-century English scientist who proposed the theory of evolution by natural selection*, he already had a brilliant career as geologist, naturalist, and world traveler long before he proposed his famous theory (Dewsbury, 2009). In fact, when he sailed from England in 1831, Darwin still accepted the Biblical story of creation. But after his experiences traveling around the world, he came to realize that tale just couldn't be true.

Photo 2.1
Portrait of Charles Darwin

Two Questions

In the early nineteenth century, most scientists assumed there was no conflict between science and religion (Burghardt, 2009). They generally accepted the Genesis account that God had created the Earth with all its plants and animals around 6,000 years ago in their current state. In other words, the ways things are now was the way they'd always been.

As scientists looked closely at the world, however, they found anomalies that appeared to contradict Genesis (Burghardt, 2009). For example, geologists observed seashell fossils in rocks far from the ocean. And naturalists discovered remains of animals that had gone extinct long ago. These anomalies were explained in terms of a theory known as **catastrophism**. This is *the idea that the Earth's geological features were formed during a small number of major cataclysms during the last few thousand years.* In particular, it was believed that the Great Flood could explain these oddities. The rising waters washed seashells to the mountaintops, and any animals not on board Noah's Ark were of course drowned in the flood.

However, some scientists were already beginning to question the accuracy of this account (Burghardt, 2009). In particular, they asked two questions:

- Is the Earth young or old?

- Do species change or remain the same?

Biblical scholars interpreted the Bible as saying that the Earth was young and that species were immutable. Yet the accumulating geological and fossil evidence suggested otherwise.

Among the doubters was **Charles Lyell** (1797–1875), an *early nineteenth-century geologist who argued that the Earth was very old* (Dewsbury, 2009). In his 1830 book *Principles of Geology*, he presented his theory of **uniformitarianism**, which is *the idea that the Earth's geological features were formed gradually over hundreds of millions of years through uniform processes still occurring today.* According to Lyell, the surface of the Earth was built up by volcanos and earthquakes and worn away by erosion from wind and water. Darwin read the *Principles of Geology* on board the *Beagle*, and the geological formations he encountered during his voyage accorded with Lyell's descriptions. While in South America, he even experienced an earthquake that changed the local landscape. By his return to England, he was convinced that the Earth was very old and that its features had changed slowly over time (Figure 2.1).

During his voyage on the *Beagle*, Darwin also became a convert to another theory, this one about biology rather than geology (Buss, 2009). When he left England, he still subscribed to **creationism**, which is *the idea that the various species existing today were created in their present form.* However, evidence from fossils suggested that species had changed over time, with some going extinct while others arose anew, and several theories of evolution had already been proposed to explain these observations. The term **evolution** refers to *the idea that species change over time as they adapt to new environments and challenges.* In fact, Charles's grandfather Erasmus Darwin (1731–1802) had proposed just such a theory.

At the time, the most widely accepted account of speciation was the one developed by French naturalist Jean-Baptiste Lamarck (1744–1829; Burghardt, 2009). Known as

Figure 2.1   Voyage of the *Beagle*

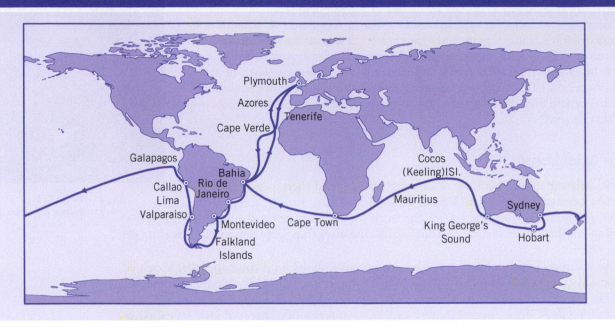

Lamarckism, this was *a theory of evolution proposing that characteristics acquired during an organism's lifetime can be passed on to its descendants*. For example, it was believed that giraffes had evolved from earlier deer-like creatures. But how did they get such long necks? The Lamarckian explanation was that the first generation stretched their necks slightly to reach leaves on higher limbs. Their offspring were then born with slightly longer necks, which they stretched even more. In this way and through many generations, giraffes acquired the long necks they have today. Although still a doubter of evolution when he departed on his journey, Darwin changed his mind as his careful study of plant and animal specimens around the world convinced him that some sort of evolution had to be taking place. And since he was already a convert to Lyell's uniformitarianism, there certainly was plenty of time for Lamarckian evolution to have occurred.

Natural Selection

After his return to England, Darwin continued thinking about the evidence for evolution he'd observed during his travels and in the specimens he'd sent back (Burghardt, 2009). He was amazed by the seemingly infinite variety of life forms, and he was also impressed by how well each species was suited to the environment it inhabited. In his notebooks, he drew diagrams and jotted down ideas as they came to mind. Traditionally, naturalists had organized species according to a Ladder of Life, with the least developed creatures at the bottom and humans, of course, at the top. However, Darwin began to think in terms of a Tree of Life. All currently existing species were like the leaves on a tree, but if you traced the history of each species, you would eventually find that all of them had evolved from a single life form in the distant past.

Still, there was the question of what drove species to change (Buss, 2009). One piece of the puzzle clicked into place when Darwin read *An Essay on the Principle of Population*, which the English economist Thomas Malthus (1766–1834) had published in 1798. According to Malthus, poverty was inevitable because a population would always grow beyond its ability to produce food. When food was scarce, there would be a struggle for existence, and only the strongest would survive the inevitable famines, wars, and plagues. Although Malthus was specifically talking about human populations, Darwin understood the same principles would apply to species living in the wild.

Darwin found another piece of the puzzle in the practices of plant and animal breeders (Darwin, 1859/2002). For example, there are many breeds of dogs, each with certain characteristics. Some are good at hunting, while others are good at herding. But to preserve those traits, you have to in-breed the animals. Through the process of **artificial selection**, or *the intentional breeding of desired characteristics in domestic animals and plants*, you get future generations with even stronger traits—better hunters or herders. In fact, all domesticated plants and animals have been intentionally bred to produce the tangiest peaches and the tastiest tomatoes, the fattest pigs and the fastest horses.

Putting these pieces together, Darwin came to understand that species are constantly adapting to their environments through a process he called **natural selection** (Dewsbury, 2009). This is *a theory of evolution proposing that individuals which are better suited to current circumstances are more likely to survive and reproduce*. The theory of evolution by natural selection has three interlocking components:

- *Variability*: individual members of a species range widely in a large number of characteristics.

- *Competition*: in any population, far more offspring are born than can survive to maturity, so there's a constant competition for resources.

- *Heritability*: those individuals which survive to reproduce will pass on their advantageous features to the next generation.

In this way, species are reshaped over time in response to environmental changes (Figure 2.2).

Figure 2.2 Darwin's Finches

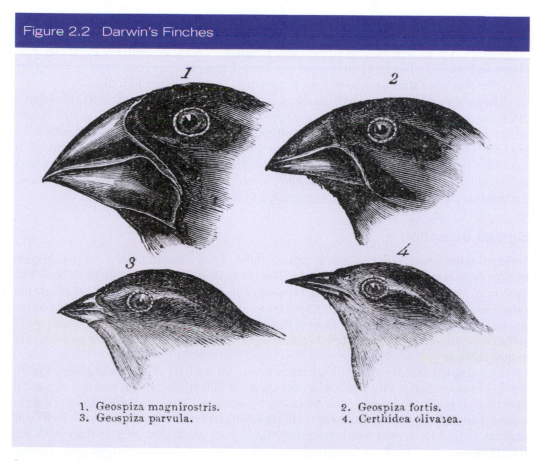

1. Geospiza magnirostris.
2. Geospiza fortis.
3. Geospiza parvula.
4. Certhidea olivasea.

Source: John Gould, from "Voyage of the Beagle," via Wikimedia Commons.

For two decades, Darwin struggled to fit the pieces of evolution together (Dewsbury, 2009). Although he published widely on other subjects in the meantime, he presented nothing about natural selection to the public. However, he did circulate a number of manuscripts outlining his ideas to his close colleagues, so it was generally known in scientific circles what problem Darwin was working on and which direction his thinking was headed.

There were two reasons Darwin hesitated to publish (Dewsbury, 2009). The first, of course, was concern about the response of the religious elite. After all, any theory of evolution would contradict a literal interpretation of the Bible. But that wasn't the most pressing issue, since it was the approval of his scientific colleagues and not the approbation of church officials that Darwin sought. The second, and more important, reason why Darwin delayed publication of his theory was that there was still a missing piece. Namely, he couldn't explain how parental traits were transmitted to offspring. Ironically, the Austrian monk Gregor Mendel (1822–1884) was working out the principles of genetics with his famous pea-plant experiments right around the same time. But Darwin never knew about Mendel's findings.

On June 18, 1858, a letter arrived from Malaysia (Dewsbury, 2009). It was from **Alfred Russel Wallace** (1823–1913), a *nineteenth-century British naturalist who was working on the problem of natural selection around the same time as Darwin.* Although Wallace didn't use Darwin's terms, and his theory wasn't fleshed out in as much detail, the essential principles were the same. Darwin was distraught that he hadn't established his priority by publishing sooner. But he was an honest man, and he gave Wallace's essay to Charles Lyell, who by now had become a dear friend. Lyell arranged a joint reading of Wallace's essay with one of Darwin's manuscripts at the Linnean Society the following month, even though neither Wallace nor Darwin was in attendance. Wallace was still abroad, and Darwin was mourning the death of his baby son.

During the following year, Darwin assembled his various manuscripts into the work he's best known for today, his 1859 book *On the Origin of Species* (Burghardt, 2009). In this volume, Darwin laid out his theory of evolution by natural selection, making the case by analogy to artificial selection. He also supported his argument with ample evidence from his *Beagle* collection as well as from farmers and hobbyists who selectively bred domesticated plants and animals. The first edition sold out immediately, and the book became a popular bestseller that went through six editions. It continues to be widely read today.

The religious backlash wasn't nearly as severe as Darwin had anticipated (Dewsbury, 2009). In part, this was because the idea of evolution was already familiar to educated British audiences, which had an overall favorable attitude toward scientific progress and were willing to interpret Genesis as allegory rather than history. Additionally, Darwin was careful in the *Origin* not to discuss the evolution of humans. That way, he wouldn't offend readers who were willing to accept that other species had evolved even if humans had not. Nevertheless, the implication of human evolution was evident to anyone willing to consider it.

Sexual Selection

Perhaps emboldened by the positive reception of the *Origin*, Darwin fleshed out his ideas on human evolution in two additional books (Shields & Bhatia, 2009). In his 1871 book *The Descent of Man*, he openly argued that humans evolved from earlier primates through the same process of natural selection that applied to all other species. However, he also introduced a new type of evolutionary process that he called **sexual selection**. This is *a theory of evolution proposing that traits can be selected through competition for mates and the preferences of mating partners.*

The classic example of sexual selection is the tail feathers of peacocks (Buss, 2009). The extravagant feathers that male peacocks sport are difficult to explain in terms of natural selection. After all, the bright colors are easy for predators to spot, and the excessive weight makes it difficult for them to escape. According to natural selection, peacocks with big bright feathers should have died out, leaving only those with small dull ones to mate with the female peahens. But that's not what happened. As it turns out, peahens are very picky about who they mate with, and only peacocks with the gaudiest tail feathers will do as father for their baby peachicks. Of course, it doesn't matter what peahens prefer if the best and brightest peacocks have already become somebody else's dinner. Instead, the brightly colored tail feathers serve as an honest signal of health and strength. It's almost as if the peacocks were saying: "Look at me! Even with my big heavy tail, I can still escape any predator. I'm just that good!" Apparently, peahens find that very sexy.

Examples of sexual selection abound in nature (Shields & Bhatia, 2009). The horns or antlers of many male quadrupeds developed in this way. Likewise, the males of many songbird species are brightly colored to attract mates, while the females are drab to avoid predation. Horns and coloration serve the same purpose as peacock tail feathers. Darwin believed that many of the sex differences we see in humans, such as the contrast in body shape and size, are due to sexual selection.

Photo 2.2
Peacock tail feathers

In 1872, Darwin published *The Expression of the Emotions in Man and Animals* (Hess & Thibault, 2009). In *Origin* and *Descent*, he'd focused mainly on the natural selection of physical traits. However, in this third book he emphasized the idea that natural selection can shape behaviors as well. He introduced this idea by exploring the various ways mammals display emotions, showing that they're quite similar from one species to another. Consider your relationship with your pet dog: Can you read her emotions from her facial expressions? And can she read yours? Most dog owners have deep emotional bonds with their pets.

Darwin argued that facial expressions of emotion evolved from behaviors that typically accompany that emotion (Hess & Thibault, 2009). Imagine a bug has just flown into your mouth. What do you do? You purse your lips, protrude your tongue, and spit the damned thing out. And how do you feel? Most people will say "disgusted." Now imagine your friend is telling you about a recent trip to Beijing, where he ate a local delicacy—deep-fried scorpions on a stick. If this sounds disgusting to you, pay careful attention to the facial expression you're making right now—pursed lips, protruding tongue, almost spitting. Your facial expression of disgust mimics the behaviors you would engage in to remove something disgusting from your mouth.

The full impact of Darwin's theory of evolution by natural selection wasn't felt until half a century after his death (Buss, 2009). Although Darwin could see that natural and sexual selection were the driving forces behind long-term changes in species, he was always troubled by the fact that he couldn't explain *how* traits were passed on to offspring. At the time, it was assumed that children inherited a mixture of their parents' traits. But if that were the case, each generation should become more homogeneous, and there was no way to explain the variation that can be seen in each generation. In fact, the mechanics of particulate genetics was being worked out around the same time by the Austrian naturalist Gregor Mendel. However, Darwin and his contemporaries never learned of this work. Well into the early decades of the twentieth century, scientists debated the relative merits and weaknesses of Darwinian and Lamarckian evolution.

It wasn't until the 1930s and 1940s that scientists began to see the connection between Darwin's and Mendel's work (Dewsbury, 2009). This led to the **modern synthesis**, which was *an explanation of Darwinian evolution in terms of Mendelian genetics*. In brief, traits are transmitted to offspring by means of the genes that encode them. Over all, you're a mixture of your parents' traits. However, each trait that you have is either from your mother or your father, not a mixture of both. In this way, traits are passed on to the next generation with enough variation for natural selection to do its part. Those with traits suitable to the current environment prosper and reproduce, while those with unsuitable traits do not. Today, we can even read and manipulate these genes, creating a genetic selection process far more efficient than nature could ever have devised.

In sum, Darwin's work provided important conceptual foundations for a scientific psychology. After all, rats running mazes and pigeons pecking keys would tell us nothing about human behavior if they didn't have nervous systems that were evolutionarily related to those in humans. Darwin's demonstration that humans evolved from primate ancestors and that all species have a common origin in the distant past greatly motivated the development of experimental psychology in the late nineteenth century. Darwin's theory has also forced us to rethink our position in the world and our relationship with it. No longer were we the special product of divine creation, graced with an immortal soul and striving for redemption in an afterlife. Instead, we were creatures of this world, caught in the struggle for survival and striving to pass our traits to the next generation.

Photo 2.3
Francis Galton

Francis Galton

Francis Galton and Charles Darwin were cousins (Fancher, 2009). Both were grandsons of Erasmus Darwin, Charles on his father's side and Francis on his mother's side. The extended Darwin family was financially well off and extraordinarily talented, and many of Erasmus's descendants—both men and women—had notable careers in a variety of fields. As one of the great polymaths of this period, **Francis Galton** (1822–1911) gained his fame as a *nineteenth-century English scientist who developed data gathering and analysis methods and who coined the term "nature and nurture."*

Excellence was simply expected in the Darwin-Galton extended family, but young Francis especially looked to his older cousin Charles as a role model (Fancher, 2009). In his youth, Darwin had made a name for himself as a world traveler, writing about his adventures for the popular press. After that, he'd settled into the career of a gentleman scholar, rising to eminence as a man of science. Galton was determined to pursue a similar life course for himself. In his early adulthood, he personally financed an exploratory expedition to Africa. On his return to England, he published popular and scientific accounts of his travels, thus establishing himself as a public figure and distinguished scholar. Although they corresponded and visited occasionally, there was no collaboration between the cousins, as their scholarly interests had little in common.

Galton and Darwin also differed in their personalities and work habits (Fancher, 2009). On the one hand, Galton excelled at mathematics, whereas Darwin had always been weak with numbers. On the other hand, Darwin was a methodical worker who patiently gathered overwhelming evidence before stating his case, while Galton quickly jumped to radical conclusions from relatively meager data. Thus, Galton can be considered the more controversial of the two.

Galton's "Religious" Conversion

Well into his late thirties, Galton jumped from topic to topic without a coherent research plan (Fancher, 2004). But all that changed when he read Darwin's *On the Origin of Species*. Before that, he had been a devout Anglican who believed in Genesis as historical fact. When Galton read *Origin*, though, he had something of a religious conversion. Rejecting the darkness of religion and reveling in the light of evolution, Galton decided to devote his career to applying the principles of natural selection to the benefit of humankind.

As already mentioned, the extended Darwin-Galton family displayed exceptional talent, and Galton noticed that talent seemed to cluster in other families as well (Fancher, 2004). Gathering data from an encyclopedia of eminent men in British history, he performed a statistical analysis to demonstrate that intellectual eminence clustered in families to a greater extent than would be expected by chance. Applying Darwinian logic to the problem, Galton came to the conclusion that intelligence must be a trait that can be passed down from parents to offspring. Galton published this analysis in an article in 1865, but he knew the data were too meager to be convincing. So he extended his investigations to include the family relationships of current eminent men. This led to the publication of his book *Hereditary Genius* in 1869.

The book was remarkable not only for its content but also for the statistical methods Galton developed to analyze his data (Fancher, 2009). Influenced by the Belgian statistician Adolphe Quetelet (1796–1874), who'd demonstrated that inherited physical traits such as height and weight ranged along a "bell curve," Galton asserted that psychological characteristics such as intelligence must be normally distributed as well. This was the first application of a normal distribution in a psychological study. Galton also demonstrated that the inheritance of features—whether physical or psychological—was a matter of probability and not certainty.

Galton believed that science could be used to improve the human condition, and he wasn't satisfied with simply explaining how the inheritance of intelligence worked (Simonton, 2003). Rather, he wanted to apply this knowledge to increase the overall intellectual capacity of humankind. If humans were subject to the laws of natural selection, Galton argued, then they were also amenable to artificial selection. He believed that if the most intelligent men married the most intelligent women, and if they bore plenty of children, the average intelligence of the human population would increase over the course of a few generations.

The idea that the human race can be rapidly improved through artificial selection techniques came to be known as **eugenics** (Fancher, 2004). Galton only advocated for *positive eugenics*, which involved the provision of government subsidies to couples of high intelligence to encourage them to have more children. However, some scholars and politicians picked up the idea and called for *negative eugenics*, that is, the elimination of "undesirables" from the population. In the early decades of the twentieth century, many countries, including the United States, enacted eugenics laws that mandated the forced sterilization of criminals and the mentally disabled, and the Nazis carried negative eugenics to its logical conclusion. Although he was an ardent eugenicist, Galton would never have approved of such deplorable measures.

Nature and Nurture

Galton was convinced that intelligence was inherited, but the received wisdom was that education and family environment were far more important factors in developing the intellect (Simonton, 2003). Still, he pressed forward and collected more data. For his next book, he distributed questionnaires to around 200 top British scientists, asking about their upbringing, education, and family relationships with other eminent men. This was the first time a questionnaire had been used to gather data for a psychological study.

In his 1874 book *English Men of Science*, Galton coined the expression **nature and nurture** as *a catchphrase to describe the respective impact of biological inheritance and environmental upbringing on human development* (Simonton, 2003). He conceded that nurture also played a role, but he asserted that biology influenced intellectual outcomes far more than upbringing or education. To this day, the question of the relative contributions of nature and nurture is an important and hotly debated issue in psychology.

Next, Galton turned his questionnaire method to the study of twins (Fancher, 2009). He understood the biological difference between identical and fraternal twins, and he reasoned that identical twins should have very similar levels of intelligence while fraternal twins would be no more similar than any other siblings. He also understood that carefully devised twin and adoption studies could be used to tease out the separate influences of nature and nurture. Today, these are standard techniques in psychology for studying the hereditary and environmental contributions to intelligence, personality, and other traits.

It's obvious that identical twins are more similar to each other than fraternal twins, and likewise with siblings compared to cousins, but Galton puzzled over how to quantify the degree of similarity for any given trait (Fancher, 2004). He found that he could lay out the corresponding values on a two-dimensional

Photo 2.4
Identical twins

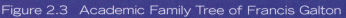

Figure 2.3   Academic Family Tree of Francis Galton

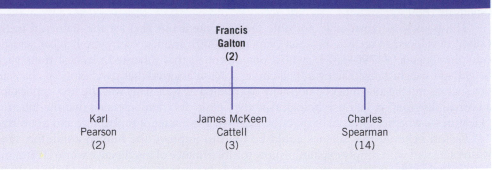

graph, creating what is now known as a scatterplot. A "best-fitting" regression line could then be drawn through the points on the scatterplot, and the slope of the line provided a numerical value for the degree of relatedness ranging from 0 to either –1 or +1. These ideas were then fleshed out by Galton's student **Karl Pearson** (1857–1936), the *British statistician who developed the methods of correlation and regression.* These are still standard statistical techniques for analyzing data in psychology today.

During these years, Galton further developed his thoughts on eugenics (Fancher, 2004). If we could arrange for eminent men and women to intermarry, he reasoned, the average intelligence of the human race would increase. However, there was a problem in that people marry and bear children in early adulthood, but eminence doesn't appear until much later, after people have developed their careers. What was needed was a test of natural ability administered in youth that would predict later accomplishments in life.

Galton assumed that intelligence was a product of brain size and efficiency, so he speculated that measurements of head size, reaction time, and sensory acuity would be good predictors of native intelligence (Fancher, 2004). However, to test this hypothesis, he would need data from lots of people. To this end, he set up an "Anthropometric Laboratory" at London's South Kensington Museum. For a small fee, people could undergo a series of tests that would measure their physical and mental characteristics. The participants got a personal data sheet, and Galton got data on thousands of people. Afterward, Karl Pearson calculated the correlations on these data sets, but he found them to be quite weak. It seemed that simple physical and behavioral measurements weren't good predictors of intelligence after all. Nevertheless, Galton sparked interest among many psychologists in measuring individual differences and in developing tests that would be good predictors of intelligence (Figure 2.3).

In sum, Francis Galton was a great innovator who made significant contributions to the concepts and methods of experimental psychology (Diamond, 1998), as follows:

- *Normal distributions* to describe data

- *Questionnaires* to collect data

- *Nature and nurture* as the interaction of heredity and environment

- *Twin studies* to explore the relative contributions of nature and nurture

- *Scatterplots* to represent correlated data

- *Correlation and regression* to analyze data

- *Test batteries* to assess individual differences

Francis Galton is clearly one of the founders of experimental psychology. He invented many of the research methods and statistical analyses that are a standard part of the psychologist's toolkit today. In this way, he helped lay the foundation for the scientific study of the human mind.

Psychophysics

Inspired by Darwin's theory of evolution by natural selection, Galton developed methods for measuring individual differences and statistical tools for analyzing these data. Meanwhile in Germany, the approach to psychology was undertaken by way of physics and **physiology**, which is *a subfield of biology that studies the processes and functions of living organisms*. In this section, we'll learn about the development of **psychophysics**, which is *the study of the relationship between physical stimuli and the sensations associated with them*. By demonstrating that sensations could be rigorously measured, the psychophysicists demonstrated that psychological phenomena could be studied in a scientific fashion after all, contrary to the sentiments of the day.

Gustav Fechner

In the early 1820s, a series of satirical pamphlets circulated around the campus of Leipzig University in Germany (Marshall, 1987). The essays mocked the foibles and follies of the medical faculty, penned by an unknown author calling himself "Dr. Mises." As it turned out, this Dr. Mises was none other than **Gustav Fechner** (1801–1887), a disgruntled medical student at the university. Although Fechner passed his exams and earned his medical degree, he never practiced medicine. He just didn't have the stomach for it. Today, Gustav Fechner is known by psychologists as the *nineteenth-century German scientist who founded the field of psychophysics*.

After giving up medicine, Fechner wrote a dissertation in philosophy on the concept of "organism," hoping to get a professorship, but none was forthcoming (Marshall, 1990). Instead, he made a living translating physics and chemistry textbooks from French to German. As he translated these books, he also performed the experiments they described so he could understand them for himself. In doing so, he taught himself the natural sciences, and he even published the results of his own experiments in physics. He developed a reputation as an expert on electricity, and occasionally he was called on to teach science courses.

When he was thirty-three years old, Fechner was finally offered a professorship in physics at Leipzig, Germany's premier university (Meishner-Metge, 2010). He'd just gotten married, and now he was financially secure, doing work he loved. So life was good. But Fechner was a workaholic, and the strain of teaching, research, publishing, and editing took its toll. He'd also taken an interest in the study of vision, and in the process he nearly destroyed his own.

Exhausted from overwork and unable to stand bright light, Fechner retreated to his darkened room (Balance & Bringmann, 1987). He stayed there for three years. Although he had only been a professor for six years, the university provided a generous disability pension for the rest of his life. As his health gradually returned, he lectured part-time to show his appreciation for his pension. But he no longer lectured about physics.

During the years of his "mysterious malady," Fechner's thoughts had turned to a new direction—the mind-body problem (Arnheim, 1985). He viewed his convalescence as a spiritual rebirth, and his thinking was imbued with religion, but not of the traditional type. He was impressed by Spinoza's double-aspect monism, in which the physical and the mental were but two views of the same natural world. Accordingly, Fechner took on *the belief that all things in the universe, whether animate or inanimate, have consciousness*, a stance known as **panpsychism**.

In the cumbersome three-volume *Zend-Avesta* that Fechner published in 1851, he laid out his views that the entire universe and everything in it was conscious, from pebbles to plants and from people to planets (Meishner-Metge, 2010). The book was a financial flop. Even more disappointing to Fechner, his colleagues dismissed it as the rantings of a madman, since it accorded with neither orthodox religion nor the materialist worldview. However, near

Photo 2.5
Gustav Fechner

the end of this expansive work, Fechner offers a glimpse of what would become his most important contribution to psychology.

The Weber-Fechner Law

The eighteenth-century German philosopher Immanuel Kant (Chapter 1) had famously proclaimed that psychology would never become a natural science because there was no way to measure mental processes (Adler, 1993). However, Fechner believed he'd found a method for measuring the mind. According to the double-aspect monism he espoused, the physical and the mental were always related. If only you knew the exact relationship between the two, you could measure the mind indirectly by observing its physical correlates. The work of one of his colleagues showed him the way to do this.

Ernst Weber (1795–1878) was a German physiologist best known for his discovery that human sensory systems are limited in their ability to detect differences (Murray, 2000). One phenomenon he studied was the **two-point threshold** (Figure 2.4). This is *a measure of skin sensitivity in which two points are gradually brought closer together until they are experienced as a single point.* Using a compass, Weber found that different parts of the body had different sensitivities. For instance, two points on the back are still felt as a single point at a much greater distance than two points on the palm of the hand.

Another phenomenon Weber studied was the **just-noticeable difference** (JND; Murray, 2000). This is *the amount a stimulus has to be increased or decreased before a change in the stimulus can be detected.* What he found was that the JND increases in proportion to the original stimulus. Imagine we're asking a person to judge the weight of two objects placed in the hand. Let's say the first item weighs 40 grams, the second item weighs 41 grams, and the participant can just notice that the second is heavier than the first. We might say the person has detected a 1-gram difference. However, if we try this again with an 80-gram weight, we'll have to increase the second one to 82 grams before the difference can be detected. Thus, the just-noticeable difference is always a proportion of the original stimulus and not an absolute value (Figure 2.5).

What Fechner saw in Weber's work was a passageway from the physical to the mental (Meischner-Metge, 2010). After all, the distance between two points and the weight of an

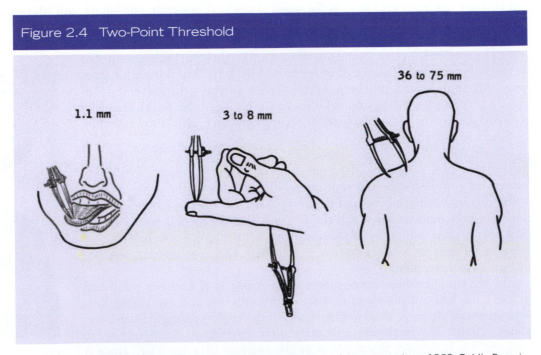

Figure 2.4   Two-Point Threshold

1.1 mm

3 to 8 mm

36 to 75 mm

Source: By House, Earl Lawrence. Pansky, Ben. - A functional approach to neuroanatomy 1960, Public Domain, https://commons.wikimedia.org/w/index.php?curid=30977875.

Figure 2.5 Just-Noticeable Differences

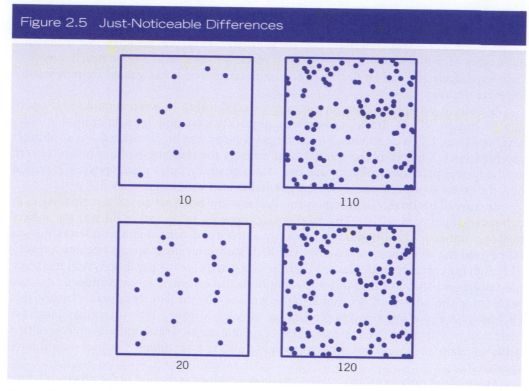

10   110

20   120

Source: MrPomidor via Wikimedia Commons.

object were physical quantities, and yet they were always accompanied by mental sensations. Weber had collected vast amounts of data on the JND, using a wide range of stimuli and testing a variety of sensory modes. *The finding that the just-noticeable difference is always a proportion of the original stimulus* occurred throughout Weber's data, and Fechner dubbed this **Weber's law**.

Working from Weber's law, Fechner derived a mathematical relationship between the physical stimulus and the mental sensation (Adler, 1993). **Fechner's law** is *the proposal that the intensity of the sensation is related by a logarithmic function to the intensity of the stimulus*. In plain English, this means that the intensity of the sensation increases at a much slower rate than the intensity of the stimulus. The classic example of Fechner's law is the perception of octaves in music. Here, the pitch is the sensation and the frequency in Hertz is the stimulus. In modern tuning, the A above middle C (called A_4) is set at 440 Hz. The octave below (A_3) is 220 Hz, while the octave above (A_5) is 880 Hz. In other words, each higher octave doubles in frequency, and yet the perception is that all octaves are equally spaced on the pitch scale.

Thus was born the science of psychophysics, demonstrating that psychological phenomena could in fact be studied in a scientific fashion (Robinson, 2010). Fechner conducted numerous experiments testing various stimuli and sensory modalities to garner evidence for his law. Since Weber's and Fechner's laws are related, most psychophysicists today group them together as the Weber-Fechner law. This foundation of psychophysics remained unchallenged for nearly a century, until the American psychologist S. S. Stevens (Chapter 11) proposed a revision to it now known as Stevens' power law.

Photo 2.6
Ernst Weber

Elements of Psychophysics

In 1860, Fechner published his best-known work, the *Elements of Psychophysics* (Murray, 1990). In this book, he describes the methods of psychophysics that he and others had developed. These methods inspired a generation of experimental psychologists, most notably Wilhelm Wundt (Chapter 3), who established the first psychology laboratory in the world at Leipzig University two decades later. However, Fechner also included a discussion of a distinction between "outer psychophysics" and "inner psychophysics." This was largely ignored by Fechner's contemporaries, but it has gained more relevance in recent decades.

By outer psychophysics, Fechner meant the relationship between stimulus and sensation (Robinson, 2010). Traditionally, psychophysicists have only been interested in outer psychophysics. Likewise, stimulus-response psychology can be considered a part of outer psychophysics. We control the stimulus and measure the response without much concern for the mental processes mediating the two. More generally, outer psychophysics looked at how the external physical world and the internal mental world were related.

Because of his double-aspect monism, Fechner saw brain activity and mental states as correlated (Robinson, 2010). This relationship between brain and mind was the subject matter of inner psychophysics. He certainly understood that such an undertaking was far beyond the technology of his time, but he hoped someday it would become a reality. Although his contemporaries hailed Fechner as a genius for his psychophysical methods, they dismissed his notion of inner psychophysics as eccentric fantasy. Indeed, it's only been since the advent of neuroimaging technology in the late twentieth century that Fechner's dream of inner psychophysics has become a reality. Neuroscientists often say their goal is to find the "neural correlates" of mental states. This emphasis on correlation between brain and mind, as opposed to causation, is a sentiment Fechner would have approved of.

Much of the early experimental research in psychology at the end of the nineteenth century was built on the psychophysical methods Fechner developed (Murray, 1990). However, even in his day, there was a lot of debate about the validity of Fechner's law. While it works fairly well within normal ranges of stimulation, it usually fails at the high and low extremes. From Fechner's time until the present, the debate has largely centered on whether a logarithmic function or a power function better describes the psychophysical relationship between sensation and stimulus.

Incidentally, Fechner claims that his great insight for psychophysics came in a dream on the morning of October 22, 1850 (Murray, 1990). He was still working on the *Zend-Avesta* at the time, and so he tacked it on at the end. Today the date is celebrated as "Fechner Day" by psychophysicists around the world as the inauguration of their field.

For the rest of his life, Fechner continued performing experiments in psychophysics, mainly to address challenges from rivals (Meischner-Metge, 2010). But even though he was a rigorous experimentalist, this doesn't mean he gave up his philosophy of panpsychism. In 1879, he published the book *The Day-View Opposed to the Night-View*, in which he clearly and concisely laid out his reasons for believing the entire universe and everything in it was conscious. By "night-view," Fechner was referring to the atheistic materialism of nineteenth-century science. He believed that such a worldview was far too limiting, as it blinded people from seeing the true beauty of the world. Instead, he called on his readers to "Wake up!" from their slumbers and experience the world from the "day-view" of panpsychism, which revealed the universe in all its splendor.

Scientists adopted atheistic materialism to protect their model of the universe as a closed mechanical system from the threat of orthodox religion (Chalmers, 2014). After all, if miracles can occur, what value do the laws of physics have? But Fechner maintained that his day-view with its Spinozan "God-as-nature" was entirely compatible with empirical science. Few scientists in Fechner's time or in our own have accepted Fechner's panpsychism. However, the idea of a conscious universe is still considered a possibility by some philosophers and scientists.

In sum, Fechner was a pioneer in experimental psychology, establishing methods that would enable a laboratory-based study of the mind (Meischner-Metge, 2010). Fechner molded the shape of late nineteenth-century psychology, influencing the thinking of contemporaries such as Hermann von Helmholtz, whom we'll meet next, as well as nurturing the careers of young psychologists such as Wilhelm Wundt, whom we'll meet in Chapter 3. As a philosopher, Fechner developed a rich theory of universal consciousness, which still has some adherents today. In addition, we shouldn't forget Fechner the prankster as his alter ego "Dr. Mises." He began his literary career as a disgruntled medical student under that pen name. So it seems only fitting that his final publication—a satirical essay about a new fountain in Leipzig—was also signed "Dr. Mises."

Early Experimental Psychology

Until the mid-nineteenth century, it was easy for scientists to simply ignore questions of the mind. According to Descartes (Chapter 1), the universe was divided into two worlds—the physical, which was the purview of science, and the spiritual, which could only be understood through religion and philosophy. However, as physiologists began studying the structure and function of the nervous system, it was only natural that they would broach questions about the relationship between mind and body. In this way, physiology set the stage for psychology.

Hermann von Helmholtz

As the paramount polymath of the nineteenth century, **Hermann von Helmholtz** (1821–1894) made foundational contributions in virtually every field of science (De Kock, 2014). The physicists saw him as one of their own for his work on energy physics and electrodynamics. The mental philosophers recognized him as the great successor to Berkeley and Kant (Chapter 1). And practitioners of the newly emerging experimental psychology hailed him as the founder of their discipline for his work on the physiology of sensation. Helmholtz did employ psychological notions in that work, but he saw psychology as belonging to the realm of philosophy, not natural science. Today we know Helmholtz as a *nineteenth-century German scientist who made important contributions to the physiology of the nervous system and the senses.*

Helmholtz's contributions to early psychology come indirectly through his work in physiology (Turner, 2000). In the 1850s, he studied muscle movement and the conduction of neural impulses. Using a dissected frog leg, Helmholtz measured the speed of electrical transmission in the nerve. Although he found it to be quite fast, this finding contradicted the general assumption that neural conduction was instantaneous or nearly so. The relevance to psychology is the fact that mental processes take time, and so the measurement of reaction time has been an important tool for experimental psychologists since the beginning of the field.

Photo 2.7
Hermann von Helmholtz

Helmholtz then turned his attention to the physiology of the sensory organs, especially the eye and the ear. He was an early advocate of the three-receptor theory of color vision (De Kock, 2014). First proposed by English scientist Thomas Young (1773–1829), this model of color vision argues for three color receptors in the retina—red, green, and blue. Today it's known as the Young-Helmholtz theory. For years, Helmholtz engaged in a bitter rivalry with fellow German physiologist Ewald Hering (1834–1918), who argued that color vision took place through an opponent process—red opposing green and yellow opposing blue. As we'll see shortly, his American student Christine Ladd-Franklin developed an evolutionary theory of vision that incorporated both the three-receptor and the opponent-process theories.

Certainly Helmholtz's greatest contribution to psychology was the modern conceptualization of the relationship between sensation and perception (Epstein, 1991). In the Cartesian worldview that still dominated nineteenth century science and philosophy, thinking about these concepts was muddled. On the one hand, sensation—detecting objects and events

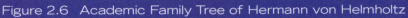

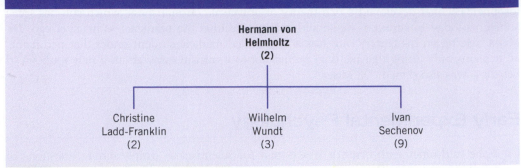

Figure 2.6 Academic Family Tree of Hermann von Helmholtz

in the environment—was a process of the material body. On the other hand, perception—conscious awareness of those objects and events—was a process of the immaterial soul. However, Helmholtz was committed to the materialist worldview from early adulthood, so he snatched perception from the soul and placed it squarely within the brain.

Helmholtz also challenged the received wisdom that perception was an accurate representation of reality (De Kock, 2014). The sense organs have no direct access to objects or events in the environment. Rather, they detect energy—in the form of light or sound, for instance—that's given off by those objects or events. The sense organs convert this environmental energy into nervous energy, which is then transmitted to the brain. Thus, sensation isn't a faithful copy of the original but rather is symbolic of the real world.

Helmholtz argued that perception is a constructive process (Epstein, 1991). Based on previous experience, the brain interprets the sensory input as symbolic of something it's experienced before. Here, he both agrees and disagrees with his intellectual predecessor, Kant, who argued that we construct perception on the basis of innate categories. Helmholtz agrees that perception is a constructive process, but he also maintains that it's learned in infancy, much as Berkeley had argued. The question of which aspects of perception are acquired or innate is still a contentious issue for psychologists in the twenty-first century.

Furthermore, Helmholtz maintained, perception isn't just a passive process of receiving sensory inputs, as was generally believed (Turner, 2000). *Helmholtz's position that perception is a rational process of finding the best interpretation of the sensory input* is known as **unconscious inference**. In other words, we don't have direct access to objects and events in the world. Rather, all we have is elemental sensations such as lights of various colors and brightness, and from this information we make our best guess about what's out there in the world. Thus, perception works just like any other reasoning process, except that it operates entirely at an unconscious level.

Helmholtz's ideas on sensation and perception have had a significant impact on psychology into the twenty-first century. Not all of his contemporaries agreed with his views, but there was a resurgence of interest in Helmholtz with the cognitive revolution during the last half of the twentieth century (Chapter 11). He also inspired those who worked with him (Figure 2.6). As we'll see, he was a mentor for both Hermann Ebbinghaus (next section) and Wilhelm Wundt (Chapter 3). As one of the great polymaths of the nineteenth century, physicists, philosophers, and psychologists all count him as one of their own.

Christine Ladd-Franklin

In the nineteenth century, a woman's place was in the home, and if a woman were ambitious enough to pursue a career, she had to forsake marriage and family (Furumoto, 1992). But Christine Ladd-Franklin (1847–1930) wanted to have it all. Today we know her as the *early American psychologist who developed the modern evolutionary theory of color vision.*

Christine Ladd grew up in an affluent family that encouraged education for its daughters, and several women relatives were active members of the suffragette movement (Furumoto, 1995). After earning a bachelor's degree from Vassar, Ladd was permitted to attend graduate courses at Johns Hopkins as a nondegree-seeking student. Although she completed all the requirements for a Ph.D. in mathematics, the university refused to award her a degree for the simple reason that she was a woman. She did, however, find a husband in her math professor Fabian Franklin, adding his last name to her maiden name.

At that time, marriage spelled the end of a woman's career, but Ladd-Franklin's husband held liberal views about gender equality, and he did all he could to encourage and support his wife's interest in doing research (Furumoto, 1992). For many years, she held an unpaid lectureship at Columbia University, where her husband was on the faculty. Despite the insult of not receiving a salary for her services, the position did provide her access to the university's facilities, which she could use for her research. Although Ladd-Franklin had completed her dissertation on the mathematics of optics, her interest shifted to the physiology of color vision. So when her husband spent his sabbatical year (1891–1892) in Germany, she had the opportunity to work in Helmholtz's lab. During this and other visits to Germany, she conducted the research that resolved the Helmholtz-Hering debate.

Photo 2.8
Christine Ladd-Franklin

As you recall, Helmholtz favored Young's three-receptor theory of red-green-blue color vision, whereas Hering argued that color vision worked through an opponent process that contrasted red with green and blue with yellow (Furumoto, 1995). Ladd-Franklin's solution to this debate was to propose that both theories were correct, in that each described a different stage in visual processing. By applying evolutionary theory to the problem of color vision, she was able to demonstrate how such a two-stage process could have evolved in order to produce the full range of color vision in humans. Ladd-Franklin spent decades promoting her theory by presenting at conferences and publishing theoretical articles. At the time, few of her (almost all) male colleagues were convinced of her solution to the problem, instead preferring to bicker about the relative merits and faults of the Helmholtz-Young three-receptor theory and the Hering opponent-process theory. Nevertheless, her theory aligns well with modern thinking on the mechanics and evolution of color vision, even though her role in its development is often still overlooked.

Despite institutionalized prejudice against women, Ladd-Franklin's accomplishments came to be recognized (Scarborough, 1988). In a 1903 review, she was listed as one of the top fifty American psychologists. Toward the end of her life, she finally got the recognition she deserved. In 1926, Johns Hopkins awarded her doctorate, and an aging Christine Ladd-Franklin attended the ceremony to accept the degree, forty-four years after she'd earned it.

Hermann Ebbinghaus

Young **Hermann Ebbinghaus** (1850–1909) had a Ph.D., but he had no job prospects in his German homeland (Traxel, 1985). So he traveled to England for a couple of years, hoping to brush up on his English while supporting himself by tutoring. He wanted to become a professor at one of the great German research universities, but in those days you had to write two dissertations—one theoretical and another presenting original research—to qualify for a position. Eventually, Hermann Ebbinghaus built his reputation as a *nineteenth-century German psychologist whose memory research demonstrated that higher mental processes could be studied using rigorous experimental methods*.

Ebbinghaus's theoretical dissertation had been a philosophical essay on the nature of memory (Traxel, 1985). But he wondered what kind of research he could do on that topic. Browsing through the second-hand book stalls in London, Ebbinghaus found a copy of *Elements of Psychophysics*. In that book, Fechner had shown that mental processes could

**Photo 2.9
Hermann Ebbinghaus**

be studied experimentally by observing just-noticeable differences in sensory tasks. Likewise, Ebbinghaus would study memory by observing people's behavior in learning tasks.

As Ebbinghaus explored the active use of memory in various situations, he hit upon a laboratory technique that seemed to yield valid measurements of learning and forgetting (Slamecka, 1985). The task involved learning lists of nonsense syllables. For this purpose, Ebbinghaus constructed all possible consonant-vowel-consonant combinations in the German language, about 2,300 altogether, and wrote each on a separate card. He put all the cards into a container, and he drew as many as needed to create a random list. The rationale for using nonsense syllables is that they're largely meaningless. Ebbinghaus knew from his early investigations that meaningful material is more easily memorized than meaningless sequences, and he wanted to eliminate the confounding variable of meaningfulness from his experiments. Incidentally, lists of nonsense syllables are still commonly used in memory research today, and even your humble textbook author used them in his dissertation research.

Ebbinghaus also sought to avoid the creation of incidental meaningful relationships among the list items by reciting them at the steady pace of two and a half syllables per second (Tulving, 1985a). At this speed, he found it impossible to think of anything but the current item, so there was no time left for any memory-enhancing strategies. He would read the list several times, repeating it until he could recite it smoothly and error-free from memory. According to his reports, the procedure was tiresome, and it often gave him a headache. In collecting his data, he memorized thousands of lists over tens of thousands of trials. There's no question about Ebbinghaus's dedication to his research program.

Ebbinghaus's famous forgetting curve is a staple in introductory psychology classes (Slamecka, 1985). He'd memorize a list and put it away for a predetermined period of time. Then he'd test himself to see how much of the list he remembered, finding that recall of the list decayed steeply at first but then tapered off. However, this wasn't his main finding. After all, any college student already knows the forgetting curve from personal experience. You cram for the test, but most of the knowledge is gone shortly after handing in your exam paper.

For Ebbinghaus, a more important phenomenon was what's called **savings during relearning** (Nelson, 1985). This is *a process that occurs when a person learns something, forgets it, but then learns it again at a faster rate*. You've no doubt experienced this as well. Let's say you took Spanish in high school. Since then, you feel you've forgotten everything you learned, but now that you're on vacation in Mexico, those words and expressions are coming back. Ebbinghaus understood that active recall is a conscious process, but with the savings-during-relearning technique he could examine unconscious memory.

To measure savings during relearning, Ebbinghaus first studied a list until he could recite it perfectly, counting the number of trials (Nelson, 1985). He set it aside for a given time, and then he relearned it a second time. This usually took fewer trials, and this was the savings during relearning. He also found that each subsequent relearning accrued even greater savings. When he used this technique with stanzas of poetry, he had the poem permanently memorized after a few relearning sessions. This was the first demonstration of the effectiveness of distributed practice over massed practice. For example, it's more effective to study a little each day rather than cram the night before the exam. (I know, you still cram anyway.)

In 1880, Ebbinghaus presented his early data in the form of a research dissertation, with Hermann von Helmholtz as the dissertation adviser (Bringmann & Early, 2000). This got him a part-time lectureship at Berlin University. But he kept collecting data with himself as the only subject. He published his book *On Memory* in 1885, after which Berlin University offered him an untenured professorship. He later accepted a tenured position at a provincial university, but with a heavy teaching load he had little time for research. Or maybe he was just tired of memorizing lists.

Although Ebbinghaus had few graduate students to carry on his legacy, his work nevertheless inspired generations of psychologists (Bahrick, 1985). In the late nineteenth century, introspection, or self-report, was still the gold-standard technique of psychology. However, Ebbinghaus had shown that the experimental rigor of the natural sciences could be applied to psychology as well. Ebbinghaus's work was much praised during his lifetime, and it's still held up as the benchmark for rigor in experimental psychology.

Looking Ahead

In the middle of the nineteenth century, scientists from England, Germany, and other countries laid the groundwork for a scientific psychology. In England, Darwin convinced us, with his theory of evolution, that humans are also part of the natural world and therefore an appropriate subject for a nature science. Meanwhile, Galton established methods for studying individual differences and the role of nature and nurture in development. In Germany, Fechner and Helmholtz showed that mental processes could be measured with the methods of psychophysics and physiology. And then Ebbinghaus pushed the envelope, demonstrating that even higher mental functions like memory could be studied with rigorous experimental methods.

During this time, psychology began taking shape. Of course, these pioneers weren't psychologists by training. Rather, they were eminent researchers in other fields who also had interests in psychology. These polymaths applied methods from their original fields to study human behavior and mental processes, often with no clear intention of creating a new science of the mind. But when they applied rigorous experimental procedures to important questions in psychology, they got meaningful answers in return. Early successes encouraged these proto-psychologists to journey even deeper into uncharted territory.

Many of the research methods developed during the nineteenth century are standard procedures of the experimental psychologist in the twenty-first century. Darwin's comparative methods are the stock in trade for animal research, and they inspired the development of evolutionary psychology in the late twentieth century. Galton taught us how to gather data and analyze them with the proper statistics. Fechner's psychophysics is an active area of research today, and the questions he posed are still debated. As we'll see in Chapter 11, the mid-twentieth-century psychologist S. S. Stevens continued Fechner's line of research, proposing a revision to the Weber-Fechner law that is now called the Stevens power law. Likewise, Helmholtz and Ebbinghaus have had a great influence on modern psychology, especially in the fields of cognitive psychology and neuroscience.

The groundwork had been laid, but no single edifice of experimental psychology was built upon it. As we'll see in Part II, experimental psychology fractured into several competing schools. Each had its pet questions and favored methods. And each saw itself as the "true" experimental psychology. Many psychologists toed the line of their favorite school, but some—the truly great thinkers—rose above the divisiveness to see the strengths and weaknesses of each approach. It was also open-minded thinkers who reunified psychology after World War II.

In the next seven chapters, we'll get acquainted with the different schools of psychology that arose around the turn of the twentieth century. In Chapter 3, we learn about Wilhelm Wundt and the first systematic approach to studying the mind. In Chapters 4 and 5, we consider two early American schools, functionalism and behaviorism. We then return to Germany in Chapter 6, where we encounter a group calling themselves Gestalt psychologists. In Chapter 7, we move to Austria, where we meet Sigmund Freud and the psychoanalysts. After that, we go the French-speaking world of France and Switzerland in Chapter 8, where we learn about Jean Piaget, whose work inspired the disciplines of developmental and cognitive psychology after World War II. Finally, we go to Russia in Chapter 9 to explore the unique brand of psychology that Ivan Pavlov and his compatriots developed. Today, each of these schools provides a leg that modern psychology stands on.

CHAPTER SUMMARY

In the early nineteenth century, scientists had come to understand that the story of Genesis in the Bible could not possibly be literally true. Geological evidence demonstrated that the Earth was millions—not thousands—of years in age, and fossil evidence indicated that species of the past were quite different from their current forms. Although several theories of evolution had been proposed, it was Charles Darwin who finally discovered the mechanisms driving it, namely natural and sexual selection. Darwin's cousin Francis Galton experienced a "religious" conversion when he read *On the Origin of Species*, inspiring him to a career of measuring the individual differences among humans that were the raw material for evolution. We credit Galton with developing a number of empirical methods and statistical analyses that are still widely used in psychological research today.

In Germany, the psychophysicists Ernst Weber and Gustav Fechner demonstrated that psychological processes could be studied in an experimental manner, as they mapped out the relationship between physical stimuli and their reported sensations. Hermann von Helmholtz, one of the great polymaths of the nineteenth century, explored the physiology of color vision and developed a theory of perception as unconscious inference. His student Christine Ladd-Franklin furthered this research by developing an evolutionary theory of color vision that resolved a long-standing debate in the field. Extending the work of the psychophysicists, Hermann Ebbinghaus demonstrated the even "higher" mental processes such as learning and memory could be studied in an experimental manner, developing techniques that are still used today.

DISCUSSION QUESTIONS

1. Compare and contrast the British and German models of doing science, considering the advantages and disadvantages of each approach. What is the standard model today?

2. Explain the two big questions that Darwin and his colleagues were wrestling with in the first half of the nineteenth century. How did Charles Lyell and Thomas Malthus influence Darwin's thinking?

3. Explain the differences between Lamarckism and Darwinism, especially with respect to the two metaphors for speciation, the Ladder of Life and the Tree of Life.

4. Discuss the three interlocking components of natural selection and how they work together to produce changes in species over time. Apply these components to the three types of Darwinian selection: artificial, natural, and sexual.

5. Why was Darwin hesitant to publish his theory of natural selection? What was the issue between Alfred Russel Wallace and Charles Darwin, and how did Charles Lyell resolve it?

6. Describe the studies that Galton conducted to test his idea that intelligence is an inherited trait.

7. Discuss the differences between positive and negative eugenics. Contrast eugenics as it was proposed by Galton and the way it was practiced in the early twentieth century.

8. What exactly is meant by the expression "nature and nurture"? Describe the design of a twin study, explaining its rationale.

9. Discuss the development of the Weber-Fechner law and Fechner's distinction between outer and inner psychophysics. Explain how psychophysics is relevant to psychology more generally.

10. What was the controversy between Hering and Helmholtz? How did Ladd-Franklin resolve the dispute? What were the consequences?

11. What is the difference between sensation and perception? Explain what Helmholtz meant by his conceptualization of perception as unconscious inference.

12. Describe the procedure Ebbinghaus used to study memory, considering why he focused on savings during relearning in his experiments. What was Ebbinghaus's impact on psychology?

ON THE WEB

On YouTube, you can find videos describing the lives and careers of the people discussed in this chapter. These videos are of variable quality, so watch with a skeptical eye.

Early Schools of Psychology

B y the middle of the nineteenth century, science was having a clear impact on the Western world. As scientists came to understand the workings of nature, they applied this knowledge to improving the well-being of society. Technology was progressing rapidly, and wealth was being created at an unprecedented pace. It was within this intellectual ferment that psychology was born in the last decades of the nineteenth century. The "great person" in this story is the German physiologist Wilhelm Wundt, who is credited as the founder of experimental psychology because he established the first psychology laboratory at Leipzig University in 1879. However, the idea that the time was ripe for a scientific approach to psychology was clearly part of the "spirit of the times," and soon psychology labs sprang up across the European and North American continents like mushrooms after a spring shower.

From ancient times, philosophers had divided themselves into schools according to their assumptions about the nature of the world and the approaches they adopted to explore it. As an offshoot of philosophy, early psychology quickly congealed into a number of independent schools, each with its unique characteristics. In Part II, we survey a number of these early schools. Chapter 3 provides an overview of structuralism, which had its roots in Wundt's laboratory but was quickly transplanted to North America. Shortly thereafter, two other North American schools emerged as competitors to structuralism, namely functionalism and behaviorism, described in Chapters 4 and 5, respectively. In the German-speaking world, two important rivals to Wundt's approach to experimental psychology were Gestalt psychology and psychoanalysis, and these are the topics of Chapters 6 and 7. Finally, we consider two schools operating outside the mainstream that eventually had a major impact on psychology in the last half of the twentieth century. These are the clinical approach of the French-speaking world (Chapter 8) and a unique style of experimental psychology practiced in the Soviet Union (Chapter 9).

Part II spans the period from the late nineteenth century to the end of World War II. This was a time of great scientific and intellectual progress, but it was also an era of tremendous political and social upheaval. At the midpoint of the twentieth century, much of Europe lay in ruins and a new world order had emerged. The same could be said for psychology, whose contentious divisions into schools gave way to a reorganization of the field by discipline. That will be the topic of Part III.

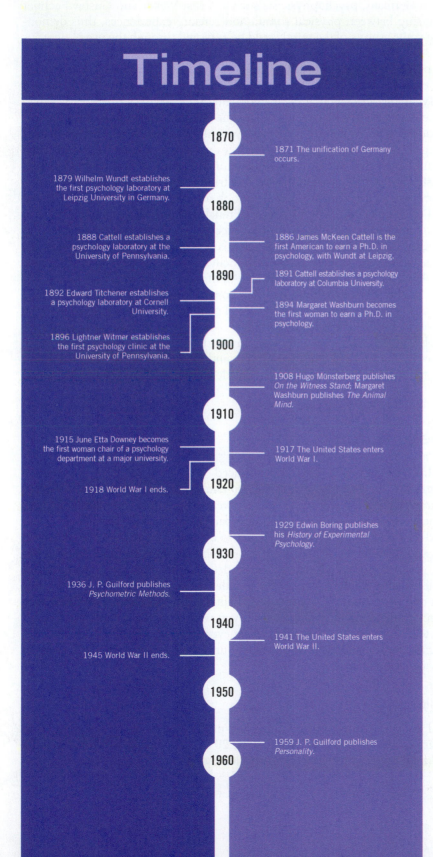

Timeline

- 1871 The unification of Germany occurs.
- 1879 Wilhelm Wundt establishes the first psychology laboratory at Leipzig University in Germany.

1880

- 1888 Cattell establishes a psychology laboratory at the University of Pennsylvania.
- 1886 James McKeen Cattell is the first American to earn a Ph.D. in psychology, with Wundt at Leipzig.

1890

- 1891 Cattell establishes a psychology laboratory at Columbia University.
- 1892 Edward Titchener establishes a psychology laboratory at Cornell University.
- 1894 Margaret Washburn becomes the first woman to earn a Ph.D. in psychology.
- 1896 Lightner Witmer establishes the first psychology clinic at the University of Pennsylvania.

1900

- 1908 Hugo Münsterberg publishes *On the Witness Stand*; Margaret Washburn publishes *The Animal Mind*.

1910

- 1915 June Etta Downey becomes the first woman chair of a psychology department at a major university.
- 1917 The United States enters World War I.
- 1918 World War I ends.

1920

- 1929 Edwin Boring publishes his *History of Experimental Psychology*.

1930

- 1936 J. P. Guilford publishes *Psychometric Methods*.

1940

- 1941 The United States enters World War II.
- 1945 World War II ends.

1950

- 1959 J. P. Guilford publishes *Personality*.

1960

Learning Objectives

After reading this chapter, you should be able to:

- Appraise the contributions of Wilhelm Wundt to the establishment of psychology as an experimental science.

- Evaluate the contributions of Wundt's students, in particular James McKeen Cattell, Lightner Witmer, James Mark Baldwin, and Hugo Münsterberg.

- Critique Edward Titchener's structural approach to psychology.

- Assess the contributions of Titchener's students, in particular Margaret Washburn, Edwin Boring, J. P. Guilford, and June Etta Downey.

Looking Back

By the last half of the nineteenth century, the scientific world was ready for an experimental approach to psychology. Although many philosophers had argued that psychology could never be a science because mental states couldn't be directly observed, John Stuart Mill broke ranks with his colleagues and maintained that the mind could be studied in a scientific fashion. In Germany, psychophysicists such as Ernst Weber and Gustav Fechner studied the relationship between physical stimuli and sensory experiences, thus demonstrating that at least some aspects of the mind could be explored through the use of rigorous scientific methods.

Experimental psychology was born in Germany, an event that was by no means accidental. When we examine the circumstances of the late nineteenth century, it's easy to understand why psychology arose as an independent field of science in Germany rather than in other scientific centers such as France, England, or the United States. First, Germany was only united as a nation in 1871. Before that time, it was divided into a number of smaller states, all competing with the others for dominance over the Germany-speaking world. Each of these smaller states sponsored one or more research institutions, so that when Germany was unified, it boasted a university system that far outstripped any of its rivals.

A second reason was that German researchers took a broader view toward the scope of science than did their European counterparts. In French and British academia, the term "science" was strictly applied only to the natural sciences, such as physics, chemistry, and physiology. From early on, however, German academia recognized a distinction between the natural sciences and the social sciences—which included not only psychology but also sociology, anthropology, musicology, and linguistics. All of these fields were considered scientific, in that their methods were rigorous and their conclusions were based on repeatable observations. The only difference was that experimental methods were only amenable to the natural sciences, not their social counterparts.

In sum, Wilhelm Wundt was a revolutionary in his demonstration that at least some psychological processes, such as perception, attention, and memory, could be studied under laboratory conditions. It's for this reason that we consider him the founder of experimental psychology.

Photo 3.1
Wilhelm Wundt

Wilhelm Wundt

Wilhelm Wundt (1832–1920; pronounced *VILL-helm VOONT*) is generally recognized as the *German physiologist who established the world's first psychology laboratory in 1879*. But for much of the twentieth century, his reputation was tarnished. As a student, I was told his approach to psychology was ill conceived. Trained as a physiologist, Wundt wanted to dissect the mind—to break it into pieces and discover its structure. It was a noble attempt at establishing a scientific psychology, but ultimately doomed to failure. However, newly found documents tell a different story of the founder of our field (Araujo, 2012). They yield a rich description of Wundt's personality and reveal a remarkably modern approach to experimental psychology. If you want to be a psychologist, Wundt would tell his students, you need to forget everything you know (Baldwin et al., 1921). The same can be said if you want to understand Wundt, both as a person and as a psychologist.

Physiological Psychology

Wundt first earned an M.D. degree, but he found the practice of medicine distasteful and he preferred doing medical research instead (Araujo, 2012). He did postdoctoral training with the noted German physiologist Hermann von Helmholtz, which greatly benefitted his career. He also picked up Helmholtz's interest in the psychological aspects of physiology, in particular sensation and perception. However, his relationship with Helmholtz was strained, and Wundt eventually established himself as an independent researcher, supporting himself and his work by writing best-selling textbooks. His most important work from this time was his *Principles of Physiological Psychology* (Wundt, 1873/1912). In this book, he demonstrated how the scientific methods of physiology could be applied to the study of conscious experience, hence the title. He also pointed out the dangers of relying solely on **introspection**, or *the careful observation of one's own mental states*, which was the favored method of psychologically oriented philosophers.

Shortly after he published the *Principles*, Wundt was offered a professorship at Leipzig University, Germany's premier research institution (Benjamin et al., 1992). In 1879, he opened the world's first psychology laboratory, and students from around the world came to Leipzig to learn Wundt's experimental techniques. He also served as mentor to the first generation of experimental psychologists. By the turn of the twentieth century, there were over forty psychology labs in universities across the United States, many of them founded by students who'd learned experimental methods from Wundt or one of his students. The Leipzig facility also set the standard for the modern psychology laboratory. Before, experimental psychology had largely been a one-man operation. But Wundt's lab was a research factory where he directed the activities of a dozen or more graduate students at a time (Baldwin et al., 1921). The lab churned out research reports, and many were published in the journal *Philosophical Studies*, which Wundt established and edited.

Life in the Leipzig Lab

Accounts from Wundt's students give us an intimate view of day-to-day life at the Leipzig lab (Nicolas & Ludovic, 1999). This was the age of **brass instrument psychology**, *an early period in experimental psychology when stimuli were presented and responses were recorded by mechanical means*. Three brass instruments in particular were standard equipment in early psychology laboratories. One was the tachistoscope (pronounced *tuh-KISS-tuh-scope*), which was used to present visual stimuli for brief time periods. Another was the rotating memory drum, which presented visual stimuli at regular intervals. And a third was the gravity chronometer, which measured reaction time to the **millisecond**, or *a thousandth of a second*. Instruments such as these continued to be used in psychology laboratories until well after World War II, when they were replaced by computers performing at similar levels of accuracy. In every respect, the Leipzig lab was state of the art, with many of its instruments even powered by electricity, still rare back then.

By all accounts, there was a high degree of camaraderie among the graduate students as well as a strong sense of mission (Baldwin et al., 1921). Wundt was formal but friendly with his students, and he often invited them to his home for Sunday dinner. But as director of the laboratory, Wundt wasn't involved in conducting experiments. Rather, he assigned research projects to his graduate students, counseled them on the design of their experiments, and checked their progress. He spent his afternoons making the rounds of the laboratory, visiting his advisees at their stations. He listened to their reports, examined their experimental setups, and gave suggestions for improvements. Nowadays, experimental psychologists mainly recruit research participants from introductory psychology classes. But back then, there were no subject pools. Instead, the graduate students served as participants in each other's experiments. In fact, Wundt believed that only those who were trained in psychology could be trusted to give reliable responses.

Two people claim to have been Wundt's first American student (Benjamin et al., 1992). One candidate is G. Stanley Hall (Chapter 4), who spent the 1878–1879 academic year at Leipzig University as a postdoctoral student. Although he claims to have collaborated on some experiments in Wundt's lab, he was never officially one of his students. Rather, his official mentor at Leipzig was the physiologist Carl Ludwig. Hall was a relentless self-promoter, and his claim to have been Wundt's first student, while often repeated even today, is dubious. The

**Photo 3.2
Wilhelm Wundt
in the Leipzig lab**

other candidate is James McKeen Cattell, who earned his Ph.D. with Wundt in 1886. In fact, other Americans had earned a Ph.D. with Wundt before Cattell, but these were in philosophy. Cattell is unquestionably the first American student to earn a Ph.D. in psychology.

In a memorial that Wundt's American students published after his death, Cattell described the warm working relationship he had with his mentor (Baldwin et al., 1921). Wundt was seeking general laws of human mental processes, and so the reaction times of the research participants were averaged to create composite scores. One day, Cattell suggested it might be interesting to study individual differences in reaction time, to which Wundt replied, "*Ganz amerikanish!*"—so American! Back in the United States, Cattell spent much of his academic career studying individual differences. However, Cattell also made a lasting impression on his mentor. He'd brought along a typewriter, a newfangled American invention still unknown in Germany at the time. Wundt was smitten with the device, so Cattell had one sent over for him. After that, Wundt did all his writing at the machine. Years later, other American students commented on Wundt and his two-finger typing. It's been estimated that Wundt averaged two pages a day during his career, and this prodigious output has been attributed to the speed with which he could compose his ideas at the keyboard.

Völkerpsychologie

Wundt understood that the experimental methods he'd developed at Leipzig were of limited application in the study of human psychology (Guski-Leinwand, 2009). These methods were suitable for investigating mental processes within the individual, but Wundt believed a full understanding of humanity could only be obtained by studying how people interact with each other in particular social, cultural, and historical contexts. This field of study, which arose in Germany in the last decades of the nineteenth century, was known as *Völkerpsychologie*, and Wundt was one of its major proponents. Although Wundt expressed an interest in this field from early in his career, it was only during the last twenty years of his life that he turned his full attention to it, producing a series of ten volumes on the subject.

There's been much discussion of how to properly translate the term *Völkerpsychologie* into English (Greenwood, 2003). His student Edward Titchener was the major translator of Wundt's works in the early twentieth century, and he rendered the term as "social psychology." On the surface, this translation is reasonable, but Titchener had only known Wundt in the early days of the Leipzig lab, and he wasn't aware of the full scope of the field. Wundt also protested against the term, since the equivalent German expression, *soziale Psychologie*, referred to sociology, a quite different field. Others have translated the term as "folk psychology," "cultural psychology," or "ethnic psychology," but these expressions can refer to disciplines that have little in common with Wundt's project. Many authors simply keep the term in the original German.

Language and culture are what distinguish humans from all other animals, and understanding the mental processes operating at the group level and over historical time periods was the goal of Wundt's *Völkerpsychologie* (Wong, 2009). Although Wundt was famous for developing experimental methods to test hypotheses about psychological processes within individuals, he recognized that these were inappropriate at the cultural and historical level. This assertion has been a point of misunderstanding for a century. Wundt's American students tended to narrowly view the scientific method as limited to experiments performed in the laboratory. For this reason, they had little interest in what they viewed as their mentor's pastime in old age; as a result, much of his *Völkerpsychologie* remains untranslated even today. However, Wundt thought in terms of the German distinction between natural and social sciences. In his view, individual psychology was a natural science amenable to experimental methods, but *Völkerpsychologie* was a social science that used the methods of naturalistic observation and comparative analysis instead. Both were sciences, even though their methods differed.

In his ten-volume series, Wundt proposed that *Völkerpsychologie* consisted of three major areas of research (Wong, 2009). The first area was language, and Wundt is often credited with being the first psycholinguist. His interests in this area centered on the social aspects of language—how it's acquired and how it's used to organize and guide social behaviors. He called the second area mythology, by which he included the arts, myths, and religion. Finally, the third area was what he called custom, and this included both cultural norms and established laws. Wundt viewed all of these as the mental products of a collective consciousness, which he saw as rising above the individual consciousness of each person but also running in parallel to it. In fact, he saw the three divisions of *Völkerpsychologie*—language, myth, and custom—as the social equivalents of individual cognition, emotion, and intentional behavior.

As we'll see in coming chapters, the cultural-historical approach to psychology flourished in early twentieth-century Europe. For example, Carl Jung was an avid student of culture and mythology, believing these to be the keys to understanding the human psyche. Likewise, Lev Vygotsky emphasized the need to study psychology within its cultural and historical contexts, a point of view that was adopted by many of his colleagues during the Soviet era. In contrast, North American psychologists saw little need for Wundt's *Völkerpsychologie*. No doubt the American emphasis on individualism played a role, as did the strong preference for practical applications over abstract theoretical discourse. Only in recent decades have psychologists on this side of the Atlantic begun to understand the importance of taking the cultural and historical context into account.

Legacy

Wundt's physiological psychology was revolutionary in two respects. First, it proposed a dynamic theory of the mind as a set of mental processes that worked together to create conscious awareness. Second, it provided a rigorous set of experimental techniques for testing hypotheses. Furthermore, Wundt saw psychology as an important experimental science with no need to justify its usefulness.

American culture, however, has always favored the practical over the theoretical. So American students came to Leipzig to learn Wundt's method, and they were less concerned with his theory. They did the master's bidding while in the master's lab, but back in their home country, they turned his methods to practical problems their mentor would never have approved of.

Wundt's legacy to experimental psychology is his set of research methods, but his theory hasn't fared well. First, his American students simply weren't ready for it. Instead, they were more interested in solving practical problems. Although they assumed there were mental processes guiding behavior, their attention just wasn't focused on questions of the mind. Second, Wundt's ideas have been misrepresented. His student Edward Titchener, who translated many of Wundt's works into English, made his mentor's ideas appear more similar to his own than they really were. Furthermore, when Titchener's student Edwin Boring published his *History of Experimental Psychology* (1929), he accepted his mentor's account wholesale. Boring's description of Wundt—warped through the lens of Titchener—was taught to generations of psychology students, your textbook author included.

Wundt's Students

Wundt's legacy was greater in North America than in Germany, where there were few academic positions for freshly minted Ph.D. holders. Even a brilliant scholar like Wilhelm Wundt was forty-two years old before he got his first professorship. Yet the story was quite different in the New World, where the American university system was rapidly expanding. New universities were cropping up across the mid-West and elsewhere, while established institutions were redesigning themselves on the German research model. By the first decades

Figure 3.1   Academic Family Tree of Wilhelm Wundt

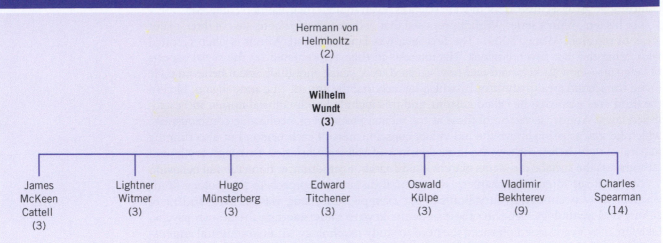

Hermann von
Helmholtz
(2)

Wilhelm
Wundt
(3)

| James McKeen Cattell (3) | Lightner Witmer (3) | Hugo Münsterberg (3) | Edward Titchener (3) | Oswald Külpe (3) | Vladimir Bekhterev (9) | Charles Spearman (14) |

of the twentieth century, most American universities had psychology laboratories, and this expansion was largely fueled by the belief that applied psychology could yield positive improvements for society. As a result, many of Wundt's students—whether American or European—pursued their careers in the United States (Figure 3.1).

Photo 3.3
James McKeen Cattell

James McKeen Cattell

As the son of a wealthy and well-educated family, great things were expected of **James McKeen Cattell** (1860–1944). His father was a college president who pulled strings to get his son the best educational opportunities. Furthermore, his family financed his extensive studies in Europe, including France, Switzerland, and Germany. Cattell spent three years working with Wundt in the Leipzig lab, and the two men had a close working relationship. Recognizing his student's skill in designing and conducting experiments, Wundt made him his assistant. In this capacity, Cattell supervised other Americans working in the lab. Thus, we know James McKeen Cattell as an *early American psychologist who brought experimental methods from Germany and pioneered the field of mental testing*.

As a star student, Cattell also had some influence on his mentor's thinking about experimental methods (Sokal, 1995). Wundt recognized the importance of behavioral measurements such as reaction time in testing hypotheses. Whereas Wundt saw behavioral data as corroborating evidence from introspective reports, Cattell insisted that introspection was too unreliable to be of any value. In Cattell's case at least, Wundt allowed his student to report only behavioral data in his dissertation without also including the standard introspective reports.

After Leipzig, Cattell spent two years as a lecturer at Cambridge University (Sokal, 2009). There, he got to know Francis Galton, who greatly influenced the direction of Cattell's career. At Leipzig, Cattell had toyed with the idea of studying individual differences, but Wundt wouldn't have it. From Galton, however, he got not only encouragement but also a rationale for pursuing the project. As Charles Darwin's cousin, Galton was a strong promoter of Darwinian evolution, and he saw individual differences as the building blocks of natural selection. Cattell visited Galton's Anthropometric Laboratory in London and was impressed by the array of physiological tests used to gather data on human variation. He even suggested some psychological tasks to include in the battery. Cattell may have learned experimental methods from Wundt, but Galton had more influence on Cattell's thinking.

On his return to the United States, Cattell's father arranged a position for him at the University of Pennsylvania, where he established the school's first psychology laboratory in 1888

(Pillsbury, 1947). In 1891, Cattell was invited to establish a new department of psychology at Columbia University. By hiring some of the best experimental psychologists in the country, Cattell built the department into one of the nation's top programs. Under his leadership, more psychology doctorates were awarded at Columbia than any other school in the country.

At Columbia, Cattell set out to replicate and extend Galton's work (Sokal, 1995). He and his graduate students subjected all Columbia undergraduates to two series of test batteries, once as freshmen and again as seniors. Within a few years, they'd amassed far more data, using a wider range of measures, than Galton had ever collected. The goal was to create a mental test—that is, *an indirect assessment of intelligence based on simple measurements such as reaction time and memory span*. As we saw in Chapter 2, Galton's disciple Karl Pearson had analyzed the anthropometric data and found no correlations with other indicators of intelligence. Galton had mainly gathered physiological data such as visual and auditory acuity, but Cattell also collected data on psychological tasks. Furthermore, he made his measures with greater precision than Galton. Cattell had high hopes that his mental tests would be good indicators of intelligence. Still, his results were no different from Pearson's. This failure put an end to Cattell's mental testing program. It also turned Cattell into a bitter man, and he fell into patterns of self-destructive behavior that would eventually sabotage his career.

Cattell had always been a man of strong opinions, which led to a number of altercations with other academics and administrators (Sokal, 2009). First, he'd gotten involved in social-ism during his student years in Germany, but his socialist views weren't well received when he returned to the United States. Second, he was a strong believer in Galton's positive eugenics—and he practiced what he preached. Cattell knew he was from a family of eminence and he married a woman of good stock, with whom he had seven children. However, many American intellectuals favored negative eugenics—or forced sterilization of "undesirables"—and they advocated for the passage of eugenics laws in several states. Cattell opposed such an inhumane approach to population control, thus setting him at odds with his colleagues. Finally, Cattell had idealized the German idea of *Lehrfreiheit*, or academic freedom, which he believed to be the very essence of a university. He was constantly bickering with Columbia's president, who in Cattell's eyes was running the institution like a corporation. At first, his colleagues supported him, but Cattell seemed unable to discern friends from enemies, and he picked fights with allies who then turned against him.

Things came to a head with the U.S. decision to enter World War I in 1917 (Sokal, 2009). Cattell had anti-war attitudes and pro-socialist sentiments. Moreover, his son was a conscientious objector, but conscription policies made no allowances for pacifists. When Cattell sent a letter of protest to Congress, the Columbia administration declared it an act of treason and fired him. Never one to walk away from a fight, Cattell sued Columbia. The university settled out of court by paying him a yearly sum for the rest of his life. With that income, Cattell established the not-for-profit Psychological Corporation, which offered test-ing services for government, corporate, and educational clients. The company floundered under Cattell's leadership but flourished once his partners took control. To this day, Cattell is hailed as a martyr for academic freedom. However, it's important to keep in mind that his attacks on his colleagues also violated their academic freedom. There are no saints in this saga, as both Cattell and Columbia acted recklessly.

Cattell believed that a scientific psychology needed to be built on observations of behav-ior and not speculations about mental processes (May, 1949). Resonating with an American bent toward pragmatism, he always maintained that the goal of psychological research should be to improve the human condition (Figure 3.2). In this way, Cattell set the tone for two American schools of psychology—functionalism, which we'll read about in Chapter 4, and behaviorism, the topic of Chapter 5.

Lightner Witmer

While Cattell was still at the University of Pennsylvania, a student by the name of Lightner Witmer approached him about doing a doctorate with him (McReynolds, 1987). So Cattell gave him a project to work on, but then Cattell got the invitation from

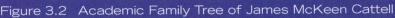

Figure 3.2 Academic Family Tree of James McKeen Cattell

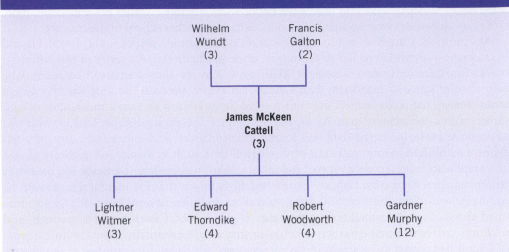

Columbia. Although Witmer could have followed his advisor to New York, Cattell had an even better plan. Witmer would travel to Leipzig for one year to complete his Ph.D. with Wundt and then return to fill the position at Pennsylvania that Cattell vacated. Today we know **Lightner Witmer** (1867–1956) as an *early American psychologist who pioneered the field of clinical psychology*.

Between his two mentors, Witmer was more influenced by Cattell than Wundt (McReynolds, 1996). Like Cattell, he believed that psychological research should be focused on individual differences and have practical applications. Yet he went even further, insisting that psychology should have relevance in individual lives.

One area where Witmer thought psychology might be of practical value was in education, and he offered courses to local schoolteachers (McReynolds, 1987). One such student mentioned a boy in her class with a severe deficiency in spelling. Although the boy did quite well in some classes, he performed poorly in those requiring lots of reading. Witmer invited the teacher to bring the boy to his lab, and this case was a turning point in his career. He interviewed the boy and subjected him to the standard battery of sensory-motor tasks developed by Galton and Cattell. He found the youth to have good reasoning skills and above-average intelligence (Witmer, 1907/1996). He also had strong spoken language abilities, but his spelling difficulties were extreme. Only by slowly sounding out each letter could the boy sometimes discern the word's pronunciation. Today, we'd diagnose this as a case of dyslexia, but the condition was unknown in 1896.

After that, Witmer saw other children with educational difficulties in his lab (Routh, 1996). Looking back, he marked March 1896 as the start of a new field he called clinical psychology. With support from the University of Pennsylvania and private donors, Witmer established the world's first psychology clinic. There, he worked with children who had a wide variety of problems, ranging from dyslexia to speech impediments and from autism to birth defects. He divided these children into two categories. The *mentally retarded* were children who'd been held back in school due to poor performance, whereas the *morally retarded* were those who exhibited behavioral problems. Although these terms are unacceptable today, it's important to understand that he used the term *retarded* in the sense of "developmentally delayed."

At that time, it was generally believed that academic or behavioral problems were due to biological defects (Fagan, 1996). Initially, Witmer accepted this explanation, but as he gained clinical experience, he began thinking more in terms of environmental causes of academic and behavioral problems. He did, of

Photo 3.4
Lightner Witmer

course, understand that brain damage could lead to irreversible mental deficits. However, Witmer believed that most learning difficulties could be remediated. Furthermore, he denied the existence of a so-called "criminal instinct." Instead, he insisted that issues in the home, neighborhood, or school underlay behavioral problems. So he also worked with parents and teachers to make environmental changes to support desired behaviors.

Witmer also set up a curriculum of graduate study to train the next generation of clinical psychologists (Fagan, 1996). These students worked in the clinic as part of their training. This served a practical purpose as well, because the clinic's caseload was rapidly increasing. At first, Witmer and his students used a hit-and-miss approach to treatment. But as they learned from experience what seemed to work, Witmer saw the need for publishing cases and he established the journal *Clinical Psychology*.

With the spread of universal education around the turn of the twentieth century, Witmer had hit upon a practical application of psychology with mass appeal (McReynolds, 1996). If all children were to be educated, then some would need special help. Furthermore, clinical psychology was one area where women psychologists could find work, and Witmer welcomed female students and staff members into his clinic. Many of Witmer's students joined the clinic's staff, while others established similar clinics in other parts of the country.

Over the decades, however, Witmer isolated himself from the rest of the psychology community (Baker, 1988). He had a domineering personality, and he demanded total loyalty from his students and staff. Outside the lab, he was highly critical of psychologists whose approach, in his view, was less scientific than his. At the same time, however, there were few quantitative analyses in any of the case studies published in his journal. In fact, he rejected statistics as dehumanizing. He also believed that intelligence tests told nothing about an individual's true intellect, which he defined as the ability to solve problems.

Witmer strongly believed that psychology should have practical benefits in the lives of ordinary people. After World War II, however, clinical psychology took a direction quite different from what Witmer had envisioned (Taylor, 2000). Today, clinical psychologists mainly work with adults who are experiencing emotional problems or relationship issues, although they sometimes work with children. The field that Witmer and his students developed is now called *school psychology* instead. It's largely through the work of his many students that the idea of psychology as a "helping profession" has become so prevalent today.

James Mark Baldwin

A South Carolina native, **James Mark Baldwin** (1861–1934) was educated at Princeton (Cairns, 1994). He spent a graduate year abroad, including a semester working with Wundt, but he returned to Princeton to complete his Ph.D. in philosophy. For more than two decades, Baldwin was a leader of the new experimental psychology, establishing laboratories at the University of Toronto, his alma mater Princeton, and Johns Hopkins University in Baltimore. He also founded several journals, was one of the charter members of the American Psychological Association, and served as its sixth president. During his career, Baldwin established himself as an *early American psychologist who was a pioneer in the fields of developmental and comparative psychology.*

Baldwin made two contributions that influenced modern psychology. The first was his thinking on evolutionary theory (Wozniak, 2009). At the time, there was a great debate between supporters of Lamarckian and Darwinian evolution. Lamarck maintained that acquired traits could be passed on to offspring, but Darwin's theory of evolution by natural selection stated that only the parents' innate traits could be inherited. Baldwin found a way to synthesize the two approaches. He made *the observation that even though learned behaviors of parents cannot be inherited by offspring, the ability to quickly learn adaptive behaviors can be.* Over several generations, then, the new behavior spreads through the population. Thus, what appears to be a Lamarckian process is in fact Darwinian in nature. This remarkable insight is now known as the **Baldwin effect**.

Photo 3.5
James Mark Baldwin

His second contribution stems from his studies on infant and child behavior. G. Stanley Hall (Chapter 4) had done early survey research on childhood development, but Baldwin was the first to approach developmental questions from an experimental perspective (Wozniak, 2009). He was a pioneer in the study of early childhood cognitive development. Baldwin argued that children's minds develop through a series of mental restructurings as they interact with their environment, especially with the adult caregivers around them. In this way, he laid the groundwork for modern theories of cognitive development as systematized by researchers such as Jean Piaget (Chapter 8) and Lev Vygotsky (Chapter 9).

Baldwin was an ambitious and arrogant man who quickly retaliated against any perceived threat to his position of dominance in psychology (Wozniak & Santiago-Blay, 2013). Although he collaborated with James McKeen Cattell in founding the influential journal *Psychological Review*, they soon became bitter enemies. For a few years, they alternated editorship, but eventually Baldwin bought out Cattell's share to have sole control. He also picked fights in print and in public with other leading psychologists. Over the years, Baldwin made few friends and many enemies.

And then came the fateful event that changed his life forever (Wozniak & Santiago-Blay, 2013). One June evening in 1908, Baldwin went out for a stroll in his neighborhood. As he passed a doorway, a young woman standing outside suggested he come in for a moment. Baldwin later claimed he had no idea it was a "bawdy house," an entertainment establishment with liquor and music on the first floor and ladies for hire upstairs. Baldwin insisted he'd done nothing immoral, which is probably true, since the police raided the joint shortly after he arrived. He was arrested but released without charge. No one else knew about the event, and he told no one. That summer he traveled to Europe. When Baldwin returned to Johns Hopkins in the fall, he met his new colleague, John Watson (Chapter 5), from the University of Chicago. The following year, Baldwin was nominated for a position on the Baltimore School Board. That's when the bordello incident came to light and the Hopkins administration demanded his resignation. Watson assumed directorship of the psychology laboratory and editorship of the *Psychological Review*.

None of Baldwin's colleagues came to his defense (Wozniak & Santiago-Blay, 2013). He'd simply made too many enemies, who now took pleasure in seeing this tall poppy cut to size. Baldwin then moved to Paris. He was quickly forgotten in the United States, but his ideas on genetic epistemology were favorably received in Europe. He befriended the early French psychologist Pierre Janet (Chapter 8), through whom both Piaget and Vygotsky learned about Baldwin's theory of cognitive development. Piaget and Vygotsky are now considered pioneers in developmental psychology. However, it's only been recently that Baldwin's early contribution to this field has been recognized.

Hugo Münsterberg

Hugo Münsterberg was a showman, in life and in death. A flamboyant character who always needed to be the center of attention, Münsterberg was despised by his colleagues and adored by his students. He was also one of America's most popular psychologists—that is, until he became public enemy number one. Today we know **Hugo Münsterberg** (1863–1916) as an early German-American psychologist who was a pioneer in applied branches of psychology.

A wonder child of the new experimental psychology, Münsterberg completed a Ph.D. with Wundt and then earned an M.D. degree as well (Kinlen & Henley, 1997). He got an untenured position at Freiburg University but longed for a professorship. When William James (Chapter 4) offered Münsterberg a three-year appointment at Harvard, he had no better alternative so he accepted. James had set up a psychology laboratory at Harvard, but his heart wasn't in it. He needed someone extraordinary to build a premier lab worthy of the nation's premier university. During his first three years at Harvard, Münsterberg did just that. When his appointment was over, Harvard offered him a tenured position but he still hoped for a professorship back home. Harvard gave him two years to think about it. Münsterberg searched but to no avail, so he returned to Harvard, where he nurtured many members of the next generation of top-tier psychologists, among them Mary Calkins and Robert Yerkes

(Chapter 4) as well as Gordon Allport (Chapter 14), who all expressed admiration for his creativity, vitality, and warmth.

During his first years at Harvard, Münsterberg focused on basic research, but by 1900, his attention had shifted toward applied psychology (Benjamin, 2006). In contrast to basic research, which seeks knowledge for its own sake, **applied psychology** is *a field that uses psychological research to solve practical problems in daily life*. There's a lot of speculation about this shift in interests. On the one hand, Münsterberg just wasn't getting the accolades he thought he deserved, so pure research must have lost its appeal. On the other hand, professors' salaries were low, and there was money to be made in applied research. Early in his career, Münsterberg criticized his American colleagues for their pursuit of practical applications. But once he got into the applied-psychology game, he quickly became the master.

Münsterberg made important early contributions in several applied fields (Landy, 1992). One area was **forensic psychology**, which is *the application of psychological principles to the legal system*. His 1908 book *On the Witness Stand* lays out many of the issues that are still important in the field, such as the fallibility of memory, the unreliability of eyewitness testimony, principles of lie detection, and methods of jury persuasion. He also invented an early polygraph device, which in his usual bombast he called the "truth-compelling machine." Another area was **industrial and organizational psychology**, or I/O psychology for short. This is *the application of psychological principles to business, manufacturing, and other large-group settings*. Münsterberg published numerous books and articles on advertising, personnel selection, vocational guidance, and management techniques. He also did workplace studies of sea captains, trolley operators, and telephone workers to develop aptitude tests for these jobs. Although he acquired a number of lucrative consultancies, his colleagues often criticized his experimental rigor.

A third area where Münsterberg left his mark was psychotherapy (Landy, 1992). He was especially critical of Sigmund Freud (Chapter 7), who had posited unconscious conflicts as the origin of psychological disorders. Münsterberg denied the existence of any unconscious mental processes other than the physiological operations of the nervous system. He also dismissed the idea of consciousness as the driver of behavior. Rather, he took *the position that consciousness is nothing more than a byproduct of brain activity*. It was the brain that processed the sensory input and programmed motor responses, so there was no need to propose a willful agent. Instead, consciousness was like the heat given off by an engine—a mere byproduct with no function. This approach to the mind-body problem is known as **epiphenomenalism**, a view that was also embraced by John Watson and the behaviorists (Chapter 5).

At the turn of the twentieth century, many Americans thought of psychologists as psychics and mind readers (Benjamin, 2006). Early experimentalists thus felt a responsibility to educate the public. But none were more prolific in writing for the popular press than Münsterberg. He wrote popular articles and books about the new scientific psychology, extolling its virtues for improving human life, as well as pieces debunking pseudoscience such as séances and the occult. In addition, he was popular lecturer, and he clearly enjoyed the limelight. With his European suits, waxed moustache, and German accent, he played the role of "science expert" to a T. He was also an avid social commentator and he liked to expose the foibles of American life, especially compared with "obviously superior" German culture. These comments garnered more negative than positive attention, but Münsterberg thrived on controversy.

With his thin skin, sharp tongue, and swollen ego, Münsterberg eventually alienated most of his American colleagues (Kinlen & Henley, 1997). As war erupted in Europe, anti-German sentiment spread rapidly. Münsterberg had never become a naturalized citizen, and he maintained his vocal support for his homeland during this time. He was branded a spy in the media, and there were calls for his deportation. He even received hate mail addressed to "Dr. Monsterbug." Clearly the stress was wearing him down. Just months before the United States entered the Great War, Münsterberg was lecturing when he stumbled and fell, dying on the spot from a cerebral hemorrhage. Even his last act in life was a public performance.

Photo 3.6
Hugo Münsterberg

Figure 3.3   Academic Family Tree of Hugo Münsterberg

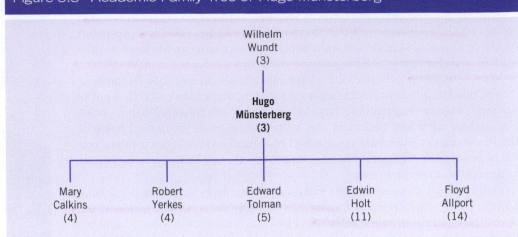

Much hated at the time of his death, Münsterberg's legacy was all but forgotten. It was only late in the twentieth century that the value of his work was once again recognized (Figure 3.3). However, today Münsterberg is recognized as a pioneer in the fields of forensic and I/O psychology.

Edward Titchener

**Photo 3.7
Edward Titchener**

As a student of philosophy at Oxford, **Edward Titchener** (1867–1927) absorbed the ideas of the British empiricists we learned about in Chapter 1 (Araujo & Marcellos, 2017). Although John Stuart Mill had declared it was time for psychology to become a natural science, Oxford wasn't ready for that. So Titchener traveled to Leipzig to learn the "new psychology" from Wilhelm Wundt. The young Englishman developed a close relationship with his advisor, even spending Christmas vacations with the Wundt family. During his two years in the lab, Titchener mastered experimental methods from Wundt, but his thinking was still influenced more by the British empiricists. With no jobs for experimental psychologists back home, Titchener accepted an offer from Cornell in 1892, where he stayed for the rest of his life. There, he built his reputation as the *early British-American psychologist who developed a school of experimental psychology known as structuralism.*

His Kingdom at Cornell

Titchener never adjusted to American culture or the rustic life of upstate New York, and he viewed himself as a British expatriate living in a foreign land (Gregory, 1982). But he built his kingdom at Cornell and he was the overlord in the lab, demanding absolute loyalty from his graduate students.

Titchener's domineering personality was legendary. Margaret Washburn, Titchener's first graduate student, remarked that he still displayed human warmth and could laugh at his own mistakes in the early days (Washburn, 1932). But later students, like Edwin Boring, have described Titchener's pompous and overbearing character at length (Boring, 1952). Titchener lectured in his academic gown, which may have been the custom at Oxford but certainly not at Cornell. When Boring asked him about it, Titchener replied: "It gives me the right to be dogmatic!" As Titchener built Cornell into one of the leading psychology labs in the country, he had numerous graduate students and junior faculty members working under him. When Titchener gave his general psychology lectures, he expected all of his underlings to process into the lecture hall behind him, ordered by rank—junior faculty, postdocs, and then graduate students (Abel, 1978). He also held a weekly seminar at his home. He assigned the topics, and attendance was mandatory. Titchener was a night owl, and the seminar usually went until 2:00 a.m.

Even after they'd graduated and established their own careers, Titchener's students still felt the domination of their mentor (Boring, 1952; Washburn, 1932). For instance, Titchener co-edited the *American Journal of Psychology* with his former student and junior colleague Karl Dallenbach (1887–1971) for many years. On one occasion, Titchener demanded a change in policy that would have been costly. Dallenbach had always been a devoted follower, but he'd also assumed full financial responsibility for the journal, and the changes were just too expensive. Deeply offended, Titchener resigned as co-editor and severed all contact with Dallenbach. As Boring (1952) commented, Titchener could be very generous to those with unquestionable loyalty, but any transgression, no matter how small, meant eternal banishment from the privileged circle.

In addition to his kingdom at Cornell, Titchener had considerable influence over other psychologists working in the northeastern United States (Goodwin, 2005). At first, he'd been a member of the fledgling American Psychological Association, but he felt the APA gave too much attention to applied psychology and not enough to pure research. Titchener thus formed his own group called the Experimentalists. At their yearly meetings, the members discussed their ongoing research, all of which fell under the purview of what Titchener considered "true" experimental psychology. The Experimentalist meetings were informal, cigar-smoking affairs—and unlike the APA, no women were allowed.

Titchener's attitudes toward women were complicated (Proctor & Evans, 2014). On the one hand, about half of his graduate students were female, largely because Cornell was one of the few universities that would grant them doctorates. On the other hand, his comments about women in general could be quite condescending. In recent decades, Titchener has been vilified as a misogynist, especially by feminist historians. Yet it's important to understand the man within the time period that he lived. He certainly held benevolent-sexist attitudes toward women, and that's why he thought they needed to be protected from the smoking, drinking, and ribald banter of his all-male gatherings. Along with many of his male colleagues, Titchener also bought into what was then called the variability hypothesis. In this view, White men were superior to women and people of color on average, but some members of these groups were exceptional in their talents and should be nurtured to reach their full potential. As offensive as this attitude sounds by current standards, it was considered quite progressive at the turn of the twentieth century. We'll learn more about the variability hypothesis and the studies that challenged it in Chapter 4.

Structural Psychology

Although Titchener recognized that applied psychology had its value, it certainly wasn't "true" experimental psychology (Araujo & Marcellos, 2017). Greatly influenced by the British empiricists, he saw the proper subject of his field as the study of conscious experience. According to philosophers like Locke, Hume, and Mill, consciousness was built up through the associations of basic sensory elements. The job of the experimental psychologist then was to uncover the building blocks of the mind. Titchener referred to his approach as structural psychology. But with the rise of functionalism around the same time, it became known as **structuralism** in contrast. Titchener and his followers thus belonged to *an early school of psychology that sought to decompose consciousness into its component parts.*

The preferred method of the structuralists was introspection, or self-reports of mental states (Gregory, 1982). Philosophers have used introspection for centuries, with little advance in our understanding of the nature of consciousness. The problem, Titchener thought, was that they weren't trained to introspect properly. Instead, his highly trained "observers" engaged in **systematic introspection**, which is *a method of accurately reporting* *sensory experiences under carefully controlled experimental conditions*. This was necessary to avoid what Titchener called the **stimulus error**, which is *the error of describing the object of perception instead of the conscious experience of that object*. Let's say I show you an apple and ask you to report your experience. If you say that you see an apple, you're committing the stimulus error—you've reported the apple itself and not your experience of it. To engage in systematic introspection, you have to report the color, shape, luminance, and so on.

There's a circularity to this approach that Titchener seemed oblivious to (Leahey, 2014). He was seeking to find the elements of consciousness, and yet he trained his observers to report exactly those elements. While the Cornell lab got consistent results with this method, rival labs did not. The apparent inconsistency of introspection gave impetus to the behavioral revolution. However, the real problem wasn't with introspection, which is still a standard technique in psychology, but rather with Titchener's analytical approach to consciousness.

Titchener also had difficulty accepting the validity of any result that contradicted his theory (Leahey, 2014). A famous case is the **imageless thought controversy**. This was *an extended debate between Titchener and his rivals about the nature of consciousness*. Because Titchener believed that consciousness was built from elementary sensations, he insisted that all thought had to be accompanied by sensory imagery. But introspect a bit yourself. Do images always accompany your thoughts? **Oswald Külpe** (1862–1915), an *early student of Wundt who was one of the founders of experimental psychology in Germany*, claimed to have evidence of thinking without images. However, Titchener dismissed these reports as stimulus error. Other psychologists joined the fray, providing their own examples of imageless thought. But Titchener remained unconvinced, and his detractors turned to more interesting questions.

Legacy

During his lifetime, Titchener had his group of loyal followers (Araujo & Marcellos, 2017). But when he died, so did the school he'd founded. His student Edwin Boring (1952) remarked on the mixed emotions of guilt and relief he felt when Titchener passed away. While his mentor was alive, Boring dared not contradict him, even though his thinking had long ago moved away from structuralist dogma. No doubt, many of his other students had similar feelings. In the United States, functionalism (Chapter 4) was morphing into behaviorism (Chapter 5). And in Europe, a school of psychology known as Gestalt (Chapter 6) was gaining ascendancy. Structuralism was ultimately a failure, but nevertheless Titchener had an important influence on psychology in the early twentieth century. This impact came in two ways. First, he published a series of lab manuals that were used to train a generation of students on the methods of experimental psychology. Second, he nurtured nearly sixty graduate students, many of

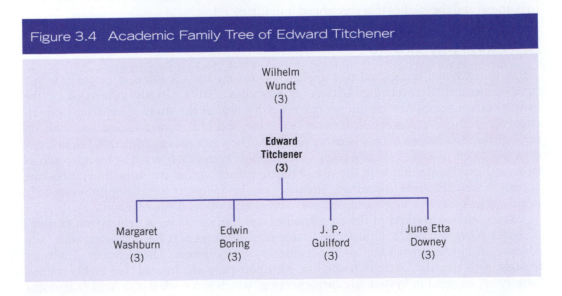

Figure 3.4 Academic Family Tree of Edward Titchener

Wilhelm Wundt (3)

Edward Titchener (3)

Margaret Washburn (3) | Edwin Boring (3) | J. P. Guilford (3) | June Etta Downey (3)

whom had illustrious careers of their own (Figure 3.4). Although these students abandoned the structuralist approach, they'd come to him to learn experimental methods, which they used to build a solid structure of psychology.

Titchener's Students

Although structuralism died with its creator, many of Titchener's students went on to illustrious careers as founders of modern psychology in the first half of the twentieth century. In this section, we'll meet four of his students, two women and two men. Each of these persons made important contributions to psychology, and each of the women broke through gender barriers as well.

Margaret Washburn

The only child of a New York businessman and an heiress, **Margaret Washburn** (1871–1939) was doted on by her parents, who encouraged her to pursue her intellectual interests (Washburn, 1932). She entered Vassar College when she was only sixteen, and she graduated with a desire to find a career that would combine her deep interests in philosophy and science. The new experimental psychology fit the bill. Today she's known as an *early American psychologist who was the first woman to earn a Ph.D. in psychology and a pioneer in animal research.*

When Washburn heard that Cattell was setting up a psychology laboratory at Columbia, she went to visit him (Washburn, 1932). Cattell assumed the young woman was interested in psychics and séances, but when she explained that she'd taught herself German by translating Wundt's *Physiological Psychology*, he was impressed. A lifelong advocate for gender equality, Cattell put Washburn to work in his laboratory and let her attend his seminars. Unfortunately, the Columbia administration wasn't as tolerant. When it became clear they'd never give her a doctoral degree, Cattell suggested she transfer to Cornell, which had just hired his Leipzig colleague Edward Titchener.

Photo 3.8
Margaret Washburn

Washburn and Titchener arrived in Cornell around the same time (Washburn, 1932). She was his first—and for a while his only—graduate student. At this point, Titchener was still very much influenced by Wundt's thinking, and he only had a general outline for his structural psychology. Washburn reports that during the two years she spent as his student, their thinking was quite similar. Both were devoted experimentalists who viewed psychology as the study of consciousness. She liked his analytical approach, and she agreed with him that introspection was a valuable tool for exploring the mind. When she finished her dissertation, Titchener sent it to Wundt, who had it translated into German and published in his journal *Philosophical Studies*. It was the first foreign article to be published in that journal.

Washburn earned her Ph.D. in psychology in 1894, the first woman to do so (Johnson, 1997). She accepted a professorship at nearby Wells College, but for the next six years she spent one day a week back in Cornell doing research. Then she took a position as "warden" of the women's dormitory at Cornell so she could devote more time to research. Two years after that, she accepted a one-year appointment at the University of Cincinnati.

In 1903 came the call from Vassar College, her alma mater, where she remained for the rest of her career (Woodworth, 1948). Vassar was an all-women's college, but Washburn built a psychology laboratory rivaling those at many research universities. Under her leadership, Vassar became one of the premier undergraduate psychology programs in the nation, and many of her students went on to graduate school and distinguished careers in psychology. Despite a heavy teaching load, Washburn found a way to keep doing research. Using her students as undergraduate assistants, she conducted a series of investigations that she wrote up as "Studies From the Vassar Laboratory." Nearly seventy of these "minor studies" were published during her career, with her students listed as co-authors.

Washburn's best-known work is *The Animal Mind* (1908), the first comprehensive textbook on comparative psychology (Johnson, 1997). The book went through four editions and remained the standard text in the field for a quarter of a century until the behaviorist approach came to dominate animal studies. In the book, Washburn takes the stand that we should assume an animal has consciousness if it has similar brain structures and behaviors to humans.

As an indication of her influence on psychology, Washburn was elected president of the American Psychological Association in 1921 (Scarborough, 2000). In her presidential address, Washburn insisted that the proper study of psychology was consciousness. She defended introspection as a valid experimental technique, and she chastised the growing behaviorist movement for trying to rid psychology of all things mental.

Washburn was never under Titchener's thumb the way his other students were (Washburn, 1932). In part, this was because she showed a high degree of self-confidence, and she always treated her male colleagues as equals even when they weren't willing to return the courtesy. And since Titchener excluded Washburn from his inner circle because of her sex, he also held less power over her. The two maintained a cool but professional relationship. At one of his seminars, Washburn read a paper that criticized aspects of his theory. Titchener unleashed a tirade of abuse as his minions cowered speechless, but afterward one of them privately expressed his sympathy. In her indomitable manner, she reflected: "It had not occurred to me to be depressed by Titchener's criticisms; it was exciting to 'draw blood' from him" (Washburn, 1932, p. 344). One has to wonder if Titchener kept her at arm's length because she intimidated him.

Titchener had excluded Washburn from his men-only Experimentalists (Goodman, 1979) but after his death, the group reorganized as the Society of Experimental Psychologists (SEP) and decided to let women into their clubhouse. They invited Washburn to join, and later they elected her as their chair.

Although there were other women already working in psychology, Margaret Washburn was the first woman in the field to be awarded a Ph.D. (Scarborough, 2000). Barred from male-only research universities, she nevertheless built a leading psychology laboratory at Vassar College using undergraduate research assistants. Despite rampant gender discrimination, Washburn had an extraordinarily productive career spanning more than four decades. Washburn's success as a female psychologist can be attributed to at least two factors beyond the drive and determination required of any successful scientist, whether man or woman. First, she showed no interest in marriage or children, so she wasn't confronted with the marriage-or-family choice other women had to contend with. Second, she kept close ties with her parents, and they in turn supported her career. During her lifetime, she was considered one of the top fifty most influential psychologists, and more recently she was ranked among the top 100 psychologists of the twentieth century (Haggbloom et al., 2002).

Edwin Boring

"Boring is my best student," Titchener proclaimed (Stevens, 1973). It was some reputation to live up to. Edwin Boring (1886–1968) first met Titchener in an elective psychology class. He found Titchener's lectures "magic" (Boring, 1952, p. 31). And Titchener even commented on his exam paper: "*You* have the psychological point of view!" But Boring was an engineering major, and he had to work in the field before he learned he didn't like it. When Boring returned to Cornell, he found his way to Titchener's lab. Over a long career, Boring built his reputation as an *early American psychologist who was a noted historian of psychology.*

You get a sense of the devotion Boring felt for Titchener by considering some of the research projects he worked on (Stevens, 1973). In one, he had to swallow a rubber bladder so liquids of varying temperatures could be poured down his throat. (They were testing the sensitivity of the digestive tract.) In another, Boring severed a nerve in his forearm to observe the time course of nerve regeneration. (It took four years to recover complete sensibility.)

Another devoted graduate student was Lucy Day, soon to be Lucy Boring (1886–1996; Furumoto, 1998). Before the wedding, Titchener gave Boring unsolicited wedding advice. And while the couple was on honeymoon, he wrote to remind them when they were due back in the lab (Boring, 1952). Lucy had a brief teaching career that ended when she gave birth, since women were expected to sacrifice career for family. Incidentally, their first child was born on Titchener's birthday, which he took as a compliment, and he forgave Boring for arriving late to his all-male party.

When the United States entered World War I, Boring joined Robert Yerkes (Chapter 4), who was directing the intelligence testing of Army recruits (Hilgard, 1986). After the war, Yerkes brought him to Washington to compile the data. Boring then accepted an offer from G. Stanley Hall (Chapter 4) at Clark University. Three years later, Boring answered a call to Harvard, where he stayed for the rest of his career.

Boring's foremost student—and later colleague—was S. S. Stevens (Chapter 11). Together, they worked out an important principle for experimental psychology known as **operationalization**. This is *the practice of defining variables in terms of the way in which they will be measured* (Boring, 1952). Although operationalization had long been practiced in physics, psychologists were still using concepts without adequately defining them. For example, when his colleagues quibbled about the nature of intelligence, Boring's reply was: "Intelligence is what the tests test." That is to say, intelligence is operationally defined by the instrument used to measure it. Since psychological concepts are abstract and can't be observed directly, operational definitions are essential to good research.

Another important contribution was Boring's *History of Experimental Psychology*, which he published in 1929 and revised in 1950 (Stevens, 1973). For more than three decades, psychologists learned the history of their field from this book. In this work, Boring introduces his readers to the concept of **Zeitgeist**, which is *the German expression for "spirit of the times," referring to the currency of ideas in a given time period.* History is often presented as the accomplishments of "Great Men," but Boring showed how certain ideas seem to be "in the air." A classic example of Zeitgeist is the case of Darwin and Wallace arriving at the theory of evolution by natural selection around the same time. Likewise, Wundt is credited with establishing the first psychology laboratory, but within a few years other German psychologists were setting up labs of their own. The Zeitgeist concept suggests that some discoveries are

Photo 3.9
Edwin Boring

Photographer unknown; image courtesy of Dr. Edwin Boring

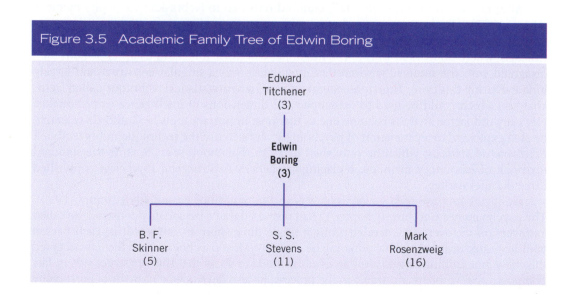

Figure 3.5   Academic Family Tree of Edwin Boring

Edward
Titchener
(3)

Edwin
Boring
(3)

B. F.
Skinner
(5)

S. S.
Stevens
(11)

Mark
Rosenzweig
(16)

inevitable because so many different people are thinking about and working on the same problems during a given time period.

In recent decades, Boring's *History* has been criticized for its inaccurate depiction of Wundt and his theories (Araujo, 2012). Boring accepted Titchener's description of Wundt at face value. It's likely that Titchener portrayed Wundt as a structuralist to lend support to his own theory. The two did agree on many things, such as consciousness being the proper study of psychology and introspection as a valid experimental technique. However, historical research since then has shown that Wundt conceived of the mind in terms of dynamic processes and not static structure.

In sum, Edwin Boring played an important role in establishing experimental psychology as a legitimate science. With his student-turned-colleague S. S. Stevens, he advocated for operational definitions to make experimental psychology more rigorous (Figure 3.5). Although he did little research, he was an active organizer and intermediary who helped resolve many of the interpersonal problems that arose during the early years of American experimental psychology. Although Boring was loyal to Titchener, his interests in psychology were wide ranging, including intelligence testing and even psychoanalysis. For these reasons, Robert Yerkes dubbed him "Mr. Psychology," a sentiment shared by many.

J. P. Guilford

With only a bachelor's degree, **Joy Paul Guilford** (1897–1987) was put in charge of the psychology clinic at the University of Nebraska (Guilford, 1967). There, his main duty was administering intelligence tests to children with academic or behavioral problems. At the time, it was standard practice to calculate either a mental age or an intelligence quotient (IQ) for each child, but Guilford felt that a single number didn't adequately represent the full range of abilities. In particular, he noticed that the children he worked with excelled at some tasks while performing poorly on others. This experience piqued his interest in the study of individual differences, and this became the theme of his career. Thus, J. P. Guilford's reputation was established as the *American psychologist who proposed the structure-of-intellect theory*.

After completing his master's degree at Nebraska, Guilford was offered an assistantship at Cornell (Guilford, 1967). All work in Titchener's lab was directed toward building his theory of consciousness, and this dimensional approach clearly influenced Guilford when he later developed his own theory of intelligence. Guilford was also greatly influenced during this time by the Gestalt psychologist Kurt Koffka, whom we'll meet in Chapter 6. As we'll see, Gestalt psychologists were interested in mental processes such as problem solving, which became central to Guilford's own theory building.

After he earned his Ph.D. in 1927, Guilford returned to Nebraska as a faculty member (Hunt, 1992). He also returned to his initial interest in intelligence testing and the question of multiple intelligences. In 1935, he was a visiting professor at the University of Chicago, where he worked with L. L. Thurstone, whom we'll meet in Chapter 4. Both men disagreed with the received wisdom that intelligence was a singular construct and largely innate. During this time, Thurstone taught Guilford a new statistical technique called factor analysis, which could be used to tease apart the dimensions of intelligence or personality. Not only did factor analysis become one of the most important tools in Guilford's research, he also explained to a generation of psychologists how to use the technique in his textbook *Psychometric Methods*, which he published in 1936. This book soon became the standard textbook of laboratory methods, replacing Titchener's *Experimental Psychology*, published three decades earlier.

Guilford's first use of factor analysis was an exploration of personality (Comrey, 1993). The psychoanalyst Carl Jung (Chapter 7) had proposed that a personality construct he called extraversion-introversion extended along a single dimension. In other words, each person could be rank-ordered by how outgoing he or she is. Most psychologists of the day accepted this view, but Guilford used factor analytic methods to show that this construct was in fact composed of several distinct traits. In the process, he also developed a number of personality tests that were widely used during that time. Although it was interrupted by World War II, Guilford's research on personality structure culminated in his 1959 book *Personality*.

Guilford's work was well received, and in 1940, he accepted an offer from the University of Southern California, where he stayed for the rest of his career (Comrey, 1993). The only exception to this was the period from 1942 to 1946, when he served in the U.S. Army Air Corps. There, he directed a unit that developed psychological tests for the screening of pilots, navigators, and bombardiers. Although Guilford was convinced that intelligence could be broken down into quite a few distinct mental abilities, he had no theory predicting how many there were. Because of this conviction, he separately scored each respondent's performance on a large battery of tests rather than assessing overall intelligence. By the time the war had ended, Guilford and his team had identified twenty-five distinct mental abilities and had devised tests to measure them.

After the war, Guilford continued his research on mental abilities (Comrey, 1993). Over the following decades, his **structure-of-intellect theory**, or SOI, took shape. This was *the proposal that mental abilities could be organized in three dimensions, depending on the kinds of operations, contents, and products involved.* Guilford identified six kinds of mental operations, such as association ("dog" and "bone") and categorization ("dog" and "animal"). He divided the information content of a mental ability into five types, including not only a division between visual and auditory information but also between semantic and social knowledge. Finally, he considered six different products of mental abilities, such as identifying relations and implications. When these three dimensions are arranged in a cube, the 6 × 5 × 6 structure suggested the existence of 180 distinct mental abilities. This theory then guided Guilford in the search for other mental abilities and suggested ways to test for them. By the end of his career, Guilford claimed to have identified and devised tests for over a hundred of these.

Guilford became something of an international celebrity when he applied the structure-of-intellect theory to education (Hunt, 1992). The theory was appealing for a number of reasons. First, it proposed that mental abilities are honed through experience rather than being set by genetics, and so there was an important role for education to play in developing the intelligence of each child. Second, his theory laid out mental abilities in a systematic fashion, giving educators a framework for developing curricula and even specific instructional materials. Advocates of Guilford's ideas formed the International Society of Intelligence Education, which promoted educational practices based on the structure-of-intellect theory. Although the popularity of Guilford's model has waned in recent decades, his work has shown that intelligence is far more complex than what was originally believed in the early twentieth century.

June Etta Downey

A Wyoming native, **June Etta Downey** (1875–1932) spent most her life in the town of Laramie (Uhrbrock, 1932). She taught philosophy at the University of Wyoming, but she spent the summer of 1901 at Cornell studying with Titchener, and this experience changed the course of her career. Although she eventually completed her Ph.D. at the University of Chicago with James Rowland Angell (Chapter 4), she always credited Titchener as her first mentor in psychology. During a time of severe gender discrimination, June Downey broke through social barriers by becoming the *American psychologist who was the first woman chair of a psychology department at a major university.*

At Chicago, Downey wrote a dissertation on the relationship between handwriting and personality, a theme that would continue through the rest of her career (Hogan & Broudy, 2000). She continued in this line of research when she returned to the faculty of Wyoming in 1907. In 1915, Downey was named chair of the newly established Department of Philosophy and Psychology, a position she held for the rest of her life. Her interest in individual differences led to the development of the Individual Will-Temperament Test, which assessed

Photo 3.10
June Etta Downey

personality on the basis of handwriting samples and observations of involuntary motor reactions. Scores from these tests were plotted on a graph to create a visual representation of the test-taker's personality profile. Although the test was popular in the early twentieth century, a number of issues concerning its validity and reliability began to emerge, most important of which was the subjective nature of the assessments, and the test fell out of favor.

A colorful episode in Downey's life illustrates her devotion to the practical application of psychology (Hein, 2018). In 1916, a prisoner in a Wyoming jail was charged with the murder of his guard. During the trial, Downey was called as an expert witness. In front of the judge and jury, she administered an intelligence test recently developed by French psychologist Alfred Binet (Chapter 8). She demonstrated that the defendant had a mental age of only 6 or 7; as a result, he was remanded to the Wyoming State Hospital instead of prison. This was one of the first instances of a psychologist influencing the outcome of a trial, thus setting a precedent for the important role that psychologists would come to play in the criminal justice system.

Looking Ahead

In 1879, Wilhelm Wundt established the first laboratory of experimental psychology in the world at Leipzig University. Soon, researchers at other German universities followed suit by opening their own psychology labs. The students who learned the new experimental psychology at these Germany institutions came not only from across Europe but also from around the world, and especially from North America. It can be said that Wundt's most important contribution to psychology was a set of research methods, as his theories have little currency today. These research methods were brought to the United States by many of his American and European students, the most notable of which was Edward Titchener. Although Titchener's structuralism died with him, his greatest contribution to psychology was the nurturing of the next generation of experimental psychologists.

Thus, we can say that the most important legacy of Wundt and Titchener lies not in their theories but in their dissemination of the experimental approach to psychology. Because of the rapidly expanding university system in the United States, the new experimental psychology flourished there more so than in Europe. However, the European penchant for abstract theorizing exhibited by Wundt and Titchener was at odds with the American preference for practical applications. Soon, a "home-grown" approach to studying the mind arose in the United States. Known as functionalism, this approach viewed the mind as a set of functions or processes rather than structures, hence the name. As we'll see in the next chapter, functionalism was built on the ideas of William James, a philosopher who understood the value of experimental psychology.

In fact, even the name "functionalism" comes from Titchener. He needed a way to distinguish his analysis of consciousness from the mostly applied work of his American colleagues, so he called his school *structural psychology* and theirs *functional psychology*. The applied psychologists gladly co-opted the name for themselves, shortening the terms to *structuralism* and *functionalism*.

The two schools also differed in terms of their attitude toward the mind-body problem. Both Wundt and Titchener seemed to accept a Cartesian dualism of mind and body. To them, the domain of psychology was clearly limited to the study of the mind. In contrast, the functionalists were greatly influenced by Darwin and his theory of natural selection. To them, mental processes had evolved because they help us survive. Thus, the functionalists took a monistic view toward the relationship between mind and body. More precisely, the functionalists viewed the mind as the output of the brain, which drove behavior as the output of the body. It was also this assumption of a direct link between brain and behavior that helped lay the groundwork for what became the major American school of psychology in the mid-twentieth century, namely *behaviorism*, which we'll read about in Chapter 5.

CHAPTER SUMMARY

In 1879, Wilhelm Wundt established the first psychology laboratory at Leipzig University, which soon became a mecca for aspiring young scholars eager to learn the methods of this new science of the mind. A physiologist by training, Wundt understood that the mind arose from the activity of the nervous system, and therefore it could be studied in a scientific fashion. He developed many basic laboratory techniques that are still used by cognitive psychologists today. In his later years, he turned his attention toward the social, cultural, and historical aspects of human psychology. Although Wundt nurtured many of the next generation of psychologists, many of his students working in North America were less interested in his theories than in his methods. They were nevertheless the pioneers in American psychology, establishing the first psychology labs and clinics on this continent. His most noted student was Edward Titchener, a British student of philosophy who earned his degree in psychology with Wundt before accepting a position at Cornell. Like his mentor, Titchener mentored many rising psychologists. However, his structural approach to psychology was quite different from Wundt's. Although his students swore allegiance to structuralism during their mentor's lifetime, the school was abandoned after his death. Despite Titchener's benevolent-sexist attitude toward women, about half of his graduate students were female, including Margaret Washburn, who was the first woman to receive a Ph.D. in psychology.

DISCUSSION QUESTIONS

1. Introspection was an important experimental method in early psychology, but it's still used today. Can you think of some examples?

2. What were some of the reasons why early American psychologists were interested in measuring individual differences? Why were Wundt and others opposed to this approach?

3. What are mental tests? What was the problem with them? How are mental tests different from intelligence tests?

4. Discuss the development of clinical psychology. How does the original conception differ from today?

5. Discuss Baldwin's two important contributions, the Baldwin effect and genetic epistemology. Who was influenced by his ideas?

6. Discuss Hugo Münsterberg's contributions to applied psychology.

7. Explain epiphenomenalism and how it relates to other approaches to the mind-body problem.

8. Discuss the differences between structural and functional psychology. What were the major antecedents for each approach?

9. Explain what Titchener meant by systematic introspection and the stimulus error. What was the imageless thought controversy all about?

10. Discuss Washburn's reasoning on consciousness in animals.

11. What is meant by "operationalization"? Why is it so important? If you have some research experience, explain how your variables were operationalized.

12. What is meant by "Zeitgeist"? Can you come up with examples besides those in this chapter?

ON THE WEB

The psychologists we met in this chapter all lived and worked at a time when film making was still in its infancy, so there are no video clips of any of these persons on the internet. However, they are all important pioneers in psychology, and there are numerous clips on YouTube describing their life and work. Many of these videos are made by amateurs, so keep a skeptical mind when watching them.

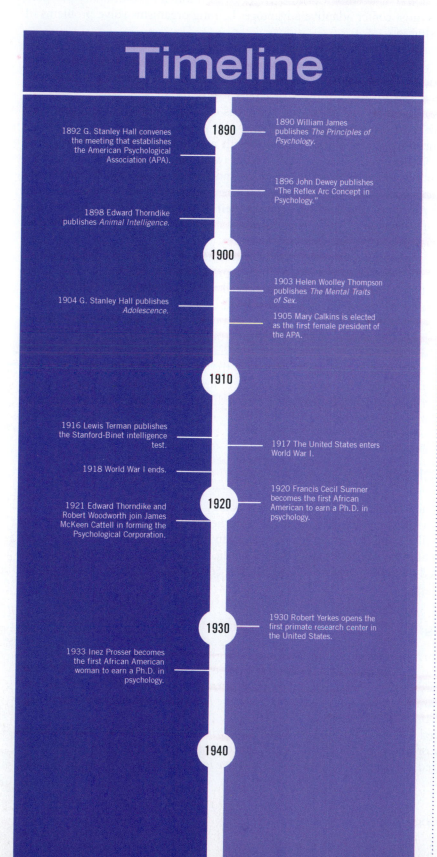

Timeline

1892 G. Stanley Hall convenes the meeting that establishes the American Psychological Association (APA).

1898 Edward Thorndike publishes *Animal Intelligence*.

1904 G. Stanley Hall publishes *Adolescence*.

1916 Lewis Terman publishes the Stanford-Binet intelligence test.

1918 World War I ends.

1921 Edward Thorndike and Robert Woodworth join James McKeen Cattell in forming the Psychological Corporation.

1933 Inez Prosser becomes the first African American woman to earn a Ph.D. in psychology.

1890

1900

1910

1920

1930

1940

1890 William James publishes *The Principles of Psychology*.

1896 John Dewey publishes "The Reflex Arc Concept in Psychology."

1903 Helen Woolley Thompson publishes *The Mental Traits of Sex*.

1905 Mary Calkins is elected as the first female president of the APA.

1917 The United States enters World War I.

1920 Francis Cecil Sumner becomes the first African American to earn a Ph.D. in psychology.

1930 Robert Yerkes opens the first primate research center in the United States.

Learning Objectives

After reading this chapter, you should be able to:

- Assess the contributions of the Harvard school in terms of William James's pragmatism.

- Demonstrate how the Clark school laid the foundations for the modern discipline of developmental psychology.

- Evaluate the contributions of the Chicago school in terms of its strong emphasis on conscious mental activities as the core of psychology.

- Appraise the contributions of the Columbia school, particularly in its focus on learning and education.

Looking Back

In the late nineteenth century, Darwinism was more accepted in the English-speaking world than elsewhere. American psychologists tended to think in terms of natural selection, but this wasn't the case for their European counterparts. Whereas Wundt simply saw consciousness as a product of physiology, American contemporaries like William James pondered the question of why consciousness had evolved. From an evolutionary perspective, consciousness must confer adaptive advantage, helping organisms solve problems of survival and reproduction.

This Darwin-inspired American approach had no name in the late 1800s until Titchener gave it one (Green, 2009). In biology, Titchener argued, there's a difference between anatomy and physiology, and you can't study function until you understand structure. Likewise in psychology, he claimed, structuralism was the true path to understanding the mind, and functionalism was misguided. His American colleagues didn't buy the argument, but they gladly accepted the name for their approach.

The label "functionalism" was first associated with a group of psychologists working at the University of Chicago around the turn of the twentieth century (Chaplin, 2000). Under the leadership of John Dewey and James Rowland Angell, **functionalism** developed as *an early American school of psychology that studied mental processes in terms of their adaptive value*. Soon, other American psychologists realized their thinking was similar and considered themselves functionalists as well. Thus, functionalism became the default school of American psychology during the early twentieth century.

In this chapter, we consider four centers of functionalism. First we visit Harvard, where William James laid the foundation for a Darwinian approach to psychology. Next we go to Clark University, where James's student G. Stanley Hall applied Darwinism to the study of development. Then we swing by the "Chicago school," where Dewey and Angell formalized the functionalist approach. Finally, we stop at Columbia, where James McKeen Cattell's students Edward Thorndike and Robert Woodworth built a psychology of learning and motivation.

Functionalism was an all-American approach to the new psychology. Although functionalism was inspired by Darwinian theory, it sought to find practical solutions to everyday problems. By this criterion, functionalism was a resounding success, and it laid the groundwork for the disciplines we're familiar with today.

Harvard School

William James argued for a dynamic theory of psychology that was grounded in evolutionary theory. This perspective influenced others who studied or worked with him at Harvard, including Mary Calkins and Robert Yerkes. We can even include Hugo Münsterberg in this school, especially after he turned his attention to applied psychology. These psychologists may not have called themselves functionalists, but they certainly took a functional approach to their research.

William James

Although he earned a medical degree, William James never practiced medicine. He was attracted instead to the new scientific psychology arising in Germany, and he even built his own lab at Harvard. But he didn't like doing experiments, preferring philosophy instead. Today, **William James** (1842–1910) is recognized as the *Harvard philosopher who inspired the first generation of American psychologists*.

James achieved this status through his 1890 book *Principles of Psychology*, which defined the field (Crosby & Viney, 1993). In that work, he challenged the British empiricists (who had in turn inspired Titchener's structuralism). When we look at an apple, James maintained, we don't experience redness, shininess, or curviness. Rather, we're conscious of the apple as a whole. And not just that. We see the apple in a bowl with other fruit sitting on a table covered with a lace cloth. In other words, our experience is holistic and not built out of simpler parts. William James's *philosophical stance that we don't just perceive sensations but rather objects in relations with other objects* is known as **radical empiricism**. This dynamic view of the mind was fundamentally different from Titchener's conception, but it presaged the Gestalt approach (Chapter 6) that emerged after James's death.

Unknown via Wikimedia Commons

Photo 4.1
William James

If something is directly experienced, according to James, it can't be dismissed just because it doesn't fit a preferred theory (Croce, 2010). James spent much of his career studying exceptional mental experiences such as hypnosis, hallucinations, drug-induced states (with himself as the subject), multiple personality disorder, and even paranormal phenomena. Most scientists of the day dismissed these as fakery or theoretically uninteresting. But James insisted they were real experiences, and as such they were legitimate topics of investigation for a psychologist.

James was one of the founders of an American school of philosophy known as **pragmatism** (Strube, Yost, & Bailey, 1993). This is *the philosophical stance that the truth of an idea should be judged according to its practical consequences.* James talked about the "cash value" of an idea—that is, the extent to which it helps us make accurate predictions as we interact with the world.

In James's view, consciousness arose through natural selection (Nielsen & Day, 1999). By providing organisms with information about the world that they can act on, consciousness helps them survive and reproduce. In his commerce metaphor, consciousness has cash value. Furthermore, different species have different quantities and qualities of consciousness, depending on their environment and the complexity of their interactions with it. Thus, the conscious experience of a bat, which navigates by echolocation, would be different from that of a bird, which navigates by vision. And the consciousness of a fish, swimming in the sea, would be quite unlike that of a bat or a bird.

James criticized the British empiricists for treating the mind as a static structure. In the *Principles*, James offered *a conception of the mind as a continuous, dynamic process* that he called the **stream of consciousness**. Like a river, our thoughts flow one into another, sometimes lingering, sometimes rushing forward. This idea greatly influenced twentieth-century literature, as novelists began writing in a first-person style that mimicked internal thought processes. One such author was Gertrude Stein (1874–1946), who'd studied with William James in the 1890s.

For James, selective attention is an important aspect of consciousness (Crosby & Viney, 1993). We aren't aware of everything around us. Rather, the mind is like a sculptor working on a piece of stone, cutting off large parts while highlighting others. Thus, our mind focuses on what it deems important and disregards the rest. Likewise, our consciousness isn't always of the same intensity. Sometimes we're fully aware with strained attention, and at other times we barely notice our surroundings. Yet even in sleep, when consciousness is reduced to a minimum, we can still be roused by a sudden noise.

James acknowledged that the brain's physiological processes weren't accessible to consciousness, but he rejected the idea of unconscious mental events. This doesn't mean all thoughts are available to consciousness at all times. If you stop and listen carefully, you'll notice certain environmental sounds—the hum of the air conditioner, the tick-tock of a clock, the rustle of leaves outside your window—that you didn't "hear" while your attention was focused elsewhere. This is but one example of **subliminal consciousness**, which is what James called *cognitive processes occurring below the threshold of awareness* (Schooler, 2011). However, James dismissed Freud's theory of a dynamic unconscious.

Emotion played a central role in James's psychology. Challenging the widely held assumption that emotion and reason are at odds with each other, he insisted that there can be no thought without emotion (Crosby & Viney, 1993). It's emotion that guides our attention in selecting what to think about, determines the amount of cognitive effort we'll put into a problem, and lets us know whether we've hit upon a reasonable solution or not.

Figure 4.1   Academic Family Tree of William James

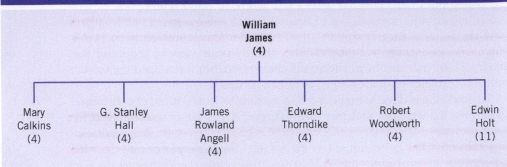

James also challenged the received wisdom on how emotions work. Imagine you're walking through the woods when you encounter a bear. What happens next? You'll probably say that you feel afraid and run, but James says you have the order wrong. Rather, he maintains that you become aroused by the sight of a bear and then interpret that arousal as fear. In other words, we don't run because we're afraid, but instead we're afraid because we run.

The idea that emotional experience is an interpretation of bodily arousal within a given situation is known as the **James-Lange theory** (Averill, 1993). Because Danish physician Carl Lange independently proposed a similar theory around the same time, both men get credit. Many current models of emotion are intellectual descendants of this theory, including the two-factor theory of emotion proposed by Stanley Schachter (Chapter 12) and the transactional model of stress proposed by Richard Lazarus (Chapter 16).

In the *Principles*, James devoted considerable space to a discussion of habits and instincts (Dewsbury, 1993). He thought of an **instinct** as *a complex behavioral response to a specific stimulus or situation that doesn't require learning*. Although instincts are innate, they may not be exhibited at birth. Rather, they appear and disappear over the course of development. According to James, instincts serve a clear evolutionary function, in that they bias the organism to behave in particular ways that increase its chances of survival and reproduction. James also pointed out that there's no clear distinction between instincts and emotions, since emotional expressions are instinctive reactions and each event that triggers an instinct also elicits an emotion.

In James's view, the purpose of instincts is to help us develop habits (Dewsbury, 1993). Both instincts and habits are complex patterns of behavior, but whereas an instinct is hard-wired, a **habit** is *a behavioral pattern that develops as the nervous system reorganizes through repeated action.* Instincts then bias us toward developing particular habits. However, James also believed we can cultivate behaviors, and much of the "self-help" advice that he sprinkled throughout his writings is based on the idea of grooming healthy habits.

James is traditionally called the father of American psychology (Figure 4.1). However, some historians of psychology maintain that it would be better to think of him in terms of the wise old uncle who advised and chastised the younger generation of experimental psychologists as they struggled to build an experimental science of the mind (Croce, 2010). Although James's ideas were largely ignored after his death, there's been a renewed interest in them in recent decades.

Mary Calkins

Mary Calkins (1863–1930) was an *early American psychologist who is best known as the first female president of the APA.* Elected in 1905, just thirteen years after its founding, this honor indicates the great respect her (mostly male) colleagues had for her. Yet today we rarely hear about her pioneering research that made her one of the most prominent psychologists of the early twentieth century. In fact, many of her discoveries were forgotten, and only recently has her priority in these fields been recognized.

After she graduated from Smith College, Calkins was offered an instructorship of Greek at Wellesley in 1887 (Calkins, 1930). When the Wellesley administration thought it would be good to offer some courses in the new psychology, Calkins was asked to get some graduate training so she could teach the subject. No university in the Boston area would accept a woman as an advanced student, but she obtained permission from Harvard to attend William James's seminars, and she also arranged privately with Edmund Sanford (1859–1924) to work in his lab at Clark University. With Sanford's help, she also established a psychology lab at Wellesley. She was making plans to travel to Freiburg, Germany, to study with Hugo Münsterberg when he got the invitation from Harvard. From 1892 to 1894, she worked as his unofficial graduate student, since Harvard still refused to admit her because of her sex.

During her first seminar at Harvard, Calkins found herself alone with James—all of the male students dropped the course when they found a woman was attending (Calkins, 1930). The two met by the library fireplace to discuss his newly published *Principles of Psychology*. This one-on-one with James deeply impressed Calkins.

Psychological thinking in the 1890s was still greatly influenced by the British empiricists, who conceived of thought processes as associations of ideas (Wentworth, 1999). James suggested Calkins experimentally test the proposed laws of association, and she undertook this project with Münsterberg. For this purpose, she invented a laboratory procedure now known as the **paired-associates task**, which is *a test of learning in which the participant memorizes pairs of unrelated words*. For example, you might be asked to remember associations such as SHOE-HOUSE and CAT-LEAF. Later, when you're prompted with SHOE, you respond with HOUSE. This has long been a standard laboratory task, but only recently has Calkins been recognized as its inventor.

At Clark University, Calkins also did groundbreaking research with Sanford on dreams (Calkins, 1930). Calkins and Sanford used an alarm clock to wake them at random intervals through the night, and they each recorded their dreams and later analyzed the content. In his 1900 work *The Interpretation of Dreams*, Sigmund Freud (Chapter 7) cites this research as evidence supporting his theory of dreams. However, Calkins maintained that her data in fact contradicted his notion of dreaming as wish fulfillment.

In 1895, Calkins presented her published work on paired-associates learning as a dissertation and passed a doctoral exam (Madigan & O'Hara, 1992). Although James and Münsterberg strongly recommended she be granted a Ph.D., the Harvard administration refused. In 1902, the university offered her a Ph.D. from its "little sister," Radcliffe College, but she refused. Shortly before her death, a group of Harvard graduates—including Robert Yerkes, Edward Thorndike, and Robert Woodworth—petitioned the university to award her the degree, but the request was rejected (Young, 2010). Harvard also ignored a petition campaign in 2002 to have Calkin's degree conferred posthumously.

After the turn of the century, Calkins became disillusioned with the direction American psychology was headed, especially the behaviorist denial of consciousness. She stopped experimenting and devoted herself instead to building a theoretical framework she called **self-psychology**. This is *the position that the proper subject of psychology is the study of conscious selves as they interact with their social and physical environments* (Wentworth, 1999). By emphasizing the conscious self, Calkins shows the great impact James had on her thinking. Perhaps because of her shift toward philosophy in later years, her early contributions to experimental psychology were largely forgotten.

Robert Yerkes

In his youth, he dreamed of being a country doctor, but an unexpected loan from a relative gave **Robert Yerkes** (1876–1956; pronounced *YUR-kees*) the chance to study at Harvard (Yerkes, 1932). Working with Hugo Münsterberg, Yerkes discovered his passion for animal psychology and earned a Ph.D. in 1902 with a dissertation on the nervous system of the jellyfish. Today, Yerkes is known as an *early American psychologist who was a pioneer in the fields of comparative psychology and intelligence testing.*

**Photo 4.2
Robert Yerkes**

After graduation, Yerkes was hired at Harvard, where he conducted much of his groundbreaking research on animal behavior and intelligence, ranging from studies of learning in earthworms (yes, they can!) to problem solving in primates (Hilgard, 1965). He collaborated with many of the leading American psychologists of the time, including Edward Thorndike (this chapter) and John Watson (Chapter 5). In Russia, Ivan Pavlov (Chapter 9) credited Yerkes with the insight that led to the discovery of conditioned reflexes; in return, Yerkes published a paper in 1909 introducing Pavlov's method to American psychologists.

In 1908, Yerkes published an article with his graduate student John Dodson that would eventually become one of his most cited works (Corbett, 2015). In this paper, they described a study on discrimination learning under threat of electric shock in Japanese dancing mice. They found that the mice learned best when the level of shock was moderate, as compared to mild or severe shocks. This finding led to what is now called the Yerkes-Dodson law, which is *the observation that there is an optimal level of arousal, neither too high nor too low, for best performance on a complex task*. This law is often presented as an inverted U-shaped curve, which you've no doubt seen in other textbooks. However, Yerkes and Dodson also found that performance improved in a linear fashion as arousal increased when the task was simple. The Yerkes-Dodson law is now considered one of the classic studies in the field, even though some psychologists in recent years have questioned whether it's truly applicable to human performance in all situations.

Harvard didn't approve of Yerkes's animal research, so they wouldn't promote him or give him a salary increase (Carmichael, 1957). Yerkes had just accepted a more lucrative position at the University of Minnesota when the United States entered World War I. Uncle Sam needed Yerkes, so he joined the Army instead. Because he already had some experience in intelligence testing, Yerkes was put in charge of the Army's program to assess the intelligence of all its recruits. Working with other psychologists, Yerkes guided the development of the Army Alpha for those who could read and the Army Beta for those who couldn't. His staff of over 400 persons then administered these tests to 1.7 million recruits.

After the war, Yerkes remained in Washington, DC, to compile a report on the Army's intelligence testing program (Hilgard, 1965). In addition, he chaired several committees with the goal of promoting and funding psychological research. He also championed for unpopular causes, such as the Committee for Research in Problems of Sex, which supported Alfred Kinsey (1894–1956), a pioneer in the study of human sexuality.

In 1924, Yerkes was offered a professorship at Yale (Yerkes, 1932). The university's president, James Rowland Angell (this chapter), was one of the founders of the Chicago school of functionalism, and he was very much interested in establishing the primate research center that Yerkes had been promoting for years. With university and external funding, Yale acquired land for this in Orange Park, Florida. Yerkes opened the facility in 1930 and remained its director until his retirement in 1942. His hand-picked successor, Karl Lashley (Chapter 10), then assumed directorship. Later, Yale transferred ownership of the Yerkes National Primate Research Center to Emory University, which moved the facility to Atlanta.

Although Yerkes's own research focused on animal behavior, he opposed the behaviorism that had come to dominate psychology. As a researcher of both human and animal intelligence, Yerkes (1932) found it "wholly indefensible, and extremely unprofitable" (p. 396) to reject the scientific study of conscious experience. Still, he respected colleagues who were convinced behaviorism was the right direction for psychology.

Clark School

In the early decades of the twentieth century, Clark University was a powerhouse for research in psychology. Its president, G. Stanley Hall, had earned his Ph.D. with James at Harvard and then done postdoctoral research at Leipzig University. We'll also consider his two most noted students, Lewis Terman and Arnold Gesell, who were pioneers in developmental psychology.

G. Stanley Hall

Although he was an expert on adolescent psychology, **G. Stanley Hall** (1846–1924) suffered from father issues all his life. He'd attended seminary, but he rejected his father's pious beliefs only to become obsessed with religion again later in life. He was a student of the two great "fathers of psychology," William James and Wilhelm Wundt, but for most of his career he belittled them both, insisting he was a much better psychologist than either of them. His vanity was legendary and his ambitions grandiose, but these qualities also drove him to excellence. It's only fitting that G. Stanley Hall, the eternal teenager, is remembered today as the *early American psychologist who pioneered developmental psychology*.

Frederick Gutekunst, via Wikimedia Commons

Photo 4.3
G. Stanley Hall

In 1878, Hall completed a Ph.D. with James at Harvard (Bringmann, Bringmann, & Early, 1992). He then spent a couple of years in Germany, including a brief period in Wundt's lab at Leipzig but also interaction with Helmholtz, Fechner, and Weber. After Hall returned to the United States, he taught at Johns Hopkins, where he established a psychology lab and began publishing the *American Journal of Psychology*.

Johns Hopkins had just recently been established on the German research university model (White, 2002). Hall found himself at the center of a revolution in American higher education, which became the focus of his life's work. So when he was asked to serve as the first president of Clark University, he gladly accepted.

Clark was also designed on the German model, and Hall visited the great universities of Europe, gathering ideas (White, 2002). He had a grand vision for Clark as a renowned research center, but the first years were touch and go. There were "town-gown" issues, and Jonas Clark, the university's sole benefactor, lost interest in the project. Worst of all, there was competition from the better-funded University of Chicago. Two-thirds of Clark's faculty and graduate students were lured to Chicago with promises of better salaries and stipends. Hall also suffered a deep personal tragedy when his wife and daughter were killed in an accident. Nevertheless, Hall persisted, building Clark into one of the major centers of psychological research in the early twentieth century.

After Clark University had become firmly established, Hall played the role of statesman for psychology (Arnett & Cravens, 2006). Two contributions are especially noteworthy. In 1892, he organized the American Psychological Association and was elected its first president. And in 1909, Hall invited Sigmund Freud and Carl Jung to Clark, where they gave speeches that popularized psychoanalytic ideas among the American public.

Hall had long been interested in the **Child Study Movement**, which was *a late nineteenth-century campaign to reform educational practices based on the scientific study of child development* (Arnett & Cravens, 2006). So he decided to make Clark University a center for child research. This was remarkable at the time, since many early psychologists thought nothing interesting could be learned from studying children. However, Hall attracted top-notch students with interests in the Child Study Movement.

Although Hall supervised a wide range of research projects on child development, he's best known for his questionnaire studies (Brooks-Gunn & Johnson, 2006). Hall and his students distributed surveys to hundreds of teachers and principals, collecting data on about 100,000 children altogether. The reports that issued from these questionnaire studies were criticized by other psychologists as unscientific. Many early American psychologists believed the proper approach to their science was the testing of hypotheses through experiments. But Hall engaged in "theory-free" data collection, so there was supposedly no way to interpret the results. Nevertheless, Hall's data painted a picture of childhood development that's generally consistent with what's known today.

In 1904, Hall published his greatest work, *Adolescence* (Arnett & Cravens, 2006). In the book, Hall broaches topics never before discussed in print, such as teenage masturbation and premarital sex. Both were to be suppressed at all costs, he insisted, but the mere fact that he openly discussed these issues was a significant step forward.

Hall favored ideas that seem odd from a modern perspective, even though they reflected the scientific thinking of his time (Graebner, 2006). For example, Hall believed in **recapitulation theory**. This is *the idea that a developing organism repeats all the stages of the evolution of its species.* Today we understand that some evolutionary vestiges may appear during the course of development, but the organism certainly doesn't recapitulate its entire evolutionary history. Likewise, he subscribed to both Darwinian and Lamarckian evolution, a common position at the time. He warned that bad habits acquired in adolescence, such as excessive sexuality, could lead to physical or mental defects in the next generation. (He was terrified of masturbation because his father had told him his nose would fall off if he touched himself.) Hall was a man of his times, and we can't blame him for that.

Because of his strong reliance on evolution as an explanation for development, Hall insisted that intelligence was inherited and that education did little to improve a child's abilities (Brooks-Gunn & Johnson, 2006). Instead of subjecting all children to the same curriculum, he argued, education should be tailored to the needs of the child. Gifted children should be prepared for a university education, while those of meager abilities should be trained as farmers or laborers.

Like many of the male psychologists of the early twentieth century, Hall had contradictory ideas concerning women and education (Diehl, 1986). He believed a woman's place was in the home, having babies and caring for children. Nevertheless, he mentored many women scholars who were attracted to the Child Study Movement. At the time, most psychologists—Hall included—subscribed to the **variability hypothesis**. This was *the notion that men display more extremes in high and low intelligence, whereas women tend to cluster around average abilities.* With its quasi-statistical approach, the theory supposedly explained why there were far more eminent men than women. In Hall's view, these rare exceptional women, who wouldn't find husbands anyway, might as well devote their careers to the "nurturing" professions. But it was women psychologists like Helen Thompson Woolley and Leta Hollingworth who then challenged the variability hypothesis, arguing that the constraints against women were social and not biological.

Many of Hall's ideas are out of touch with modern sensibilities. Yet his legacy to psychology is the impact he had on the rising generation of experimental psychologists. One of his Hopkins students, John Dewey, made significant contributions to pedagogical theory. And his Clark students Lewis Terman and Arnold Gesell, to name just two, were pioneers in developmental psychology. Hall applied the variability hypothesis to people of color as well, and so he agreed to mentor Francis Cecil Sumner, the first African American to earn a Ph.D. in psychology (Figure 4.2). Although Hall's ideas were forward-looking in many respects, he never quite freed himself from his nineteenth-century worldview.

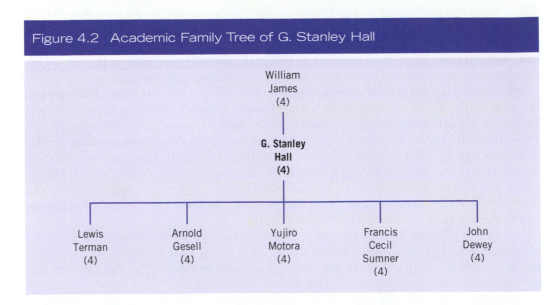

Figure 4.2   Academic Family Tree of G. Stanley Hall

Lewis Terman

In his early days, Lewis Terman taught in a one-room schoolhouse (Terman, 1932). But he was attracted by the Child Study Movement, so he did his doctorate at Clark. During his long career at Stanford, Terman built the psychology department into one of the top programs in the nation. Today, Lewis Terman (1877–1956) is known as an *early American psychologist who popularized the use of intelligence tests and performed landmark studies on gifted children.*

As we've already seen, there was a push in the early twentieth century to develop tests to measure the intelligence of children and young adults. However, the mental tests of Galton and Cattell had failed to correlate with other indicators of intelligence. In France, psychologist Alfred Binet and his assistant Théodore Simon (Chapter 8) developed an intelligence test that successfully identified schoolchildren needing remedial education. Rather than assessing basic abilities, as Galton and Cattell had done, they asked children to solve problems. The Binet-Simon, published in 1905, became the first practical test of intelligence.

Photo 4.4
Lewis Terman

Terman reworked the Binet-Simon for the English language and American culture. Published in 1916, the **Stanford-Binet** was *the first successful English-language test of intelligence* (Minton, 2000b). In revised form, it's still widely used today. Terman also extended the work of Binet and Simon by including an IQ score so that individuals could be compared against their group norms. The German psychologist William Stern (Chapter 6) had developed the concept of an **intelligence quotient**, or IQ, as *the ratio between the mental age and the chronological age of the test taker*. However, the Stanford-Binet was the first time IQ was incorporated into a published intelligence test.

Because of the Stanford-Binet's success, Terman was quickly regarded as an expert in intelligence testing (Hegarty, 2007). So when the United States entered World War I in 1917, Yerkes asked Terman to join his team, where he helped develop the Army Alpha and Beta tests. The original intention of the tests was to sort out those who were unfit for military duty. But Terman understood they could also identify bright young men who would make good officers, and this insight led to the project that consumed the rest of his career.

During the 1920s, Terman used the Stanford-Binet to identify over 1,500 children of high intelligence (Colangelo, 1997). The purpose of the study was to test several common beliefs about gifted children. First, the group contained roughly equal numbers of boys and girls, calling the variability hypothesis into question. Second, Terman wanted to challenge the common notion that gifted children were physically weak, so he gave them physical exams and found they were healthier than their classmates.

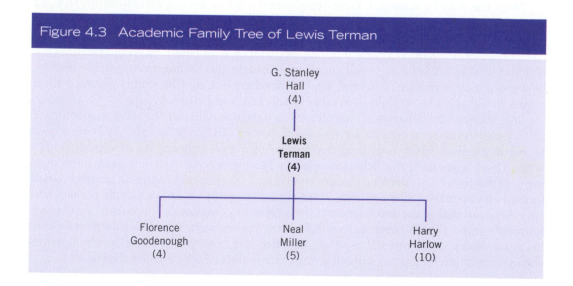

Figure 4.3 Academic Family Tree of Lewis Terman

G. Stanley
Hall
(4)

Lewis
Terman
(4)

Florence
Goodenough
(4)

Neal
Miller
(5)

Harry
Harlow
(10)

Terman followed this group into adulthood, testing them at regular intervals (Minton, 2000b). As the group entered mid-adulthood, they continued to test in the top 1%, and many of them—especially the men—had significant career achievements. (Terman recognized that social norms prevented many women from entering the workforce.) Furthermore, the group as a whole maintained high levels of health, and they had a much lower incidence of psychological disorders or alcoholism.

When Terman died, his associates continued the study (Novotney, 2011). This was the first large-scale longitudinal study ever conducted in psychology, and the data gathered in this massive project are still being mined for useful information today. The project had another impact on psychology as well. Lee Cronbach (Chapter 13) was one of the "Termites," as the group members called themselves (Figure 4.3). Inspired by Terman, Cronbach became one of the leading experts on psychological testing, ranking among the 100 most influential psychologists of the twentieth century (Haggbloom et al., 2002).

Arnold Gesell

Before attending Clark, Arnold Gesell worked as a teacher and principal. He was attracted to the Child Study Movement, so he went to Clark to study with Hall. Today, **Arnold Gesell** (1880–1961) is remembered as an *early American psychologist who measured developmental norms in infants and young children.*

In 1911, Gesell was hired at Yale, where he stayed for the rest of his career (Thelen & Adolph, 1992). There, he set up a clinic similar to Witmer's at Pennsylvania. Gesell was ambitious and wanted to stake out his own turf. Witmer worked with delayed children, Terman studied gifted children, and fellow Clark graduate Henry Goddard (1866–1957) was a specialist in the feeble-minded. What was left was the normal child, and that's where Gesell focused his research.

Gesell felt his psychology degree left him ill-prepared for studying childhood development (Harris, 2011). So he pursued a medical degree, specializing in pediatrics. During the 1930s and 1940s, he built up the world-renowned Yale Clinic of Child Development with generous funding from the university and external agencies.

The central task of Gesell and his associates was a detailed description of the developmental process (Benzaquén, 2001). Thousands of infants and toddlers were brought into the clinic, where their performance on tasks like grasping and walking was meticulously recorded. In addition to written records, over 12,000 children were photographed or filmed. Gesell even had a large observation dome with one-way vision screens set up in the lab so that students and visitors could unobtrusively watch him and his assistants conduct what he called "behavioral interviews." The laboratory amassed a huge collection of photographs—many of which were published in a series of popular books—and an outstanding film library.

With the data he collected, Gesell established a set of developmental norms that are still in use today (Thelen & Adolph, 1992). Furthermore, the common notion that there's a typical timeline for the onset of behaviors comes from Gesell's work. Recent years have seen some criticism of his developmental norms, in that they were based on White, middle-class children from intact families. Gesell intentionally sought this homogeneous sample because he wanted a clear picture of normal, healthy development, and he simply assumed these norms would apply to children from other social classes and ethnic groups.

In contrast to the behaviorists, who emphasized the role of the environment in shaping the child, Gesell insisted that genetics was far more important (Thelen & Adolph, 1992). He argued for **maturationism**, which is *the belief that development unfolds according to a set schedule of milestones.* Gesell maintained that behaviors appear when the nervous system is ready to produce them. In this respect, his thinking was similar to that of Jean Piaget (Chapter 8), although Gesell focused on observable behaviors while Piaget studied cognitive processes. Gesell's position also ran counter to that of the psychoanalysts, who came to dominate developmental psychology toward the end of Gesell's career. As a result, his contributions were neglected in the decades after his death. Today, developmental psychologists often take concepts like developmental norms and maturationism for granted without giving credit to the one who originated these ideas.

Yujiro Motora

Japan's first experimental psychologist was the son of a samurai, so swift was the nation's transformation from a feudal to an industrial society (Sato & Sato, 2005). **Yujiro Motora** (1858–1913) worked with G. Stanley Hall at Johns Hopkins University, and he was the *first Japanese psychologist to earn his doctorate at an American university* (Sato et al., 2016).

Returning to Japan in 1888, Motora was appointed professor of psychology at Tokyo Imperial University (Oyama, Sato, & Suzuki, 2001). Working with his younger colleague Matataro Matsumoto (1865–1943) who'd studied with Wundt in Leipzig, Motora established Japan's first psychology lab, equipped with state-of-the-art "brass instrument" technology. Motora and Matsumoto then trained the first generation of Japanese experimental psychologists.

Motora was especially interested in the process of attention (Takeda, Ando, & Kumagai, 2015). Japan was expanding its school system, and Motora saw an educational application for his attention research. Like Witmer in Philadelphia, Motora opened a clinic in Tokyo for underachieving school-children. He insisted that these children weren't mentally deficient but rather had difficulty inhibiting distractions. He developed tasks to teach them how to focus their attention. After treatment in his clinic, many of these children showed improved performance in school. In sum, Motora found ways to treat what we now call attention-deficit disorder.

Motora nurtured a number of graduate students, who formed the first generation of experimental psychologists in Japan. Indeed, the son of a samurai was the father of Japanese psychology.

Photo 4.5
Yujiro Motora

Francis Cecil Sumner

His parents didn't think he could get a good education in the segregated schools, so **Francis Cecil Sumner** (1895–1954) was homeschooled instead (Sawyer, 2000). In 1911, he was admitted to Lincoln University—he was only 15 at the time. He graduated four years later, as class valedictorian. Sumner stayed at Lincoln to do his master's degree, but he had difficulty finding a doctoral program that would accept him. So he wrote to G. Stanley Hall (this chapter), president of Clark University, stating that he wanted to study "race psychology."

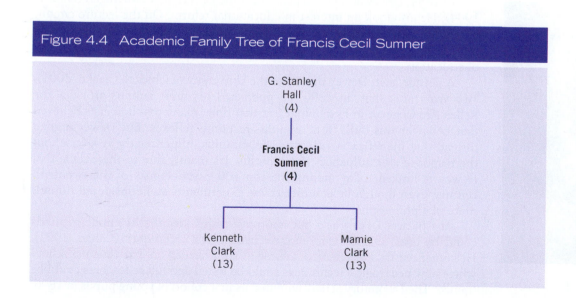

Figure 4.4 Academic Family Tree of Francis Cecil Sumner

G. Stanley
Hall
(4)

Francis Cecil
Sumner
(4)

Kenneth
Clark
(13)

Mamie
Clark
(13)

Hall was impressed and admitted him. Three years later, in 1920, Sumner become the *first African American to earn a Ph.D. in psychology.*

In 1928, Sumner was called to Howard University to build a department of psychology there (Sawyer, 2000). Under his directorship, Howard became a leading bachelor's and master's program in psychology, producing more Black psychologists than all other colleges and universities combined (Guthrie, 2000). Sumner's most famous students were the husband-and-wife team of Kenneth Bancroft Clark and Mamie Phipps Clark (Chapter 13). The Clarks went on to Columbia University to earn their doctorate degrees, and they conducted research that the Supreme Court cited in their 1954 *Brown v. Board of Education* decision declaring school segregation unconstitutional (Figure 4.4). Sumner died four months before the landmark ruling, but he was proud that his students were fighting to end the segregation that had kept him out of school (Sawyer, 2000).

Chicago School

Although William James had first proposed a psychology based on Darwinian principles, it was John Dewey and James Rowland Angell at the University of Chicago who fully developed this approach (Chaplin, 2000). Defining psychology as the study of how mental activities aid the organism in adapting to its environment, they gladly accepted the label "functionalism" as the name for their school.

John Dewey

His life spanned nearly a century—from the mid-nineteenth to the mid-twentieth—but most of the contributions John Dewey (1859–1952) made to psychology were in his early years. As Dewey matured in his career, he was dismayed by the field's enthusiasm for behaviorism, and he turned to other disciplines in which he also made significant contributions. Today, Dewey is recognized as an *early American psychologist who, with James Rowland Angell, was one of the founders of the Chicago school of functionalism.*

Dewey studied philosophy at Johns Hopkins University, but he some took psychology courses with G. Stanley Hall (Backe, 2001). He also befriended James McKeen Cattell, who'd studied with Hall before working with Wundt in Leipzig. Although Dewey considered himself a philosopher, these two acquaintances impressed him with the idea that psychology could be approached in a scientific manner.

In 1884, Dewey accepted a position at the University of Michigan (Barone, 1994). He also took an interest in educational reform. On the lecture circuit, he argued that experimental psychology provided methods for discovering more effective pedagogical techniques, and he developed an influential theory of education.

A decade later, Dewey moved to the University of Chicago (Backe, 2001). Two years after that, in 1896, he published his most famous article, "The Reflex Arc Concept in Psychology." At that time, many psychologists believed that behavior was built from stimulus-response reflexes. But Dewey argued instead that the reflex is a circuit. The stimulus influences the response, but the response also influences the stimulus. It's mainly due to this article that Dewey is ranked today among the top 100 psychologists of the twentieth century, even though he conducted few experiments and considered himself more of a philosopher.

At Chicago, Dewey also put into practice his idea that scientific methods could be used to find more effective pedagogical techniques (Cahan, 1992). He convinced the University of Chicago that it needed an experimental school where new pedagogical techniques could be tested and future teachers could be trained. The Laboratory School admitted its first cohort of young pupils in 1896.

Photo 4.6
John Dewey

Its teachers were all graduate students in Dewey's program, and he used the school to try out new pedagogical techniques as he developed his theory of education.

Dewey's educational reforms were met with considerable resistance (Barone, 1994). At the beginning, the university administration gave Dewey free rein, but later it wanted more oversight. For three years, Dewey fought for the independence of the Laboratory School, but the administration seized control while he was away on a lecture tour. When Dewey returned, he saw no option but to resign and thus ended his decade at the University of Chicago.

Cattell arranged a professorship for Dewey at Columbia, where he continued to develop his theory of education (Pillsbury, 1957). An early advocate for student-centered learning, Dewey believed that the traditional view of children as receptacles into which teachers poured their knowledge was flawed. Instead, he viewed learning as a problem-solving process, and he called for the use of structured tasks in which children learned through experience. The teacher's role, then, was to act as a facilitator of learning, not as an authority who handed down wisdom from on high. Half a century later, the humanistic psychologist Carl Rogers (Chapter 15) would pick up Dewey's idea of facilitated learned and popularize it.

Dewey used his growing influence to champion for human rights (Barone, 1994). In 1916, he helped establish the American Civil Liberties Union. He also defended Cattell when he was fired, one of the few who did. Recognizing the need for a safe haven for faculty members who expressed unpopular views, Dewey and other prominent academics founded the New School for Social Research in 1919. Many German psychologists fleeing Nazism in the 1930s found refuge at the New School.

Psychology claims John Dewey as one of its founders. But many other fields, such as philosophy, educational theory, social activism, and secular humanism all claim him as one of their own. It's hard to think of a twentieth-century figure who contributed so much to so many fields as John Dewey.

James Rowland Angell

James Rowland Angell (1869–1949) was an undergraduate at the University of Michigan when he first met Dewey, who encouraged him to stay for a master's degree (Angell, 1936). After that, Angell spent a year at Harvard working with William James before going to Germany. He was almost done with his dissertation when he got an offer from the University of Minnesota. Stay and finish the thesis, or take the job? There was a sweetheart back home, but he needed a decent income to marry her, so he left without his degree. Nevertheless, he soon developed a reputation as an *early American psychologist who, with John Dewey, was one of the founders of the Chicago school of functionalism.*

Angell only spent a year at Minnesota (Hunter, 1951). Dewey was now chair of psychology at Chicago, and he wanted Angell to work with him. Dewey and Angell quickly built Chicago into one of the nation's leading centers for psychology. Among the noted graduates of the program during this time were Helen Thompson Woolley and L. L. Thurstone (this chapter) and John Watson (Chapter 5).

Titchener had used the term "functional psychology" as a loose term for any approach that didn't fit into his structural psychology (Tolman, 2000a). But during the years around the turn of the twentieth century, Dewey and Angell worked to define functional psychology in terms of James's pragmatism. In fact, it was James who dubbed their approach "the Chicago school." Dewey's 1896 "Reflex Arc" article had set the agenda for a pragmatic, functional psychology, but it was Angell's presidential address to the APA in 1906 that laid out the goals and methods of functionalism.

According to Angell, functionalism used both introspection and objective observations of behavior to study how the organism adapts to its environment (Hunter, 1951). Functionalists viewed consciousness as an interface between

Photo 4.7
James Rowland Angell

organism and environment that had evolved to solve complex problems which simpler reflexes, instincts, and habits couldn't handle. Consciousness then was an adaptation that helped the organism survive. Thus, we can see the approach was deeply grounded in Darwinian principles.

In 1921, Angell accepted the presidency at Yale, where he expanded the existing psychology program into the Institute of Human Relations (Hunter, 1951). He included Gesell's clinic as part of this institute and supported its phenomenal growth. He also enticed Yerkes to Yale with the promise of a primate research facility. Additionally, he brought psychiatry and social psychology into the institute, making it one of the nation's most comprehensive research centers for the social sciences.

During his busy career, Angell never returned to Germany to finish his dissertation. Nevertheless, the man who gave up his Ph.D. for the woman he loved guided the doctoral research of many of psychology's next generation of leaders, including five presidents of the APA (Tolman, 2000a). In his role as administrator at Chicago and Yale, Angell significantly raised the prestige of psychology as a legitimate and important science (Figure 4.5).

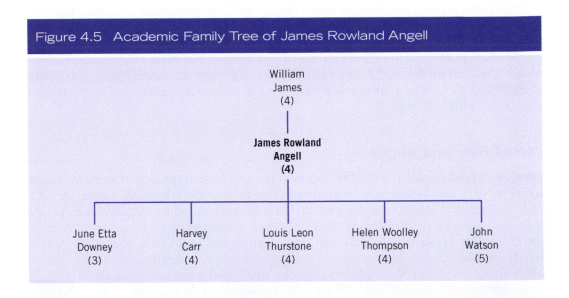

Figure 4.5 Academic Family Tree of James Rowland Angell

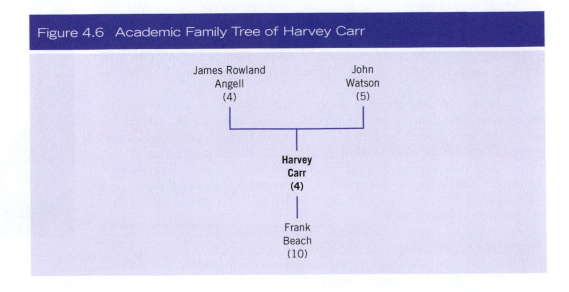

Figure 4.6 Academic Family Tree of Harvey Carr

Harvey Carr

After the departure of Dewey and Angell, **Harvey Carr** (1873–1954) assumed the leadership of the Chicago school (Tolman, 2000b). As a graduate student at Chicago, he'd considered both Angell and John Watson (Chapter 5) as his mentors, and he adopted a philosophical stance halfway between the two. Angell emphasized the centrality of conscious mental processes in psychology, whereas Watson denied their importance. In the middle stood Carr, who never rejected the assumption of underlying mental processes but who also believed that the careful observation of behavior was the core of psychology, particularly in the study of animals. He contributed little to the field in terms of theory, but he was a mentor to many notable psychologists of the mid-twentieth century (Figure 4.6). Thus, Harvey Carr is seen as the *early American psychologist who led the functionalist movement during its transition into behaviorism*.

Helen Thompson Woolley

In the early twentieth century, women were seen as the "weaker sex," not just physically but also mentally (Milar, 2010). **Helen Thompson Woolley** (1874–1947) challenged that assumption, both in her research and in her own life. She was the first woman to receive a Ph.D. from the University of Chicago, outperforming her classmate John Watson, who admitted being envious for years. We remember Woolley as an *early American psychologist who made important contributions to the psychology of women and child development*.

Woolley published her dissertation as the book *The Mental Traits of Sex* (1903). This was the first systematic study of gender differences (Minton, 2000a). In her research, she tested men and women on a battery of sensory, motor, and cognitive tasks. The differences she found were small, disputing the assumptions of the variability hypothesis. Furthermore, she challenged the received wisdom that gender differences were biological, arguing instead for environmental factors such as training or social expectations.

In 1909, Woolley moved to Cincinnati with her husband and baby daughter. There she directed a large study conducted by the city's school district to investigate the effects of child labor on later development (Milar, 1999). The results of this massive project led to important changes in laws concerning child labor and compulsory education. Like many women psychologists through much of the twentieth century, Woolley made important contributions to psychology even though she was effectively barred from academia because of her sex.

L. L. Thurstone

As an undergraduate, **Louis Leon Thurstone** (1887–1955) studied engineering at Cornell (Thurstone, 1952). But he also attended lectures by Titchener, which led to an interest in human-machine interaction. After college, Thurstone worked in the laboratory of the famous inventor Thomas Edison, but he eventually left to pursue his doctorate at Chicago, earning his degree in 1917 with Angell as his mentor. Even before completing his degree, he was offered a position at Carnegie Institute of Technology in Pittsburgh. In 1923, he moved back to Chicago, where he stayed for the rest of his career. Among his many contributions, we remember L. L. Thurstone mainly as the *early American psychologist who proposed that intelligence can be broken down into seven primary mental abilities*.

Thurstone was a pioneer in the field of **psychometrics**, which is *the field involved in the measurement of an individual's psychological characteristics* (Guilford, 1957). As such, he made important early contributions to the development of personality, intelligence, and scholastic aptitude tests. He also developed effective means for assessing attitudes, which many of his contemporaries believed to be unmeasurable. Nowadays, attitude measurement is a common feature in psychological research, both in theoretical areas such as social and personality psychology as well as in applied areas such as marketing and industrial/organizational psychology. Yet Thurstone was the first to demonstrate that attitude assessment could be done in a valid and reliable manner.

Table 4.1 Thurstone's Seven Primary Mental Abilities

Primary Mental Ability	Description
Space	Ability to perceive complex spatial relations
Perceptual speed	Ability to detect visual details quickly
Number	Ability to make mental and other numerical computations
Verbal comprehension	Ability to understand the meaning of spoken and written language
Word fluency	Ability to retrieve and use vocabulary rapidly
Memory	Ability to store and retrieve information efficiently
Reasoning	Ability to induce a general rule from a few instances

No doubt, Thurstone is best known for his work on intelligence (Guilford, 1957). Early in the twentieth century, British psychologist Charles Spearman (Chapter 14) promoted his theory of general intelligence, which held that there was a single intellectual basis for all cognitive abilities. He arrived at this conclusion through the use of *a statistical technique for reducing a large number of observed variables to a small number of underlying variables*. Spearman is generally credited with having invented this method, which he called **factor analysis**. Thurstone developed his own version of factor analysis, but when he applied it to his data sets, he found he couldn't reduce intelligence to a single variable. Instead, his analyses suggested seven factors, which he called the **primary mental abilities** (Table 4.1). These are *the seven basic forms of intelligence proposed by Thurstone*. As we learned in Chapter 3, Thurstone taught J. P. Guilford how to do factor analysis, and this eventually led to Guilford's structure-of-intellect theory with its proposal of 180 mental abilities.

Supporters of Spearman and Thurstone engaged in an extended debate regarding the nature of intelligence and the proper methods of factor analysis. British psychologists tended to prefer Spearman's approach to factor analysis, which consistently supported the theory of general intelligence. In contrast, opinion among American psychologists was divided. On the one hand, many of the early pioneers in intelligence testing, such as Lewis Terman, Robert Yerkes, and Edwin Boring, favored the notion of a general intelligence that could be represented by a single number such as mental age or intelligence quotient. On the other hand, quite a few different theories of multiple intelligences have been proposed by American psychologists. While these theorists all agree that there isn't just one kind of intelligence, they still haven't reached a consensus on just how many there are. A century after it began, the debate over general intelligence versus multiple intelligences is still going strong, with no resolution in sight.

Columbia School

Although James McKeen Cattell had been a student of Wundt, his thinking was more in line with the functionalists. This can be seen not only in Cattell's own work but also in the research of those he mentored, such as Edward Thorndike and Robert Woodworth. Later joining Cattell as faculty members at Columbia, these two psychologists applied experimental methods to problems in education and industry. Together, they built Columbia as yet another center of the functionalist movement.

Edward Thorndike

In 1897, Edward Thorndike (1874–1949) headed to New York with his "two most educated chickens" (Thorndike, 1936, p. 265). As a student at Harvard, he'd kept his chickens in his room until his landlady protested. William James offered space in his lab but Harvard forbade animals on campus, so James let Thorndike use his basement instead, much to the annoyance of Mrs. James. The problem was solved when Cattell offered Thorndike a fellowship at Columbia and space in his lab for the birds. The following year, Thorndike completed his doctoral dissertation, which he published as *Animal Intelligence*. This book revolutionized the field of comparative psychology by demonstrating that the experimental methods of psychology could be applied to non-human animals as well. Today, Thorndike is known as an *early American psychologist who pioneered learning theory and educational psychology*.

To test animal intelligence, Thorndike constructed a device he called a **puzzle box.** This was *an enclosure from which a test animal can escape if it performs the correct behavior* (Beatty, 1998). He then put a hungry cat into the puzzle box and some food outside. In the "amazing animal" tales that were common in the late nineteenth century, dogs and cats supposedly used rational problem solving to overcome barriers. But this wasn't what Thorndike observed. Instead, the animals thrashed wildly about, eventually undoing the latch by accident. And when they were put back in the puzzle box, they seemed to have no idea how they'd escaped before. Instead, over many repetitions and through a process of trial and error, the animals learned how to open the door.

These studies led Thorndike to devise three laws of learning (Galef, 1998). While they had a significant influence on educational theory, as Thorndike had intended, they also helped shape the behaviorist movement of the following decades. Although Thorndike saw all three laws as important (Table 4.2), different factions of behaviorism tended to latch onto one or another of the three laws as the key principle of learning:

Photo 4.8
Edward Thorndike

- **Law of readiness.** This is *the observation that individuals learn best when they are motivated and prepared to do so.* For educational theory, this law indicates the need to provide students with a clear purpose for learning. It was also viewed as the key law of learning among neo-behaviorists such as Clark Hull, who made motivation the center of his drive theory of learning.

- **Law of exercise.** This is *the observation that learning increases with the number of repetitions.* For educational theory, this law emphasizes the need for drill and practice in acquiring a new skill. It was also the key law of learning that underlay John Watson's theory of conditioned emotional responses.

- **Law of effect.** This is *the observation that learning is strengthened when it is accompanied by a pleasant feeling and weakened when it is accompanied by an unpleasant feeling.* For educational theory, this law recognizes the importance of a pleasant learning experience, and it also shows that the threat of punishment can be detrimental to learning. The law of effect also became the basis for B. F. Skinner's operant conditioning.

We'll revisit Thorndike's three laws of learning in Chapter 5 when we discuss behaviorism.

Thorndike grouped these three laws under a general theory of learning called **connectionism** (Woodworth, 1952). This was *the view that learning is fundamentally about forming new associations or connections.* He also claimed that connectionism accounted for learning in all organisms, from the simplest animals to humans. The only difference was in the ability to form new connections rapidly. For example, he found that a monkey could escape from a puzzle box faster than a dog or cat, but it still went through the same trial-and-error process. Although Thorndike never tried the experiment on humans, introspect for a moment: What would you do if you were put inside a human-sized puzzle box?

After graduation, Cattell arranged a position for Thorndike at Columbia Teachers College, where he stayed for the rest of his long and productive career (Beatty, 1998). At this point, he abandoned animal research and applied his connectionist theory of learning to the

Popular Science Monthly, Volume 80, via Wikimedia Commons

Table 4.2 Thorndike's Three Laws of Learning

Law	Definition	Application
Readiness	Individuals learn best when they are motivated and prepared to do so.	Clark Hull's drive reduction theory
Exercise	Learning increases with the number of repetitions.	John Watson's conditioned emotional response
Effect	Learning is strengthened when it is accompanied by a pleasant feeling and weakened when it is accompanied by an unpleasant feeling.	B. F. Skinner's operant conditioning

educational process instead. With his colleague Robert Woodworth, Thorndike embarked on a series of experiments that tested the **transfer of training**. This is *the idea that learning in one subject will aid learning in a different subject*. For instance, it was believed that instruction in Latin or geometry fortified a student's faculty of reasoning. Thorndike and Woodworth showed this wasn't the case. Some transfer of training does occur when two tasks are very similar, but when the tasks have few elements in common, little transfer of training takes place. Learning Latin simply doesn't improve your ability to think rationally, and few high schools or colleges teach it anymore.

Influenced by Cattell, Thorndike became interested in test development (Woodworth, 1952). He devised tests for assessing children's progress in various school subjects. During World War I, he kept his civilian status but he still participated in the intelligence testing of Army recruits. Later, he devised one of the first college entrance exams. Thorndike and Woodworth also joined Cattell in forming the Psychological Corporation in 1921, where they constructed personality and vocational tests for educational, industrial, and governmental clients.

Thorndike was a man of strong beliefs, and although he was never combative toward contrary opinions, he always stood fast in his own (Woodworth, 1952). His work had set the stage for the behaviorist movement, but he firmly rejected its dismissal of mental processes. He also believed that intelligence and other individual differences were largely due to hereditary factors, in line with the thinking of his academic forebears Cattell and Galton. So he also opposed the behaviorist emphasis on experience over inheritance.

Figure 4.7 Academic Family Tree of Edward Thorndike

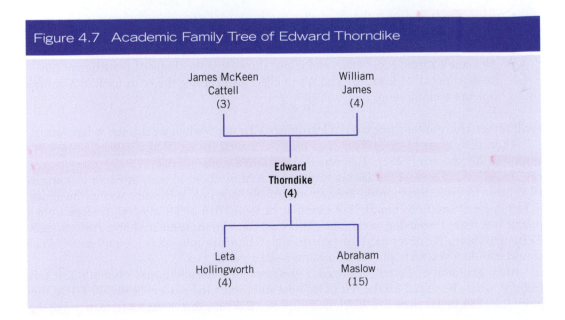

Finally, Thorndike maintained that psychological research should be driven by data and not theory. He believed in exact measurement and in letting the data speak for themselves. There was no need for a grand theory to explain the data, nor did he need theory to guide his research. In this sense, he was the quintessential functionalist, finding solutions to practical problems. Woodworth (1952) remarked that Thorndike would often say: "All that exists, exists in some amount and can be measured" (p. 217). With over 500 publications spanning a career of five decades, Thorndike certainly measured many things (Figure 4.7).

Popular Science Monthly, Volume 74, via Wikimedia Commons

Photo 4.9
Robert Woodworth

Robert Woodworth

A classmate at Harvard with both Edward Thorndike and Walter Cannon (Chapter 10), **Robert Woodworth** (1869–1962) nurtured his friendship with these two colleagues for the rest of his life (Graham, 1967). They also represented his two divergent fields of interest—Thorndike in psychology, and Cannon in physiology. Woodworth earned his Ph.D. in psychology with Cattell at Columbia, but then he worked with noted physiologist Charles Sherrington (1857–1952) in England. An offer from Cattell brought Woodworth back to Columbia, where he spent the rest of his career at Teachers College. Today Woodworth is remembered as an *early American psychologist whose dynamic psychology emphasized the role of motivation in behavior*.

As we've already seen, Woodworth collaborated with Thorndike to test the transfer of training (Graham, 1967). Their findings had a major impact on American educational practices, as pedagogical thinking shifted from strengthening mental faculties to teaching useful content. Woodworth also joined Cattell and Thorndike in establishing the Psychological Corporation.

With colleagues like Cattell and Thorndike, it's not surprising that Woodworth would become interested in measuring individual differences (Gibby & Zickar, 2008). In 1917, he got involved in the war effort, but not in the testing of intelligence. Instead, he was asked to develop a test of emotional stability. Many young men were coming back from the front lines with a condition then known as "shell shock." Symptoms included heart palpitations, insomnia, and uncontrollable weeping, which rendered the sufferers incapable of performing their military duties. Because Woodworth had experience working in mental hospitals, he was able to devise a questionnaire to detect susceptibility to what we now call post-traumatic stress disorder. He was still calibrating the test when the war ended, so it was never put to its intended use.

After World War I, there was great interest in applying the methods of psychology to improving business practices (Gibby & Zickar, 2008). It was generally believed that the productivity of the whole group could be dragged down by a few disgruntled employees who fomented discontent among their fellow workers. Managers wanted a simple and effective test for sorting out these "bad eggs." So Woodworth reworked his test for shell shock by targeting emotional instability more generally and marketed it as the Woodworth Personal Data Sheet. The WPDS was the first objective personality test ever devised, and it's generally viewed as the "grandfather" of all personality inventories. As a member of the Psychology Corporation, he developed additional educational and vocational tests.

From early in his career, Woodworth took an interest in the problem of motivation (Woodworth, 1932). His view of motivation was broad, ranging from basic biological drives like hunger and sex to complex personal motives like ambition and altruism. Furthermore, he felt that the behaviorist emphasis on stimulus-response (S-R) links as the explanation for learning left out the most important element—the organism itself. Instead, he proposed a stimulus-organism-response (S-O-R) model of psychology. **Dynamic psychology** was the name he gave to *the position that behavior can only be explained if the motivations of the organism are first understood*.

In sum, Woodworth's view of psychology was colored by his early interest in physiology. For him, learning wasn't about abstract connections between stimuli and responses. Rather, he saw learning as taking place within an organism as it adapts to its environment.

As we'll see in Chapter 5, Woodworth's S-O-R model had considerable influence on the neo-behaviorists, especially Clark Hull and Edward Tolman, who viewed Watson's theory of conditioned responses as too simplistic.

Leta Hollingworth

Leta Hollingworth (1886–1939) earned her doctorate thanks to the Coca-Cola Company (Silverman, 1992). Her husband Harry Hollingworth (1880–1956) was a young psychologist at Columbia. Coca-Cola was being sued and needed evidence that caffeine wasn't harmful. Harry accepted the lucrative assignment and hired Leta to direct the study. The experience turned her into a seasoned experimentalist, and the proceeds paid her tuition. She completed her Ph.D. under the mentorship of Edward Thorndike, who then offered her a position at Teachers College, where she remained for the rest of her career. There, she built her reputation as an *early American psychologist known for studies on the psychology of women and gifted children*.

Early in her career, Hollingworth focused on the psychology of women (Silverman, 1992). For her thesis, she disproved the myth that women are emotionally and physically incapacitated during menstruation. Challenging the variability hypothesis, she found more men than women in asylums, but only because mentally handicapped women were kept at home to perform menial tasks. She also found no support among birth records for the variability hypothesis.

Later in her career, Hollingworth turned her attention toward gifted children (Shields, 2000). Her work paralleled Terman's, but while Terman believed giftedness was hereditary and would unfold regardless of circumstances, Hollingworth emphasized the need to nurture talent to reach its full potential. In her own longitudinal study of giftedness, she found that when bright children exhibited social adjustment issues, it was due to lack of challenge or inept treatment.

Leta Hollingworth was one of the few women in the early twentieth century to hold an academic position at a research institution. This meant that she also had the opportunity to mentor the next generation of psychologists (Figure 4.8). Her most prominent student was the humanistic psychologist Carl Rogers, whom we'll meet in Chapter 15.

Florence Goodenough

Florence Goodenough (1886–1959) was an *early American developmental psychologist who pioneered field methods for studying children's behavior over time* (Johnson, 2015). She earned her master's degree at Columbia with Leta Hollingworth and completed her Ph.D. at Stanford

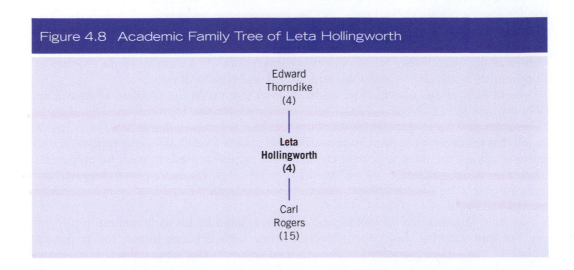

Figure 4.8 Academic Family Tree of Leta Hollingworth

Edward
Thorndike
(4)

**Leta
Hollingworth
(4)**

Carl
Rogers
(15)

with Lewis Terman. She was then hired at the University of Minnesota, where she remained for her entire career. Having worked with Terman on intelligence testing, she sought ways to extend testing to preschool children. The result was her Draw-a-Man test, which assessed youngsters' intelligence on the basis of pictures they drew.

At a time when most developmental research was performed in the laboratory, Goodenough maintained that a complete understanding of childhood could only be gained through extensive observation of children in daily life (Thompson, 2000). She trained mothers to record information about their children at regular intervals, thus amassing large sets of behavioral data for each child. This method is now known as time sampling, but Goodenough pioneered the technique long before it was commonly used in psychological research.

Goodenough was remarkably productive during her relatively short career (Johnson, 2015). She was 39 when she was hired at Minnesota, and she retired twenty-two years later due to illness. Nevertheless, she published several books and numerous articles in the span of two decades. She was also one of the few women psychologists of her time who supervised doctoral students, and she mentored many of the next generation of women psychologists (Figure 4.9). She firmly believed that women could have both a career and a family life, and she encouraged her students not to give up one for the other.

Photo 4.10
Florence Goodenough

Ruth Howard

The youngest of eight children, **Ruth Howard** (1900–1997) was the daughter of an influential Protestant minister in Washington, DC (Saltzman, 2001). Experience with her father's congregation led her to an interest in disadvantaged populations. Today she's recognized as the *second African American woman to receive a Ph.D. in psychology.*

As a social worker in Cleveland, Howard was dismayed to find that so many of her colleagues showed little empathy for the plight of those they were serving (Held, 2010). More generally, she found people to have little understanding of other cultural groups due to preconceived notions. She decided to study psychology to better understand the dynamics of racial attitudes.

Starting her graduate work at Columbia Teachers College, Howard transferred to the University of Minnesota, where she earned her doctorate in 1934 (Saltzman, 2001). For her dissertation, she investigated the relative contributions of nature and nurture in 229 sets of triplets, comparing three siblings from the same egg, three siblings from different eggs, and

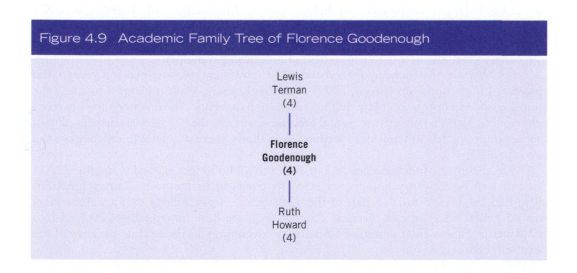

Figure 4.9   Academic Family Tree of Florence Goodenough

Lewis
Terman
(4)

Florence
Goodenough
(4)

Ruth
Howard
(4)

two siblings from one egg with a third from another. Although this was the largest study of triplets at that time, her research wasn't published until 1946.

After graduation, Howard married fellow psychologist Albert Beckham and set up a private practice with him (Held, 2010). She also served on the faculty of a school that trained African American nurses. Later, she pursued postdoctoral studies at the University of Chicago with Carl Rogers (Chapter 15). When she lost her husband in 1964, she continued their private practice until retirement, after which she returned to her native Washington, DC, where she died in 1997.

Inez Prosser

Howard is often recognized as the first African American woman psychologist, but recent historical research shows that distinction actually goes to **Inez Prosser** (1895–1934; Benjamin, 2008). We know very little about Prosser, and even her date of birth is a mystery. A Texas native, Prosser taught in the state's "colored" schools for a number of years. Because that state's universities were segregated, she had to travel to Colorado to do her master's degree and then to the University of Cincinnati for her doctorate, which she earned in 1933. Thus, we now recognize Prosser as the *first African American woman to earn a doctorate in psychology*.

For her dissertation, Prosser compared Black students in segregated and integrated schools (Benjamin, 2008). She found that those in segregated schools experienced fewer psychological and social issues than those in integrated schools. Students in segregated schools had higher self-esteem and better relationships with their teachers, classmates, and families. In contrast, Black students in integrated schools felt inferior, were less happy with their relationships, and wanted to leave school sooner.

Her research was much discussed in the years leading up to the *Brown v. Board of Education* decision in 1954 (Benjamin, 2008). Although integration was viewed as a future ideal, some African American educators recognized that segregated schools provided a more supportive environment for Black children. This was thought to be especially true when White teachers in integrated schools held prejudicial attitudes.

Unfortunately, Prosser didn't live to see the influence of her work (Benjamin, 2008). Just a year after she earned her degree, her life ended tragically in an automobile accident. But during her short life, she helped many African American students obtain funding to extend their education to college and graduate school.

Looking Ahead

Functionalism, the Darwin-inspired approach to psychology, evolved rapidly during the first half of the twentieth century. As psychologists applied its methods of observing behavior under experimentally controlled conditions to a variety of problems, the modern disciplines of psychology began to take root and flourish. By the 1930s, functionalism had morphed into behaviorism, the new dominant school of American psychology.

John Watson, the founder of the behaviorist movement, was trained at Chicago, the epicenter of functionalism (Green, 2009). In his early years, Watson claimed to study the animal *mind*, and only later did he shift his emphasis to *behavior*. The functionalists observed behavior but assumed underlying mental processes, whereas the behaviorists dispensed with that assumption. Yet, in terms of experimental methods, there was little to differentiate the two schools.

By mid-century, functionalism as a distinct school no longer existed (Chaplin, 2000). But this isn't because psychologists rejected its tenets or its methods. Rather, functionalism had become so much a part of the mainstream of psychology that a unique label was no longer necessary. In the next chapter, we'll see how functionalism evolved into behaviorism, which then dominated American psychology in the middle decades of the twentieth century.

CHAPTER SUMMARY

Functionalism is an American school of psychology that developed around the turn of the twentieth century. Functionalists rejected the perceived sterility of Titchener's structuralist movement, instead viewing psychology as the study of mental functions that arose in Darwinian fashion. Harvard philosopher William James is generally recognized as the founder of functionalism, in that he nurtured the first generation of this approach to psychology. The functionalist movement had centers at four different universities, each with somewhat different perspectives. Harvard functionalists were influenced by James's pragmatic approach and included noted psychologists such as Mary Calkins, Robert Yerkes, and Hugo Münsterberg. James's student G. Stanley Hall built Clark University into an important research institution for developmental psychology, fostering the academic growth of scholars such as Lewis Terman, Arnold Gesell, Yujiro Motora, and Francis Cecil Sumner. The Chicago school was founded by James Rowland Angell, a student of James, and John Dewey, who studied with Hall. Among its most prominent students were Helen Thompson Woolley, Louis Leon Thurstone, and Harvey Carr. John Watson, the founder of the behaviorist movement, was also a student of the Chicago school. The final center of functionalism was at Columbia and included important contributors to psychology such as Edward Thorndike, Robert Woodworth, and Leta Hollingworth. In the early decades of the twentieth century, functionalism stood in contrast to both structuralism and behaviorism. By mid-century, the term "functionalism" was no longer in use, even though the questions this school pursued are still at the heart of psychology today.

DISCUSSION QUESTIONS

1. What is functionalism? What were its antecedents?

2. Consider how James's philosophy inspired functional psychology. How does his approach differ from Wundt's?

3. Discuss the ways in which Calkins's early research influenced psychology. Can you relate her self-psychology to any modern approaches you've learned about?

4. Consider the ways in which Yerkes contributed to psychology. How did his approach to animal research differ from that of his behaviorist colleagues?

5. How did Hall advance the Child Study Movement? Explain recapitulation theory and the variability hypothesis, considering why these ideas would have had wide support at the turn of the twentieth century.

6. Discuss Terman's contributions to intelligence testing. What myths were dispelled by his research on gifted children?

7. Consider Gesell's work in developmental psychology. Explain the concept of maturationism and how it fit into his work.

8. Why do we consider Dewey one of the founders of functionalism? How did he influence educational theory?

9. Describe how Angell worked with Dewey to define functionalism as a distinct school. What other contributions did he make, and in what capacity?

10. Explain Thorndike's theory of connectionism and describe how he developed it. Can you think of ways his puzzle-box studies are relevant to human behavior?

11. Discuss Thorndike and Woodworth's transfer of training studies and their relevance to modern education.

12. Discuss Woodworth's contributions to psychology. Explain his concept of dynamic psychology.

ON THE WEB

YouTube hosts videos on the lives and contributions of nearly all of the psychologists we read about in this chapter. Many of these videos are created by amateurs, so keep a skeptical mind as you watch them. Some of the films created in Arnold Gesell's laboratory are also posted on YouTube.

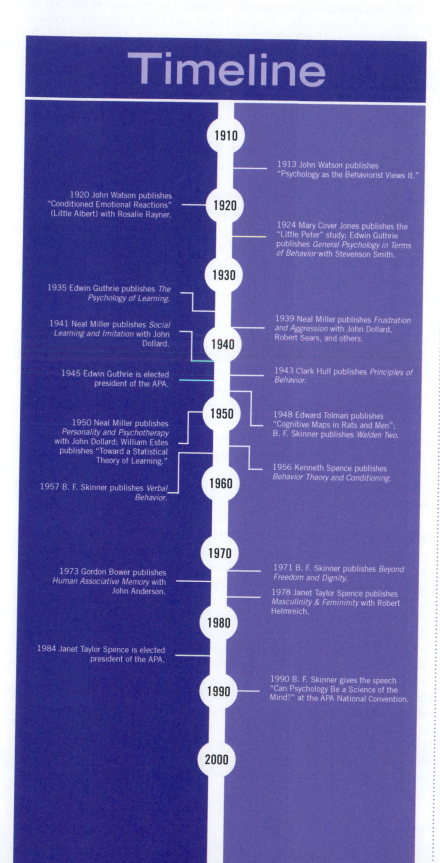

Timeline

1910

1913 John Watson publishes "Psychology as the Behaviorist Views It."

1920 John Watson publishes "Conditioned Emotional Reactions" (Little Albert) with Rosalie Rayner.

1920

1924 Mary Cover Jones publishes the "Little Peter" study; Edwin Guthrie publishes *General Psychology in Terms of Behavior* with Stevenson Smith.

1930

1935 Edwin Guthrie publishes *The Psychology of Learning.*

1939 Neal Miller publishes *Frustration and Aggression* with John Dollard, Robert Sears, and others.

1941 Neal Miller publishes *Social Learning and Imitation* with John Dollard.

1940

1945 Edwin Guthrie is elected president of the APA.

1943 Clark Hull publishes *Principles of Behavior.*

1950

1948 Edward Tolman publishes "Cognitive Maps in Rats and Men"; B. F. Skinner publishes *Walden Two.*

1950 Neal Miller publishes *Personality and Psychotherapy* with John Dollard; William Estes publishes "Toward a Statistical Theory of Learning."

1956 Kenneth Spence publishes *Behavior Theory and Conditioning.*

1957 B. F. Skinner publishes *Verbal Behavior.*

1960

1970

1973 Gordon Bower publishes *Human Associative Memory* with John Anderson.

1971 B. F. Skinner publishes *Beyond Freedom and Dignity.*

1978 Janet Taylor Spence publishes *Masculinity & Femininity* with Robert Helmreich.

1980

1984 Janet Taylor Spence is elected president of the APA.

1990 B. F. Skinner gives the speech "Can Psychology Be a Science of the Mind?" at the APA National Convention.

1990

2000

Learning Objectives

After reading this chapter, you should be able to:

- Examine the evolution of methodological behaviorism from its origins in positivism, pragmatism, and functionalism, as well as its reaction to structuralism.

- Assess the similarities and differences among the various approaches to neo-behaviorism, in particular those of Clark Hull, Edward Tolman, and Kenneth Spence.

- Evaluate the impact on contemporary psychology of the contributions made by the radical behaviorist B. F. Skinner.

- Outline the trends following World War II that led to a transition of behaviorism into the modern disciples of psychology.

Looking Back

During the second decade of the twentieth century, a Behavioral Revolution swept through American psychology (Virues-Ortega & Pear, 2015). By the 1920s, a new school known as behaviorism had come to dominate the field. Rejecting the notion that psychology was the study of the mind, behaviorists redefined psychology as a science of behavior. The revolution was led by the young and charismatic John Watson, but it was only successful because he tapped into concerns that many of his generation had about the field. In particular, psychologists of that time period felt insecure about the status of psychology: Was it a social science or a natural science? Watson's answer was that psychology *could* be a natural science, but only if it jettisoned the notion of unobservable mental states and focused instead on observable behavior. As radical as the idea sounded at the time, its roots in fact extended back nearly a century.

In the 1820s, the French philosopher Auguste Comte (1798–1857; *pronounced* oh-GOOST KOHNT, *rhymes with "don't"*) proposed a new philosophy of science he called positivism (Pearce, 2015). This was *the philosophical stance that scientists can only know what they can directly observe through their senses or instruments*. In other words, science progresses only by careful observation and measurement and not by making inferences about underlying causes that can never be observed or measured directly. Comte's purpose was twofold. First, he wanted to make a clear distinction between science and philosophy. According to Comte, true knowledge could only be gained by means of the scientific method, not through idle philosophical speculations. Second, he wanted to provide a pathway for the newly emerging social sciences, such as sociology and anthropology, to become as rigorous as the natural sciences, like physics and chemistry. In fact, Comte is often considered to be the founder of sociology.

Positivism had a significant impact on the conduct of both science and philosophy throughout the nineteenth century (Kincheloe & Tobin, 2009). It also influenced the growth of psychology, especially in the United States. For instance, the pragmatic philosophy that William James and John Dewey subscribed to was an offshoot of positivism. According to the pragmatists, a statement was true if it "worked." In other words, truth came from observation, not abstract reasoning. And since the functionalist school of psychology was built on pragmatic philosophy, it's not surprising that functionalists tended to agree with the tenets of positivism.

An important forerunner of the Behavioral Revolution was the functional psychologist Edward Thorndike (Malone, 2014). While Thorndike never denied the reality of mental states, he avoided using them as explanations for observable behaviors. This positivist stance is apparent in his three laws of learning, which explain changes in behavior as a result of the organism's current and past experiences. As we'll see in this chapter, Thorndike's laws set the foundation for behaviorist learning theories. Especially when it came to animal behavior, Thorndike expressed strong reservations about attributing mental states. However, he still had hesitations about completely abandoning cognitive explanation of human behavior. For this reason, we count Thorndike as a precursor to behaviorism but not as one of its founders.

As we saw in Chapters 3 and 4, American psychology in the early twentieth century was split between two schools, structuralism and functionalism (Malone, 2014). The behaviorists dismissed the structuralist definition of psychology as the study of conscious experience and rejected the method of introspection as invalid. The roots of behaviorism are clearly in the functionalist tradition. Yet the young followers of this new movement, with their positivist perspective, insisted that psychology could only become a natural science if it set aside the mind as an object of study or as an explanation for behavior. In sum, the behaviorists believed that the only way to make psychology more rigorous was to limit the scope of the field to that which could be directly observed and measured.

Photo 5.1
Auguste Comte

Methodological Behaviorism

It's a mistaken notion to think that behaviorists denied the existence of conscious experience. Rather, they simply agreed that the mind was beyond the purview of psychology as a natural science. In its simplest form, this philosophy of science meant **methodological behaviorism**, which is *the position that psychology should ignore questions of consciousness and focus on behavior instead.* The early behaviorists tended to take this agnostic stance toward the mind, simply searching for correlations between stimuli and responses in organisms.

John Watson

A young professor and his graduate student at the University of Chicago were training rats to race down a long corridor to find a piece of food at the end. After the training session, the experimenters shortened the corridor. This time, the rats bypassed the food and slammed into the wall. The so-called "kerplunk" experiment (Carr & Watson, 1908) tested the hypothesis that rats navigate through reflexive behaviors. Both men went on to illustrious careers in psychology. The graduate student, Harvey Carr (Chapter 4), assumed leadership of the Chicago school of functionalism after the departure of Dewey and Angell. And the professor, **John Watson** (1878–1958), became the *American psychologist best known as the founder of the behaviorist movement.*

The Johns Hopkins Gazette, via Wikimedia

**Photo 5.2
John Watson**

At Chicago, Watson developed a dislike for human-subjects research, preferring to work with animals instead (Watson, 1936). In particular, he felt introspective studies were too artificial, but with animals he could simply observe behavior. Trained in the functionalist school, he still thought he was using behavior to make inferences about animal mentality, but within a few years he'd dispensed with discussions of consciousness altogether. Watson was then hired at Johns Hopkins in 1908 and given freedom to pursue whatever research he wished. The following year, when James Mark Baldwin was dismissed, Watson became chair of the department and editor of the *Psychological Review*. Although Watson was only in his early thirties, he was a rising star in the field of psychology.

In 1913, Watson gave a talk titled "Psychology as the Behaviorist Views It." This lecture is considered the beginning of the behaviorist revolution that quickly swept through American psychology. The positivist perspective is clear from the opening sentences:

> Psychology as the behaviorist views it is a purely objective experimental branch of natural science. Its theoretical goal is the prediction and control of behavior. (Watson, 1913/1994, p. 248)

Thus, the method of psychology is the observation of behavior, with the purpose of learning how to control it for the benefit of humankind (Harzem, 2001).

Watson (1913/1994) started with the observation that biology makes no categorical distinction between humans and animals. Therefore, the methods developed by comparative psychologists should be applied to humans as well. Consciousness was a private experience, so there was no way to tell whether introspective reports were accurate. Only outward behavior could be publicly observed and verified. This argument resonated with the rising generation of functional psychologists, who were already relying on behavioral measures in their experiments.

However, Watson's position has also been misunderstood. He never claimed that the mind didn't exist, only that it was irrelevant to the study of behavior:

> One can assume either the presence or the absence of consciousness . . . without affecting the problems of behavior . . . and without influencing in any way the mode of experimental attack upon them. (Watson, 1913/1994, p. 249)

In other words, Watson argued for methodological behaviorism (Horowitz, 1992). He had no qualms with the everyday use of terms like "mind" and "consciousness," only with the idea that these were things that could be studied scientifically. The beauty of a behavioral approach to psychology, in Watson's view, was that it simply sidestepped the mind-body problem.

As a student at Chicago, Watson had suffered an anxiety disorder lasting several weeks (Watson, 1936). This experience made him receptive to the ideas of Sigmund Freud (Chapter 7), which were becoming popular in the United States. Although Watson rejected Freud's concept of an unconscious mind, he did think Freud made good observations of human behavior that could be tested in the laboratory.

Freud believed that even normally functioning adults displayed the same emotional maladjustments—although to a lesser degree—as did those with full-blown psychological disorders (Rilling, 2000). This observation helped Watson understand the panic attacks of his student years. Around this time, Robert Yerkes published an article introducing Pavlov's method of conditioned reflexes. Watson thought that conditioning, in which a reflexive behavior becomes associated with a previously neutral stimulus, could be a way of explaining everyday psychopathologies without recourse to a Freudian unconscious (Gewirtz, 2001).

One psychoanalytic phenomenon that caught Watson's attention was **transference**, or *the placing of feelings for one person or object onto another* (Rilling, 2000). For example, it's common for patients to develop emotions toward their therapist that are similar to those they feel for their parents. Freud believed this was an unconscious process, but Watson thought it could be explained in terms of Pavlov's conditioned reflexes. In Freudian theory, transference typically involves sexual feelings. But Watson believed the process was more general, shaping each individual's pattern of likes and dislikes—in other words, their personality.

Conditioned Emotional Responses

Since Freud argued that personality developed in infancy, Watson would have to study babies. Conveniently, Watson's lab was connected to the university's hospital, where there was an ample supply of infants. Watson also reinterpreted Freud's concept of infant sexuality as the emotion *love*, which was a pleasant sensation elicited by being touched, caressed, or cuddled (Watson & Rayner, 1920/2000). He also added two more innate emotions—*rage*, which infants expressed when their movements were confined, and *fear*, which was elicited by loss of support or a loud noise.

Pavlov's technique required an innate reflex as a starting point, and Watson believed he'd found one in the infant's fear response (Watson & Rayner, 1920/2000). Following the laws of classical conditioning, Watson reasoned that an infant could develop a phobia for a specific object if it were consistently paired with a loud noise that elicited fear. In other words, the fear of the loud noise would transfer to the object. He called this a **conditioned emotional response**, which is *a process in which a person develops an emotional reaction to a previously neutral stimulus*. He also believed that conditioned emotional responses account for many of the emotional disturbances of adulthood.

Early in 1920, Watson and his graduate student Rosalie Rayner began working with an 11-month-old infant they called "Albert B." (Watson & Rayner, 1920/2000). "Little Albert," as he came to be known, lived at the hospital where Watson did his research. His mother worked as a wet nurse, and so the boy spent his days in the hospital nursery. Among the available children, they chose Albert because he had a calm temperament and didn't startle easily.

Watson and Rayner (1920/2000) brought the boy into the lab and let him play with a white lab rat, which Albert gladly accepted. When Watson made a sudden loud noise, Albert cried and let the rat go, but then he calmed down and accepted the rat again. However, after several pairings of the rat and the noise, Albert pushed himself away when the rat was placed before him. They brought Albert back to the lab on several subsequent occasions, and each time he showed fear toward the rat. In addition, he also became fearful of other objects that resembled the rat, such as a rabbit, a white fur coat, and a Santa Claus mask. Watson interpreted these as further examples of transference. At that time, he was unaware of the work Pavlov was doing on the generalization of conditioned responses (Rilling, 2000). Watson had intended to reverse Albert's fear of white furry objects, but around this time the boy and his mother left the hospital, and no one knows if the boy ever overcame his phobia (Digdon, 2017).

The **Little Albert experiment**, which was *a case study in which John Watson demonstrated a conditioned fear in a young boy*, was the most famous piece of research in Watson's career (Beck, Levinson, & Irons, 2009). It was also his last academic publication. The rising star of psychology was about to fall.

The affair began around the time they were working with Little Albert (Benjamin, Whitaker, Ramsey, & Zeve, 2007). Both Watson's wife and Rosalie Rayner were from prominent families, so the divorce was sensationalized in the press and Watson was asked to resign. He searched for another academic position, but none was forthcoming. After the divorce, Watson married Rosalie. With his new bride twenty years his junior, Watson moved to New York City, where a friend introduced him to the J. Walter Thompson advertising agency. Within two years, Watson had risen to the rank of vice president. By all accounts, the marriage was a happy one (Beck et al., 2009). They had two sons, William and James. Naturally, this has led to all sorts of speculation about whether the names were intended to honor the father of American psychology.

Husband and wife also collaborated on a popular book, *The Psychological Care of Infant and Child*, which they published in 1928 (Bigelow & Morris, 2001). Although most of the book consisted of common-sense childcare advice, Watson was heavily criticized for advising parents not to hug or kiss their children too much lest they develop into needy adults. However, in his autobiography, Watson (1936) expressed his regret for having given such ill-founded advice, confessing: "I did not know enough to write the book I wanted to write" (p. 280). There's also no evidence he or Rosalie followed such advice in raising their own children.

In addition to his advertising career, Watson (1936) published popular articles and books on various topics in psychology, and he was sought after as a lecturer (Figure 5.1). He seemed happy in his new life—until tragedy stuck (Larson, 1979). Rosalie contracted a fever and died after returning from a trip to the West Indies. She was only 36. Watson was devastated by the loss, and he withdrew from public life and spent most of his free time at his country estate. Just before he died, he burned all of his private papers. Thus, the man who changed the course of American psychology remains much of a mystery to historians today.

Now he fears even Santa Claus

Via Wikimedia Commons

Photo 5.3
John Watson and Rosalie Rayner with little Albert

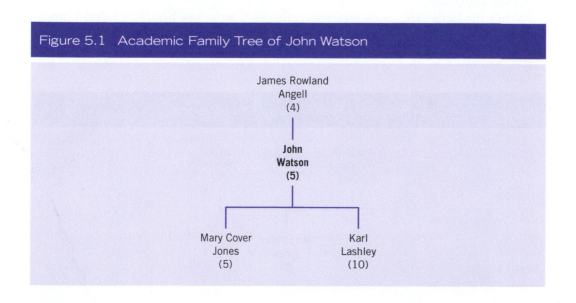

Figure 5.1   Academic Family Tree of John Watson

James Rowland
Angell
(4)

John
Watson
(5)

Mary Cover
Jones
(5)

Karl
Lashley
(10)

**Photo 5.4
Mary Cover Jones**

Mary Cover Jones

As a friend of Rosalie Rayner, **Mary Cover Jones** (1896–1987) got to know John Watson after he and Rosalie married and moved to New York (Jones, 1974). She was working on her Ph.D. at Columbia at the time. When Jones attended one of Watson's public lectures in which he described the Little Albert study, she wondered if the same conditioning techniques could be used to remove a fear. With Watson's guidance, she successfully helped a little boy overcome a phobia for animals. Thus, Mary Cover Jones acquired a reputation as the *American developmental psychologist who pioneered behavior modification therapy*.

Mary Cover had studied psychology at Vassar, where she worked with Margaret Washburn (Chapter 3; Mussen & Eichorn, 1988). This was also where she got to know Rosalie Rayner. In 1919, she moved to New York to begin graduate studies at Columbia University. But the following year was seminal for her, in that she met the two people who would have the most influence on her life and career. The first was Harold Jones, a fellow classmate at Columbia and soon to be her husband. The second was John Watson, who guided her on the research project that would make her name in the field.

When Jones mentioned her idea of removing a fear through conditioning, Watson offered his support (Rutherford, 2010). She located a three-year-old named Peter who was afraid of animals. Using a white rabbit in a cage as the fear-evoking object, she tried out a variety of methods to help the boy overcome his phobia. The procedure that eventually worked was to pair the rabbit with Peter's favorite food. At snack time, Jones brought the rabbit into the room but kept it at a "safe" distance. On each successive occasion, she placed the animal a little closer to the boy as he ate. Eventually, Peter was willing to touch and even play with the rabbit. Watson advised Jones throughout the process and even stopped by to observe her efforts with the boy (Jones, 1974). He also helped her write up an article describing the "Little Peter" study, but he declined to add his name as coauthor, explaining that she still had a reputation to build and so he wanted her to have all the credit. The study was published in 1924.

In 1927, Mary and Harold Jones accepted positions at the University of California, Berkeley, where they remained for the rest of their careers (Mussen & Eichorn, 1988). There, they initiated a longitudinal project known as the Oakland Growth Study, which Mary continued working on until her death in 1987 at the age of 90. (Harold had passed away in 1960.) This project spawned more than a hundred articles investigating such topics as the long-term consequences of physically maturing late versus early and the developmental precursors of alcoholism.

While the Little Peter study was frequently cited, Jones saw herself as a developmental rather than clinical psychologist, and she didn't pursue further research on the subject (Mussen & Eichorn, 1988). It wasn't until the 1950s that clinical psychologists such as

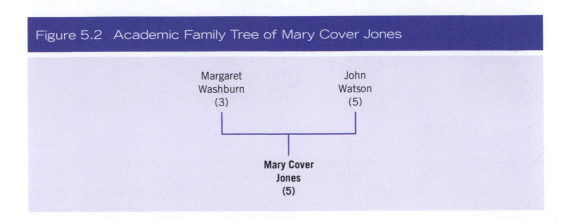

Figure 5.2 Academic Family Tree of Mary Cover Jones

Margaret
Washburn
(3)

John
Watson
(5)

**Mary Cover
Jones
(5)**

Hans Eysenck (Chapter 14) began promoting various forms of behavior modification therapy. Then psychologists began to recall the Little Peter study that had been done three decades before, and Mary Cover Jones was retroactively recognized as "the mother of behavior therapy," a title she proudly accepted (Figure 5.2).

Edwin Guthrie

The young **Edwin Guthrie** (1886–1959) was an unlikely psychologist, and the few psychology courses he'd taken in college had given him a strong distaste for the subject (Clark, 2005). He'd earned his degree in mathematical philosophy, but at the University of Washington he befriended psychologist Stevenson Smith (1883–1950), and they collaborated on *General Psychology in Terms of Behavior* (1924), the first textbook to present behaviorist contributions on an even footing with the traditional topics of psychology. The book was well received and established Guthrie's reputation as a psychologist. In this way, Edwin Guthrie became well known as an *American behaviorist who explained learning in terms of contiguity theory and the recency principle.*

Via Wikimedia Commons and Guthrie Genealogy

Photo 5.5
Edwin Guthrie

While completing his doctorate in philosophy at the University of Nebraska, Guthrie also worked with Harry Kirk Wolfe (1858–1918), the second American student to earn his degree with Wilhelm Wundt (Clark, 2005). Perhaps on account of his limited formal training in psychology, Guthrie viewed learning differently from other behaviorists. In particular, he felt that the current theories of learning were too complex. Because he had no graduate students and limited research facilities, Guthrie did few experiments during his career. Instead, he examined the theories and reanalyzed the data of other learning theorists, searching for a common thread that would tie all learning phenomena together.

In his 1935 book *The Psychology of Learning*, Guthrie presented his **contiguity theory**, which is *the proposal that stimulus-response associations are created in a single instance when the stimulus and response co-occur at about the same time* (Prenzel-Guthrie, 2000). He believed that other learning theorists had missed this simple principle of temporal contiguity either because the complexity of their experiments masked this basic underlying process or else because they sought to explain behavior in terms of neurological or cognitive processes.

Guthrie agreed with Watson that the study of learning should rely solely on observable behavior without recourse to inferences about mental states (Coleman, 2010). And like Watson, he defined behavior in terms of muscle movements and glandular secretions. He also argued that it was misleading to treat the stimulus as a unit, since at any given moment the environment was filled with all sorts of stimuli. Likewise, large-scale behaviors are built up from the movements of many different muscles, and each microbehavior can become associated with a different microstimulus.

However, Guthrie disagreed with Watson on Thorndike's law of exercise, which Watson saw as the best explanation for learning (Clark, 2005). Guthrie dismissed the idea that stimulus-response pairs were created through repetition. Instead, his contiguity theory posited that learning occurred on a single trial. He did agree that recent behaviors are more likely to be repeated, but not because earlier associations had faded from memory, as Watson believed. Instead, Guthrie made *the proposal that a familiar stimulus will evoke the most recent response to it*, which he called the **recency principle**.

Guthrie illustrated his recency principle with a classic example (Prenzel-Guthrie, 2000). If a child throws her coat on the floor when she arrives home from school, the parent can eliminate this undesired behavior by making the child put her coat back on and step outside. The child is then instructed to come back in and hang her coat in the closet. This way, the desired behavior is the last one performed in the situation, and so it will be the most likely behavior to occur the next time the child comes home.

When *Conditioned Reflexes* by Ivan Pavlov (Chapter 9) became available in English, Guthrie published a theoretical paper that reinterpreted conditioning in terms of his contiguity theory (Sheffield, 1959). In the traditional example, the researcher rings a bell and gives a dog a piece of food, which produces a salivary response. After a number of repetitions, the dog also salivates when the bell is rung even if it gets no food. Pavlov interpreted this situation as the dog having associated the bell with the food. In other words, the dog salivates to the bell because it expects food. But Guthrie insisted instead that the association is between the bell and the saliva. Since the dog salivated the last time it heard the bell (because it received food), this same salivating response will occur when it hears the bell again. This article became famous because Pavlov responded to it with the only paper he ever published in an American journal. Pavlov interpreted conditioning in terms of changes to the nervous system, but Guthrie insisted on studying behavior at the level of behavior without recourse to hidden processes.

Guthrie also took issue with Thorndike's law of effect (Clark, 2005). In one of the few experiments Guthrie undertook during his career, he and a colleague replicated Thorndike's famous study of trial-and-error learning. This time, however, they filmed the cats as they escaped from the puzzle box, and they analyzed the cats' behaviors frame by frame. They found that each cat had its own unique way of opening the latch, which it repeated every time it was placed in the puzzle box. This finding supported Guthrie's law of contiguity and his recency principle. That is, whatever configuration of behaviors the cat engaged in as the door opened on the last occasion was then repeated the next time it found itself inside the puzzle box. Thus, Guthrie maintained, reinforcement wasn't necessary for learning to occur. However, he did concede that when a behavior is reinforced, the organism is unlikely to perform any other response—once the door opens, the cat stops trying to get out. So, it is recency and not reinforcement that makes the behavior likely to occur again.

Although Guthrie made his name by confronting the prevailing theories of learning, he wasn't combative with his colleagues (Clark, 2005). He had a reputation for being an inspirational teacher, and his writing was famous for its clarity and liberal use of humor. Nevertheless, Guthrie believed he had seen the unifying simplicity that underlay the complex learning theories of his day. As an indication of the high regard his colleagues had for him, Guthrie was elected president of the APA in 1945, a remarkable choice given that he spent his career at a teaching college rather than a research university (Figure 5.3). But from his armchair, Guthrie challenged his fellow psychologists to think critically about their pet theories, and in the process he earned their deep respect.

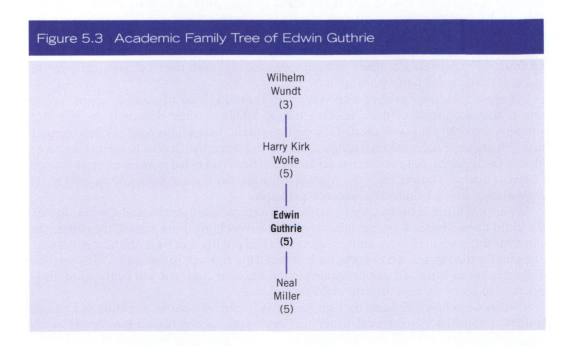

Figure 5.3 Academic Family Tree of Edwin Guthrie

Wilhelm
Wundt
(3)

Harry Kirk
Wolfe
(5)

Edwin
Guthrie
(5)

Neal
Miller
(5)

Neo-Behaviorism

By the 1930s, it was clear that Watson's vision of behavior was too limited. Not all behaviors seemed to be elicited by stimuli in the environment, and responses weren't as predictable as Watson had expected. **Neo-behaviorism** was *an approach that sought to explain behaviors that could not be described as conditioned responses*. The neo-behaviorists borrowed from Robert Woodworth's dynamic psychology, which proposed that various internal states of the organism mediated between stimulus and response. They were also influenced by the Gestalt psychologists, which we'll read about in the next chapter. While they differed in their approaches, they all recognized the need to move beyond methodological behaviorism.

Clark Hull

Stricken with polio in early adulthood, **Clark Hull** (1884–1952) could only walk with the aid of a cane and a special leg brace he designed himself (Hull, 1952). Hull was a critical thinker, and he was famous for "cussing" and shaking his cane at any student who slipped into shoddy reasoning (Beach, 1959). Admiring the simple elegance of Newton's laws of motion, Hull sought to create a similar set of laws to describe behavior. Although his theory eventually collapsed under its own weight, his greatest legacy was his students, many of whom rose to the top ranks of twentieth-century psychology. Clark Hull is now remembered as the *American neo-behaviorist who emphasized the role of drives and motivation in learning*.

Via Wikimedia Commons, Free Art License

Photo 5.6
Clark Hull

Hull earned his Ph.D. at Wisconsin with Joseph Jastrow (1863–1944), a functionalist who'd studied with G. Stanley Hall (Beach, 1959). After joining the faculty at Wisconsin, Hull took a keen interest in the ongoing debate between the behaviorists and the Gestalt psychologists, and he arranged for Kurt Koffka (Chapter 6) to spend a year at Wisconsin. At first, Hull favored Gestalt psychology, but eventually he became more sympathetic to the behaviorist cause. Hull felt that Watson hadn't made a sufficiently strong case for behaviorism. Watson's approach had been based on second-hand reports of the work that Pavlov and his Russian contemporaries were doing on classical conditioning. But when Pavlov's *Conditioned Reflexes* became available in English, Hull read it and was greatly impressed.

During his years at Wisconsin, Hull built a reputation as a first-rate experimenter (Hovland, 1952). In 1929, he was offered a position at Yale. Although he had no teaching responsibilities, Hull offered a weekly seminar that became known as the "Monday Night Meetings." These seminars attracted many graduate students and faculty members, and they largely dealt with the relationship between behaviorism and psychoanalytic theory. These meetings inspired many of his students to seek ways of integrating behaviorism and psychoanalysis, mainly by reinterpreting psychoanalytic concepts in behavioral terms, just as Watson had done.

Hull gave considerable attention to the process of learning (Smith, 2000b). Watson believed learning resulted from the repetition of a stimulus-response association, but Hull thought this too simplistic. Thorndike's law of effect maintained that learning occurred when a pleasant or unpleasant state occurred after a behavior had been performed, but Hull saw this as backward cause and effect. Instead, Hull maintained, the organism needed motivation to learn. Thus, he developed his **drive reduction theory**, which is *the proposal that learning occurs when a behavior is impelled by an unpleasant state that is reduced after that the behavior is performed*. For example, a rat will run a maze for food, but only if it's hungry. It's easy to see how drive reduction works in the case of appetitive behaviors such as eating, drinking, or sex, but it's not clear that all learning involves the reduction of some sort of unpleasant internal state.

Over a span of two decades, Hull sought a law of behavior that could be expressed as a mathematical function (Beach, 1959). In so doing, he advocated for the use of the

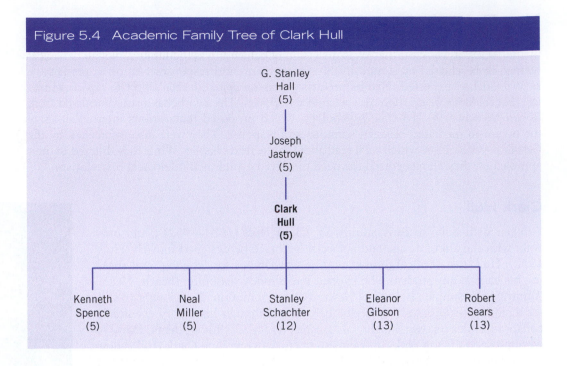

Figure 5.4 Academic Family Tree of Clark Hull

G. Stanley
Hall
(5)

Joseph
Jastrow
(5)

**Clark
Hull
(5)**

| Kenneth Spence (5) | Neal Miller (5) | Stanley Schachter (12) | Eleanor Gibson (13) | Robert Sears (13) |

hypothetico-deductive method, which is *the scientific approach of generating falsifiable hypotheses that are then tested in experiments*. As Hull built his law of behavior, he set his students to work conducting experiments to test hypotheses derived from his theory.

Hull published his most famous work, *Principles of Behavior*, in 1943 (Beach, 1959). In that book, he put forth his law of behavior, expressed in the form of a mathematical equation:

$$_sE_R = {_s}H_R \times D \times V \times K$$

This formula incorporates key concepts from Hull's theory that he believed were determinants of stimulus-response behavior, such as *habit strength*, *drive strength*, and *stimulus intensity*.

After the publication of *Principles of Behavior*, Hull continued refining his theory (Beach, 1959). Although he'd hoped to find a simple law of behavior, the equation grew ever more complex. When experiments failed to support the theory, he added more variables to the equation to get it to match the data. After his death, it became clear the equation was too cumbersome, so Hull's theory of learning was abandoned. Nevertheless, his theory inspired vast amounts of research and as a result, we now have a much better understanding of how learning works.

Hull's theory is also important because it resurrected Woodworth's S-O-R psychology, namely the idea that internal states of the organism mediate between stimulus and response (Smith, 2000). This position broke sharply with Watson's S-R behaviorism, in which all discussion of internal states was banished. As the proponent of the most prominent learning theory of the time, Hull was the "king of the hill" that other theorists tried to knock down. Thus, even in its failure, Hull's theory inspired the development of new and better approaches to learning and behavior (Figure 5.4).

Edward Tolman

Twice in his career, **Edward Tolman** (1886–1959) was fired for his political views (Tolman, 1952). As a young assistant professor, he was dismissed from Northwestern University for his opposition to the United States entering World War I. Late in his career, he lost his professorship at Berkeley because he refused to sign an anti-Communist loyalty oath. But by this time,

Tolman was one of the most distinguished scientists in the United States. He sued and won back his job, only to retire shortly thereafter. He's been hailed as a hero in the cause of academic freedom ever since. Today, Edward Tolman is known as the *American neo-behaviorist who studied latent learning and cognitive maps in rats*.

Tolman studied human memory with Hugo Münsterberg (Chapter 3) at Harvard (Tolman, 1952). But he was also introduced to Watson's behaviorism in a course in comparative psychology with Yerkes. Additionally, he spent time in Germany learning Gestalt psychology with Kurt Koffka (Chapter 6). At Berkeley, Tolman was asked to propose a new course, and he suggested comparative psychology. This choice was fateful, as he shifted his research from humans to rats.

During the early Berkeley years, Tolman's neo-behaviorist thinking took shape (Tolman, 1952). He agreed with Watson and Hull that Thorndike's law of effect seemed to imply backward causation. Instead, he advocated for what he called **purposive behaviorism**, which is *the position that organisms engage in behaviors to achieve particular goals*.

Tolman also rejected Watson's definition of behavior as glandular secretions and muscle contractions, a position he mocked as "twitchism" (Tolman, 1952). In his view, large-scale behavior wasn't built out of combinations of elementary movements but rather occurred as a whole. To clarify his thinking on the nature of behavior, Tolman borrowed the terms *molecular* and *molar* from chemistry to explain the difference between Watson's approach and his own (Hilgard, 1948). Thus, **molecular behavior** refers to *the movements of the individual muscles that make up a behavior*, whereas **molar behavior** refers to *the behavior of the organism as a whole, especially as directed toward a particular purpose*. Although biologists may be interested in molecular behavior, he argued that the purview of psychology was molar behavior. After all, various configurations of muscles can be engaged to perform the same action. In his insistence on studying behavior as a whole, we can clearly see Koffka's influence.

Likewise, Tolman took issue with Watson's insistence that all discussion of mental processes should be banned from psychology (Garcia, 1997). He interpreted the idea of methodological behaviorism as a recognition of the fact that the only data available to the psychologist were the observable behaviors of organisms. Still, Tolman had no doubt that his rats had rich mental lives, and he believed he could make inferences about their cognitive processes on the basis of observed behaviors.

Like Hull, Tolman believed that behavior and learning cannot be understood unless *the internal states of the organism mediating between stimulus and response* are taken into account (Innis, 2000). He called these internal states **intervening variables**. In Tolman's theory, intervening variables included beliefs about how the world works and the current motivational state of the organism. Unlike Hull, who proposed noncognitive intervening variables such as drive and habit strength, Tolman was unabashed about attributing mental states such as beliefs and expectations to his rats.

Of all the research Tolman conducted with his students, the best known is his work on place learning (Tolman, 1948). In "Cognitive Maps in Rats and Men," Tolman showed that learning involves more than just stimulus-response pairs, and also that neither reward nor drive reduction is necessary for learning to take place. In one classic experiment, Tolman found that rats first allowed to freely explore a maze were then able to learn the location of a food reward faster than those trained to navigate to it.

Tolman (1948) introduced two important concepts to explain these results. First, he argued that his rats were building a **cognitive map**, that is, *a mental model of the spatial layout of a location*. The rats who were rewarded with food each day built a narrow cognitive map of left and right turns to the goal. However, the rats who'd wandered freely through the maze had built a broad cognitive map, so when they later discovered the food reward, they knew exactly where to find it again. Second, he argued that these rats had built their cognitive maps through a process he called **latent learning**, which is *a type of learning that occurs without reward or drive reduction and without any overt expression of behavior*. At the time, learning

Photo 5.7
Edward Tolman

was conceptualized as the creation of stimulus-response pairs, but in his demonstration of latent learning, Tolman showed that complex knowledge could be acquired even though it was of no immediate use to the organism.

As another example of the rich mental life of rats, Tolman (1948) investigated a phenomenon known as vicarious trial and error, or VTE. This is *the hesitation that occurs when an organism is uncertain which choice to make*. When a rat is learning a maze, it will often pause at a choice point, looking left and right several times before proceeding. For Tolman, the analog with human behavior was obvious. The idea is that organisms—whether rats or humans—play out mental simulations of each alternative before deciding which route to take. In other words, the trial-and-error learning takes place mentally and not in the real word, and in this sense it's "vicarious."

Tolman never mentored as many graduate students as Clark Hull. But unlike Hull, Tolman's theory has stood the test of time. Whereas Hull sought to reduce all behavior to a single formula, Tolman embraced the complexity of behavior and proposed underlying cognitive processes to explain it. Many of his contemporaries resisted his efforts to bring the mind back into psychology. Nevertheless, Tolman's ideas blazed the trail for later generations of psychologists who rallied to the Cognitive Revolution in the 1960s (Figure 5.5).

Zing-Yang Kuo

While still an undergraduate at Berkeley, Zing-Yang Kuo (1898–1970) published a paper arguing that invoking instincts to explain development stifles further research (Blowers, 2001). This paper set off a firestorm as prominent psychologists responded in defense, among them his adviser Edward Tolman. Kuo completed his Ph.D. with Tolman in 1923, and during his career he conducted groundbreaking experiments to support his anti-nativist position. Zing-Yang Kuo thus developed a reputation as the *Chinese behaviorist who rejected the concept of instinct and maintained that development occurs through an interaction of nature and nurture.*

In one series of experiments, Kuo tested the idea that cats have an instinct to kill mice (Honeycutt, 2011). Of course, cats kill mice in the wild, but when he raised kittens with mice, he found they had no inclination to kill them. Instead, the kittens developed an emotional attachment to the mice, playing with them and searching for them when they were removed from the cage.

Perhaps Kuo's most notable research was his studies of embryonic development in chicks (Gottlieb, 1972). He invented a method for creating windows in chicken eggs so he could observe the embryos without killing them. He found that many behaviors young chicks engage in first appear while they're still in the shell. For instance, newly hatched chicks peck

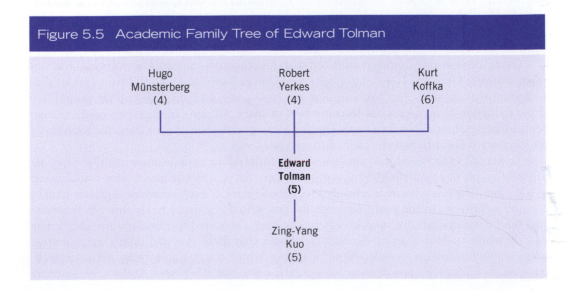

Figure 5.5 Academic Family Tree of Edward Tolman

Hugo Münsterberg (4)

Robert Yerkes (4)

Kurt Koffka (6)

Edward Tolman (5)

Zing-Yang Kuo (5)

for food by bobbing their heads up and down. Kuo found that this behavior started in the egg, where the head rested on the breast, and the beating heart lifted it up and down. Furthermore, hatchlings peck in a rhythmic manner, picking up whatever they encounter on the ground, be it a speck of grain, a small pebble, or even their own feces. Of course, they spit out nasty items, but it takes a day or so for them to learn to discriminate food from nonfood items. Thus, Kuo argued, there's nothing instinctual about food-pecking behavior in chicks.

These and other experiments demonstrated that behaviors many believed to be instincts actually depended on the way the developing organism interacted with its environment (Greenberg, 2016). Today, psychologists understand that nature and nurture aren't separate factors in development. However, Kuo's interactionist perspective was many decades ahead of its time. As a result, his early contributions to behavioral development are often overlooked.

Photo 5.8
Zing-Yang Kuo

Kenneth Spence

As a graduate student at Yale, **Kenneth Spence** (1907–1967) worked on visual perception in chimpanzees (Amsel, 1995). He earned his Ph.D. in 1933 and continued working on this problem for several years at the primate lab Yerkes had set up in Florida. However, during his time at Yale, Spence also developed a close relationship with Clark Hull and pursued a separate line of research testing his theory of learning. After leaving Yale, Spence and Hull maintained an extended correspondence, and in his 1943 *Principles of Behavior*, Hull credited Spence as a major influence on the shaping of the theory. Thus, Spence became known as the *American neo-behaviorist who was the major proponent of Hull's drive reduction theory*.

Spence's career took off after he accepted a professorship at the University of Iowa, where he stayed for more than a quarter of a century, with most of those years as department chair (Amsel, 1995). Spence had a domineering personality and was said to rule with an iron hand, but he also built Iowa into one of the most important centers for the behaviorist movement. He hired faculty members who shared his neo-behaviorist perspective and mentored scores of graduate students and postdoctoral fellows, who then spread what had become known as the Hull-Spence system to universities across the United States.

The Hull-Spence system was an ambitious project to develop a general theory of behavior by deducing the laws of learning using the hypothetico-deductive method (Kendler, 1967). Both Hull and Spence shared a molecular view of learning, and they saw the classical conditioning of stimulus-response pairs as the basic building block of all behavior. They also agreed that drive reduction was the basis for reinforcement. That is, an organism learns when a biological drive, such and hunger or thirst, is relieved. Additionally, they agreed that rate of learning was a function of both *drive strength*—for instance, how much hunger the rat was experiencing—and what they called *incentive motivation*—that is, how attractive the stimulus is. Thus, a hungry rat will work hard for any kind of food, but a rat that's not hungry will only go after tasty food. But Hull and Spence did have their points of disagreement as well. For instance, Hull multiplied drive strength and incentive motivation in his equation, but Spence insisted the two terms should be added. As insignificant as this difference may seem from our modern perspective, it was quite a hot topic among behaviorists at the time.

Although Spence was committed to Hull's theory, he was also open to the ideas of other behaviorists (Hilgard, 1967). In particular, Spence was impressed with Tolman's concept of intervening variables as an operationally defined construct linking stimulus and response, and he helped shape the way Hull thought about the terms in his equation. For example, Hull originally thought of drive purely in terms of physiological needs, but Spence convinced him to think of it operationally instead. That is to say, a hunger drive could simply be defined as time elapsed since the organism's last meal without recourse to any sort of physiological state that couldn't be directly observed anyway. In a nutshell, the Hull-Spence system described behavior at the level of behavior with an agnostic stance toward both mental and internal bodily processes, in line with the positivistic view that we can only know what we can directly perceive.

Before moving to Iowa, Spence's research focused on **discrimination learning** in animals, especially primates (Amsel, 1995). This is *the process of learning to respond differently to stimuli that differ in some particular aspect*. For example, a pigeon can learn that it can peck a key to get a pellet of food when a green light comes on but not when the light is red. The Gestalt psychologist Wolfgang Köhler (Chapter 6) had done some early research on discrimination learning that seemed to challenge behaviorist assumptions about the process. In one series of experiments, Köhler trained hens to respond to a light-gray square but not to one that was a darker shade. He then presented the hens with two squares that were different shades of gray, but this time the lighter of the two was the same shade as the darker one in the previous task. If hens learned to respond to a particular stimulus, as behaviorist theory would predict, they shouldn't respond to either of the squares. Instead, they responded to the lighter of the two squares regardless of the exact shade. Köhler interpreted this result as suggesting that the hens had learned to respond to a color relationship ("the lighter of the two") rather than to a specific stimulus. Spence developed a complex mathematical formula that supposedly explained Köhler's results in terms of the Hull-Spence system, but no doubt most psychologists today would see the Gestalt explanation as more parsimonious.

At Iowa, Spence devoted most of his time to the study of a phenomenon known as **eyelid conditioning** (Wiseman, 2000). This is *a classical conditioning procedure in which a light or tone is paired with a puff of air to the eye, causing the subject to blink*. Eyelid conditioning had been used with animals such as rabbits, but Spence built a lab in which he could study eyelid conditioning in humans. Behaviorist dogma claimed that the laws of learning that were found in other animals applied equally well to humans. In practice, however, humans posed special problems for classical conditioning, and Spence thought this was because language enabled them to second-guess the purpose of the experiment. However, blinking is a largely automatic behavior, and he believed he could circumvent the language problem with this task. Many of the dissertations produced under Spence's supervision used eyelid conditioning to test hypothesizes about motivation and learning. Spence's 1956 book *Behavior Theory and Conditioning* was also a product of the research conducted in his eyelid conditioning lab.

Through his mentoring of the next generation of psychologists and his editorial control over important journals, Spence became one of the most influential psychologists of the mid-twentieth century (Wiseman, 2000). His list of publications was prodigious, and during the last decade of his career he was one of the most highly cited authors in psychology. Although Spence's ideas have lost favor and his work is much less frequently cited today, his legacy has continued into the current century, with many of his academic children, grandchildren, and even great-grandchildren making important contributions to the field today (Figure 5.6).

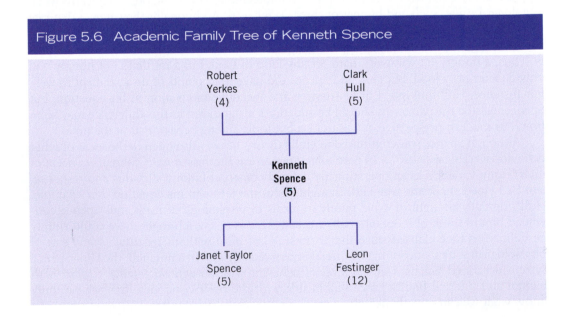

Figure 5.6 Academic Family Tree of Kenneth Spence

Janet Taylor Spence

Janet Taylor started her doctoral work in the clinical psychology program at Yale, where she got to know Clark Hull, but after a year she left for a clinical internship in New York (Deaux, 2016). She then traveled to Iowa to work with Kenneth Spence. In her 1949 dissertation, Taylor tested the idea of anxiety as a personality trait using the eyelid conditioning paradigm. After graduation, she became the first woman psychologist at Northwestern University in Chicago. But Spence, now divorced, kept in touch with his young ambitious student, and over the next decade a romance blossomed between them. In 1959, Taylor married Spence, resigned her position at Northwestern, and moved back to Iowa. At first, her marriage hampered her career, but after overcoming many obstacles, **Janet Taylor Spence** (1923–2015) built a reputation as an *American clinical psychologist who was a leader in gender studies during the last half of the twentieth century.*

As a student at Iowa, Janet Taylor developed a questionnaire for assessing people's level of general anxiety, which she called the Manifest Anxiety Scale, or MAS for short (Wiseman, 2000). Kenneth Spence saw the score on the MAS as a good operational definition for drive, and studies correlating MAS scores with rate of learning in eyelid conditioning appeared to support this hypothesis. These experiments, which served as the basis for Taylor's dissertation, also served as an example of how the Hull-Spence system could be put to practical use. Taylor continued her work on the MAS during her decade at Northwestern.

But when Janet Taylor Spence married, her career was thwarted (Deaux, 2016). Nepotism laws prevented her from working at the university. Instead, she found a position at the local Veterans Administration hospital studying motivation in schizophrenics. Five years later, Kenneth Spence was lured to the University of Texas to build the psychology program there, and Janet followed her husband. Once again, nepotism laws prevented her from a faculty position in the psychology department, but when Kenneth threatened to leave, the rules were bent and she was given a position in the separate educational psychology program. The Spences' time together at Texas was brief. In their third year there, Kenneth contracted a sudden illness and died at the young age of 59.

Although Janet was devastated by her husband's death, she was also now free of nepotism restrictions (Deaux, 2016). She was offered Kenneth's vacant position, and within a few years she rose to chair of the department. At first, she was the only woman in the department, but as chair she made it a priority to hire women psychologists. Moreover, the women's liberation movement was then flourishing in the United States, and her research interests turned to gender studies. With her Texas colleague Robert Helmreich, she published the book *Masculinity & Femininity* in 1978. This work looked at how personal attributes, self-esteem, and gender attitudes account for differences in achievement motivation between men and women. The authors concluded that there was no gender difference in degree of achievement motivation, only the directions in which it was applied.

During the last two decades of the twentieth century, Janet Taylor Spence became an organizational leader for the field of psychology as a whole ("Janet Taylor Spence, PhD," 2019). In 1984, she was elected president of the American Psychological Association (APA), the sixth woman to hold that position. She was also one of the founders of the Association for Psychological Science (APS), serving as its first president in 1988. During her long and productive life, she blazed the path for a whole generation of women psychologists who finally were able to stand on equal ground with their male colleagues.

Radical Behaviorism

René Descartes believed that the mind and the body were two different kinds of stuff, one spiritual and the other physical, and this Cartesian dualism dominated Western philosophy and psychology until the twentieth century. Methodological behaviorism dealt with the mind-body problem by banishing unobservable mental events from the realm of scientific inquiry. In contrast, the neo-behaviorists acknowledged the need to take internal states of the organism into account, but they redefined these in terms of quantifiable variables. A third approach, known as radical behaviorism, took a completely different approach to the mind-body problem, in that it simply denied that there was any difference between the two. In other words, radical behaviorism was *the philosophical stance that internal experiences of the organism are behaviors just like outwardly observable actions*.

B. F. Skinner

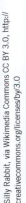

Photo 5.9
B. F. Skinner

He called it his "Dark Year" (Skinner, 1967). Graduating with a degree in English, Burrhus Frederic Skinner (1904–1990) dreamed of a career as a novelist. So he moved into his parents' attic, but when he sat before his typewriter, he found he had nothing to say. Meanwhile, he'd been reading Watson and Pavlov, so he went to Harvard to earn his Ph.D. in psychology. B. F. Skinner would become a *prominent American psychologist who is best known for developing the methods of operant conditioning and for promoting radical behaviorism*.

Skinner was something of an oddball at Harvard (Fallon, 1992). His reading of Watson and Pavlov had sparked his interest in psychology, but Edwin Boring dominated Harvard psychology, and he was strongly opposed to behaviorism. Furthermore, the Harvard faculty came from a structuralist-functionalist tradition that emphasized hypothesis testing as the appropriate scientific method for psychology. However, Skinner had read two philosophers of science who'd given him a vision for an alternative approach to science.

In his youth, Skinner had read the works of Francis Bacon (Chapter 1), which convinced him that the inductive method of gathering data without prior hypotheses was the proper approach to understanding the natural world (Benjamin & Nielsen-Gammon, 1999). Instead of proposing hypotheses and testing them with experiments, Bacon argued that scientists should make careful and extensive observations before making tentative theories to explain their data. Moreover, Bacon emphasized the value of applied research aimed at improving technology, and this could only be accomplished by learning how to predict and control nature. This data-driven approach contrasted with the theory-driven method that had been the hallmark of psychological science since the days of Wundt.

Another early influence on Skinner was the German physicist and positivist philosopher Ernst Mach (1838–1916), who'd argued against the Newtonian concept of force as an explanation for cause-and-effect relationships (Chiesa, 1992). Newton had seen the world as a chain of impact events, such as when one billiard ball strikes another and transfers its motion to it. But Mach argued that we can't always observe such a chain of cause and effect, nor should we always assume it exists. Instead, Mach argued that cause and effect was a functional relationship between independent and dependent variables. For example, we observe that patients get better when they're given an active drug but not when they're given a placebo, so we say that the drug causes the patient's condition to improve, even though we can't identify a direct link between the two. This Machian view of cause and effect as a functional relationship is more widely accepted in psychology today, but it was still a radical idea in Skinner's time. Nevertheless, Mach's concept of functional relations served as a cornerstone for Skinner's approach to research.

As a student, Skinner benefited from the fact that the faculty was too occupied with academic politics to pay much attention to him (Overskeid, 2007). Instead, he found his mentor in the biology department with physiologist William Crozier (1892–1955). In turn, Crozier had been inspired by his reading of Jacques Loeb (1859–1924), who had also influenced John Watson as a student at Chicago. In a nutshell, Loeb maintained that you can only understand an organism by studying it as a whole, rather than by breaking it down into its component parts. Loeb was particularly interested in the behavior of the organism, but he also emphasized that behaviors should be viewed holistically and not as a collection of individual muscle movements and glandular secretions. He also rejected the use of mentalistic language in explaining behavior. Although Loeb influenced the development of Watsonian behaviorism, we can see that Skinner's approach was in fact truer to Loeb's original intention.

Skinner quickly rose through the ranks of psychology (Fowler, 1990). After earning his Ph.D. in 1931, he remained at Harvard another five years as a research fellow. He then spent nine years at Minnesota and three at Indiana before being called back to Harvard as a full professor. There he remained for the rest of his life.

Operant Conditioning

Skinner had originally been drawn to psychology by reading Pavlov and Watson, who maintained that all behavior occurs as a response to some stimulus in the environment. Pavlov had trained a dog to salivate to the sound of a bell, and Watson had trained Little Albert to fear a white lab rat. In each case, the behavior—whether salivating or crying—was elicited by some stimulus—either a bell or a rat.

Early in his career, however, Skinner observed behaviors that didn't seem to be responses to environmental stimuli (Iversen, 1992). For instance, he found that he could train a rat to press a lever to get food. The lever press didn't seem to be a response to any stimulus in the environment. Rather, it seemed to originate from within the rat. A Cartesian dualist would say the action was initiated by the will of the rat. But Skinner rejected mentalistic explanations, instead maintaining that the rat pressed the lever because it had learned the consequences of its behavior. In this way, Skinner traced the origin of the behavior back to the environment.

Skinner believed his fellow behaviorists had missed the fact that there are two types of behavior (Delprato & Midgley, 1992). **Respondent behavior** is *an action that is performed by an organism in response to a stimulus*. Behaviors such as salivating to a bell or crying at the sight of a rat are examples of respondent behavior. But a behavior such as pressing a lever for food is *an action that is performed by an organism without being elicited by a stimulus in the environment*. Skinner called this **operant behavior** because the animal operates on its surroundings. In a sense, the organism provides the stimulus and the environment the response. Additionally, he maintained that operant behavior is far more important than respondent behavior in terms of the organism learning to adapt to its environment.

Although operant behavior appears to originate from within the organism, Skinner insisted that the ultimate source of the behavior is still in the environment (Leão, Laurenti, & Haydu, 2016). Organisms explore their surroundings, and in the process they learn the consequences of their behaviors. The first lever press may have been accidental, but when a pellet of food dropped into the dispenser, the rat learned the consequence of that behavior and so is likely to repeat it. Likewise, if the rat receives an electric shock when it presses the lever, it's not likely to produce that behavior again. Skinner used the term **operant conditioning** to refer to the *process of an organism learning about the consequences of its behavior*.

Skinner also saw a parallel between operant conditioning and natural selection. At the species level, the environment selects which individuals will survive and reproduce, whereas at the individual level, the environment selects which behaviors will be acquired. It does this by providing **reinforcement**. That is, the environment provides *a consequence of a behavior that increases the likelihood it will be repeated*. The concept of reinforcement is frequently misunderstood. It's not getting food on this occasion that reinforces the rat's lever-pressing behavior. Instead, it's the rat's **reinforcement history**—that is, *an organism's past experience with a behavior and its consequence*—that determines the animal's behavior in the current moment.

Skinner came to understand the importance of reinforcement history quite by accident. He'd developed a device that not only dispensed food pellets when the rat pressed the lever but also recorded the time of each lever press (Iversen, 1992). One day when he returned to the lab, he found the pellet dispenser had jammed. Skinner expected the rat would have pressed the lever a few times and then given up, just as Pavlov's dog stopped salivating at the bell when it no longer received food. Instead, the rat had pressed the lever many times, stopped for a while, and then pressed the lever some more. This observation made it clear to Skinner that behavior isn't determined by future consequences but by past outcomes—in other words, the organism's reinforcement history.

According to Skinner, the goal of psychology is the prediction and control of behavior (Catania, 1992). If you know the organism's reinforcement history, you can predict its behavior. Additionally, you can control behavior by *arranging the consequences so that desired behaviors are reinforced*. Skinner called this process shaping. Complex behaviors can be built through shaping in a step-by-step manner, by first reinforcing simpler forms of the desired behavior and then gradually leading the organism to more complex actions. If you've ever seen a dolphin show at an aquarium, you've witnessed the power of shaping in training animals to perform significant feats.

Skinner recognized that operant conditioning was an extension of Thorndike's law of effect (Iversen, 1992). However, at that time the mechanism behind it wasn't well understand, and Watson, Tolman, and Guthrie all rejected it as unimportant for explaining behavior. Only Hull was convinced by Skinner's explanation of Thorndike's law in terms of operant conditioning, and he even incorporated it into later versions of his theory.

Although Skinner worked mainly with rats and pigeons, he was mostly interested in human behavior (Holland, 1992). In 1957, he published what he considered his most important book, *Verbal Behavior*, a work that had taken two decades to complete. In this book, he attempted to explain the unique phenomenon of human language in terms of operant conditioning. Skinner believed that every way in which humans are uniquely different from all other animals comes down to language, or as he preferred to call it, verbal behavior. Nevertheless, language itself isn't a uniquely different form of behavior, he insisted. Rather, it's simply another variety of operant behavior.

Skinner assiduously avoided using mentalistic language, but that doesn't mean he denied the existence of internal experiences such as thoughts and feelings (Delprato & Midgley, 1992). Instead, he distinguished between *public events*, that is, outward behaviors that are observable by others, and *private events*, which are only accessible to ourselves. However, he didn't think public and private events were two different kinds of things. Instead, both were varieties of behavior. Furthermore, he rejected the notion that mental processes cause outward behaviors. Rather, both public and private events have their source in the organism's reinforcement history. For example, your conscious decision to drink some coffee and your outward behavior of reaching for your coffee cup are both driven by your reinforcement history of experiencing the pleasure of coffee drinking.

Radical behaviorism enabled Skinner to view the environment-organism interaction in a far more complex and subtle fashion than methodological behaviorism allowed (Rutherford, 2017). Watson had viewed the organism as a passive entity that was acted on by the environment and that responded in predictable ways. In other words, methodological behaviorists treated the organism like a mindless machine, and mechanical metaphors such as telephone switchboards linking stimulus and response were common. Skinner, in contrast, saw the organism as an active entity that operated on its environment and learned about the consequences of those actions. Instead of just responding to stimuli in the present moment, the organism is guided in its behaviors by its reinforcement history, the accumulation of all its experiences as it has interacted with its environment in the past.

Skinner the Popular Psychologist

Skinner, like his hero Francis Bacon, believed technology should benefit humankind by freeing people from drudgery and making their lives more enjoyable. To that end, Skinner invented devices to make life easier in the lab, home, and school.

To streamline his work, Skinner invented a machine to dispense food when an animal pressed a lever (Rachlin, 1995). He also created a device for recording those lever presses, which he called the cumulative recorder. Putting these together, he developed what he called an operant conditioning chamber, so that all he had to do was put the animal into the box at the beginning of the experiment and take it out at the end, letting the device dispense food and record presses on its own (Figure 5.7). Clark Hull and his students adopted the operant conditioning chamber for their own experiments, calling it a Skinner box. This became the common way of referring to the chamber, much to its inventor's chagrin.

Figure 5.7　Operant Conditioning Chamber

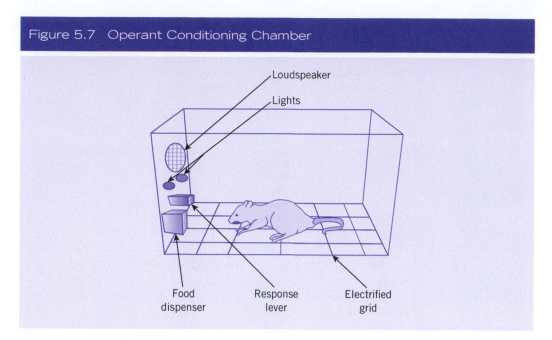

Loudspeaker

Lights

Food dispenser　Response lever　Electrified grid

Source: Andreas1 via Wikimedia Commons.

When Skinner's wife told him she wouldn't mind having a second child but didn't like the extra housework, he set to work on a solution (Benjamin & Nielsen-Gammon, 1999). The result was a new type of crib he called the baby tender. It consisted of an insulated enclosure with a safety-glass front, a mattress of stretched canvas, and a heater below. The baby tender provided a climate-controlled environment in which the baby slept wearing only a diaper, and it was large enough to also serve as a playpen and bassinet. For the first two years of her life, Skinner's daughter Deborah slept and played in the baby tender. Her mother was pleased with the device, as it eliminated much of the laundering of bedsheets, blankets, and pajamas that usually went with early childcare, giving her more free time to interact with her new baby.

Thinking about marketing the baby tender, Skinner submitted an article describing it to the popular magazine *Ladies Home Journal* (Benjamin & Nielsen-Gammon, 1999). The reaction was mixed. Some parents wanted one for their babies, but others thought of it as an operant conditioning chamber for humans and were appalled. Skinner's attempts to market the baby tender eventually failed, although he tried out several brand names, including "air crib" and "heir conditioner." In large part, the failure was largely due to rumors about the psychological damage inflicted on poor Deborah from being confined to a box for her first two years. Various accounts either placed her in a mental institution or marked her as a victim of suicide. In reality, though, Deborah Skinner grew up to be a successful artist with no history of mental illness.

Once when Skinner visited his daughter's school, he was appalled by the methods the teachers were using, as they violated all that was known about reinforcement (Rutherford, 2017). So he invented a teaching machine that broke down material into easy-to-learn steps. It also gave students reinforcement for correct answers and helpful feedback for wrong responses. Skinner had hoped to revolutionize American education, but he met with vehement protest from teachers, parents, and students alike who thought Skinner was trying to replace humans with machines. For his part, Skinner saw the machines as teaching aids and not as teacher replacements, but once again popular opinion was against this labor-saving device.

Skinner enjoyed being in the public eye and finding himself in the middle of controversy (Dinsmoor, 1992). He challenged the received wisdom and basked in the attention he received when the powers-that-be and the people-at-large attacked his iconoclastic views. As a result, Skinner became a household name in the last half of the twentieth century, standing as the image of the scientific psychologist who was both revered and reviled.

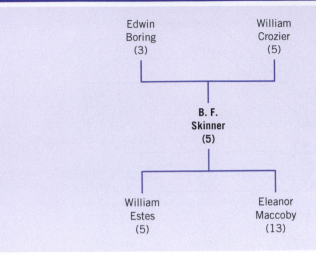

Figure 5.8 Academic Family Tree of B. F. Skinner

Edwin Boring (3)

William Crozier (5)

B. F. Skinner (5)

William Estes (5)

Eleanor Maccoby (13)

Early in his career, Skinner demonstrated the power of operant conditioning by putting on displays of his well-trained animals, with rats playing slot machines and pigeons playing ping pong (Rutherford, 2017). During World War II, he even proposed a method for training pigeons to guide missiles, but the Army didn't take him seriously. People marveled at his abilities to train animals to perform amazing tricks, and his methods are still widely used in animal shows today (Figure 5.8). At the same time, the public feared that such powerful methods of behavior control, when applied to humans, would lead to totalitarianism.

Much of Skinner's fame resulted from two books he wrote for the popular press, *Walden Two* in 1948 and *Beyond Freedom and Dignity* in 1971. The first was a novel describing a utopian society that employed behavioral technology to increase the happiness of its inhabitants, and the second was a nonfiction work in which he argued against the notion of free will. At first, few people read *Walden Two*, but by the 1960s college professors began assigning it to promote class discussion of social issues, and millions of copies have now been sold (Rutherford, 2000). In contrast, *Beyond Freedom and Dignity* was an instant bestseller, and Skinner even got his face on the cover of *Time* magazine. In this book, he argued that free will is an illusion because our behavior is determined by our reinforcement history. However, he maintained, we can increase human happiness by controlling the reinforcers in our environment instead of allowing our behavior to be guided haphazardly. This book evoked the kind of heated controversy Skinner reveled in.

Legacy

Skinner retired from Harvard in 1974, but he continued to walk the two miles between home and office for many years after that (Fowler, 1990). In November 1989, he learned he had leukemia and was given two months to live. But Skinner kept up his spirits, and by the following summer he was still active. On August 10, 1990, he gave the speech "Can Psychology Be a Science of Mind?" at the American Psychological Association national convention. He revised it for publication during the following week and sent it off to the publisher the day before he died.

B. F. Skinner left his mark not only on psychology but on American society as a whole. With the development of operant conditioning, he spawned a whole new discipline known as behavioral analysis, which has had a tremendous impact on psychotherapy and education. Furthermore, almost all of the animal research conducted today depends on Skinner's methods. In addition, many of the ideas for improving human happiness that he presented in *Walden Two* and *Beyond Freedom and Dignity* have been incorporated into the field of positive psychology.

Skinner's impact on the discipline is indicated by the fact that he ranked number 1 in a survey of the most eminent psychologists of the twentieth century (Haggbloom et al., 2002). He was also a controversial public figure, standing with Sigmund Freud as one of the few psychologists familiar to the general public in the twentieth century.

Behaviorism in Transition

A fundamental premise of behaviorism was that the laws of learning derived from observations of animal behavior applied equally well to humans. By the middle decades of the twentieth century, however, a new generation of behaviorists were beginning to challenge that assumption. Unlike other animals, humans live in complex social networks supported by language and culture. Moreover, new techniques for studying brain functions were being developed, and so these young learning theories also jettisoned the standard behaviorist practice of treating the brain as a "black box." Finally, the advent of the computer after World War II provided a new metaphor of the behaving organism as an information processor. This was a time when American behaviorism was beginning to transition into the disciplines of psychology we know today.

Neal Miller

When James Rowland Angell (Chapter 4) became the president of Yale University in 1921, he built the Institute of Human Relations (IHR) to encourage interdisciplinary collaboration among psychiatrists, psychologists, and other social scientists (Coons, 2014). As Freudians and behaviorists interacted, they began to ask whether there was any way to bridge these two seemingly disparate approaches to understanding human behavior. This was the heady atmosphere in which Neal Miller (1909–2002) found himself as a doctoral student. Miller had already come under the influence of two great psychologists, Edwin Guthrie as his undergraduate adviser and Lewis Terman, who'd supervised his master's thesis. At Yale, he gravitated toward Clark Hull and his learning theory, but at the same time his curiosity was piqued by discussions of psychoanalytic theory. During his long career, Miller became known as the *American learning theorist who sought to redefine Freudian concepts in behavioral terms*.

Photo 5.10
Neal Miller

Psicoterapiaintegrativa.com via Wikimedia Commons

In his doctoral research, Miller pointed out a similarity between Sigmund Freud's (Chapter 7) concept of *repression* and Ivan Pavlov's (Chapter 9) proposed process of *inhibition* (Coons, 2002). This connection led him to the belief that a synthesis of the Freudian and behavioral approaches was possible, but first he needed to learn more about psychoanalysis. So after he earned his Ph.D. in 1935, he obtained a fellowship to spend the following year at the Vienna Psychoanalytic Institute studying under Anna Freud (Chapter 7). He underwent a training analysis and became adept at Freudian theory, but his only regret was that he declined a session with Sigmund Freud because he felt the hourly rate of $20 was too expensive. Nevertheless, he returned to Yale, this time as a faculty member, and he began his program to integrate the two theories.

At the IHR, Miller engaged in a longtime collaboration with sociologist John Dollard (1900–1980; Miller, 1982). Dollard had undergone psychoanalytic training in Berlin, and he'd also done a sociological analysis of racial oppression in the rural South. Likewise, Miller had witnessed the rise of fascism during his year in Europe—Hitler was already in power in Germany, and many Austrians were sympathetic to the Nazi cause. Since Freud viewed aggression as a drive, it seemed a logical place to begin their Freudian-behavioral synthesis. They first posited what they called the frustration-aggression hypothesis. This is *the proposal that people turn to aggression when they are frustrated in reaching their goals*. In his earlier work, Dollard had already proposed that criminal activity results from social deprivation, and Miller had observed the frustration of Germans and Austrians at the economic hardships due to heavy reparations that had to be paid after losing World War I as well as the aggressions they were perpetrating against Jews. These observations, they believed, lent credence to the hypothesis, and a series of animal studies provided additional support. Several of their Yale colleagues, including Robert Sears (Chapter 13), joined in this project, and the result was the 1939 book *Frustration and Aggression*.

Miller and Dollard were now working with a version of learning theory that had shed the shackles of methodological behaviorism (Miller, 1982). That is, they saw no need to refrain from making inferences about internal mental states. Their emphasis was still on learning and behavior, but their explanations had taken on a cognitive flavor, much like the approach Tolman had adopted. They also turned their attention to the social nature of human life, with the understanding that the environment shaping human behavior consisted of complex interactions with other people rather than the buzzing tones, flashing lights, and electric shocks endured by rats in cages. This line of research led to the 1941 book *Social Learning and Imitation*. In this work, Miller and Dollard argued that imitation of others was an important learning process for humans. They also found that even rats learn through imitation when they're allowed to live together and form social groups as opposed to being housed in individual cages. This research eventually led to the development of social learning theory by Robert Sears, Albert Bandura (Chapter 13), and others after World War II.

Both Miller and Dollard served in the military during World War II. When they returned to Yale, they resumed their project to synthesize Freudian and behavioral theories (Bower, 2011). Just after the war, Miller had done some animal studies on **approach-avoidance conflict**. This is *a situation in which an organism simultaneously experiences a drive to obtain a desired object and a fear compelling it to flee the object*. For instance, if a rat is trained to retrieve a piece of food in a specific portion of a maze but also receives a shock each time it takes the food, it will experience approach-avoidance conflict. It will rush down the alleyway but then halt before arriving at the food, and just where it stops depends on the attractiveness of the food and the severity of past shocks. Miller believed he saw a parallel between this and the Freudian defense mechanism known as reaction formation, in which an unpleasant emotion is expressed as its opposite tendency. For instance, if you don't get accepted at your dream school, you may decide that you didn't really want to go there anyway. In a similar manner, Miller and Dollard linked phenomena from animal behavior studies with other defense mechanisms in psychoanalytic theory. The result was the 1950 book *Personality and Psychotherapy*.

In the mid-1950s, Miller turned his research interests toward an exploration of the brain mechanisms responsible for physiological drives (Coons, 2014). James Olds and Peter Milner (Chapter 16) had just discovered the reward center of the brain, and the race was on to use their technique of surgically implanting electrodes to stimulate specific neural structures. Miller explored the role of the hypothalamus in regulating the hunger drive, and he also found early evidence for the role of the neurotransmitter dopamine in promoting reward.

As technology for monitoring and manipulating brain activity advanced, Miller explored a question he'd long pondered, namely whether autonomic responses could be brought under voluntary control (Coons, 2014). Specifically, he asked whether people could learn to regulate their own heart rate. He worked with a population of human patients whose spinal cords had been severed, leaving them paralyzed. When these patients were lifted to an upright position, they often passed out. Ordinarily, our heart rate automatically increases when we sit or stand up to ensure sufficient blood flow to the brain, but this wasn't happening in these patients. Miller let them view the readout from a heart monitor as they attempted to mentally manipulate

Photo 5.11
Biofeedback training program for PTSD symptoms

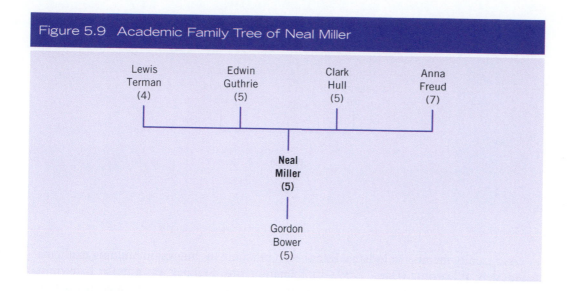

Figure 5.9 Academic Family Tree of Neal Miller

Lewis Terman (4)   Edwin Guthrie (5)   Clark Hull (5)   Anna Freud (7)

Neal Miller (5)

Gordon Bower (5)

their heart rate. Some patients found they could do this through exciting—and often erotic—imagery. Thus was born the method of **biofeedback**, which is *the process of gaining insights into physiological functions with the assistance of instruments that monitor them*. Biofeedback is often depicted in the popular press as a medical miracle, but the truth is that its effectiveness is far more limited. However, medical researchers have found biofeedback helpful in the treatment of some disorders, such as migraine.

Although Neal Miller never gained the level of public notoriety that B. F. Skinner enjoyed, his contribution to psychology was at least as great (Coons, 2002). Whereas Skinner steadfastly held on to his radical behaviorism, denouncing the rise of cognitive psychology unto his death, Miller's interests grew along with the development of new ideas and research techniques. Trained as a Hullian behaviorist, Miller found ways to empirically test concepts from Freudian theory as psychoanalysis grew in popularity at mid-century. Later in his career, he turned his attention to issues in physiological psychology as well as in the budding field of neuroscience. By breaking down the walls that separated the early schools, Miller became one of the major architects of the newly reorganized psychology in the second half of the twentieth century (Figure 5.9).

William Estes

As a graduate student at the University of Minnesota, **William Estes** (1919–2011) was interested in "learning and memory," but every time he used that phrase in a paper, his mentor B. F. Skinner would strike out the words "and memory" (Estes, 1989). After finishing his dissertation in 1943, Estes was inducted into the military, but after World War II, Skinner offered him a faculty position at Indiana University where he was now the department chair. Once again, Estes had to be careful not to mention the naughty "M-word," and it took years for him to get out from under Skinner's thumb. Eventually, however, Estes established a reputation as the *American psychologist who developed influential mathematical models of learning and memory*.

During the Blitz (1940–1941), the Germans bombed London and other English cities on an almost daily basis (Gluck, 2011). When Londoners heard a missile approaching, they froze on the spot and until they heard the explosion in another part of the city, after which they went about their business as normal. Skinner and Estes thought they could replicate this behavior in rats, which they trained in an operant conditioning chamber to press a lever for a pellet of food. However, the chamber also had a buzzer and an electrified floor. The rats soon learned the buzzer meant a jolt of electricity was on its way, and they froze on the spot until the shock ended, after which they went to the lever for more food. This procedure became known as the conditioned emotional response paradigm, and it was commonly used in animal learning experiments during the 1940s and 1950s.

Figure 5.10   Academic Family Tree of William Estes

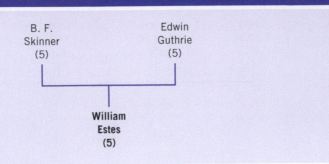

As a faculty member at Indiana, Estes began pursuing his interest in building mathematical models of learning (Estes, 1989). In Tolman's terms, Skinner was a molar behaviorist, treating behaviors as holistic movements of the organism. However, Estes was greatly influenced by a careful reading of the works of Edwin Guthrie, a molecular behaviorist who broke down both the stimulus and the response into component parts. If a stimulus is composed of many elements, Estes reasoned, then on any given trial, the organism is only likely to perceive a small subset of these. For example, a green light can be broken down into its brightness, hue, size, shape, duration, and so on. Likewise, if behaviors can be decomposed into individual muscle movements, then not all of them need to be performed during a given response. Estes also agreed with Guthrie that learning occurs during a single stimulus-response pairing. That is to say, some element of the stimulus may become associated with some element of the response on a single trial, but it takes many trials to pair the bulk of stimulus elements with those of the response.

Estes presented this idea in his watershed article "Toward a Statistical Theory of Learning," which he published in 1950 (Healy, Gluck, Nosofsky, & Shiffrin, 2012). In this work, he presents *the proposal that stimulus-response associations are learned in a statistical, not absolute, manner,* and he called this idea **stimulus sampling theory**. Estes saw an analogy between natural selection and learning, in which the organism selects elements of the stimulus and response, discarding those that don't lead to positive outcomes on future occasions and keeping those that do. It's possible that Estes's thinking was influenced by his mentor in this regard, since Skinner had also seen a Darwinian analogy with operant conditioning. Stimulus sampling theory was widely hailed because it explained diverse phenomena such as generalization and discrimination as well as variability in performance even in highly trained organisms.

Over the next decade, Estes became deeply involved in a new movement called mathematical psychology, and he was recognized as one of its founders (Gluck, 2011). This was *an approach to explaining learning and memory by constructing mathematical models of these processes*. In a sense, this was an extension of Hull's attempt to construct equations to describe and predict behavior. In building their models, however, this new generation of theorists employed fields of mathematics far more complex than Hull could have mustered. In 1962, Estes was invited to Stanford University to help establish a program of mathematical psychology. There, he joined the younger Gordon Bower, with whom Estes had already been collaborating for several years (Figure 5.10).

Gordon Bower

As an undergraduate, **Gordon Bower** (born 1932) became enthralled with Clark Hull's learning theory (Bower, 2008). But when he arrived at Yale in 1955 for graduate training, his mentor Neal Miller had already moved beyond learning theory to an exploration of drive systems in the brain. Bower learned how to surgically implant electrodes in rats, but Miller could see his heart wasn't in it, and in the end he encouraged his student to pursue his passion in learning theory with other professors. In his second year as a graduate student, Bower attended a summer workshop at Stanford on mathematical psychology. There he developed a close intellectual relationship with William Estes, still at Indiana, who became a mentor at a distance. With a good word from Miller to his former Yale colleague Robert Sears, now the chair at Stanford, Bower was offered a faculty position in 1959, and there he remained for the rest of his career. Bower started off as an animal behaviorist but transitioned his research focus according to the changing spirit of the times to become an *American psychologist who developed influential mathematical and computational models of human learning and memory.*

When Bower first arrived at Stanford, he set up an animal learning lab and began a very traditional behaviorist research program (Bower, 2007). But a few years later, Estes was brought on board to help build a program in mathematical psychology, and they rekindled their old working relationship. Once again Bower's interest in mathematical models of learning was piqued, but he also needed far more data than could be obtained from animal research, so he shifted to using human subjects instead. He began working in an area known as **verbal learning**, which was *a behavioral field of study that investigated the retention and recall of language-based materials such as word lists and word pairs.* In a few years, the Cognitive Revolution would be under way, and Bower could freely say that he was studying human memory. But for the time being, he and others of his generation had to assiduously avoid the taboo "M-word."

During the 1960s, Bower attended conferences and workshops on computational modeling, where he interacted with founders of the cognitive movement, such as George Miller and Herbert Simon (Chapter 11; "Gordon H. Bower," 1980). Bower created mathematical models of information processing in short-term memory, which served as foundational components of the modern theory of human memory. With his student John Anderson, he also built an influential computational model of human long-term memory. Known as HAM for short, the computer model mimicked the way people make inferences based on the information they already have available. *Human Associative Memory*, published in 1973, became one of the most highly cited works in cognitive psychology. From this point onward, he made a number of important contributions to the study of human memory. Gordon Bower started his career as an animal behaviorist and became recognized as one of the founders of cognitive psychology.

Both Estes and Bower are representatives of the generation of behaviorists trained just before or after World War II that laid the groundwork for the Cognitive Revolution of the 1950s (Fuchs, 2012). They differed from their forebears in a number of respects. First, they were far more interested in studying humans than animals, challenging the assumption that laws of behavior observed in rats applied equally well to people. Second, they were unabashed in making inferences about underlying cognitive processes from the behaviors they observed. And third, they approached their research with an unprecedented level of mathematical sophistication, bolstered by the computation power of the newly invented computer (Figure 5.11).

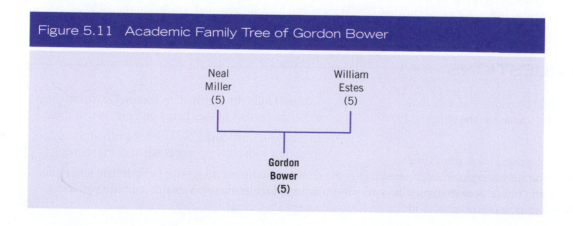

Figure 5.11 Academic Family Tree of Gordon Bower

Looking Ahead

In the early decades of the twentieth century, John Watson rallied a generation of psychologists to abandon inferences about underlying mental processes and turn their attention instead to formulating laws of observable behavior. The hope of this positivist approach was that it would give psychology the rigor it needed to become a natural science. The irony of this endeavor is that physics was abandoning its adherence to positivism at just the time that psychology was adopting it. Just after the turn of the century, physicists had come to the conclusion that the universe could only be understood by making inferences derived from careful observations. For instance, no one could see inside an atom, but scientists could deduce its structure from other evidence. As we'll see in the following chapters, two schools of psychology were emerging in Germany and Austria at around the same time as behaviorism was developing in the United States. Neither the Gestalt psychologists (Chapter 6) nor the Freudian psychoanalysts were reluctant to draw inferences about internal mental processes on the basis of observed behavior. By the 1930s, however, war clouds were gathering in Europe, and as psychologists there fled to the United States, they insisted on bringing the mind back into psychology.

CHAPTER SUMMARY

John Watson argued that psychology could become a natural science if it shifted its focus to observable behavior and avoided explanations in terms of unobservable mental states, a position known as methodological behaviorism. He's best known for his Little Albert study, in which he induced a conditioned fear of lab rats in a young boy. He later assisted Mary Cover Jones in helping another boy known as Little Peter overcome a fear of animals using classical conditioning techniques. Edwin Guthrie argued against Thorndike's three laws of learning, the foundation of behaviorist learning theories, maintaining instead that stimulus-response associations are created in a single instance. Whereas Watson and Guthrie insisted on describing direct relationships between stimuli and responses, the neo-behaviorists recognized the need to posit intervening variables representing internal states of the organism. Clark Hull is best known for his drive theory of motivation and his attempt to create an equation describing all behavior. Among all the behaviorists, Edward Tolman pushed closest to a cognitive explanation of learning with his studies of latent learning and cognitive maps in rats. Meanwhile,

his student Zing-Yang Kuo was a vocal critic of the notion of instinct. As a student of Hull, Kenneth Spence was a strong proponent of a learning theory that became known as the Hull-Spence system, and his wife Janet Taylor Spence applied this system to the study of anxiety. B. F. Skinner introduced a new form of learning that he called operant conditioning, built on Thorndike's law of effect, in which the organism learns about the consequences of its behavior. Skinner's solution to the mind-body problem was to claim that even mental processes were behaviors. Neal Miller led a group of post-World War II learning theorists who attempted to integrate behaviorism with Freudian theory. Skinner's student William Estes developed a statistical theory of learning that was a forerunner of computational modeling. Likewise, Miller's student Gordon Bower began his career as an animal-learning theorist but shifted to the study of human memory under the influence of William Estes. Thus, by the 1960s, mainstream American psychology was transitioning back to a cognitive orientation much like that of the functionalists, against which Watson and his followers had rebelled in the 1920s.

DISCUSSION QUESTIONS

1. Explain methodological behaviorism and its roots in positivism. How does it relate to the mind-body problem?

2. Discuss how Watson integrated ideas from Pavlov and Freud in formulating his concept of conditioned emotional response. Can you think of examples of conditioned emotional responses in everyday life?

3. Explain Hull's drive reduction theory. Give examples of behaviors that fit the theory and others that don't.

4. Discuss Hull's hypothetico-deductive method. How does it contrast with Skinner's approach to doing science?

5. Compare Tolman's purposive behaviorism and Hull's drive reduction theory. Which theory do you find more convincing?

6. Explain Tolman's distinction between molecular and molar behavior. Classify Watson, Hull, Tolman, Guthrie, and Skinner as molecular or molar behaviorists.

7. Explain Skinner's distinction between respondent and operant behavior. How does Tolman's latent learning relate to these other two types of learning?

8. Explain how Guthrie recast Pavlovian conditioning in terms of his contiguity theory.

9. Discuss why Guthrie rejected Thorndike's law of exercise in favor of the recency principle.

10. Hull, Tolman, and Guthrie contended that reinforcement implies backward causation. Why would they argue this? How would Skinner reply?

11. Explain Skinner's distinction between public and private events. How does radical behaviorism relate to the mind-body problem?

12. Discuss Miller's concept of approach-avoidance conflict. Give some examples from everyday human life.

ON THE WEB

On YouTube, you can find video clips of the **Little Albert experiment** by John Watson and Rosalie Rayner. You can also find a half-hour interview with **Janet Taylor Spence**. YouTube hosts interviews with **B. F. Skinner** as well as demonstrations of **operant conditioning**. You can also find an hour-long interview with **Gordon Bower**. There are also a number of videos on YouTube describing the work of each of the psychologists we met in this chapter. These videos are of variable quality, so watch with a critical eye.

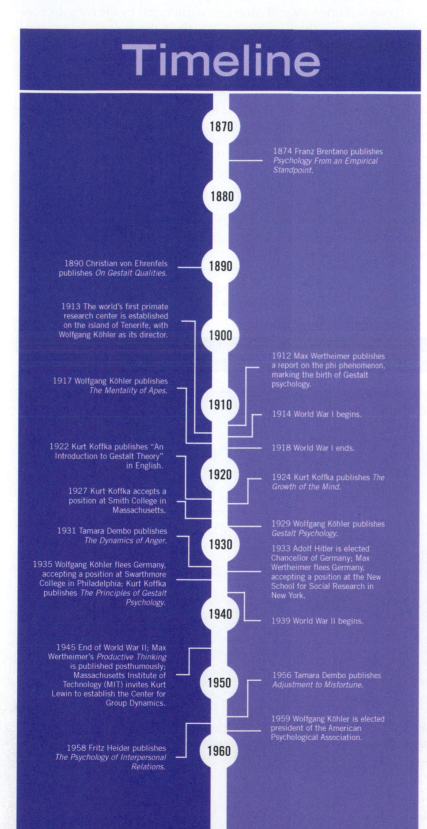

Timeline

1870

1874 Franz Brentano publishes *Psychology From an Empirical Standpoint.*

1880

1890 Christian von Ehrenfels publishes *On Gestalt Qualities.*

1890

1913 The world's first primate research center is established on the island of Tenerife, with Wolfgang Köhler as its director.

1900

1912 Max Wertheimer publishes a report on the phi phenomenon, marking the birth of Gestalt psychology.

1917 Wolfgang Köhler publishes *The Mentality of Apes.*

1910

1914 World War I begins.

1922 Kurt Koffka publishes "An Introduction to Gestalt Theory" in English.

1918 World War I ends.

1920

1924 Kurt Koffka publishes *The Growth of the Mind.*

1927 Kurt Koffka accepts a position at Smith College in Massachusetts.

1929 Wolfgang Köhler publishes *Gestalt Psychology.*

1931 Tamara Dembo publishes *The Dynamics of Anger.*

1930

1933 Adolf Hitler is elected Chancellor of Germany; Max Wertheimer flees Germany, accepting a position at the New School for Social Research in New York.

1935 Wolfgang Köhler flees Germany, accepting a position at Swarthmore College in Philadelphia; Kurt Koffka publishes *The Principles of Gestalt Psychology.*

1940

1939 World War II begins.

1945 End of World War II; Max Wertheimer's *Productive Thinking* is published posthumously; Massachusetts Institute of Technology (MIT) invites Kurt Lewin to establish the Center for Group Dynamics.

1950

1956 Tamara Dembo publishes *Adjustment to Misfortune.*

1959 Wolfgang Köhler is elected president of the American Psychological Association.

1958 Fritz Heider publishes *The Psychology of Interpersonal Relations.*

1960

Learning Objectives

After reading this chapter, you should be able to:

- Identify the contributions of Franz Brentano, Carl Stumpf, and Christian von Ehrenfels in the development of Gestalt psychology.

- Outline the development of the Berlin school of Gestalt psychology through the work of Max Wertheimer, Wolfgang Köhler, and Kurt Koffka.

- Evaluate the contributions of Kurt Lewin and his students to the development of social psychology and group dynamics.

- Assess the contributions of Fritz Heider to both cognitive and social psychology.

Looking Back

Experimental psychology has its origins in Europe, where Wilhelm Wundt established the first psychology laboratory at Leipzig University in 1879. Yet many of his students—both European and American—built their careers in the United States, where an expanding university system provided ample employment opportunities for this first generation of experimental psychologists. In the New World, Wundt's approach was modified to suit the more practical and less theoretical orientation of American science, and by the early decades of the twenty-first century there were three competing schools of psychology—structuralism, functionalism, and behaviorism. Likewise in the Old World, groups of psychologists coalesced that challenged Wundt's physiological psychology, both on theoretical and methodological grounds. Among these, the most important rival to the Leipzig school was Gestalt psychology (pronounced *guh-SHTALT*, rhymes with *default*), mainly centered in Berlin but with another important group working in the Austrian city of Graz.

The map of Europe at the turn of the twentieth century looked much different than it does today. Some of the countries of Western Europe, such as France, Spain, and Italy, still have roughly the same borders today as they did then. But the middle of the continent was dominated by two large German-speaking countries (Figure 6.1). To the north, the German Empire extended through much of modern Poland as far as Lithuania, while the southern Austro-Hungarian Empire included the modern Czech and Slovak Republics as well as territory that now belongs to a number of other countries. This German-speaking "Middle Europe" dominated the culture—both the arts and the sciences—of the continent in the late nineteenth and early twentieth centuries. Thus it should come as no surprise that this region was the birthplace not only of the first school of experimental psychology but also of a number of other historically important schools of psychology. Among these, Gestalt psychology will be the topic of this chapter, and psychoanalysis the focus of Chapter 7.

Figure 6.1   Map of Europe in 1914

Source: Department of History, United States Military Academy.

Early approaches to experimental psychology tended to be analytical in their approach, breaking down cognitive and behavioral processes into their component parts. This was certainly the mindset of the German physiologist Wilhelm Wundt, who attempted to apply the methods of physiology to the study of human psychology. However, the Gestalt psychologists viewed consciousness as an emergent phenomenon that is different from the sum of its parts. In fact, **Gestalt** is the *German word for "configuration."* Early texts referred to this school as configurational psychology, but the term is much richer in meaning than this translation suggests, so by mid-century the original German name was adopted into English. Today there are no researchers who would call themselves "Gestalt psychologists." Nevertheless, this movement built the foundations on which the modern disciples of cognitive, social, and developmental psychology rest today.

Forerunners of Gestalt Psychology

Many of the early schools of psychology had a founder who promoted that particular discipline and recruited followers. But Gestalt psychology was different. Instead, it arose through the work of a loosely knit group of researchers who thought in similar ways about the proper approach to building a science of the mind. In this section, we'll look at the contributions of the philosopher Franz Brentano and two of his students, Carl Stumpf and Christian von Ehrenfels.

Franz Brentano

Franz Brentano (1838–1917) started his career as a Catholic priest, but he got involved in a protest against the doctrine of papal infallibility; as a result, he resigned from the priesthood (Whalen, 2005). He was hired as an assistant professor of philosophy at the University of Vienna, but in a strongly Catholic country like Austria, his status as an ex-priest haunted him for the rest of his career and hampered his hopes for promotion. Nevertheless, he was the university's academic superstar. With his fiery rhetoric, Brentano lectured to standing-room-only audiences, and he gathered around him a group of devoted students. Among them were founders of Gestalt psychology, such as Christian von Ehrenfels and Carl Stumpf, whom we'll meet shortly, as well as the leader of the psychoanalytic movement, Sigmund Freud, whom we'll meet in Chapter 7. Franz Brentano is recognized today as the *Austrian philosopher who advocated for a scientific approach to studying the mind that he called act psychology.*

M. Wacker, via Wikimedia Commons

Photo 6.1
Franz Brentano

Brentano's major work was the book *Psychology From an Empirical Standpoint*, which he published in 1874 (Meyer, Hackert, & Weger, 2018). This was a year after Wilhelm Wundt (Chapter 3) published his *Principles of Physiological Psychology*. While it would be an exaggeration to call these two men enemies, each was a vocal critic of the other's work. Nevertheless, Brentano did praise Wundt's establishment of a psychology laboratory at Leipzig in 1879. In fact, Brentano had also attempted to set up a lab around the same time, but his request for space and equipment was blocked by the university's administration, which seemed to hold a grudge against the "fallen" priest. Brentano argued that psychologists needed to approach their subject in a scientific manner, but he also believed that the experimental methods of the natural sciences were limited to the study of perception, attention, and working memory (to use the modern terms for these processes). The higher mental processes, such as imagination, judgment, and reasoning, would need to be approached in a different manner. To this point, Brentano's and Wundt's views are very similar. After all, Wundt devoted the last two decades of his life to his *Völkerpsychologie*, which was an extensive description of language and culture around the world.

Brentano's approach to the study of the mind became known as **act psychology** (Polkinghorne, 2003). This was *an early school of psychology which held that mental phenomena are active rather than passive processes.* This position should remind you of William James's view of consciousness as a set of mental functions rather than structures, and certainly Brentano and James were influenced by many of the same philosophers. However, Brentano also took aim at psychophysicists such as Ernst Weber and Gustav Fechner (Chapter 2). While conceding that sensation may be a passive process of taking in stimuli from the environment, as the psychophysicists viewed it, Brentano insisted that active processes of organization and interpretation were necessary to give meaning to sensory impressions. In other words, thinking was a kind of act, hence the name for the school. Brentano noted that mental phenomena have a unique quality that distinguishes them from physical phenomena, and he called this characteristic feature **intentionality**. In Brentano's sense, this term has nothing to do with motivation or purpose. Rather, he uses it in a different sense that refers to *the quality of being about something*. When you think, you have a thought *about* something. When you remember, you have a memory *about* something. And when you experience an emotion, you have a feeling *about* something. In contrast, physical phenomena aren't about anything—a rock simply is.

Furthermore, Brentano distinguished three types of intentionality—imagination, judgment, and emotion (Polkinghorne, 2003). In Brentano's framework, imagination is the most basic mental act, and it involves bringing a thought into consciousness, drawing from either current perception or past memory. For example, you look at a piece of abstract art, recognizing various shapes and colors. Judgment occurs when you make a rational assessment of the object in imagination. For instance, you decide that the work has been executed with a high level of artistic technique. Finally, emotion involves an appraisal of the object as good-and-desirable or else bad-and-undesirable. So even though you know the artist is skilled, you just don't like the painting.

An important distinction in Brentano's *Psychology From an Empirical Standpoint* is that between outer and inner perception (Meyer et al., 2018). Sensation and perception, in the modern usage of these terms, comprise outer perception, which involves a conscious awareness of the physical environment around us. Brentano was greatly influenced by his reading of the British empiricists (Chapter 1), and he agreed with them in contending that our perception of the external world is indirect. In other words, we don't have direct access to the environment outside of our bodies but rather only the incomplete information provided by our senses. But inner perception, or the awareness of our thoughts and feelings, is different. Internal experiences are perceived directly, without mediation of any sense organs. This distinction also delineates the limit of what the experimental method can tell us about human psychology. Wundt's physiological psychology was limited to studies of outer perception. But the truly interesting parts of psychology, such as thinking and feeling, were beyond the purview of the experimental method. Instead, Brentano insisted, we need a science of psychological experience.

This is why Brentano uses the term "empirical" rather than "experimental" in the title of his book (Polkinghorne, 2003). An empirical standpoint is one in which knowledge is gathered through our interactions with the real world. It includes experimental methods but isn't limited to them. Brentano was greatly influenced by his reading of Aristotle (Chapter 1), who emphasized observation and data collection over experimentation and hypothesis testing. To study inner perception, psychologists would have to use empirical but not experimental methods. Here, Brentano makes a distinction between inner perception and inner observation. For example, if you feel angry right now, you are experiencing an inner perception. However, if you try to observe your anger as an outsider, your attention shifts instead to the objective qualities of that emotion, and the feeling dissipates. This, according to Brentano, was the problem with introspection as used by the philosophers as well as by experimental psychologists such as Wundt—when you observe an internal state, you no longer experience it. What an empirical psychology needed, then, was subjective descriptions of internal experiences, not objective introspections of them.

Franz Brentano was clearly one of the founders of scientific psychology, ranking along with Wilhelm Wundt, William James, and Sigmund Freud, and during his lifetime he was just as well known as these contemporaries (Meyer et al., 2018). After his death, his ideas lived on in a school of philosophy known as phenomenology, but he was largely forgotten by psychologists. In America, Brentano's approach simply didn't resonate with the behaviorist movement that was underway. And in Europe, both the Gestalt and the psychoanalytic movements, even though they had their foundations in act psychology, moved far beyond what Brentano had imagined for a science of the mind.

However, Brentano's ideas, passed down through the phenomenologist philosophers (Figure 6.2), inspired the humanistic psychologists (Chapter 15) of the post-War United

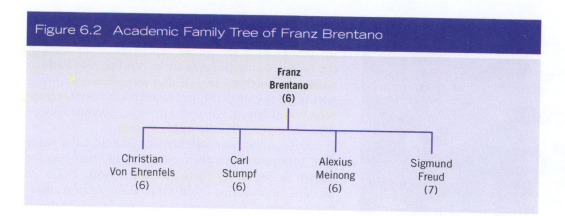

Figure 6.2   Academic Family Tree of Franz Brentano

Franz Brentano (6)

- Christian Von Ehrenfels (6)
- Carl Stumpf (6)
- Alexius Meinong (6)
- Sigmund Freud (7)

States (Polkinghorne, 2003). Humanism represented a reaction against both the sterility of behaviorism and the pessimism of psychoanalysis by proposing a middle way that viewed humans as active constructors of their lives. Furthermore, with the advent of cognitive psychology in the last half of the twentieth century, Brentano's concept of intentionality has regained currency. But more immediately, we'll shortly see that Brentano laid the groundwork for Gestalt psychology, an important empirical approach to the study of the mind in the first half of the twentieth century. And in turn, Gestalt psychology laid the groundwork for many of the modern disciplines of psychology that we see today.

Carl Stumpf

Carl Stumpf (1848–1936; pronounced *SHTOOMPF*) came under the sway of the young Franz Brentano when he enrolled at the University of Würzburg in Germany as a law student (Reisenzein & Sprung, 2000). When Brentano resigned from the priesthood, he also gave up his professorship at Würzburg to accept a new position in Vienna. Stumpf then took over his position at Würzburg, but after a series of career moves, he ended up at the University of Berlin, where he remained for the next quarter of a century. Although Stumpf was a philosopher by training, he established the Berlin Institute of Psychology, which became one of the largest experimental laboratories of psychology in the world and a major rival of Wundt's lab in Leipzig. Today, Carl Stumpf is mainly remembered as the *German philosopher who trained the first generation of Gestalt psychologists.*

Stumpf was an accomplished musician, and much of his research centered on the psychology of music (Ruckmick, 1937). He published two large volumes that are considered foundational works on the study of music perception. However, he didn't limit himself to research on Western music. Over his long career, he amassed a collection of some 10,000 phonographic recordings of music around the world, many of them made by Stumpf and his students as they traveled the globe. These were housed at the Berlin Institute, making it the greatest library of world music at that time. Thus, Stumpf is often credited as one of the founders of the field known as ethnomusicology.

Another important contribution was Stumpf's cognitive theory of emotion, which was remarkably similar to currently accepted models (Reisenzein & Sprung, 2000). At the time, the two rival theories were those of Wilhelm Wundt (Chapter 3) and William James (Chapter 4). Wundt had proposed a three-dimensional model in which emotions were distinguished as either pleasant or unpleasant, tense or relaxed, and excited or depressed. James rejected this structural model, focusing instead on physiological arousal and behavioral responses. As you recall from Chapter 4, James said you don't run from the bear because you're afraid, but rather you're afraid because you run from the bear. Stumpf considered James a friend and was far more sympathetic to his work than to that of his rival Wundt,

Via Wikimedia Commons

Photo 6.2
Carl Stumpf

**Photo 6.3
Clever Hans**

but he thought James's theory was missing a vital cognitive component. Specifically, Stumpf proposed that the physiological arousal we experience at the sight of the bear not only prompts us to run but also leads to a cognitive interpretation of that arousal as fear. Much later in the twentieth century, social psychologist Stanley Schachter (Chapter 12) would provide experimental evidence to support this theory of emotion.

Early in the twentieth century, Stumpf led a panel that investigated a phenomenon that has become known as the Clever Hans incident (Lewin, 1937). At the time, animals that could supposedly perform amazing intellectual feats were popular spectacles. Many of these had simply been trained to perform tricks so their owners could charge admission from gullible audiences. But Hans the horse was different. His owner was a high-school math instructor, and he really believed the horse could do arithmetic. If you gave Hans a math problem, he would tap out the correct answer with his hoof. Furthermore, Hans's owner never sought to earn money from the horse. Instead, he invited the scientific community of Berlin to investigate. Eventually, Stumpf's student Oskar Pfungst (1874–1933) uncovered what was going on. Hans was reading subtle changes in his owner's facial expressions and body posture that let him know when to start and stop tapping his hoof. If he couldn't see his owner, his math abilities disappeared. In the end, Hans was indeed a clever horse, but his intelligence was more of a social than quantitative sort.

No doubt, Stumpf's greatest legacy to experimental psychology was his active promotion and organization of the field (Reisenzein & Sprung, 2000). In addition to the world music library he created at the Berlin Institute, he also lobbied government agencies to provide funding to establish the world's first primate research facility. This was set up on Tenerife in the Canary Islands off the Atlantic coast of North Africa. In the next section, we'll read about the important studies on problem solving in primates that his student Wolfgang Köhler conducted there (Figure 6.3).

Christian von Ehrenfels

Franz Brentano had inspired a generation of psychologists and provided them with a framework that he called act psychology. His student Carl Stumpf then trained the first cohort of researchers that would eventually call themselves Gestalt psychologists. Finally, it was another of Brentano's students who gave the school its name. This was Christian von Ehrenfels (1859–1932), the *Austrian philosopher who introduced the concept of Gestalt quality*.

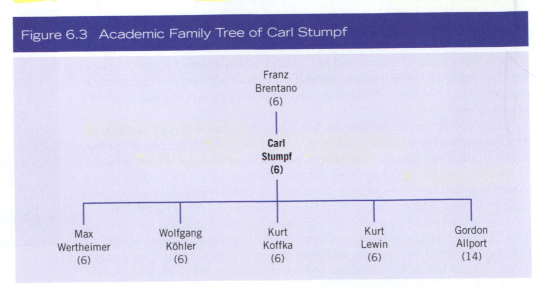

Figure 6.3   Academic Family Tree of Carl Stumpf

Franz
Brentano
(6)

Carl
Stumpf
(6)

| Max Wertheimer (6) | Wolfgang Köhler (6) | Kurt Koffka (6) | Kurt Lewin (6) | Gordon Allport (14) |

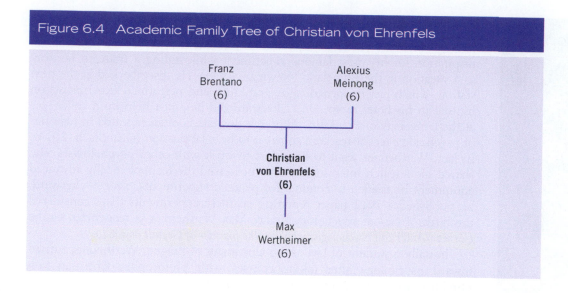

Figure 6.4 Academic Family Tree of Christian von Ehrenfels

Franz
Brentano
(6)

Alexius
Meinong
(6)

**Christian
von Ehrenfels
(6)**

Max
Wertheimer
(6)

Ehrenfels's most famous work is his 1890 book *On Gestalt Qualities*, in which he challenged prevailing theories of perception (Wertheimer, 2003). At the time, the prevailing belief was that perception was built up from the combination of sensory elements, a point of view sometimes referred to as "mental chemistry." It was this perspective, for example, that led Edward Titchener (Chapter 3) with his structural approach to attempt a deconstruction of conscious experience into its elemental sensations. However, Ehrenfels challenged the notion of mental chemistry, insisting instead that the perceptual whole is more than just a sum of its parts. One example was that of a square, which is composed of four equal lines and four right angles. But there's also an additional quality about the figure—its "square-ness." If you shorten or lengthen the four lines equally, you still have a square, even though the elements making it up are now different. And if you rotate the figure by 45 degrees, you no longer have a square but a diamond, even though the elements haven't changed. He called the square-ness of this figure its **Gestalt quality**, meaning that it was *an aspect of a configuration as a whole that none of its parts possesses*.

An even more compelling example of a Gestalt quality for Ehrenfels was that of a melody (De Vecchi, 2003). The classic definition of a melody is that it's a series of notes. However, if you change the key, every note will change, even though the melody as a whole still sounds the same. In other words, a melody has an overall form independent of the elemental notes that comprise it. This overall form, Ehrenfels said, is the melody's Gestalt quality. The melody example became a favorite demonstration among the Gestalt psychologists (Figure 6.4). In fact, it also illustrates that Gestalt qualities aren't just *more* than just an assemblage of elements. Rather, this example shows something of fundamental importance in perception: namely, the whole is *different* from the sum of its parts. This statement would become the motto of the Gestalt school.

Berlin School

It was at the University of Berlin, located in the capital of the German Empire, that Gestalt psychology was born. In particular, three of Carl Stumpf's students—Max Wertheimer, Wolfgang Köhler, and Kurt Koffka—are credited as the founders of Gestalt psychology. For a while, Berlin was one of the major centers of experimental psychology in the world. But with the rise of Nazism in the 1930s, these three founders and many of their students fled to the New World, where they challenged the sterility of behaviorism and prodded American psychology to reorganize itself in the modern disciplines we see today.

Max Wertheimer

Photo 6.4
Max Wertheimer

Max Wertheimer (1880–1943) told his colleague Edwin Newman that he got inspiration for his most famous experiment while riding a train on his way to a vacation in the Rhineland (Newman, 1944). He disembarked at the next station, which just happened to be Frankfurt, and performed experiments on himself in his hotel room. Only afterward did he enlist help from colleagues at the University of Frankfurt. Although this tale is often repeated in histories of psychology, recent research shows it to be a fabrication (Grundlach, 2014). In fact, Wertheimer went to Frankfurt to work with other psychologists who shared his research interests and who possessed the technologically advanced equipment he needed to conduct his planned experiments. Shortly afterward, he published a 1912 paper reporting on these experiments that's considered the birth of Gestalt psychology. Today, Max Wertheimer is recognized as the *German-American psychologist who was the founder of Gestalt psychology*.

Initially a student of law at the University of Prague, Wertheimer turned toward psychology after taking courses with philosopher Christian von Ehrenfels, who argued against the prevailing analytical accounts of perception (Wertheimer, 2014). At the University of Berlin, Wertheimer studied with Carl Stumpf, who was another forefather of Gestalt psychology. He then transferred to Würzburg University, where he completed his Ph.D. with Oswald Külpe (Chapter 3). In 1910, he arrived at Frankfurt, where he conducted the series of experiments that launched the Gestalt movement. There, he also became friends with Wolfgang Köhler and Kurt Koffka, the other two founders of Gestalt psychology.

Wertheimer was interested in the problem of apparent motion (Stock, 2014). When two lights next to each other turn on and off in quick succession, it looks as though a single light moves from the first to the second position. *The apparent motion of stationary but rapidly changing objects is known as the* **phi phenomenon**. You experience the phi phenomenon every time you watch a movie, which is, after all, just a series of still pictures flashing rapidly one after another. Wertheimer chose to work with Schumann in Frankfurt because he had a state-of-the-art **tachistoscope**, which is *an instrument that displays images for precise durations of time* (pronounced *tuh-KISS-tuh-scope*).

Wertheimer's studies of the phi phenomenon led him to a deeper understanding of what it meant for a perceptual configuration to be a Gestalt (Wagemans et al., 2012). Von Ehrenfels had said the whole is greater than the sum of its parts, but this wasn't quite true in the case of the phi phenomenon. The stimulus (that is, the parts) consisted of two blinking lights, but the perception (that is, the whole) consisted of the apparent movement of a single light. Thus, Wertheimer concluded, the whole isn't just more than the sum of its parts. Rather, the whole is *different* from the sum of the parts. Wertheimer's analysis of the phi phenomenon marked the beginning of Gestalt psychology as an experimental science.

After this, Wertheimer accepted a position at the University of Berlin, where he published a series of papers outlining the Gestalt principles of perception (Wagemans et al., 2012). The elements of the visual field are colors, lines, and curves, and yet we perceive Gestalten—objects and events (Figure 6.5). The **principles of perceptual grouping** are *descriptions of how features such as similarity and proximity guide the organization of sensory elements into Gestalten*. We also make *the distinction between foreground and background*, a process known as **figure-ground organization**. These processes can all be subsumed under one general principle of perception, the **law of Prägnanz**. This is *the assertion that perceptual organization will be as good as the prevailing conditions allow*. (*Prägnanz* is German for "conciseness.")

The Gestalt principles of perceptual organization aren't just limited to the laboratory (Wagemans et al., 2012). In fact, they guide perception in the real world as well. Consider the following example. When you're typing and can't find your cursor, what do you do? You jiggle the mouse to make the cursor move. You've just taken advantage of **common fate**, which is *the Gestalt principle that items moving together are perceived as a single object*. When the cursor is stationary, it blends in with the other letters on the page, but when it moves it jumps out visually. Common fate also explains why we perceive schools of fish and flocks of birds as single objects. Once you understand the Gestalt principles, you see them in operation everywhere.

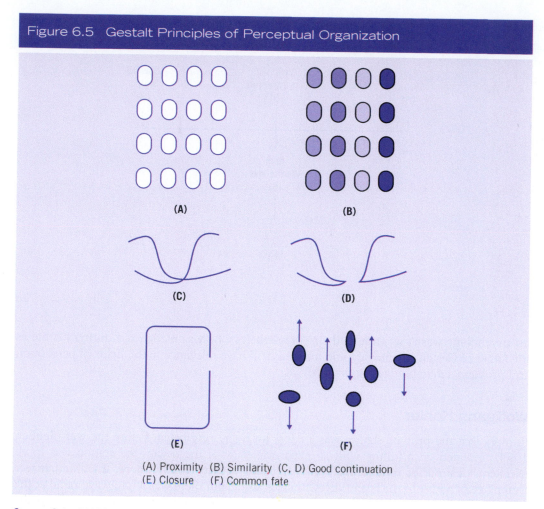

Figure 6.5 Gestalt Principles of Perceptual Organization

(A) Proximity (B) Similarity (C, D) Good continuation
(E) Closure (F) Common fate

Source: Galotti (2018).

In 1929, Wertheimer accepted a professorship at Frankfurt, taking over the position of his former mentor Friedrich Schumann (King, Wertheimer, Keller, & Crochetière, 1994). But he only stayed four years. When Hitler came to power, Wertheimer knew he had no future in Nazi Germany because of his Jewish ancestry, so he accepted an offer from the New School for Social Research in New York City. He and his family immigrated to the United States in 1933, where he remained for the rest of his life.

Wertheimer spent the next decade working on a new project (King et al., 1994). His goal was to apply Gestalt principles to the process of thinking as well. He believed that meaningful comprehension was only achieved when the thinker had grasped the interrelatedness of the details, and he called this process productive thinking. As part of his research on productive thinking, he conducted extensive interviews with his longtime friend Albert Einstein to understand how he'd constructed his theory of relativity. Wertheimer had just finished the manuscript of his book *Productive Thinking* when he died suddenly of a heart attack in 1943. The book was published in 1945, and it had a profound impact on the psychology of thinking and problem solving.

For Wertheimer, as well as for his followers, Gestalt theory was more than just an approach to studying perception and problem solving (Newman, 1944). It was a way of doing science and understanding the world around us. "You need to approach the problem from above, not below," Wertheimer would say. By this, he meant that if we approached it from below, all we would see is the parts. Only if we approached the problem from above would we be able to see how the parts "hang together." Wertheimer never published as much as his colleagues Wolfgang Köhler and Kurt Koffka, so by objective standards his influence

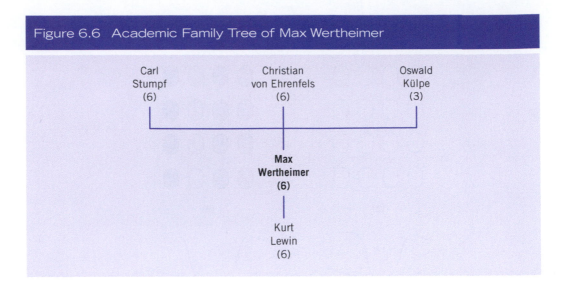

Figure 6.6 Academic Family Tree of Max Wertheimer

Carl Stumpf (6)   Christian von Ehrenfels (6)   Oswald Külpe (3)

Max Wertheimer (6)

Kurt Lewin (6)

on psychology wasn't as great as theirs. Nevertheless, he was recognized during his life as the father of Gestalt psychology, and his ideas still have relevance in the fields of perception and problem solving today (Figure 6.6).

Wolfgang Köhler

Rumors that the primate station was a cover for a spy ring began before the war (Teuber, 1994). Situated on a hilltop with an expansive view of the ocean, the station was in an excellent location for monitoring British shipping activity. Furthermore, the chimpanzees weren't even native to the island. Eyewitnesses also claim there was a longwave radio at the station that the director, **Wolfgang Köhler** (1887–1967), used to communicate with the German mainland (Ley, 1997). Still, the evidence for espionage is only circumstantial, and Köhler certainly hadn't gone to Tenerife with the purpose of spying, even if he'd heeded the call to duty after he arrived. More importantly, during the six years he spent on the island, he conducted groundbreaking research and established his reputation as one of the world's leading psychologists. Today, we remember Wolfgang Köhler as the *German-American Gestalt psychologist who studied intelligence and problem solving in chimpanzees.*

At the University of Berlin, Köhler had studied field physics with physicist Max Planck before he completed his Ph.D. in psychology with Carl Stumpf (Asch, 1968). Throughout his career, he kept one foot in physics and the other in psychology, and his lifelong goal was to reconcile psychological experience with the laws of physics. His first academic position was at Frankfurt, where he befriended Max Wertheimer and Kurt Koffka. In 1913, Köhler published one of the first papers laying out the new Gestalt theory. In this article, he maintained that conscious experience was constructed from innate organizational principles rather than being built up from elements of sensation, as Wundt, Titchener, and others believed. Around this time, Carl Stumpf asked Köhler to direct the primate station on Tenerife, even though he had no experience working with animals.

Tenerife is one of the Canary Islands, a Spanish territory lying off the Atlantic coast of North Africa (Teuber, 1994). Although the Germans had a colony in nearby Cameroon, Tenerife was already a well-developed tourist destination. So the Germans brought chimpanzees from Cameroon, and they hoped scientists from around the world would come to work at the world's first primate research station. In fact, Robert Yerkes (Chapter 4) had already planned to spend a sabbatical year at the station in 1915, but then war broke out and he had to cancel the trip.

Köhler arrived with his family in December 1913 (Teuber, 1994). He quickly set to work because he was only planning to stay for a year. When World War I began in July 1914, he wanted to return to Germany to do his military duty. But no ship would carry

German passengers through waters controlled by the British fleet, so he was forced to wait out the war on the island. Still, he was very productive during his six years on the island, and the research he conducted there established his career.

Köhler was especially interested in studying how primates solve problems (Neisser, 2002). He placed some food in sight of the animal but just out of reach. He also provided sticks, ropes, and boxes that could be used to retrieve the food. His reports show the chimpanzees used insight to solve these problems. That is, they seemed to first visualize how the pieces of the problem fit together, and then they acted. In other words, the problem-solving behaviors that Köhler observed were fundamentally different from the trial-and-error learning that Edward Thorndike (Chapter 4) had observed in cats escaping from puzzle boxes. If there was any trial and error going on, it was within the minds of the apes. They may not have been able to reach a solution right away, but once they'd gained insight into the structure of the problem, they quickly acted to accomplish their goal.

Problem solving by insight challenged a basic tenet of behaviorism (Teuber, 1994). Behaviorists viewed thinking as nothing more than subvocalized speech—that is to say, quietly talking to yourself. And since nonhuman animals don't have language, they shouldn't be able to think. However, Köhler's experiments clearly showed that thought processes were taking place in animals even without language. In other words, thinking didn't depend on language, as the behaviorists had asserted.

Some of Köhler's chimps were better problem solvers than others (Teuber, 1994). Among the seven apes in the colony, the young male Sultan was the brightest, solving problems that stumped the others. But even Sultan didn't always find the best solution. In one experiment, Köhler hung a basket of fruit from a rope that ran through a pulley with its end tied to a tree branch. The best solution was to untie the rope and let the basket fall, but instead Sultan shook the rope violently until the fruit dropped out of the basket.

On other occasions, the chimps showed creative solutions to problems (Sharps & Wertheimer, 2000). For example, they'd learned to stack boxes and climb on them to reach hanging fruit. One time, however, the fruit was already in place, but no boxes had yet been brought into the enclosure. Sultan was getting impatient, so he led Köhler by the hand until he was standing under the hanging basket, and then he climbed onto his shoulders to reach the fruit. Behaviors like these convinced Köhler that his animals were learning the structure of problems and not just superficial solutions. Although he was accustomed to climbing on boxes to get the fruit, Sultan understood that other objects—including a human being—could be climbed on as well.

Köhler's 1917 book *The Mentality of Apes*, in which he described these studies, established his reputation as a Gestalt psychologist, but it wasn't his only project while on Tenerife (Neisser, 2002). He also wrote a book demonstrating that Gestalt structures aren't limited to psychological experience but occur in the physical world as well. This was an important point to make, because Köhler and other Gestalt psychologists took a strong monist stance toward the mind-body problem. It was the brain that produced conscious experience, and if mental activity was organized in Gestalten, then the underlying brain processes must be as well. Because the book relies heavily on complex mathematics and concepts from physics, it's rarely read by psychologists. Nevertheless, writing the book helped Köhler think out the research program that would occupy him for the rest of his career.

World War I ended as a disaster for Germany, leaving the country in political and economic disarray (Kressley-Mba, 2006). With no funds available to maintain the primate station, Köhler shipped his family and the chimpanzees back to Germany. The chimps went to the Berlin zoo, and Köhler accepted a professorship at the University of Berlin.

Carl Stumpf was ready to retire, and Köhler replaced him as the director of the university's Psychological Institute (Henle, 1978). For more than a decade, he and his students published research on learning, memory, and problem solving as well as perception. His reputation continued to grow, and he was frequently sought out as a guest speaker, both in Germany and abroad. He also published the book *Gestalt Psychology* in 1929, thus establishing himself as the leader of the Gestalt movement.

Photo 6.5
Testing chimpanzee intelligence at the Tenerife Primate Lab

In January 1933, the Nazis came to power in Germany, and one of their first acts was to remove all Jewish professors and students from the universities (Henle, 1978). Few of his colleagues protested, but Köhler did. Because his ancestry was purely German, he could have cooperated with the Nazis, but instead he used his position to help victims of Nazi oppression. He tried in vain to get Jewish colleagues reinstated, and he challenged the random raids of his classes in search of students who'd been labeled as Jews, Communists, or other undesirables.

When the government ordered all professors to begin their lectures with the Nazi salute, Köhler complied in a mocking fashion that clearly signaled where his sympathies lay (Henle, 1978). But as the Nazis consolidated their grip on political and academic life, it became clear things wouldn't go well if he remained in Germany. In 1935, he accepted a professorship at Swarthmore College near Philadelphia, and he remained there for the rest of his career. Köhler was able to bring some, but not all, of his research assistants with him. Many of those who stayed behind suffered dire fates at the hands of the Nazis. Thus the golden age of Gestalt psychology came to an end in Germany, although it experienced a rebirth when it was transplanted in the United States.

At Swarthmore, Köhler continued to do research with his students, and his scholarly interests can be roughly grouped into two categories (Asch, 1968). One academic endeavor was his strident criticism of behaviorism. While conceding that behaviorism had added rigor to experimental psychology, he also believed it was too confining. By defining psychology as the study of behavior, it banished too much of what was interesting in the field, namely the mental life of humans and other animals. He also maintained that science shouldn't be defined by its methods. Rather, a wide variety of methods should be employed so as to survey the field in its entirety.

A second academic endeavor involved the concept of **isomorphism** (Neisser, 2002). This is the *idea that the structure of conscious experience is mirrored by similarly structured physical events in the brain.* Köhler had already been thinking along these lines while working with Wertheimer in Frankfurt, but by the 1940s new technologies enabled him to develop tests of this theory. Using electroencephalography (EEG) to measure electrical activity in the brain, Köhler believed he'd found support for his isomorphism hypothesis, but neuroscientists today think there are better explanations for his findings.

Köhler remained at Swarthmore until his retirement in 1958, when he moved to New Hampshire near Dartmouth College, which provided him with research facilities (Neisser, 2002). In 1959, he was elected president of the American Psychological Association, indicating the high degree of respect he'd garnered from his American colleagues. Even though his theory of isomorphism didn't pan out, his contributions over a span of six decades are nevertheless considered invaluable to the development of psychology. Köhler's ideas still pervade the fields of visual perception and attention as well as comparative research (Figure 6.7).

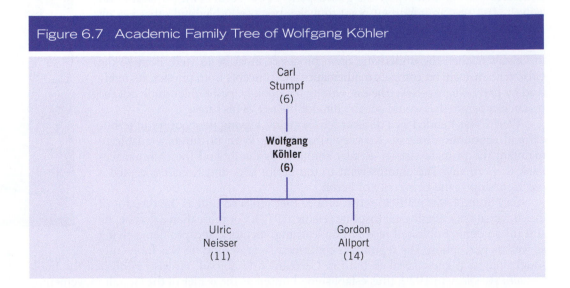

Figure 6.7   Academic Family Tree of Wolfgang Köhler

Kurt Koffka

Kurt Koffka (1886–1941) grew up with a British nanny, so unlike his Berlin colleagues Wertheimer and Köhler, he could communicate his ideas directly in English (Harrower-Erickson, 1942). As a result, Koffka became the face of Gestalt psychology for American and British psychologists in its early years. Having earned his Ph.D. in 1908 with Carl Stumpf, Koffka quickly absorbed Wertheimer's ideas when he worked with him in Frankfurt. Although his contributions ranged widely, today he's known as the *German-American psychologist who introduced Gestalt theory to English-speaking psychologists.*

The following year, Koffka received an appointment from the University of Giessen (Köhler, 1942). The pay was low with no prospect of tenure, but it gave him the opportunity to work with graduate students and do research. In 1922, Koffka published "An Introduction to Gestalt Theory" in English. This article was the first exposure many American psychologists had to this new movement in psychology coming out of Germany. Because the Gestalt principles are easiest to explain as they apply to perception, this is what the article focused on. As a result, many American psychologists were led to the false belief that Gestalt psychology was limited to the study of perception, a misconception still held today.

Two years later, Koffka published *The Growth of the Mind*, in which he applied Gestalt principles to developmental psychology (Köhler, 1942). It also presented one of the most thorough overviews of the research that had been conducted so far within the Gestalt framework. The book challenged the behaviorist view of the child born as a blank slate. Instead of learning to respond to stimuli in a piecemeal fashion, Koffka argued, the child is born with Gestalt principles already in place to guide it through its interactions with the world. This was one of the first clear articulations of the position that Gestalt principles are innate processes and not acquired through early childhood experiences.

Having become the face of Gestalt psychology in the English-speaking world, Koffka was invited to a series of visiting professorships (Harrower-Erickson, 1942). The last of these was an invitation from Clark Hull (Chapter 5) to spend a year at Wisconsin. As Hull (1952) explains in his autobiography, he was initially attracted to Gestalt theory and wanted to learn more about it from the master. The relationship between Hull and Koffka started off pleasant but quickly soured, as Hull rejected Gestalt theory for neo-behaviorism.

In 1927, Koffka accepted an offer from Smith College in Northampton, Massachusetts, and there he stayed for the rest of his life (Sokal, 1984). An undergraduate women's college may seem an unlikely place for a major researcher like Koffka, but in many respects Smith had made him an offer he couldn't refuse. His teaching load was light, he was given ample funds for research, he could invite some of his assistants from Europe, and his salary was quite generous. At Smith, Koffka organized a master's program in which he nurtured the careers of a number of women psychologists, among them Molly Harrower and Tamara Dembo, whom we'll meet in this chapter, as well as Eleanor Gibson, whom we'll meet in Chapter 13. Ironically, after completing a master's degree with Koffka, Eleanor Gibson then went to Yale to do her Ph.D. with Hull.

The position at Smith also provided Koffka with access to the east coast cities, where he was frequently invited to speak (Köhler, 1942). He also made two extensive trips abroad during this time. In 1932, he traveled to Russia to conduct research with Alexander Luria (Chapter 9). And in 1939, he spent a sabbatical year as visiting professor at Oxford University in England.

The Russian expedition involved an extended visit to rural Uzbekistan in Central Asia (Harrower, 1978). The Soviet government had funded this project because it intended to establish schools in the area, and it wanted an assessment of general intellectual abilities of the native population for planning purposes. However, shortly after his arrival, Koffka contracted a fever that required his evacuation. Although he couldn't contribute to the project, he began writing the first draft of a general textbook on Gestalt psychology during his long recovery.

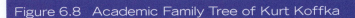

Figure 6.8 Academic Family Tree of Kurt Koffka

Carl
Stumpf
(6)

**Kurt
Koffka
(6)**

Molly
Harrower
(6)

When Koffka returned, he completed *The Principles of Gestalt Psychology* (Harrower-Erickson, 1942). This book, published in 1935, constituted the most systematic presentation of Gestalt theory to date, and it argued convincingly that Gestalt principles applied not only to perception but also to the entire extent of psychology. He hoped that a full exposition of Gestalt theory would clarify misunderstandings and leave his new compatriots with a more positive attitude toward the approach.

Koffka spent the 1939–1940 academic year at Oxford (Harrower-Erickson, 1942). In general, his ideas were much better received in England than they were in America. The Gestalt insistence on keeping the mind as the focus of psychology was much more to the liking of his British colleagues than was the "mindless" psychology of Watson. At Oxford, Koffka renewed an old interest in the cognitive deficits of patients with brain injuries. He planned to present the data from these studies in a book, but shortly after his return to Smith he suffered a heart attack and died, so the book was never completed.

Although Koffka's life was short, he played an important role in introducing Gestalt theory to English-speaking psychologists. Through his interactions with his American colleagues, he helped spread acceptance of Gestalt principles in this country. His influence on Hull was subtle, moving him toward a neo-behaviorist stance. But his effect on the neo-behaviorist Edward Tolman (Chapter 5) was more profound. Tolman had spent time with Koffka in Germany, and he made ample use of Gestalt ideas in his own theories of learning. In the end, we see that Koffka's ideas have achieved a sort of immortality, in that they lived on in the work of the next generation of psychologists (Figure 6.8).

Molly Harrower

While studying psychology at the University of London, **Molly Harrower** (1906–1999) longed to experience life in the United States, and she accepted a position as research assistant for Kurt Koffka at Smith College in 1928 (Dewsbury, 1999). Even though Smith had no doctoral program, it awarded her a Ph.D. in 1934 for her work with Koffka, and her dissertation committee included such notables as Edwin Boring (Chapter 3) and Arnold Gesell (Chapter 4). Today, Molly Harrower is remembered as a *British-American clinical psychologist best known for her study of Nazi personality.*

When a friend experienced a radically altered personality after surgery, Harrower's interests turned to clinical psychology (Dewsbury, 2000). She did a postdoctoral fellowship with noted neurologist Wilder Penfield (Chapter 10) in Montreal, and after World War II she moved to New York, where she opened a private practice. She became especially interested in the Rorschach inkblot test as a diagnostic for psychological disorders, and she developed a form of the test that could be administered to groups.

After World War II, psychologists had administered Rorschach tests to Nazi leaders as they awaited trial in Nuremburg (Joyce, 2009). At the time, it was believed these Nazis must have had pathological personalities. But Harrower suspected situational factors played a role, so she compared the Nazi Rorschach data with results from groups of clergymen and mental patients. She found no evidence for a consistent Nazi personality type. Rather, the Nazis exhibited the same range of personality traits as the general American population, providing support for her situational hypothesis.

Harrower spent her last decades on the faculty of the University of Florida, where she devoted herself to writing. In 1983, she published a biography of her mentor Kurt Koffka based on the more than 2,000 letters she exchanged with him during his lifetime. Thus, Harrower became a major source of information about the life of Koffka.

Kurt Lewin and His Students

If you were looking for Professor **Kurt Lewin** (1890–1947; pronounced *luh-VEEN*), you'd likely find him in the Schwedensche Café chatting with his students (Ash, 1992). Lewin was different from other professors, who kept interactions with students distant and formal. Nor did he demand loyalty to his particular point of view. During these informal discussions, he encouraged his students to offer any idea that came to mind, and as a group they worked out its merits. Although he and his students worked on a wide range of topics, today Kurt Lewin is recognized as the *German-American Gestalt psychologist who was one of the founders of experimental social psychology*.

Field Theory

Kurt Lewin completed his doctoral degree in 1916 with Carl Stumpf at the University of Berlin (Berscheid, 2003). He then remained as an instructor, and during this time he was influenced by Wertheimer and Köhler. But whereas his Gestalt colleagues focused on cognitive processes studied in the laboratory, Lewin wanted to explore them in real-life social settings. For example, when his student Bluma Zeigarnik, whom we'll meet shortly, noticed the waiter at the café could remember what everyone in her group ordered without writing it down, Lewin encouraged her to investigate further. She found the waiter remembered his customers' orders until they paid their bill, after which he promptly forgot. Reproducing this scenario in the laboratory, she discovered what's now called the **Zeigarnik effect**, which is *the observation that the details of uncompleted tasks are better remembered than are those of completed tasks.* You experience the Zeigarnik effect each time you cram for a test—the answers are fresh in your mind during the exam, but you forget them soon afterward. This study was typical of the kind of research on ordinary life situations conducted by Lewin's group during the Berlin years.

Lewin was intrigued by Köhler's proposal that brain activity involved electromagnetic fields, and he applied the concept of field metaphorically to what he called the **life space** of the individual (Van Elteren, 1992). This was *Lewin's term referring to the totality of forces acting on an individual, including personality and motivation as well as social and environmental influences.* In physics, a field is a region of space and time through which a force extends, and the behavior of a particle within this field is influenced by this force. In the classic example, iron filings on a sheet of paper self-organize into contour lines when a magnet is brought below. Thus, Lewin saw the life space as a force field, and *Lewin's idea that an individual's behavior is determined by personal and situational forces* is known as **field theory**.

Lewin's important insight was that behavior is driven by the interaction of multiple factors, some arising from within the person and others arising from the situation (Dunn, 2011). Personality psychologists focused on the role of individual differences in determining behavior, whereas behaviorists emphasized the

Photo 6.6
Kurt Lewin

influences of the environment. However, Lewin insisted that both personality and situation are important. As a useful mnemonic, he created what's known as **Lewin's equation**, written as $B = f(p,E)$, meaning that behavior (B) is a function (f) of both personal (P) and environmental (E) variables. The purpose of Lewin's equation is not to explain behavior but rather to remind psychologists to include both sets of variables in their research. Furthermore, Lewin wasn't insisting that both are equally important in all cases. Instead, the conditions of a person's life space at a given moment determine whether personal or environmental factors will dominate.

Lewin's research designs challenged the limits of what was considered possible in experimental psychology, and he made use of the latest technology (Van Elteren, 1992). In his developmental studies, for example, he used hidden cameras to capture in real time the evolving behavior of children as they struggled to accomplish tasks or overcome difficulties. At the Ninth International Congress of Psychology at Yale University in 1929, he showed a short film of children solving problems. This movie challenged behaviorist learning theory and made a great impression on the audience. After that, Lewin received invitations to visit the United States and even Japan.

Lewin was lecturing at Stanford when Hitler came to power, and he quickly understood he had no future in Germany as a Jew (Bargal, 1998). Cornell University was able to offer him a two-year contract. After that he accepted a professorship from the University of Iowa, where he stayed for the next decade.

Action Research

Iowa was a bastion of behaviorism, and Lewin incurred considerable criticism from his fellow psychologists (Ash, 1992). But he deftly handled the conflict with his personal charm and characteristic friendliness. His group was treated as an independent unit, so he had freedom to pursue research topics of his own choosing. During his decade at Iowa, he attracted capable graduate students with whom he conducted groundbreaking research, and many of these went on to illustrious careers in psychology.

One such student was Tamara Dembo, who'd previously worked with him in Berlin and with Koffka at Smith (Ash, 1992). Together, they conducted a series of studies on how children deal with frustration. One important finding from this research was the discovery that ultimate success on a difficult task depends less on ability than level of aspiration, that is, by how much the person wants to complete the task. They also observed how children respond to hopeless conflict, such as by rolling into the fetal position to make themselves smaller or by engaging in flights of fantasy. Seeing a connection between their findings and the concept of regression as developed by Sigmund Freud and Alfred Adler (Chapter 7), they remarked on the general tendency of both children and adults to revert to a more immature state when overwhelmingly frustrated. We'll learn more about Dembo shortly.

Working with his graduate student Ronald Lippitt, Lewin conducted one of his most frequently cited pieces of research, a study on the effects of leadership style (Billig, 2015). Two groups of children in an after-school program were engaged in a project lasting several weeks in which they constructed theatrical masks. With one group, Lippitt acted as a "democratic" leader, providing instructions in the form of alternatives that the group could choose from and providing technical advice only when asked. In the other group, he acted as an "authoritarian" leader, giving specific instructions on how to proceed and negative feedback when mistakes were made. Using hidden cameras and trained observers, they found much higher levels of aggression and scapegoating in the authoritarian group and higher levels of cooperation in the democratic group. This project demonstrated the feasibility of studying large groups, and it's now considered a benchmark study in leadership research. It also marked a shift in Lewin's research interests from childhood development to applied social research.

During World War II, the United States experienced a meat shortage, and the government asked Lewin to find ways to encourage Americans to consume less meat (Coghlan & Brannick, 2003). Lewin began by asking why people eat what they eat, and he came to the conclusion that people generally ate whatever was served at the family dinner table. Thus, it was mainly housewives who made food decisions for the rest of the family. He called these women "gatekeepers" in the food-decision process, and so they were the ones who had to be targeted if eating habits were to be changed. He also found that people's habits tend to be stable, but they can be changed if people perceive a real need to do so. By providing housewives with information about the need to conserve meat for the war effort as well as giving them ideas for meals that used less meat, Lewin and his team were able to change eating habits.

This research led to the **three-step model of change**, which was *Lewin's process for reshaping the culture of a group by changing the attitudes and behaviors of its members* (Coghlan & Brannick, 2003). The first step was to *unfreeze* the culture by making the need for change apparent to members of the group, especially the gatekeepers. He also found that it was more effective to ease the forces resisting change than it was to encourage the forces pushing for change. This could be done by decreasing the sense of threat and increasing the feeling of safety among group members. The second step was to *move* the culture by introducing the desired changes. However, Lewin understood that changes in habit are generally temporary, with a tendency to revert to old ways. Thus, the third step was to *refreeze* the culture by reinforcing the new habits until they become the established norm for the group.

This three-step model of change was integrated into what Lewin called **action research** (Coghlan & Brannick, 2003). This involves *experimental investigations aimed at finding effective methods for social change*. Action research focuses on real problems in social systems in order to improve the quality of life for the members of the group. To effect social change, it's necessary to go through repeated cycles of problem identification, planning, action, and evaluation. Furthermore, social change cannot solely be implemented from above. Rather, all members of the group need to get involved, and this generally involves a process of *re-education* so that the group members understand the need for change and what has to be done to solve the problems they face. For re-education to be effective, the members of the group need to be involved in the problem identification and planning process so that they can understand the need for change and have the willingness to follow through with planned changes.

Group Dynamics

The primary goal of action research is to find practical solutions to pressing social issues, but at the same time it contributes to our understanding of **group dynamics** (Burnes, 2004). Lewin coined this term to refer to *the ways in which social organizations respond to changing circumstances*. In his view, groups are constantly in a state of flux, but like the flow of a river, sometimes that change is slow and sometimes rapid. Thus, the way to understand the dynamics of a particular group is to introduce a change and then observe how the group reacts. During his Iowa years, Lewin used action research to find solutions a number of practical problems, such as resolving a labor dispute at a rural Virginia factory and helping to integrate Black and White staff at a New York department store. These and other projects solidified Lewin's reputation as a social psychologist.

In 1945, the Massachusetts Institute of Technology (MIT) invited Lewin to establish the Center for Group Dynamics (Berscheid, 2003). By the end of World War II, it had become clear that there was a need for a greater understanding of the psychological processes underlying social phenomena as well as effective tools to implement positive social change. The rise of fascism in Europe had led to the deadliest war in history, and the world was under the threat of nuclear annihilation in its wake. Meanwhile, racial tensions in the United States were rising, and effective methods of dealing with prejudice and discrimination had to be found. These were all urgent issues that had to be dealt with.

The establishment of the center gave credence to the idea that group dynamics was a legitimate area of research (Berscheid, 2003). Until that time, the received wisdom was that groups were nothing more than convenient fictions, especially among behaviorists. Rather, all that existed were the individual group members who held attitudes and engaged in behaviors toward other group members. The Gestalt notion of a group as a whole that could have properties different from those of the individual members was rejected by most American psychologists. This attitude began to change after one of the nation's most prestigious universities opened a center specifically for the purpose of studying group dynamics.

One of the tasks of the Center for Group Dynamics was to develop a Ph.D. program in social psychology (Coghlan & Brannick, 2003). This was the first of its kind in the nation,

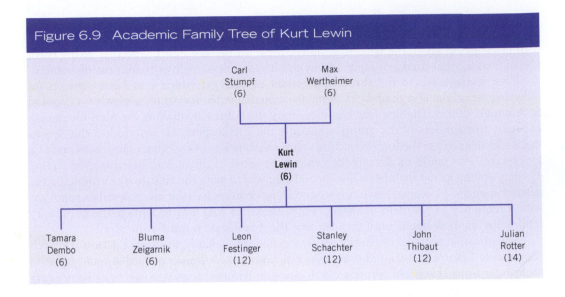

Figure 6.9 Academic Family Tree of Kurt Lewin

and it attracted a number of gifted students who went on to become the leaders in social psychology. Among those who studied with Lewin were Leon Festinger, Stanley Schachter, and Harold Kelley, all of whom we'll meet in Chapter 12. The center showed great promise for developing a body of scientific knowledge that would aid in the solution of real-world problems. But just two years after his arrival at MIT, Lewin died of a heart attack at the age of 57. MIT quickly lost interest in supporting the Center for Group Dynamics, and the University of Michigan took over the enterprise. As a result, Michigan became a major site for research in social psychology.

Kurt Lewin's contribution to psychology is enormous. He demonstrated that rigorous experimental research could be conducted on large-scale groups. Furthermore, he showed that the results of these studies had practical applications. Thus, he's rightly called the founder of experimental social psychology. Furthermore, by mentoring dozens of graduate students over the years, he nurtured the next generation of leading social psychologists, who then groomed the following generation, and today many social psychologists can trace their academic ancestry back to Lewin (Figure 6.9). With his endearing personality, genuine warmth, and unflagging energy, Kurt Lewin demonstrated in his own career how social activism can have a profound positive influence on the lives of so many others.

Tamara Dembo

Two circumstances in the childhood of **Tamara Dembo** (1902–1993) foreshadowed her future research interests. She grew up in a Jewish family in Russia and experienced discrimination from an early age (Cherry, Unger, & Winston, 2010). She also suffered from a childhood illness that restricted her mobility for years, so she understood firsthand the experience of disability (Hodgson, 2004). In her career, she developed a reputation as a *Russian-American psychologist who was a pioneer in the field of rehabilitation psychology*.

When she was nineteen, Dembo traveled to Germany to enroll at the University of Berlin. She wanted to study engineering, but she wasn't allowed to because she was a woman (Wright, 1993). So she joined Kurt Lewin's research group, completing a dissertation that she later published as *The Dynamics of Anger* in German in 1931. She then accepted a research position with Kurt Koffka at Smith College. As the political situation in Europe deteriorated during the 1930s, she decided to build her career in the United States rather than return home.

Dembo rejoined Lewin in Iowa, where she worked with him on a study looking at the relationship between frustration and regression in children (Van der Veer, 2000). Later, Dembo held a series of temporary positions before landing a tenured professorship at Clark University.

During those years, she conducted a long-term study of war veterans who'd lost limbs or suffered other disfigurements, which she published as *Adjustment to Misfortune* in 1956.

At Clark, Dembo continued her research in rehabilitation psychology, maintaining that it wasn't the physical disability itself that handicapped the individual but rather it was the environment that hampered mobility (De Rivera, 1995). She conducted studies of children with cerebral palsy and other cognitive disabilities, demonstrating that when social attitudes and the physical environment are altered, "handicapped" persons can become self-sufficient. Thanks to the work of Dembo and her colleagues, many people with disabilities can now lead productive lives.

Bluma Zeigarnik

When she was just 19, **Bluma Zeigarnik** (1901–1988) traveled to Germany to enroll in the University of Berlin (Kostyanaya, 2014). She joined Kurt Lewin's group around the same time as Tamara Dembo. After noticing the remarkable memory abilities of the waiter at the café where Lewin's group met, she completed a dissertation on what is now called the Zeigarnik effect. Today, she's mainly known as a *Russian psychologist who studied memory for completed and uncompleted tasks,* but she had a long and often turbulent career after her return to Russia.

Zeigarnik and her husband were sympathetic to the Communist cause, and they moved to Moscow in 1931 (Kostyanaya, 2014). There, she worked with Lev Vygotsky and Alexander Luria (Chapter 9). Her interests had already shifted toward clinical psychology during her time in Berlin, and during World War II she investigated techniques for rehabilitating soldiers with brain injuries. The 1940s and 1950s were a turbulent time for Zeigarnik. When her husband was arrested on charges of espionage, she was left alone to care for their two children. Later, she lost her job during an anti-Semitic campaign. Luria and other psychologists provided her with financial assistance from their own pockets.

By the 1960s, relative political stability had returned to the Soviet Union, and Zeigarnik's career flourished once more (Zeigarnik, 2007). Because her German Ph.D. wasn't recognized in the Soviet Union, she earned a second Ph.D. and was appointed professor of psychology at Moscow State University. There, she continued her research on the rehabilitation of patients with brain damage. Although she traveled to several international conferences after this, she was unable to accept an award for lifelong accomplishments because of political tensions between the United States and the Soviet Union. Nevertheless, Bluma Zeigarnik showed what a dedicated researcher can accomplish in spite of discrimination and political oppression.

Photo 6.7
Bluma Zeigarnik

Via Wikimedia Commons

Fritz Heider

Fritz Heider was a late bloomer. Although he earned his Ph.D. in his early twenties, he continued taking classes as a student for years afterward, only accepting a faculty position at the age of 30 (Heider, 1989). Relatively unknown for most of his career, he published a book in his early sixties that revolutionized social psychology. Today, **Fritz Heider** (1896–1988) is known as the *German-American Gestalt psychologist who pioneered the field of social cognition with his attribution theory and balance theory.*

Object Perception

Heider did his doctorate with philosopher **Alexius Meinong** (1853–1920) at the University of Graz (Heider, 1989). Meinong had been a student of Franz Brentano, and he gained a reputation as the *Austrian philosopher who founded the Graz school of Gestalt psychology.* For a number of years, Meinong and his students were seen as rivals to the Berlin school, but eventually there was a merging of the two early approaches to studying Gestalt phenomena.

Fritz
Heider

Photo 6.8
Fritz Heider

One of Meinong's early students had been Christian von Ehrenfels, who then had an important influence on Max Wertheimer.

For his dissertation, Heider tackled a problem that Meinong had proposed (Heider, 1989). Imagine you're looking at a house. The only reason you can see the house is because sunlight bounces off it and into your eyes. In other words, you don't have direct contact with the house but only with the sunlight. Yet you say "I see the house" and not "I see the sun." Meinong asks: Why is the house the focus of our attention and not the sunlight?

To answer Meinong's question, Heider said that we need to distinguish between *thing* and *medium* (Wieser, 2014). In this view, a thing is any object or event in the real world that we perceive. However, we only know about things because some medium transmits information about them to our sense organs. We then use this information to make inferences about the identities and natures of those things. Here, Heider was relying on Helmholtz's theory of perception as unconscious inference. But whereas Helmholtz (Chapter 2) believed that we learned to perceive through experience, Heider argued that innate Gestalt principles guided the inferences we make.

Heider's next step was to consider the qualities of things and media (Reisenzein & Rudolf, 2008). A thing is a relatively stable entity that influences other entities in its vicinity, but a medium is transitory and ever-changing. In other words, we focus on the thing because it has an impact on our lives, whereas the medium is nothing more than a channel of information about the thing.

After Heider completed his doctorate, he wandered around Europe for several years (Heider, 1989). Eventually he arrived at the University of Berlin, where he attended lectures by Wertheimer and Köhler and seminars by Lewin. Of the three, Lewin was particularly influential on Heider's thinking, and the two developed a close friendship that continued even after both had immigrated to the United States.

In 1927, **William Stern** (1871–1938) offered him an assistant professorship at the University of Hamburg (Lamiell, 2000). A student of Hermann Ebbinghaus (Chapter 2), Stern was the *German psychologist who developed the concept of intelligence quotient, or IQ*. Shortly thereafter, Lewis Terman (Chapter 4) incorporated the IQ into his Stanford-Binet, and it's become the standard measure of general intelligence ever since. Stern and his wife Clara conducted extensive diary studies of their three children, which they published in a series of influential books. As a result, he became one of the most influential developmental psychologists of the early twentieth century. Stern also disagreed with many of the positions of the Gestalt psychologists, but Heider profited from exposure to a different point of view (Figure 6.10).

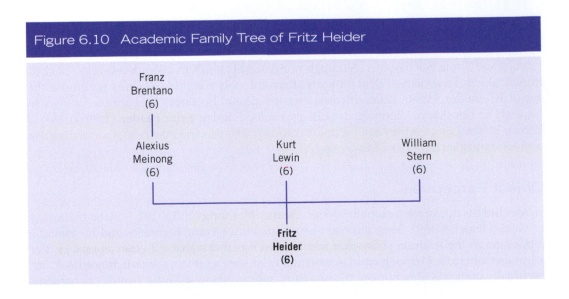

Figure 6.10 Academic Family Tree of Fritz Heider

Franz
Brentano
(6)

Alexius
Meinong
(6)

Kurt
Lewin
(6)

William
Stern
(6)

Fritz
Heider
(6)

When Koffka told Stern he was looking for an assistant, he recommended Heider, who gladly accepted the position. He'd long wanted to immigrate to America, and in the summer of 1930, he realized that dream.

Social Cognition

When Heider arrived in Northampton, Massachusetts, one of the first persons he met was Grace Moore (Heider, 1989). Grace was working on her master's degree with Koffka, and he asked her to help the new arrival get settled. To everyone's surprise, Fritz and Grace fell in love and were married by the end of the year. Theirs was a very special marriage, lasting more than fifty years. They often collaborated on research, and they supported each other in their endeavors.

Heider's duty was to conduct research at the Clarke School for the Deaf, which was affiliated with Smith College (Schmidt, 2017). Grace Moore Heider was also involved in this project. Her mother was a noted educator of the deaf, and her sister had been a student at Clarke. Over the next few years, the two Heiders collaborated on a series of groundbreaking studies in the psychology of deafness. However, their conclusions were very much at odds with the attitudes of the school's administrators and teachers.

In their observations of deaf children in their day-to-day interactions, the Heiders found they were just as sociable as hearing children (Schmidt, 2017). Furthermore, they recognized that the sign languages of the deaf were well developed communication systems. At the Clarke School, the children were forbidden to use sign language, but they did so anyway among themselves, and they much preferred signing to speaking and lip-reading. In the end, the Heiders concluded that deafness was a social rather than physical handicap. That is, while deafness isolated these children from interactions with the mainstream hearing society, they nevertheless formed engaging social relationships and vibrant sign-language communities. While the Heiders' conclusions were unacceptable to those who ran the Clarke School, it did lay the groundwork for psychosocial studies of the deaf over the next few decades.

This emphasis on the social aspects of deafness led Heider to think more about social interactions in general (Heider, 1967). In the 1940s, he published a series of papers exploring the idea of **social cognition**, that is, *the typical thought patterns that people engage in as they interact with others*. In our interactions with others, we're constantly making inferences about the contents of their minds, and without this ability, we'd be unable to coordinate our behaviors. In 1944, Heider and his student Marianne Simmel (1923–2010) created a short stop-motion animation in which three simple geometric shapes seem to take on personality characteristics and engage in intentional behavior.

At Smith College, Heider had a heavy teaching load and only a few graduate students to work with him (Rudolph & Reisenzein, 2008). Thus, he was left with little time to develop his theory of social cognition. But then in 1947 he got an offer from the University of Kansas, which he gladly accepted. There, his teaching load was light, and he had graduate students to run the experiments needed to develop his theory. Still, it took another decade for his ideas to become fully formed. But when he finally published *The Psychology of Interpersonal Relations* in 1958, he revolutionized the field of social psychology.

Psychology of Interpersonal Relationships

When Heider first started thinking about the psychology of interpersonal relationships, he tried to use Lewin's field theory but found it inadequate (Heider, 1989). Lewin had focused on how the social environment affects the individual, but Heider was interested in social situations where each person in the group influenced the others. He needed to come up with a formalism to capture interpersonal relationships.

Heider began by looking at how people think about human behavior and motivations (Malle, 2008). By analyzing plays and stories as well as making casual observations, Heider worked out *the set of beliefs about human behavior that people use to guide their interactions with others*, which he called **commonsense psychology**. The point wasn't to catalog all possible social cognitions, but rather to gather a collection of examples from which he could extract a small set of underlying patterns or laws. It was this analysis, conducted over a number of years, which led to the core concepts in *The Psychology of Interpersonal Relations*. This book presented two ideas that became hot topics in social psychology in the following decades, namely attribution theory and balance theory. Although social psychologists have treated these as two separate theories, Heider viewed them as interdependent.

Attribution theory is *a framework for explaining the types of inferences people make about the causes of behavior* (Malle, 2008). Heider contended that humans want to know why things happen, both in the physical world of objects and in the social world of people. For each event we observe, we automatically generate an **attribution**, which is *an inference about the cause of a behavior*. Heider divided attributions into two types, impersonal and personal. We make attributions of impersonal causality for naturally occurring events, such as leaves falling or the wind blowing. In such cases, we attribute the event to the workings of nature. But when we observe human behavior, attribution becomes more complex. This is because we think of persons as intentional agents. If we see a person call a friend or leave the room, we assume these acts were done on purpose. In such cases, we make attributions of personal causality, inferring that the person meant to perform the action. But we don't always make personal attributions of people's behavior. For instance, when people sneeze or slip on a wet floor, we assume it was unintentional and make an impersonal attribution instead. Attribution theory tries to tease out the conditions under which we make personal or impersonal attributions about others' behaviors. Later theorists modified Heider's personal-impersonal distinction into one between dispositional and situational factors.

Heider believed social perception operated according to the same Gestalt principles as object perception (Crandall, Silvia, N'Gbala, Tsang, & Dawson, 2007). In particular, he saw the principle of Prägnanz as an organizing principle in our cognitions about our relationships with other people. Thus, the ways we think about those we interact with tend to be as simple and stable as possible. This is especially true in terms of our sentiments about other people. **Balance theory** then is *a description of how people adjust their sentiments toward others to achieve a stable cognitive state*.

Balance theory is often illustrated in terms of a POX model, a formalism that Heider invented to represent the forces that lead to balance in interpersonal relationships (Wright, 1989). In this model, P stands for the focal person, O stands for the other person that P has a relationship with, and X stands for some object, event, or even another person that both P and O have a sentiment about (Figure 6.11). These entities are connected by three sentiment relationships, namely P→O, P→X, and O→X, each of which is either positive ("like") or negative ("dislike"). To determine whether the sentiment relations are balanced, you multiply the three signs together. If the product is positive (either three pluses or two minuses and a plus), then they're balanced, otherwise they're not.

When the sentiment relations aren't balanced, P experiences an uncomfortable cognitive state. Consider the situation in which Paul likes Olivia, and Olivia likes Xavier, but

Figure 6.11   POX Model

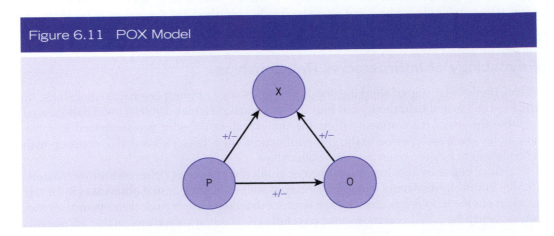

Paul dislikes Xavier. According to balance theory, the sentiment relations aren't balanced, so Paul must feel uncomfortable. To ease the tension, Paul has to change either his feelings about Olivia ("She can't be a nice person if she's friends with Xavier") or his feelings about Xavier ("If Olivia likes him, he must not be so bad after all"). In sum, people strive for cognitive consistency, because maintaining inconsistent social cognitions requires effort.

Fritz Heider's contribution to social cognition stands as his greatest achievement. The idea that people act as naïve psychologists in their interactions with others was a novel concept at the time, and it challenged accepted approaches to social psychology. Yet today the field takes commonsense psychology as a given. Heider's influence is all the more remarkable in that it rests mainly on a single theoretical book published late in his career. Nevertheless, that book provided a wealth of ideas that inspired social psychologists for the next half century.

Looking Ahead

Gestalt psychology has had a significant impact on modern psychology. Wertheimer's principles of perceptual organization are still a mainstay of cognitive psychology. Köhler's work on problem solving in apes set the standard for modern comparative research, and Koffka showed how Gestalt principles can be applied to developmental psychology. Lewin devised methods of studying groups that are essential to social psychology, while Heider provided foundational theories for the field. In coming chapters, we'll see how Gestalt theory has had a lasting influence on psychology. Rejecting the "mindlessness" of behaviorism, Gestalt theorists returned the mind to center stage in psychology. In the next chapter, we'll see how Sigmund Freud and his followers went beyond the study of conscious experience to explore the unconscious processes that drive our thoughts and behaviors.

CHAPTER SUMMARY

A contemporary of Wilhelm Wundt, Franz Brentano proposed an alternative approach to the scientific study of the mind that he called act psychology. One of his students, Carl Stumpf, established a major psychology lab in Berlin, while another, Christian von Ehrenfels, proposed the concept of Gestalt quality, thus giving the field its name. Stumpf's students then formed the Berlin school of Gestalt psychology. Max Wertheimer launched the Gestalt approach to experimental psychology with his study of the phi phenomenon, and Wolfgang Köhler studied problem solving in apes at the world's first primate research center. Kurt Koffka introduced Gestalt psychology to the English-speaking world, and he was also the first to immigrate to the United States, where he had considerable influence on many of the key psychologists of the mid-twentieth century. A later member of the Berlin school, Kurt Lewin, is known today as one of the founders of experimental social psychology, and in particular the study of group dynamics. He also nurtured a great number of students, both in Europe and in the United States. Among these, the most notable was Fritz Heider, who developed both attribution and balance theory, two key pillars of social psychology in the last half of the twentieth century.

DISCUSSION QUESTIONS

1. Compare and contrast the differing approaches to experimental psychology proposed by Wilhelm Wundt and Franz Brentano. Which do you think is more in line with modern thinking in the field? Explain.

2. Carl Stump and Christian von Ehrenfels are often considered the grandfathers of Gestalt psychology. Trace their influence on the psychologists presented in this chapter.

3. What is a Gestalt? Explain how the concept applies to Ehrenfels's example of a melody and Wertheimer's example of the phi phenomenon.

4. Ehrenfels said the whole is *more than* the sum of the parts, but Wertheimer insisted the whole is *different from* the sum of the parts. What exactly is the distinction between these two conceptualizations of a Gestalt?

5. Compare Köhler's experiments on problem solving in apes with Thorndike's studies of cats escaping from puzzle boxes. Why might these two researchers have come to such different conclusions about the nature of problem solving in animals?

6. What is meant by Köhler's concept of isomorphism? Explain how it relates to the mind-body problem.

7. Compare the effect Koffka had on the thinking of the neo-behaviorists Clark Hull and Edward Tolman.

8. What is the Zeigarnik effect? Two examples are given in the chapter, but can you think of others?

9. Explain field theory and the concept of life space in terms of Lewin's equation.

10. How did Lewin change the way social psychologists thought about their field?

11. Explain Heider's attribution theory, giving examples of impersonal and personal attributions. Why do we make attributions?

12. Work out the various combinations of positive and negative sentiment relations in a POX model. Determine whether each is stable or unstable.

ON THE WEB

On YouTube, you can find original footage of chimpanzees solving problems that Wolfgang Köhler filmed at the primate research center in Tenerife. Search **Wolfgang Kohler chimpanzee experiment**. The site also hosts original film footage of Kurt Lewin's experiment on leadership style. Search **Kurt Lewin leadership experiment**. Finally, you can find a famous stop-motion animation produced by Fritz Heider and Marianne Simmel illustrating how easily we attribute intentional behavior even to inanimate objects. Search **Heider Simmel animation**.

Psychoanalysis

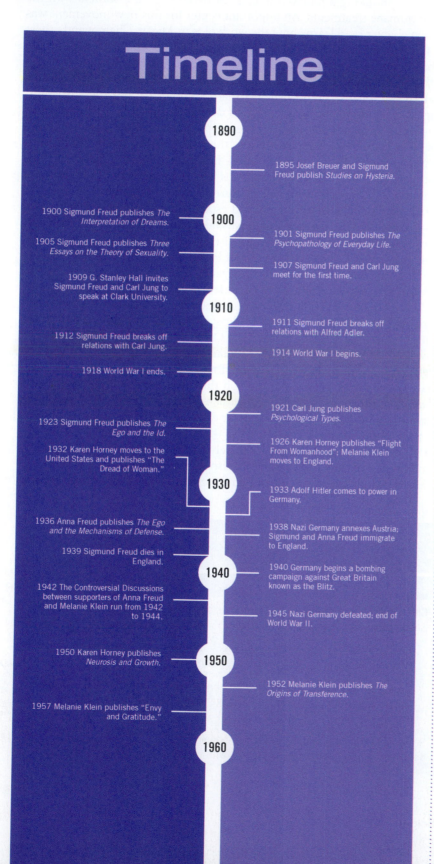

Timeline

1890

1895 Josef Breuer and Sigmund Freud publish *Studies on Hysteria*.

1900 Sigmund Freud publishes *The Interpretation of Dreams*.

1900

1905 Sigmund Freud publishes *Three Essays on the Theory of Sexuality*.

1901 Sigmund Freud publishes *The Psychopathology of Everyday Life*.

1907 Sigmund Freud and Carl Jung meet for the first time.

1909 G. Stanley Hall invites Sigmund Freud and Carl Jung to speak at Clark University.

1910

1911 Sigmund Freud breaks off relations with Alfred Adler.

1912 Sigmund Freud breaks off relations with Carl Jung.

1914 World War I begins.

1918 World War I ends.

1920

1921 Carl Jung publishes *Psychological Types*.

1923 Sigmund Freud publishes *The Ego and the Id*.

1926 Karen Horney publishes "Flight From Womanhood"; Melanie Klein moves to England.

1932 Karen Horney moves to the United States and publishes "The Dread of Woman."

1930

1933 Adolf Hitler comes to power in Germany.

1936 Anna Freud publishes *The Ego and the Mechanisms of Defense*.

1938 Nazi Germany annexes Austria; Sigmund and Anna Freud immigrate to England.

1939 Sigmund Freud dies in England.

1940

1940 Germany begins a bombing campaign against Great Britain known as the Blitz.

1942 The Controversial Discussions between supporters of Anna Freud and Melanie Klein run from 1942 to 1944.

1945 Nazi Germany defeated; end of World War II.

1950 Karen Horney publishes *Neurosis and Growth*.

1950

1952 Melanie Klein publishes *The Origins of Transference*.

1957 Melanie Klein publishes "Envy and Gratitude."

1960

Learning Objectives

After reading this chapter, you should be able to:

- Evaluate the strengths and weaknesses of Sigmund Freud's theories within the social context of the early twentieth century.

- Consider the ways in which Alfred Adler's individual psychology and Carl Jung's analytical psychology diverged from traditional psychoanalysis.

- Explain the psychoanalytic perspectives of Melanie Klein and Karen Horney and the influence they have had on contemporary psychology.

- Appraise Anna Freud's contributions to developmental psychology.

Looking Back

For centuries, persons with psychological disorders were often treated inhumanely, subjected to cruel exorcisms or brutal treatments intended to chase out demons or frighten the patients back to reality. If deemed incurable, they were locked away, either at home or in an asylum, usually under appalling conditions. In the last decades of the nineteenth century, medical professionals began taking a renewed interest in psychological disorders with the goal of creating more humane treatments. An important center for this new movement was France, and in the next chapter we'll learn about the work of Jean-Martin Charcot and others in developing new forms of psychotherapy. However, in this chapter we'll first consider the contributions of Charcot's most famous student, the Austrian neurologist Sigmund Freud. *Freud's theory of the origin of psychological disorders and his method for curing them* became known as **psychoanalysis**. Because Freud believed that psychological disorders in adulthood have their origins in childhood trauma, he delved deep into the earliest experiences of his patients. For this reason, psychoanalysis and related approaches are also known as depth psychology. Freud's ideas had intuitive appeal, and by the middle of the twentieth century, the psychoanalytic movement had spread widely across Europe and North America.

As we'll see in this chapter and the next, Freud was less of an innovator than he was a synthesizer and promoter of ideas that were already current during his time. The image of Freud as the maverick battling against an entrenched establishment—a self-image that he himself promoted—is certainly false. In fact, Freud was taken quite seriously by other psychologists, and as we saw in Chapter 5, even behaviorists tried to reconcile psychoanalytic concepts with learning theory. Thus, it's best to think of Freud not as a pioneer but rather as a focal point for the turn-of-the-twentieth-century Zeitgeist.

Before we begin this chapter, we also need to consider the terminology used to describe mental illness at the end of the nineteenth century. The modern classification of psychological disorders had not yet been developed, and instead psychologists and psychiatrists made a two-way distinction in terms of severity (Table 7.1). On the one hand, a **neurosis** was *a relatively minor psychological disorder that interferes with the patient's ability to lead a happy and productive life but without a loss of contact with reality.* Today's mood and anxiety disorders would have been labeled neuroses in Freud's time. On the other hand, a **psychosis** was *a severe psychological disorder involving hallucinations, delusions, and a general loss of contact with reality.* Today's schizophrenia and some forms of bipolar disorder would have been classified as psychoses at the turn of the twentieth century.

It's not just that psychologists and psychiatrists merely had an incomplete understanding of the nature of mental illness at that time. Rather, it's also the case that forms of psychological disorders prevalent in a population can depend on the culture of a society at a given time

Table 7.1	Categorization of Psychological Disorders in the Early Twentieth Century	
Disorder	**Description**	**Modern Terms**
Neurosis	Chronic distress but without hallucinations or delusions. Subtypes are *neurasthenia* and *hysteria*	Depression, anxiety
Neurasthenia	Condition with symptoms such as fatigue, headache, heart palpitations, anxiety, and depressed mood	Depression, anxiety
Hysteria	Condition with symptoms such as numbness and paralysis even though there's no damage to the nervous system	Conversion disorder
Psychosis	Severe disorder with symptoms such as hallucinations, delusions, and a general loss of contact with reality	Schizophrenia, bipolar disorder

period. One common form of neurosis was called **neurasthenia**, which is *an antiquated diagnosis for patients suffering from symptoms such as fatigue, headache, heart palpitations, anxiety, and depressed mood.* The term itself comes from the Ancient Greek and means "weakening of the nerves." In common parlance, the condition was often referred to as a "nervous breakdown." We now know that weak nerves have nothing to do with the condition, and today we view the term as a general category for depression and anxiety.

Another common form of neurosis was **hysteria**. This is *an antiquated diagnosis for patients suffering from symptoms such as numbness and paralysis even though there is no damage to the nervous system.* It was a particularly common diagnosis among women, and even the name for the disorder comes from the Greek word for uterus—*hystera*, as in *hysterectomy*, or removal of the uterus. Today, we understand hysteria as a psychological reaction to the social and sexual repression of women in Western society during that time period. As Western women have gained independence, the incidence of hysteria has declined dramatically. Moreover, hysteria has now been relabeled as conversion disorder, with the recognition that both men and women can suffer from this now uncommon ailment. Also note that the common usage of the word *hysteria* today is completely different from its meaning in the nineteenth century.

As we'll see in this chapter and the next, hysteria became the center of attention for those who were interested in developing effective psychotherapies. First, it was a common disorder, so there was a pressing need for treatments that worked. Furthermore, hysterics often responded well when psychotherapists treated them humanely and showed them genuine concern. Indeed, Freud built his career—and his theory—working mainly with patients with hysteria. By extrapolating from the detailed analyses of the thought processes of these patients, Sigmund Freud tried to build a theory of the mind that was applicable to all humans.

Sigmund Freud

Vienna was his beloved city, and he spent nearly his entire life there. **Sigmund Freud** (1856–1939; pronounced *FROYD*) wanted to be a professor of physiology at the University of Vienna, and he even spent several years there as a research assistant. But academic positions were hard to come by—especially for Jews—so he earned a degree in medicine, specializing in **neurology**, which is *the branch of medicine that treats disorders of the nervous system.* Early in his career, Freud was awarded a fellowship to study at the Salpêtrière, a famous mental hospital in Paris. There, he came under the influence of the neurologist Jean-Martin Charcot and the psychologist Pierre Janet, both of whom we'll meet in Chapter 8. At that time, Charcot was considered the world's leading expert on hysteria, a disorder that Freud was already developing an interest in. Freud was especially impressed with Charcot's attempts to help his patients by letting them talk about their problems and concerns. Charcot also influenced Freud's thinking on the origin of psychological disorders by suggesting that repressed sexuality lay at the root of neurosis. Today, Sigmund Freud is known as the *Austrian neurologist who developed the theory and therapy known as psychoanalysis.*

Max Halberstadt, via Wikimedia Commons

Photo 7.1
Sigmund Freud

Talking Cure

On his return from Paris, Freud began working with **Josef Breuer** (1842–1925; pronounced *YOH-seff BROY-er*), a well-known *Austrian neurologist who pioneered the use of the cathartic method to treat hysteria* (Grünbaum, 2006). Breuer was instrumental in helping young Freud set up his psychotherapy practice, and he was an important influence in Freud's early thinking on the origin of psychological disorders. Freud and Breuer worked with a hysteric patient known as Anna O. Among Anna's symptoms was an extreme phobia of water. Breuer already suspected that hysteria was caused by traumatic events that had been repressed from memory. Under hypnosis, Anna O. recalled seeing a dog drink from a glass of water. Disgusted by the sight, she developed a fear of drinking water that might be contaminated. Once this memory was brought to light, the phobia went away. Breuer and Freud described the experience as a catharsis, meaning *the release of pent-up emotions that cause psychological distress.* If you've ever felt better after talking with someone about your problems, you've experienced catharsis.

In 1895, Breuer and Freud co-authored *Studies on Hysteria*, in which they described the cases of Anna O. and several other hysterics (Grünbaum, 1992). They proposed that hysteria is caused by repression, which is *the exclusion of an unwanted or traumatic memory from consciousness.* Although the patient no longer consciously remembers the event, the memory lingers in an unconscious part of the mind, from which it creates the symptoms of hysteria. To cure the disorder, the repressed memory needs to be brought back into consciousness so the patient can deal with the painful emotions associated with it. Only then will the symptoms of hysteria go away. This book was important for two reasons. First, it provided a theory that explained the cause of hysteria, and by extension other psychological disorders. Second, it offered a treatment for the disorder that seemed to work.

After this, Freud began using the talking cure in his private practice (Grünbaum, 1992). But not all patients could be hypnotized, so instead he developed a method he called free association. This is *a psychotherapy technique in which patients are encouraged to say whatever comes to mind without attempting to censor their thoughts.* When patients became reluctant to discuss a particular topic, Freud believed this resistance showed they were approaching the repressed memory, and he urged them to talk more about it. Once the repressed memory was identified, the patient showed an improvement in symptoms. However, the relief was usually only temporary, and either the symptoms returned or new ones appeared in their place.

To find the root cause of hysteria, Freud had to dig deeper (Kupfersmid, 1992). Instead of focusing on traumatic events of adulthood, he asked his patients to free associate about their childhood. And as they did so, he discovered something quite shocking. Many of his patients reported vague memories of sexual molestation as young children. This finding led him to put forward his seduction theory, which is *the proposal that psychological disorders in adulthood are caused by sexual abuse in childhood.* But soon after Freud presented this idea to his colleagues, he backtracked on it. First, medical authorities doubted that childhood sexual abuse was as rampant as seduction theory suggested. Furthermore, there was no corroborating evidence for most of these reported cases of abuse. And finally, when Freud performed a self-analysis, he uncovered vague childhood memories of his own father molesting him and his siblings, although he doubted these events had actually occurred.

Eventually Freud concluded that while some of his patients' memories of childhood sexual abuse were factual, most of them were fantasies instead (Emde, 1992). But where could these imagined memories have come from? At the time, it was assumed that children were sexually innocent until puberty. But influenced by his friend Wilhelm Fliess (1858–1928), who had unorthodox sexual views, Freud began to see babies as sexual beings from birth. Although they were incapable of reproductive acts until adolescence, they still delighted in sensual bodily experiences and harbored strong sexual desires. These infantile yearnings then became the basis for the memories of childhood sexuality his patients reported.

Interpretation of Dreams

Meanwhile, Freud (1900) had expanded his clinical repertoire to include a discussion of his patients' dreams. Calling dreams "the royal road to the unconscious," he believed sleep was a time when the censors of consciousness were relaxed, letting repressed thoughts and memories rise to the surface. *The Interpretation of Dreams* (Freud, 1900) is considered his most important work, and in it he laid out many of the ideas he's most noted for today. Dreaming was a hot topic of research at the turn of the twentieth century, and as we saw in Chapter 4, Mary Calkins did important early studies on the topic that Freud cited in this work. Still,

Freud was the first to propose a comprehensive theory of dreams that incorporated their known features into his developing psychoanalytic theory.

Freud (1900) proposed that dreams occur on two levels. The **manifest content** is *the narrative of a dream as recalled by the dreamer on awakening*. But underlying this is the **latent content**, which is *the unconscious meaning of the dream*. Freud insisted that the latent content of a dream involved sexual urges that had been disguised with symbols to make them nonthreatening. Other researchers had already observed that most dreams contain elements from the previous day's thoughts or activities. Freud called this the day residue, but he also insisted that the selection of items was far from random. Instead, they were intentionally selected for their symbolic value. This is why the interpretation of dreams became such an important therapeutic tool for Freud.

In *The Interpretation of Dreams*, Freud (1900) provided an explanation for infantile sexual fantasies by relating the Ancient Greek story of Oedipus, who unknowingly kills his father and marries his mother. He speculates that this story reveals a universal truth about the human condition. Specifically, he offers *the proposal that all young children develop a sexual longing for their opposite-sex parent and a sexual jealousy toward their same-sex parent*. In his later writings, he calls this infantile love triangle the **Oedipus complex**.

In Freud's theory, the resolution of the Oedipus complex became a key event in the child's psychosexual development (Josephs, Katzander, & Goncharova, 2018). Children learn to relinquish their sexual longing for the opposite-sex parent, mainly because they fear the same-sex parent will harm them in retaliation for their amorous desires. By around age six, they've repressed all thoughts of sex, which disappear until puberty. Although adults have no conscious memories of infantile sexuality, the Oedipus complex still has an impact on how they conduct their sexual relationships. While most people learn to transfer their desire for their opposite-sex parent to appropriate persons, unresolved oedipal issues lead to neuroses in adult relationships.

Freud argued that psychopathology occurs along a continuum, and that even normally functioning adults can be affected in adverse ways by repressed memories (Josephs, 2015). In other words, all of us are plagued by psychological issues, largely benign in most people but seriously impacting the lives of those we label as "abnormal." Following *The Interpretation of Dreams* was one of his most popular works, *The Psychopathology of Everyday Life*, which he published in 1901. In this book, Freud explored a phenomenon he called parapraxis, but which is more commonly known as a **Freudian slip**. This is a *lapse of memory or an error in speech due to interference from a repressed memory*. Although some instances of forgetting or slips of the tongue are inadvertent, others seem to be driven by unconscious processes. For example, forgetting a dreaded dental appointment could be seen as an example of motivated forgetting.

Around this time, Freud also proposed that the mind consists of a series of levels (Grünbaum, 1992). At the top was consciousness, that is, whatever you're currently aware of. Just below that was the preconscious, which consists of all memories that can be readily brought into consciousness. Repressed memories are pushed down to the third level, the unconscious, which is a dynamic system teeming with drives and desires that influence our conscious thoughts and behaviors without our awareness. Furthermore, the unconscious actively represses unpleasant memories because of the pain they would cause.

Psychosexual Development

In his *Three Essays on the Theory of Sexuality*, Freud (1905) laid out his theory of infantile sexuality and psychosexual development. He began with his argument that infants are sexual creatures from birth. Furthermore, he maintained that babies are born bisexual, that is, they're equally attracted to members of both sexes. Through the socialization process, most people learn to direct their amorous attentions to the opposite sex, but some develop same-sex attraction, while others either maintain a bisexual orientation in adulthood or else adopt different orientations depending on the circumstances.

Thus, Freud (1905) rejected the idea that homosexuality was an innate perversion, insisting on the importance of early childhood experiences and dismissing the notion that it

Photo 7.2
Freud's couch

was abnormal. While acknowledging that homosexuality was highly stigmatized in Western society, he pointed to ancient Greek culture, where it was widely practiced. Moreover, he observed that the first sexual activities of many adolescents are with members of the same sex, even when they become strictly heterosexual in adulthood. Likewise, heterosexual men in prison often resort to homosexuality.

It was also in this work that Freud (1905) introduced his theory of **psychosexual development**, which was *the proposal that infants progress through a series of stages, each centered on a body part that is a source of sensual pleasure*. By early adulthood, most people have progressed into mature sexuality. But those with psychological disorders develop a fixation on one of these body parts, leading to particular symptoms.

In Freud's theory, psychosexual development begins with the **oral stage**. This is *a time in psychosexual development when an infant derives pleasure from nursing at the breast or bottle*. Freud (1905) observed that the facial expressions of a suckling baby are similar to those of an adult experiencing orgasm. After the infant is weaned, it seeks out substitutes such as thumb-sucking. Kissing before, during, or after sexual intercourse hearkens back to the oral stage, but in a healthy way. However, others develop an **oral fixation**, which is *a behavior involving the mouth that is engaged in to relieve anxiety*. Smoking, biting nails, and chewing gum are examples. Given his cigar habit, Freud clearly suffered from an oral fixation.

After weaning, the child then enters the **anal stage**, which is *a time in psychosexual development when a child derives pleasure from the anus and buttocks*. Toilet training occurs during this period. The social interaction of this process can give children a sense of pleasure as they leave a present in the potty for mommy, but they can also develop a sense of power by withholding that present. Light, playful spanking can be exciting for children at this age (and for adult lovers as well). Furthermore, toddlers often scratch or rub their anus, apparently to relieve anxiety.

From age three to six, children are in the **phallic stage**, which is *a time in psychosexual development when a child derives pleasure from rubbing the genitals*. Freud noted that many children enjoy touching themselves, but usually their parents stop them. The Oedipus complex occurs during this time as well, the resolution of which leads to the repression of infantile sexuality.

Table 7.2	Freud's Stages of Psychosexual Development		
Stage	**Age**	**Description**	**Fixation as Adult**
Oral	0–1	Pleasure from nursing	Chewing gum, smoking, eating
Anal	1–3	Pleasure from bowel and bladder elimination	Obsessively neat or compulsively disorganized
Phallic	3–6	Pleasure from touching genitals	Oedipus complex; unresolved sexual issues with parents
Latent	6 to puberty	Dormant sexual feelings	Lack of interest in sexuality
Genital	Puberty onward	Mature sexual interests	Frigidity, impotence, and unsatisfactory relationships

Figure 7.1 Iceberg Metaphor

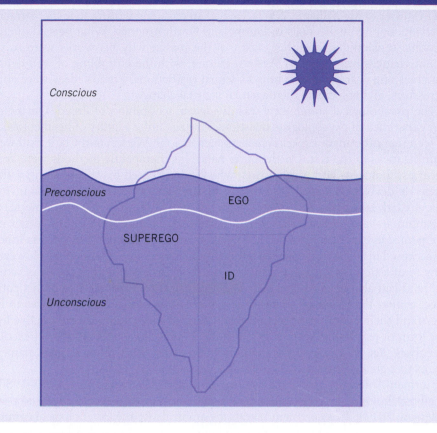

Source: Historicair via Wikimedia Commons.

These events introduce the **latency stage**, which is *a time in psychosexual development when a child's sexual feelings remain dormant*. The child's interests turn instead to friendships, hobbies, sports, and school. However, the onset of puberty leads to the **genital stage**, which is *the period of mature psychosexual development in adulthood*. For well-adjusted adults, sexual intercourse becomes the means for relieving sexual tension, but stimulation of the other erogenous zones is still included as a part of foreplay.

Freud's theory of psychosexual development is important for two reasons (Table 7.2). First, it represented a pioneering attempt at describing the development of both normal and abnormal personality within a single framework. And second, the idea of development progressing through clearly definable stages provided inspiration for other stage models, such as the theory of cognitive development proposed by Jean Piaget (Chapter 8) and the eight stages of psychosocial development posited by Erik Erikson (Chapter 15).

In *The Ego and the Id*, Freud (1923) further developed his theory of the structure of personality. Present at birth is a component called the **id**, which is *the repository of innate drives or instincts*. It operates on the pleasure principle, meaning that it demands immediate satisfaction of its urges, even though it has no means of doing so. During childhood, a second component appears. This is the **ego**, which is *the sense of self or agency*. The ego operates according to the reality principle, meaning that its role is to find realistic ways of satisfying the needs of the id. Finally, a third component emerges with the resolution of the Oedipus complex. This is the **superego**, which is *an internalization of social and moral rules*. It also contains our ego-ideal, that is, the image we maintain of the person we'd like to be. These three components—id, ego, and superego—compete with each other, and adult personality results from the compromise that's achieved from this interaction. Freud's theory of personality is often represented by the iceberg metaphor, in which most of its components are submerged below consciousness (Figure 7.1).

Legacy

Freud wrote extensively, and he continuously revised his theory over the course of his career (Messer & McWilliams, 2003). He had an engaging writing style that attracted a large readership among intellectuals in Europe and North America. What he said often offended traditional sensibilities, and this is part of the reason why his works were so controversial. But changes were afoot in Western culture, with the crumbling of well-defined social hierarchies and a gradual loosening of sexual restrictions. Freud's ideas were appealing to progressives, giving focus to their agenda of social change.

The psychological community was divided in its opinion of Freud. On the one hand, many experimental psychologists questioned the scientific validity of his theories. But we've also seen that prominent experimentalists such as John Watson and Clark Hull were willing to put his ideas to the test. On the other hand, his therapeutic methods were appealing to clinical psychologists and psychiatrists, who often accepted his theory along with his techniques. He developed a loyal following in Europe, and after G. Stanley Hall invited him to speak at Clark University in 1909, he garnered many followers in North America as well.

Ambitious and authoritarian, Freud desired above all else to be the leader of a major movement. He expected absolute obedience from his followers, but he was kind to those who accepted his ideas and deferred to him as the father of psychoanalysis. However, anyone daring to question his authority was banished from his circle with no hope of return.

Freud can also be considered the father of psychotherapy. He treated his patients with respect, rather than viewing them as deviants, and his therapeutic goal was to help them understand their underlying psychological issues so they could lead productive lives. Every other form of psychotherapy can be considered either an extension of or a reaction to psychoanalysis. Yet all forms of psychotherapy have the same ultimate goal, namely to lead patients to a greater insight of their own condition.

German-American psychoanalyst and philosopher Erich Fromm (1900–1980) claimed that all psychologists need to understand Freud, even though everything he said was wrong (Anderson, 2017). This comment reveals the ambivalence the psychological community has toward Freud. His theories are compelling but vague, so they're hard to test. Nevertheless, he was a keen observer of human behavior, and it's easy to see how his ideas relate to our own lives. Freud had a fruitful imagination, and even when his theories extend far beyond what's warranted by the data, his many case studies and anecdotes challenge us to rethink our assumptions about human nature (Figure 7.2).

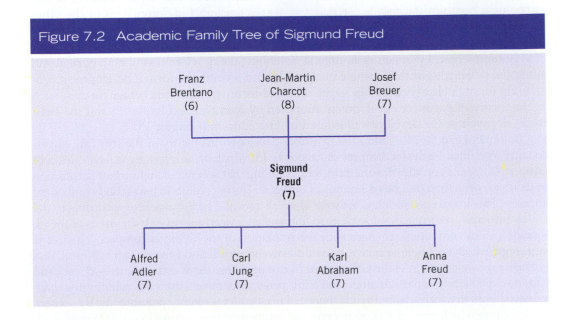

Figure 7.2   Academic Family Tree of Sigmund Freud

First Generation

Freud gathered a number of disciples around him, who adopted his theory and techniques in their own clinical practices. He was also an ambitious man who hoped to start a movement that would outlive him, so he needed an heir after he was gone to keep psychoanalysis going in the direction he envisaged. His first choice was Alfred Adler, but when the disciple challenged the master, he was banished from the group. His next choice was Carl Jung, but again Freud would tolerate no dissent, and the second heir was ousted as well. While both Adler and Jung benefitted from their early association with Freud, each raised valid concerns about the standard theory. And it was only after breaking free of their mentor that they were able to make their most important contributions to psychology.

Alfred Adler

Alfred Adler (1870–1937) suffered from rickets as a child, so he couldn't walk until he was four. This early experience of struggling with a disability taught him a lot about how people deal with a profound sense of inferiority. Some persons succumb to psychological disorders as they grapple with their disability. Others, like himself, see it as a challenge that provides an opportunity for growth. Later in life, Alfred Adler became known as an *Austrian psychologist who emphasized overcoming feelings of inferiority and maintaining active social interest as the keys to mental health.*

Like Freud, Adler was a secular Jew with a medical degree from the University of Vienna, and he was one of Freud's first followers (Ansbacher, 2004). Freud saw Adler as an important ally, placing him in key positions within the movement and treating him as his heir. During the years of his association with Freud, Adler published on the nature of psychopathology, and he was a popular lecturer. Thus, he saw his relationship with Freud as one of equals. But for Freud there were no equals—he was the master, and Adler the disciple. At first, Freud tolerated Adler's diverging views as long as he continued to use standard methods of psychoanalysis in the clinic. However, the break finally came in 1911, when Freud insisted his followers accept the doctrine of sexual repression as the root of all psychological disorders.

Adler's approach differed from Freud's in many ways (Hirsch, 2005). First, Adler discounted infantile sexuality and repression as important psychological mechanisms. Furthermore, he challenged the notion of a dynamic unconscious. Instead, he maintained that there were parts of people's psyches that they were generally unaware of but could come to know with the proper guidance. He also dismissed Freud's theory of the Oedipus complex as nothing more than sexual mythology. In addition, he chafed at Freud's misogynistic views of inherent male superiority.

As a socialist, Adler advocated for gender equality and women's rights (Hirsch, 2005). He accepted the notion of innate bisexuality, but whereas Freud viewed the concept in terms of sexual orientation, Adler considered it from the aspect of gender identity. He felt that much distress stemmed from the fact that men suppressed their feminine side to live up to unrealistic standards of manliness, and likewise women were denied the opportunity to express their masculine traits. Moreover, he changed the arrangement of his clinic. Instead of sitting behind the reclining patient, as Freud did, he sat face-to-face with his client.

Adler rejected Freud's view of each person as a seething mass of conflicting drives and motives (Barton-Bellessa, Lee, & Shon, 2015). Instead, Adler argued that people's behaviors could only be understood by considering them within their social environments. In particular, he maintained that you could assess people's mental health by observing how they responded to the demands of the three main spheres of social life—work, friendship,

Photo 7.3
Alfred Adler

and family. Well-adjusted individuals navigated these realms skillfully, actively engaging with others and finding effective solutions to problems. In contrast, those who were maladjusted tended to respond rigidly to social challenges, such as acting overly fearful, dependent, or domineering.

Because of his concern with the ways the individual adjusts to the demands of society, Adler called his approach **individual psychology** (Overholser, 2010). This was *Adler's version of psychotherapy that emphasized the centrality of social functioning in mental health*. For the rest of his career, Adler built individual psychology as a comprehensive model of psychological health and illness.

For Adler, the key to emotional health was **social interest**, by which he meant *active engagement in meaningful relationships with others and a desire to make positive contributions to society* (Clark & Butler, 2012). He noted that people with neuroses tend to focus on their own fears and frustrations without proper regard for the needs of those around them. In fact, he often told his patients to do things to make other people happy instead of ruminating over their own unhappiness, with the expectation that doing so would improve their own emotional state.

Adler believed a person's level of social interest was determined by positive or negative social experiences in early childhood (Karrel & Gill, 2002). Children growing up in loving, supportive families became well-adjusted adults, whereas those reared in dysfunctional homes exhibited maladjusted behaviors in later life. Adler maintained that level of social interest generally remained steady throughout life, but troubled individuals could learn to raise theirs by gaining insight into the nature of their poorly adjusted behaviors and thought patterns.

Although Adler sometimes talked about personality, he preferred the term **lifestyle** (Karrel & Gill, 2002). This was *Adler's term for an individual's typical approach to dealing with the world*. In this view, people don't *have* psychological disorders, but rather they *behave* in socially ineffective manners. For instance, the hysteric patient acts in ways that gain the attention and sympathy of others, but the hysteric lifestyle hinders the successful navigation of life's challenges. Adler also noticed that people suffering from neuroses often strive to protect their self-image rather than facing problems head on. For example, people with social anxieties set up barriers between themselves and others instead of facing their fears. Likewise, a person can use symptoms of depression to avoid difficult social situations they'd rather not deal with.

In the clinic, Adler probed his patients' childhood experiences, just as Freud did, and hence his approach is considered a form of depth psychology (DeGree & Snyder, 1985). However, Adler's aim was to demonstrate to his patients that their lifestyle was ineffective and that they needed to change their attitudes and behaviors if they wanted to lead a fulfilling life. Adler disagreed with the notion that traumatic experiences caused psychological disorders. Rather, distressed persons use painful memories to maintain their ineffective lifestyle. This may sound like blaming the patient, but Adler insisted that lifestyle choices aren't made consciously, and that's why they feel inevitable. His goal was to show his patients that they had the power to take control of their lives. With self-awareness, people can shed their maladaptive behaviors and lead a healthy and fulfilling lifestyle instead.

Adler saw an underlying sense of inferiority in his patients that drove their maladaptive behavior (Barton-Bellessa et al., 2015). He identified three different sources of inferiority:

- *Organ inferiority.* This refers to physical comparisons with other persons. As children, we all feel inferior because the adults in our lives are so much bigger and stronger than we are. But the child who isn't as good at sports or in school as his peers will also feel inferior. As Adler knew from personal experience, physical handicap is also a source of inferiority because you're unable to do things others take for granted.

- *Societal influences.* In Adler's time, women were taught from an early age that they were inferior to men. So it was little wonder that so many women sought treatment for hysteria and other problems. Likewise, racial prejudice created feelings of inferiority. As a Jew, Adler understood the pernicious effects of racism first hand. In addition to discrimination, he pointed to poverty, religion, and education as other sources of inferiority.

- *Family dynamics*. Adler is well known for his studies on the effects of birth order, noting that first-born, second-born, last-born, and only children each had typical lifestyles they assumed based on their position within the family structure.

The way parents treated their children was also important (Barton-Bellessa et al., 2015). When parents raise their children in loving, supportive homes, they provide effective models of problem solving that their children adopt to resolve their own feelings of insecurity. However, other parenting styles are ineffective. Some parents pamper their children, meeting all their needs and shielding them from life's challenges. These children grow up expecting to always get their way, and they're resentful when they can't get what they want. Despite their sense of entitlement, there's still an underlying feeling of insecurity because they have no effective means of resolving problems in life. Other parents neglect or abuse their children, who feel inferior because they sense they're not loved. As adults, they tend to feel isolated and distrustful of others. They may also believe they're entitled to special treatment to compensate for the emotional emptiness of their childhood.

According to Adler, all of us experience feelings of inferiority, but the key is how we respond (Hirsch, 2005). Some people are motivated to overcome inferiority in a process he called **striving for superiority**. This is *Adler's term for people's natural desire to improve themselves*. Striving for superiority meshes with social interest, because people can only be their best when they're integrated into their social networks of work, friends, and family. Other people assume *a lifestyle dominated by a sense of helplessness and unworthiness,* which Adler called an **inferiority complex**. Rather than striving to improve themselves, these people act in ways that confirm their sense of being inferior or worthless, such as by failing to achieve goals that are clearly within their reach. Still others compensate by developing a **superiority complex**. This involves *a lifestyle dominated by a sense of being better than other people*. People with a superiority complex are constantly in competition with others rather than cooperating with them, because their first priority is to demonstrate their superiority in order to compensate for their underlying sense of inferiority.

After the devastation of World War I, Adler looked to the United States as a country more likely to achieve his dream of social equality than his native Austria (Hirsch, 2005). Starting in 1926, he spent half of each year as a visiting professor in America. He'd learned English and acclimated to American culture, and he was ready to call the United States his new home if need be. But he died suddenly in 1937 while on a lecture tour in Scotland, less than a year before the Nazis invaded Austria.

Since his death, Adler's ideas have been incorporated into our current thinking on psychological disorders and their treatment. In fact, modern clinical methods resemble Adler's much more than Freud's. We can see the impact of his thinking on many of the modern approaches to psychotherapy, particularly those that focus on cognitive and behavioral change. Furthermore, his concept of striving for superiority was an early formulation of the notion of self-actualization that humanistic psychologists developed after World War II. Nowadays, however, Adler often goes unrecognized for his contributions. Far from following in Freud's footsteps, Adler was a pioneer who blazed the trail for modern thinking on personality formation, psychopathology, and psychotherapy.

Carl Jung

He first learned of Freud's theory when he read *The Interpretation of Dreams*, and it left a profound impression on him (Alexander, 1982). **Carl Jung** (1875–1961; pronounced *YOONG*) was working as a psychiatrist at the Burghölzli (pronounced *BOORG-hult-slee*), a famous mental hospital in Zurich, and he'd just conducted research on unconscious complexes in psychiatric patients. After reading the book, he understood that repression was the mechanism for creating these complexes. Jung's relationship with Freud was quite intense, and eventually they had a falling out. In the aftermath of this breakup, Carl Jung developed a reputation as a *Swiss psychologist noted for his theory of personality types and his idea of the collective unconscious.*

Photo 7.4
Carl Jung

A common psychiatric concept at the time was **complex**, which was an *interrelated set of unconscious memories and emotions on a common theme*. Freud had proposed the Oedipus complex, and Adler the inferiority and superiority complexes. Jung explored possible complexes underlying psychiatric disorders, and he did this with a word association task (Wertheimer, King, Peckler, Raney, & Schaef, 1992). In this procedure, he read a list of 100 words one at a time to his patient, who responded to each with the first thought that came to mind. Words with delayed responses supposedly indicated something about the complex. He even used the technique to catch a thief. These studies established Jung as a promising young psychiatrist.

In 1907, Jung and Freud finally met (Ireland & Pennebaker, 2010). They quickly developed a deep friendship, but it was also one of mutual benefit. Freud was concerned that psychoanalysis was perceived as a Jewish school, but Jung as a Protestant would lend credence to the movement. Furthermore, there were growing tensions with Adler, who insisted on being treated as an equal. But Jung, who was just starting his career, saw himself as the intellectual son to the father figure of Freud—at least at first. Freud began calling Jung his heir, a title once reserved for Adler.

However, Jung was an ambitious young man, and within a few years he began asserting his independence (Alexander, 1982). The first cracks in the relationship occurred in 1909, when G. Stanley Hall invited both Freud and Jung to speak at the twentieth-anniversary celebration at Clark University. To pass the time on board the ship, they analyzed each other's dreams, but when Jung probed too deep, Freud stopped the discussion. They had several other quarrels over the next few years. By 1912, Jung could no longer tolerate Freud's dogmatic attitude, and he also had doubts about the Oedipus complex and the sexual origin of psychological disorders. After an exchange of spiteful letters, they severed their relationship and never spoke to each other again. From Freud's point of view, an oedipal drama had played out right before his eyes. The son (Jung) was in love with the mother (psychoanalysis) and wanted her all to himself, but to do that, he would first have to kill the father (Freud). Instead, the father banished the son.

The break with Freud was so painful that Jung couldn't bear to think about it directly (Davis & Mattoon, 2006). Instead, he focused his attention on the earlier break between Freud and Adler. Jung thought he perceived an important difference in the personalities of these two men that was also reflected in each of their theories. On the one hand, Freud was an introspective type who was reluctant to reveal his innermost thoughts, and this personality style was reflected in his theoretical approach, which looked inward to understand the psyche. On the other hand, Adler was a "people person"—outgoing and sociable—and he looked outward to the social environment for answers to the riddles of the mind. Perhaps, Jung proposed, Freud and Adler represented two basic attitudes toward the world. He called Freud's inward-looking attitude *introversion* and Adler's outward-looking attitude *extraversion*.

The distinction between introversion and extraversion seemed a fundamental aspect of personality (Davis & Mattoon, 2006). However, Jung found this division wasn't sufficient to account for the whole range of individual differences. In his 1921 book *Psychological Types*, he laid out his theory of personality. In addition to the two attitudes, Jung also proposed that people differ in the way they take in information (perceiving functions) and the way they make decisions (judging functions). The dimensions of personality then are as follows:

- *Attitudes*: People with a dominant *extraversion* attitude are outward looking and seek breadth of knowledge, whereas people with a dominant *introversion* attitude are inward looking and seek depth of knowledge.

- *Perceiving functions*: People with a dominant *sensation* function are interested in the objective reality of facts and things, whereas people with a dominant *intuition* function are interested in the subjective reality of patterns and possibilities.

- *Judging functions*: People with a dominant *thinking* function use logic to make decisions, whereas people with a dominant *feeling* function use emotions instead.

Table 7.3   Carl Jung's Personality Typology

Each person has one of two dominant attitudes and one of four dominant functions, for eight personality types.

Dimension	Type 1	Type 2
Attitude *How you deal with the world*	Extraversion *Outward looking; seek breadth of knowledge*	Introversion *Inward looking; seek depth of knowledge*
Perceiving functions *How you take in information*	Sensation function *Interested in objective reality of facts and things*	Intuition function *Interested in subjective reality of patterns and possibilities*
Judging functions *How you make decisions*	Thinking *Use logic to make decisions*	Feeling *Use feelings to make decisions*

According to Jung, both attitudes and all four functions occur in every individual. But each person has one dominant attitude and one dominant function, so there are eight personality types altogether (Table 7.3).

Unlike Freud, who viewed the unconscious as a dynamic system of repressed memories and urges, Jung saw it as a vast expanse containing not only personal memories but also ideas we all have in common from our evolutionary past. *Jung's approach to depth psychology emphasizing the role of the collective unconscious and archetypes* came to be known as **analytical psychology**.

Jung proposed that the mind consists of three levels (Zayed & Mook, 1999). At the top is the **personal conscious**—that is, *the part of the mind that a person is aware of*—consisting of two entities. The ego is the sense of self, while the **persona** is *Jung's term for the self that each person presents to others*. In other words, there are things about yourself that you keep private, and others that you display publicly.

Below this is the **personal unconscious**, which is *a repository of repressed memories accumulated over a lifetime* (Corrington, 1987). In this aspect, Jung's theory is similar to Freud's, with the exception that Jung discounted the influence of repressed sexual urges. Several entities reside within this layer. One is the **shadow**, which is *an unconscious entity in Jungian theory that contains those aspects of the self which the person doesn't like and so represses*. Even though we're unaware of our shadow, we tend to project its traits onto other people. If deep down we're distrustful of others, we'll assume that others don't trust us. An important aspect of Jungian psychotherapy is to help patients become aware of their shadow and the unconscious influence it has on them.

Like Freud and Adler, Jung accepted the idea of innate bisexuality, and he posited a male and female aspect in the personal unconscious of each individual (Carter, 2011). The **animus** is *the ideal masculine image*, while the **anima** is *the ideal feminine image.* In a man, the animus guides his endeavors toward manliness while the anima leads him in the selection of a mate. Likewise, a woman shapes the feminine aspects of her character according to her anima and chooses a mate according to her animus.

Even deeper lies the **collective unconscious**, which is, *in Jungian theory, a storehouse of innate ideas that have been passed down through human evolutionary history* (Maaske, 2002). Jung was a world traveler, and as he experienced various cultures, he noticed many aspects of people's thoughts and behaviors that were remarkably similar wherever they lived. He referred to *the primitive ideas contained in the collective unconscious as* **archetypes**. These archetypes then accounted for common themes that occur in myths and rituals across cultures.

A more controversial aspect of Jung's theory is the concept of **synchronicity** (Marlo & Kline, 1998). This is *the idea that shared archetypes in the collective unconscious enable the*

Photo 7.5
Sigmund Freud with G.
Stanley Hall and Carl Jung
at Clark University

occurrence of meaningful coincidences. For example, synchronicity occurs when you think of a friend and then a few minutes later that friend calls. The event may be a coincidence, but the fact that it's meaningful to both of you makes it more than just a coincidence. Jung saw synchronicity as an important aspect of psychotherapy. To be effective as a counselor, you have to have empathy for your patient, and this is facilitated through the synchronicity of the collective unconscious you both share.

The goal of Jungian psychotherapy is **individuation** (Gildersleeve, 2014). This is *a process in which unconscious complexes are brought into consciousness and integrated with the ego*. For example, by unconsciously projecting elements of your shadow onto others, you damage your relationships and suffer as a result. By becoming aware of the shadow, you can change your behaviors. Furthermore, by facing those aspects of yourself that you don't like, you can make efforts toward self-improvement. Jung's notion of individuation can be seen as an early formulation of the concept of self-actualization that was developed by humanistic psychologists (Chapter 15) in the decades following World War II.

Carl Jung left an important legacy to psychology. His theory of psychological types was a major early contribution to the field, and a number of personality tests in common use today, such as the Myers-Briggs Type Indicator, are based on his theory. The theoretical aspects of analytical psychology, with mystical concepts such as collective unconscious, archetypes, and synchronicity, are often criticized by those who prefer a more rational approach to psychology. Nevertheless, Jungian psychotherapy, with its goal of individuation, is still widely practiced today.

Second Generation

As the psychoanalytic movement grew, members of Freud's inner circle took on students of their own, and thus arose the second generation of psychoanalysts. One of Freud's most faithful colleagues was Karl Abraham, who mentored two important woman psychoanalysts, Melanie Klein and Karen Horney. Perhaps because they didn't have a direct relationship with Freud, they felt no need to be loyal to his ideas, challenging his theory and reshaping it according to their own perspectives. It was also significant that they were women, and they offered an alternative worldview to the male-centric framework that Freud propounded.

Karl Abraham

As a young physician at the Burghölzli, **Karl Abraham** (1877–1925) learned about Freud's psychoanalytic theory from his supervisor, Carl Jung (Astor, 2003). However, Jung quickly grew to greatly dislike Abraham, whose cool demeanor and apparent lack of empathy for his patients made him a poor analyst in Jung's opinion. The relationship was completely ruptured the following year when Abraham openly challenged Jung's physiological theory of schizophrenia at an international conference. Nevertheless, Freud found Abraham to be a useful ally. Abraham remained loyal to Freud's theory, spending his short career studying the dynamics of the oral phase of development. As a result, Karl Abraham became known as the *German psychoanalyst who laid the groundwork for object-relations theory.*

Photo 7.6
Karl Abraham

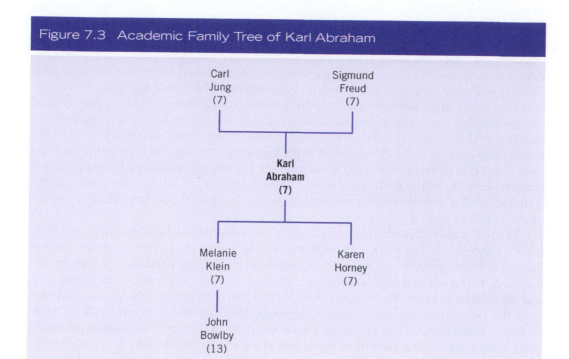

Figure 7.3 Academic Family Tree of Karl Abraham

```
   Carl              Sigmund
   Jung               Freud
   (7)                 (7)
     └────────┬─────────┘
              │
            Karl
           Abraham
            (7)
     ┌────────┴─────────┐
  Melanie             Karen
   Klein              Horney
   (7)                 (7)
     │
   John
  Bowlby
   (13)
```

Abraham presented himself as calm and unemotional, but it was only a façade he'd built to hide the depression that plagued him for his entire life (Robinson, 2017). Thus, it comes as no surprise that the thrust of his research was toward an understanding of the origin of depression. While Abraham remained true to Freud's drive theory, he emphasized the fact that these drives were directed at particular objects. Freud used the term *object* to refer to any person that the infant interacted with, particularly its mother. Abraham saw hatred and aggression as unavoidable aspects of the infant's psyche in its relation with its caregiver, who could never meet all of its demands. Furthermore, he speculated that repeated frustration in getting its needs met could then lead to depression in adulthood.

By suggesting that the root of adult neurosis lay in the first year of life, Abraham set the foundation for **object-relations theory** (Kunstreich, 2014). This is *the proposal that relationships with significant others in infancy shape patterns of relating in adulthood.* Abraham died at the young age of 52, and it's unclear how he would have developed this theory had he lived longer. The term *object relations* itself isn't even his, but rather it's a name that was chosen by the next generation of psychoanalysts who expanded Abraham's germ of an idea into a well-developed theory (Figure 7.3). Among those who Abraham most directly influenced were two women psychoanalysts who would leave a major impact on the field in the middle decades of the twentieth century—Melanie Klein and Karen Horney—and we turn to their stories next.

Melanie Klein

A series of mother-daughter conflicts extending at least three generations characterized the life of **Melanie Klein** (1882–1960; Donaldson, 1998). Her meddling mother destroyed her marriage, and her neurotic daughter nearly ruined her career. Small wonder then that she spent her adult life studying the effects of the mother-infant relationship on personality formation. With her pioneering efforts in child psychoanalysis, Melanie Klein built her reputation as the *Austrian-British psychoanalyst known for her development of object-relations theory.*

Photo 7.7
Melanie Klein

Klein was born in Vienna and dreamed of going to medical school, but family poverty led her to the financial security of an early marriage instead, and she moved to Budapest to follow her husband's career (Donaldson, 1998). Yet she struggled in her roles as middle-class housewife and mother, and she spent much of her married life in and out of various sanatoriums, where she took treatments for neurasthenia. This meant her home was dominated by her mother, who seemed to derive meaning in life from tending to the needs of her grandchildren and son-in-law. Klein was racked by conflicting feelings of love and hate after her mother's death, and she sought psychoanalysis with Sándor Ferenczi (1873–1933), a disciple of Freud's. She responded well to the treatment, and she also read up on Freudian theory, so Ferenczi recommended that she practice psychoanalysis as well by analyzing her own children. By 1919, Klein had gathered enough data to publish her first paper, which qualified her for membership in the Hungarian Psycho-Analytic Society. Thus began her career as a child analyst.

The following year, Klein met Karl Abraham at an international conference (Donaldson, 1998). Impressed by her work with child analysis, he invited her to join the Berlin Psycho-Analytical Society, where her caseload included the children of colleagues. Abraham was interested in the role of conflict during the oral phase in the development of adult neuroses, and Klein's data from her observations of young children corroborated his findings garnered from the recollections of adult patients. Although Abraham fully supported Klein's techniques of analyzing children during play sessions, most of their male colleagues dismissed child analysis as nothing more than the hobby of an uneducated housewife. However, her fellow female colleagues in Berlin, including Karen Horney, held far more favorable views of her work.

It was during the decade she spent in Berlin with Abraham that Klein refined her method of engaging in play with children as a psychoanalytic technique (Rustin, 2016). Obviously, she couldn't use adult methods such as free association and dream analysis, which required a level of linguistic skill beyond the abilities of two- and three-year-olds. But she believed that children acted out their fantasies during play, and so this could be used as a way of exploring their unconscious dynamics. She gave the children drawing materials or toys to play with, and then she interpreted their productions. When she explained the hidden meanings behind these behaviors, she found the children sometimes responded with understanding and found relief from their anxieties.

During her years in Berlin, Klein also developed a reputation as a revolutionary theorist (Donaldson, 1998). In particular, she challenged the timeline of personality formation during the early stages of psychosexual development. According to the standard Freudian theory, the superego embodying the child's sense of morality emerges with the resolution of the Oedipus complex around three to five years of age. However, Klein argued for an *infantile superego* that preceded the Oedipus complex. In Klein's view, this infantile superego came into being as young children create a fantasy-based mental representation of their mother, which she called an *internal object*. Because the id can never be fully satisfied, children harbor hateful thoughts and destructive wishes against their caregivers, and the infantile superego encapsulates their guilty feelings and their fear of being punished for having these fantasies. Thus, her therapeutic goal was to loosen the strictures of this infantile superego to relieve the inhibitions and anxieties these children experienced.

By daring to challenge Freudian orthodoxy, Klein earned the enmity of her colleagues, both in Berlin and in Vienna, the two major centers of psychoanalysis on the European continent (Donaldson, 1998). In Berlin, Abraham played the diplomat, arguing for an open exchange of ideas as a means for driving psychoanalysis forward as a science. But the Viennese attack was spearheaded by a relative newcomer with a powerful ally—Freud's youngest daughter, Anna. Rejecting both the theory and the method that Klein had proposed, Anna Freud argued instead for a more conservative approach to child psychoanalysis that hewed close to her father's theory and was based on educational rather than therapeutic interactions. She also dismissed the notion that young children could even understand, let alone benefit from, psychoanalytic interpretations of their own unconscious thoughts. As long as hundreds of miles separated the two women, their catfight was limited to pointed exchanges in journals and at conferences. Much later, they would find themselves living in the same city as members of the same psychoanalytic society, and as World War II raged around them, the battle between Melanie Klein and Anna Freud shook psychoanalysis to its foundations.

When Abraham died suddenly at the end of 1925, Klein found herself in a difficult situation, as the bulk of her colleagues lined up with Anna Freud against her (Donaldson, 1998). Around this same time, however, she found a new source of support in Ernest Jones (1879–1958), then president of the British Psychoanalytical Society (BPS). Unlike Klein's colleagues on the continent, British psychoanalysts were enthralled with her theory of early childhood psychodynamics as well as with her play method of psychotherapy. Jones invited her to set up practice in London and join the BPS, and she quickly rose through the ranks as one of its leaders.

Klein spent the rest of her life in London, where she further developed her theory of personality formation during the first few years of life (Long, Clarkson, Rockwell, & Zeavin, 2015). In her 1952 book *The Origins of Transference*, Klein emphasizes that the child is in a primary object relationship with its mother. In other words, the child's interactions with its caregiver over the first years not only serve as the center of life in early childhood but also shape the child's personality for the rest of its life. However, the object from the child's point of view isn't the mother as she really is, but rather it's a fantasy image as the child perceives her. In its simple black-white thinking, the child at first can't understand its mother as a person with both positive and negative qualities, and so it splits its fantasy image of her into two parts, one that is all good and another that is all evil. In healthy development, the child eventually reconciles its ambivalent feelings, but not so in the neurotic adult. Insight for this theory no doubt came from the contradictory emotions that Klein experienced at the death of her mother and that she worked out in analysis with Sándor Ferenczi in Budapest.

Late in her career, Klein turned her attention to the question of envy (Hunt, 2018; Likierman, 2008). In her 1957 paper "Envy and Gratitude," she distinguished the three concepts of greed, jealousy, and envy. Whereas greed is an insatiable desire to possess what you don't already have, jealousy is the fear of losing something good that you already have. In either case, the desire is to either obtain or maintain what's good for yourself. But envy is a different type of experience. Like greed, it's a desire to have something good, but if you can't have it, you then want to destroy it so no one else can enjoy it either. Klein also emphasized the fact that envy, unlike greed or jealousy, is always directed at a specific individual with whom you have a meaningful relationship. Klein believed that envy originated in the infantile defense mechanism of black-white splitting as an attempt to resolve the infant's ambivalent feelings toward its mother.

Klein's insight regarding envy may have derived from her conflict-ridden relationship with her daughter Melitta (Shapira, 2017). Following in her mother's footsteps, Melitta also became a psychoanalyst. In her early adulthood, Melitta was an ardent supporter of her mother in her ongoing battle against Anna Freud. But in the mid-1930s, Melitta entered into treatment with the prominent analyst Edward Glover, and it's generally believed they became lovers. Glover had also initially been a Klein supporter, but the two suddenly switched to an alliance with Anna Freud instead. Melitta made public statements against her mother that were both highly critical and highly personal. In response, Klein defended herself by branding Melitta as a mentally ill person who was pathologically lashing out against her mother, and she also damaged Glover's reputation with accusations of impropriety. In the end, the BPS sided with Klein, and the careers of both Melitta and Glover were destroyed. You as the reader can discern for yourself the dynamics of envy and destruction that played out in this mother-daughter confrontation.

Melanie Klein's legacy to psychology is enormous (Donaldson, 2000). For one thing, her theorizing on infantile defense mechanisms such as black-white splitting shed light on a condition now known as borderline personality disorder. But even more importantly, her development of object-relations theory lay the groundwork for attachment theory after World War II. First proposed by her student John Bowlby (Chapter 13), attachment theory has become by far the most widely accepted explanation of social and personality development since the last decades of the twentieth century. Without doubt, Klein's most enduring contribution to developmental psychology is shifting the focus from the individual child to the child within an intensely emotional relationship with its caregiver.

Karen Horney

When she promised in writing that it was the last thing she'd ever ask of him, her aging sea-captain father grudgingly agreed to pay her expenses for medical school (Garrison, 1981). Still, those student years weren't easy for **Karen Horney** (1885–1952, pronounced *HORN-eye*). She fell in love with and married a young lawyer, and she gave birth to all three of her children while still in school. But she finally earned her medical degree from the University of Berlin and decided she wanted to practice psychoanalysis, so she underwent training with Karl Abraham. While her career flourished, her marriage floundered, eventually ending in divorce. Although Horney never remarried, she openly took on a series of male lovers over the course of her life, flaunting the conventions of the day by acting as a sexually liberated woman. Today, she's known as the *German-American psychoanalyst who was a pioneer in feminist psychology*.

During the 1920s in Berlin, Horney developed a reputation as an outspoken critic of Freudian views on female psychology and personality development (Eckhardt, 2005). One of the first tenets that she attacked was the concept of **penis envy**. This was *Freud's contention that women naturally feel inferior to men because they know they lack a penis*. In support of Freud, her mentor Abraham published an essay on what he called the *castration complex*, in which women supposedly become psychologically damaged by the thought that their penis had been taken from them. In her cheeky reply, Horney freely admitted that women envied men for their penises. After all, penises are convenient for urination, and they make masturbation easier as well. However, it wasn't the lack of a penis that psychologically damaged women, but instead it was their cruel subjugation by men from an early age that was so mentally harmful to them. And why did men oppress women? Because they feared them! This was because they knew, deep down, that they couldn't bear children of their own. With no natural outlet for their creative urges, men instead pursued careers to leave their mark on posterity—a poor substitute for childbirth.

In her 1926 article "Flight From Womanhood," Horney argued that the psychology of women up to that time had been presented from a male point of view (Smith, 2007). Since men were describing women, it was obviously biased and inaccurate, more a collection of male fantasies and desires rather than an accurate depiction of feminine mentality. In particular, she challenged the received wisdom that women were merely passive receptacles of reproduction, insisting instead that they had strong sex drives just as men did. While it was true that many women acted submissive toward men and showed little interest in sex, this was only because they were following the cultural scripts that had been fed to them since they were young. She also expressed her doubts that marriage could ever lead to long-term happiness for either the husband or the wife, as it restricted the sexual freedom of both, especially the woman. At best, marriage offered a compromise arrangement that offered economic security at the cost of personal fulfillment. Given that her own marriage had just failed, it's no wonder she had a negative attitude about the institution, but in later writings she continued to point out the shortcomings of the romantic notion of marriage that most people entertained.

A final attack on the Freudian view of female psychology was Horney's 1932 article, "The Dread of Woman" (Garrison, 1981). In this essay, she turned Freudian theory upside down. It's not women who are psychologically damaged on account of their sex, she insisted. Rather, it's the men who are mentally wounded by the cultural scripts of masculinity that they've internalized. For instance, in every sexual act the man has to contend with the anxiety of not being able to maintain an erection. Since he sees sexual conquest as the defining feature of masculinity, he equates the loss of an erection with the loss of his manhood. Women, on the contrary, are ready for sex whenever they want it,

Photo 7.8
Karen Horney

and every sexual act they willingly engage in is a confirmation of their femininity. Men intuitively know this, so when they compare themselves with women they feel physically inferior.

Horney was one of the most renowned of the women psychoanalysts in the 1920s (Garrison, 1981). She was also an intelligent and engaging writer, so her ideas had to be taken seriously. In particular, she represented a new wave of feminism that was sweeping across the industrialized world, one that demanded not only political and economic equality but sexual freedom as well. Thus, she represented a major threat to the male-dominated world of psychoanalysis, and it was clear to her that any attempt to advance her career would be stymied. In particular, she hoped for an academic position, which she had little chance of obtaining in the German-speaking world. So she began looking for opportunities in the New World, and when she was offered the position of associate director at the Chicago Psychoanalytic Institute in 1932, she gladly accepted it.

Although Horney had hoped her new American colleagues would be more open to her revolutionary ideas, this was not to be the case (Eckhardt, 2005). She left Chicago after two years because of a falling out with the director. She accepted a position at the New York Psychoanalytic Institute, and she also taught at the New School for Social Research, where she was a popular lecturer. At the New School, she continued to challenge Freudian dogma, but she turned her attention away from feminine psychology, instead focusing on the development and treatment of neurosis. This line of research led to the publication of her book *New Ways in Psychoanalysis* in 1939. Her radical ideas again rankled her male colleagues, and in 1941 she was expelled from the New York Psychoanalytic Institute. This time, however, a group of loyal followers walked out with her, and together they formed the American Institute for Psychoanalysis, where she remained until her death in 1952.

Horney laid out her ideas on psychological illness and health most clearly in her 1950 book *Neurosis and Growth* (Gudan, 2008). Rejecting Freud's drive theory, which proposed that the life and death instincts of the id determined human behavior, Horney maintained instead that children are motivated by their need for emotional security (Figure 7.4). When they receive this security within a loving and nurturing family, they grow into psychologically healthy adults. But if they're neglected or abused, they become emotionally insecure, a state she called **basic anxiety**. This is *Horney's term for a profound feeling of isolation and helplessness in an uncaring world.* To cope with this basic anxiety, children adopt one of three stances. In the *compliant* stance, they seek security through ingratiating themselves with others; in the *aggressive* stance, they bully others to avoid being hurt themselves, and in the *withdrawn stance* they isolate themselves to protect themselves from harm. In any case, they've come to the conclusion that they're incapable of receiving the love they desire, at least if they present their true selves to others, so instead they fabricate an ideal self as a façade.

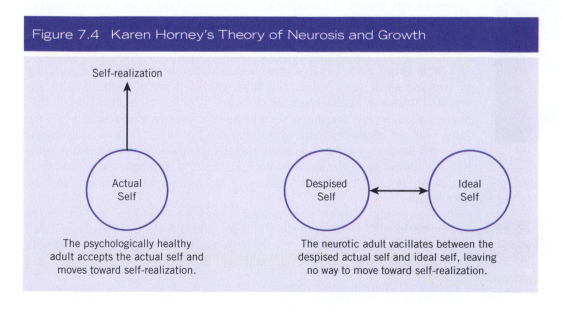

Figure 7.4 Karen Horney's Theory of Neurosis and Growth

Self-realization

Actual Self

The psychologically healthy adult accepts the actual self and moves toward self-realization.

Despised Self

Ideal Self

The neurotic adult vacillates between the despised actual self and ideal self, leaving no way to move toward self-realization.

For Horney, then, the origin of neurosis in adulthood is emotional insecurity in early childhood (Gudan, 2008). Neurotic adults bring forward the coping stances of their early years, and these have now become highly fixed patterns of behavior. Furthermore, they've fully internalized the ideal self they created in a bid for love, but this only generates further anxiety because they hold themselves to standards that are impossible to attain. This leads to the **tyranny of the shoulds**, which is *Horney's term for the tension between the real and the ideal self.* In other words, the ideal self is a set of beliefs about how you should be, as opposed to an honest understanding of who you actually are, that is, the real self.

Since neurotic adults despise the real self, they vacillate between it and the ideal self, which cannot be achieved (Gudan, 2008). Thus, they have no room for personal growth. In contrast, psychologically healthy adults accept the real self as it is, and thus they have room for a kind of personal growth she calls self-realization. The goal of therapy, then, is to help patients understand the impossibility of the ideal self and to relieve them of the anxiety generated by the tyranny of the shoulds. Once they've come to an acceptance of the real self, they can start making decisions in life based not on the need to alleviate anxiety but rather on rational plans for personal growth.

Karen Horney's legacy to psychology is threefold. First, she was a pioneer in feminist psychology who challenged the male-centric norms of the early twentieth century. Although her ideas about the nature of female sexuality and the role of culture in shaping gender identity are widely accepted today, they were radical at the time. Second, her views on the importance of emotional security in early childhood and its lasting effects into adulthood presaged key aspects of attachment theory, which was being independently developed by John Bowlby (Chapter 13) at around the same time. And third, her approach to psychotherapy influenced the thinking of humanistic psychologists such as Carl Rogers and Abraham Maslow (Chapter 15), who emphasized the importance of personal growth and what they called self-actualization. In these three respects, Karen Horney served as a transitional figure who helped guide modern psychology into its current form.

Anna Freud

Sigmund Freud needed an heir to lead the psychoanalysis movement after he was gone. But that person had to remain true to his theory, and both Adler and Jung had dared to question his authority. In the end, he found his successor right at home. His youngest child, Anna, often played on the floor during her father's meetings with his colleagues, so she grew up listening to discussions of psychoanalytic theory. She was her father's favorite child, completely devoted to him during his life and after his death. As Sigmund Freud's hand-picked successor, **Anna Freud** (1895–1982) developed a reputation as an *Austrian-British psychoanalyst who conducted pioneering research on early childhood development.*

Anna Freud made her first contribution to psychoanalysis at the early age of two-and-a-half years, when her father included some of the dreams she reported to him in his *Interpretation of Dreams* (Cohler & Galatzer-Levy, 2008). She attended her first meeting of the Vienna Psychoanalytic Society in 1918, the same year she began her training analysis with her father. Four years later, she delivered her first paper at the Society, thereby qualifying for membership. Anna had also trained as an elementary school teacher, and she applied psychoanalytic concepts to the classroom. Her publications were well received among educators, and she was popular as a lecturer.

Anna Freud also conducted direct observations of preschool children, and she established a daycare center in 1927 for this purpose (Midgley, 2007). Sigmund Freud had called for observational studies to corroborate his theory of psychosexual stages. But Anna Freud was one of the first psychoanalysts to observe childhood development in a consistent and systematic manner.

**Photo 7.9
Anna Freud**

In 1927, the American divorcée **Dorothy Burlingham** (1891–1979) arrived at Sigmund Freud's office, seeking help for her eldest son, a school-aged boy with behavioral problems (Young-Bruehl, 2004). She'd had a difficult marriage. After Burlingham left her unstable husband, she took their four children with her to Europe, hoping psychoanalysis could heal their emotional wounds. All four of her children underwent psychoanalysis, and she even underwent a training analysis with Sigmund Freud. Dorothy and Anna became intimate partners, and Sigmund Freud treated the Burlingham children as his own grandchildren. Thus, Burlingham became known as an *American psychoanalyst and partner of Anna Freud who studied early childhood development.*

Working together, Anna Freud and Dorothy Burlingham led a group of women psychoanalysts who were interested in direct observations of infant and childhood development as well as relationships between mothers and children (Young-Bruehl, 2004). Burlingham also assisted Anna Freud in her research at her daycare center, and later they opened a second one that specialized in daycare for children of poor working mothers. In addition, Burlingham developed a reputation for her work with blind children. The two women had an intense working relationship as well as a deeply emotional personal life together, and they remained life partners until Burlingham's death.

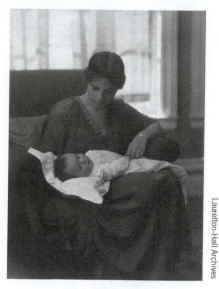

Photo 7.10
Dorothy Burlingham

Laurelton-Hall Archives

Defense Mechanisms

Meanwhile, the storm clouds of war were spreading across Europe. Hitler had come to power in Germany in 1933, and many Austrians supported him. It was during these tense years that Anna Freud produced her most important book.

In her 1936 work *The Ego and the Mechanisms of Defense*, Anna Freud extended her father's theory in significant ways (Midgley, 2007). First, she pointed out that the workings of the ego could be observed directly, as opposed to those of the id, which could only be inferred through analysis. And since the ego was the intermediary between the drives of the id and the facts of reality, much could be learned by observing a person's *unconscious responses to anxiety-provoking situations.* Sigmund Freud had mentioned these **defense mechanisms** in various writings, but Anna Freud catalogued them, describing their characteristics in more detail. She enumerated ten defense mechanisms altogether, but the following five are the most common:

- *Repression:* forcing unwanted feelings below the level of consciousness. For example, Alice is a married woman who's infatuated with another man but denies any interest in him.

- *Regression:* falling back to a less mature state that feels safer. Alice flirts with the other man, but only in a silly, childish manner so she can deny any real interest in him.

- *Projection:* denying unwanted feelings in one's self and attributing them to another person instead. Alice denies she's in love with the other man but accuses her husband of infidelity.

- *Reaction formation:* behaving in a manner that's opposite of one's true feelings. Alice tries to overcome her infatuation with the other man by being especially attentive to her husband.

- *Sublimation:* expressing unwanted feelings in socially acceptable ways. Alice remains faithful to her husband but writes romance novels so she can vicariously act out her fantasies.

These concepts are common fare in introductory textbooks and the self-help literature.

**Photo 7.11
Sigmund and Anna Freud**

During the 1930s, Sigmund Freud's health was in decline (Lacoursiere, 2008). His cigar habit had led to cancer of the mouth, and he endured many painful surgeries. Anna was drawn into the role of her father's primary caretaker, even though she was at the height of her professional career. In March 1938, the German army invaded Austria, and the Freud family homeland was absorbed into the Third Reich. With the intercession of friends in England, Sigmund Freud and his immediate family were granted permission to emigrate. If they had not done so, they would have surely died in the concentration camps, as did many of their relatives. By the time they were settled in England, Sigmund Freud's health had worsened, and he'd lost the will to live. Anna was now his constant companion. Knowing the end was near, he asked his doctor for a dose of morphine that would stop all his suffering forever. And thus the father of psychoanalysis came to the end of his life.

Although the Freud family had escaped persecution in their homeland, they soon faced the horrors of war in their new country. For eight straight months in 1940–1941, the Germans bombed London and other British cities in what became known as the Blitz. Although the British successfully resisted the attack, tens of thousands of civilians lost their lives, and many children were orphaned. Anna Freud and Dorothy Burlingham decided to do their part by opening the Hampstead Nurseries, which housed over 80 children for the duration of the war (Midgley, 2007). The nurseries also served as a natural experiment in which Freud and Burlingham could study the effects of parental loss on young children. They trained the nurses to keep detailed records of the children under their care. One of the first significant findings was the observation that providing for the children's material needs wasn't sufficient for their development. Rather, the emotional trauma of losing their parents was even more detrimental than the stress of daily air raids. Within a year, Freud and Burlingham had reorganized the nursery into artificial families, with each nurse having sole responsibility for no more than five children. Once these children formed attachments to their new "mothers," their emotional health improved rapidly.

Controversial Discussions

In the late 1920s, Anna Freud and Melanie Klein began taking potshots at each other in their publications (Shapira, 2017). The two had differing views on how to approach child psychoanalysis, and yet each believed her methodology was more faithful to Freudian theory. Klein kept psychoanalytic sessions with children as close as possible to the format used with adults, but Anna Freud insisted they needed to be more nurturing and educational because of the children's immaturity. In a sense, Klein was staying true to Freud's theory in word, but Anna had her father's full support in practice. As long as they lived in different cities, the quarrel was limited to psychoanalytic journals, but now that Anna Freud had relocated to London, the two enemies started vying for power within the same professional society.

As the Blitz drew to a close, a conflict within the BPS came to a head (Robinson, 2015). Over the years, British psychoanalysis had evolved away from the Viennese model. Its membership was largely Protestant rather than Jewish, and British psychoanalysts tended to favor Melanie Klein's approach over that of Sigmund and Anna Freud. With the rise of Nazism, many Jewish psychoanalysts on the continent had fled to Great Britain, and this created tensions within the BPS. The influx of foreign analysts threatened the livelihoods of British practitioners, and latent anti-Semitism was also an underlying issue, as were interpersonal conflicts within the BPS.

Thus began the **Controversial Discussions**, *a series of meetings of the British Psychoanalytic Society in the early 1940s that pitted supporters of Anna Freud and Melanie Klein against each other* (Robinson, 2015). The continental analysts generally sided with Freud, and most British members favored Klein, although some were sympathetic to Freud (Robinson, 2017). Eventually, the BPS reached a compromise that allowed for three divisions, one for the Freudians, a second for the Kleinians, and a third for those who wished to remain independent. While this kept the BPS from falling apart, tensions remained high well into the 1970s—that is, until all the members who'd taken part in the Controversial Discussions had passed away.

Figure 7.5   Academic Family Tree of Anna Freud

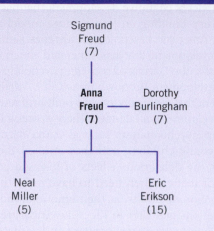

In hindsight, the differences between Anna Freud and Melanie Klein weren't as great as they appeared at the time. Later in her career, Klein became known for her work on object-relations theory, which emphasized the impact that relationships with significant others in infancy had on the formation of adult personality. Anna Freud was also keenly aware of the importance of mother-infant bonds on emotional development, but her theoretical approach was somewhat different. At any rate, both Anna Freud and Melanie Klein laid the groundwork for modern attachment theory, which was developed after World War II. Furthermore, they both emphasized the importance of observing children directly, thus setting the stage for an experimental approach to developmental psychology.

After the war, Anna Freud expanded the Hampstead Nurseries into the Hampstead Clinic, with the dual purpose of conducting developmental research and helping children with psychological problems. In 1982, the clinic was renamed the Anna Freud Centre. Today, it's one of the leading institutes devoted to child research, a fitting tribute to one of the pioneers of developmental psychology (Figure 7.5).

Looking Ahead

Psychoanalysis was both a theory of the origins of psychological disorders and also a principled approach to treating psychological disorders. As such, it's generally considered the first well-developed approach to psychotherapy. By the middle decades of the twentieth century, psychoanalysis as a movement had spread widely across Europe, North America, and other parts of the world. At the same time, it spawned a large number of splinter groups whose adherents offered alternative interpretations of Freudian theory and who bickered bitterly with members of other groups. Nevertheless, the idea that psychological disorders could be treated with some form of talk therapy became more broadly accepted, both among psychologists and the general public. In this sense, all subsequent approaches to psychotherapy can be viewed either as derivatives of psychoanalysis or else as reactions to it.

However, psychoanalysis was more than just a theory of psychopathology and an approach to psychotherapy. As we've already seen, many of the neo-behaviorists in the middle decades of the twentieth century attempted to incorporate Freudian concepts into their theories of learning. Beyond that, the influence of psychoanalysis can still be seen in many of the modern disciplines of psychology. This is because psychoanalysis was also a theory of normal human development, particularly in terms of personality and social relationships.

A case in point is Freud's theory of psychosexual stages. Even when developmental psychologists have taken issue with some of Freud's premises, they've also recognized the usefulness of conceptualizing development in terms of milestones or stages. The Swiss psychologist Jean Piaget (Chapter 8), who was strongly influenced by Freudian theory early in his career, proposed a stage model of cognitive development that has dominated the field of child psychology for half a century. Building on Piaget's stage model and his early work in moral thinking in childhood, the American psychologist Lawrence Kohlberg (Chapter 15) proposed a stage model of moral development that has generated much debate but also much more research on the topic. Finally, the German-American psychologist Erik Erikson (Chapter 15) extended the concept of development "from womb to tomb," delineating an eight-stage model of psychosocial development that incorporated and built on Freud's psychosexual stages.

Within the field of development, attachment theory owes a great debt to psychoanalysis. Second-generation women psychoanalysts such as Anna Freud and Melanie Klein made detailed observations of young children, and they studied their developing relationships with caregivers as well as the deleterious effects of losing a caregiver in early childhood. These studies made it clear that children need to have more than just their physical needs met to grow into well-functioning adults, as their emotional bonds with caregivers provide them with models for relationships later in life. Like Anna Freud, the British psychologist John Bowlby (Chapter 13) worked with war orphans and witnessed firsthand the devastating effect this emotional loss had on their social development. In the decades after World War II, Bowlby and his collaborator Mary Ainsworth (Chapter 13) built and tested attachment theory, one of the most important models of social development in the field. Around this same time, the American psychologist Harry Harlow (Chapter 10) was providing empirical support for attachment theory with his studies of monkeys raised in isolation.

Researchers in the field of personality also owe a debt to psychoanalysis. Today, Freud's dynamic theory of personality, with its three interacting components of id, ego, and superego, seems rather odd. However, Carl Jung's typology was a clear precursor to current trait theories of personality. The Myers-Briggs, a personality test widely used in counseling as well as in industrial and organizational psychology, is based on Jung's typology. Furthermore, Jung's personality types show obvious similarities to the traits of the Big Five model, today's most widely accepted theory of personality.

Finally, we need to point out the rise of humanistic psychology after World War II, which brought the striving of individuals to the forefront. Humanistic psychology was seen as a "third force" to counter the behaviorist rejection of the mind and the psychoanalytic emphasis on the dark side of human nature. With its roots in Ancient Greek philosophy, humanistic psychology asked the age-old question: "What is the nature of a good life?" Although hopes that humanistic psychology would become the leading discipline within the field never materialized, the approach has morphed over the decades into positive psychology, which employs scientific methods to understand the requirements for living a happy and fulfilling life.

Sigmund Freud has often been criticized for building complex theories that extend far beyond what a reasonable interpretation of the data would allow. However, it's also important to understand that many of the concepts we associate with Freud weren't original to him. Rather, Freud was highly attuned to the ideas that were current at the time, which he then assembled into a coherent theory. He was also a very ambitious man who promoted these ideas vigorously to promote his career. In the end, Freud's ideas are more compelling when considered within the sociocultural context in which they were developed rather than viewing them as a universal description of the human condition.

CHAPTER SUMMARY

Around the turn of the twentieth century, Sigmund Freud developed a psychotherapy for treating neurotic patients based on methods he'd learned from Jean-Martin Charcot, Pierre Janet, and Josef Breuer, among others. He also used reports from his patients to develop theories about the origins of psychological disorders as well as the development of personality. Theory and therapy as a whole were known as psychoanalysis. Freud had many disciples, among whom the most influential were Alfred Adler and Carl Jung. Eventually, both men broke away from Freud, developing their own versions of psychoanalytic theory. Among the second generation were a number of influential women psychologists, including Sigmund Freud's daughter Anna Freud, as well as Melanie Klein and Karen Horney. Although Anna Freud and Melanie Klein were bitter rivals, they both made important contributions to the study of child development. By the middle decades of the twentieth century, the psychoanalytic movement had spread through Europe and North America, extending even to developing regions of the world, such as Japan.

DISCUSSION QUESTIONS

1. Hysteria was a common disorder in Freud's time, but it's no longer recognized as one today. Why might the incidence of psychological disorders depend on the culture of a society or time period?

2. Even if you don't buy into Freudian theory, why might techniques like hypnosis, free association, and dream interpretation still be useful in psychotherapy?

3. Modern development psychology proposes that both boys and girls form a deep emotional attachment with their mothers. Explain why the Oedipus complex is difficult to reconcile with attachment theory.

4. Contrast Adler's individual psychology with Freud's psychoanalysis. Why is Adler's approach considered to be a form of depth psychology?

5. What does Adler mean when he says people don't "have" psychological disorders? Defend your position for or against this view.

6. Jung proposed eight psychological types. However, the Myers-Briggs Type Indicator, which is based on Jung's theory, specifies sixteen personality types. Research the MBTI to find out how it expanded Jung's typology.

7. The Big Five model of personality has some overlap with Jung's typology. Research the Big Five to find the similarities and differences between it and Jung's theory.

8. Compare and contrast Freud's and Jung's theories of the structure of the mind.

9. Anna Freud was criticized for having received her training analysis from her father. Evaluate the positive and negative aspects of this situation.

10. Assemble your own examples of the five listed defense mechanisms, drawing from everyday life, movies, or other sources.

11. The first generation of psychoanalysts all had medical degrees, but many in the second generation, such as Anna Freud and Melanie Klein, did not. Do you think you can be an effective psychoanalyst without medical training? Defend your position.

12. Karen Horney was one of the first psychologists to emphasize the role of culture in shaping gender roles and gender identity. Consider some of the ways that culture has this effect.

ON THE WEB

The works of Sigmund Freud are now in the public domain and are posted on various sites on the internet. The website www.sigmundfreud.net has an excellent collection of his works in English translation. You can also search **Carl Jung** on YouTube to find an interview he made with the BBC in 1959. Some online streaming services host the movie *A Dangerous Method* (Thomas & Cronenberg, 2011), which portrays the troubled relationship between Carl Jung and Sigmund Freud in a compelling and reasonably accurate fashion. However, much of the film is devoted to an alleged affair between Jung and Sabina Spielrein, whom we'll meet in Chapter 9. Historians have challenged the accuracy of this part of the movie, so keep a critical mind as you watch the film.

French Psychology

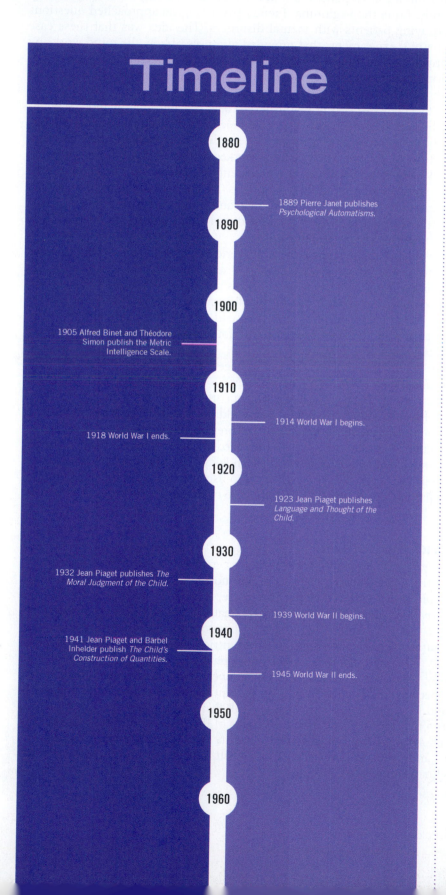

Timeline

- 1880
- 1889 Pierre Janet publishes *Psychological Automatisms.*
- 1890
- 1900
- 1905 Alfred Binet and Théodore Simon publish the Metric Intelligence Scale.
- 1910
- 1914 World War I begins.
- 1918 World War I ends.
- 1920
- 1923 Jean Piaget publishes *Language and Thought of the Child.*
- 1930
- 1932 Jean Piaget publishes *The Moral Judgment of the Child.*
- 1939 World War II begins.
- 1940
- 1941 Jean Piaget and Bärbel Inhelder publish *The Child's Construction of Quantities.*
- 1945 World War II ends.
- 1950
- 1960

Learning Objectives

After reading this chapter, you should be able to:

- Discuss the impact Jean-Martin Charcot and Pierre Janet had as mentors to many of Europe's great psychologists of the twentieth century.

- Explain how Alfred Binet's earlier research in psychology led to an interest in intelligence testing.

- Assess Jean Piaget's role as a focal point in psychology, considering both those who influenced him and those he influenced.

- Discuss the contributions of some of Piaget's key students.

Looking Back

In Germany and North America, the approach to scientific psychology was experimental from the start. Psychologists observed humans or animals engaged in specific tasks, from which they either inferred underlying mental processes, or else they sought correlations between stimuli and responses. But in the French-speaking world, psychology developed differently. From the beginning, French psychologists approached questions of the mind by studying patients with mental disorders. The idea was that these case studies provided natural experiments that provided glimpses of how the mind works by showing what happens when things go wrong. Even when French-speaking psychologists began adopting experimental methods, the clinical tradition was still evident in their work.

Psychology in the French-speaking world never coalesced into one or more schools, each with its own theoretical approach and prescribed methods. Instead, French psychology remained eclectic both in theory and in practice. Nevertheless, French-speaking psychologists around the turn of the twentieth century worked within a highly interconnected intellectual network, and mutual influences are evident in their work. Furthermore, the reach of this nexus spread well beyond French borders. In fact, two of the most important psychologists of the twentieth century, Sigmund Freud and Jean Piaget, spent time in France during their formative years and were greatly influenced in their thinking and methodology by the French psychologists who mentored them.

The story of psychology in the French-speaking world begins with Jean-Martin Charcot, who mentored many of the other psychologists we'll read about in this chapter. And as we learned in the last chapter, Charcot's most famous student was Sigmund Freud, who incorporated many of his mentor's ideas into his psychoanalytic theory. We then move on to Charcot's other two most noted students, Pierre Janet and Alfred Binet. Although these two men are not as well known today, they each had a profound impact on the development of psychology in the early twentieth century.

Our story then concludes with a visit to Jean Piaget, the French-speaking Swiss psychologist whose stage theory of cognitive development is so well known. As a student of Janet, Piaget used a mixture of clinical and experimental methods to probe the thought processes of children. Psychologists from around the world flocked to Piaget's research center to work with him, and through collaborations with scores of colleagues, research assistants, and graduate students, Piaget amassed the data he needed to support his theory. Without a doubt, Piaget is one of the pillars of modern psychology. His ideas not only gave developmental psychology the shape it has today, they also ushered in the cognitive revolution, which dominated psychology during the last half of the twentieth century.

Hysteria and Hypnosis

In the last half of the nineteenth century, one of the most advanced facilities in the world for treating psychological disorders was the Salpêtrière, a famous mental hospital in Paris (pronounced *SAL-pet-tree-AIR*). There, patients were treated humanely, and serious attempts were made to cure them. It also boasted a major laboratory for the study of neurological disorders, and it attracted researchers from many countries, including the young Sigmund Freud (Chapter 7). The Salpêtrière was a research hospital, and two important founders of French psychology, Jean-Martin Charcot and Pierre Janet, spent their careers there. These two men were especially interested in hysteria, investigating both its causes and its possible cures. Charcot and Janet developed early forms of talk therapy, and they also experimented with hypnosis as a tool for understanding the origins of the disorder. Furthermore, all the rest of the French-speaking psychologists we'll meet in this chapter are academic descendants of Charcot and Janet, and so we start in the late nineteenth century when French psychology was first getting started.

Jean-Martin Charcot

The world-renowned neurologist Jean-Martin Charcot (1825–1893; pronounced *shar-KOH*) directed the Salpêtrière during the last decades of the nineteenth century (Kumar, Aslinia, Yale, & Mazza, 2011). Charcot was a physical monist who insisted that all psychological disorders were due to disruptions in the functioning of the nervous system. For instance, Charcot and his associates conducted key studies that provided insight into the physiological basis of diseases such as Parkinson's, multiple sclerosis, and epilepsy. He also believed that the bizarre behaviors and experiences of hysterics must be due to impaired functioning in the nervous system, even though he could find no evidence of structural damage that would account for their symptoms. Today, Charcot is known as the *French neurologist who first described the symptoms and possible causes of hysteria.*

In the late nineteenth century, women led restricted lives with few rights and little economic power, and one of the few means of escape was to play the role of the sick person (Spanos, 1996). Sexual frustration was also a factor, and nymphomania was often included as a symptom of hysteria. Although Charcot was the first to suspect that repressed sexuality may be the cause of hysteria, it was his student Sigmund Freud who took that idea and weaved it into a complex theory of psychological disorders.

| Photo 8.1
Jean-Martin Charcot

During Charcot's time, the difference between hysteria and epilepsy was unclear (Faber, 1997). Because neurologists could find no consistent lesions that they could associate with either disorder, they assumed both were caused by a dysfunctional nervous system without physical damage. At the Salpêtrière, hysteric and epileptic patients were housed in the same ward. This gave hysteric patients plenty of opportunities to observe and mimic epileptic seizures, which they then added to their repertoire of symptoms. At first, Charcot bought into the hysteria-epilepsy link, but he eventually convinced himself that these were in fact two separate disorders. The method he used for demonstrating this distinction generated considerable controversy.

Although hypnosis had been popular among the general public since the 1700s, neurologists only began studying it seriously in the late nineteenth century (Bogousslavsky, Walusinkski, & Veyrunes, 2009). Charcot found that hysteric patients were easily hypnotized but not those with epilepsy. Thus, he came to the conclusion that hypnotic susceptibility was itself a symptom of hysteria, and he attributed both to a weakened nervous system. He believed he'd discovered four stages of hysteria that corresponded to four stages of hypnosis, which he demonstrated in public exhibitions. What Charcot never knew was that his assistants, in an effort to please him, coached the patients on how to behave—and the hysterics were quite happy to perform because of the attention they received.

Around this same time, a rival in the city of Nancy challenged Charcot's theory of hysteria and hypnosis (Bogousslavsky et al., 2009). Hippolyte Bernheim (1840–1919) was also investigating the use of hypnosis as a therapeutic technique for patients with mental disorders. However, he took the essentially modern view that hypnosis is nothing more than a heightened state of suggestibility and that the hypnotized subject is merely role-playing according to the demands of the hypnotist. Charcot rejected Bernheim's view on hypnosis and adamantly stuck to his own theory for the rest of his life. Moreover, none of his colleagues or students at the Salpêtrière dared challenge his ideas until after his death. Thus, we see in Charcot the power of self-deception. As a man of science who was known worldwide for his major contributions to medicine, he firmly believed in his powers of objective observation. Yet this belief blinded him to the role he himself played in shaping the behaviors of the hysteric patients he hypnotized.

Charcot was a showman, and he offered public lectures at the Salpêtrière every Tuesday morning (Gelfand, 2000). His public demonstrations of hypnosis and hysteria attracted medical researchers from around the world. The drama of these "Tuesday lectures" was captured in a group portrait by French artist Pierre Brouillet, in which a patient faints after

Photo 8.2
Portrait of a clinical lesson at the Salpêtrière

being hypnotized by Charcot. Prints of this portrait were quite popular, and Sigmund Freud had one hanging in his office.

Charcot trained many of the next generation of neurologists, including those who later turned their attention to psychological disorders and psychotherapy (Gelfand, 2000). For our purposes, his two most important students were Pierre Janet and Sigmund Freud, both of whom were instrumental in the development of psychotherapy (Figure 8.1). Some key ideas in abnormal psychology first arose in casual comments Charcot made to his students. For example, he suggested that trauma may be a trigger for hysteria, and he hinted that frustrated sexuality may lie at the root of the disorder. He also tried to help his patients by talking with them and showing them genuine concern for their welfare. As an influential researcher, Charcot shaped the thinking of early twentieth-century psychologists on both sides of the Atlantic.

Pierre Janet

As a young man, **Pierre Janet** (1859–1947, pronounced *zha-NAY*) had two very influential mentors. The first was his uncle Paul Janet, an important philosopher in a movement known as spiritualism, based on the ideas of René Descartes (Carroy & Plas, 2000). Recall from Chapter 1 that Descartes had proposed an interactive dualism between the spiritual mind and the physical body. The spiritualists studied the structure and processes of the mind mainly through introspection, and they concluded that mental activity occurs at two levels. At the voluntary level we're consciously aware of our surroundings and the reasons for our actions, but at the automatic level our perceptions, thoughts, and behaviors occur without any conscious intention or ability to control them. Examples of automatic activities include dreams, hallucinations, and hypnotic states.

The second major influence on Pierre Janet was Jean-Martin Charcot, with whom he worked at the Salpêtrière (Bühler & Heim, 2011). According to Charcot, a key feature of hysteria was anesthesia, which involved a loss of sensation or movement in a limb that couldn't be accounted for by damage to the nervous system. Janet thought he saw a connection between the automatic activities of the spiritualists and the anesthesia of hysteric patients. When he published his doctoral thesis *Psychological Automatisms* in 1889, Pierre

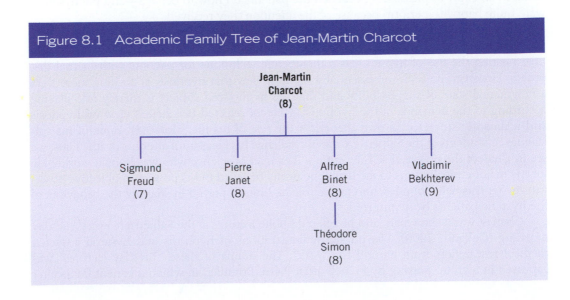

Figure 8.1   Academic Family Tree of Jean-Martin Charcot

Jean-Martin Charcot (8)

Sigmund Freud (7)   Pierre Janet (8)   Alfred Binet (8)   Vladimir Bekhterev (9)

Théodore Simon (8)

Janet bridged the gap between philosophy and science to establish himself as a *clinical psychologist who became recognized as the father of French psychology.* In the decades around the turn of the twentieth century, French scientific psychology emphasized clinical over experimental methods, following the lead that Janet established.

In the late nineteenth century, a number of cases of multiple personality cropped up in Europe and North America, typically involving women with hysteria (Brown, 2003). Janet worked with several hysterics who revealed alternate personalities under hypnosis. Interestingly, the alternate personalities displayed none of the symptoms of the main personality. These early experiences suggested to Janet that he might be able to use hypnosis to cure hysteria, an idea he pursued in his clinical work for the rest of his career.

Photo 8.3
Pierre Janet

The very notion of multiple personalities was controversial, because the self was believed to be a unitary entity (Carroy & Plas, 2000). Janet proposed that these multiple personalities were in fact parts of the same self. In healthy individuals, he argued, various experiences are united into a single sense of self that includes current thoughts and sensations as well as an autobiographical memory for the past. However, when the mind is weakened as in the case of hysteria, this synthesis fails to occur. Sensory experiences and thoughts remain disconnected, as do past and present experiences. In this way, he explained both the anesthesia and the amnesia of patients with hysteria.

Janet used the term **automatism** to refer to *a behavior that is performed without conscious awareness* (LeBlanc, 2004). Behaviors performed under hypnosis—especially when they were no longer recalled upon awakening—were examples of automatisms. Janet believed automatisms could also explain many of the symptoms of hysteria. Perhaps a patient says she feels no pain in her right arm not because her nerves are damaged but rather because she doesn't have a conscious experience of the pain.

Thinking of automatism in this way led Janet to his concept of the **subconscious** (Bacopoulos-Viau, 2012). This is *a level of consciousness in which perceptions are experienced and behaviors are performed without being aware of them*. In other words, Janet distinguished between the conscious, which necessarily entailed awareness and memory, and the unconscious, which excluded them. This two-stage model of consciousness fit well with the spiritualist philosophy that had differentiated between voluntary and automatic mental processes. It also helped explain many of the symptoms of hysteria, so it was hailed by the medical community. With the concept of the subconscious, Janet succeeded in unifying philosophical and clinical approaches to psychology in France, and it's for this reason that he's often called the father of French psychology.

In the ordinary person, Janet argued, everyday experiences are integrated into a unitary sense of self at the conscious level (Dorahy & van der Hart, 2006). In the mentally ill, however, experiences are fragmented due to **dissociation**. This is *a phenomenon in which persons become detached from their perceptions, memories, or behaviors*. As a result, people may feel no pain when injured, or they may have no conscious memory of a traumatic event. Hypnosis then was a form of dissociation as well. Janet also explained the occurrence of multiple personalities in terms of dissociation in that each personality represented a different dissociated state. This is why one personality may not be aware of the others. In fact, the experience of multiple personalities is now called *dissociative identity disorder*.

Like many psychologists at the turn of the twentieth century, Janet borrowed the concept of *energy* from physics (Bühler & Heim, 2011). In his view, people in good mental health have sufficient psychic energy to integrate life experiences into a unified sense of self. But traumatic events are difficult to cope with, and they can drain us of the psychic energy needed to integrate them, so they're left as separate pieces of experience in the subconscious. Janet referred to a *subconscious memory of a traumatic event* as a **fixed idea**. Although the fixed idea isn't consciously recalled, it still creates emotional disturbances in the person. Janet believed that fixed ideas were at the root of all hysterias. It's important to note the similarity between Janet's concept of fixed idea and that of repression developed somewhat later by Freud.

Janet was among the first to develop a systematic form of psychotherapy (Bühler & Heim, 2011). Called **psychological analysis,** this was *Janet's approach to treating psychological disorders by identifying and eliminating fixed ideas.* Since patients were unaware of their fixed ideas, Janet used hypnosis to find them. In a suggestible state, patients often related emotional issues or traumatic experiences that they were unable or unwilling to discuss when awake. Therapy could also include a discussion of recent dreams. Because dreaming is an automatic behavior, Janet believed that it can reveal aspects of fixed ideas lingering in the subconscious. However, he had no patience for dream interpretation, which he dismissed as nonsense. Only the manifest content of the dream had any meaning for the patient.

Janet explored various methods for identifying fixed ideas, but this was only the start of the therapeutic process (Bühler & Heim, 2011). Sometimes, simply bringing the fixed idea to consciousness was enough to cure the symptoms of the disorder, especially if the patient could fully experience the emotions associated with it. Often, however, Janet had to work hard with his patients to get them to accept and deal with their fixed ideas. He also used hypnotic suggestion in an attempt to reduce the potency of traumatic memories. But he also warned of the dangers of this approach, in particular the potential for the patient to become reliant on dissociative states for dealing with their problems instead of integrating these into conscious experience. Comparing hypnosis with a drug, he acknowledged that it could do great good but at the risk of doing great harm.

Janet was working at the Salpêtrière at the time Freud was studying with Charcot (Fitzgerald, 2017). Freud became acquainted with Janet's techniques, which he later adopted in his own clinical practice in Vienna. In the early years, Freud credited Janet as the source for many of his ideas. But by the turn of the twentieth century, Freud had acquired a name for himself and a group of loyal followers. Seeing his thinking as having developed far beyond that of Janet, he no longer recognized him as the source of his ideas.

Janet accused Freud of plagiarism, insisting that Freud had taken his theory and claimed it as his own (Fitzgerald, 2017). For instance, Janet called his method for treating hysteria *psychological analysis.* Freud used many of the same methods in his "talking cure," but he called it *psychoanalysis.* Janet believed hysteria was caused by *subconscious fixed ideas,* whereas Freud spoke of *unconscious repressed memories.* During therapy sessions, Janet often asked his patients to engage in *automatic speech,* in other words, speaking freely about thoughts as they come to mind. Freud used the same technique, but he called it *free association.* Both also believed that dreams could provide insights into under psychological issues in patients. Clearly, there's a lot of overlap between the methods used by Janet and Freud.

Particularly in the English-speaking world, Freud's theories dominated psychology for much of the twentieth century, while Janet's contributions were largely forgotten (Bacopoulos-Viau, 2012). In part, this was because Freud's books were translated into English, whereas Janet's works were not. However, in the last decades of the twentieth century, psychoanalytic influence waned. Moreover, there was a renewed interest in dissociation—one of the few ideas of Janet that Freud hadn't incorporated into his theory. In particular, conditions such as post-traumatic stress disorder, which receives a lot of attention these days, are better explained in Janet's terms than in Freud's. Pierre Janet was a man whose thinking was clearly ahead of its time, and his ideas resonate far more with clinicians in the early twenty-first century than they did in the mid-twentieth.

Alfred Binet

Although he trained as a lawyer and even practiced the profession for a few years, **Alfred Binet** (1857–1911, pronounced *bee-NAY*) just didn't have the heart for it (Nicolas & Ferrand, 2002). Instead, he spent much of his time reading works by the major thinkers of his time, especially John Stuart Mill (Chapter 1), which led him to an interest in the new experimental psychology. As a man of independent means, Binet didn't have to earn a living, so he was free to follow his passions. After working as an unpaid assistant to Charcot, he then took the position of unsalaried director in a laboratory of experimental psychology at the Sorbonne, one of France's most prestigious universities. Although he did groundbreaking research in many areas of psychology, Alfred Binet earned an international reputation late in his career as the *French psychologist who collaborated with Théodore Simon to produce the first reliable intelligence test*.

Abnormal Psychology

We can trace three distinct stages in Binet's career, although there's considerable overlap of interests from one to the next (Sternberg & Jarvin, 2003). During the first stage, his interests focused on psychopathology, which then dominated French psychology. He next turned his attention to experimental psychology after the German and American model. Then in his last years he shifted to the study of childhood development, culminating in the creation of the intelligence test that now bears his name.

In 1883, Binet started working with Charcot at the Salpêtrière (Nicolas & Sanitioso, 2012). At that time, experimental psychology in France was almost entirely focused on the study of psychological disorders, with the idea that these disorders represented "natural experiments," which could lead to a greater understanding of how the mind worked. Initially, Binet adopted this attitude as well, and he became enthralled with Charcot's work on hypnosis and hysteria. However, he soon became disillusioned with Charcot's ideas as well as the premise that case studies of mental disorders constituted the best approach to a scientific understanding of the mind.

Binet was also unusual among those working at the Salpêtrière in that he had a degree in law and not in medicine (Siegler, 1992). He remedied this lack of training by working in the physiology lab at the hospital and eventually earning a doctorate in natural science. Perhaps because he was an academic outsider, he was more skeptical of Charcot's approach than others. Eventually, he became convinced that the only way to understand the human mind was to study mentally healthy persons. Binet left the Salpêtrière when he got the opportunity to head the psychology laboratory at the Sorbonne in Paris, although he still collaborated with Charcot from time to time.

Photo 8.4
Alfred Binet

Experimental Psychology

Over the next two decades at the Sorbonne laboratory, Binet conducted many high-quality studies over a wide variety of topics, ranging through the modern fields of cognitive, developmental, and social psychology (Siegler, 1992). Many of these findings were forgotten after his death, only to be rediscovered in the latter decades of the twentieth century. Although he'd turned away from psychopathology, he still believed that mental functions could be best understood by comparing normal people with exceptional cases.

One such exceptional case was **synesthesia** (Nicolas & Sanitioso, 2012). This is *a perceptual phenomenon in which sensations from different modalities become automatically associated.* One common form of synesthesia involves the perception of letters or numbers as having specific colors. For example, all As may be perceived as blue, while all Bs may be perceived as red, and so on. Each person with synesthesia experiences a different letter-color association, but the particular association typically remains constant for the entire lifespan. Although Francis Galton (Chapter 2) had been the first to report systematic studies of synesthesia, Binet also did extensive work on this topic. For Binet, synesthesia was interesting because of what it showed about the way the perceptual system worked. At that time, many psychologists believed that perception was nothing more than the summation of all sensory experiences at a given moment. But Binet insisted that synesthesia showed the constructive nature of perception, because his subjects reported perceiving colors that could not have been in the sensory input. For most of the twentieth century, synesthesia was dismissed as an uninteresting phenomenon, but there's been an upsurge of interest in recent decades.

Binet also studied the workings of the perceptual system by investigating the ways in which stage magicians created illusions (Lachapelle, 2008). Although he was skeptical of the supernatural, he did take an interest in sleight-of-hand tricks. He invited magicians into his lab, who performed tricks for him. He found that no matter how many times he watched the trick, he still fell for the illusion. But once the magician explained how the trick was done, he was no longer deceived. He also used a special camera that could take a series of photos in rapid succession to decompose the trick into its basic movements. He concluded that it wasn't the eyes that were being deceived but rather the mind, as the deception was plainly visible if only one knew where to look. Through these studies, Binet came to understand the importance of attention in perception.

In other research on exceptional abilities, Binet explored the nature of memory (Nicolas & Gounden, 2011). At that time, many philosophers and psychologists assumed that memory was a singular faculty. However, Binet had been influenced by Charcot's belief that memory consisted of multiple independent functions. In one set of studies, he questioned expert chess players who could even play the game blindfolded. His subjects reported that they created a visual image of the chess board in their minds. Although these players exhibited extraordinary memories for chessboard configurations, their memory abilities on other tasks fell within the normal range, supporting his contention of multiple memory systems.

Binet continued his study of memory by examining the abilities of so-called "mental calculators" (Burman, Guida, & Nicolas, 2015). In 1892, Charcot introduced Binet to a man named Jacques Inaudi, who earned his living performing complex mathematical calculations rapidly in his head before theater audiences. For instance, Binet found that Inaudi could correctly multiply 58×15 in just 1.36 seconds! On further examination, Binet found that he did this by manipulating the sounds of the numbers in his head. Inaudi had no exceptional mathematical abilities beyond rapid mental arithmetic. In fact, he'd grown up as an illiterate shepherd who'd played with arithmetic problems in his head to while away the time, and that was how he developed his skill as a mental calculator.

Furthermore, Inaudi's exceptional memory abilities were limited to numbers (Nicolas & Sanitioso, 2012). Although he could easily repeat back a twenty-four-digit sequence, he could only repeat a series of seven or eight letters. This finding further supported Binet's belief that memory wasn't a singular faculty.

Later, Binet got to know another mental calculator named Périclès Diamandi (Nicolas & Gounden, 2011). He found that whereas Inaudi remembered numbers verbally, Diamandi did so visually. Presenting each with a 5×5 table of digits, either man could easily memorize the twenty-five numbers. However, Inaudi could only repeat the numbers in left-to-right serial order, while Diamandi could recite the numbers horizontally or vertically. Binet saw this as evidence that verbal memory and visual memory are different systems.

Child Psychology

Binet had two young daughters that he carefully observed at home (Sternberg & Jarvin, 2003). These observations then led to more formal experiments in his lab. Using children as participants, Binet challenged the notion that memories were relatively accurate portrayals of past events. After viewing a poster with six everyday objects attached to it, some participants were asked specific questions about the objects, while others were simply told to describe the objects to the best of their ability. He found that children in the guided-question condition were able to recall more information, but they often got details wrong. In contrast, children in the free-recall condition reported less information, but it was more accurate. Binet concluded that the questions had modified the children's memories through suggestion. Although Hugo Münsterberg in the United States made similar claims about the unreliability of eyewitness testimony around this same time, it wasn't until the last decades of the twentieth century that cognitive psychologists such as Elizabeth Loftus (Chapter 11) took a renewed interest in memory modification.

Binet also conducted some of the earliest research on group dynamics (Nicolas & Levine, 2012). He randomly assigned children to groups and gave them tasks to perform. First, he observed that leaders aren't intentionally selected by the other members but rather arise naturally through social interactions within the group. In the beginning, there's little group cohesion as the individual members seek solutions to the problem on their own. The first to voice a possible answer typically becomes the leader while the others orient their efforts toward him or her. Second, he found a high degree of group conformity, with members becoming quite susceptible to the suggestions of their peers and especially of the leader. This strong impulse to conform to the group would be rediscovered by social psychologists such as Solomon Asch (Chapter 12) in the second half of the twentieth century.

As Binet worked with children, his interests turned toward educational psychology (Nicolas & Sanitioso, 2012). Binet administered a number of tests to his two daughters, and he found they were quite different from each other in their personalities and intellectual styles. This study of his own children led him to develop what he called **individual psychology**, which was *Binet's term for the study of individual differences in personality and intelligence.* Contrary to the received wisdom of the day, Binet argued that children aren't just miniature adults. Rather, their thought processes are inherently different from those of grownups. Furthermore, ways of thinking evolve as children grow older, and even within a particular age group there can be considerable differences among individuals. In Binet's ideas, we see clear precursors to Jean Piaget's theory of cognitive development. Also, it's important to distinguish Binet's use of the term *individual psychology* from that of Alfred Adler (Chapter 7), who used it as the name of his version of psychotherapy.

Binet's ideas about individual differences and developmental trajectories in children resonated with early twentieth-century French society (Cicciola, Foschi, & Lombardo, 2014). Like other industrialized countries, France had recently instituted universal compulsory education. Before that time, schooling was optional. Those who did well or had family support continued their education, but it wasn't uncommon in the nineteenth century for school-age children to be working on farms or in factories. However, once all children were required to attend school for a certain number of years, a new problem arose. This was the question of how to deal with the wide range of abilities in any cohort of children. Binet was asked to join a government commission to investigate this problem.

As Binet saw it, the issue was the discrepancy between the majority of students, who were within the normal range of intelligence, and those with mental deficits that were in the "subnormal" range (Carson, 2014). While Binet clearly understood that there were considerable individual differences in intelligence, he also believed deeply in the power of education. Even high native intelligence required nurturing to reach its full potential. Likewise, children with low levels of native intelligence could be trained to be productive members of society. Furthermore, he distinguished between children who didn't do well in school because of mental deficiencies and those who struggled because of a poor upbringing. What was needed was an educational approach that was tailored to the needs of students with different abilities.

Théodore Simon

Binet was a solitary man who didn't like working with collaborators (Wolf, 1961). But he would need assistance in constructing an intelligence test and collecting norming data. That help came from the young psychiatrist **Théodore Simon** (1872–1961, pronounced *see-MOAN*), who had charge of an asylum for boys with cognitive disabilities. Working together, Binet and Simon sought to create a test that was easy to administer and that could reliably identify those children in need of special education. Thus, we know Théodore Simon today as the *French psychologist who collaborated with Alfred Binet to produce the first reliable intelligence test.*

Binet and Simon were hardly the first psychologists to devise a measure of intelligence, but their thinking was revolutionary in many respects (Beauvais, 2016). Both Francis Galton (Chapter 2) and James McKeen Cattell (Chapter 3) had attempted to use low-level processes such as reaction time as proxy measures for intelligence. But this approach had failed to be a good predictor of outcomes of intelligence, such as school performance. Ebbinghaus had also tried to sort children according to levels of intelligence by including language and memory tasks. However, Binet and Simon's revolutionary insight was

Photo 8.5
Théodore Simon

that intelligence depends far more on higher-level mental functions such as memory, problem solving, and reasoning, than it does on lower-level processes such as reaction time or visual acuity.

Galton and Cattell were attempting to measure adult intelligence, which is likely to remain stable over time (Cicciola et al., 2014). But Binet and Simon were trying to measure child intelligence, which not only varied among individuals but also within a single individual over time. Even an average six-year-old is clearly more intelligent than a bright two-year-old. However, this meant there could be no single standard of intelligence. Instead, individual children would have to be compared with their peers.

The solution was to devise a test consisting of a series of problems of ever-increasing difficulty (Beauvais, 2016). In 1905, Binet and Simon published what they called the Metric Intelligence Scale, which consisted of thirty tasks. Each task had been administered to dozens of children ranging from age two to twelve, and the researchers had determined which tests were usually solved by normal children of a given age. Let's say we administer the test to little Suzette, who completes all the tasks that a normal seven-year-old would get right. This means that she has a *mental age* of seven. But Suzette is only six years old, meaning that she has a *chronological age* of six. In other words, she's performing at a higher level than would be expected for her age. In 1908, Binet and Simon revised the test after administering it to a much larger sample of children from a wider range of backgrounds. Meanwhile, experience had shown that the test was doing a good job of identifying those children in need of special education.

Binet died suddenly in 1911 at the young age of 54, just after he and Simon had made a second revision to the test (Siegler, 1992). Thus, he had little opportunity to advocate for its widespread use in the French school system. In the meantime, Lewis Terman (Chapter 4) had adapted the test for use in America, renaming it the Stanford-Binet. This test was then modified by Robert Yerkes (Chapter 4) and others as the Army Alpha for screening soldiers in World War I. Furthermore, many intelligence tests today are derivatives of Binet-Simon. For much of the twentieth century, Binet's extensive work was largely forgotten, and his ideas on intelligence were greatly distorted. But in the last few decades, psychologists are rediscovering the over 300 articles and books Binet published during his career. Largely ignored during his own lifetime, psychologists today find his work remarkably modern and forward looking. Clearly, Binet was a man who was ahead of his time.

Jean Piaget

Photo 8.6
Jean Piaget

Jean Piaget's mother struggled with mental health issues, and as a boy he immersed himself in scientific pursuits to escape the emotional turmoil of his home (Brainerd, 1996). At age seven, he began an apprenticeship with the curator of the local museum of natural history, and he published his first scholarly work—a brief description of an albino sparrow—when he was ten. He completed a bachelor's degree in natural science when he was eighteen and a doctorate just three years later, with a dissertation on mollusks. He seemed ready for a promising career as a zoologist. But instead his interests turned to psychology. Seeking to understand the reason for his mother's mental illness, he did postgraduate work with Pierre Janet. He also took a job with Théodore Simon administering intelligence tests. In this second position, Piaget found his life's passion. Today, **Jean Piaget** (1896–1980, pronounced ZHAN pee-ah-ZHAY) is known as the *Swiss psychologist who developed a very influential theory of cognitive development.*

Clinical Method

Piaget was greatly influenced by Janet (Amann-Ganotti, 1992). Steeped in Freudian theory before arriving in Paris, Piaget also learned Janet's alternative view of psychopathology. Part of his training involved doing clinical interviews with patients in mental hospitals, a skill he'd employ in his research for the rest of his life. During this time, Janet was also developing his own ideas about an evolutionary approach to human behavior and thinking. Rather than viewing children as little adults, he argued that human behaviors develop through a series of stages from simple to more complex. Furthermore, he maintained that hysterics had child-like minds, in that both tended to view the world as operating through magic and fantasy rather than reason and logic. Likewise, he claimed, neither children nor hysterics could take an objective point of view but rather saw all events as happening to them and because of them. These ideas had a great impact on Piaget, but working with patients also taught him psychopathology wasn't the right career direction for him.

Rather, he found his life's calling in Binet's laboratory school (Brainerd, 1996). Although Binet had passed away several years before, the school continued under Simon's directorship. Piaget was hired to collect norming data for a new test, and the job was straightforward: simply administer the test to children one at a time and mark down their correct and incorrect responses. Simon was occupied with another project in a different city, so Piaget worked without supervision. As he interacted with these children, he noticed they often gave wrong responses to problems whose answers seemed quite obvious. Breaking with protocol, he began asking them why they gave the responses they did. The purpose wasn't to teach them or to guide their responses. Rather, Piaget simply wanted to understand how they thought about these problems. At his other job, he interviewed patients to gain insight into the mental processes underlying their disorders. Likewise with these children, he used *the investigative technique of asking probing questions and recording responses without judgment*. Thus was born Piaget's **clinical method**, which became the hallmark of his research for the next five decades.

Piaget understood that his clinical method was fraught with danger (Mayer, 2005). If he wasn't careful, he could easily suggest ideas to the children he was interviewing, and he could inadvertently encourage them to make up stories on the spot. While recognizing these dangers, he also believed that his clinical method had advantages over objective approaches to gathering data. Although we can objectively observe children's responses, we don't know why they solve the problems the way they do. If they give the right answer, it could be because they understand the principle behind the problem, or it could be their thinking is flawed, leading them to the correct answer for the wrong reason. Likewise, there are several reasons why children might give wrong answers. They might not have been paying attention, or maybe they misunderstood the question. But it could also be that they have a fundamentally different view of the world from adults.

Listening to children explain their thought processes, Piaget detected consistent patterns (Jahoda, 2000). Instead of viewing events in terms of logical cause-and-effect relationships, children saw a world infused with magic and dominated by emotions. Just as his mentor Janet had proposed, both the child and the hysteric saw the world as governed by forces quite different from those understood by normally functioning adults.

Piaget published his findings from the Binet lab in three separate articles. The last of these caught the attention of **Édouard Claparède** (1873–1940), the *Swiss developmental psychologist who nurtured Piaget's career*.

A decade before, Claparède had founded the Jean-Jacques Rousseau Institute for educational research in Geneva, Switzerland, and he was much impressed with the results Piaget had obtained using his clinical method (Mayer, 2005). Claparède offered Piaget a position as research director at the institute, and soon he had a team of research assistants, many of them women, using the clinical method he taught them to explore cognitive development in young schoolchildren. Soon Piaget was publishing articles and books reporting the latest findings from the Rousseau Institute. Claparède was an important mentor for Piaget during his early years in Geneva, but other psychologists also influenced his thoughts during this time.

Photo 8.7
Édouard Claparède

The Russian psychoanalyst Sabina Spielrein (Chapter 9) was already doing research at the Rousseau Institute when Piaget arrived (Vidal, 2001). Spielrein studied early childhood development from a largely Freudian perspective, and they had a mutual influence on each other during the time they worked together. Piaget even agreed to undergo psychoanalysis with Spielrein, but the experience turned him away from Freudian theory. Soon afterward, Spielrein returned to Russia, where she worked with Lev Vygotsky (Chapter 9), whose ideas have also greatly shaped modern thinking on cognitive development.

Another important influence on Piaget during this time was the American psychologist James Mark Baldwin (Chapter 3; Cahan, 1984). Baldwin had proposed a stage model of cognitive development with many of the features of Piaget's later model. After Baldwin's embarrassing dismissal from Johns Hopkins, his works were largely ignored, but Piaget found much food for thought in them. Baldwin's ideas were largely theoretical, but over the years, Piaget conducted experiments that tested those ideas and helped him flesh out the stage model he's so well known for today.

In 1923, Piaget published *Language and Thought of the Child*, in which he argued that preschool children, unlike older children and adults, use language mainly to guide their own thought processes (Beilin, 1992). In other words, most utterances in the early years aren't made for communicative purposes, and the social uses of language only come to dominate in later childhood. Moreover, he argued, even when it appears that the speech of a young child is directed at others, its social purpose is limited. This is because preschool children have *a lack of awareness that other people have points of view different from one's own*, a condition he called **egocentrism**. For instance, when three-year-old Anna has a conversation with Mommy, she only talks about what interests her and has no idea how her words influence her mother's thoughts or feelings. Real communication, according to Piaget, only occurs when we take the point of view of the person we're talking to. This book and several that followed were highly acclaimed and translated into a number of languages, so by his early thirties Piaget was well known by psychologists around the world. As we'll see in Chapter 9, Lev Vygotsky in Russia also read Piaget's early books with great interest, even though he disagreed with his interpretations.

Another of Piaget's notable early works was his 1932 book *The Moral Judgment of the Child* (Beilin, 1992). By observing how children play games, Piaget detected a shift in their thinking about morality around age ten. He found that younger children operated according to a morality of constraint, in which rules of behavior are handed down by adults. For example, they know that lying and cheating are wrong because their elders tell them so. But older children act according to a morality of cooperation and reciprocity. That is, they understand it's wrong to cheat or lie to others because they wouldn't want others to cheat or lie to them. This was as far as Piaget went with the question of moral development. But in the 1950s, American psychologist Lawrence Kohlberg (Chapter 15) continued where Piaget left off, building an influential and controversial theory of his own.

Stage Model

Piaget's early training was in biology, so he often contemplated the problem of how organisms adapt to their environment. For the most part, animals have a set of behavioral traits that enable them to thrive within their natural environments. This repertoire of flexible behaviors allows them to assimilate to minor changes in their surroundings. But when the changes to the environment are larger, organisms need to reshape their behaviors to accommodate new demands. He saw the same processes of assimilation and accommodation taking place within the cognitive development of human children.

British philosopher John Locke (Chapter 1) had argued that children were like blank slates on which the experiences of life are written (Flavell, 1996). But Piaget disagreed with this view of children as passive receivers of knowledge, maintaining instead that children are actively engaged with their physical and social environments and that they are constantly adapting their understanding of the world to changing circumstances. For example, little Billy knows that the furry, four-legged animal in the house is a "doggie." When he hears Mommy call the furry creature next door a "doggie," he learns that this name extends to other animals as well. This is **assimilation**, which is *the process whereby new information is* *incorporated into existing cognitive structures.* Then on a drive through the country, Billy points to an animal in a field and says "doggie," but Mommy tells him it's a "cow." Now Billy knows that not all furry, four-legged animals are doggies, because big ones standing in fields are cows. This is **accommodation**, which is *the process whereby new information leads to the construction of novel cognitive structures.*

In Piaget's terminology, *the process of aligning cognitive structures with current environmental conditions* is called **equilibration** (Flavell, 1996). According to Piaget, cognitive development advances through a series of cycles. Equilibration at a lower level is maintained through assimilation, but new experiences that challenge existing cognitive structures disrupt that equilibration, calling on processes of accommodation to restore the balance. Yet this new equilibration is at a higher level, meaning that these new cognitive structures better match the external world. These cycles of equilibration, disruption, and re-equilibration repeat constantly throughout the lifespan.

**Photo 8.8
Jean and Valentine Piaget**

In 1923, Piaget married Valentine Châtenay (1899–1983), a coworker at the Rousseau Institute (Fischer & Hencke, 1996). They had three children who became the subjects of some of Piaget's most important books. He and Valentine kept a detailed diary of each child, filled with rich descriptions of how his or her behavior changed over time. Piaget also had to modify his clinical method, since infants can't talk. Instead, he took a behavioral approach, giving them physical objects to manipulate and observing how they responded.

During this time, Piaget also reconsidered the nature of thinking (Fischer & Hencke, 1996). In his *Language and Thought of the Child*, he'd viewed speech as a foundation for logic and reasoning. But now he was dealing with speechless infants who acted upon the world in seemingly purposeful ways. He concluded that logical thought wasn't based on language after all but rather on action. That is to say, infancy is *a period in which babies learn how the world works by experiencing it through their own bodily sensations and muscle movements.* As Piaget developed his stage model of cognitive development, the first two years of life became known as the **sensorimotor stage**.

According to Piaget, infants in the first few months of life can't distinguish between objects and the actions they perform on those objects (Fischer & Hencke, 1996). The development of hand-eye coordination is especially important during this time. For example, an infant at first can only hit a rattle to make a noise. But over time, it learns how to grasp and shake it. Through such experiences, the infant learns that objects are more than just extensions of themselves, and furthermore it comes to view itself as an agent that can willfully act upon the world. Still, its understanding of the properties of objects is limited to what it can directly experience through its senses and motor movements. Although a six-month-old will grasp at an object it can see, it won't go searching for an object that an adult hides from it.

In Piagetian terms, we say that young infants lack **object permanence**, which is *the understanding that objects continue to exist even when out of sight.* This doesn't mean that infants believe a hidden object ceases to exist but rather that they simply have no idea what has happened to it. By around 9 to 10 months, infants reach for a toy that an adult hides from them, indicating they now understand the continued existence of objects even when not in view. In recent decades, there's been considerable criticism of Piaget's proposed milestones in sensorimotor development. However, it's important to keep in mind that he was describing a developmental sequence highly dependent upon context rather that a series of age-related milestones.

Piaget built the Rousseau Institute into a major laboratory for child research (Burman, 2012). The institute also served as a center for teacher training, and it had an excellent relationship with the local school district. This meant access to thousands of children for use as research participants, and furthermore all students at the institute were expected to do research as part of their training. At the top was Piaget, who assigned broad projects to his research assistants, mainly doctoral and postdoctoral students. In turn, these assistants directed specific experiments that the teachers-in-training conducted at local schools.

Table 8.1 Piaget's Stages of Cognitive Development

Stage	Age	Description	Milestones
Sensorimotor	0–2	Infants learn about the world through their bodily sensations and muscle movements.	Object permanence
Preoperational	2–6	Preschool children's reasoning is dominated by magical thinking rather than rational thought.	Egocentrism
Concrete operational	6–12	Grade schoolers can think logically with the aid of manipulated objects.	Conservation, reversibility
Formal operational	Postpuberty	Teenagers acquire the ability to think logically about abstract situations.	Hypothetical supposition

This mass production of research led to prodigious output, and Piaget got into the habit of calling the institute "the factory" (Burman, 2012). Likewise, all the research assistants and students called him "boss." This title was fitting. Within a few years of joining the institute, Piaget was no longer conducting research himself. Instead, he spent most of his time soliciting external funding and planning new avenues of research as well as editing research reports and assembling them into the scores of books published under his name and those of his collaborators. Many of the workers in this factory were women, most notably Bärbel Inhelder and Alina Szemińska, whom we'll meet shortly.

All work at the Rousseau Institute was conducted with the sole purpose of helping Piaget build his grand theory of cognitive development (Brainerd, 1996). The bulk of the work on this theory was completed during the 1930s and 1940s, but most of the world didn't know about it until later. As the rest of Europe sank into the turmoil of fascism, Nazism, and World War II, the Swiss simply went on with their lives. During this period of isolation, Piaget and his workers constructed the **stage model of cognitive development** that he's so well known for today. This is *Piaget's theory that children's understanding of the world goes through a series of transformations as they reorganize their mental structures to adapt to new experiences.*

A key concept in this stage theory is **operation**, which is *Piaget's term for a logical thought process* (Beilin, 1992). Early work with youngsters had convinced him that their thinking was "pre-logical," but now he described these children as being in the **preoperational stage**, which is *a period in which the reasoning of preschoolers is dominated by magical thinking rather than rational thought.* At first, he believed that school-aged children were generally capable of logical thought, but the work of Bärbel Inhelder convinced him this depended on the situation. From around age six or seven, children use logic to solve problems, but only if all the pieces are physical objects they can manipulate. Piaget said these children were in the **concrete operational stage**, which is *a period in which grade schoolers have the ability to think logically with the aid of manipulated objects.* Only after age eleven or twelve can children think rationally in abstract situations. They then enter the **formal operational stage**, which is *a period when adolescents acquire the ability to think logically about abstract or hypothetical situations.* Much of the developmental research over the last half century has been aimed at testing—and challenging—Piaget's stage theory of cognitive development (Table 8.1).

Genetic Epistemology

In his later years, Piaget turned his mind to the philosophy of science, developing a theory of knowledge acquisition he called genetic epistemology (Beilin, 1992). Recall from Chapter 1 that epistemology refers to the study of knowledge, asking questions such as what it means to know something and how knowledge is acquired. Piaget uses the term *genetic* not in the modern sense of "having to do with genes" but rather in the older sense of "having to do with origins," as in the word *genesis*. Thus, **genetic epistemology** is, *in Piaget's terms, the study of the origin of knowledge.*

Piaget saw a remarkable parallel between children's development of their understanding of the world and the history of science (Inhelder, 1989). Just as children's magical thinking is gradually replaced by reason, so has been the history of our own species as our understanding of the universe has evolved over the millennia. Thus, his stage model of cognitive development is one part of an even grander theory of genetic epistemology. Yet, whether we're talking about evolving knowledge structures within an individual person or within societies as a whole, the same processes of assimilation and accommodation take place.

Recall that philosophers of epistemology can be divided into two camps (Inhelder, 1989). On the one hand, nativists like Plato believe that knowledge is already inside the person and only needs to be drawn out through proper instruction. On the other hand, empiricists like Aristotle believe that knowledge exists in the world, ready to be discovered by the objective observer. However, Piaget took issue with both camps, insisting that knowledge is neither innate nor acquired through experience. Instead, knowledge is constructed as the individual interacts with the environment. This is true, Piaget insisted, both on the individual and the societal level. In sum, knowledge exists neither in the person nor in the world but rather in the interaction between the two.

When Piaget's theory was introduced to English-speaking psychologists after World War II, it posed a significant challenge to the dominant behaviorist approach (Erneling, 2014). Piaget had unabashedly spoken of knowledge structures, mental operations, and cognitive development. Even the neo-behaviorists, who spoke of motivation and intervening variables, dared not use such mentalistic language. And yet, Piaget's theory was built on data collected from thousands of children as they solved problems and explained their reasoning. Perhaps rats couldn't tell us all we needed to know about human learning after all. As more American psychologists read Piaget's works in translation, they began thinking it was time to bring the mind back from its Watsonian exile, and within a few years the cognitive revolution was underway. Developmental psychologists may debate what Piaget really meant by terms like egocentrism or object permanence, and whether he overestimated or underestimated children's abilities, but none treat Piaget as irrelevant. Clearly, Jean Piaget ranks along with Sigmund Freud and B. F. Skinner as one of the most important psychologists of the twentieth century (Figure 8.2).

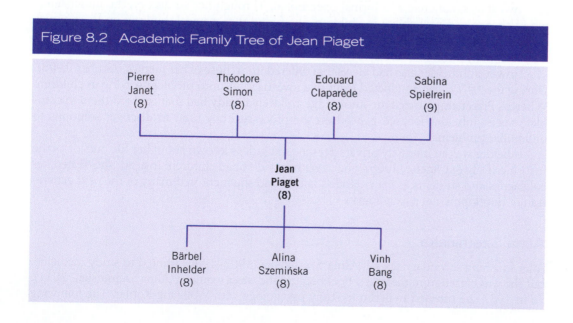

Figure 8.2 Academic Family Tree of Jean Piaget

Piaget's Students

Piaget mentored hundreds of students who traveled from all over the world to work with him in Geneva. While Bärbel Inhelder is generally considered Piaget's most important collaborator, it's also important to consider those who traveled from abroad to work with him.

Bärbel Inhelder

Although **Bärbel Inhelder** (1913–1997) worked closely with Piaget and collaborated with him on a number of projects, she also had her own research program that differed considerably from his. Today, she's recognized as the *Swiss psychologist who discovered the formal operational stage in cognitive development.*

In her early years at the Rousseau Institute, Inhelder collaborated with Alina Szemińska on several projects investigating the development of operational thought, leading to the publication of three pioneering articles on the subject (Gruber, 1998). Inhelder was planning to use data from these studies for her doctoral dissertation. But then Piaget invited her to collaborate on a project that led to the publication of their co-authored book, *The Child's Construction of Quantities*, in 1941.

It was while collecting data for this book that they developed two important concepts in Piagetian theory, conservation and reversibility (Inhelder, 1989). **Conservation** is *the understanding that the mass of a substance remains the same even when its shape changes.* Inhelder would take a ball of modeling clay and roll it into a sausage shape. Five-year-olds believed there was more clay because it was longer. By age seven, these same children now understood the amount of clay hadn't changed, explaining that you can always roll it back into the same ball that it was before. Thus, these children also displayed **reversibility**, which is *the mental undoing of a process to demonstrate conservation.*

Inhelder (1989) enjoyed working with Piaget, but she also feared he'd keep coming up with new projects for them to collaborate on and she'd never complete her dissertation. So in 1939 she returned to her hometown, where she took a position as a school psychologist working with mentally handicapped children. She believed the degree of retardation could be assessed in terms of Piaget's developmental stages, and she used these data in the writing of her dissertation, which she subsequently published.

In 1943, Inhelder (1989) returned to the Rousseau Institute, where she remained for the rest of her career, frequently collaborating with Piaget. During this time, they did the research on adolescence that convinced them of the need to divide the school-age period into two stages, concrete and formal operational. Through her studies on the understanding of chance and probability in children, she found that magical thinking on these topics continued until the beginning of the teenage years, in which the necessary abstract reasoning abilities finally became available.

However, Inhelder also had views that differed from those of her mentor (Gruber, 1998). During the 1970s, she conducted extensive investigations into problem solving in children. Whereas Piaget emphasized the knowledge children already had that enabled them to complete tasks, Inhelder focused instead on the processes they used to discover solutions to unfamiliar problems.

Inhelder was an intensely private person, and little is known about her life outside of the Institute (Daly & Canetto, 2006). She never married or had children. Instead, she treated her colleagues and students as her extended family, and she mentored many of the next generation of developmental psychologists.

Alina Szemińska

After finishing secondary school, **Alina Szemińska** (1907–1986) wanted to study medicine, but she was barred from medical school because she was a woman ("Alina Szeminska," 2011). So in 1927 she traveled to Berlin to study psychology with Wolfgang Köhler. The following year, she took Köhler's advice and went to Geneva to work with Piaget. During the decade she worked at the Rousseau Institute, Szemińska developed a reputation as the *Polish psychologist who investigated the development of mathematical knowledge in children with Piaget.*

Szemińska earned a bachelor's degree in psychology from the University of Geneva while working with Piaget and Inhelder ("Alina Szeminska," n.d.). One of her early contributions was the invention of the classic demonstration of conservation in which colored liquid is poured between glass containers of different sizes. Her collaboration with Piaget led to the eventual publication of two co-authored books, one in 1941 and the other in 1949. But by this time, she'd disappeared and was presumed dead.

When Germany invaded Poland in 1939, Szemińska returned to her home country as a member of the Red Cross ("Alina Szeminska," 2011). She also joined the resistance, but she was arrested in 1942 and later interned in the concentration camp at Auschwitz. By sheer determination, she survived these brutal years of imprisonment. After the camp was liberated in 1945, Szemińska returned to Warsaw, where she worked in a psychological clinic for children who'd been displaced by the war. She was also appointed professor of psychology at the University of Warsaw, where she conducted research on math education.

In the 1970s, political tensions had relaxed to the point that Szemińska was able to make annual trips back to Geneva to work with Piaget and others ("Alina Szeminska," 2011). In 1979, the University of Geneva granted Szemińska an honorary doctorate in recognition of her important contributions to developmental psychology and educational research.

Vinh Bang

A recognized weakness of Piaget's clinical method is its subjectivity, making it difficult to compare data from different subjects even when they're performing the same task (Dionnet, 2009). However, one researcher at the Rousseau Institute devoted much of his career to developing standardized operational tests that could be used to compare data across subjects. This was accomplished by **Vinh Bang** (1922–2008), a *Vietnamese psychologist who collaborated with Piaget and Inhelder for nearly half a century.*

Vinh Bang was born in the city of Huê in Vietnam in 1922 ("Vinh-Bang," 2018). He ran a school in Vietnam based on modern principles of education before immigrating to Switzerland in 1948. Known as "Bang" by his colleagues, his practical approach to problems and his understanding of statistical methods were quickly put to good use. While collaborating with Piaget and Inhelder, Bang continued his work toward a Ph.D., which he earned in 1955. He remained on the staff of the Rousseau Institute for the rest of his career.

In addition to devising standardized tests of operational tasks, Bang took a deep interest in educational psychology (Dionnet, 2009). He saw learning as only taking place when the student's level of operational development was in line with the structural and functional properties of the material being presented. In particular, he was interested in the development of writing skills in schoolchildren, and he recommended structuring writing tasks according to students' abilities. Perhaps Vinh Bang's most important contribution was that he was able to find practical applications for Piaget's often very abstract theories.

Looking Ahead

Psychology in the French-speaking world was built on the study of psychopathology through the clinical method. Jean-Martin Charcot, a world-renowned neurologist who made many importance advances in our understanding of the physiology of the nervous system, turned to the treatment of hysteric patients rather late in his career. It was through his studies of hysteria that Charcot crossed the boundary from neurology into the largely uncharted territory of psychology. He was also one of the first to treat psychological disorders such as hysteria as legitimate objects of study. In the end, his theories about hypnosis and hysteria were found to be untenable. Nevertheless, he served as a catalyst for the promotion of psychology as the science of the mind through his mentorship of influential twentieth-century psychologists.

Charcot's student Pierre Janet developed a form of psychotherapy that was remarkably modern in many respects. Yet through much of the twentieth century, Janet's ideas were largely forgotten as they were overshadowed by Sigmund Freud's ambitious program to promote psychoanalysis as both a theory of the mind and as an effective method of psychotherapy. Although the approaches of the two men were similar in many respects, Freud's version dominated in the English-speaking world. This was due as much to the vagaries of world events as it was to Freud's own efforts to advance the psychoanalytic cause. Without doubt, Freud was an engaging writer whose works appealed not only to professional psychologists but also the educated lay public. For this reason, more of Freud's works were translated into English than were Janet's. However, another important factor in the domination of Freudian psychoanalysis over Janetian psychological analysis was the large emigration of German-speaking intellectuals with the rise of Nazism. Finding refuge in the English-speaking world, Freud's disciples practiced psychoanalysis in their adopted homelands and promoted psychoanalytic ideas among professionals and the general public alike. Since few French-speaking psychologists immigrated to North America around this time, their important contributions went largely unrecognized. It was only in the late twentieth century that historians of psychology rediscovered Janet's work and noticed the striking parallels between his ideas and Freud's more familiar theories.

To some extent, Alfred Binet was spared the fate of having been forgotten that Janet had suffered. In an ironic twist, the Binet-Simon test was much better known in the United States than it was in France. This is because Binet died shortly after the test was developed, and so he had little opportunity to promote its use within the French school system. In North America, however, Lewis Terman saw the potential of the Binet-Simon early on, translating it into an English version known as the Stanford-Binet. We can trace the lineage of many intelligence tests in use today through the Stanford-Binet to the Binet-Simon. Thus, during the twentieth century Binet was well known as the inventor of the intelligence test, yet English-speaking psychologists were unaware of his many other contributions. It was only after cognitive psychologists independently discovered many of his findings on perception, attention, and memory that historians of psychology found that Binet had charted this territory first.

Without question, the French-speaking Swiss psychologist Jean Piaget was one of the pillars of twentieth-century psychology. Furthermore, both his approach to doing science and his thinking on psychological issues were greatly influenced by the network of Charcot's intellectual descendants who mentored him during his formative years. Returning to his native Switzerland as the clouds of war gathered on the European horizon, Piaget's research into the development of cognitive abilities in children flourished even as the Second War World ravaged the continent just beyond the borders of his homeland. Once the war had subsided and a new world order had emerged, Piaget's grand theory of cognitive development burst upon the scene fully formed. His ideas challenged the behaviorist world view, and shortly thereafter the new cognitive approach came to dominate psychology in North America.

Piaget's stage model of cognitive development is certainly one of the foundational theories of modern psychology. For more than half a century, it has provided the basic framework for research in cognitive development. This isn't to say that there's widespread agreement about the accuracy of the model, especially in its details. In fact, many notable developmental psychologists currently working in the field, such as Elizabeth Spelke and Renée Baillargeon, have built their careers testing aspects of Piaget's theory. In particular, it's been found that infants and children can often perform tasks at much earlier ages than Piaget had predicted—at least when those tasks are properly structured. Such findings may seem to challenge Piagetian theory, yet Piaget acknowledged that a child's performance depended not only on the demands of the task but also on the context in which it's performed. The important point here is not whether the theory is right or wrong in the details. Rather, its value lies in its clear structure and specific predictions that continue to inspire productive research programs.

From early in his career, Piaget's ideas were influential. Far off in Russia, a group of young Soviet psychologists were reading Piaget's books and generating their own theories of how children learn to adapt to their social and physical worlds. This is the story we turn to in the next chapter.

CHAPTER SUMMARY

Unlike the experimental psychology of Germany and North America, French psychology grew out of the study of individuals with psychological disorders. This clinical rather than experimental approach is the hallmark of psychology as practiced in the French-speaking world from even before the time of Jean-Martin Charcot. This approach is also evident in Jean Piaget's clinical method, which he and his students used well into the middle decades of the twentieth century. Although Charcot's study of hysteria was far more lacking in rigor than he ever realized, he nevertheless served as mentor and inspiration for many of France's early psychologists, among them Pierre Janet and Alfred Binet. Charcot also served as an important mentor for Sigmund Freud. The early contributions of Pierre Janet in his studies of psychopathology and of Alfred Binet in perception and memory were largely forgotten until they were rediscovered in the late twentieth century. Although Janet's ideas were eclipsed by the rise of psychoanalysis, we can clearly see his influence on the thinking of young Sigmund Freud. Likewise, Alfred Binet is well known today for the intelligence test he developed with his student Théodore Simon, even though this was only accomplished at the end of his illustrious career. Building on this legacy of French psychology, the Swiss psychologist Jean Piaget went on to build his very influential stage model of cognitive development. Using the clinical method he'd learned working with Janet and Simon, Jean Piaget and his colleagues methodologically tested the thinking processes and reasoning skills of children ranging from infancy to the teenage years. In the process, he helped usher in the cognitive revolution after World War II, making him one of the most influential psychologists of the twentieth century.

DISCUSSION QUESTIONS

1. Hysteria was a common disorder in the decades around the turn of the twentieth century. Today, it's known as conversion disorder, but it's far less common. Consider why a psychological disorder might be more prevalent in one time period or culture compared to another.

2. Janet argued that hysteria, hypnosis, and multiple personalities were all examples of dissociation. Formulate other examples of psychological phenomena that can be described in terms of dissociation.

3. Consider the parallels between Janet's and Freud's theories. To what extent is it acceptable to incorporate another person's ideas into your own theory? Did Janet have a legitimate complaint against Freud? Defend your position.

4. Given that both men had similar theories, consider the reasons why Freud became well known whereas Janet was largely forgotten.

5. At the turn of the twentieth century, French psychology was based on the premise that exceptional cases are more informative than studies of normal behavior. Consider the ways Binet continued in this mindset even after he gave up psychopathology.

6. Explain how Binet and Simon's concept of mental age is determined and interpreted. Assess the usefulness of this construct.

7. Trace the development of modern intelligence tests from Binet and Simon to Terman and Yerkes. What changes were made along the way?

8. Binet considered both personality and intelligence to be a part of individual psychology. What do these two concepts have in common?

9. Describe Piaget's clinical method. In what sense is interviewing children like interviewing mental patients?

10. Piaget made important contributions to psychology, but he had a lot of help along the way. Name the people who mentored or worked with Piaget, describing how they influenced the formation of his theory.

11. Explain how the processes of assimilation and accommodation represent a link between biology and psychology in Piaget's mind.

12. A common criticism of Piaget is that his work is based on the observations of his own three children. How would you respond to this?

ON THE WEB

YouTube hosts documentaries and presentations of varying quality on the lives and contributions of **Jean-Martin Charcot**, **Pierre Janet**, and **Alfred Binet**. View these with a critical eye if you're seeking more information about these early French psychologists. YouTube also hosts several videos in which **Jean Piaget** talks about his ideas. Note that he speaks in French, and not all of these items have English subtitles. However, the Canadian psychologist Jordan Peterson has posted a number of engaging lectures on Piaget's theory of genetic epistemology and its application to science as well as our own lives. If you would like to see demonstrations of his clinical method, search **Piaget conservation task** and **Piaget three mountain task**. Finally, the **Jean Piaget Foundation** website houses a wealth of information about Piaget and his students, including a photo album and brief biographies.

Timeline

1900

1904 Ivan Pavlov wins the Nobel Prize; Sabina Spielrein begins psychoanalysis with Carl Jung.

1912 Sabina Spielrein publishes "Destruction as the Cause of Coming Into Being."

1910

1917 The Russian Revolution takes place; Vladimir Lenin rises to power.

1914 World War I begins.

1918 World War I ends.

1923 Ivan Pavlov travels to North America and Great Britain.

1920

1924 Lenin dies; Joseph Stalin rises to power.

1926 Pavlov's biological station at Koltushi opens.

1927 Vladimir Bekhterev dies under mysterious circumstances.

1931 Alexander Luria conducts his first expedition to Central Asia.

1930

1932 Alexander Luria conducts his second expedition to Central Asia; he also publishes *The Nature of Human Conflicts* in English.

1934 Lev Vygotsky dies.

1936 Ivan Pavlov dies and receives a state funeral; Vygotsky's book *Thought and Language* is published posthumously.

1935 The Soviet Union hosts the Fifteenth International Physiological Congress.

1940

1941 The Nazis invade Russia.

1945 Nazi Germany surrenders.

1950

1960

1962 Alexander Luria publishes *The Higher Cortical Functions in Man.*

1968 Alexander Luria publishes *The Mind of a Mnemonist.*

1970

1970 Alexander Luria publishes *Traumatic Aphasia.*

1978 An edited volume of Vygotsky's articles is published in English as *Mind in Society.*

1980

1987 Evgenia Homskaya publishes *Neuropsychology.*

1990

Learning Objectives

After reading this chapter, you should be able to:

- Explain how Pavlov attempted to use the artificial conditioned reflex to study higher nervous activity.

- Contrast Bekhterev's associated motor reflex with Pavlov's artificial conditioned reflex.

- Compare Vygotsky's theory of cognitive development with that of Piaget.

- Assess Luria's contributions to neuropsychology.

Looking Back

Russian has a long history, but it was only around the turn of the eighteenth century that it began looking toward Europe as a model for becoming a modern nation-state. During the reign of Peter the Great from 1689 to 1725, Russian society underwent considerable restructuring. The government was completely reorganized, and Peter brought large-scale manufacturing enterprises into the country for the first time. He also began a series of military campaigns to extend the Russian territory. By the reign of Catherine the Great from 1762 to 1796, Russia had expanded to borders somewhat like what it has today. Furthermore, Russian industrial and military might had grown to the extent that it was now considered a European power.

The eighteenth century is often known as the Age of Enlightenment, and Russia experienced a flourishing of science and philosophy during this period as did the other nations of Europe. Most notable from this time period was Mikhail Lomonosov (1711–1765), who was a contemporary with David Hume in Britain and Immanuel Kant in Germany (Chapter 1). Lomonosov was a polymath who made significant contributions in a wide range of fields, including physics, astronomy, chemistry, and geology. In his philosophical works, he also touched on issues that would now be considered topics in social psychology. However, his most important contribution for the development of psychology in Russia was his materialist stance and insistence that the world—even that of humans—was governed by laws that could be discerned through the scientific method.

During the last half of the nineteenth century, Russia experienced another period of rapid growth in the natural sciences (Maslov, 2016). For our purposes, the most notable person from this period was **Ivan Sechenov** (1829–1905), the *Russian physiologist who argued that all behavior, no matter how complex, can be broken down into simple reflexes*. This assertion presented the possibility that human psychology could be understood in terms of the activity of the nervous system, and thus it was amenable to study through the scientific method. Sechenov had studied with Hermann von Helmholtz (Chapter 2), and it was no doubt from his mentor that he acquired this physiological approach to psychology. In turn, Sechenov inspired the work of Ivan Pavlov and other Russian scientists of the early twentieth century as they explored the conditioned reflex, and thus we can also say that he was an intellectual ancestor of American behaviorism as well.

At the turn of the twentieth century, Russia was rapidly modernizing. Meanwhile, the transition from an agricultural to an industrial society created considerable social upheaval. Its government was also becoming unstable during this time. The House of Romanov, which had included such illustrious leaders as Peter and Catherine, was now in decline. The last tsar to rule Russia, Nicholas II, was particularly inept at dealing with the social crises that plagued the nation. When World War I broke out, Russia sided with England and France against Germany and Austria, leading to devastating consequences. More than three million Russians lost their lives in the conflict, and by 1917 the people were in revolt. Nicholas II abdicated, and a provisional government ruled for a few months, but toward the end of the year a second revolt brought the Bolsheviks to power with Vladimir Lenin (1870–1924) as their leader.

It took several years for the Bolsheviks to solidify their control over the country, and during this time famine was widespread. Although he was a Communist, Lenin took a practical approach to governing the country and rebuilding the economy. Psychology flourished in the Soviet Union under Lenin, especially those fields with practical applications in education, industry, and the military. In terms of educational psychology, the goal was to create a new generation of Soviet citizenry that was forward looking and that had cast off the pernicious habits of Russia's feudal past.

When Lenin died in 1924, Joseph Stalin (1878–1953) assumed leadership of the Soviet Union. Unlike his predecessor, Stalin was far more interested in

Ilya Repin

Photo 9.1
Portrait of Ivan Sechenov

consolidating his own power than he was in building a prosperous Communist state. He was a master at dividing people and setting one group against another. Accusations of disloyalty to the Communist cause were rampant, yet no one knew how to toe the party line since Stalinist doctrine kept changing. Despite the social turmoil caused by Stalin's reign of terror as well as the disruptions of World War II, Russian psychologists still managed to make important contributions, as we'll see in this chapter.

Our story of Soviet psychology begins with Ivan Pavlov, whose discovery of the conditioned reflex led to a fruitful program of research that became the model for scientific psychology in Russia and inspired the behaviorist movement in North America. We'll also learn about Pavlov's archrival Vladimir Bekhterev and his unfortunate encounter with Stalin. Next we'll meet a trio of men who are often referred to as the "Russian troika" after the tradition of harnessing horses three abreast. These three men—Lev Vygotsky, Alexander Luria, and Alexei Leontiev—were the leaders of Soviet psychology during the middle of the twentieth century, and it was through their guidance that a community of psychologists managed to flourish in the Soviet Union despite economic hardship and political oppression.

Ivan Pavlov

The old man and his grown son boarded a train in New York's Grand Central Station one afternoon in July 1923 (Thomas, 1994). They were the first people to enter the carriage. As the son was lifting their luggage onto the overhead rack, three ruffians attacked the old man, snatching his pocketbook. The son and a porter chased after the thieves but to no avail. Inside the wallet was all the money the father and son had brought for their trip. Not knowing what to do next, the two disembarked and headed back into the city, looking for a friend.

The victim was none other than **Ivan Pavlov** (1849–1936), the *Russian physiologist who discovered the conditioned reflex* (Thomas, 1994). Pavlov was on a lecture tour through the United States and Great Britain, and his son Vladimir was accompanying him as translator, manager, and personal assistant. They got in touch with Pavlov's colleague Walter Cannon (Chapter 10), who arranged lodging and took up a collection to provide them with sufficient funds to finish their trip. It wasn't the first time that Cannon had come to Pavlov's aid in time of need. Nor was it the last time these two great psychologists from opposite ends of the world would meet.

Ivan Pavlov was born the son of a Russian Orthodox priest, and he too was preparing for the priesthood when he discovered Darwin and lost his religion ("Ivan Pavlov," 1967). Earning a degree in physiology, Pavlov undertook the line of research in physiology that would earn him the Nobel Prize in 1904. He was a skilled surgeon, and he had learned a new technique for studying the functions of the internal organs using laboratory animals. This involved creating a **fistula** (pronounced *FIST-chu-la*), which is *a surgical opening that provides access for inserting tubes into internal organs*.

For example, some of Pavlov's early investigations into the digestive process involved a procedure known as **sham feeding** (Dewsbury, 1997). This is *a process in which a fistula is cut into the throat and a tube inserted so that everything eaten is diverted from the stomach*. Another fistula was incised in the stomach so that the gastric juices could be extracted. Pavlov found that digestive fluids were secreted as soon as the dog started eating, before the food reached the stomach. From this observation, he concluded that the secretion of gastric juices was mediated by the nervous system and not initiated by the presence of food in the stomach.

By the way, if you feel that sham feeding and fistulas constitute animal abuse, you need to consider standard practices at the time. In the late nineteenth century, research in physiology still depended on **vivisection**, which involved *the cutting open of a live animal to study the functioning of its internal organs* ("Ivan

Photo 9.2
Ivan Pavlov

National Institute of Health

Pavlov," 1967). This was generally done without anesthesia, and the animals suffered horribly before they died. Pavlov's pioneering technique revolutionized the study of physiology. His dogs lived long, healthy lives, and there's every reason to believe he was genuinely concerned about their welfare.

In short order, Pavlov built a research team that could systematically study the functioning of each organ and gland of the digestive system, using the methods he'd developed (Klimenko & Golikov, 2008). By the turn of the twentieth century, Pavlov's institute was world renowned, and scientists from across Europe and even from North America came to do research there. When Pavlov was awarded the Nobel Prize in 1904, it was for two decades of research on the functioning of the digestive system (Figure 9.1). But even before he received the world's most prestigious award in science, Pavlov had already turned his attention to a new topic—the functioning of the brain. You see, he found he could do this by measuring dog spit.

Artificial Conditioned Reflex

As far back as the sham feeding experiments, Pavlov understood that digestive processes were controlled by the nervous system. *Pavlov's term for the nervous system functions that regulate the internal organs* was **lower nervous activity**, and he believed that this didn't involve the cerebral cortex (hence, "lower"). This concept was sufficient to explain how most of the digestive system worked, but it fell short when it came to explaining the first step in the process, salivation.

Salivation was also the last piece of the digestion puzzle that Pavlov worked on (Todes, 1997). Creating fistulas in salivary ducts was challenging because of their small size, but when one of his colleagues devised a technique in 1895, the study of salivation proceeded apace. The following year, one of Pavlov's students used the technique to explore the factors that influenced salivation. During his experiments, Pavlov found that his dogs would salivate at the sight of food, well before it had entered their mouth. Physiologists already knew about this so-called **psychic secretion**, or *salivation at the expectation of food*, but they discounted it as nothing more than noise in the data. Pavlov's genius was to recognize that psychic secretion provided a window into the workings of **higher nervous activity**, which was *Pavlov's term for the nervous system functions that coordinate the organism's interactions with its environment.* This, he believed, involved the cerebral cortex (hence, "higher").

During the next few years, Pavlov gave students research projects using the method of "teasing" the animal with food to test various hypotheses about the workings of higher nervous activity (Klimenko & Golikov, 2008). For example, they found that dogs with damage to certain areas of their cerebral cortex no longer produced psychic secretion. This settled a long-running debate

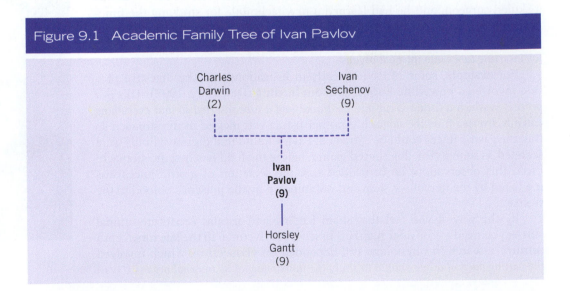

Figure 9.1   Academic Family Tree of Ivan Pavlov

in the lab over whether the phenomenon was mediated by cortical or subcortical structures. Another study in Pavlov's lab showed that virtually any stimulus in any sensory modality—whether a flashing light, a ringing bell, or even an electric shock—could elicit psychic secretion as long as the animal had learned to associate it with food. Thereafter, Pavlov called this kind of response an **artificial conditioned reflex**, which involves *the association of an innate reflex with a novel stimulus.* The artificial conditioned reflex became the mainstay of research in the Pavlov lab for the next three decades, resulting in more than 500 publications (Figure 9.2).

Pavlov won the Nobel Prize in 1904 for his work on the digestive system ("Ivan Pavlov," 1967). But at his acceptance speech, he talked mainly about the conditioned reflex that promised to be a fruitful line of research in his lab. He would have no way of knowing that conditioned reflexes would dominate his thinking for the rest of his long and productive life.

Pavlov had long expressed a curiosity about the mind and the experience of consciousness, but he rejected the subjective approaches taken by philosophers and psychologists ("Ivan Pavlov," 1967). The discovery of conditioned reflexes, however, was a game changer

Figure 9.2 Artificial Conditioned Reflex

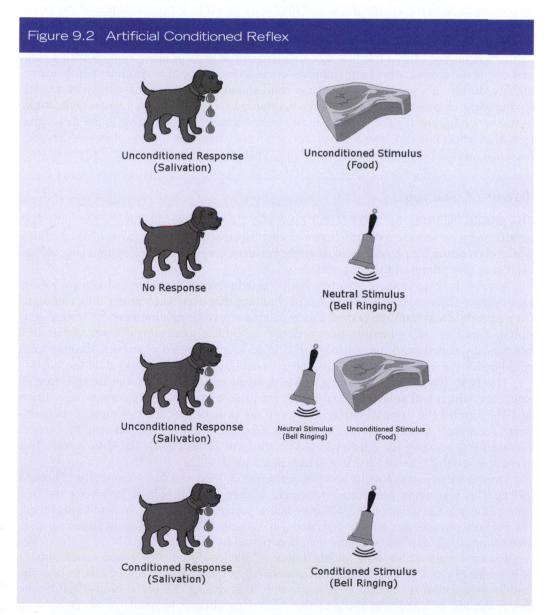

Unconditioned Response
(Salivation)

Unconditioned Stimulus
(Food)

No Response

Neutral Stimulus
(Bell Ringing)

Unconditioned Response
(Salivation)

Neutral Stimulus
(Bell Ringing)

Unconditioned Stimulus
(Food)

Conditioned Response
(Salivation)

Conditioned Stimulus
(Bell Ringing)

for Pavlov. Now he had a method for objectively studying mental processes. Over the next three decades, Pavlov and his team used this method to test his theory of higher nervous activity. Although he couldn't observe this activity directly, he could accurately measure its effects through conditioned responses. This approach was no different from the way that physicists of this time period were studying the structure of the atom. Although they couldn't directly observe electrons or nuclei, they could measure the effects they produced in experiments. However, such a speculative approach within psychology was still controversial.

In Pavlov's theory, what we call mind or consciousness is the product of biological processes in the brain (Pickering, 1997). We aren't consciously aware of these processes, but rather they're what produce our conscious experience. Thus, an introspective approach is doomed to failure. However, a biological approach, such as the method of artificial conditioned reflexes, could provide important insights. Pavlov's task, then, was to construct a theory of the nervous system that could explain the behaviors he observed.

Greatly influenced by Darwin, Pavlov believed that innate reflexes evolved to provide the organism with a set of fixed responses to common environmental situations (Ushakova, 1997). In this view, unconditioned responses—that is, innate reflexes—are elicited by direct contact with the environment, and they're mediated in subcortical areas of the brain. However, more complex organisms can respond flexibly. The **first signal system** is *Pavlov's conceptualization of conditioned reflexes as adjustments to a changing environment*. On the one hand, humans respond to this first signal system just as dogs or other animals with a cerebral cortex do. On the other hand, humans live in a unique social environment of their own making, and so they've also developed a **second signal system** to manage that constructed environment. Specifically, this is *Pavlov's conceptualization of language as a means for adjusting each other's behavior.* If I show a dog a tasty treat, its mouth waters. This is the first signal system at work. But all I have to do is mention a tasty treat like a piece of sweet, delicious chocolate, and already your mouth is watering. That's the power of the second signal system!

Tower of Silence

The decade following his 1904 Nobel Prize was a heady time for Pavlov. Not only had he attained a reputation for himself as a distinguished scientist, he'd turned his lab into a world-class center for physiological research. Furthermore, he was developing a psychological theory that promised to be revolutionary.

Always the consummate scientist, Pavlov sought ever more rigor and control for his experiments (Klimenko & Golikov, 2008). Fretting that even faint noises and vibrations from outside could taint the results, he envisioned a pristine environment for testing conditioned reflexes. With funding from a donor, he built a three-story "Tower of Silence," hermetically sealed from the outside world. In its sound-proofed chambers, Pavlov's team could conduct their experiments in complete tranquility. It was the calm before the storm.

The First World War, beginning in 1914, weakened the already declining House of Romanov, which had ruled Imperial Russia for three centuries. The February Revolution of 1917 toppled the imperial family, leading to the exile or execution of most of its members. Then the October Revolution eight months later toppled the Russian Provisional Government, bringing the Bolsheviks led by Vladimir Lenin (1870–1924) to power. This event sparked the Russian Civil War, which lasted until 1922.

During these years of social and political turmoil, food and fuel were scarce (Thomas, 1994). This was when American physiologist Walter Cannon helped Pavlov for the first time. Cannon collected about $2,000 from fellow psychologists, which he sent to his friend, the Finnish physiologist Robert Tigerstedt, in Helsinki. With the money, Tigerstedt purchased food and supplies, which he then transported to St. Petersburg.

Pavlov continued to work in his Tower of Silence despite the social chaos outside (Klimenko & Golikov, 2008). But due to a scarcity of food and a lack of fuel to heat the building, he found it impossible to work with dogs during the years 1918–1920. So he began visiting colleagues working in the various psychiatric hospitals of St. Petersburg, interviewing the doctors and observing the patients. It was during this period that Pavlov began to see how his theory of higher nervous activity could lead to a better understanding of the causes of psychological disorders, as well as their possible cures.

By 1921, social order had been restored to most of Russia, with the Bolsheviks firmly in control (Thomas, 1994). Concerned that he might not be able to obtain sufficient funding for his research under the new regime, Pavlov requested permission to emigrate. But Lenin keenly understood the political capital to be garnered by holding onto Pavlov, the Nobel laureate, the shining star of Soviet science. Pavlov was needed to help build the new Soviet Union, and his research would continue to be well funded. Lenin did grant Pavlov permission to do a lecture tour of North America and Great Britain in 1923, with travel expenses paid by the Soviet government. Most of that money, as we know, ended up in the hands of three New York thugs!

Also in 1923, the Soviet government granted Pavlov land near the village of Koltushi, just outside St. Petersburg, to establish a biological station where experimental animals could be bred and kept ("Ivan Pavlov," 1967). The station opened in 1926, and the last building was completed in 1933. Pavlov even received some primates so that his theories could be tested on animals more closely related to humans. Koltushi even became known among physiologists as the "Capital of Conditioned Reflexes," especially after the Fifteenth International Physiological Congress was hosted there and at sites in Moscow and Leningrad in 1935. (Note that Leningrad was the new name of St. Petersburg, in commemoration of the founder of the Soviet Union.)

It was at this conference that Ivan Pavlov and Walter Cannon met for the last time (Klimenko & Golikov, 2008). In his memoirs, Cannon recalled that the 86-year-old was as energetic as ever. During their walk through the Koltushi facility, Pavlov expressed gratitude to his government for its generous support, regretting only that he didn't have such opportunities twenty years earlier.

Still, Pavlov wasn't afraid to bite the hand that fed him. He considered himself a Russian patriot but not a supporter of Bolshevik policies (Windholz, 1997). Knowing that his superstar status made him untouchable, Pavlov denounced Soviet policies in his lectures. He also advocated for tolerance of religious beliefs, even though he'd lost his faith in his youth. Even thin-skinned Joseph Stalin, who'd succeeded Lenin, put up with his antics. The same could not be said for another of Pavlov's contemporaries, Vladimir Bekhterev, whose story we'll read about shortly.

Later in his career, Pavlov extended his method of conditioned reflexes to the study of human personality and psychopathology and laid important foundations for the development of new clinical techniques (Klimenko & Golikov, 2008). When Pavlov died of natural causes in 1936, he was given a state funeral. For the next few decades, Pavlov's approach was the only school of psychology sanctioned by the Russian government. As we'll see, other Soviet psychologists had to couch their research in terms of Pavlovian conditioning, whether it was relevant or not. Using such twists of logic kept Soviet scientists from political persecution, but they depended on their colleagues to read between the lines. In the end, Pavlov was an accidental psychologist. A physiologist in training and in outlook, he showed a way to move beyond dualistic thinking on the relationship between mind and brain. In this way, he demonstrated what a rigorous science of the mind could look like.

From Pavlov to Vygotsky

Hailed as the star of Soviet science, Ivan Pavlov was without doubt the most well known and most influential of Russian psychologists during the first decades of the twentieth century. Nevertheless, other psychologists in Russia were also making important early contributions to the field, and this was all the more remarkable given hardships they endured during this turbulent time in Russian history. In this section, we'll read about three notable psychologists working in the Soviet Union during its early years. The first was an American doctor who studied with Pavlov and introduced his ideas to the English-speaking world. The second was Pavlov's archrival, whose contributions to psychology were equally important, but who unwisely got on the wrong side of Stalin. And the third is a female medical doctor and psychoanalyst who worked with many of the top figures in European psychology—including Carl Jung and Sigmund Freud (Chapter 7) as well as Jean Piaget (Chapter 8). She then returned to her homeland after the Russian Revolution to help build the new Soviet state, and there she introduced the latest ideas from Europe to the next generation of Russian psychologists, most notable among them being Lev Vygotsky.

Horsley Gantt

In the first decades of the twentieth century, many aspiring psychologists from around the world traveled to Europe or North America to learn this new science of mind and behavior. However, one man traveled in the opposite direction to learn psychology. Horsley Gantt (1892–1980) was an *American medical doctor who studied conditioned reflexes with Pavlov in Russia*.

Gantt traveled to Russia in 1922 to assist with famine relief efforts (Harvey, 1995). After World War I and the Russian Revolution, there were widespread food shortages, and diseases such as cholera, typhus, and smallpox were rampant. While Gantt was in St. Petersburg, a friend introduced him to Ivan Pavlov. This surprised Gantt because he thought the Nobel Prize laureate had died several years before—the *Encyclopedia Britannica* had even published Pavlov's obituary in 1918. Gantt found that Pavlov was not only alive and well, he was also working on a project unfamiliar to Gantt—the conditioned reflex. Gantt was so fascinated by the way Pavlov was using this technique to study mental processes that he decided to stay in Russia and work with him.

Over the next seven years, Gantt learned the conditioned reflex technique from Pavlov as well as the Russian language (McGuigan, 1981). But he also suffered greatly during this period. Often going days without food, Gantt contracted pneumonia, which developed into tuberculosis. He experienced firsthand the deprivations that Russians were suffering during the early years of the Soviet Union. For example, he once had to stand in line for two hours to buy paper for recording laboratory notes—he was only allowed to purchase four sheets, the maximum ration. Nevertheless, he worked enthusiastically in Pavlov's lab, as he discovered that a problem he'd been working on back in the United States could now be solved using the conditioned reflex technique.

In 1929, Gantt returned to the United States (Harvey, 1995). He set up a lab at Johns Hopkins where he applied Pavlovian conditioning to a number of problems. But he's best known for his translations of Ivan Pavlov's and Alexander Luria's works. It was largely through Horsley Gantt that the English-speaking world came to know about the latest developments in Soviet psychology.

Vladimir Bekhterev

Pavlov is remembered today as the discoverer of the conditioned reflex. But what's not widely known is that he spent much of his career in a bitter rivalry with a fellow Russian psychologist who claimed priority for the discovery. Vladimir Bekhterev (1857–1927) was a *Russian neurologist who founded an approach to psychology known as reflexology based on the associated motor reflex*.

Although his training was in neurology, Bekhterev spent a year in the laboratory of Wilhelm Wundt (Chapter 3) learning the new experimental psychology (Araujo, 2014). During his time in Western Europe, Bekhterev also traveled to Paris to work with Jean-Martin Charcot (Chapter 8) (Figure 9.3). In 1885, Bekhterev returned to Russia to accept a professorship at the University of Kazan, where he established the first psychology laboratory in that country. At Kazan, he began research on motor reflexes in dogs, which he continued after moving to St. Petersburg. He not only discovered that his dogs flinched when they received an electric shock, he also found that they began anticipating the shock

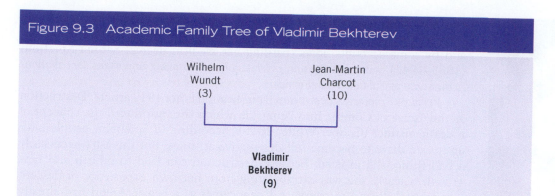

Figure 9.3 Academic Family Tree of Vladimir Bekhterev

Wilhelm
Wundt
(3)

Jean-Martin
Charcot
(10)

Vladimir
Bekhterev
(9)

and tried to withdraw. Thus, he discovered the **associated motor reflex**, which is *a muscle movement in response to a signal that a pain stimulus is about to occur*.

Both Pavlov and Bekhterev had been greatly influenced by Ivan Sechenov, who'd argued that all behavior, no matter how complex, can be broken down into simple reflexes (Maslov, 2016). Sechenov had argued that even brain processes are reflexes, that is, responses to stimuli emanating either from the environment or from within the body. Thus, *Bekhterev's approach of using associated motor reflexes to make inferences about the nature of mental processes in the brain* became known as **reflexology**.

By all accounts, both Pavlov and Bekhterev had massive egos and combative personalities (Maslov, 2016). Although each had come upon the concept of a conditioned reflex by different routes—Pavlov by way of food and the salivary response, Bekhterev by way of pain and the motor response—neither would give any credit to the other, and each claimed priority. Pavlov's award of the Nobel Prize only made tensions between the two men worse, as Bekhterev had been nominated several times but had never won. The animosity between the two giants of early Russian psychology spread to their students and collaborators as well—one simply could not claim both Pavlov and Bekhterev as mentors or colleagues.

Because of his Nobel Prize, Pavlov was the star of Soviet science, so he felt free to openly criticize the Bolshevik regime (Moroz, 1989). Bekhterev was also a vocal opponent of the government, but, unlike Pavlov, he was vulnerable. When he suggested in public in 1927 that Stalin might be paranoid, Bekhterev died suddenly the next day, even though he'd been in excellent health up to that point. It could have just been a coincidence. But then, such coincidences were a frequent occurrence under Stalin's reign.

Bekhterev's mysterious death also meant the immediate demise of reflexology (Byford, 2016). In both the Soviet Union and the United States, Pavlov was hailed as the discoverer of the conditioned reflex, and Bekhterev's contribution was forgotten. In fact, the conditioned reflex that John Watson and other early behaviorists adopted in their research was the associated motor reflex of Bekhterev, not the salivary response of Pavlov. This is because the writings of Pavlov weren't translated into English until well after the founding of the behaviorist movement. At the time, early behaviorists only knew of Pavlov's and Bekhterev's work through indirect sources, and they didn't have a clear understanding of the distinction between the two approaches.

History of Medicine (NLM), via Wikimedia Commons

Photo 9.3
Vladimir Bekhterev

Sabina Spielrein

In 1904, a young Russian woman by the name of Sabina Spielrein was admitted to the Burghölzli, the famous mental asylum in Zürich, Switzerland, with symptoms of hysteria (Kelcourse, 2015). Her doctor, Carl Jung, decided to use the new method of psychoanalysis to treat her. The treatment apparently worked, and within a year she not only was pronounced

**Photo 9.4
Sabina Spielrein**

cured but also had been accepted to medical school. For the next six years, Jung was an important presence in Spielrein's life—as her therapist, mentor, and by some accounts, lover. Earning her medical degree, **Sabina Spielrein** (1885–1942) became a *Russian psychoanalyst who made important contributions to the study of childhood development.*

Perhaps Spielrein's best-known publication is her 1912 article "Destruction as the Cause of Coming Into Being," in which she introduced the concept of a death instinct (Cooper-White, 2015). According to Spielrein, people have an innate drive to become self-destructive at times. But this isn't necessarily a bad thing, she insisted, because destruction can lead to rebirth and new growth. Clearly she was extrapolating from her own experience of descent into mental illness, recovery, and new career as a healer. Freud had already posited an innate sex drive from birth, and this could also be interpreted as a creative or life instinct. The concept of a death instinct sounding appealing as a counterpart to the life instinct, and Freud adopted it into his theory, crediting Spielrein for the idea in a footnote in his 1920 book, *Beyond the Pleasure Principle.* However, Spielrein also got caught up in the falling out between Freud and Jung, and as a result both men distanced themselves from her.

When Jean Piaget arrived at the Rousseau Institute in Geneva, Spielrein was already working as a developmental researcher there (Davis, 2006). Piaget underwent psychoanalysis with Spielrein to learn more about the process, but he was generally unimpressed with the technique. Spielrein also worked with Piaget on several research projects. In 1923, she returned to Russia, where she worked in Moscow with Vygotsky and Luria. As a child psychoanalyst who had worked with Piaget, she particularly had an influence on Vygotsky's early theorizing about cognitive development. Spielrein set up the first psychoanalytic institute in Russia, but when Stalin came to power, he banned the practice of psychoanalysis, so she went back to her hometown of Rostov, where she spent a few relatively quiet years before the Nazis occupied the city in 1942. Spielrein and her two daughters were among the 10,000 other Jewish residents who were marched out of town, mowed down with machine guns, and buried in a mass grave.

Sabina Spielrein's work had been all but forgotten until her diaries were discovered in the early 1980s (Cooper-White, 2015). In over thirty articles, she had laid out key ideas that predated, and in many cases influenced, the work of Anna Freud and Melanie Klein (Chapter 7) as well as that of Jean Piaget (Chapter 8) and Lev Vygotsky. Only recently has she begun to receive proper recognition as a pioneer in developmental psychology.

Lev Vygotsky

Lev Vygotsky was a man ahead of his time. He'd come to psychology late, and he was mostly self-taught in the subject. His career as a psychologist spanned a mere decade before his life was tragically cut short. Although he left behind some 270 manuscripts, these remained largely unpublished for decades due to political oppression (Ghassemzadeh, Posner, & Rothbart, 2013). When his works finally became available in Russia and the West, they were widely celebrated for the originality of their ideas. Today, **Lev Vygotsky** (1896–1934) is known as a *Russian psychologist who emphasized the role of social interaction in cognitive development.*

Vygotsky was born during Russia's "Golden Age," when the nation was undergoing rapid industrialization along with a restructuring of society, and he grew up in a well-educated Jewish family (Kotik-Friedgut & Friedgut, 2008). His parents sent him to Moscow to learn medicine, but he studied philosophy instead. He graduated in 1917, just before the Russian Revolution, and he was devoted to the socialist cause. Returning to his hometown, he taught school and married a local woman. But he went back to Moscow to finish his graduate studies, completing a dissertation on the psychology of art.

In 1924, Vygotsky presented a paper at a psychology conference in which he dared to criticize the star of Soviet science, Ivan Pavlov (García, 2016). Vygotsky asserted that the primary question of psychology was the nature of consciousness. He granted that both Pavlov and Bekhterev had been right to reject the introspective methods of the philosophers. Yet he also maintained that they'd gone too far by reducing psychology to the level of physiology with their focus on reflexes. This talk was well received, and as a result he was offered a research position at the Moscow Institute of Psychology. Thus began Vygotsky's career as a psychologist, which lasted until his death a decade later.

Early in his career, Vygotsky studied children with learning disabilities but later extended his research to normally developing children as well (Vassilieva, 2010). His thinking was greatly influenced by developmental theories that had been proposed by psychologists in other countries, such as James Mark Baldwin (Chapter 3), Kurt Koffka (Chapter 6), Sigmund Freud (Chapter 7), and Jean Piaget (Chapter 8). One of his early mentors was Sabina Spielrein, who'd studied with Carl Jung.

Vygotsky was also friends with Kurt Lewin (Chapter 6), whom he visited in 1925 (Yasnitsky, 2011). When Lewin's student Bluma Zeigarnik (Chapter 6) returned to Russia in 1931, she worked in Vygotsky's lab. And Lewin visited Vygotsky in Moscow in 1933 before immigrating to the United States. These foreign contacts proved to be politically costly. As Stalin tightened his grip on Soviet society, Vygotsky was accused of being "too cosmopolitan" and an "insincere Marxist." As a result, much of his writing remained unpublished during his lifetime. Although Vygotsky had struggled with tuberculosis most of his life, no doubt the stress of political censure took its toll as well.

Vygotsky's best-known work, *Thought and Language*, was published by his students in 1936, two years after his death (Ghassemzadeh et al., 2013). In this book, he lays out many of the ideas he's known for today. However, political pressures kept them from publishing his other writings. The Soviet government had banned research on child development, which effectively made all of Vygotsky's works taboo. It was decades before his writings became widely disseminated in Russia and the rest of the world.

Photo 9.5
Lev Vygotsky

Thought and Language

In *Thought and Language*, Vygotsky laid out his theory of the social origins of consciousness (Burkholder & Peláez, 2000). Because consciousness is a private experience, it's generally thought of as arising within the individual. The British empiricists (Chapter 1), as well as Edward Titchener and the structuralists (Chapter 3), saw consciousness as being assembled from the elements of sensation. Likewise, Jean Piaget (Chapter 8) viewed cognitive processes as developing through the child's interaction with the physical environment. But Vygotsky disagreed, maintaining instead that consciousness first resides in the social environment of the child, and it then becomes internalized through interactions with adults and peers. It was this revolutionary idea that made Vygotsky so influential in later decades of the twentieth century.

To understand the relationship between thought and language, we need to first comprehend Vygotsky's distinction between lower and higher mental functions (Arievitch & van der Veer, 2004). Lower mental functions include such cognitive processes as sensations, reflexes, and basic emotions. These kinds of psychological phenomena are the product of evolution by natural selection, and they were the focus of Pavlov's and Bekhterev's research programs. While their study can yield important information about human *behavior*, Vygotsky maintained, they cannot account for human *consciousness*. By contrast, higher mental functions such as conceptual thinking, reasoning, and decision making are what consciousness is all about. Moreover, these processes arise not through biological evolution but rather through social development. Although he never used the term, *Vygotsky's theoretical approach emphasizing the role of social interaction in cognitive development* became known as **cultural-historical psychology**.

In Vygotsky's view, language is what facilitates the development of higher mental functions (Damianova & Sullivan, 2011). Before children learn language, they can certainly think in terms of lower mental functions like sensations, urges, and feelings. But higher mental functions require the internalization of language. That is, children learn to use language not just to communicate but also to think. In other words, Vygotsky saw language as a tool. And just as we use tools like hammers and shovels to extend the natural limits of our physical activities, so too language provides us with a psychological tool that increases our thinking abilities far beyond what we could manage otherwise. Without language, we're merely beings that are driven by our emotions. But with language internalized as thought, we're capable of problem-solving, self-regulation, and planning for the future.

Note that this idea of complex thought as being supported by internalized language is why Vygotsky says that consciousness first resides outside the individual in the social environment (Karpov & Haywood, 1998). In the beginning, the child learns language as a tool for communication. For example, Mommy says "No!" to make baby Suzie stop pulling the cat's tail. Sometime later, Suzie tells Mommy "No!" when she tries to put her to bed. At this point, Suzie has learned that language functions as a tool for regulating the behaviors of other people. As Suzie's language skills improve, she sometimes talks to herself. Reaching for the cat's tail, she says "No!" out loud—even imitating her mother's voice—as she restrains her impulse. Now we can see that Suzie has learned the self-regulating function of language. Eventually, this self-talk will disappear, but we all know from our own personal experience that this self-directed language is still going on inside Suzie's head, because we all have the same kind of self-talk going on in our own minds. In other words, language has become internalized as a tool for higher-level thinking.

Piaget was the first to systematically observe what he called egocentric speech (Frauenglass & Diaz, 1985). While he recognized that young children talk to themselves to regulate their behaviors, he also believed this kind of self-talk eventually disappeared because children learn it isn't socially acceptable. Vygotsky replicated some of Piaget's early studies and came up with similar results, but his interpretation was different. Instead, he argued that there are three different kinds of speech. When children talk with other people, they're using *social speech*. But when they talk out loud to themselves, they're using *private speech*, in other words, Piaget's egocentric speech. Finally, when children learn to enlist language for thinking, they're using *inner speech*. Thus, self-talk never goes away, as Piaget argued. Rather, it becomes silent as it's turned inward.

As Vygotsky investigated the cognitive development of children, he used a procedure he called the **method of dual stimulation**. This is *an experimental technique in which a child is first asked to solve a problem alone and then with the help of an adult* (Van Geert, 1998). Using this technique, he could determine not only which problems children knew how to solve but also which problems they were capable of learning to solve. Furthermore, Vygotsky insisted that learning entailed far more than receiving instruction. Rather, learning takes place through the joint activity of the child and a more capable adult. Instruction beyond the capability of the child is pointless, but instruction within the child's potential is effective. Thus, the method of dual stimulation measured the child's readiness to learn.

Vygotsky called *the difference between a child's actual and potential development* the **zone of proximal development**, or ZPD for short (Van Geert, 1998). The ZPD then is what's measured in the method of dual stimulation, and it indicates the difference between what the child is capable of doing alone compared to what it can do with the help of an adult (Figure 9.4). Furthermore, Vygotsky argued that two children at the same level of development—that is, capable of solving the same problems—may have different ZPDs. This is because one may be able to complete a more difficult task with help while the other still cannot. Thus, he argued that the concept of mental age was insufficient for measuring a child's level of cognitive development, and that the ZPD painted a more accurate picture of the child's current potential for learning. The ZPD is Vygotsky's most widely known concept, and it's had a significant impact in the fields of developmental psychology and educational theory.

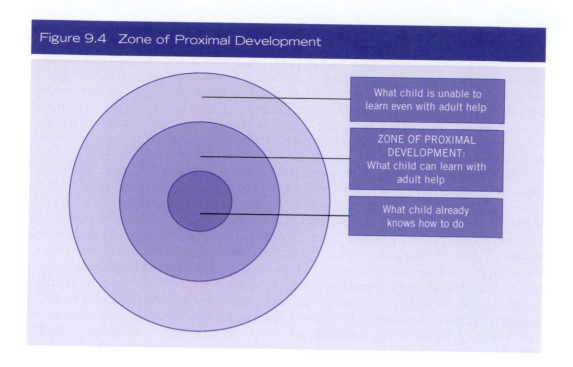

Figure 9.4 Zone of Proximal Development

What child is unable to learn even with adult help

ZONE OF PROXIMAL DEVELOPMENT: What child can learn with adult help

What child already knows how to do

Alexei Leontiev

In his early years as a psychologist, Vygotsky formed a close working relationship with two other researchers, Alexei Leontiev and Alexander Luria. The three even became known as the troika of Soviet psychology, after the traditional Russian practice of harnessing horses three abreast. They were seen as the three bright young scholars who would lead Soviet psychology to its next level, and they attracted quite a few followers.

Especially after the mysterious death of Bekhterev in 1927, their group seemed to be favored by the authorities (González Rey, 2014). But soon it became apparent that Stalin was merely pitting one group against another. To get away from the political turmoil in Moscow, Leontiev and Luria decided to move their research labs to the provincial city of Kharkov. There, they were joined by a number of their students as well as local colleagues who were sympathetic to Vygotsky's cultural-historical psychology. Vygotsky thought about joining them, but instead he accepted a second position in Leningrad in addition to the one he had in Moscow, and for the next few years he commuted regularly between the two cities. The following year, Luria returned to Moscow, but Leontiev remained in Kharkov until 1941, when he evacuated to Moscow after the German invasion at the start of World War II.

Leontiev's move to Kharkov may have also been motivated by a desire to distance himself from Vygotsky (Yasnitsky & Ferrari, 2008). Both Luria and Leontiev were more politically astute than their mentor, and they understood the dangers of remaining loyal to a theoretical framework that was coming under attack from the Soviet authorities. Luria simply turned to other interests, and we'll read about his important contributions to neuropsychology shortly. But with Luria gone, **Alexei Leontiev** (1903–1979) became the leader of the Kharkov group, and in that role he developed his reputation as the *Russian developmental psychologist who revised Vygotsky's cultural-historical psychology into activity theory*. Soviet authorities had charged that Vygotsky's approach was "too cosmopolitan" and didn't align with officially accepted Pavlovian theory. Leontiev saw the problem in Vygotsky's insistence on language as the foundation of consciousness. Instead, he took *the theoretical position that physical activity during social interactions is the basis for cognitive development*. Because **activity theory** focused on actions instead of speech, he could hew closer to the Pavlovian party line.

Although Leontiev presented himself as the intellectual successor to Vygotsky who rectified the flaws in his mentor's theory, others have criticized him as a political opportunist (Vassilieva, 2010). At any rate, discussion of Vygotsky's theories was virtually banned, whereas Leontiev with his activity theory rose to prominence. It wasn't until the 1970s that the political situation in the Soviet Union had relaxed to the point where Vygotsky loyalists felt safe to criticize the weaknesses of activity theory. For a while, there was even an attempt to unify the two approaches, but today Vygotsky's cultural-historical psychology has garnered renewed interest among developmental psychologists in Russia, whereas Leontiev's activity theory has gone into eclipse.

Around 1960, American psychologist Jerome Bruner (Chapter 11) began correspondence with Alexander Luria, whom we'll meet shortly, and this led to Bruner's visit to Moscow (González Rey, 2014). Luria was already known in the United States for his work with brain-damaged patients during World War II, and while Bruner was in Moscow, Luria introduced him to Leontiev. In his discussions with his two Soviet colleagues, Bruner learned about the ideas of their mentor. At the time, Lev Vygotsky was completely unknown to Western psychologists. Bruner arranged to have Vygotsky's *Thought and Language* translated into English, but when it appeared in 1962 it received little attention. However, when an edited volume of Vygotsky's articles was published under the title *Mind in Society* in 1978, Western psychology took notice. By this time, the cognitive revolution was in full swing, so a discussion of "higher mental functions" was completely acceptable to American psychologists. Furthermore, developmental psychologists were beginning to take issue with some of Piaget's ideas, and they found Vygotsky's fresh approach appealing.

The so-called **Vygotsky boom** was *a period in the 1980s and 1990s when both Western and Russian psychologists took a renewed interest in Vygotsky's theory of cognitive development* (Vassilieva, 2010). By the end of the twentieth century, Vygotsky's collected works were finally published in Russian and translated into English. Although Vygotsky was little known during his lifetime, he's now recognized as one of the most influential psychologists of the twentieth century (Figure 9.5). By insisting on returning the study of consciousness to the core of psychology, he demonstrated the weakness of the behavioral approaches that dominated psychology for much of the twentieth century in both the United States and the Soviet Union.

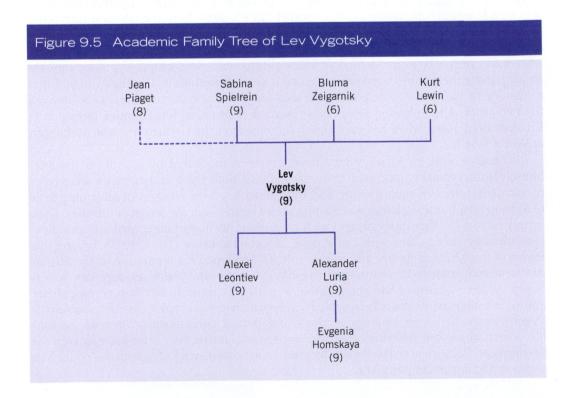

Figure 9.5 Academic Family Tree of Lev Vygotsky

Furthermore, his contention that human consciousness arises from social interaction and joint activity accorded well with the dominant views in social psychology during the second half of the twentieth century. And finally, his view of development as a continuous process rather than a series of stages was appealing to a new generation of developmental psychologists who were having difficulty reconciling their experimental findings with Piaget's theory.

Little appreciated and much abused during his lifetime, Vygotsky's works languished unpublished and unread for decades. But today, his genius is fully recognized. And his contributions to psychology are all the more remarkable given that he died at an age when most people are only beginning to make a mark in their careers. Clearly, Lev Vygotsky was a great thinker who was far ahead of his time.

Alexander Luria

As a student, Alexander Luria organized a psychoanalytic circle at his university (Christensen & Caetano, 1996). He wrote Freud a letter telling him about it and received a reply addressed to "Honorable Mr. President." Luria got quite a kick out of it—he was only seventeen years old at the time. This was just the first of many honors he received during his long and fruitful career. Today, **Alexander Luria** (1902–1977) is recognized as a *Russian psychologist who was one of the pioneers in neuropsychology*.

Photo 9.6
Alexander Luria

The Russian Revolution had just occurred when Luria entered Kazan University (Horton, 1987). The educational system was in disarray, and he found he could design his own course of study. His father, a noted physician, wanted him to go into medicine. But young Luria chose psychology as his major, although he did honor his father's wishes some years later when he eventually earned a medical degree. He found Freud's theories fascinating, although he was also drawn to the experimental psychology that was being developed in the German universities as well as to the work of Pavlov and Bekhterev.

Luria remained at Kazan University to complete his doctorate degree (Cole, 1978). Working at a psychiatric hospital, Luria experimented with Jung's word-association method as he interviewed his patients. As you recall, this procedure involves measuring the subject's responses to various words, with the idea that longer reaction times indicated ideas associated with underlying emotional complexes. However, Luria found it difficult to measure reaction times accurately, so he devised a new approach he called the **combined motor method**. This is *an experimental procedure in which participants squeeze a rubber bulb as they give word-association responses*. He found that the more emotionally laden the word, the less force the participant used to grip the bulb. And since the amount of air squeezed from the bulb could be accurately recorded, he had a precise measurement of emotionality in word associations.

With his new device, Luria measured inner emotional conflict with a variety of populations (Cole, 1979). He used it on students waiting to find out their scores on a major exam, observing that they squeezed with much less force to words such as "fail" or "expelled," which clearly indicated what they were worried about. He also used it on criminals awaiting interrogation, finding they squeezed with less force as they responded to words associated with the crime. Luria even hailed his device as the world's first lie detector. More importantly, he'd come up with a way of indirectly observing mental states by observing outward behavior. The result of his extensive research using the combined motor method was *The Nature of Human Conflicts*. This book was finally published in English in 1932, which made him famous internationally.

In 1923, Luria accepted a position at Moscow University, and in a few years he got to know Vygotsky and Leontiev (Akhutina, 2003). This was the beginning of the Russian "troika." Luria was impressed by Vygotsky's cultural-historical theory and the role of social interaction in the development of speech and consciousness. Vygotsky also got Luria interested in the study of brain-damaged patients, a field of research that he devoted much of his career to. During this time, Luria and Vygotsky collaborated on studies of **aphasia**, or *loss of language functions due to brain damage*. The thinking was that aphasic adults were in a sense like prelinguistic infants, and that perhaps by using external supports, some speech functions could be recovered. They also studied patients with Parkinson's disease, testing ways in which environmental support might help them regain control of their motor functions.

Central Asia

A point of contention between Piaget's and Vygotsky's theories of cognitive development was the relative contributions of nature and nurture to the child's developing mind. Piaget saw logical reasoning as unfolding according to a maturational schedule, and he even assigned age ranges to his stages of development. In contrast, Vygotsky saw the child's thought processes as developing within a social and cultural context. This meant that people in other parts of the world may not reason in the same way as those who'd received a Western education. Luria decided to test this hypothesis by organizing two expeditions to Central Asia in 1931 and 1932. (As you recall from Chapter 6, Kurt Koffka traveled from the United States to join Luria on this second expedition, but he soon became gravely ill and had to be evacuated.)

Luria and his research team visited remote villages in Uzbekistan and Kirghizia (Karpov, 2007). Instead of administering standardized tests, the team made friends with the villagers and conversed with them in their own language through interpreters. In the course of discussion, they posed problems of logical reasoning and observed how the local people responded. Because schools had only just recently been introduced in these areas, the researchers could examine the performance of those with a few years of education and those with no formal schooling. They found that those who'd attended school responded similarly to people back in Moscow, but unschooled villagers approached these reasoning problems in a completely different way.

Some of these logic problems involved categorization (Horton, 1987). For example, villagers were shown a set of four cards depicting a hammer, saw, log, and hatchet, and they were asked which three go together. Educated villagers responded the way schoolchildren in Moscow would respond, namely by grouping the hammer, saw, and hatchet together as tools. But the uneducated villagers grouped the items contextually, putting the saw, log, and hatchet together instead. When asked if the hammer, saw, and hatchet could be grouped as tools, they dismissed the notion as nonsense.

Others involved the use of a **syllogism**, which is *a logical argument that uses deductive reasoning to reach a conclusion* (Horton, 1987). For example, the team asked the villagers to respond to syllogisms such as: "Cotton only grows in warm climates. England has a cold climate. Does cotton grow in England?" Although the villagers were cotton farmers and knew a lot about cotton, they refused to answer the question. "How would I know?" they'd respond. "I've never been to England." It wasn't that they didn't understand the format of the problem. Rather, the issue was cultural, as these people believed it was inappropriate to make an assertion that was beyond their personal experience.

For Luria, these results were clear evidence that Vygotsky's cultural-historical theory was correct (Cole, 2002). Piaget's theory might hold in the case of children growing up in Western culture, but those from different cultures would have different developmental experiences. Luria was also quite excited by the results, since he believed in the potential of the new Soviet man to learn how to live in harmony with his fellow citizens, and his data showed the power of education to mold thought processes in particular ways. He assumed the Soviet authorities would be pleased with his studies as well, but they weren't. Instead, they viewed his experiments as insulting to indigenous peoples by suggesting they were mentally inferior to Westerners. As Stalin was grappling with the problem of holding together a multiethnic Soviet Union, he saw the potential political backlash if the indigenous populations of the

Soviet republics were portrayed as "uncivilized" or "mentally deficient." Luria had only said that the people he interviewed were cognitively different, not cognitively deficient, but this wasn't how the government interpreted it.

Back in Moscow, Luria conducted a series of studies on identical twins to further investigate Vygotsky's cultural-historical theory (Luria, 1974). In these studies, he would give one twin special training, while the other twin received no training. If cognitive development unfolded according to a maturational schedule, the special training should have no effect, and both twins should acquire a new cognitive ability at the same time. Instead, Luria found that the twin with special training moved ahead of the other twin. Again, the results provided support for Vygotsky's theory. And again, the Soviet authorities weren't pleased.

Neuropsychology

By the late 1930s, a reign of terror was sweeping across Russia (Horton, 1987). Luria felt it was becoming unsafe to do research, since his findings could always be used as political ammunition against him. His mentor had died, and now Vygotsky's ideas were being criticized by authorities as straying too far from Pavlovian theory, which had been declared the official Soviet psychology. Better lay low for a few years, Luria thought. So he quit the research lab and enrolled as a medical student, thus granting his father's wish that he become a physician. By the time World War II erupted, he'd completed his medical studies and was ready to serve the war effort. In the process, he made groundbreaking discoveries concerning the relationship between brain and mind.

Since Luria already had experience studying patients with brain injuries, he decided to specialize in neurology (Akhutina, 2003). When World War II began, he spent much of his time treating soldiers who'd come back from the front with head wounds. Meticulously cataloging the location of the brain injury and the loss of abilities for each patient, Luria amassed copious amounts of data relating specific brain areas to specific behavioral or cognitive functions. For nearly a century, doctors had been documenting case studies of brain-injured patients, but Luria's data far exceeded what had been collected so far.

For Luria, these data seemed to suggest a three-part model of brain functioning (Christensen & Caetano, 1996). According to his model, the first functional unit is the brainstem, which regulates levels of activity and vigilance. This part of the brain maintains the physiological functions that keep the organism alive, and it modulates states of arousal and sleep. The second functional unit is the back half of the forebrain, which processes information coming from the senses, thus providing the organism with knowledge about both the external environment and its internal states. Finally, the third functional unit is the front half of the forebrain, which is tasked with planning and executing motor movements. Although our knowledge of the brain is far more developed today than it was in Luria's time, his three-part model of brain functioning is largely consistent with currently accepted theories.

With these data on brain injuries and functional loss, Luria became a pioneer in the field of **neuropsychology** (Bodrova, Leong, & Akhutina, 2011). This is *a field of study that seeks to find connections between brain locations and behavioral or cognitive functioning.* Yet what distinguished Luria from other neuropsychologists of the time was his insistence on the functional organization of the brain in terms of Vygotsky's cultural-historical theory. Brain functions aren't just simply laid down according to a maturational plan, Luria insisted. Rather, the brain organizes itself as the child engages in social and cultural interactions with parents and other significant persons.

Vygotsky had argued that functional links in the brain are laid down as the organism engages with the environment (Hazin & da Rocha Falcão, 2014). This line of thought led Luria to the idea that perhaps lost functions could be regained if patients were provided sufficient external support to relearn those tasks. Although the area of the brain that had previously performed the function was destroyed, Vygotsky's theory suggested that other brain regions could learn to take on that function with external aids. Much of the rest of Luria's career was devoted to finding ways to rehabilitate patients with a loss of behavioral or cognitive functioning due to brain injury. This research led to a number of books that were translated into English, including *The Higher Cortical Functions in Man* in 1962 and *Traumatic Aphasia* in 1970, in which Luria laid out his ideas.

Luria (1974) maintained that intellectual operations such as reading, writing, counting, and even speech itself could be restored at least to a certain degree if the investigator helped the patient find new ways to perform these tasks. Vygotsky had maintained that any complex cognitive function is built up from simpler functions, and so if some of these are lost due to brain damage, the higher mental process can be rebuilt by recruiting other components that are still intact. This was accomplished by "externalizing" the process until it could be reinternalized. For instance, if an aphasic patient had difficulty perceiving speech, Luria would show the patient the written word as he spoke it. That is, the written word served as a crutch until the functional system for spoken word perception could be reorganized. The successful rehabilitation of many patients with brain damage, Luria believed, lent support to Vygotsky's ideas about the dynamic organization of higher cognitive functions in the brain.

In evaluating his patients, Luria (1974) developed a method he called **syndrome analysis**. This is *the process of breaking down higher cognitive functions into their component parts.* For example, we may have a patient who has lost the ability to speak fluently because of a brain injury. To simply say this patient suffers from aphasia, that is, a loss of language faculty, doesn't get at the root of the problem. The complex function of speaking is composed of many simpler component functions, any of which, if destroyed, will disrupt the patient's ability to speak. By using syndrome analysis, Luria sought to isolate the impacted function that was root of the disorder. The results of this examination likewise provided insights for formulating a rehabilitation plan. In one famous case study, he also applied syndrome analysis as he investigated the abilities of a man with extraordinary memory skills, which he reported in his 1968 book *The Mind of a Mnemonist*.

Throughout Luria's long career, we can detect a common theme in all of his research (Cole, 2002). Specifically, this is the question of how the brain organizes its basic functions to produce complex behavioral and cognitive tasks. Greatly influenced by the thinking of his mentor Lev Vygotsky, Luria emphasized the idea that the cognitive organization of the brain proceeds from the outside to the inside. That is, thought processes occur first in social interaction and only later are they internalized, in accordance with Vygotsky's cultural-historical theory. Although his research activities landed him in trouble with Soviet authorities on several occasions, Luria deftly navigated the political minefield of Stalinist Russia, and as a result he also received great accolades for his work. Moreover, he was permitted to travel abroad and to interact with scientists from other countries, a rare privilege at that time. In the West, Luria became the face of Soviet psychology after the passing of Pavlov. Long before the advent of brain imaging technology, Luria pioneered the field of neuropsychology, greatly advancing our understanding of how the brain produces the mind.

Evgenia Homskaya

Alexander Luria had many students over his long career, but his most famous one, both in Russia and the West, was **Evgenia Homskaya** (1929–2004; Glozman & Tupper, 2006). As a *Russian neuropsychologist known for her studies on the role of the frontal lobes in regulating behavior*, she was Luria's most devoted student and colleague for a quarter of a century. She began working with Luria as a research assistant after graduating from Moscow University, and several years later she defended a Ph.D. dissertation that tested one of her mentor's ideas about the role of speech in normally and abnormally developing children.

After Luria's death in 1977, Homskaya continued in her line of research that tested hypotheses derived from his theory of the functional organization of the brain (Glozman & Tupper, 2006). Throughout her career, she strove to integrate Luria's neuropsychology with Vygotsky's cultural-historical theory. She also employed new technologies, such as EEG, to the study of brain functioning and its relationship to thought and behavior. Like her mentor, she applied what she learned in the clinic to improving methods of rehabilitating patients with brain damage. And her 1987 textbook *Neuropsychology* was considered the standard Russian textbook in the field for nearly two decades. Altogether, she published over 300 articles and books in Russian, English, and other languages.

Homskaya was a quiet person who was totally devoted to her work (Glozman & Tupper, 2006). She never married, but for many years she lived with her ill mother, who she cared for until her death. Her closest living relative was a nephew, and she treated him as her son. For Homskaya, her work truly was her life. She continued her active research program until the very end, giving her last lecture at Moscow State University on the day she died.

Looking Ahead

Russia has long had an ambivalent attitude toward the West, yearning to reshape itself along the European model on the one hand and yet clinging nostalgically to its ancient traditions on the other hand. We see this same ambivalence playing out in Russian psychology. At the turn of the twentieth century, the nation seemed well on the path toward integration with Western culture, and its scientists interacted as equals with their colleagues in Europe and North America. Ivan Pavlov was a perfect example of the international Russian scientist who was respected as much abroad as he was at home.

Yet with the new Soviet order, Russia turned inward once again, this time to protect the fledgling Communist state from damaging outside influences. With the goal of producing the "new Soviet man," the natural sciences—including psychology—were supported by the state. Yet the price was that researchers had to fit their science within the strictures of Marxist theory. The rise of Joseph Stalin and his reign of terror turned the practice of science into a political balancing act, as the fate of Vladimir Bekhterev so clearly demonstrated. Meanwhile, the Russian troika of Lev Vygotsky, Alexander Luria, and Alexei Leontiev served as the hub around which a Soviet psychology was built. In spite of economic hardships and political oppression, these three had a significant impact not only at home but also in the West. Despite living behind the Iron Curtain, psychologists like Pavlov, Vygotsky, and Luria made a significant impact on the development of psychology during the twentieth century, and their influence is still felt today.

During the 1980s, Soviet premier Mikhail Gorbachev announced a new period of *glasnost* and *perestroika*—openness and restructuring. The Soviet Union was sorely in need of political and economic reform, and it was Gorbachev's hope that an open discussion of the country's problems and their possible solutions would revitalize the Communist state. Instead, it led to the dissolution of the Soviet Union, as its ethnic-minority regions broke free from Russian domination. In the ensuing chaos, government funding for science dwindled (Mironenko, 2014). Psychologists scrambled for sources of income through the practice of applied psychology. Among their customers were politicians hoping psychologists could help them win elections and businessmen who wanted to apply psychological techniques to increase sales and productivity.

By the turn of the twenty-first century, many Russian psychologists had learned to do the sorts of statistical analyses so commonly practiced in Western experimental psychology (Hakkarainen, 2013). These had been largely unknown in Russia during the Soviet era, but there was also the belief that Russian psychologists wouldn't be taken seriously by their international colleagues otherwise. Nevertheless, there still remains the perception that the quality of contemporary Russian research fails to meet the standards of its Western counterparts. This disappointment on the international stage has led some Russian psychologists to turn inward, advocating for an indigenous Russian psychology that follows its own path rather than integrating with the Western world.

Today in Russia, we can see psychologists divided into three groups (Mironenko, 2014). The first group continues to work within the tradition of Leontiev's activity theory, and its attitude is neutral toward Western psychology. The second group strives to reform Russian psychology along Western models so that it can gain acceptance on the international scene.

And the third group has turned completely inward, rejecting Western ideology and aligning itself with the Russian Orthodox Church and traditional Russian culture.

Despite the fracturing of modern Russian psychology, the stars of the Soviet era still shine brightly in the Western world. Pavlov's classical conditioning technique is a basic tool in animal research, and Vygotsky's theory continues to grow in popularity among developmental psychologists as a counterpoint to Piaget. Moreover, Luria's work with brain-damaged patients is still frequently cited in the neuroscience literature. These pioneers blazed the trail that scientific psychology has followed into the twenty-first century.

CHAPTER SUMMARY

Because of the country's unique cultural history and its relative isolation during the twentieth century, Russian psychology took a separate path from that followed by Western Europe and North America. Ivan Pavlov is generally credited as the founder of Russian psychology, and yet he wasn't a psychologist by training. Rather late in his career, however, he stumbled upon the artificial conditioned reflex, now more commonly known as classical conditioning, which became a powerful tool for investigating the ways in which organisms learn about the contingencies in their environment. Because his materialistic perspective on psychology was in line with the Marxist ideology of the new regime, Pavlov's research was well supported, and it was held up as the model for Soviet psychology. Pavlov's archrival Vladimir Bekhterev discovered what he called the associated motor reflex around the same time, but he died in a political intrigue shortly after criticizing Stalin. Also notable during this time was Horsley Gantt, the American physician who studied with Pavlov and translated his works into English. Among the generation of psychologists just starting their careers at the beginning of the Russian Revolution, three stand out as the key players in Soviet psychology. Lev Vygotsky's theory of cognitive development is very influential today, although it wasn't known in the West until long after his death. An important early influence for Vygotsky was Sabina Spielrein, who'd worked with Piaget in Switzerland before returning to her Russian homeland. Alexander Luria made important contributions to neuropsychology, and these were recognized in North America even during his lifetime. His research program in neuropsychology was continued by his most noted student, Evgenia Homskaya. The third member of the so-called Russian troika, Alexei Leontiev, modified Vygotsky's cultural-historical theory into a form he called activity theory. By shifting emphasis from social interaction to individual behavior, Leontiev's theory hewed closer to Pavlovian dogma, thus making it more acceptable to the Stalinist regime.

DISCUSSION QUESTIONS

1. Pavlov's methods of animal research were considered quite humane by the standards of that time. Explain why this was the case. Defend your own position on the ethics of animal research.

2. Pavlov called conditioning the first signal system and language the second signal system. What sort of parallel did he see between conditioning and language? Consider carefully what the purpose of each system is.

3. Contrast Pavlov's conditioned reflex with Bekhterev's associated motor reflex. Which was more useful for behavioral research?

4. What does Vygotsky mean when he maintains that consciousness first resides in the social environment of the child? Why is this notion still considered radical today? (Consider the commonsense view of consciousness.)

5. Explain the method of dual stimulation and the zone of proximal development, illustrating with real-life examples.

6. Contrast Vygotsky's theory of cognitive development with that of Piaget.

7. Contrast Leontiev's activity theory with Vygotsky's cultural-historical theory. Explain why activity theory was more acceptable in Stalinist Russia.

8. Compare Jung's method of word association with Luria's combined motor method. What is the theory behind these two methods?

9. Describe the studies that Luria conducted in Central Asia and his interpretation of the results. Explain why the Stalinist regime considered this study politically dangerous.

10. If you've taken a class in neuroscience, assess how well Luria's three-part model of brain functioning accords with what we currently know.

11. Despite political oppression, Soviet psychology—at least in approved areas—developed rapidly through the twentieth century. Consider the ways in which Pavlov, Vygotsky, Leontiev, and Luria dealt with government authorities and the consequences of their actions.

12. Sabina Spielrein published papers that presaged ideas later attributed to Sigmund and Anna Freud, Jean Piaget, and others. Why do you think they got the credit and not her?

ON THE WEB

YouTube has some short videos on the **Ivan Pavlov dog experiment** that include original footage or reenactments accompanied by an explanation of the process. You can also find some short instructional videos demonstrating **Lev Vygotsky's zone of proximal development** in the classroom. In addition, there's an engaging interview with noted British neurologist Oliver Sacks as he discusses his relationship with **Alexander Luria** and the impact he had on his own career. As mentioned in Chapter 7, the movie *A Dangerous Method* (Thomas & Cronenberg, 2011) portrays the alleged affair between Sabina Spielrein and Carl Jung, but while it is good drama, the accuracy of the story has been questioned by historians.

Modern Disciplines of Psychology

World War II was a watershed event, changing the course of human history. For the last several centuries, Europe had led the scientific revolution that was fundamentally changing life on this planet. But in the aftermath of the war, much of Europe lay in ruins, and most of its brightest minds had immigrated to North America. As a result, the United States took the lead as the world's scientific and technological leader. For this reason, Part III is devoted largely to the history of psychology in the United States from the end of World War II up to the present day.

A new generation of psychologists after the war had a grand vision for the direction that a scientific psychology should go. They broke down the barriers that separated the old schools, exploring specific topics of interests and using whatever research tools were available in their work. In this way, psychology reorganized itself into the set of interlocking disciplines we know today.

As a student of psychology, you should find the titles of the chapters in Part III familiar. These are the disciplines of psychology that became established after World War II, and you've probably taken a course in each of them. While many of the concepts presented in Part III will likely be familiar, the people behind these concepts—as well as the intellectual networks in which they worked—may be unknown to you. This is the story that's presented in Part III.

We begin Part III with Chapter 10, looking at some loosely interconnected groups of researchers who worked outside the confines of the traditional schools during the middle decades of the twentieth century. We then move to Chapter 11, which surveys the rise of cognitive psychology from practical research conducted for the war effort. Chapter 12 looks at social psychology, which arose in response to the human devastation of World War II, with the hope that a better understanding of human nature may help us avoid such a tragedy again in the future. Likewise in Chapter 13, we see how psychologists working with the millions of children orphaned by the war led to our modern understanding of early childhood development. Next, we see in Chapter 14 how an interest in measuring individual differences in the early 1900s led to the blossoming of personality research in the last half of the twentieth century. World War II also left a psychological toll on millions of people, driving the need for new and more effective methods of psychotherapy and for promoting mental health, and this is the story of Chapter 15. We then wrap up Part III with Chapter 16 on neuroscience, which holds the promise of finally solving the mind-body problem. Whether that promise can be fulfilled is a question we ponder as we bring the book to a close.

CHAPTER

10

Physiological and Comparative Psychology

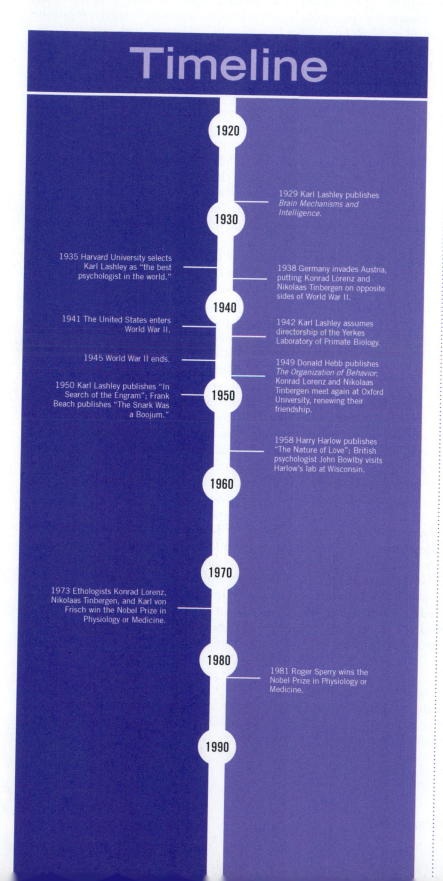

Timeline

1920

1930

1929 Karl Lashley publishes *Brain Mechanisms and Intelligence.*

1935 Harvard University selects Karl Lashley as "the best psychologist in the world."

1938 Germany invades Austria, putting Konrad Lorenz and Nikolaas Tinbergen on opposite sides of World War II.

1940

1941 The United States enters World War II.

1942 Karl Lashley assumes directorship of the Yerkes Laboratory of Primate Biology.

1945 World War II ends.

1949 Donald Hebb publishes *The Organization of Behavior*; Konrad Lorenz and Nikolaas Tinbergen meet again at Oxford University, renewing their friendship.

1950 Karl Lashley publishes "In Search of the Engram"; Frank Beach publishes "The Snark Was a Boojum."

1950

1958 Harry Harlow publishes "The Nature of Love"; British psychologist John Bowlby visits Harlow's lab at Wisconsin.

1960

1970

1973 Ethologists Konrad Lorenz, Nikolaas Tinbergen, and Karl von Frisch win the Nobel Prize in Physiology or Medicine.

1980

1981 Roger Sperry wins the Nobel Prize in Physiology or Medicine.

1990

Learning Objectives

After reading this chapter, you should be able to:

- Assess the contributions of Walter Cannon, Karl Lashley, and John Garcia in their search for the brain basis of behavior.

- Appraise the contributions of Donald Hebb, Brenda Milner, and Roger Sperry toward our understanding of the relationship between brain and mind.

- Interpret Harry Harlow's work with monkeys in terms of human development.

- Evaluate the relevance of the ethological studies of Konrad Lorenz and Nikolaas Tinbergen to human development and behavior.

223

Looking Back

In the middle decades of the twentieth century, behaviorism dominated in North America, turning psychology into the study of outwardly observable behavior rather than of inferred but unobservable mental states. The focus of research was on learning, which was viewed as a general process of all organisms with a nervous system, meaning observations of learning in one species could be applied to any other species. Since rats were inexpensive and easy to handle, they became the species of choice for learning research. However, organisms themselves were viewed as "black boxes" that somehow linked stimuli with responses, and speculations about mental processes or brain functions were discouraged.

As Europeans fled to America to escape the rise of fascism in the 1930s, two other schools exerted an influence. One of these, Gestalt psychology, was in many respects the polar opposite of behaviorism. It emphasized innate as opposed to learned processes, and it concerned itself with mental states inferred from outward behavior rather than viewing behavior as an end in itself. Gestalt psychologists also built theories of brain functioning and tested them with the available technology. Thus, Gestalt psychology was a science of both the mind and the brain. The other European school of psychology that rose in influence before World War II was psychoanalysis. Like Gestalt psychology, psychoanalysis acknowledged human consciousness as its primary focus of study. However, it also posited a complex set of mental mechanisms that were largely outside of conscious awareness. Freud's theories were compelling, and they demanded a scientific response.

During the first half of the twentieth century, not all psychologists adhered to a particular school. Although there was considerable overlap in the interests of these scientists, we can roughly divide these researchers into two approaches, depending on the questions they asked and the methods they used.

The first approach was known as **physiological psychology**, and its members were interested in *the study of how behavior is generated and guided by the nervous system*. They used behaviorist methods, but they rejected the behaviorist moratorium on discussing mental processes. We also need to clarify the meaning of the term *physiological psychology* as it's used here. In the late nineteenth century, Wilhelm Wundt used this term to refer to his approach to the science of the mind, meaning he would use the experimental methods of physiology to test hypotheses about psychological processes. By the early decades of the twentieth century, the term had acquired its present meaning. This approach can be traced all the way back to René Descartes, who first described the reflex arc. Another pioneer in physiological psychology is Charles Darwin. In his books, Darwin argued that not only biological traits but also behaviors were shaped by natural selection, based on the assumption that the biological nervous system was responsible for psychological behavior.

The second approach was called **comparative psychology**, and its focus of interest was *the study of the origin, control, and consequences of behavior across a wide range of species*. Behaviorists experimented on rats, pigeons, and a few other species, and they simply assumed that their findings extended to humans. In contrast, comparative psychologists observed a much wider range of species, often in natural settings. They also rejected the assumption that virtually all behavior was acquired through experience, leaving it as an open question whether behavior was innate, learned, or developed through an interaction of nature and nurture. Even in the early twentieth century, psychologists such as Margaret Washburn, Robert Yerkes, and Wolfgang Köhler followed a comparative approach in their research.

In many ways, the physiological and comparative psychologists of the mid-twentieth century set the stage for experimental psychology as it is practiced today. They kept the methods and the rigor of the behaviorist approach, but they greatly expanded the range of research topics that could be explored. Many of the questions they posed are just now being answered as the technology driving neuroscience advances.

In this chapter, we begin by tracing the development of physiological psychology through the middle of the twentieth century. We start with Walter Cannon, whose concept of fight-or-flight is now well known even among the general public. We then turn to Karl Lashley and his many students. Lashley was particularly interested in how memories are formed in the brain, and in his work he demonstrated that the widely accepted theories of his day were untenable. However, it was his student Donald Hebb who built the theory of brain-based learning and memory that is still accepted today. Hebb's student Brenda Milner then extended this research on the biological basis of memory with studies of brain-damaged humans. Another noted student of Lashley, Roger Sperry, went even further to explore the question of how the brain creates consciousness.

We then turn to the contributions of comparative psychologists working in the mid-twentieth century. First we meet Harry Harlow, whose work on social isolation in monkeys has had a profound impact on the study of human social development. As we'll later see in Chapter 13, his findings helped explain the causes of psychological and social disorders observed in orphaned children during World War II. The chapter then ends with a discussion of ethology, a comparative approach developed in Europe that emphasized the need for studying a wide range of species in their natural environment. In the last half of the twentieth century, this approach has had an important impact on the thinking of North American psychologists.

Brain and Behavior

For much of the twentieth century, the functioning of the brain was largely a mystery. Since the nineteenth century, doctors had been collecting data on the behavioral anomalies of patients with brain damage, and this information provided some insight into what faculties the various parts of the brain were responsible for. In the twentieth century, doctors began using invasive procedures on nonhuman animals to systematically test hypotheses about the relationship between brain and behavior. This approach came to be known as physiological psychology.

Walter Cannon

As an undergraduate, **Walter Cannon** (1871–1945) was torn between biology and psychology (Quick, 1990). Although he took courses with William James and admired him deeply, in the end Cannon chose biology and medicine. After earning his M.D. degree, he joined the faculty of Harvard, where he remained for the rest of his career, building his reputation as an *American physiological psychologist best known for his concepts of flight-or-flight and homeostasis*.

Cannon's first research project as a graduate student involved the use of X-rays, which had just been discovered (Robinson, 2018). He induced a dog to swallow a button and used X-rays to follow its movement down the dog's throat and through its digestive tract. Later, he mixed heavy-metal salts with food, making it opaque to X-rays so he could observe the entire digestive process. He discovered that food is moved through the gut by waves of muscular contractions. But he also found that these waves stopped if the animal was frightened or angered. This finding led to Cannon's lifelong interest in the relationship between emotional experiences and the internal functioning of the body.

In particular, Cannon was interested in what he called the "fighting emotions," that is, how animals respond to perceived dangers (Quick, Quick, Nelson, & Hurrell, 1997). He'd already found that digestion shuts down in these situations, but he came to understand that this was just one part of *the body's arousal reaction to a dangerous situation*. He called this the

Photo 10.1
Walter Cannon

fight-or-flight response, meaning that the organism is preparing to either defend itself or to run away. Identifying the sympathetic nervous system as the regulator of the fight-or-flight response, he also discovered the role that the hormone adrenaline plays in arousing the body for action.

After serving in World War I, Cannon resumed his research on bodily responses to fear and trauma (Robinson, 2018). Although it was generally understood that organisms were self-regulating, he described *the processes by which the body maintains stable internal conditions*, which he called **homeostasis**. In this view, homeostasis works through information from the senses and negative feedback from the autonomic nervous system. For instance, your sense organs indicate that the room is cold. In response, your autonomic nervous system activates various processes to conserve or generate heat, such as raising goose bumps and inducing shivering. Various internal conditions of the body are regulated in a similar manner.

Later in his career, Cannon developed a theory of emotions that challenged the James-Lange theory, which proposed that bodily reactions lead to emotional experiences (Lang, 1994). Although that theory was widely accepted at the time, Cannon maintained that there were significant problems with it. In particular, he claimed that bodily arousal happens too slowly for it to be the cause of emotional experiences, which have a rapid onset. Furthermore, he demonstrated that emotions still occur even when all bodily sensations are blocked by severing the spinal cords of cats and exposing them to threatening stimuli. The cats still hissed and showed facial expressions of fear or rage, leading Cannon to the conclusion that bodily reactions cannot be the cause of emotional experiences.

Working with his graduate student Phillip Bard, Cannon proposed *the theory that stimulation of the thalamus leads to both physiological arousal and the psychological experience of emotion* (Lang, 1994). This is known as the **Cannon-Bard theory**. Although Cannon and Bard pointed to some legitimate weaknesses of the James-Lange theory, their proposal hasn't fared well either. It's now known that the thalamus isn't the brain's emotional center. Furthermore, Cannon and James were talking about emotions at two different levels. James's

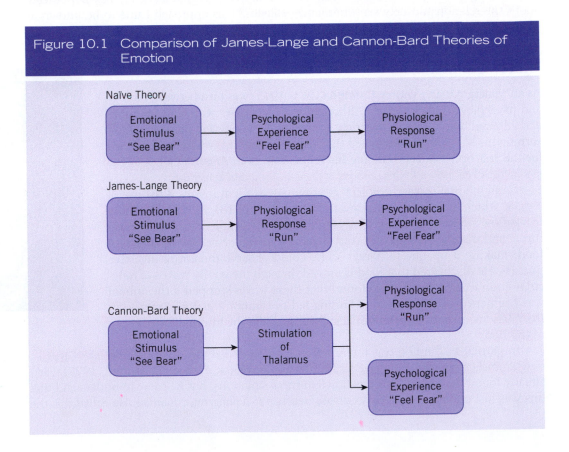

Figure 10.1   Comparison of James-Lange and Cannon-Bard Theories of Emotion

focus was on the psychological experience of emotion, whereas Cannon looked at only physiological responses to emotional situations. Even if we're unaware of our body's internal states, as Cannon argued, we're certainly aware of our body's outward reactions, such as shivering and heavy breathing. Psychologists debated the merits of the two theories for years (Figure 10.1).

The first half of the twentieth century was a turbulent era around the world, full of wars and revolutions, and Cannon was involved in several of the great political struggles of the day (Yerkes, 1946). First, he organized a medical expedition to provide assistance during the Spanish Civil War. Second, he spent a year as a visiting professor in China during a time when the country was beset by civil war and foreign invasion. Third, he organized a relief effort for Ivan Pavlov (Chapter 9) during the Russian Revolution, hosted him in the United States, and visited him in the Soviet Union. Because of his connections with Pavlov and other Soviet scientists, Cannon was accused of being a Bolshevik sympathizer. In fact, Cannon disapproved of Communism, but he was a realist who understood the need to deal with the powers that be. In addition to his important scientific contributions, Cannon was also a public figure who spoke his mind and did what he could to make the world a better place.

Karl Lashley

Karl Lashley had come to Johns Hopkins to study zoology, but he also worked with John Watson on several projects involving animal behavior both before and after receiving his Ph.D. (Bartlett, 1960). In one study, they traveled together to the coast of North Carolina to observe the nesting and mating behaviors of sea birds. They then took some of the birds to Alabama and released them—the birds made it back home. It was his work with Watson that lured him to psychology. Although they remained friends for life, **Karl Lashley** (1890–1958) later became a strident critic of behaviorism as his reputation grew for being an *American physiological psychologist whose studies on how memories are formed in the brain led to his laws of equipotentiality and mass action.*

Lashley quickly made a name for himself (Beach, 1961). After a few years at Minnesota, he accepted an offer from Chicago, where he did the research he's most known for today. These studies concerned the location of memories in the brain, which he reported in his 1929 book *Brain Mechanisms and Intelligence*. To the extent that behaviorists thought about the brain at all, they generally assumed that the stimulus and response pathways in the nervous system linked up at a specific point, perhaps even a single cell or a small cluster of neurons. However, Lashley provided evidence that memories—especially for complex tasks—were widely distributed across the cerebral cortex.

To find the **engram**, or *the hypothetical location in the brain where a memory is stored*, Lashley trained rats to navigate a maze, and then he performed brain surgeries on them (Dewsbury, 2002). In each rat, he excised a small but different portion of the cerebral cortex. If the engram for navigating the maze was located in a small area, he reasoned, at least one of the rats would no longer remember the task. However, none of the lesioned rats showed a decrease in performance. Next, Lashley trained rats to navigate the maze, but this time he varied the amount of tissue removed from each. This time, post-surgery performance depended on how much brain tissue had been removed. Those with small lesions generally performed well, while those with larger lesions did not.

These findings led Lashley to formulate two laws (Bruce, 2001). The first law was called **equipotentiality**, which is *the observation that any part of a functional area of the brain is able to carry out the function of the whole area*. In other words, damage to one part doesn't disrupt the ability of the rest of the brain region to perform its task. If engrams were located at specific points in

Wikimedia Commons

Photo 10.2
Karl Lashley

the cortex, this wouldn't be the case. The second law was called **mass action**. This is *the observation that an impairment in functioning depended on the amount of brain tissue destroyed*. Within a given functional area, a small lesion may have minimal impact, but as the lesion gets larger, performance gets worse. The results of these studies supported Lashley's contention that memories are widely distributed across the cerebral cortex.

It's important to note that Lashley didn't claim that the laws of equipotentiality and mass action applied to the brain as a whole or for all memories (Bruce, 2001). It was already known that some areas of the brain had specific functions. The point was that complex tasks couldn't be decomposed into chains of stimulus-response links, as the behaviorists had proposed. Instead, many different areas of the brain get involved in all but the most basic reflexes.

Going on the attack against prevailing theories of learning as the building of stimulus-response connections, Lashley engaged in debates with some of the biggest names in the field, including Ivan Pavlov and Clark Hull (Dewsbury, 2002). Even though he had no specific theory to replace the reflex model of learning, his argument that current thinking on the issue was too simplistic resonated with many psychologists. Lashley was building a reputation as a bold and critical thinker who was nudging psychology from its behaviorist slumbers.

In 1935, the president of Harvard decided he wanted to hire "the best psychologist in the world," and he instructed Edwin Boring (Chapter 3) to set up a search committee (Beach, 1961). After deliberation, the committee unanimously agreed to invite Karl Lashley to join the Harvard faculty. This came as a surprise to Lashley, since he hadn't applied for the position, but he accepted anyway. He was given ample laboratory space, a light teaching load, and freedom to engage in whatever research he wanted. At Harvard, he continued his investigation into the relationship between brain and behavior, examining various theories and finding deficiencies in all of them.

In 1942, Lashley was invited to take over the directorship of the Yerkes Laboratory of Primate Biology (Beach, 1961). Even though the primate facility belonged to Yale, Harvard kept Lashley on its faculty as well, with the only obligation being that he return to campus once a year to conduct a two-week graduate seminar on a topic of his choice. Such was Lashley's status as a physiological psychologist.

At the Yerkes lab, Lashley shifted from working with rats to studying primates instead (Bartlett, 1960). Nevertheless, the theme of his research program remained unchanged, namely an understanding of the relationship between the brain and learning. In the process, he challenged the behaviorist status quo in two ways. First, he chided his colleagues for ignoring the brain in their theories of learning. Second, he spoke freely of mental states and consciousness at a time when such terms were considered taboo. He had no qualms about attributing thoughts and feelings to the primates he worked with, much to the chagrin of behaviorists who visited his lab.

Lashley had spent his career trying to formulate a brain-based theory of learning, but his goal seemed forever out of reach (Bruce, 2001). In 1950, he gave a speech at Cambridge University that he later published as the essay "In Search of the Engram." He chastised his generation of psychologists for their simple-minded theories of learning, pointing out that they were little different from the ideas René Descartes had proposed in the seventeenth century. All you had to do, Lashley said, was replace Descartes's term "animal spirits" with the modern concept of neural impulses, and you had the same reflex-arc model of learning. At one point in the speech he commented that the available evidence suggested learning simply wasn't possible. Of course he didn't mean it, but he was expressing his frustration at his inability to make headway on this problem.

Some psychologists—even his own students—have criticized Lashley for being the great destroyer of theories without ever building any of his own (Beach, 1961; Hebb, 1980). In fact, he did propose brain-based theories of learning, but he always tested his own ideas with the same rigor he applied to those of other people, and in every case he found his own ideas weren't supported by the evidence. He may not have found the answers he was looking

Figure 10.2 Academic Family Tree of Karl Lashley

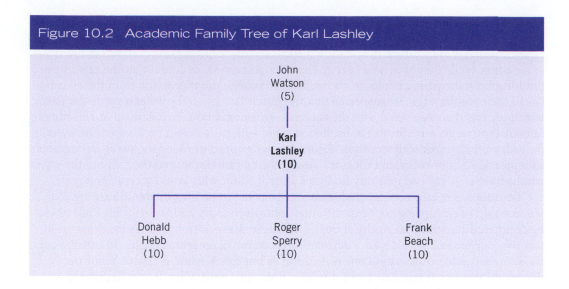

for, but at least he was asking the right questions. His bold thinking about brain and mind helped usher in the cognitive revolution that took off shortly after his death (Figure 10.2). But Karl Lashley's work had even greater repercussions, in that many of the questions that he asked in the middle of the twentieth century are the ones neuroscientists are now trying to answer in the early twentieth-first.

John Garcia

Have you ever gotten sick after eating a favorite food, and then later you found you now have a strong dislike for it? If so, you've experienced **conditioned taste aversion**, which is a *learned avoidance of a food associated with illness* (Garcia, 1981). This phenomenon had been observed by philosophers and scientists for centuries, but it was only recognized by psychologists in the last half of the twentieth century. Conditioned taste aversion was studied extensively by **John Garcia** (1917–2012), and for this reason it's sometimes called the Garcia effect. For much of his career, he fought the behaviorist establishment, which rejected his findings because they supposedly violated the laws of learning. However, today John Garcia is known as the *first Hispanic-American psychologist and discoverer of conditioned taste aversion.*

One reason why Garcia's ideas weren't taken seriously at first was that he lacked the proper credentials ("Awards," 1980). He was born among the California vineyards to uneducated farm workers who'd emigrated from Spain. He pursued higher education at Berkeley on the G.I. Bill after World War II. However, Garcia struggled with the demands of school and his need to support his growing family while doing the research that would eventually make him famous. He finally earned his Ph.D. at the age of 46, and over time his research gained acceptance as behaviorist domination of American psychology waned.

According to classical conditioning theorists, the conditioned stimulus needs to be immediately followed by the unconditioned stimulus (Garcia, 1981). In the case of Pavlov's dog, the bell (CS) comes right before the food (US). In this way, the dog associates the bell with the response of salivating. But in the case of conditioned taste aversion, the tainted food (CS) may be consumed half an hour or more before stomach distress (US) occurs. Furthermore, Pavlov's dog needed several trials before it began to salivate to the bell. But you only have to get sick from a particular food once to develop a strong dislike for it. Because it didn't fit with accepted behavior theory, many psychologists rejected it as impossible, and Garcia even had difficulty getting his papers published. Nevertheless, he persisted in his research.

While working on his Ph.D., Garcia took a job at the U.S. Naval Radiological Defense Laboratory in San Francisco ("Awards," 1980). There he led a research team investigating the biological effects of radiation. In one study, Garcia and his colleagues exposed rats to low doses of radiation while they were in a special chamber. Afterward, he found that the rats stopped drinking from the plastic bottles in the radiation chamber, but they drank from the glass bottles in their regular cage. He suspected that the plastic had given the water a particular flavor, which the rats then associated with the nausea from the radiation. To follow up on this hunch, he replaced the glass bottles in the habitation cages with plastic, and he flavored the water in the radiation chamber with saccharin. Again, the rats stopped drinking the sweet-tasting water after getting ill from radiation exposure. Clearly, the rats had associated the flavor of the water with getting sick. He had difficulty finding a journal editor who would accept his reports.

Because his results contradicted what was believed to be known about learning, Garcia was accused of employing poor experimental controls (Garcia, 2003). So for his Ph.D. thesis, he countered these arguments by showing a **double dissociation**. This is *the demonstration that two independent variables have different effects on two dependent variables.* In other words, we show a double dissociation when A causes X but not Y while B causes Y but not X. In this study, the rats learned to avoid drinking from the spout when it was flashing to avoid an electric shock but not nausea (from radiation). Conversely, they learned to not drink sweetened water to avoid nausea but not to avoid an electric shock. Again, he had a hard time publishing these studies.

Working with his students, Garcia tested real-life applications of conditioned taste aversion (Garcia, 2003). In one field study on a ranch in Utah, they tried a novel approach to keep wolves and coyotes away from sheep herds. The researchers put poisoned lamb meat under sheepskins. The predators ate the meat and got sick, after which they avoided the sheep. Although predation rates went down drastically, government agencies disapproved of the method. However, replications in Canada and California confirmed the effectiveness of this technique. A similar study was also conducted in Kenya, where farmers were vexed by baboons raiding their vegetable gardens. The technique worked there as well, but again local authorities were resistant to the idea.

By the late 1970s, reports of species-specific learning abilities challenged the received wisdom that conditioning was a general learning principle (Garcia, 2003). The behaviorist monolith was crumbling, and now conditioned taste aversion was accepted as yet another example of biologically based learning. Garcia was also finally recognized for his decades of hard work. He then used his new fame to go on the attack against behaviorism. He called out the behaviorists for banishing the brain as well as the mind from psychology—pointing in particular to B. F. Skinner, who was still alive. Looking back to the roots of behaviorism, Garcia reminded his fellow psychologists that Pavlov had always used the conditioning technique as a tool for studying how mental processes occur in the brain, and never as an end itself. Garcia also insisted that behavior cannot be explained without recourse to the brain, nor can it be understood without assuming mental states on the part of the organism. While his mentor Edward Tolman (Chapter 5) had cracked the door to cognitive psychology ajar, John Garcia pushed it wide open.

Thanks to the work of John Garcia and others like him, psychologists today clearly understand that there are biological constraints on learning (Davidson & Riley, 2015). Evolution has shaped organisms to learn behaviors that promote survival. Conditioned taste aversion quickly teaches animals to avoid foods that have made them sick and could possibly kill them if eaten again. And this is a life lesson far more important than learning to salivate to a bell.

Brain and Mind

As we learned in Chapter 1, the mind-body problem is an ancient one. However, the materialistic worldview of nature science pushed most experimental psychologists from the earliest days of the field to take the monistic position that the mind is somehow the product of brain activity. Exactly how that worked, though, was anyone's guess, but as we've already seen in previous chapters, many proposals had been put forth. Still, it was only around the midpoint of the twentieth century that physiological psychologists gained significant insights that have led to our current understanding of the relationship between brain and mind.

Photo 10.3
Donald Hebb

Donald Hebb

Reading Freud got Donald Hebb interested in psychology (Hebb, 1980). He applied to the master's program at McGill University, but his undergraduate grades were too low to qualify for financial aid. So he took night classes, and he worked during the day as the principal of a Montreal elementary school in a working-class neighborhood. Student performance was poor, and teachers spent more time disciplining than teaching. Hebb decided on a new approach. He announced that from now on schoolwork was considered a privilege, and those who misbehaved in class would be sent to the playground as punishment. To his surprise, the strategy worked, and students' performance improved dramatically. As he finished his master's degree, he faced a dilemma: Should he make a career of educational administration, or go on for the Ph.D. in psychology? In the end, he accepted an invitation from Karl Lashley to come to the University of Chicago. Today, **Donald Hebb** (1904–1985) is known as the *Canadian physiological psychologist who developed a highly influential theory of how learning takes place in the brain*.

At McGill, Hebb had worked with a student of Ivan Pavlov, and he was thoroughly indoctrinated in the belief that all behavior consisted of learned responses (Beach, 1987). But as he worked with Lashley, he began to temper his views. When Lashley was invited to Harvard, he brought Hebb along. For his thesis, Lashley suggested he compare rats raised in darkness with normal rats on some visual discrimination tasks to see whether visual perception was innate or learned. Both groups of rats succeeded at the tasks, and so Hebb concluded that visual perception was innate. In his rush to publish his findings, he failed to see an important pattern in the data. When Hebb revisited the work many years later, he found that the dark-reared rats had taken much longer to learn the task, suggesting instead an interaction between innate and learned abilities. By this time, however, he'd already come to the conclusion that all behavior depends on both nature and nurture.

After earning his Ph.D. from Harvard, Hebb accepted a fellowship at the Montreal Neurological Institute (Snyder & Whitaker, 2013). There, he worked with **Wilder Penfield** (1891–1976), the noted *Canadian neurosurgeon who mapped the somatosensory cortex*. Penfield had developed a new technique for treating intractable epilepsy with brain surgery, performed while the patient was awake. Using an electrode, he tested various areas of the brain to find the focus of the lesion to avoid removing any more tissue than necessary. In the process, however, he learned the layout of the sensory and motor cortices as well as other functional areas of the brain. As a teaching aid, he developed the **somatosensory homunculus**, which is *a diagram illustrating how specific areas of the brain map onto specific body parts* (Figure 10.3).

Photo 10.4
Wilder Penfield

Hebb's job was to administer a battery of tests to patients before and after surgery to check for any loss of cognitive ability as a result of their operation (Milner & Milner, 1996). As expected, patients usually had some reduction in cognitive abilities after surgery. But this wasn't always the case. In particular, patients with frontal-lobe surgeries often showed improved performance on intelligence tests. Penfield and Hebb surmised that the epileptic seizures had been interfering with the proper functioning of the surrounding brain tissue. With an end to the seizures, the rest of the brain returned to its normal level of performance.

Figure 10.3 Somatosensory Homunculus

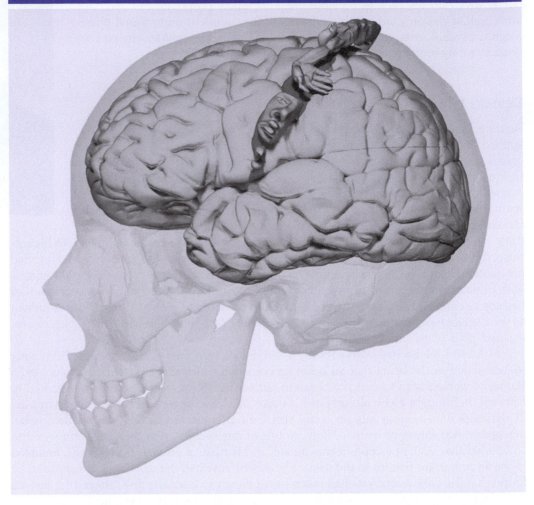

Source: Database Center for Life Science, via Wikimedia Commons, CC BY-SA 2.1 JP https://creativecommons
.org/licenses/by-sa/2.1/jp/deed.en.

Hebb's experiences working with Penfield significantly impacted his thinking on the nature of intelligence (Klein, 1999). At the time, most psychologists viewed intelligence as innate, but Hebb thought experiences—especially those in early childhood—could also play an important role. He devised a complex maze that could be used to test the intelligence of rats reared in various environments, and he found that the more enriched the early environment was, the better the rats performed on the test. After this, Hebb advocated for the establishment of early enrichment programs for underprivileged children such as Head Start.

When Lashley took over the directorship of the Yerkes Laboratory of Primate Biology in 1942, he invited Hebb to join him (Hebb, 1980). Lashley trained the animals on various learning and problem-solving tasks, while Hebb studied their emotional and personality characteristics. For nearly five years, Hebb spent most days interacting with the chimpanzees, and he was deeply impressed with the wide range of personalities he observed. Furthermore, their emotional expressions and personality quirks were no different from those of humans.

While he was in Florida, Hebb also had the opportunity to study dolphins (Milner, 1993). Although the dolphins appeared to be quite intelligent, there was no standard for assessing the problem-solving skills of an animal that had no limbs and so couldn't manipulate objects. In the end, he came to the conclusion that play was a good measure of intelligence across species. That is, the more complex the playful behavior, the more intelligent the animal is likely to be.

At the Yerkes lab, Hebb also began working on the book that would eventually make him famous (Hebb, 1980). He invited Lashley to join him in the project, thinking the book was more likely to be accepted with a well-known name on the cover. The goal was to develop a biologically plausible account of how learning takes place in the brain. Although this was a question Lashley had mulled over for decades, he dismissed Hebb's ideas as unreasonable and refused to work with him. Hebb was hurt by the rejection, and he told others Lashley was no longer interested in building theories but only tearing down the work of others. Clearly, it was time for them to part ways.

The Organization of Behavior

In 1947, Hebb accepted a position at McGill and returned to Montreal (Ghassemzadeh et al., 2013). There, he was tasked with rebuilding the psychology department, which had all but shut down during the war. He re-established his connection with Wilder Penfield and arranged for his graduate students to work with him. In a few years, Hebb built McGill into a major center for neuropsychological research, attracting brilliant students who went on to become pioneers in the new field of neuroscience that developed later in the twentieth century.

Hebb was still working on the manuscript he'd started at the Yerkes lab, and it wasn't complete until 1949, when he published it as *The Organization of Behavior* (Sejnowski, 2003). In this book, he argued that theories of brain and behavior needed to be biologically plausible. Behaviorists spoke of switchboard models in which stimulus inputs were connected to response outputs. Gestalt psychologists tried to explain consciousness in terms of electrical fields in the brain. And almost everyone thought of information as flowing through the brain in a feedforward manner, that is, in one direction. None of these models were plausible, Hebb insisted, especially in light of what was already known about the biology of the brain.

Hebb's theory is based on three main points (Posner & Rothbart, 2004). First, he made *the proposal that when two adjacent neurons are repeatedly activated at the same time, the connection between them is strengthened.* According to the theory, this is how learning takes place in the brain, and today the idea is known as **Hebbian learning**. At the time, he was simply making a conjecture, and it took a quarter of a century for scientists to demonstrate Hebbian learning in the nervous system.

Second, Hebb asserted that memories are distributed widely across the brain, not at specific points as the switchboard model suggests (Posner & Rothbart, 2004). Building on his first point, he proposed that *a group of neurons that tend to fire together* form what he called a **cell assembly**. Because of their complex connections, these cell assemblies have feedback loops that can keep them active even after the stimulating event has ceased. Connecting brain with mind, Hebb says that these cell assemblies represent our ideas or concepts.

Finally, Hebb proposed that the activation of one cell assembly can spread to another one that's related to it, and so on (Posner & Rothbart, 2004). This sequence of cell assemblies becoming activated one after another represents the thought process. The take-home message of the book was that both behavior and mind can be explained in terms of plausible biological processes occurring within the brain.

The Organization of Behavior was well received, and it made Hebb famous among psychologists (Klein, 1999). Certainly, the book had come out at just the right time. Behaviorism was already in decline, and cognitive approaches to psychology were becoming more acceptable. But the book also had significant influence on the future trajectory of psychology, making it respectable to study the relationship between brain and mind. The book also inspired a vast amount of research that led to the much better understanding of the brain-in-action that we have today. Although many of the details in Hebb's theory have been proven wrong, the overarching ideas have survived the test of time.

Figure 10.4 Academic Family Tree of Donald Hebb

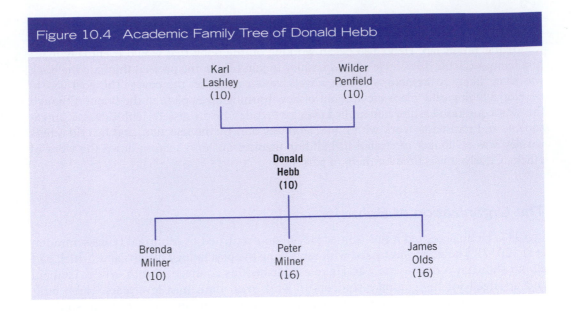

It's no exaggeration to call Donald Hebb the grandfather of modern neuroscience (Milner & Milner, 1996). *The Organization of Behavior* set the agenda for behavioral neuroscience, which took off rapidly once brain imaging technology became available. He also trained many of the pioneers in that field (Figure 10.4). But Hebb's theory has also had a major impact in a field he would never have thought of. The first computers were just being developed as Hebb wrote *The Organization of Behavior*. Because the theory was so speculative, it wasn't just a proposal for how learning could take place in the brain. Rather, its abstract formulation meant it was applicable to machine learning as well. In the field of artificial intelligence, Hebbian learning has had wide application and underlies much of the "smart" technology we have today.

Brenda Milner

Brenda Milner (born 1918) was born in England and received her master's degree in psychology at Cambridge University (Birchard, 2011). During World War II, she traveled to Canada to administer aptitude tests to servicemen who were training as pilots. After the war, she studied with Hebb and Penfield. In testing patients with frontal-lobe lesions, she found that although they performed within the normal range on standard intelligence tests, they also exhibited changes in personality that profoundly affected their lives. She remained an active researcher well into her nineties, but she's best known as the *British-Canadian psychologist who studied memory in patients with brain damage*.

Because she'd also published studies on damage to the temporal lobe, a Connecticut neurosurgeon contacted Milner about one of his patients, who was suffering unexpected memory loss after surgery (Carey, 2017). The young man, known as H.M. in the literature, had areas of the hippocampus in both left and right temporal lobes removed to treat his epilepsy. Although he no longer had seizures, he now had a strange form of amnesia. When Milner tested H.M., she found that his memories from before the surgery were still intact, but he remembered nothing afterward. This finding was quite remarkable, because until that time it was assumed that no specific area of the brain was responsible for memory. Since H.M. still had his presurgery memories but no new ones, Milner inferred that the hippocampus was somehow responsible for creating long-term memories but not for storing them.

As Milner continued to work with H.M., she found his amnesia was more complicated than she'd initially thought (Birchard, 2011). One day, she asked H.M. to try to draw a star while looking in a mirror. Although this task is difficult at first, people quickly learn to reverse their movements according to the reflected image. Since H.M. was unable to form any new long-term memories, she assumed he'd be unable to learn the task. To her surprise, he showed a normal learning curve. Milner reasoned that there must be two different memory systems, an explicit system for names, faces, and personal events, and an implicit system for procedures like playing a musical instrument or driving a car. Furthermore, the hippocampus only seemed to be involved in encoding explicit memories, which was why H.M. was still able to learn the mirror-drawing task.

In recent decades, Milner's work has focused on how the two hemispheres coordinate their activities (Birchard, 2011; Carey, 2017). She's also kept up with advances over her long career, for example adopting brain imaging equipment such as MRI in her research. In fact, researchers recognize her as one of the pioneers of cognitive neuroscience (see Figure 10.5). Over the years, Milner has received many awards and cash prizes for her ground-breaking discoveries. She then used this prize money of around a million dollars to establish the Brenda Milner Foundation to fund postdoctoral research in neuroscience. Without a doubt, this centenarian psychologist has made a lasting impact on the field and will continue to do so well into the future.

Photo 10.5
Brenda Milner

Roger Sperry

Roger Sperry liked to say that he was "imprinted on the mind-body problem" early in life when he happened to read a book by William James in grade school (Sperry, 1995, p. 505). On the first page of his notes for his introductory psychology course in college, Sperry wrote two questions:

- Where does behavior come from (nature vs. nurture)?

- What is the purpose of consciousness?

Sperry pursued these two questions for the rest of his life. Although he made many important discoveries during his long career, **Roger Sperry** (1913–1994) is best known as the *American psychologist who won the Nobel Prize for his research on split-brain patients.*

Sperry did his Ph.D. in zoology at the University of Chicago (Voneida, 1997). He learned surgical techniques with his mentor, and for his dissertation research he transposed the nerve fibers joining the hind-leg muscles of rats. Most scientists, his mentor included, assumed that the rat would simply learn the new nerve-muscle configuration and return to normal—but it didn't.

After Sperry earned his Ph.D. in 1941, he worked with Lashley at the Yerkes lab (Voneida, 1997). There, Sperry extended the research he'd done for his dissertation, this time working with newts. Severing the optic nerve from eye to brain, he rotated each eye 180 degrees. In humans, such an operation would have caused permanent blindness, but Sperry understood newts have the capacity to regenerate damaged neural tissue. In a month, the newts could see again. But their visual world had turned upside-down. When Sperry dangled a fly above the newt, it lunged downward. And when he enticed it from below, it jumped upward. Left and right were also reversed, just as would be expected from eyes that had been rotated a half-circle. Apparently, the two ends of each severed nerve had somehow reconnected, even though they'd been jumbled during the operation.

Sperry suspected some sort of chemical signal had guided the two severed ends back together again (Sperry, 1995). He also thought this was how the nervous system got wired during fetal development. *The idea that developing nerve tracts find their destinations by following chemical trails* is now known as

Photo 10.6
Roger Sperry

the **chemoaffinity hypothesis**. This theory greatly influenced the thinking of researchers who were interested in the question of how the nervous system developed. Furthermore, it challenged the received wisdom that the nervous system was shaped through experience rather than heredity.

Next, Sperry wondered whether the connections within the brain might also be hard-wired (Voneida, 1997). Working with various animal species, he and his students severed the **corpus callosum**, which is *the band of nerve fibers connecting the left and right hemispheres of the cerebrum*. Subsequent behavioral changes weren't as dramatic as they'd expected, but certain quirks did show up in the research. For instance, a behavior that the animal learned to perform with only one side of its body didn't transfer over to the other side, which had to be separately trained. Yet both sides showed similar learning curves. It was almost as if the animal now had two brains, one for the left side of its body and another for the right.

In 1960, a neurosurgeon approached Sperry about the possibility of cutting the corpus callosum in epileptic patients (Puente, 1995). The idea was that seizures starting on one side of the brain couldn't spread to the other side, thus reducing their impact. One of the neurosurgeon's patients was suffering around twenty seizures a day, and so he performed the operation. The frequency and severity of the patient's seizures were greatly reduced, and so the procedure was done on other patients as well.

These patients then served as research participants in Sperry's lab (Voneida, 1997). In daily interactions, they displayed no behaviors that were obviously out of the ordinary. But in carefully controlled experiments, Sperry and his students soon came to understand that these patients in effect had two separate streams of consciousness, one controlled by the left hemisphere and the other by the right. The researchers also learned for the first time about hemispheric specialization. That is, the functions performed by the two hemispheres aren't always mirror images of each other. In broad terms, the left hemisphere performed better at tasks requiring analytical or sequential processing, whereas the right hemisphere excelled at holistic processing and spatial abilities. Furthermore, only the left hemisphere had language, and whatever information went through the right hemisphere was processed in a nonlinguistic format.

These discoveries caught the popular imagination (Root-Bernstein, 2005). According to pop psychology, left-brainers think logically like scientists while right-brainers think intuitively like artists. In fact, this isn't at all what Sperry and his students found. The two lobes do indeed process information differently, but each of us needs both halves to function. We're all dual-brain thinkers, and there's no such thing as left-brain people and right-brain people.

Work with split-brain patients had provided Sperry with new insights into the age-old problem of the relationship between body and mind (Rychlak, 1997). Challenging the received wisdom that mind is nothing more than a by-product of neural activity, he contended that mind is an entity that emerges from brain activity. Thus, while the brain causes the mind, the mind also influences the brain. This may sound like Cartesian dualism, but the important difference in Sperry's theory is that both brain and mind are physical, so there isn't the difficulty of explaining how the two interact. Sperry's theory is highly speculative, and few psychologists even today give it much credence. It's simply too early to tell whether Sperry had glimpsed the future of psychology or slipped into abstract philosophy in his old age.

There's no greater acknowledgment for a lifetime of scientific achievement than receiving the Nobel Prize in Physiology or Medicine (Berlucchi, 2006). In 1981, Sperry became the first American psychologist to win the award in that category. (Pavlov had earned the same award many years earlier, but for his work on digestion, and his work in psychology came afterward.) Although Roger Sperry may not be a household name, his work is certainly familiar to the layperson. His findings on differences in left and right hemispheric specialization have taken on a life of their own in popular psychology. Nevertheless, Sperry's contributions count as early contributions in neuroscience (Figure 10.6). Furthermore, he dared to remind his fellow psychologists that they need to keep the mind front and center in their research.

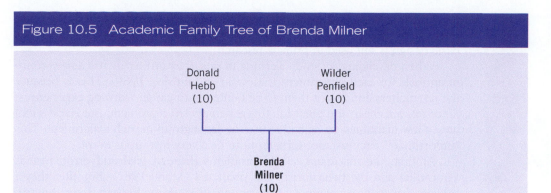

Figure 10.5   Academic Family Tree of Brenda Milner

Donald
Hebb
(10)

Wilder
Penfield
(10)

**Brenda
Milner
(10)**

Nature of Love

In 1958, the comparative psychologist Harry Harlow published an article entitled "The Nature of Love." This article shocked both professionals and the lay public alike for two reasons. First, it challenged the received wisdom that infants form a deep emotional bond with their mothers because they provide them with nourishment, arguing instead that contact comfort is the basis of this bond. Second, it described a series of experiments that illustrated the devastating effects of social isolation on newborn monkeys, and the implications for humans were obvious. As heart-wrenching as these studies were, they changed forever our understanding about the nature of love.

Harry Harlow

Harry Israel did his Ph.D. at Stanford, working with Lewis Terman among others (Gluck, 1997). His mentors thought highly of his work, but they were concerned he'd have difficulty finding a university position for a couple of reasons. First, his last name sounded Jewish, and given the anti-Semitism of the time, they feared no one would hire him. Even though he wasn't Jewish, he heeded their advice and changed his name to Harlow. Second, he was extremely introverted because of a speech impediment. Even in graduate school, his fellow students teased him when he said "wat" instead of "rat." Eventually he overcame his shyness and honed his pronunciation, such that in his later years he was highly sought after as a public speaker. But this was only after **Harry Harlow** (1905–1981) had built a reputation as an *American comparative psychologist best known for his studies on the effects of social isolation in monkeys.*

Harlow was hired to run the animal facilities at the University of Wisconsin, but when he arrived he was told the building had burned down (Sidowski & Lindsley, 1989). His colleagues suggested he work with the animals at the local zoo, so that's what he did. Two years later, the university gave him a dilapidated house for his lab, and together with his graduate students he renovated it into Wisconsin's first primate lab.

At the time, psychologists were split on the issue of animal learning (Sidowski & Lindsley, 1989). Behaviorists generally agreed with Thorndike that animals can only learn through trial and error, but Gestalt psychologists argued that primates can learn through insight as well. Many psychologists also believed only humans were capable of abstract thought, but Harlow wasn't convinced. He had access to a small group of macaques at the zoo, and he gave them various tasks in which they sorted objects by size, color, or shape. If they solved these problems, it would be evidence of abstract, categorical thinking. At the same time, he could look for evidence of insight learning.

Harlow and his students designed and built a piece of laboratory equipment known as the Wisconsin General Test Apparatus (Sidowski & Lindsley, 1989). The device consisted of a chamber to contain the primate and a board to hold objects to be manipulated by the subject.

Shantanu Kuveskar via Wikimedia Commons

**Photo 10.7
Macaque**

It enabled the experimenter to interact safely with the primate and allowed other researchers to observe the monkey's behavior in an unobtrusive manner. This basic design is still used in primate research.

When psychologists study learning in rats, they ordinarily use a new group of animals for each experiment (Sidowski & Lindsley, 1989). This is because the researchers don't want them to be tainted with earlier learning experiences. Since rats are cheap and plentiful, this generally isn't a problem. But Harlow had only a few macaques, so he had to use the same group in each experiment. This "unfortunate" circumstance turned out to be a very fortuitous event.

At first, the macaques solved problems through trial and error, just as Thorndike and the behaviorists had predicted (Sears, 1982). But after they'd solved a few of the same type of problem, their behavior changed. Instead of trying solutions in a random fashion, they took a more methodological approach. To Harlow, it appeared as though they were testing hypotheses. Once they started doing this, they were able to solve problems much more rapidly. Harlow called this *understanding of how to approach a solution to a particular type of problem* a **learning set**. Here was clear evidence that the animals were capable of both insight learning and abstract thought. In the end, it was fortunate that Harlow had to reuse the same monkeys, since they could only develop learning sets after solving several similar problems. In retrospect, Harlow also believed the situation with his monkeys more closely resembled learning in human children than did any one-off experiment with rats.

Many behaviorists agreed with Clark Hull (Chapter 5) that learning needed to be motivated through the reduction of a drive, such as hunger or thirst (Sears, 1982). But Harlow soon found reason to question this notion as well, at least as far as his macaques were concerned. He noticed hungry monkeys weren't especially motivated to solve puzzles, but when they were well fed, they approached the tasks with enthusiasm. And if they were given food as rewards for correct responses, they usually just stuffed them in their cheek pouches so they could enjoy the treats later. When Harlow's team stopped reinforcing the macaques, they kept performing the tasks—apparently, the monkeys enjoyed solving puzzles. They would also work very hard for the opportunity to peek through a small window, just to get a glimpse of a toy electric train running around its track.

Clearly, primary drives like hunger and thirst weren't sufficient to explain the motivation of these macaques (Sidowski & Lindsley, 1989). Harlow proposed instead that the behaviors of his monkeys were guided by **curiosity and manipulation drives**. By this, he meant that the animals had *motivation to seek out novel experiences and explore new things*. In other words, the monkeys were naturally curious about the world around them, and they didn't need to be motivated by hunger or thirst to solve problems. No doubt, the same can be said about humans and many other species as well.

Raising Primates in Isolation

Harlow was becoming famous for his rigorous studies on primate learning and the unexpected results they'd produced (Sidowski & Lindsley, 1989). In 1953, the University of Wisconsin provided him with a much larger building for his laboratory, so Harlow decided to establish a breeding colony for primates. Macaques are warm-climate animals, and Wisconsin is too cold for them to go outside for most of the year. This meant that they would have to be kept indoors, but many of the macaques imported from India were already sick with tuberculosis. The question was how to prevent the spread of this deadly disease to the next generation. No one had ever raised macaques in a cold climate before, so they were just going to have to use trial and error until they found a way that worked.

The final decision was to separate the infants from their mothers and raise them in a disease-free environment (Harlow, 1958). Baby macaques are usually born at night, but early the next morning lab assistants would take them away and place them in sterile cages. Infant mortality plummeted, and the bottle-fed babies were physically much healthier than those raised with their mothers. But Harlow's team also observed bizarre behaviors in the infants. In particular, the babies clung tightly to the cloth pads that lined the bottoms of their cages, and they threw tantrums when the cloths were removed for cleaning. Harlow remarked that the baby macaques' need for contact comfort was just like that of baby humans, who cling to favorite blankets or stuffed animals.

When the isolated infants grew up, they exhibited other bizarre behaviors as well (van der Horst, LeRoy, & van der Veer, 2008). Instead of playing with their peers, they remained aloof. As they matured and it came time to mate, they didn't know how to do it. Females that were artificially inseminated became abusive mothers, and they would surely have killed their babies if they hadn't been taken away. Apparently, interaction with a caregiver is vital for taking on healthy adult roles. This may seem obvious from our twenty-first-century perspective, but none of the theories at the time would have predicted it.

In the middle of the twentieth century, there were two theories explaining why infants develop a deep emotional bond with their mothers, and both made similar predictions (Harlow, 1958). According to the psychoanalytic view, the mother is a reliable source of nutrition, so the baby associates her with the pleasurable experience of a full belly. The behaviorist theory proposed that hunger is a primary drive that mother's milk satisfies. The affection or love the infant then feels for her is a secondary drive that is learned through association with the primary drive. From either perspective, milk from the mother's breast is the reason why infants develop emotional bonds with their mothers.

Harlow (1958) suspected there was more to infantile attachment than a full belly. After all, his baby macaques reared in isolation were well fed, and yet their social development was stunted. At this point, Harlow referenced the founder of behaviorism, John Watson (Chapter 5). According to his concept of conditioned emotional responses, there had to be some innate emotions as the starting point. In particular, positive responses were supposedly built on the innate emotion of love, which was elicited in the infant by skin contact. Harlow was also familiar with the work of British psychiatrist John Bowlby (Chapter 13), who'd worked with orphans during World War II. Although these children had had all their physical needs met, their social development was stunted, just like Harlow's isolated macaques.

Harlow (1958) and his team were trying to develop a breeding colony, but they were caught in a dilemma. Either they let infants be raised by their natural mothers and lose many of them to disease, or else they had to find a way to meet the social as well as physical needs of infants raised in sterile environments. Harlow wondered if a mechanical mother that provided milk and contact comfort would be good enough for the baby macaques. So his team covered a metal frame with brown terrycloth, installed a rack for a bottle of milk, and inserted a small heater for warmth. In fact, the baby macaques treated mechanical mom as if it were their real mother.

The mechanical mothers provided Harlow (1958) with the opportunity to test two competing hypotheses. Namely, did infants develop emotional bonds with their mothers because of the nutrition or the comfort they provided? Baby macaques were provided with two "mothers," one a cold metal frame with a bottle of milk, and the other a warm, cloth-covered frame that provided no milk. Although the babies fed from the cold metal mother, they spent most of their time clinging to the warm cloth mother. Watson and Bowlby were right, it was contact comfort that was most important. And the psychoanalysts and behaviorists were wrong.

Harlow (1958) tested additional hypotheses about the role the mother plays in the life of her infant. First, he proposed that the mother provides a *safe haven* for the infant, such that when it's frightened, it seeks out and clings to its mother for protection. In a series of studies, Harlow and his team exposed young isolation-raised macaques to frightening experiences he called the *strange situation* (p. 679). When they were put alone in a small chamber with a mechanical toy bear, the baby macaques cried out and curled themselves into balls. But when the wire and cloth mechanical mothers were also present, the babies sought out and

**Photo 10.8
Baby Macaque With
Mechanical Mother**

clung to the cloth mothers. Second, he believed that mothers provide a *secure base* from which the infant can go out and explore the world. When babies were placed alone in a room full of attractive toys, they tended to stay put. But when the cloth mother was in the room with them, they ventured away from her to explore, periodically returning to her for comfort and encouragement.

At first, Harlow (1958) thought he'd solved the problem of raising healthy macaques in captivity. The babies raised by mechanical mothers seemed reasonably well adjusted. But as they matured, they still showed signs of social and sexual immaturity. Harlow reasoned that the mechanical mothers were too good. They were always available, infinitely patient, and they never grew irritated with their babies or pushed them away. Although real mothers serve as a secure base, they also actively encourage their children to interact with their peers. But the mechanical mothers never did this, so the infants remained immaturely attached.

In the late 1950s, Harry Harlow and John Bowlby began corresponding (van der Horst et al., 2008). Bowlby saw firsthand the emotional devastation experienced by war orphans raised in large institutions. He believed that attachment to a caregiver was vital for healthy emotional development, and now Harlow had experimental evidence with a species quite similar to humans. In 1958, Bowlby traveled to the United States and visited Harlow's primate lab. As he toured the facilities and saw the macaques in their individual cages, he was struck by how similar their self-soothing behaviors were to those of the orphans he'd observed back in England.

During these years, Harlow collaborated extensively with his wife Margaret Kuenne Harlow (1918–1971), who was a child psychologist (Sidowski & Lindsley, 1989). Working together, they established two types of relationships that a developing macaque (and presumably a developing human) needed to grow into a well-functioning adult. First, it had to have an emotional attachment with a caregiver. And second, it needed to form friendships with peers. These two sets of relationships then provide the social experiences necessary to thrive in adult interactions, sexual relations, and parenting.

Harlow's experiments on isolation in infancy quickly became famous both within the psychological community and among the general public (Gluck, 1997). Professionals and laypersons alike were impressed with the clear demonstrations of the need for contact comfort, maternal attachment, and peer relations. After all, his studies provided scientific evidence for what so many people already intuitively understood. At the same time, Harlow has often been condemned for the intense emotional distress he inflicted upon helpless baby monkeys. Whether you deem the emotional harm to his animals justifiable or not, there's no question that Harry Harlow deepened our understanding of ourselves as humans by studying our close cousins, the macaques.

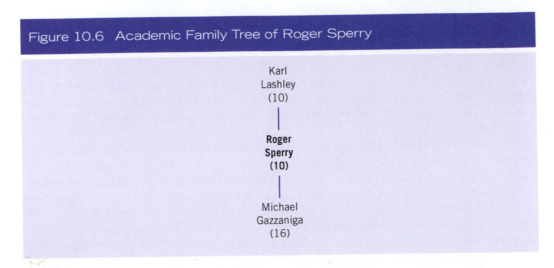

Figure 10.6 Academic Family Tree of Roger Sperry

Karl
Lashley
(10)

**Roger
Sperry
(10)**

Michael
Gazzaniga
(16)

Ethology: Konrad Lorenz and Nikolaas Tinbergen

Laboratory-based comparative psychology was a North American phenomenon (Dewsbury, 1990). But in the years before World War II, a small group of European researchers argued for a different approach. They practiced **ethology**, which they saw as *the study of animal behavior in natural settings*. The two leaders of the field were Konrad Lorenz and Nikolaas Tinbergen.

Konrad Lorenz (1903–1989) was an *Austrian ethologist best known for his studies of imprinting in birds* (Vicedo, 2009). Born into a wealthy family, Lorenz grew up on a country estate outside of Vienna.

Photo 10.9
Nikolaas Tinbergen and Konrad Lorenz

Lorenz's father was a famous physician, but he indulged young Konrad's hobby of collecting and caring for wild animals. However, he did insist his son study medicine. Lorenz obeyed, but as soon as he'd earned his M.D. degree, he pursued a Ph.D. in comparative anatomy. Even in his twenties and thirties, he continued living at home, tending his menagerie of animals. But during this time he also published influential papers on animal behavior in which he developed his ideas on instinct.

In particular, Lorenz became well known for his vivid descriptions of **imprinting** in geese (Brigandt, 2005). This is *a behavioral phenomenon in which a newly hatched chick identifies the first moving object as its mother*. Ordinarily, chicks imprint on their birth mother and follow her wherever she goes. However, Lorenz discovered that goslings (baby geese) would imprint on other animals, moving toys, or even his wading boots! Geese that had imprinted on Lorenz showed no interest in the company of other geese and only wanted to mate with his boots.

Nikolaas Tinbergen (1907–1988) was a *Dutch ethologist best known for his field studies on the nature and function of instinctive behaviors* (Dewsbury, 1990). He earned his Ph.D. in biology and accepted a faculty position at the University of Leiden in 1933. Tinbergen met Lorenz three years later when Lorenz gave a seminar in Leiden, and the two quickly became friends. The following year, Tinbergen and his wife spent several months at Lorenz's family estate. The two men studied bird behaviors, such as egg-rolling in greylag geese, which led to their only jointly authored paper.

Although Tinbergen credited Lorenz with inventing the field of ethology, many psychologists today understand it was a joint effort (Dewsbury, 1990). Because of his charismatic, flamboyant personality, Lorenz was the public face of ethology. He regaled his audiences with amusing anecdotes of bizarre animal behavior, and he spun grand theories based on a few observations from his menagerie. In contrast, the unassuming Tinbergen ran well-designed field experiments to test hypotheses about the functions of species-specific behaviors. He's best known for positing **Tinbergen's four questions**, which were *a set of guidelines for interpreting observations of animal behavior* (Table 10.1).

Lorenz and Tinbergen had similar views about the nature of instinct (Brigandt, 2005). In their view, instincts are innate behaviors that first appear fully formed without learning. Furthermore, instincts are fixed-action patterns, meaning that they're always performed the same way and can't be modified by experience. Likewise, instinctive behaviors were always triggered by some particular stimulus in the environment. Finally, they saw instincts as species-specific behaviors that had evolved to promote survival.

World War II found the two friends on opposite sides of the conflict (Bateson, 1990). Lorenz welcomed the unification of Austria with Germany in 1938. He even joined the Nazi Party and worked as a military psychologist for Hitler's Army. He was then sent as a doctor to the Eastern front, where he was captured by the Russians and put in a prisoner-of-war camp. He wasn't released until 1948, three years after the war had ended. Shortly after the German army invaded Austria, Lorenz had published an article praising the eugenic policies

Table 10.1	Tinbergen's Four Questions
Category	**Question**
Mechanism (causation)	How does the structure work?
Function (adaptation)	What survival or reproductive problem does the structure solve in the current environment?
Ontogeny (development)	How does the structure develop within the individual?
Phylogeny (evolution)	How did this structure evolve over many generations?

of the Nazis. After he saw the full extent of Nazi atrocity, he recanted his views and expressed remorse for joining the Nazi Party, but the damage to his reputation had already been done.

Tinbergen's fate during the war was in some ways similar but also quite different (Dewsbury, 1990). The Nazis invaded the Netherlands in 1940, and Tinbergen protested when Jewish faculty members were removed from his university. For this, he was arrested and spent the remainder of the war in a detention camp. So both men became prisoners, but one had joined the Nazis whereas the other had defied them.

In 1949, Tinbergen immigrated to England to join the faculty at Oxford University (Dewsbury, 1990). That same year, Lorenz was invited to give a talk at Oxford, and the two friends were reunited after a decade apart. At first, Tinbergen was hesitant to renew his friendship with Lorenz because of his pro-Nazi stance during the war. But in the end he forgave him for the sake of continuing the development of ethology. Both wanted to spread their ideas to the English-speaking world.

Lorenz made several trips to the United States, where he popularized his ideas about instincts (Vicedo, 2009). Although he'd only worked with birds, Lorenz's observations about the importance of mother-infant bonding for normal adult development struck a chord with his American audiences. At this same time, John Bowlby was reporting on his observations of war orphans in London, and Harry Harlow was publishing his studies on monkeys raised in isolation. These findings seemed to support the "common-sense" notion of the time that mothers should stay home with their children and not enter the workforce.

Comparative psychologists in America, however, were not as receptive to the tenets of ethology, especially as presented by Lorenz (Dewsbury, 1990). As we've seen in this chapter, physiological and comparative psychologists in the mid-twentieth century took a midway position in the nature-nurture debate, reacting against both the extreme empiricism of the behaviorists and the extreme nativism of the Gestalt psychologists. Instead, they tended to view behavior as an interaction between heredity and environment. In contrast, the ethologists maintained that there were two kinds of behavior, one instinctive and the other learned, and they rejected the notion that instincts could be modified by experience. American psychologists were also turned off by Lorenz's flamboyant style, but Tinbergen acted as a diplomat behind the scenes to help Americans and Europeans find common ground.

Another important figure during this time was **Frank Beach** (1911–1988), an *American comparative psychologist who was instrumental in helping the European ethologists gain acceptance in North America* (Glickman & Zucker, 1989). Beach had studied with Lashley at Chicago and Harvard, and he eventually accepted a position at Yale, where he conducted important research on animal sexuality and behavioral endocrinology. Beach was also a vocal critic of his field, and in particular he had two concerns. First, he took issue with the fact that most research in comparative psychology was conducted on just a few species, making it difficult to generalize findings. Second, he expressed his concerns about a dependence on laboratory studies and the general lack of field research. In his famous 1950 article, "The Snark Was a Boojum," Beach took his fellow psychologists to task for focusing their research efforts on the rat, arguing that comparisons of rats

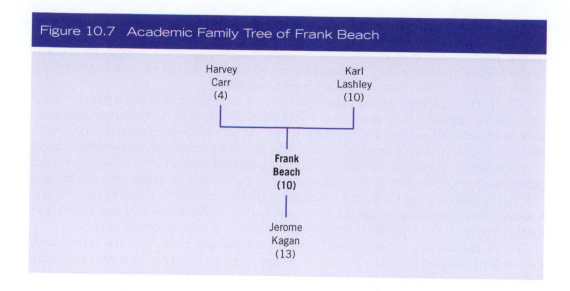

Figure 10.7 Academic Family Tree of Frank Beach

Harvey
Carr
(4)

Karl
Lashley
(10)

**Frank
Beach
(10)**

Jerome
Kagan
(13)

and humans were insufficient to constitute a comparative psychology. Instead, he praised Lorenz and Tinbergen, who studied a wide range of species in their natural habitats. As a result of Beach's efforts, many American students of animal behavior traveled to Europe in the 1950s and 1960s to study the ethological approach (Figure 10.7).

The contributions of Lorenz and Tinbergen were recognized with the Nobel Prize in Physiology or Medicine in 1973 (Vicedo, 2009). They shared this award with **Karl von Frisch** (1886–1982), the *Austrian ethologist noted for his work on perception and communication in bees*. This was the same category of Nobel Prize that had been awarded to Ivan Pavlov (Chapter 9) sixty-nine years earlier, although his was in recognition for his work on the digestive system. This time, however, the prize was awarded for work on animal behavior, which, the Nobel committee believed, also shed light on the human condition.

Looking Ahead

After World War II, psychology in North America began reorganizing itself from a set of schools into an array of disciplines. In the first half of the twentieth century, schools such as behaviorism, psychoanalysis, and Gestalt psychology dominated psychology. The questions each school asked ranged widely across topics, but what distinguished each was a particular set of initial assumptions and methods of inquiry. With the reorganization of psychology into disciplines, topics of research were narrowed, but practitioners were free to choose their assumptions and methods.

Physiological and comparative psychology of the mid-twentieth century can thus be seen as part of a transition from the earlier period of schools to the current era of disciplines. Working outside the strictures of the established schools, these physiological and comparative psychologists challenged assumptions and questioned accepted norms within the schools. A case in point would be the ardent empiricism of the behaviorists and the steadfast nativism of the Gestalt psychologists. In contrast to these viewpoints, the physiological and comparative psychologists tended to look at both nature and nurture as contributors to behavior.

Physiological psychology asked many of the same questions that neuroscience explores today, yet its practitioners had to work within the technological limits of their time. Thus, we can see that many of their students—or their students' students—became the pioneers of neuroscience. For example, we see this in the case of Brenda Milner, whose academic lineage extends back through Donald Hebb, Karl Lashley, and John Watson. Early in her career, her research relied on case studies of individuals with brain damage, but later on she took advantage of the developing brain imaging technology. Likewise, Lashley's student Roger Sperry was still a traditional physiological psychologist, in that much of his human research relied on case studies of brain-surgery patients. However, his student Michael Gazzaniga, whom we'll meet in Chapter 16, also incorporated brain imaging techniques into his research program as they became available.

Comparative psychology continues to be a robust area of research, and it has also had a considerable impact on other disciplines. For example, the work of Harry Harlow with monkeys raised in social isolation has had a significant impact on developmental psychology. As we'll see in Chapter 13, the work of John Bowlby and Mary Ainsworth on the development of attachment in childhood was given important empirical support by Harlow's studies. In particular, Bowlby was struck by the similarities of the psychological symptoms of the war orphans he observed and the bizarre behaviors of Harlow's monkeys. The work of ethologist Konrad Lorenz also drove home the point that healthy relationships between infants and their caregivers are essential for normal social and sexual development into adulthood.

In the last decades of the twentieth century, comparative psychology has turned from the study of complex behaviors in natural environments to the study of animal cognition. Early in the twentieth century, psychologists such as Margaret Washburn, Robert Yerkes, and Wolfgang Köhler argued that animals, especially primates, were capable of complex thought processes. At mid-century, Harry Harlow conducted studies of learning and memory in macaques, but these results have largely been forgotten in the wake of his even more notable studies of social isolation in primates. However, by the end of the twentieth century, a number of researchers had again picked up the question of primate cognition. For example, Tinbergen's student Beatrix Gardner, working with her husband Allen, taught the rudiments of American Sign Language to the chimpanzee Washoe, thus demonstrating the ability of primates to learn complex communication systems. Around the same time at the Yerkes Laboratory of Primate Biology, David Premack was studying the ability of primates to make causal inferences. Finally, we need to mention the work of Sue Savage-Rumbaugh at the Iowa Primate Learning Sanctuary with the bonobo Kanzi, who can communicate with humans using an artificial language known as Yerkish, in honor of Robert Yerkes.

The physiological and comparative psychologists worked outside of the established schools of the first half of the twentieth century. In spite of this, or perhaps because of this, they were able to make contributions that helped reshape psychology in its present form. As we'll see in the following chapters, their influence reaches to the present day.

CHAPTER SUMMARY

In this chapter we explored the careers of several researchers working during the early and middle decades of the twentieth century who thought of themselves as physiological or comparative psychologists. Rather than adhering to any particular school, physiological psychologists asked questions about the relationship between brain and behavior and between brain and mind. Likewise, comparative psychologists emphasized the need to expand research beyond the common lab rat to understand how organisms adapt to their natural environments. The early-twentieth-century physiologist Walter Cannon studied phenomena such as fight-or-flight and homeostasis, which are common fare in introductory psychology textbooks today. He also introduced an important theory of emotion. One of the most notable psychologists of the mid-twentieth century was Karl Lashley, whose concepts of mass action and equipotentiality laid bare the weaknesses

of current theories. Lashley's student Donald Hebb went on to develop a biologically based theory of how learning and thought take place in the brain. In turn, Hebb's student Brenda Milner explored the relationship between brain and memory, especially in her work with the patient known as H.M. In the middle decades of the twentieth century, comparative psychologists in North America and ethologists in Europe observed complex behavioral patterns across a wide range of species. These findings also provided us with a better understanding of human behavior as well, especially in the realm of social development. In particular, we can point to Harry Harlow's studies of social isolation in monkeys and Lorenz's work on imprinting in birds as key findings that provided a deeper understanding of human social development, particularly when coupled with the research on orphans during World War II that we'll discuss in Chapter 13.

DISCUSSION QUESTIONS

1. Consider how Cannon's concepts of fight-or-flight and homeostasis are related to the mind-body problem.

2. Compare the common-sense notion of how emotions work with the James-Lange and Cannon-Bard theories.

3. Describe the rationale behind Lashley's experiments with brain-lesioned rats, judging whether the results warrant his postulation of the laws of equipotentiality and mass action.

4. Discuss the evolution of thinking on the nature of learning from the behaviorist model to Lashley's search for the engram and to Hebb's *The Organization of Behavior*.

5. Outline the evidence Hebb took into consideration in creating a biologically plausible theory of how learning occurs in the brain.

6. Hebb's theory also had a great impact on the field of artificial intelligence. Can you think of some "smart" technologies that likely use Hebbian learning?

7. Describe Sperry's experiments with newts and explain why they support the hypothesis that the nervous system is wired according to an innate plan.

8. In split-brain patients, the two hemispheres of the brain can no longer directly communicate with each other. Propose some ways they might communicate indirectly. How would you test these hypotheses?

9. Discuss how Harlow's studies of learning sets in monkeys challenged behaviorist theory and extended the work of Wolfgang Köhler (Chapter 6) on insight learning in primates.

10. Outline the results of Harlow's studies on primates raised in isolation. In your opinion, does the importance of this work for humans justify the emotional distress imposed on these animals? Defend your position with arguments and evidence.

11. Explain how Milner's observations of the behavior of H.M. led her to the concepts of memory consolidation and explicit versus implicit memory.

12. Compare the results of Harlow's experiments on social isolation in monkeys and Lorenz's studies of imprinting in birds. What are the implications of these findings?

ON THE WEB

YouTube hosts instructional videos illustrating **Walter Cannon**'s concepts of **fight-or-flight** and **homeostasis** as well as **Karl Lashley**'s concept of **equipotentiality**. However, the quality of these items is inconsistent, so think critically as you view them. If you search for **Donald Hebb**, you can find brief footage of him talking about his theory of brain and memory as well as a short documentary on his career. His student **Brenda Milner** is still alive and active in the internet age, and you can find her TED Talk and other recorded interviews on the web. YouTube also hosts short documentary videos on the **split-brain experiment**, most of them featuring Roger Sperry's student Michael Gazzaniga, who is now a highly respected cognitive neuroscientist. You can also find short documentaries about and original footage from the **Harry Harlow monkey experiment**. If you search **Konrad Lorenz**, you can find a short documentary on **imprinting** as well as an interview (in German) with the great ethologist.

Cognitive Psychology

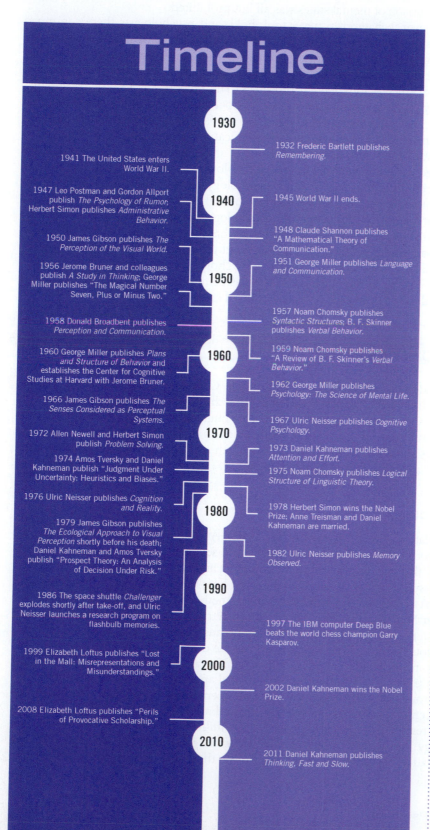

Timeline

1930

1932 Frederic Bartlett publishes *Remembering.*

1941 The United States enters World War II.

1947 Leo Postman and Gordon Allport publish *The Psychology of Rumor*; Herbert Simon publishes *Administrative Behavior.*

1940

1945 World War II ends.

1948 Claude Shannon publishes "A Mathematical Theory of Communication."

1950 James Gibson publishes *The Perception of the Visual World.*

1951 George Miller publishes *Language and Communication.*

1956 Jerome Bruner and colleagues publish *A Study in Thinking*; George Miller publishes "The Magical Number Seven, Plus or Minus Two."

1950

1957 Noam Chomsky publishes *Syntactic Structures*; B. F. Skinner publishes *Verbal Behavior.*

1958 Donald Broadbent publishes *Perception and Communication.*

1960 George Miller publishes *Plans and Structure of Behavior* and establishes the Center for Cognitive Studies at Harvard with Jerome Bruner.

1960

1959 Noam Chomsky publishes "A Review of B. F. Skinner's *Verbal Behavior.*"

1962 George Miller publishes *Psychology: The Science of Mental Life.*

1966 James Gibson publishes *The Senses Considered as Perceptual Systems.*

1967 Ulric Neisser publishes *Cognitive Psychology.*

1972 Allen Newell and Herbert Simon publish *Problem Solving.*

1970

1973 Daniel Kahneman publishes *Attention and Effort.*

1974 Amos Tversky and Daniel Kahneman publish "Judgment Under Uncertainty: Heuristics and Biases."

1975 Noam Chomsky publishes *Logical Structure of Linguistic Theory.*

1976 Ulric Neisser publishes *Cognition and Reality.*

1980

1978 Herbert Simon wins the Nobel Prize; Anne Treisman and Daniel Kahneman are married.

1979 James Gibson publishes *The Ecological Approach to Visual Perception* shortly before his death; Daniel Kahneman and Amos Tversky publish "Prospect Theory: An Analysis of Decision Under Risk."

1982 Ulric Neisser publishes *Memory Observed.*

1990

1986 The space shuttle *Challenger* explodes shortly after take-off, and Ulric Neisser launches a research program on flashbulb memories.

1997 The IBM computer Deep Blue beats the world chess champion Garry Kasparov.

1999 Elizabeth Loftus publishes "Lost in the Mall: Misrepresentations and Misunderstandings."

2000

2002 Daniel Kahneman wins the Nobel Prize.

2008 Elizabeth Loftus publishes "Perils of Provocative Scholarship."

2010

2011 Daniel Kahneman publishes *Thinking, Fast and Slow.*

Learning Objectives

After reading this chapter, you should be able to:

- Assess the contributions of British psychologists and the New Look movement to the development of cognitive psychology.

- Appraise the importance of the computer metaphor in sustaining the Cognitive Revolution.

- Compare and contrast the ecological and social approaches to cognition with the information-processing approach.

- Illustrate how judgment and decision-making theorists Daniel Kahneman and Amos Tversky extended the early work of Herbert Simon.

Looking Back

The very word *psychology* means "the study of the mind," and this was its understood meaning by both philosophers and experimental psychologists until the early decades of the twentieth century. Influenced by the positivist movement, which insisted that scientists can only study what they can directly observe, John Watson redefined psychology as "the study of behavior." By the beginning of the 1930s, behaviorism had come to dominate American psychology, and discussion of mental states was all but prohibited.

In Europe, however, behaviorism never took hold, and psychologists there continued to view the mind as their object of study. With the rise of fascism, many German-speaking psychologists immigrated to North America, bringing with them two schools of psychology that were clearly mentalist in nature. The first was psychoanalysis, which explained human behavior in terms of unconscious mental processes. The second was Gestalt psychology, which studied many of the same phenomena, such as perception and problem solving, that cognitive psychologists would take up starting in the 1960s. The roots of cognitive psychology can be found in the computational and communications technologies that emerged at the end of World War II. But once it was established as an independent discipline, cognitive psychology absorbed the findings of the Gestalt psychologists as part of its own literature.

Although the cognitive approach pointed psychology back to the study of the mind, many view behaviorism as a course correction that brought needed rigor to the field. Like their behaviorist forebears, the early cognitive psychologists understood that they couldn't observe the mind directly. Nevertheless, they believed that they could use behavioral data to make inferences about underlying mental processes. But unlike the free-ranging hypothesizing of the psychoanalysts, the theories of cognitive psychology were constrained by the view that human minds worked in much the same ways as computers. The computer metaphor thus became the lodestar guiding the first generation of cognitive psychologists.

Early Approaches

Although we traditionally mark the beginning of the Cognitive Revolution from the late 1950s, there were in fact precursors to this paradigm shift in psychology in the preceding couple of decades. One of these approaches arose in England as British psychologists contributed to the effort to defend their country from invasion by Nazi forces. The second arose in the United States shortly after World War II, in which a group of American psychologists took a "New Look" at the process of perception.

British Psychology

Psychology came late to Great Britain (Costall, 1992). At its two great universities, Oxford and Cambridge, both the philosophers and the natural scientists distrusted the new experimental psychology that was developing on the continent and across the Atlantic. The received wisdom was that psychology, as the study of the mind, was the province of philosophy—and it certainly couldn't be studied through experimental methods.

Even **William McDougall** (1871–1938), the *early twentieth-century British psychologist and pioneer in social psychology*, left Oxford in 1920 because he felt a keen lack of acceptance from his compatriots (Jones, 1987). As it turned out, he didn't get along any better with his colleagues at Harvard, many blaming this on his argumentative personality. He spent his last years at Duke University in North Carolina, where he'll appear once again in our story.

Despite the strong British antipathy toward experimental psychology in the early decades of the twentieth century, attitudes changed during and after World War II. This was when a small group of researchers working for the British military developed a uniquely British form of psychology. Furthermore, it was decidedly cognitive in its outlook, as opposed to the behaviorist orientation of American psychology during that same time period. Thus, we can say that modern cognitive psychology was born from the efforts of British scientists to save their country from German invasion. We turn first to Sir Frederic Bartlett, generally considered to be the founder of British psychology.

At Cambridge University, **Frederic Bartlett** (1886–1969) studied a field called moral science, but one of his teachers suggested he pursue a career in experimental psychology (Collins, 2006). Cambridge was just opening the first psychology lab in the country. Shortly after that, England entered World War II, and the director of the lab went off to fight. Because of health problems, Bartlett was rejected by the army, and instead he became director of the laboratory, where he led research for the military. By the time he retired in 1952, he'd built the Applied Psychology Unit at Cambridge University into a major research center. In his own country, Bartlett is known as the father of British psychology. But he's also noted as an important *early twentieth-century British psychologist who argued for the reconstructive nature of memory*.

Bartlett is best known for his 1932 book *Remembering*, in which he described an experiment that has become one of the classics of cognitive psychology (Collins, 2006). First, he asked his participants to read what was supposed to be a Native American folktale called "The War of the Ghosts." This story was very unusual in both structure and content from what English speakers of the early twentieth century would have expected. Afterward, the participants wrote down the story from memory. Bartlett observed that these retellings of the folktale were reshaped to fit British expectations for how a story should be told.

Photo 11.1
William McDougall

Today *Remembering* is considered a classic, but it wasn't well received at the time it was published (Costall, 1992). On the one hand, there was still considerable antipathy toward psychology in England. Bartlett was using the tools of science to encroach on the turf of philosophy, and neither the scientists nor the philosophers approved. On the other hand, behaviorists in North America stood firmly against his mentalist approach to what they considered to be the science of behavior. It wasn't until the Cognitive Revolution of the early 1960s that Bartlett's work on memory was rediscovered.

As a pilot during World War II, **Donald Broadbent** (1926–1993) noticed that many of the problems he and his fellow pilots encountered when they were flying their aircraft were due to psychological rather than technological issues (Broadbent, 1980). Machines simply weren't designed with human limitations in mind, so pilots made thoughtless—and sometimes deadly—errors even though they knew their planes well. After the war, he entered Cambridge to study engineering, but then he met Bartlett and was attracted to the kind of research being conducted at the Applied Psychology Unit. Today, Broadbent is known as the *British psychologist who developed the filter model of attention*.

Broadbent joined the Applied Psychology Unit in 1949, and his early research was supported by the British Navy, which wanted to know more about the effects of noisy environments on work performance (Craik & Baddeley, 1995). He found that loud noise had little effect on cognitive abilities, but it did interfere with communication. In other studies, he examined the performance of air traffic controllers, and he also investigated communication over radio frequencies in which multiple speakers were broadcasting at the same time. What all of these projects had in common was the question of attention, a topic that was of great interest in the early days of psychology but which had lost favor during the behaviorist era.

The fruit of these labors was Broadbent's 1958 book, *Perception and Communication* (Craik & Baddeley, 1995). In this work, he presented the vision of the human being as an information-processing system. He incorporated the idea of feedback loops into his theory, thus portraying humans as being far more complicated than the simple input-output models the behaviorists had proposed. Furthermore, Broadbent challenged the very idea of an environmental stimulus eliciting an organismal response. It's not the *actual* stimulus, he argued, but the *perceived* stimulus that guides behavior. This is because perception isn't just a copy of the external world, but rather it's also shaped by expectations and past experience. Furthermore, humans are limited in their capacity to process information. Since there's more

Figure 11.1   Dichotic Listening Task

Source: Galotti (2018).

stimulation in the environment than the organism can take in at any given moment, it somehow needs to decide what to pay attention to. All else fails to be processed at any meaningful level and therefore never reaches awareness.

Perception and Communication outlines the **filter model**, which is *Broadbent's description of attention as a bottleneck that limits the amount of information coming into the organism* (Broadbent, 1980). In other words, we're constantly bombarded by multiple streams of information from the environment, and the purpose of attention is to filter out all but one of these streams for further processing. Broadbent developed this model after he and his colleagues had conducted studies in **dichotic listening** (pronounced *die-COT-ik*). This is *a laboratory task in which the participant hears two different streams of speech through left and right headphones and is asked to only attend to one of them* (Figure 11.1). The participants had good recall of the attended stream but virtually no memory of the unattended stream. While initial results from dichotic listening tasks supported the filter model, studies from a newly established psychology lab at Oxford soon challenged aspects of the theory.

Anne Treisman (1935–2018) was working on her Ph.D. in clinical psychology at Oxford when Broadbent's *Perception and Communication* was published ("Anne Treisman," 1991). She was fascinated by his filter model, and she conducted her own dichotic listening experiments. In the end, she abandoned counseling for a career in attention research, and she's known today as the *British psychologist who proposed the attenuation model and the feature integration theory of attention.*

At Cambridge, Broadbent and his colleagues had found that participants in dichotic listening tasks remembered virtually nothing from the unattended ear ("Anne Treisman," 1991). Treisman replicated these results, at least when the unattended stream had no contents that were personally meaningful. *The ability to focus on one environmental stimulus while ignoring others* is referred to as the **cocktail party effect**. This comes from the fact that at a party you need to focus your attention on the conversation you are having and ignore all the other conversations going on around you. Even so, if someone across the room calls your name, you'll likely hear it. Likewise, Treisman found that when she

Photo 11.2
Anne Treisman

included instances of the participants' name in the unattended speech stream, they reported afterward that they'd heard it. She also found plenty of other instances of meaningful information leaking through the filter that was supposedly blocking the unattended stream.

Clearly, Broadbent's filter theory needed some revision (Craik & Baddeley, 1995). Instead of thinking about attention as a filter that blocked the unwanted stimulus, Treisman proposed instead that attention worked like the volume knob on a radio. Imagine you have several radios playing different stations at the same time. If the volume is turned high on all of them, you won't understand anything. But if you keep just one on high volume and turn the others down low, you'll be able to listen to that broadcast while monitoring the others in case they report something important. On this analogy, she proposed the **attenuation model**, which is *Treisman's proposal that attention increases the intensity of a wanted stimulus and decreases the intensity of an unwanted stimulus*. (The name of this model comes from the word *attenuate*, which means "to reduce the force of something.") Broadbent was quite magnanimous in Treisman's challenge, acknowledging that all theories are tentative and need to be revised as new data come in.

After this, a number of other researchers proposed different models of attention ("Anne Treisman," 1991). In the 1970s, during the heyday of the Cognitive Revolution, Treisman as well abandoned her attenuation model in favor a new perspective on attention, which she called **feature integration theory**. This is *Treisman's proposal that the role of attention is to bind features of objects, such as color or shape, into coherent wholes*. If you're looking for a single can of Coca-Cola in a refrigerator full of Sprite, it's easy. That one red can seems to pop out from the array of green cans. But if the refrigerator is stocked with a wide variety of beverages, many of which come in red cans, you'll have to pay careful attention to the details of the Coke can to find it. In other words, searching for an item based on a single feature like color doesn't require attention, but searching for an item based on multiple features does require sustained attention. Among the various models of attention in currency today, Treisman's feature integration theory is one of the most widely accepted.

British psychology was born of wartime necessity. It grew out of the problem of how to design complex machines so that humans could use them effectively. Researchers viewed human-machine interactions as a problem of information flow, and they extended principles of information-processing machinery to describe the mental processes that must be going on within humans as well. In the years after World War II, the work of these British researchers inspired a new generation of American psychologists to cast aside the strictures of behaviorism, bringing their field back to the study of the mind. Thus, we can say that British psychology of the mid-twentieth century laid the foundations for the Cognitive Revolution.

New Look

Revolutions are rarely successful the first time around. Often, there's one or more aborted attempts to change the system before the status quo is finally overturned and a new order established. Such was the case with the Cognitive Revolution. In the years after World War II, a movement called the "New Look" challenged established views on perception, arguing for the important role that mental states play in our view of the world. After a brief fit of excitement, interest died out. But the leader of the New Look movement, Jerome Bruner, regathered his forces, and with a new set of colleagues he helped lead the Cognitive Revolution just a few years afterward.

When **Jerome Bruner** (1915–2016) started as an undergraduate in psychology, behaviorism dominated the field (Gardner, 2017). He studied at Duke University with William McDougall, the British psychologist who'd fled Oxford because of the unwelcoming attitude of his colleagues. McDougall was adamantly opposed to the mindlessness of behaviorism. This attitude rubbed off on Bruner, and when he went to Harvard for his Ph.D., he worked with Gordon Allport (Chapter 14), the social and personality psychologist. He graduated just before the United States entered World War II, which he spent working on propaganda and intelligence for the military, including some time in Paris. This introduction to

**Photo 11.3
Jerome Bruner**

European culture had a profound impact on him. After the war, Bruner was hired at Harvard, where he developed his reputation as an *American developmental psychologist who was one of the founders of the Cognitive Revolution*.

Returning to Harvard as a faculty member after World War II, Bruner demonstrated in a series of experiments that emotional factors can influence perception (Bruner & Goodman, 1947). Participants were asked to estimate the size of coins by adjusting the width of a beam of light projected on a screen. Bruner speculated that the subjective value of the coins would lead to a perception of them being bigger than they actually were. As a further test of this hypothesis, he compared three groups—college students, children from well-to-do families, and children from poor families. Even the adult students overestimated the size of the coins, but the well-to-do children made larger overestimations, and the poor children—for whom the coins had the most value—made the largest overestimations of all.

These studies caught the attention not only of other psychologists but also the popular press (Haste & Gardner, 2017). The following year, fellow Harvard graduate Leo Postman returned as a faculty member, and the two collaborated on a number of other studies exploring the role of emotion and expectation in perception. Thus began the "New Look" movement of the late 1940s.

Born in Russia just after the Bolshevik Revolution of 1917, **Leo Postman** (1918–2004) immigrated to the United States as a young child (Brown, 2005). As part of the war effort, Postman conducted research with his advisor Gordon Allport (Chapter 14) on the origin and dissemination of rumors. This work resulted in their joint publication of *The Psychology of Rumor* in 1947. He also collaborated with Bruner on the perception research that came to be known as the New Look. After that, he accepted a position at Berkeley, where he spent the rest of his career doing research on memory. Today, Leo Postman is known as the *American cognitive psychologist who developed the interference theory of forgetting*.

In one of their most noted studies, Bruner and Postman (1949) investigated the role of expectation in perception. Using a tachistoscope, they flashed images of playing cards at increasing intervals, ranging from 10 to 1,000 milliseconds. The trick was that half of the cards had their colors reversed, for example a black heart or a red spade. It took on average four times longer for participants to identify the incongruous cards as it did the normal ones. Furthermore, participants often misidentified them, either not noticing the color change or else changing the suit to match the color, such as perceiving a red spade as a heart. When participants did finally identify an incongruous playing card, they often acted with surprise, after which they became faster at identifying new ones. Bruner and Postman compared this finding with Wolfgang Köhler's concept of insight learning, such that participants learned to generate a new expectancy of playing cards with their colors switched.

In retrospect, Bruner (1992) viewed the New Look as the first attempt at a cognitive revolution in psychology. At the midpoint of the twentieth century, American psychology still wasn't quite ready for a cognitive approach. The New Look movement, which gained so much attention early on, soon petered out. However, Bruner and Postman weren't alone at this time in their emphasis on the effects of mental states on behavior. For instance, the work of Edward Tolman (Chapter 5) on cognitive maps in rats was published around the same time that the New Look was flourishing. Already, there were cracks in the behaviorist edifice, but it would still take several more blows before it would fall.

In 1950, Leo Postman left Harvard for Berkeley, where he remained for the rest of his career (Bruner, 1992). There, he pursued a line of research known as verbal learning, which was still behaviorist in approach even though it was cognitive in its content. In particular, he focused on the learning and forgetting of word lists, much as Hermann Ebbinghaus had done more than half a century before. However, Postman challenged Ebbinghaus's notion that forgetting was due to decay, arguing instead that it was due to interference of similar items in memory. Postman's interference theory is still the most widely accepted explanation for forgetting. In a sense, Postman began practicing cognitive psychology before it was even called that.

Meanwhile, the information-processing approach of the British psychologists was starting to make an impact on their American counterparts (Bruner, 1980). In 1955, Bruner spent a semester at Cambridge, where he interacted with Frederic Bartlett and Donald Broadbent. He also traveled to Switzerland, where he met with Jean Piaget. The result of this sabbatical was Bruner's 1956 book *A Study in Thinking*, which Piaget enthusiastically praised. As Bruner continued his correspondence with Piaget, his research interests gradually shifted toward cognitive development. It was also around this time that Bruner began interacting with his Harvard colleague George Miller, which we'll explore in the next section.

Cognitive Revolution

The guiding symbol of the Cognitive Revolution was the **computer metaphor** (Crowther-Heyck, 1999). This was *the notion that the mind is an information-processing device much like an electronic computer*. The computer metaphor gave cognitive psychologists a new way of looking at mental processes, and the computer itself was also a model for the human mind that could be used to test hypotheses about perception, memory, problem solving, and decision making. Thus, the study of the mental processes could be conducted in a rigorous fashion, and the behaviorist moratorium on discussion of the mind was no longer valid. Such was the thinking of a number of psychologists in the late 1950s, but the central figure in the rise of cognitive psychology was a recent Harvard graduate by the name of George Miller.

George Miller

During World War II, Harvard psychologist **Stanley Smith Stevens** (1906–1973) was asked to do research for the U.S. Air Force that was similar to what Donald Broadbent was doing for the British military (Stevens, 1974). But unlike Broadbent, Stevens took a dim view of the information-processing ideas that were current after the war. Well versed in both physics and physiology, Stevens believed that only the study of sensation and perception fit within the scope of experimental psychology. And like his mentor Edwin Boring (Chapter 3), he dismissed any research of a social nature as nonscientific. Instead, Stevens built his reputation as an *American psychologist who developed the power law in psychophysics and an influential theory of scales of measurement*.

Stevens is especially known for two contributions to psychology (Miller, 1975). The first contribution is known as **Stevens' law**, which is *the observation that a power function best*

Table 11.1　Stevens's Theory of Scales

Scale	Definition	Examples
Nominal	Classifies each data point according to a predetermined set of categories	Male vs. female, Democrat vs. Republican, freshman vs. senior
Ordinal	Rank orders the data, but does not indicate intervals between them	Taste preferences (chocolate, vanilla, strawberry); opinions (completely agree, somewhat agree, somewhat disagree, completely disagree)
Interval	Indicates a degree of difference among data points but not an absolute difference; an interval scale may have an arbitrary zero but no absolute zero	Fahrenheit and Centigrade scales of temperature, where zero is arbitrary
Ratio	Indicates an absolute degree of difference among data points; a ratio scale has an absolute zero	Kelvin scale of temperature, which has an absolute zero; height, weight, and age are all scales with absolute zero

**Photo 11.4
George Miller**

describes the relationship between physical stimuli and psychological sensation. Many psychophysicists now consider Stevens's power law to be a better fit to the data than the logarithmic law that Gustav Fechner had proposed a century earlier. The second contribution is Stevens's **theory of scales**. This is *the argument that scales of measurement should be categorized by the types of mathematical operations that can be performed on them.* Any psychology major should be familiar with Stevens's four scales—nominal, ordinal, interval, and ratio. Although his theory of scales is widely accepted within psychology, it has been criticized by statisticians who've proposed alternative classification systems.

Although Stevens's research during World War II was quite similar to that of Donald Broadbent, it didn't lead him to a cognitive point of view. However, it was quite a different story for his student, **George Miller** (1920–2012), who'd been tasked with developing radio jamming techniques for the military (Miller, 1989). This work served as his doctoral dissertation, but because it was classified, only Stevens could read it. According to Miller, the dissertation defense was touch-and-go, since another member of the committee was Gordon Allport (Chapter 14), who was a bitter enemy of Stevens. In the end, though, the committee approved the "secret thesis," and Miller got his degree. Within a few years, Miller became known as the *American psychologist who led the Cognitive Revolution with his description of the mind as a limited-capacity information processor.*

Miller continued at Harvard after earning his degree, and in 1948 Stevens showed him an article that changed the direction of his career (Pinker, 2013). This was Claude Shannon's 1948 article "A Mathematical Theory of Communication," which demonstrated how to quantify the amount of information in a message. A key concept was the **bit**, or "binary digit," as *the basic unit of information in communication and computing.* This paper also introduced Miller to the idea of information processing in machines, and he quickly saw the parallels with human behavior. Until this time, Miller had been a strict behaviorist, but now he saw that behavior could only be explained if the mental processes of the organism were understood. Thus, he was converted to a cognitivist perspective, which he laid out in his 1951 book *Language and Communication.* Over the next few years he found a number of like-minded colleagues.

In 1955, Miller was invited to give a talk at the Eastern Psychological Association (Miller, 1989). None of his current research projects yielded enough material for an hour-long presentation, so instead he talked about three separate topics that seemed to cohere around the theme of the mind as a limited-capacity information processor. First, studies showed that people can keep no more than about seven categories in mind when making absolute judgments, as for example when identifying different pitches. Perhaps then it's no coincidence that the musical scale consists of seven tones. Second, he'd found that people can generally hold no more than seven items, such as digits or common words, in immediate memory. This is why we break up long series of digits like telephone and credit card numbers into smaller groups. Third, research indicated that people can accurately detect the number of objects in a group up to about seven items. For example, it's easy to see the difference between a group of three and a group of four, but not if the two groups have ten and eleven items. The common theme running through these various data sets was the "magical number seven," an expression Miller had intended in jest.

The following year, Miller (1956) published this talk as the article "The Magical Number Seven, Plus or Minus Two," and it quickly became the manifesto of the Cognitive Revolution. In the paper, Miller demonstrated that we have a limited ability to take in and retain information in what soon became known as short-term memory. Although he made use of Shannon's information theory, he found that capacity limitation isn't determined but the number of bits or individual items but rather by a larger unit he called a **chunk**. This was the term he used to refer to *a meaningful unit of information held in short-term memory.* For example, if I ask you to repeat back the twelve-letter string LFNIBFAICASU after hearing it one time, you won't be able to do it. But if I read the string to you backward (USACIAFBINFL), you'll likely notice that it consists of four common acronyms, and you'll repeat the list easily. By grouping chunks into larger and larger meaningful structures, we can process lots of information quickly despite our limited capacity. This is how language works, and it's probably true for thought in general.

Noam Chomsky

Photo 11.5
Noam Chomsky

Noam Chomsky (born 1928) earned his doctoral degree in linguistics from the University of Pennsylvania in 1955 (Miller, 1989). But when he tried to publish his dissertation as the book *Logical Structure of Linguistic Theory*, publishers rejected it as too unconventional. One even recommended that he first make himself famous before trying to publish such a book—and that's exactly what he did. *Logical Structure of Linguistic Theory* was eventually published two decades later, in 1975, by which time Noam Chomsky was quite well known as the *American linguist who helped start the Cognitive Revolution by demonstrating that language cannot be learned through operant conditioning alone.*

In 1957, Chomsky published a shortened version of his dissertation as *Syntactic Structures* (Radick, 2016). At that time, linguists and psychologists believed that sentences were constructed as a series of words like beads on a string. Chomsky contended first that people don't construct sentences in this manner and second that such a grammar would be impossible to learn. Instead, he argued that sentences are produced by first grouping words into phrases and then grouping those phrases into sentences according to a set of rules he called phrase-structure grammar. Furthermore, he argued, this phrase-structure grammar—or syntax—operated independently of the meaning, or semantics. As an example, he offered the sentence "Colorless green ideas sleep furiously," which is clearly grammatical even though it is nonsensical (Figure 11.2).

Chomsky pushed his argument even further by contending that phrase-structure grammar alone isn't enough to account for how people produce and comprehend sentences (Chomsky, 1957). First, he noted that people rarely recall what they hear verbatim. Instead, they remember the gist in the form of basic sentences. In Chomsky's theory, basic sentences are constructed according to phrase-structure grammar, but they can also be modified by transformational rules. For instance, the sentence "The student ate the pizza" can be transformed in various ways, such as making it into a question ("Did the student eat the pizza?") or a negative ("The student did not eat the pizza"). These modified sentences aren't generated by phrase-structure rules but rather by transformational rules that change basic sentences according to consistent patterns. Taken together, Chomsky had proposed *a theory of sentence structure based on phrase-structure and transformational rules*, which he called **transformational-generative grammar**.

Figure 11.2   Sentence Tree for "Colorless Green Ideas Sleep Furiously."

```
                        S
               ┌────────┴────────┐
              NP                 VP
          ┌────┼────┐        ┌────┴────┐
         ADJ  ADJ   N        V        ADV
          │    │    │        │         │
      Colorless green ideas sleep   furiously
```

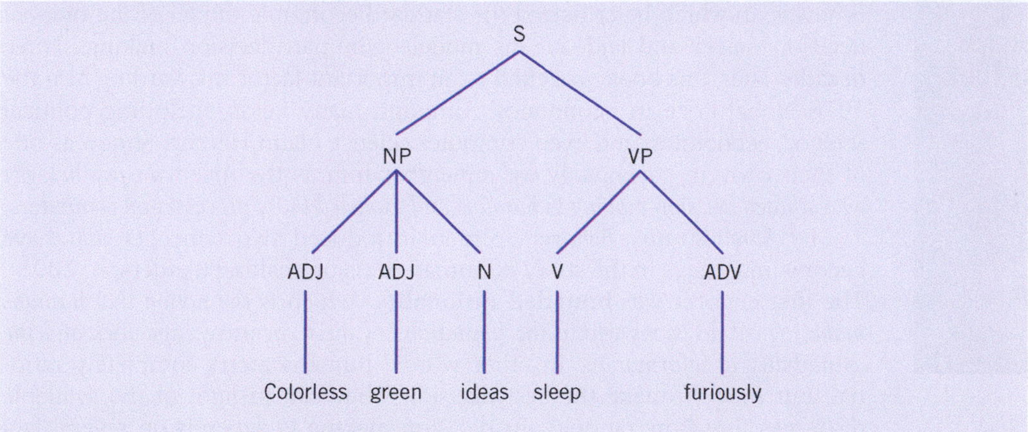

Miller clearly saw that Chomsky's phrase-structure grammar was an instance of chunking, with words grouped into meaningful phrases that are then combined into sentences (Miller, 1989). In this way, we can produce and comprehend sentences longer than just a few words. He also saw in Chomsky's transformational rules a sort of computer program that manipulated symbols. Clearly, no behaviorist approach could ever explain language production or comprehension. Instead, a mind capable of powerful computational processes would be needed.

Over the next few years, Miller and his students conducted a series of experiments designed to test the psychological reality of Chomsky's transformational-generative grammar (Pinker, 2013). Specifically, they tested the hypothesis that sentences with more transformations would be more difficult to recall. The results initially seemed to support the theory, but other psychologists soon pointed out confounds in the procedures that left the data uninterpretable. Eventually, psycholinguists came to the conclusion that transformational-generative grammar is a useful formalism for demonstrating syntactic structures but doesn't explain how humans actually process language.

In 1957, B. F. Skinner published *Verbal Behavior*, in which he outlined his views on language learning and language use within a behaviorist framework (Radick, 2016). Two years later, Chomsky (1959) published a lengthy review of the book in which he challenged Skinner's contention that language is learned through reinforcement. He pointed out that young children acquire language with very little feedback as to whether their sentences are grammatically correct or not. Furthermore, he argued, children master the grammar of their language within five or six years, not nearly enough time for that "verbal behavior" to have been shaped through operant conditioning. Instead, he argued that infants have an innate understanding of universal linguistic structure that guides the language acquisition process. Cognitive psychologists often point to Chomsky's "Review" as the manifesto of the Cognitive Revolution.

Over the next half century, Chomsky made numerous modifications to bring it more in line with the psychological evidence. Nevertheless, his view of the mind as a sort of computer specifically designed to rapidly and efficiently process complex linguistic structures has remained a cornerstone of cognitive psychology.

Herbert Simon and Allen Newell

Herbert Simon (1916–2001) got his Ph.D. in political science at the University of Chicago in 1942 (Leahey, 2003). Convinced that politics could only be understood if economic factors were taken into account, he delved into the literature of that field. But soon he became disillusioned with economics, which assumed that people always make rational decisions. In the real world, Simon believed, people have neither the cognitive capacity nor the relevant information to make perfectly logical choices. Instead, they make decisions that are good enough. In 1947, Simon published the book *Administrative Behavior*, in which he criticized the standard economic model of the rational decision maker and laid out his model of human decision making. Three decades later, this book was cited as an important factor in awarding him the 1978 Nobel Prize in Economics. Although many fields, including political science, economics, and even computer science claim Herbert Simon as one of their own, in psychology we remember him as the *American psychologist who studied decision making in humans and modeled those processes on computers.*

In *Administrative Behavior*, Simon introduced two concepts that have become mainstays in the study of human decision making (Anderson, 2001). The first concept was **bounded rationality**, which is *the notion that humans make logical decisions within the limitations of their cognitive capacities and the availability of information.* In other words, humans aren't completely rational, but they do make the best decisions they can in light of the available resources. Just how rational our decision making is depends on several factors. One has to do with our level of expertise or experience, and another has

**Photo 11.6
Portrait of
Herbert Simon**

to do with the amount of time or the information that's available. Although our decisions aren't perfectly rational, they're usually good enough to meet our needs.

The second concept was introduced in *Administrative Behavior*, but it wasn't until a decade later that Simon gave it a name (Leahey, 2003). In that book, he describes how even major corporations don't act in ways that maximize their profits, as economists assume. Instead, they pursue satisfactory—but not optimal—returns on their investments. This is because companies, like the individuals who make them up, have limited cognitive resources and available information. Later, Simon called this phenomenon **satisficing**, which is *the practice of making choices that are good enough for current needs*. At the individual level as well, we satisfice in our decision making, for example when ordering from a menu or deciding on a movie to watch.

Although Simon thought of himself as an economist and political scientist, in a sense he'd been doing psychology all along. He just didn't realize this until he met Allen Newell, with whom he enjoyed a long-time and fruitful collaboration.

Allen Newell (1927–1992) had studied physics and math, but he'd quit graduate school to take a job at the RAND Corporation, a think tank funded by the Air Force to study human organizational behavior as it related to military strategy (Simon, 1993). One project involved the study of group dynamics in air traffic control, and Newell used a simple computer to simulate blips on a radar screen—one of the first computer simulations ever implemented. The success of this project set the trajectory for the rest of his career, and Newell became known as an *American psychologist who used computer simulations to study human problem solving*.

In 1952, Carnegie Tech psychologist Herb Simon was brought to RAND as a consultant (Simon, 1993). Although Simon's early work was in economics and political science, he'd recently taken an interest in the new information-processing models of human cognition. When Newell and Simon met, they quickly found they'd been thinking along the same lines. Of particular importance was the common attitude they held toward the new electronic computing devices that were just being developed. Although most people saw computers as nothing more than number crunchers, both Newell and Simon had come to understand that computers could also be used to process information. And if both computers and humans were information processors, then the former could be used to model the thought processes of the latter. In other words, they both believed it was possible to write programs that would make computers think.

Simon convinced Newell to come to Carnegie Tech (now Carnegie Mellon), where they could collaborate on research projects while Newell finished his Ph.D. ("Allen Newell," 1986). Newell then stayed on at Carnegie Tech as a professor of psychology and computer science. Their first project was the Logic Theorist, a computer program that could discover proofs for geometric theorems. This was one of the first demonstrations that computers could do more than crunch numbers, as they could also be programmed to solve complex problems. The Logic Theorist helped establish the field of artificial intelligence, but it also demonstrated that computers could be used to model human thought processes.

Although it was very effective at the task it was designed for, the Logic Theorist didn't solve problems the same way humans did (Anderson, 2001). This meant that it wasn't a good model for human problem solving. Instead, Newell and Simon realized that they first had to gather data on how humans solve problems, and then they could design computer programs that solved those problems in the same way. In a series of experiments on human problem solving, they developed the **think-aloud protocol**, which was *a laboratory procedure in which participants verbally reported their thought processes as they solved puzzles*.

Humans employ a number of strategies in problem solving, but Newell and Simon found that one common approach was **means-ends analysis** (Anderson, 2001). This is *the problem-solving method of searching for ways to close the distance between the current state and the goal state*. Let's say you want to order a pizza. That means you'll have to call your favorite pizzeria, but first you need to find your phone. And once you've done that, you'll have to see whether you've saved the phone number. If not, you'll have to do a quick internet search. You call, and when they answer, you'll have to give them your order. When the pizza arrives, you pay the delivery person and give her a tip, and she hands you the pizza. Finally, the problem is solved. But at each step along the way, you set up a subgoal that helped you get closer to the solution.

With a grasp of how humans use means-ends analysis, Newell and Simon wrote a computer program to solve problems in a similar manner (Anderson, 2001). The result was the General Problem Solver, which used means-ends analysis to solve problems. Despite the name, the General Problem Solver could only solve a limited number of puzzles, and most problems that humans deal with on a daily basis were beyond its reach. In 1972, Newell and Simon published the book *Problem Solving*, which outlined the means humans use to solve problems as well as their attempts to get computers to model human thought processes.

Newell and Simon were pioneers in the field of artificial intelligence (Anderson, 2001). Although the Logic Theorist and the General Problem Solver were simple programs compared with the multitude of smart devices we enjoy today, these two men were among the first to see the wide range of possible uses that computers could be put to. In 1957, Simon prophesied that in ten years the world's chess champion would be a computer. Although it took much longer than he expected, in 1997 the IBM computer Deep Blue beat the world chess champion Garry Kasparov.

Harvard Center for Cognitive Studies

As the year 1960 approached, the cognitive movement reached critical mass (Bruner, 1980). In 1956, Bruner and colleagues had published *A Study of Thinking*, in which they described the ways humans go about solving problems in terms of the hypotheses they generate and the solutions they consider. This was followed in 1960 by *Plans and the Structure of Behavior*, which Miller had written with several colleagues. But Bruner and Miller were frustrated with the state of psychology at Harvard, which reflected the state of the field in general. The psychology department had fractured into multiple fiefs that were no longer talking to each other. For instance, the tension between S. S. Stevens and B. F. Skinner, with labs at opposite ends of the same building, was palpable. And the social psychologists, including Jerome Bruner, had split with psychology and were now allied with sociology. Miller and Bruner believed a cognitive approach could unify disparate fields, and in 1960 they established the Center for Cognitive Studies at Harvard.

The center attracted scholars from a wide range of disciplines, including philosophy, linguistics, anthropology, and computer science (Crowther-Heyck, 1999). What these fields had in common was the question of how humans use their minds to solve problems and to guide their interactions with the world. Other early figures in the Cognitive Revolution, such as Chomsky, Newell, and Simon, were frequent visitors. Likewise, the center attracted a number of graduate students who then spread the Cognitive Revolution to other psychology departments across the country. Within a few years, the cognitive approach had gained widespread acceptance, and in 1962 Miller felt confident enough to title his new textbook *Psychology: The Science of Mental Life*.

Ecological and Social Approaches

Although the computer metaphor provided a framework for conceptualizing mental processes, it also had its limitations. Both humans and computers may be information processors, but there was one important difference that had been neglected. Unlike computers, humans process information in order to interact with their physical and social environments. Therefore, any well-developed theory of human cognition would have to take these factors into account.

James Gibson

Trains, planes, and automobiles—things that move people through the world—played a central role in the life of **James Gibson** (1904–1979). As a boy, he often rode in trains with his father, who worked for a railroad company, and he marveled at how the world before him seemed to expand outward from the horizon as the engine rolled down the tracks (Gibson, 1967). During World War II, Gibson trained pilots for the Army Air Force, and he wondered what visual cues they were using to land their planes without crashing. And as an eligible bachelor professor at an all-women's college, he used to court his female students by taking them for rides in his Model T Ford—until one of them fell in love with him and married him. Despite his early playboy lifestyle, Gibson eventually built a reputation as a revolutionary thinker in the field of visual perception. Today we remember him as the *American cognitive psychologist who developed the theory of direct perception.*

Gibson earned his Ph.D. in psychology at Princeton in 1928 (Hochberg, 1994). He worked with **Edwin Holt** (1873–1946), an *early twentieth-century American psychologist who proposed the motor theory of consciousness.* Holt rejected Cartesian dualism, insisting that the mind was a part of the physical world. More specifically, he maintained that consciousness arose from the activity of the nervous system as the organism moved through and acted on its surroundings. This emphasis on organism-environment interaction in the evolution of consciousness deeply impacted Gibson's thinking throughout his career (Figure 11.3).

After graduation, Gibson accepted a position at Smith College, where three people greatly influenced his thinking (Neisser, 1981). The first influence was the Gestalt psychologist Kurt Koffka (Chapter 6), who'd just arrived at Smith the year before. For Koffka, the most important question in psychology was: "Why do things look the way they do?" He believed that perception was shaped by the innate structure of the nervous system. Although Gibson agreed that the problem of perception was the central question of psychology, he disagreed with the Gestalt account that innate organizational principles explain why the world looks the way it does.

The second influence was Fritz Heider (Chapter 6), who came to Smith a couple of years after Gibson (Hochberg, 1994). Heider introduced him to the distinction between distal and proximal stimuli, that is, the object in the world versus the image on the retina. He also impressed Gibson with the idea that light is the medium that transmits information about objects in the environment to the organism. Gibson disagreed with his emphasis on the retinal image, but Heider's conceptualization of light as a medium for transmitting information about the environment played a central role in Gibson's theory.

The third influence was Eleanor Jack, the student at Smith that he married in 1932 (Neisser, 1981). Known as Jimmie and Jackie to their friends and colleagues, the couple enjoyed a relationship of mutual support and admiration, even though they found it difficult

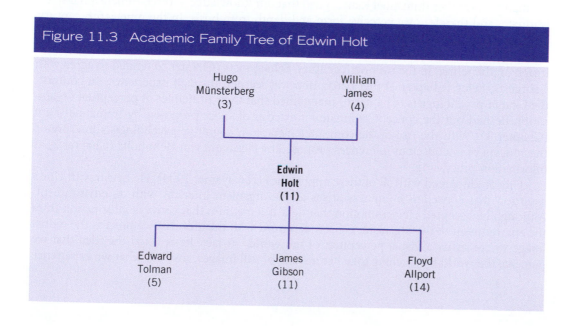

Figure 11.3 Academic Family Tree of Edwin Holt

to collaborate with each other. During the late 1930s he encouraged her to pursue her Ph.D. at Yale with Hull, and during the war years she played the role of housewife and stay-at-home mom while her husband built his career as a vision researcher through his work for the Army Air Force. Later at Cornell, they pursued separate research programs, even though they clearly influenced each other's thinking. We'll learn more about Eleanor Gibson's career in Chapter 13.

Despite the heavy teaching load at Smith, Gibson managed to publish several papers on visual perception that attracted attention (Gibson, 1967). Disenchanted with traditional approaches, which asked people to respond to still images, Gibson emphasized the process of people perceiving their environments as they move through them. One of these studies analyzed the visual cues that drivers use to keep their cars on the road and avoid obstacles. Another investigated a circus act in which a motorcyclist performed loop-the-loops inside a spherical metal cage. Based on this research experience, Gibson was assigned director of a motion picture unit tasked with producing training films for cadets learning how to fly. Before his arrival, training mainly proceeded through the use of photos and line drawings, but Gibson made films by putting cameras in the cockpits of experienced pilots so that the training experience could be as realistic as possible. This was also the time during which he began pondering the question of what visual cues a pilot uses to land a plane without crashing it.

Direct Perception

After the war, the Gibsons returned to Smith College, where James published the aviation research he'd conducted during the war (Hochberg, 1994). This attracted the attention of psychologists at major research universities, and in 1949 he accepted an offer from Cornell, where he and Eleanor remained for the rest of their careers. During those years, James Gibson published numerous articles and three books that outlined his revolutionary theory of **direct perception**, which is *the argument that we perceive the world as it is without having to process the sensory stimulus.*

To understand just how radical Gibson's approach was, we need to review traditional theories of visual perception (Hagen, 1985). You should recall from Chapters 1 and 2 that European philosophers and scientists from the eighteenth century onward have debated whether form and depth perception are innate or learned from experience. On the one hand, the British philosopher George Berkeley argued that we learn to perceive shape and distance as we correlate tactile experiences with visual input. On the other hand, the German philosopher Immanuel Kant argued that our knowledge of three-dimensional space is innate, and therefore we perceive form and depth from birth. In the nineteenth century, German physiologist Hermann von Helmholtz maintained that we need to make unconscious inferences about the three-dimensional world on the basis of the two-dimensional image on the retina. In the twentieth century, behaviorists (Chapter 5) tended to agree with George Berkeley (Chapter 1) that perception was learned through experience. In contrast, the Gestalt psychologists (Chapter 6) maintained that their principles of perceptual organization fleshed out the concept of innate knowledge of space proposed by Immanuel Kant (Chapter 1). With the rise of the computer metaphor, cognitive psychologists interpreted the concept of unconscious inferences proposed by Hermann von Helmholtz (Chapter 2) as information processing.

Gibson disagreed with all of these approaches (Nakayama, 1994). He began with Holt's assertion that conscious awareness arises as the organism interacts with its environment. Although he accepted Heider's notion that light is a medium that conveys information from the environment to the organism, Gibson disagreed with the idea that we process the retinal image to construct a visual perception of the world. In fact, he rejected the idea that we perceive the world by stitching together a series of still images. Instead, what we experience is a world in flux as we move through it, and it's this interplay between what changes and what remains constant that constitutes perception. According to Gibson, there's no need to interpret or process the light coming into our eyes because it's already so rich in information about the world around us. In other words, there's no stimulus to process, and instead what we do is merely pick up information from the light. While such a way of thinking was counterintuitive to most psychologists at the time—and even today—Gibson spent the next three decades fleshing out his theory of direct perception.

In *The Perception of the Visual World*, Gibson (1950) lays out two important concepts in his theory. The first concept involves *the observation that the visual scene appears to expand from a central point in front of a moving observer*, and he called this **optic flow** (Figure 11.4). Drivers use optic flow to steer their cars by keeping the center of expansion on the road ahead of them. Likewise, pilots use optic flow to land their planes by targeting the center of expansion on the point where they want to touch down. Optic flow also provides us with information about how fast we're approaching an object, or how quickly it's approaching us. Gibson contended that there's no need to calculate distance or speed. Rather, optic flow provides us with plentiful information for navigating through the world.

The second concept is **texture gradient**, which is *a repeating pattern in the environment that conveys information about distance and relative size* (Gibson, 1950). The same object appears smaller in the distance than it does up close. This isn't a trick of the eye, Gibson insists, but rather the nature of the physical world. The farther away an object is, the less light there is from it that reaches our eyes, and so it appears smaller. Our environment is replete with texture gradients, such as trees, pebbles, and blades of grass, that are each of a more or less consistent size. Even our man-made world is filled with texture gradients such as floor and ceiling tiles as well as doors and windows in walls. These texture gradients provide a grid that allows us to directly perceive the size and distance of objects in our environment.

In *The Senses Considered as Perceptual Systems*, Gibson (1966) introduced a third key concept in his theory of direct perception. According to the received wisdom, the purpose of visual perception was to identify objects in the environment. In Gibson's view, however, we don't identify objects per se but rather what we can do with them. For instance, a squirrel doesn't see a tree but rather something to climb, and a robin doesn't see an earthworm but rather something to eat. Gibson referred to *what the environment offers to an organism as*

Figure 11.4   Optic Flow

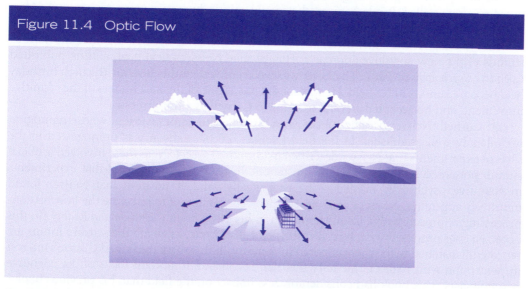

Source: Galotti (2018).

an **affordance**. Identifying affordances is different from identifying objects, in that what the environment affords depends on the perceiving organism. For example, as I walk through the woods with my dog, I find a fallen tree to sit on. But my canine companion sits on the ground, since logs don't afford sitting for dogs. Gibson (1979) further developed his concept of affordances in *The Ecological Approach to Visual Perception*. In that book, he also emphasized that an affordance is a relationship between the organism and its environment. This book was published just months before he succumbed to cancer.

In response to Koffka's question of why things look the way they do, Gibson's response was that we see the world as it actually is. Instead of constructing a mental representation from an ambiguous and impoverished input, we perceive our environments directly because all the information we need is already "in the light." Gibson not only challenged traditional theories of perception, he also rejected the information-processing approach of his contemporaries. Although Gibsonian concepts such as optic flow, texture gradients, and affordances are now part of the vocabulary of cognitive psychology, many vision researchers remain unconvinced even today that we can perceive the world directly without processing the sensory input. Nevertheless, Gibson did influence the thinking of some psychologists, in particular his colleague at Cornell, Ulric Neisser, who we turn to next.

Ulric Neisser

Cognitive psychologist **Ulric Neisser** (1928–2012) was plagued with a false memory for much of his life (Neisser, 2007). He recalls learning about the Japanese attack on Pearl Harbor while listening to a baseball game on the radio. The only problem, he later realized, was that no one plays baseball in December. Still, baseball was an important component of Neisser's self-concept. Having immigrated to the United States from Germany as a young boy, he asserted his new American identity by becoming a baseball fan. Later, he came to understand that it was football and not baseball he was listening to when news of the attack was announced. Nevertheless, the unreliability of memory remained an important theme in his career. Today, Ulric Neisser is remembered as the *German-born American cognitive psychologist who investigated the unreliability of flashbulb memories.*

Neisser completed his undergraduate and doctoral degrees at Harvard, working mainly with George Miller during the time when Miller was developing his ideas about cognition as information processing (Cutting, 2012). In 1960, Neisser published an account of a computer program called Pandemonium that could mimic human pattern recognition. After this, Neisser received a number of research grants and an appointment at the University of Pennsylvania. At the time, there was no book in the field that tied together the various strands of the new cognitive approach. This became Neisser's next goal, and he published *Cognitive Psychology* in 1967. The book was well received, and before his thirtieth birthday he'd become famous in his field. He was sought out as one of the new leaders of the cognitive movement, and he accepted an offer to come to Cornell as a full professor.

At Cornell, Neisser became friends with his colleague James Gibson, whose reputation was already well established in the field (Neisser, 2007). Gibson was uninterested in the sorts of experiments that Neisser described in *Cognitive Psychology*, as these involved artificial stimuli presented under artificial circumstances. Instead, Gibson insisted that experiments in cognitive psychology needed to be ecologically valid, a position that Neisser found intuitively appealing. Neisser's next project involved an attempt to integrate the information-processing approach with Gibson's approach in his 1976 book *Cognition and Reality*. In this book, Neisser proposed what he called the perceptual cycle, in which the sensory inputs are repeatedly matched with schemas stored in memory. In this work, he linked Gibson's interest in perception with issues in memory that had become an important focus of the cognitive psychologists. This book had considerably less impact on the field than his previous book.

Despite the lackluster reception of his second book, Neisser continued to extend Gibson's ecological approach to the question of memory (Neisser, 2007). At a conference, Neisser presented the paper "Memory: What Are the Important Questions?" in which he concluded that "if X is an interesting or socially important aspect of memory, then psychologists have hardly ever studied X" (p. 289). Neisser also took an interest in the testimony of John Dean, White House counsel to Richard Nixon during the Watergate incident. Since Nixon had recorded all conversations in the Oval Office, Neisser could compare Dean's testimony with the actual recordings. What Neisser found was that although Dean was correct in the overarching themes of his conversations with Nixon, his details were mostly wrong. This led Neisser to surmise that personal memories aren't accurate depictions of past events but rather reconstructions based on fragments of past recollections combined with current knowledge. He presented these ideas in his 1982 book *Memory Observed*. He also noted the spate of recovered memories about childhood sexual abuse that were racking the country at that time. We'll pick up this issue again in the next section on Elizabeth Loftus, who pursued this question in far greater detail.

NASA

Photo 11.7
***Challenger* explosion**

The next year, Neisser moved to Emory University in Atlanta, where he could attend major league baseball games on a regular basis while continuing his research on the unreliability of personal memories (Neisser, 2007). On January 28, 1986, the space shuttle *Challenger* blew up shortly after take-off. The event had been televised live, and the nation was stunned. The next morning while taking a shower—according to his admittedly unreliable memory—it occurred to him that the *Challenger* disaster provided the perfect opportunity to study a phenomenon that had become known as **flashbulb memory**. Several years before, Harvard psychologist Roger Brown (Chapter 13) had found that it's common for people to report *a vivid and detailed recollection of events after an emotionally charged experience*. Neisser quickly worked up a questionnaire and distributed it to his freshman psychology class, asking them to describe in as much detail as possible where they were and what they were doing when they learned about the disaster. Three years later, he tracked down 44 of these students—now seniors—and asked them the same questions again. Although a few people's later recollections matched their initial reports, the large majority were completely different, even though they felt very confident about their recollections. The so-called *Challenger* study became the paradigm for studying flashbulb memories.

When the San Francisco earthquake struck in 1989, Neisser once again took the opportunity to test the reliability of flashbulb memories (Neisser, 2007). This time he collaborated with colleagues at Berkeley and Santa Cruz to form two groups of participants, those in California who'd experienced the earthquake directly and those at Emory who'd only heard about it on the news. As it turned out, later recollections of the West Coast group were far more accurate than those of the East Coast group. Apparently, autobiographical memories are more likely to be accurate when those events are personally meaningful.

With his student Ira Hyman, Neisser explored an effect that came to be known as **inattentional blindness** (Neisser, 2007). This is *a phenomenon in which persons fail to see something directly in front of them because their attention is focused elsewhere*. In this study, participants viewed a video of players passing a basketball and were instructed to count the number of times the ball was passed. In the middle portion of the video, a woman carrying an umbrella strolled among the players. Afterward, few participants reported seeing the woman, but the rest were quite surprised when they viewed the video again and saw they'd missed something that was seemingly so obvious.

Neisser's legacy to cognitive psychology is his integration of the rigors of the information-processing approach of George Miller with the ecological validity of James Gibson (Belardinelli, 2012). He showed that carefully designed field experiments could be used to study socially relevant aspects of perception, attention, and memory. His first book defined the field of cognitive psychology when it was still in its infancy, and throughout his career he nudged his colleagues to work on topics that could have a meaningful impact on society. For these reasons, he's often credited as the father of cognitive psychology.

Photo 11.8
Elizabeth Loftus

Elizabeth Loftus

As an undergraduate, **Elizabeth Loftus** (born 1944) did a double major in math and psychology (Loftus, 2007). When she learned about Stanford's doctoral program in mathematical psychology, she thought it would be the perfect fit, but she was soon disillusioned. To get the math to work, her professors had to make simplifying assumptions about human behavior that Loftus found implausible. She was so bored in her seminars that she spent her time hemming her skirts or writing letters, and her classmates secretly voted her "least likely to succeed." Late in her doctoral program, she collaborated with the young faculty member Jonathan Freedman on a series of experiments investigating the structure of semantic memory, and her passion for psychology was rekindled. Today, Loftus is known as an *American psychologist who studies the unreliability of eyewitness testimony and personal memories.*

After graduation, Loftus continued to collaborate with Freedman and others, and with them she published a series of articles that have become seminal works on the topic (Zagorski, 2005). **Semantic memory** refers to our *knowledge of facts and concepts about the world in general*, as opposed to memories about the events of our lives. Loftus and colleagues explored the way that these facts are organized in semantic memory by giving participants prompts such as "Name a bird that is small" and measuring their reaction time. The researchers assumed that shorter reaction times reflected concepts that were more closely linked in semantic memory. These studies now are standard fare in cognitive psychology textbooks.

Although the studies on semantic memory had renewed her interest in psychology, Loftus soon longed to do research that had social relevance ("Elizabeth F. Loftus," 2003). From a young age, she'd been fascinated by true and fictionalized stories of crime and the courtroom. Seeking a way to tie this interest in legal issues to her work on memory, she pondered the reliability of eyewitness testimony, leading her to the work that she's most famous for today.

In the early 1970s, Loftus conducted a series of experiments examining the reliability of eyewitness accounts of traffic accidents (Loftus, 2007). In one study, participants viewed a short film of an automobile collision. Afterward, they were asked a series of questions, including "How fast were the cars going when they *hit* each other?" Other participants got a slightly altered question: "How fast were the cars going when they *smashed into* each other?" As expected, those who heard "smashed" estimated a higher speed than those who heard "hit." Furthermore, they were also more likely to say there was broken glass, when in fact there was none. This and similar experiments demonstrate what Loftus calls the **misinformation effect**, namely *the distortion of memory due to exposure to false or misleading information after the event.* Loftus and colleagues explored the misinformation effect in a wide range of circumstances. She also demonstrated that people can feel quite certain these false memories are true, even betting money on them.

Around this same time, Loftus assisted a public defender with a murder case that hinged on eyewitness testimony (Loftus, 2007). The female defendant was charged with murdering her boyfriend, but she claimed it was in self-defense. With Loftus's help, the woman was acquitted. Shortly after that, Loftus published an article in the popular magazine *Psychology Today*, in which she described the case as well as her research on eyewitness testimony. Soon she was inundated with requests from lawyers around the country who were hoping she could help them with their cases. Over the decades, her work in the lab and in the courtroom became intertwined, as cases suggested new experiments, and as evidence from her lab was brought into the courtroom. She's also served as an expert witness in a number of high-profile cases you might have heard of, including the Oklahoma City bombing and the Michael Jackson case.

In the 1980s, there was a rash of cases in which young adults accused family members of sexual assault during their childhood (Loftus, 2007). In each case, the plaintiff claimed that the traumatic memory had been repressed only to be recovered later during psychotherapy. In the early twentieth century, Sigmund Freud (Chapter 7) had popularized the idea that memories of traumatic events can be repressed; some psychotherapists still believed they could help their patients by getting them to recover the repressed memories of childhood trauma. As a result, however, innocent people went to prison and families were destroyed. In a survey of the literature, Loftus found no experimental evidence for repressed memories, and instead she suspected that memories recovered during therapy had in fact been unintentionally implanted in the patients by therapists and others.

To test this idea, Loftus developed *a laboratory procedure for implanting false memories* that became known as the **lost-in-the-mall technique** (Loftus, 1999). Participants read four accounts of person events from their childhood that had been provided by family members. They were asked whether they could recall each event, and if so, whether they could provide more information. Unknown to the participants, one of the four events was false. About a quarter of the participants stated that they remembered the false event, and many of these were able to provide additional details. Other researchers have used this technique to implant false memories from childhood such as knocking over a punchbowl at a wedding or nearly drowning and being saved by a lifeguard. A common criticism of this technique has been that the participants may be confusing these plausible false memories with similar actual events in their lives. In response, researchers have also succeeded in implanting impossible false memories, such as shaking hands with Bugs Bunny at Disneyland. (This can't be true because Bugs Bunny is a Warner Brothers character, not part of the Disney cast.)

The assertion that memories of traumatic childhood events recovered during psychotherapy are likely false has earned Loftus quite a few enemies among clinicians who practice memory-recovery therapy as well as among their clients (Loftus, 2008). In what became known as the "Jane Doe case," a young woman who had accused her mother of sexual assault as a child sued Loftus for invasion of privacy. Although Loftus had investigated the case and reported on it, she hadn't disclosed any identifying information. In fact, she was unaware of the alleged victim's identity until she was served notice of the lawsuit. After years of litigation that went all the way to the California Supreme Court, Loftus's insurance company paid out a nuisance settlement of $7,500, while the plaintiff was ordered to pay all legal fees, totaling nearly half a million dollars. In her 2008 article "Perils of Provocative Scholarship," Loftus contends that too many psychologists avoid socially important but potentially controversial topics for fear of frivolous lawsuits. Likewise, she maintained that universities are reluctant to support their faculty against such threats to scholarship, as happened in her case.

For over four decades, Elizabeth Loftus has championed those who have been falsely accused on the basis of unreliable eyewitness testimony or dubious recovered memories of the long past. According to Loftus (2007), the theme of her career has been "science for justice." Often attacked for her assertions that personal memories are unreliable, she nevertheless takes solace in the knowledge that the justice system is now paying attention to the science of memory, and it's beginning to change the way it evaluates personal recollections. Perhaps more than anyone else in her generation, Elizabeth Loftus has shown that psychological science can have real-world relevance and tackle important social issues.

Judgment and Decision Making

Herbert Simon's early work on bounded rationality led to his receipt of the Nobel Prize in Economics in 1978. Although his ideas had an important impact on cognitive psychology, most economists continued to assume that humans were perfectly rational decision makers. Subsequently, Simon and his colleague Allen Newell turned instead to the field of artificial intelligence. A new generation of young psychologists then picked up the idea of bounded rationality and fleshed out its complexities in a series of papers they published in the 1970s.

Daniel Kahneman and Amos Tversky

In the 1970s, the dynamic duo of decision-making research consisted of two young psychologists from Israel. The first of these was **Daniel Kahneman** (born 1934), known today

**Photo 11.9
Daniel Kahneman**

as the *Israeli psychologist who won the Nobel Prize for his work on the heuristics and biases approach to judgment and decision making.* His partner in this endeavor was **Amos Tversky** (1937–1996), remembered as the *Israeli psychologist who collaborated with Daniel Kahneman on the heuristics and biases approach.* As Kahneman (2002) acknowledged, the Nobel Prize was awarded for work that he and Tversky had completed together. But the Prize isn't awarded posthumously, and by the time the value of their work had been acknowledged, his long-time collaborator and dear friend had passed away.

Daniel Kahneman spent his childhood in France, the son of immigrants from Lithuania (Kahneman, 2002). As Jews, the family kept on the move to avoid the invading Nazi forces. His father died of untreated diabetes just weeks before D-Day, but after the war young Kahneman and the rest of his family immigrated to the British mandate of Palestine, which was soon to become the state of Israel. After completing a Ph.D. in psychology at Berkeley, he returned to Israel as a professor of psychology at Hebrew University. In the early years of his career, Kahneman focused on his teaching and did little research. But then he met Amos Tversky, a young researcher in the field of decision making. They quickly became best friends, and together they embarked on a collaborative program of research that lasted more than a decade.

Amos Tversky was born in the territory that would become the state of Israel after World War II (Kahneman & Shafir, 1998). After receiving his Ph.D. in psychology at the University of Michigan, he accepted a position at Hebrew University, where he got to know Kahneman. Unlike his colleague, Tversky was already making a name for himself as a researcher in the field of decision making. However, as the two became friends, they found that ideas flowed easily between them, and they were soon spending several hours a day working together. Tversky understood the prevailing theories in decision making, and Kahneman had already developed intuitions about the often irrational nature of human thinking during his years serving as a military psychologist in the Israeli Defense Forces.

Kahneman and Tversky jointly published a number of articles during the 1970s, but the first to catch widespread attention was their 1974 piece "Judgment Under Uncertainty: Heuristics and Biases" (Tversky & Kahneman, 1974). In the field of decision making, the term **judgment** refers to *the estimation of the likelihood of an event.* For example, you need to decide whether to read the next chapter in psychology tonight, and your decision depends on how likely you think it is that there will be a pop quiz in psychology tomorrow. Although there are mathematical models for estimating the probability of events, Tversky and Kahneman argued that people rely instead on **heuristics**, that is, *intuitive decision-making processes that are fast and easy but prone to error.* Although heuristics usually bring us to good-enough decisions, they can also lead us to predictable errors in thinking, which are called biases.

Tversky and Kahneman (1974) described three examples of heuristics that people rely on in making judgments. The first example is the **representativeness heuristic**, which is *a way of judging the probability of an event by how typical it appears.* For instance, in a series of five coin flips where heads (H) and tails (T) are noted, people judge the sequence HTHHT as very likely to occur. However, they judge the sequence HHHHH as very unlikely, even though both sequences have the same probability, namely 1 in 32. If the coin is fair, we know any sequence it produces will be random, but five heads in a row just doesn't look random.

The second example is the **availability heuristic**, which is *a way of judging the probability of an event by how easily examples come to mind.* For instance, Tversky and Kahneman (1974) asked participants to judge whether more English words have the letter R in the first position (like *road*) or in the third position (like *carton*). If you guessed first position, you're like most of the participants in this study. Since it's easier to think of words beginning with R, you judge them to be more frequent. You're wrong, by the way—more English words have R in the third position.

Finally, the third example is a heuristic called **anchoring and adjustment** (Tversky & Kahneman, 1974). This is *a way of estimating a value by moving away from a potentially arbitrary starting point.* In one experiment, the experimenters asked participants to spin a wheel numbered from 1 to 100. After the wheel had stopped on a particular number, they were asked to estimate how many countries there are in Africa. When the wheel landed on a small number, their estimates were smaller than when it landed on a large number. This suggests that they'd used the arbitrary number on the wheel as an anchor or starting point from which they adjusted their final answer. Anchoring and adjustment plays an important role in negotiations, as the person who makes the initial offer sets the anchor from which all other bids are adjusted.

Prospect Theory

In their next major collaboration, "Prospect Theory: An Analysis of Decision Under Risk," Kahneman and Tversky (1979) investigated decision making in situations involving potential losses or gains. Consider the following problem:

- Would you prefer (A) a 50% chance of winning $1,000 with a 50% chance of winning nothing, or (B) a 100% chance of winning $450?

If you're like most people, you'll go with the sure bet rather than a chance at much more, but with the risk of gaining nothing. However, according to *the standard mathematical model of decision making under risk*, known as **expected utility theory**, the risk is worth taking. The point of the article is that economics makes predictions about human decision making that don't line up with the way people actually behave. And because Kahneman and Tversky published this article in a major economics journal, rather than one in psychology, economists paid attention. Eventually, so did the Nobel Prize committee.

Prospect theory is a *model of human decision making under risk that is based on evidence from experimental psychology*, and it challenges expected utility theory in a number of ways. Traditional theory proposes that people should weigh potential gains and losses equally. However, Kahneman and Tversky (1979) found that people are impacted more by losses than by gains. For example, if you discover an extra $20 bill in your wallet, you'll be happy. But you'll be much more disappointed if you find out that a $20 bill is missing. And although we're reluctant to take risks to gain something, we're quite willing to take risks when losses are involved. Consider this problem, which is the reverse of the one above:

- Would you prefer (A) a 50% chance of losing $1,000 with a 50% chance of losing nothing, or (B) a 100% chance of losing $450?

Again, if you're like most people, you'll take the 50% chance of losing a lot over the certainty of losing a smaller amount. In sum, whereas expected utility theory proposes that we should weigh potential gains and losses equally, prospect theory shows that we prefer to avoid risks in the case of potential gains but are quite open to risk in the case of potential losses.

Another important element of prospect theory is what Kahneman and Tversky (1979) called the **framing effect**, which is *the observation that the way a problem is presented influences the decision that is made*. Consider this scenario:

- A deadly disease has infected 1,000 people. If doctors use a new experimental drug, 200 will live. Should they use the drug?

Most people respond that the doctors should use the drug. But consider the same scenario framed in the opposite manner:

- A deadly disease has infected 1,000 people. If doctors use a new experimental drug, 800 will die. Should they use the drug?

Now, most people say the doctors shouldn't use the drug. Although the outcomes are the same in both cases (that is, 200 people live and 800 people die), the way the question is framed influences the decisions people make. Framing effects are often used in marketing. For example, an ice cream that's "3% fat reduced" may sound healthy, but it's probably not.

At the end of the 1970s, the two collaborators were each offered positions at North American universities, Tversky at Stanford and Kahneman at Vancouver (van Raaij, 1998). No longer able to spend hours together bouncing ideas off each other, they found it much more difficult to collaborate, and they pursued different research interests. Tversky did important research on judgments of preferences. For instance, Sam prefers mint chocolate chip ice cream to rocky road, and she prefers rocky road to butter pecan. However, she prefers butter pecan to mint chocolate chip. Written in quasi-mathematical form, this would be:

$$Mint\ chocolate\ chip > rocky\ road > butter\ pecan$$

$$Butter\ pecan > mint\ chocolate\ chip$$

As illogical as this series of preferences sounds, it's actually quite common.

Even during the time he was collaborating with Tversky, Kahneman was also turning his attention to attention, so to speak (Kahneman, 2002). He'd met Anne Treisman at a conference in 1967, and she inspired him to do the research that led to his 1973 book *Attention and Effort*. Kahneman and Treisman kept in touch with each other, and twelve years after their first meeting, they were married. Conceptualizing attention as an effortful process also led Kahneman to re-evaluate the heuristics and biases approach and prospect theory that he and Tversky had developed. Many people interpreted their theories as implying that humans are inherently bad at decision making, but Kahneman insisted this wasn't the case. First, heuristics usually give us good-enough solutions and only sometimes fail. Furthermore, if we put in the effort to pay attention, we can avoid the traps of these heuristics and think logically instead. He summed up his dual-process approach to decision making in his bestselling book *Thinking, Fast and Slow* (Kahneman, 2011).

Although Herbert Simon was awarded the Nobel Prize in Economics in 1978, his idea of bounded rationality had little effect on theory in that field. Amos Tversky and Daniel Kahneman further developed Simon's idea that human reasoning is limited with their heuristics and biases approach and their prospect theory. By the late twentieth century, however, economists were interested in developing psychologically driven models of human decision making. In recognition of this contribution to economics, Daniel Kahneman was awarded the Nobel Prize in 2002. But as Kahneman (2002) acknowledges, at least half the credit belonged to his friend and collaborator Amos Tversky, who didn't live to see the value of his contributions recognized.

Looking Ahead

By the 1970s, the cognitive approach had come to dominate psychology. The computer metaphor provided an especially fruitful model for studying human cognition, and research programs tended to run human-subjects research in parallel with computer modeling. Early computer simulations of human cognition were typically based on symbol manipulation, which reflected the way that traditional computers were built rather than portraying a biologically plausible model of human thought processes. The development of parallel processing in computers during the 1980s led to new models called neural networks that were believed to more accurately depict how the brain handles cognition. Notable among the modelers using neural networks was **David Rumelhart** (1942–2011), an *American psychologist who developed the parallel distributed processing model of perception* (Violino, 2011). Much of the artificial intelligence we are accustomed to today, such as voice and face recognition, is based on the neural network approach developed by Rumelhart and others.

The cognitive approach also influenced other disciplines in psychology. Although social and developmental psychology had remained more cognitive in nature during the behaviorist era, the Cognitive Revolution gave researchers in this field license to speculate more extensively regarding the underlying thought processes that drove the behaviors they observed. Even clinical psychology was influenced by the Cognitive Revolution, and practitioners added cognitive-modification techniques to the set of behavioral methods already in their toolkit. Thus we see the rise of cognitive-behavioral therapies that take a double-pronged approach to treating psychological disorders.

The cognitive approach predominated in psychology for the rest of the twentieth century, but the rise of new brain-imaging technologies has challenged this dominance in the twenty-first century. While cognitive psychologists paid lip service to the notion that brain activity underlies mental processes, their focus of study was specifically the mind, not the brain. Even the supposedly biologically plausible neural network models were only vaguely related to the way the brain actually functioned. In contrast, brain-imaging techniques such as positron emission tomography (PET) and magnetic resonance imaging (MRI) enabled a new group of psychologists calling themselves neuroscientists to observe the brain in action, allowing them to correlate cognitive processes with brain activity for the first time. We'll read more about this endeavor in the final chapter of this book.

CHAPTER SUMMARY

Modern cognitive psychology arose after World War II and was tied to the new communication and computational technologies that emerged during that time. In England, Frederic Bartlett demonstrated the reconstructive nature of memory, and Donald Broadbent proposed an information-processing model of perception and attention. In the United States, Jerome Bruner and Leo Postman led a short-lived movement known as the New Look, which showed that perception was impacted by emotional factors. A few years later, Bruner joined his colleague George Miller in creating the Center for Cognitive Studies at Harvard, which is often seen as the start of the Cognitive Revolution. Among the early contributions to the field were Noam Chomsky's work on transformational-generative grammar and the work by Herbert Simon and Allen Newell on the computer modeling of human problem solving. James Gibson was one of the most important critics of the information-processing approach, contending instead that cognitive psychologists should conduct studies—preferably in the field—that had ecological validity. A new generation of psychologists, including Ulric Neisser and Elizabeth Loftus, heeded Gibson's call for an ecological and social approach to cognition. Finally, the judgment and decision-making paradigm of Daniel Kahneman and Amos Tversky fleshed out the limits of human reasoning, showing that although human thought processes aren't always rational, they are nevertheless predictable.

DISCUSSION QUESTIONS

1. Although experimental psychology came late to England, British psychologists were among the first to advocate for the information-processing view of cognition. Speculate on the historical and social factors that led to these ideas arising first in Great Britain rather than North America.

2. Compare and contrast the main ideas of the New Look movement with those of neo-behaviorist Edward Tolman. Why were these two approaches perceived as a threat to established psychology in North America?

3. The mantra of the Cognitive Revolution was the computer metaphor. Consider the ways in which the human mind is like a computer, and also enumerate the ways in which the two are different.

4. Both Donald Broadbent and George Miller saw the human mind as a limited-capacity information processor, but they saw the bottleneck as occurring in different places along the information flow. Compare Broadbent's and Miller's models, considering how the two might be reconciled.

5. Although Noam Chomsky is a linguist, he's considered one of the founders of the Cognitive Revolution because of his review of Skinner's *Verbal Behavior*. Contrast Chomsky's and Skinner's views on language acquisition, evaluating the merits and weaknesses of each.

6. Simon and Newell's think-aloud protocol was criticized as a form of introspection, which had been discredited by the behaviorists as a

legitimate form of data in experimental psychology. Considering both the strengths and weaknesses of self-reports, evaluate the validity of introspective methods.

7. Herbert Simon and Allen Newell's attempts to model human problem solving on computers met with only limited success. Propose some ways in which humans and computers differ in their approach to problem solving, considering the strengths and weaknesses of each.

8. Contrast James Gibson's theory of direct perception with the major philosophical and psychological theories of visual perception that had been proposed to that point.

9. Trace the development of Ulric Neisser's view of cognitive psychology as he was influenced by his two most important mentors, George Miller and James Gibson.

10. Elizabeth Loftus has repeatedly shown that personal memories are often inaccurate and that recovered memories are almost certainly false. Consider the social and psychological reasons why her research is so controversial.

11. Many people have interpreted the work of Daniel Kahneman and Amos Tversky as suggesting that human decision making is inherently faulty. Explain why this is not the case.

12. Contrast the strengths and weaknesses of the information-processing approach to cognition with the ecological and social approaches. The concepts of internal and external validity may be helpful in this discussion.

ON THE WEB

On the internet, you can find video interviews with many of the people we met in this chapter, including **Anne Treisman** and **Herbert Simon**. In online interviews, the elderly **Jerome Bruner** discusses his later theories on education and cognitive development, which he turned to after becoming disillusioned with the information-processing approach. YouTube has demonstrations of the **red spade experiment** by Bruner and Postman, which was one of the key studies of the New Look movement. YouTube also hosts numerous interviews with **Noam Chomsky**, some on his theory of language acquisition, but mostly in his later role as a political scientist. Search **inattentional blindness** for many demonstrations of this effect that was first explored by Ulric Neisser and his students. There are many videos online of **Elizabeth Loftus** discussing her research and its application to current events, including a couple of TED Talks. Likewise, **Daniel Kahneman** has a significant presence on the internet in addition to his TED Talk.

Social Psychology

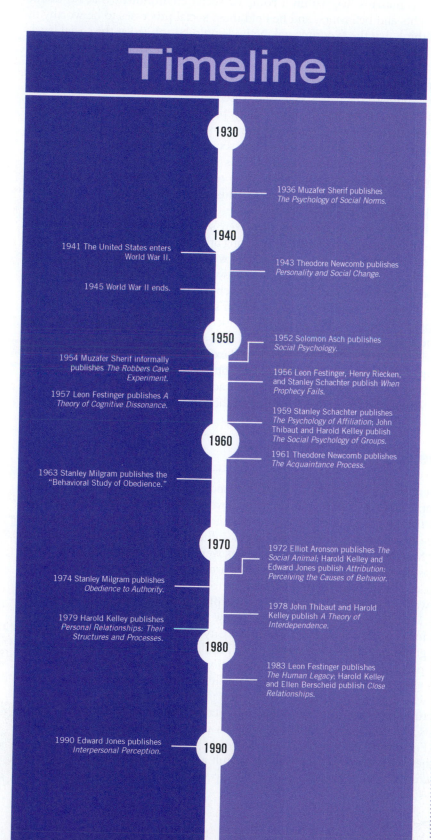

Timeline

- 1930
- 1936 Muzafer Sherif publishes *The Psychology of Social Norms.*
- 1940
- 1941 The United States enters World War II.
- 1943 Theodore Newcomb publishes *Personality and Social Change.*
- 1945 World War II ends.
- 1950
- 1952 Solomon Asch publishes *Social Psychology.*
- 1954 Muzafer Sherif informally publishes *The Robbers Cave Experiment.*
- 1956 Leon Festinger, Henry Riecken, and Stanley Schachter publish *When Prophecy Fails.*
- 1957 Leon Festinger publishes *A Theory of Cognitive Dissonance.*
- 1959 Stanley Schachter publishes *The Psychology of Affiliation;* John Thibaut and Harold Kelley publish *The Social Psychology of Groups.*
- 1960
- 1961 Theodore Newcomb publishes *The Acquaintance Process.*
- 1963 Stanley Milgram publishes the "Behavioral Study of Obedience."
- 1970
- 1972 Elliot Aronson publishes *The Social Animal;* Harold Kelley and Edward Jones publish *Attribution: Perceiving the Causes of Behavior.*
- 1974 Stanley Milgram publishes *Obedience to Authority.*
- 1978 John Thibaut and Harold Kelley publish *A Theory of Interdependence.*
- 1979 Harold Kelley publishes *Personal Relationships: Their Structures and Processes.*
- 1980
- 1983 Leon Festinger publishes *The Human Legacy;* Harold Kelley and Ellen Berscheid publish *Close Relationships.*
- 1990 Edward Jones publishes *Interpersonal Perception.*
- 1990

Learning Objectives

After reading this chapter, you should be able to:

- Appraise the value of the social influence research conducted by Muzafer Sherif, Solomon Asch, and Stanley Milgram.

- Propose common themes running through the work of social cognition psychologists Leon Festinger, Stanley Schachter, and Elliot Aronson.

- Evaluate the work of the social perception psychologists in understanding the attribution process and the dynamics of interpersonal relationships.

- Critique the work of the social psychologists at the University of Michigan, particularly Theodore Newcomb and Robert Zajonc.

Looking Back

Since its inception in the last decades of the nineteenth century, psychology has been viewed as scientific study of individual thought processes and behavior. Wilhelm Wundt maintained that the experimental method could only be applied to individual participants, and even then only when testing lower-level psychological processes such as perception and attention. Wundt recognized that humans live within a complex social environment that no doubt influences their thoughts and behaviors, and he held these social processes to be worthy of study. He just didn't think that the experimental method could be applied at the social level. In his multivolume *Völkerpsychologie*, he took up the study of human social interactions and culture, but only at the descriptive level. For Wundt, science lacked the power to explain social or cultural forces, but he could observe and describe them in great detail, much as the naturalists of his time did with the new species they discovered.

Until the middle of the twentieth century, many psychologists agreed with Wundt's opinion that social interactions were beyond the purview of experimental psychology. For the structuralists, functionalists, and behaviorists, the social context was seen as little more than the stimulus to which the individual reacted. This was the viewpoint that even those few social psychologists of the early twentieth century took, in that they studied how the individual behaved within a specific social context. Thus, the focus of early work in social psychology was still on the individual.

During the first half of the twentieth century, there were some psychologists who viewed the social environment as more than a mere stimulus impinging upon the individual. Rather, they saw it as a dynamic system in which thoughts and behaviors were shaped through reciprocal influences. A good example of this approach was the Soviet psychologist Lev Vygotsky (Chapter 9), whose cultural-historical approach greatly influenced psychology in Russia. However, his work was largely unknown in the West until the 1960s, well after social psychology had found its feet.

Modern social psychology traces its origins to the work of Kurt Lewin (Chapter 6) on group dynamics during the war years of the mid-twentieth century. Lewin was the master at creating complex social situations that could be manipulated experimentally to observe how group behavior emerges out of the interactions of individuals. Thus, it comes as no surprise that many of the social psychologists we'll meet in this chapter can trace their intellectual lineage to Lewin, and most of them acknowledge the influence he had on their thinking and methodology.

Social Influence

We like to think that we act of our own accord, but social psychologists have long maintained that the people around us have great influence over our behavior. The field of **social influence** looks at *the ways in which the social situation shapes a person's behavior*. In this section, we meet three psychologists who studied social influence—Muzafer Sherif, Solomon Asch, and Stanley Milgram. These three psychologists were key players in the early development of social psychology, but each of these owes a debt to the same mentor who first inspired them to take an experimental approach to the topic of social influence.

This mentor was none other than **Gardner Murphy** (1895–1979), who earned his Ph.D. with James McKeen Cattell (Chapter 3; Hartley, 1980). He then remained on the Columbia faculty for two decades before moving to City College of New York. Although he left behind no grand theories or key experimental findings, he made his mark on mid-twentieth-century psychology as a mentor and inspirational role model. In fact, a survey of American psychologists in 1957 ranked Gardner Murphy second (behind Sigmund Freud) as the one person who'd most influenced their decision to enter the field. He was renowned as an engaging lecturer and as a devoted teacher and mentor, but he also inspired a generation of cognitive, social, and personality psychologists with two dozen books and over a hundred articles (Figure 12.1).

Through all these endeavors, Gardner Murphy built a reputation as the *American social psychologist who advocated for a biosocial approach to personality* (Hartley, 1980). During a time when personality and social psychologists staked out extreme positions on the nature-nurture debate, Murphy took an interactionist position on both personality formation and social behavior. It would take half a century for psychologists in these two fields to reconcile their differences, very much along the lines that Murphy had envisioned. It can be argued that Murphy was just as important to the development of social psychology as Kurt Lewin, and yet he's barely remembered today. This is likely due to personality differences. Both were inspirational leaders, but whereas Lewin's students glowed in the reflected brilliance of their mentor, Murphy provided the warmth and passion his students needed to shine on their own.

Photo 12.1
Gardner Murphy

Muzafer Sherif

Born to a wealthy family in Turkey, **Muzafer Sherif** (1906–1988; pronounced *moo-ZAH-fer sha-REEF*) was sent abroad on a government scholarship as part of his country's modernization efforts (Russell, 2016). He earned a master's degree at Harvard working with Gordon Allport, traveled to Berlin to study with Wolfgang Köhler, and then earned his doctorate with Gardner Murphy at Columbia. His published dissertation made him famous, and he was highly productive throughout his career despite suffering political persecution in both Turkey and the United States. Today, Muzafer Sherif is known as the *Turkish psychologist who studied the spread of social norms and the dynamics of intergroup conflict.*

Sherif's dissertation, published as *The Psychology of Social Norms* in 1936, examined the ways that people's perceptual judgments are influenced through social interactions (Harvey, 1989). It made use of *a perceptual phenomenon in which a stationary point of light on a dark background appears to move*, known as the **autokinetic effect**. Participants view the point of light in a darkened room and shout out whenever it appears to move. When tested individually, estimates of distance and direction vary widely from person to person and within individuals from one time to the next. Likewise, when people are tested in groups, initial reports greatly differ from each other. However, over time all participants begin reporting apparent movement in the same direction and with the same magnitude, even though there was no discussion among them other than hearing what the others had reported. This demonstration of social influence on perceived motion challenged accepted theories, which held perception to be a reasonably accurate representation of the physical world. It was also one of the findings that led Jerome Bruner and his colleagues to initiate the New Look movement after World War II.

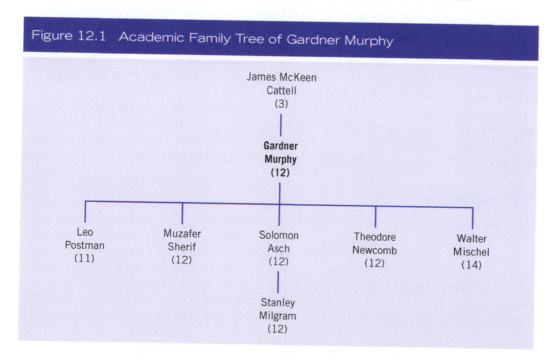

Figure 12.1 Academic Family Tree of Gardner Murphy

James McKeen Cattell (3)
Gardner Murphy (12)
Leo Postman (11)
Muzafer Sherif (12)
Solomon Asch (12)
Theodore Newcomb (12)
Walter Mischel (14)
Stanley Milgram (12)

After earning his Ph.D., Sherif returned to Turkey, where he set up a small laboratory at Ankara University (Russell, 2016). There, he and his students translated a number of key psychology texts into Turkish. They also administered a Turkish version of the Stanford-Binet that they'd created to adolescents in urban and rural areas to test the effects of exposure to modern technologies on intelligence.

During World War II, Turkey remained neutral, but the government was sympathetic toward the Nazi regime in Germany (Harvey, 1989). Having seen the Nazis firsthand while studying in Berlin, Sherif wrote a book criticizing Nazi racial doctrines as scientifically unfounded and socially dangerous. He also got involved in an underground Communist movement, which resulted in his arrest in 1944, when he was placed in solitary confinement for four months. Gordon Allport, his mentor at Harvard, implored the U.S. State Department to intercede on his behalf, and in 1945 Sherif was brought to the United States as a visiting scholar. At the same time, his Turkish citizenship was revoked, and he never returned to his homeland again.

In 1949, Sherif accepted a permanent position at the University of Oklahoma, where he conducted the second research project that he's well known for today (Harvey, 1989). In the Robbers Cave experiment, Sherif studied the processes that lead to conflict and cooperation among groups of boys attending a summer camp. Conducted over a series of summers, the procedure involved arousing animosity between two groups through a series of highly competitive activities. Sherif and his colleagues observed increasing acts of conflict—such as bullying and vandalism—between the two groups over the course of the program. To de-escalate the violence, Sherif created a situation in which the two groups had to cooperate, such as by telling them the food truck had broken down and needed to be pushed into the camp. In 1954, Sherif printed the technical report *Intergroup Conflict and Cooperation: The Robbers Cave Experiment*, which circulated widely among social psychologists, but it wasn't formally published until 1988.

During the years of the Robbers Cave study, Sherif's personal life was also filled with conflict (Russell, 2016). Although he'd been granted political asylum in the United States, he knew he couldn't apply for U.S. citizenship because of his previous activities with the Communists in Turkey. During the time that Senator Joseph McCarthy was accusing people in government, academia, and entertainment of being Communist sympathizers, Sherif was arrested and deportation proceedings were initiated. Again, his colleagues intervened on his behalf and he was released.

For the rest of his career, Sherif was highly productive, often collaborating with his wife Carolyn Wood, who was a prominent psychologist as well (Harvey, 1989). However, Sherif also struggled with bipolar disorder. Although he received many honors and awards during his career, he sometimes fell into paranoid states in which he claimed that his work hadn't received the recognition it deserved. His depression deepened when his wife died in 1982, and he attempted suicide on at least one occasion. He'd just recovered from that depressive episode when he was struck by a fatal heart attack.

Despite his frequent self-doubt, Sherif was an important shaper of modern social psychology. Although he made important contributions to many topics, he's best known for his work on the diffusion of social norms and the Robbers Cave experiment. These two studies are standard fare in textbooks, perhaps the greatest testament of Muzafer Sherif's impact on psychology.

Solomon Asch

Using the autokinetic effect, Muzafer Sherif had shown that people's perceptions can be influenced by social norms. In highly ambiguous situations, many eyes can see more than just a single pair, so it makes sense to go along with the crowd. But will people still conform even when the situation is unambiguous? Suppose you're shown two lines marked A and B. It's obvious that A is longer than B, but six other people say line B is longer. When it's your turn to respond, will you go with the group or stand your ground? **Solomon Asch** (1907–1996) believed that most people would remain independent and tell what they believe to be the truth regardless of what the rest of the group says. Today, we remember Asch as the *Polish-American social psychologist who studied conformity in a series of famous experiments*.

Asch was born in Poland but immigrated to the United States with his parents as a teenager (Gleitman, Rozin, & Sabini, 1997). He received his Ph.D. from Columbia University in 1932 working with Gardner Murphy. However, another important mentor during this time was the Gestalt psychologist Max Wertheimer, who was teaching at the New School for Social Research, where Asch worked part-time. There, he was greatly influenced by Wertheimer's insistence on studying real-life phenomena, and he came to think of himself as a Gestalt psychologist. This self-concept was further developed during nearly two decades at Swarthmore College, where he was a close colleague of the Gestalt psychologist Wolfgang Köhler.

Like his Gestalt mentors, Asch was mainly interested in questions of perception and memory, but he also pondered how social situations influence these processes (Gleitman et al., 1997). In one early study, he found that people interpret a quotation as positive or negative depending on who it's attributed to. For instance, participants read items such as: "I hold it that a little rebellion, now and then, is a good thing, and as necessary in the political world as storms are in the physical." Those who were told it was written by Thomas Jefferson endorsed it, whereas those who thought it was from Vladimir Lenin rejected it. Even their paraphrases of the quote differed depending on who they thought the author was. In another study, Asch looked at impression formation by presenting participants with descriptions of hypothetical people. For example, Person A was described as "intelligent and warm," while Person B was said to be "intelligent and cold." Asch found that people interpreted intelligence differently in the two cases, in line with the Gestalt motto that the whole is different from the sum of its parts.

Asch is best known for his series of conformity experiments, which had a major impact on thinking in social psychology (Levine, 1999). In the original experiment, participants were told they'd be taking part in a visual perception experiment along with several other people. These others were in fact not participants, but rather each was a **confederate**, that is, *a collaborator with the experimenter whose job it is to create a specific social situation in which to observe the participant's behavior*. On a given trial, the group saw a standard line X and three comparison lines A, B, and C, and their task was to determine which of these three was the same length as the standard. Each member of the group responded in turn, with the actual participant always going last. When all the others gave the wrong answer, Asch observed whether the participant gave the right answer or went with the group.

At the time, most psychologists were impressed with Sherif's findings, and they believed conformity was a general social process (Levine, 1999). But because the situation was unambiguous, Asch believed few participants would conform. In fact, he was surprised by the degree of conformity he observed. He found that people went along with the group about a third of the time. While this was more than he'd expected, it was still far less than what Sherif had found. Overall, Asch believed his hypothesis that people only conform in ambiguous situations was largely supported. After all, there was no conformity on two-thirds of the trials, and a quarter of the participants never went along with the group. In debriefings, most of the participants who conformed said they'd done so because they began to doubt that they understood the task correctly. In other words, they conformed because the situation had become ambiguous to them.

To explore the determinants of conformity, Asch conducted a long series of variations on this central theme (Levine, 1999). He found that the size of the group matters, at least up to about half a dozen people. That is, participants were much less likely to go along with just one or two people who consistently gave wrong answers, but they were more likely to go with a group of six or seven. Perhaps the most important factor was having one other person who broke from the group. In fact, even when that person gave incorrect answers, as long as they were different from those of the rest of the group, participants almost always gave the correct response.

Asch presented a full account of his conformity experiments in his 1952 textbook *Social Psychology* (Levine, 1999). He also laid out his general theory of social interaction in this work.

Photo 12.2
Solomon Asch

In Asch's view, independence and conformity aren't opposites, but rather they're two separate forces that work together to shape social processes. In other words, we don't just sheepishly follow the group, nor do we insistently maintain our position regardless of what others think. Instead, we each share our own perspective with the group, but we're also influenced by the views of other people, and working together we construct a social reality we can all agree on.

Solomon Asch was one of the foundational figures of modern social psychology. His influence on the field also continued through the work of his most noted student, Stanley Milgram, whose infamous experiments on obedience to authority were directly derived from Asch's conformity studies. This is the story we turn to next.

Stanley Milgram

Harvard Department of Psychology

**Photo 12.3
Stanley Milgram**

As an undergraduate, **Stanley Milgram** (1933–1984) studied political science, but he was discontented with the philosophical approach to the field. When he learned about Harvard's Department of Social Relations, he saw that he could explore questions about human interactions in a scientific manner (Martin, 2016). At Harvard, Gordon Allport (Chapter 14) took Milgram under his wing, and he also interacted a great deal with Jerome Bruner. But his real mentor was Solomon Asch, who was then a visiting professor at Harvard (Figure 12.2). After working with Asch on his conformity experiments, Stanley Milgram quickly developed a reputation as the *American social psychologist who conducted controversial experiments on obedience to authority.*

As Jews, both Asch and Milgram wondered how such a tragic event as the Holocaust could have happened (Brannigan, 2013). During the Nuremberg trials, the standard defense of Nazi officials was that they were just following orders, and some scholars speculated that the Germans must be more susceptible to authoritarianism than other people. For his dissertation, Milgram traveled to Europe and conducted the conformity study in several countries, including Germany, but he found no notable differences compared with Americans. Perhaps, he thought, obedience to authority is part of the universal human condition, and he began devising a laboratory procedure to test this hypothesis.

When he arrived at Yale in 1960 as an assistant professor, Milgram got straight to work on setting up the experiment that would make him famous (Sabini, 1986). He did this by creating a situation in his laboratory in which an authority figure commanded the participant to administer a potentially lethal dose of electricity to another human being. When he polled his colleagues, they doubted anyone would obey such an order. But if Nazis could

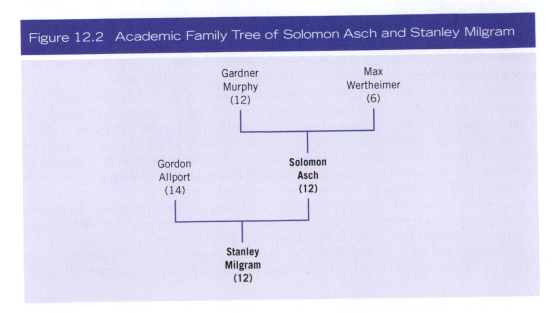

Figure 12.2 Academic Family Tree of Solomon Asch and Stanley Milgram

kill millions of people just because they were following orders, perhaps he could induce average Americans to shock people they'd just met.

In 1963, Milgram published the article "Behavioral Study of Obedience," in which he reports on the studies which made him famous. Milgram (1963) recruited participants from the surrounding community under the guise of a memory experiment. When the participant arrived at the lab, he met two other men—the experimenter dressed in a lab coat and a middle-aged man that was supposedly another participant. In fact, both were amateur actors serving as confederates. The experimenter asked the two men to draw straws to decide who would take the role of the learner and the teacher. Of course, the drawing was rigged so that the real participant was always assigned the role of teacher. The two were then led to an adjoining room, where the learner was strapped into an "electric chair." The teacher was also given a test shock to "prove" that the equipment was real, and he was also told the shocks he would administer to the learner would be painful but cause no tissue damage. The teacher was then led to another room, where he was seated in front of a console marked "Shock Generator" with a bank of thirty switches ranging from 15 to 450 volts, and with labels ranging from "Slight Shock" to "Danger: Severe Shock."

For the memory test, the teacher read lists of words via an intercom (Milgram, 1963). If the learner responded incorrectly, the experimenter told the teacher to administer a shock, with the voltage increasing after each error. At the 300-volt level, the learner pounded on the wall and then no longer responded. The experimenter told the teacher to read the next list and count a no-response as an error. If the teacher hesitated, the experimenter urged him to continue with the following prods, always in the same order:

- Please go on.

- The experiment requires that you continue.

- It is absolutely essential that you continue.

- You have no other choice, you *must* continue.

The dependent variable in this experiment was the shock level at which the teacher refused to comply with the experimenter (Milgram, 1963). All teachers continued with the experiment at least to the 300-volt level, when the learner pounded the wall. Five of forty participants quit at this point, and nine others quit after administering a few more shocks. The rest—two-thirds of the participants—continued to the end of the experiment. Contrary to the expectations of Milgram's colleagues, all participants administered potentially lethal doses of electricity and most continued with the shocks long after the learner had stopped responding, simply because the experimenter had told them to. This doesn't mean they did so gladly, and in fact they showed considerable agitation and distress. When the experiment had ended, the learner entered the room and greeted the teacher, assuring him that he was all right and that no shocks had actually been received.

Over the course of a year, Milgram conducted nearly two dozen versions of this basic experiment, involving a total of 780 participants (Martin, 2016). The general pattern of results extended to most replications, although some situations influenced the degree of obedience. For instance, when there were two experimenters, one telling the teacher to go on and the other telling him to quit, not one participant finished the experiment. Some of these results were published during the 1960s, but it wasn't until 1974 that Milgram presented the full array of experiments in his book, *Obedience to Authority*. In this work, he theorized that participants had undergone what he called an **agentic shift**, which is *a process in which individuals transfer responsibility for their own actions to an authority figure*. In other words, they were just following orders. Not all psychologists agree with Milgram's concept of agentic shift, but nevertheless his experiments are clearly important as a demonstration of the human predilection for obeying authority figures.

The obedience studies left an important mark on social psychology for several reasons (Brannigan, 2013). First, they called for a review of the ethical treatment of human subjects. Although the participants in Milgram's experiments were reassured they'd done no harm,

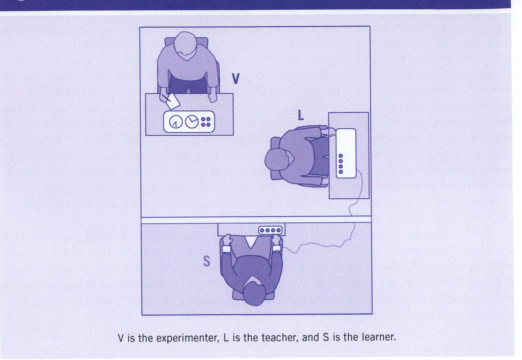

Figure 12.3 Setup for Milgram's Obedience Experiment

V is the experimenter, L is the teacher, and S is the learner.

Source: Wikimedia Commons.

follow-up studies found that many of them had suffered from some degree of psychological distress afterward. Second, the experiments helped solidify the attitude in social psychology that the situation is the main determinant of behavior, with personality playing little or no role. After all, none of the participants had quit before potentially harming the learner. And third, Milgram demonstrated that carefully scripted scenarios in the laboratory can be used to test interesting hypotheses about social behavior in humans.

Afterward, Milgram conducted a number of creative experiments that still have some currency in popular culture (Sabini, 1986). For instance, he tested the idea that all humans are connected to each other within six degrees of separation. Likewise, he popularized the concept of familiar stranger, that is, the person you regularly see during your daily routine even though you've never interacted with them. Although his later experiments were highly original and addressed everyday issues in social psychology, they've all remained in the shadow of his study on obedience to authority. Stanley Milgram was still an active and creative experimenter when he suddenly died of a heart attack at the young age of 51, but he left behind a legacy that has shaped social psychology to the present day.

Social Cognition

In the second half of the twentieth century, American psychologists returned to the study of mental processes. But we live within complex social networks, and surely our transactions with others influence the way we think. As we learned in Chapter 6, social cognition refers to the typical thought patterns that people engage in as they interact with others. Social cognition, then, is what drives our social behaviors.

Leon Festinger

As an undergraduate at City College of New York, **Leon Festinger** (1919–1989) was enthralled with the work of Kurt Lewin (Aronson, 1991). So the city boy traveled to the

Midwest to study with the master at the University of Iowa. After earning his Ph.D., Festinger served as a military psychologist during World War II, and then he joined Lewin as a faculty member in the Research Center for Group Dynamics, which had just been established at MIT. When Lewin suddenly died two years later, Festinger assumed leadership of the center. Thus began the illustrious career of Leon Festinger, known today as the *American social psychologist who developed social comparison theory and cognitive dissonance theory*.

When Lewin died, MIT was unwilling to maintain the Research Center for Group Dynamics without a prominent researcher as its director, so Festinger negotiated with the University of Michigan to take on the program (Schachter, 1994). Festinger brought with him a massive amount of data that Lewin and his students had collected at MIT. As part of a larger research project on architecture and city planning, the university had asked Lewin's group to conduct surveys of the residents in its married-study housing complex. In addition to asking for the residents' opinions on various aspects of the housing project, the researchers also measured social relationships with questions such as "Which people here do you see most often socially?" In sifting through these data, Festinger and his colleagues found that residents who interacted frequently with each other held very similar opinions about the housing project.

An analysis of the data from the MIT housing project led Festinger to develop his first theoretical contribution, namely **social comparison theory**. This is *the proposal that people evaluate their own opinions and abilities by comparing themselves to other people who are similar to them*. In his first major article, Festinger (1950) reasoned that people shape their own opinions by comparing their thoughts with the stated attitudes of those around them, adjusting their own beliefs so they fall in line with the group. But there's more than just conformity going on, he insisted, and instead people are trying to determine how reasonable their opinions are through social comparison. In a follow-up article, Festinger (1954) extended social comparison theory to people's evaluations of their own abilities. For example, how well you think you play basketball depends on your standard. Compared with the NBA pros, you're very bad, but compared with your friends at the gym, you're pretty good. Without a standard for comparison, any rating of an ability is meaningless. More generally, social comparison enables us to create a social reality we can all agree on.

Festinger's next research project showed his flair for the dramatic (Gazzaniga, 2006). In 1954, a Chicago housewife announced that she was in telepathic communication with space aliens who'd informed her that the Earth would be destroyed at the end of that year. However, they were sending a flying saucer to rescue her and any believers before the cataclysm occurred. She'd gathered a group of followers, who'd left their spouses, quit their jobs, and given up all their earthly possessions so they could be transported to the planet Clarion. Festinger wondered how these people were going to react when the appointed hour came with no end of the world and no flying saucer to rescue them. So to find out, he, Stanley Schachter, and Henry Riecken joined the group! Although the followers remained distressed throughout that fateful night, early the next morning their leader received a new message: The God of Earth had been so moved by their devotion that he decided to spare the world. Rejoicing at their salvation, they began an active campaign to recruit more members to their new religion. Festinger, Riecken, and Schachter (1956) wrote up their experiences in the classic book *When Prophecy Fails*.

This study also marks the introduction of Festinger's most important contribution to social psychology, namely the theory of **cognitive dissonance** (Nisbett, 2000). This is *the mental discomfort that occurs when a person holds contradictory beliefs or when there is a mismatch between attitudes and behaviors*. The members of this millennial group deeply believed that they would be rescued by a flying saucer just before the end of the world, so they must have experienced a great deal of cognitive dissonance when neither event came to pass. To relieve the intense mental discomfort, they had to create a new belief—that their faith had saved the world—to relieve the dissonance. They were simply too invested to admit they'd been wrong, and they even began proselytizing to confirm their beliefs. Festinger published these ideas in his 1957 book *A Theory of Cognitive Dissonance*.

One famous demonstration of cognitive dissonance is the so-called "boring task" experiment (Festinger & Carlsmith, 1959). In this experiment, Festinger and his student James Carlsmith had participants perform repetitive tasks such as turning screws and filling trays with spools for an hour, after which they were divided into one of three groups. Participants in the first group were offered $1 if they would tell another person—supposedly the next person in the experiment—that the task they were about to perform was interesting. Participants in the second group were offered $20 for lying about the experiment to the next person. And participants in the third group served as a control. All three groups were then interviewed, with the key question being: "How interesting was the task you just performed?" Those in the control group verified that the task was indeed boring. But the crux of the experiment was the ways in which the two paid groups responded. Reinforcement theory predicts that those who were paid $20 would change their attitude more than those paid only $1. In contrast, Festinger predicted—and found—that those paid only $1 said the task was interesting, while those paid $20 found it boring. The rationale goes this way: People generally believe that lying is wrong. Those who lied for $20 can justify the transgression with the large amount of money they received, whereas those who lied for only $1 couldn't do so. Instead, they had to convince themselves the task really was interesting, in which case they hadn't really lied.

On closer inspection, we can see that dissonance theory is related to Fritz Heider's balance theory (Schachter, 1994). According to Heider, mismatched attitudes between two persons in a relationship had to be brought into agreement to relieve the tension between them. But in Festinger's dissonance theory, the mismatched attitudes or behaviors were within a single person. The framework has proven especially fruitful in generating research, and we'll encounter another example when we discuss Festinger's student Elliot Aronson. Furthermore, dissonance theory makes predictions about human behavior that directly contradict reinforcement theory. And since the data generally support dissonance theory, the applicability of reinforcement theory as a model of human behavior has been called into question.

As Festinger's fame rose, he followed one job offer after another—from Michigan to Minnesota, and then to Stanford. But Festinger was a restive soul, and although he approached new research projects with enthusiastic abandon, he soon grew tired of them. By the mid-1960s, he'd given up research in social psychology altogether, taking up studies in visual perception instead. And then he shocked his colleagues by accepting a position at the New School for Social Research. Although the job brought him back to his beloved New York City, it was a definite step downward in terms of academic prestige. The New School was also the institute where he spent the bulk of his career. Although he came as a researcher in visual perception—and he even made important contributions to the field—he soon abandoned it for archeology. This new pursuit led to the 1983 book *The Human Legacy*, in which he deduced important changes in prehistoric societies that led to the rise of modern civilizations. That project complete, he next turned his attention to the history of religion, and he was putting together a manuscript on this subject when cancer ended his life at the age of seventy.

Kurt Lewin had first demonstrated that important questions in social psychology could be answered through the experimental method (Zajonc, 1990). But it was his student Leon Festinger who showed a generation of social psychologists how to construct dramatic social situations in the laboratory to test important hypotheses about human behavior. He also impacted the field by training students in the art of social psychology experimentation, and these in turn nurtured the next generation of researchers (Figure 12.4). In the next two sections, we'll meet two of Festinger's most accomplished students, Stanley Schachter and Elliot Aronson. Festinger's bold approach to studying human behavior in dynamic social settings has now become the norm for social psychology research.

Stanley Schachter

As the son of Jewish immigrants from Eastern Europe, **Stanley Schachter** (1922–1997) was expected to attend a laundry college in the Midwest and then take over the family business in New York City (Schachter, 1989). Instead, he attended Yale, where he got hooked on psychology with Clark Hull. After working as a military psychologist during World War II, he joined Kurt Lewin's first cohort of students at MIT. However, Lewin died shortly after

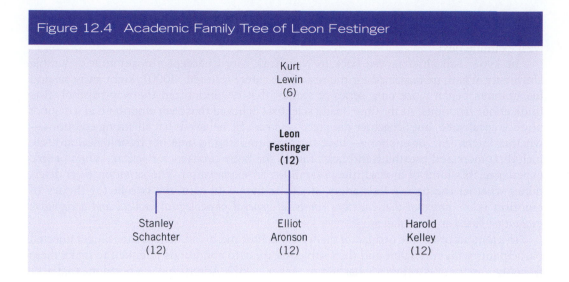

Figure 12.4 Academic Family Tree of Leon Festinger

Kurt Lewin (6)

Leon Festinger (12)

Stanley Schachter (12) Elliot Aronson (12) Harold Kelley (12)

his arrival, and Leon Festinger became his mentor. Stanley Schachter conducted creative research on a wide range of topics, but he's best known as the *American social psychologist who developed the two-factor theory of emotion*.

Schachter took part in the same MIT housing study that had led Festinger to develop his social comparison theory (Nisbett, 2000). One important finding of that project was that those respondents with divergent opinions tended not to associate with the other residents of the community. Schachter wondered if they'd been rejected because of their views, and this became the topic of his dissertation.

In this study on deviation from group standards, Schachter (1951) recruited college students on the pretext of forming a club. As part of a supposed ice-breaking activity, the experimenter—posing as the organizer of the club—gave them a case study of a juvenile delinquent named Johnny Rocco to discuss. Their task was to come to a consensus on what to do about the boy. The report was written in a way to bias the reader toward leniency, and this is the position that the participants took. However, Schachter had embedded three confederates in the group. The first, called the *mode*, voiced the average opinion of the group. The second, called the *slider*, first advocated for harsh discipline but let himself be convinced to agree with the lenient stance of the group. The last, called the *deviate*, took a position for harsh discipline and remained unmoved throughout the discussion. At first, the group members devoted considerable effort toward convincing the deviate, but eventually they gave up and ignored him altogether. After the discussion, the group members rated each other on a number of characteristics, with the mode and the slider being judged far more favorably than the deviate. It's important to note here that even though the slider originally disagreed with the group, after he changed his mind he was welcomed back and received high ratings from the other group members. Thus, the reward for conforming is acceptance into the group.

Later, Schachter traveled to Europe, where he replicated the deviation study in a number of countries (Wesselmann et al., 2014). Although the researchers found small differences from country to country, they still observed the same general tendency to ostracize those with deviant opinions and welcome those who change their minds to conform to the group.

Schachter worked on two other major projects during the 1950s. The first was his participation with Festinger in the millennial cult they described in their 1956 book *When Prophecy Fails*. The second was a study that led to *The Psychology of Affiliation* (Schachter, 1959). In this book, Schachter describes how people naturally congregate when the situation becomes ambiguous and potentially threatening. People do this because they're uncertain of their own emotional states, and so they use the reactions of others to develop a better understanding of how they themselves feel. The idea that people evaluate their emotions on the basis of situational cues led Schachter to develop the theory he's best known for, which we'll examine next.

In 1961, Schachter moved back to New York City to accept a position at Columbia University, where he remained for the rest of his career (Nisbett, 2000). Right away, he and his students began work on a series of studies that revolutionized the way psychologists think about emotions. At the time, many scientists believed that each emotion had a distinct physiological state, but Schachter disagreed. Instead, he believed that all strong emotions—whether anger, fear, or euphoria—have the same underlying state of physiological arousal, including increased breathing and heart rate as the body prepares for action. When people experience this kind of arousal, they search for an explanation. The situation then determines whether the person feels angry, afraid, or happy. In sum, the **two-factor theory of emotion** is *the proposal that emotions consist of general physiological arousal and a cognitive evaluation based on the situation.*

In a famous test of the two-factor theory, Schachter and his student Jerome Singer injected participants with adrenaline and then subjected them to conditions intended to make them feel either angry or euphoric (Schachter & Singer, 1962). Adrenaline is a hormone that activates the sympathetic nervous system, causing the symptoms of physiological arousal. The participants were told the shot was a vitamin supplement, but half were also warned that side effects may include heavy breathing and heart palpitations, whereas the others were warned of a different, false set of side effects. After that, they filled out a questionnaire with another person who was actually a confederate. For half of the participants, the confederate acted in a playful manner and encouraged the participant to join in the fun. For the other half of the participants, the confederate was grumpy and irritable, and he encouraged the participant to get angry at the very inappropriate personal questions on the survey. This session was followed by an interview in which most of the participants reported an increased heart and breathing rate. Those warned of the side effects attributed the symptoms to the injection. But the others believed these were due to the emotions of either euphoria or anger that they were feeling. Although the theory has its dissenters, it has nonetheless become one of the most influential theories of emotion.

Throughout his career, Schachter conducted experiments on everyday problems and came up with solutions that were often surprising or counterintuitive (Nisbett, 2000). One example was his study on obesity and eating (Schachter, 1968). He found that normal-weight people eat when they're hungry and stop when they're full, but obese people are insensitive to these internal cues. Instead, they eat when food is available. Moreover, they often let themselves go hungry because they're trying to lose weight, and as a result they overindulge when they encounter tasty food. Another example was his study of nicotine addiction in cigarette smokers (Schachter, 1977). At the time, many psychologists still believed that cigarette smoking was simply a well-learned habit, but Schachter was a smoker, and he suspected that nicotine was an addictive substance. So he gave his smoking friends unmarked cartons of cigarettes with either high or low levels of nicotine and asked them to record how many they smoked. As expected, the participants smoked more of the low-nicotine cigarettes, suggesting that they were trying to regulate their nicotine intake.

Schachter had a major impact on the shaping of social psychology in the last half of the twentieth century (Nisbett, 2000). He demonstrated that it was possible to construct tightly controlled experiments in the lab that still retained ecological validity. He also showed that considerable progress can be made by positing theories in what has been termed the "middle range." And finally, he nurtured a number of graduate students who went on to become the next generation of social psychologists, many of whom are still active researchers today (Figure 12.5). As the intellectual grandson of Kurt Lewin, Schachter followed the great Gestalt psychologist's admonition to do tough-minded research on tender-hearted issues.

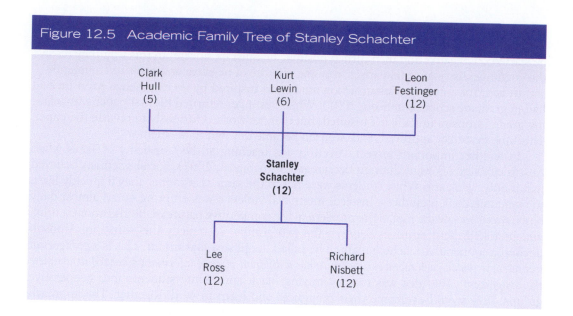

Figure 12.5 Academic Family Tree of Stanley Schachter

Clark
Hull
(5)

Kurt
Lewin
(6)

Leon
Festinger
(12)

**Stanley
Schachter
(12)**

Lee
Ross
(12)

Richard
Nisbett
(12)

Elliot Aronson

As a boy growing up in a working-class neighborhood of Boston, **Elliot Aronson** (born 1932) often got roughed up by bullies simply because he was Jewish (Aronson, 2007). In college, he was attracted to psychology by the humanistic psychologist Abraham Maslow (Chapter 15), who lectured on the causes of prejudice and discrimination. He also learned from Maslow that psychology could have good effects on society, but it wasn't until he worked with Leon Festinger at Stanford that he learned how to do good experiments. Thus, the theme of his career was to do good experiments that would help make the world a better place. Today, Elliot Aronson is known as the *American social psychologist who has used cognitive dissonance theory for the purpose of effecting positive social change.*

Aronson's first experiment as a graduate student looked at the processes shaping people's attitudes toward the groups they belong to (Aronson & Mills, 1959). In particular, he asked why people who go through severe initiations, such as those for joining fraternities or the Marine Corps, become so dedicated to those groups. To explore this question, the experimenters recruited female college students to take part in a discussion about sexual issues. The students were told that they had to pass a test about sexual attitudes before they could join the discussion. In the mild initiation condition the test consisted of reading a list of sexually related words out loud, whereas in the severe initiation condition participants had to read aloud graphic descriptions of sexual acts. After being told that they'd passed the test, they then joined in a discussion that was set up to be as boring as possible. In follow-up interviews, the participants in the severe initiation condition said the discussion was much more interesting than those in the mild initiation condition. Aronson explained this finding in terms of cognitive dissonance theory. Specifically, the participants who'd undergone the severe initiation had to justify their embarrassment by convincing themselves that the discussion was worthwhile.

Next, Aronson applied cognitive dissonance theory to explore processes of interpersonal attraction (Aronson & Linder, 1965). Reinforcement theory predicts that we should like people who consistently say good things about us. But when Aronson arranged for participants to overhear an evaluator's comments about their performance, they rated as more likeable the speakers who first made negative comments about them before making an

Photo 12.4
Elliot Aronson

overall positive assessment. Aronson speculated that the participants reasoned as follows: If the evaluator said only good things about me, then maybe he's just trying to be nice. But if he started off negative and then turned positive, he must be sincere. In this way, they resolve the cognitive dissonance that arises from the mixture of negative and positive comments.

In fact, the interpersonal attraction study was inspired by an experience Aronson had had in graduate school (Aronson, 2007). When Festinger returned his first paper with a failing grade, Aronson initially felt insulted, but then he worked furiously to rewrite the paper. This time Festinger approved, and Aronson became devoted to his mentor.

In another important project, Aronson was teaching at the University of Texas when Austin city schools went through desegregation (Aronson, 2007). Social scientists believed that if only Black and White students were put in the same classrooms, they'd quickly learn to overcome their prejudices. Instead, interracial violence was erupting on an almost daily basis. Aronson saw the root of the problem in the competitive nature of the classroom setting, which stoked racist attitudes between the two groups. To remedy this situation, Aronson devised a cooperative teaching method he called the **jigsaw classroom**. This is *a pedagogical technique in which each member of a group has a different piece of information needed to complete the assignment*. The idea was that by mixing Black and White students into cooperative groups, they would overcome their prejudices and learn to work together. The approach proved to be successful, and today it's a widely used approach in public education.

Much of Aronson's work has explored methods for changing people's counterproductive behaviors (Aronson, 1999). Noting that direct persuasion techniques rarely work, Aronson's approach has been to induce people to persuade themselves that they want to change. This is usually accomplished through the use of **counter-attitudinal advocacy**, which is *a self-persuasion technique in which people are asked to take a public position on an issue that differs from their privately held beliefs*. When people are only offered minimal incentives for doing so, cognitive dissonance kicks in, and they start to change their inward beliefs to match their outward expressions. The technique is especially effective when people can be made to feel hypocritical for their inward beliefs or past behaviors, because we all want to believe we're moral people.

Two examples illustrate the counter-attitudinal advocacy approach. In the first, Aronson and his students induced sexually active college students to use condoms to prevent AIDS by having them produce educational videos about safe sex (Aronson, Fried, & Stone, 1991). In the second, they encouraged people to take shorter showers during a California drought by having them sign a publicly displayed poster outlining common water-wasting habits (Dickerson, Thibodeau, Aronson, & Miller, 1992). Follow-up assessments indicated that both of these attempts at self-persuasion had lasting effects.

In addition to being an innovative researcher, Aronson has also been an inspirational teacher to graduate and undergraduate students alike (McNulty, 1999). He's received many awards for his teaching, and his textbook *The Social Animal*, first published in 1972, has become a classic in the field, going through numerous editions and still being widely used in the twenty-first century. Although retired, Aronson continues to write books that engage professionals and laypersons alike in the excitement of doing social psychology for the good of society (Figure 12.6).

Social Perception

As we navigate our interactions with other people, we build expectations about how they're going to behave, and we alter our own behavior in response. **Social perception** refers to *the ways we make inferences about the motivations and intentions of those we interact with*. Much of the work in the field of social perception builds on Fritz Heider's attribution theory, and during the 1970s and 1980s there was a major push in research toward understanding the factors that influence the attribution process. And since attributions guide our interactions with others, social psychologists began looking at the dynamics of interpersonal relationships as well.

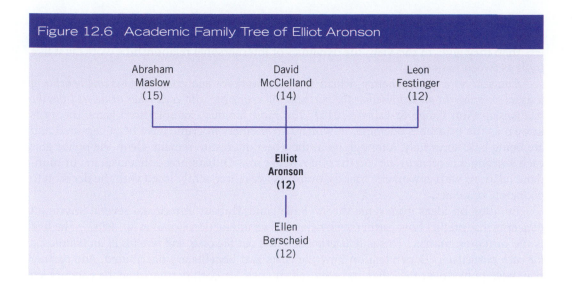

Figure 12.6 Academic Family Tree of Elliot Aronson

Abraham Maslow (15)

David McClelland (14)

Leon Festinger (12)

Elliot Aronson (12)

Ellen Berscheid (12)

Harold Kelley

After completing his bachelor's and master's degrees in psychology at Berkeley under the guidance of Edward Tolman, **Harold Kelley** (1921–2003) then served as a military psychologist during World War II (Raven, Pepitone, & Holmes, 2003). After the war, he joined the inaugural class of Kurt Lewin's Research Center for Group Dynamics at MIT. For his dissertation, he followed up on Solomon Asch's classic experiment on how being told that someone was "cold" or "warm" affected people's attitudes and behaviors toward that person. The thesis became a classic in the newly emerging field of social perception. Over a long and productive career, Harold Kelley built his reputation as an *American social psychologist who played important roles in developing interdependence theory and attribution theory.*

During his time at MIT, Kelley became close friends with fellow student **John Thibaut** (1917–1986, pronounced *tee-BOW*), with whom he continued to collaborate for several decades, even as each pursued careers at different universities (Jones, Kelley, & Schopler, 1987). Thibaut also formed a close working relationship with Edward Jones, whom we'll meet in the next section. Today Thibaut is mainly known as the *American social psychologist who collaborated with Harold Kelley on interdependence theory and with Edward Jones on attribution theory.* Despite his great learning and intellect, Thibaut was painfully shy in public, and so he yielded the limelight to his collaborators. As a result, it was Kelley and Jones who got most of the credit for the two major theories that Thibaut had played an instrumental role in building. Nevertheless, both Kelley and Jones have counted Thibaut among their intellectual mentors.

Although Kelley and Thibaut had worked together on several previous projects, their first major collaboration was the 1959 book *The Social Psychology of Groups* (Thibaut & Kelley, 1959). This was followed nearly two decades later by their 1978 book *Interpersonal Relations: A Theory of Interdependence.* In these two works as well as in a number of articles and book chapters, Kelley and Thibaut laid out interdependence theory and the evidence to support it. In a nutshell, **interdependence theory** is *a description of how the costs and benefits of particular interactions lead to decisions about whether to cooperate or compete and whether to continue or leave the relationship.* The theory is based on the assumption that human behavior can be understood only if the social context in which it occurs is taken into account.

Kelley and Thibaut built interdependence theory by borrowing two important theories from economics and mathematics (Van Lange & Balliet, 2015). The first is **social exchange theory**, which is *the view that people enter into relationships in order to trade goods and services for mutual advantage.* Extending the concept of "goods and services," Kelley and Thibaut also included psychological needs such as praise, companionship, love, and so on. Social exchange theory predicts that two persons will remain in a relationship as long as each perceives the benefits as outweighing the costs, and they'll leave when they feel they get less than they give. In this view, the dynamics of interpersonal relationships works just like trade between nations.

The second is **game theory**, which is *a framework for analyzing the costs and benefits of a social exchange to predict whether the partners will cooperate with each other or defect from the relationship* (Van Lange & Balliet, 2015). The most famous example from game theory is known as the prisoner's dilemma, in which two partners in crime have been captured and are being held separately. Although it's in their best interest to remain silent, the police give each a strong incentive to "rat" on the other. Kelley and Thibaut noted that even in our mundane relations with coworkers, friends, or lovers, we're frequently faced with the decision to cooperate or defect.

Building on ideas from game theory, Kelley and Thibaut introduced several important concepts that predict how partners will behave in an interaction (Jones et al., 1987). The first is the **outcome matrix**. This is *a diagram that lays out the costs and benefits of an interaction for each participant*. Depending on how the costs and benefits are distributed, one partner may have power over the other and seek selfish goals, or both partners may be encouraged to compromise so that each gets something he or she wants. As partners engage in repeated interactions, they make decisions about whether to stay or leave the relationship. First, they decide based on the **comparison level**, which is *a consideration of the quality of the relationship in the current interaction as compared with past interactions*. We tend to stay when the relationship is at least as good as it was in the past, and we're tempted to leave when interactions are no longer satisfying. But this doesn't mean that partners always break up when things go bad, because they also have to consider the **comparison level of alternatives**. This is *a consideration of the other relationship options available to each partner*. We're more likely to leave if other potential partners are available, or if we think we'd be better off alone, but we're more likely to stay in a bad relationship if we judge the alternatives to be worse.

Even though Kurt Lewin passed away just a year after Kelley and Thibaut entered MIT as his graduate students, his influence on interdependence theory is evident (Van Lange & Balliet, 2015). Recall Lewin's equation $B = f(P, E)$ from Chapter 6. By this, he meant that behavior is a function of both the person and the environment. Kelley and Thibaut expanded this equation by acknowledging that behavior takes place between persons within a social context. Thus, they proposed what's become known as the SABI equation, or $f(S, A, B) = I$. This can be read out as: A function of the Situation, person A, and person B determines the outcome of a social Interaction.

Kelley and Thibaut remained close friends and frequent collaborators until Thibaut's death from cancer in 1986 (Raven et al., 2003). After that, Kelley continued to refine interdependence theory for the rest of his life, publishing his final work on the subject, *An Atlas of Interpersonal Situations*, in 2003, shortly before his death. In this book, he and his collaborators analyzed nearly two dozen common interaction types, considering how both situational and personality factors determine the outcomes in each case.

In the 1960s, Kelley also took an interest in Fritz Heider's work on attributions after John Thibaut had done an earlier study on this topic (Raven et al., 2003). As you recall from Chapter 6, Heider proposed that we seek explanations for other people's behavior to guide our interactions with them. These attributions can explain behavior in terms of either personal factors ("Joe flunked the test because he isn't good at math.") or situational factors ("Joe flunked the test because it was too hard.") However, Heider didn't explore in depth the reasons why we make personal or situational attributions. This was the task that Kelley undertook.

In a series of publications, Kelley laid out his **covariation model**, which was *the proposal that people make attributions by considering which potential cause best predicts the behavior* (Hewstone & Jaspars, 1987). In his theory, Kelley expanded Heider's model by proposing three potential causes for a behavior. The first is the personal characteristics of the *person* we're making an attribute about ("Harry yelled at Sally because he's a grumpy person."). The second involves *entities*, or other people that make up the social situation ("Harry yelled at Sally because she was rude to him."). And the third is what he called *time-modality*, by which he was referring to the characteristics of the specific situation in which the behavior is taking place ("Harry yelled at Sally because he's under a lot of stress right now.")

According to Kelley, we attribute to the behavior the potential cause that best explains it (Hewstone & Jaspars, 1987). More specifically, we look for the potential cause that only occurs when the behavior occurs. For example, if only Harry is yelling at Sally, he yelled at her in the past, and he often yells at other people, we attribute his anger to his grumpy personality. In contrast, if Harry doesn't usually yell at people, we may attribute his anger to the situation—either Sally did something to make Harry angry, or maybe Harry is just under a lot of stress.

In the covariation model, Kelley viewed social perceivers as amateur scientists testing various hypotheses about the causes of other people's behavior (Kollock, 2000). Some experimental evidence supports the notion that people look for covariation when making attributions, at least when they have sufficient motivation and the information is available. Kelley recognized that covariation theory was a **normative model**, meaning that it's *a description of how people should act rather than how they really behave*. However, Kelley recognized that most of the time people rely on heuristics to make attributions in a quick and effortless manner, much like those Daniel Kahneman and Amos Tversky had proposed for judgment and decision making (Chapter 11). In 1972, Kelley collaborated with Edward Jones and others on the edited volume *Attribution: Perceiving the Causes of Behavior*. This book sparked widespread interest in studying the attribution process. As we'll see shortly, Jones was one of the key figures in uncovering the built-in biases we have in making attributions.

Ellen Berscheid

During the 1970s, Kelley worked on interdependence theory and attribution theory in parallel (Raven et al., 2003). While these theories helped explain how people behave in a variety of social interactions, the two together had clear implications for an important aspect of human life that psychology had up to that point shied away from, namely intimate relationships. The depth of emotion between lovers leads to an intensity of interdependence rarely seen in other kinds of relationships. Furthermore, the attributions that people make about their intimate partners can have profound effects—for good or bad—on the quality of the relationship. Thus, Kelley began studying the ways that young couples resolved conflicts, and the result was the 1979 book *Personal Relationships: Their Structures and Processes*.

This interest in applying interdependence and attribution theories to the study of intimate relationships also led Kelley to a collaboration with **Ellen Berscheid** (born 1936), an *American social psychologist who studies the dynamics of close interpersonal relationships* (Berscheid, 2003). Berscheid had been a student of Elliot Aronson at the University of Minnesota, where she later joined the faculty as its first woman psychologist. Kelley and Berscheid, leading a group of social psychologists, published the edited volume *Close Relationships* in 1983. This book led to a growing consensus among social psychologists that romantic relationships were a legitimate topic for research, and its publication marked the beginning of a new subdiscipline of social psychology known as relationship science.

As unremarkable as the study of romantic love may seem today, Berscheid found herself embroiled in controversy when she first proposed the topic for a National Science Foundation grant in the early 1970s (Berscheid, 2003). She was awarded the grant, but soon William Proxmire, a senator from Wisconsin, learned of it. Proxmire was on a campaign to censure the supposedly frivolous spending of taxpayer money on worthless science projects. When he nominated her for a sarcastic "Golden Fleece Award," Berscheid and her study of romantic love became front-page news around the world. She received death threats from anonymous callers, but she also received a number of marriage proposals—mostly from lonely men in prison, but also one from a wealthy Arabian sheik! She also received lots of mail from everyday folks asking for advice on how to save their marriages—people really did want to know how romantic love worked after all. Eventually the scandal subsided, and following her collaboration with Kelley, she went on to become a recognized leader in the field of relationship science.

Edward Jones

As a student of Jerome Bruner during the New Look movement, **Edward Jones** (1926–1993) believed that perception was rooted in social interaction (Gilbert & Lindzey, 1994). Although he finished his Ph.D. in clinical psychology, he spent the rest of his career as a social psychologist. While at Harvard, he also collaborated on a top-secret study for the Navy on the psychological vulnerabilities of living and working on a submarine. It was during this project that Jones got to know John Thibaut, who later introduced him to Fritz Heider's attribution theory as well as the work of Kurt Lewin, Leon Festinger, and others at the Research Center for Group Dynamics. Today, Edward Jones is known as the *American social psychologist who developed correspondent inference theory and discovered the correspondence bias.*

Jones's first academic position was at Duke University, where he remained on the faculty for nearly a quarter of a century (Gilbert & Lindzey, 1994). Meanwhile, his friend and mentor John Thibaut had moved to nearby University of North Carolina, and the two remained in frequent contact. One of Jones's first projects at Duke was a study of *the kinds of behaviors people engage in to get others to like them*, or what he called **ingratiation**. Although people engage in a wide range of ingratiation techniques, Jones was impressed by how readily observers take those behaviors at face value. When someone compliments us, we tend to assume it's because they're a genuinely nice person, and we rarely consider that they could be acting that way for other reasons. Jones didn't know at first what to make of this observation. But as he learned more about attribution theory through his interactions with Thibaut and others, he gradually saw a connection between our gullibility to ingratiation in particular and the typical errors we make when attributing the causes of others' behaviors in general.

In 1965, Jones and his student Keith Davis published their **theory of correspondent inferences** (Gilbert, 1998). This was *a normative description of the circumstances in which we should make personal rather than situational attributions about another's behavior.* First, it states that if we know an actor has a choice, we should infer that the behavior was intentional. Furthermore, if the actor's behavior is directly relevant to us, we should be highly motivated to understand the reason for it. The theory then proposes that we should assume a behavior corresponds to a personal disposition unless the behavior was performed accidentally or the person was coerced in some way. While these rules of attribution sound like common sense, Jones soon found that they're not commonly followed.

Early tests seemed to confirm the predictions of correspondent inference theory, but two years later Jones and one of his students published a study that had yielded unexpected results (Jones & Harris, 1967). They asked participants to read an essay that either supported or opposed Fidel Castro's regime in Cuba, and they were told either that the writer had been given a choice of which position to take or that the writer had been compelled to take the position expressed in the essay. The participants were then asked to rate the degree to which they believed the writer actually believed what he'd written. According to correspondent inference theory, the participants should make a dispositional attribution when they were told the writer was free to choose a position ("The essay reflects the beliefs of the writer.") but a situational attribution when they were told the position had been assigned to then ("The writer was forced to express these views and doesn't necessarily agree with them."). But this isn't what Jones found. Instead, the participants made dispositional attributions in both cases, although they were somewhat stronger in the free-choice than compelled condition.

Although this result fails to support correspondent inference theory, Jones interpreted it as a significant finding, dubbing it the **correspondence bias** (Gilbert, 1998). This is *the tendency to assume that behaviors reflect the true intentions of the people who perform them.* In other words, we tend to make dispositional attributions even when we have reason to believe the behavior was dictated by the situation. Jones spent much of the rest of his career teasing out the conditions under which the correspondence bias would occur or go away. Overall, he found it to be quite a robust effect that persisted despite virtually all attempts to make the coercive nature of the situation salient. In other words, we find it hard to believe other people would act against their true beliefs, despite the fact that we can all think of instances when we've either been compelled to act against our will or have intentionally deceived another person. This is where Jones's earlier observation on ingratiation became relevant, in that people generally take behaviors at face value.

Around this same time, another psychologist was also looking at similar biases in attribution (Gilbert, 1998; Ravindran, 2012). **Lee Ross** (born 1942) had been a student of Stanley Schachter, and he'd taken an interest in attribution processes. Today he's known as the *American social psychologist who discovered the fundamental attribution error*. A tenet of social psychology is that the social situation is an important factor in driving behavior. Like Jones, Ross was intrigued by *the tendency to discount situational factors and to assume that behavior is driven by personal dispositions*. Ross called this bias the **fundamental attribution error**— an error because situational factors are ignored even when they're important for explaining the behavior and salient to the observer. Although some psychologists claim there's a subtle difference between the correspondence bias and the fundamental attribution error, most see these two terms as referring to the same phenomenon. In fact, even Jones referred to the effect as the fundamental attribution error, quipping that he wished he'd thought of that name for it!

Photo 12.5
Lee Ross

Although the correspondence bias or fundamental attribution error—whichever you want to call it—is ubiquitous, Jones did find an interesting case in which people prefer to make situational over dispositional attributions (Jones, 1979). At the time, he was collaborating with **Richard Nisbett** (born 1941), the *American social psychologist known for his studies of cognition across cultures*. Nisbett had also been a student of Stanley Schachter along with Lee Ross. Jones and Nisbett observed that we don't just make attributions about other people's behaviors. Oftentimes, we have no clear idea why we behaved the way we did, and so we have to make attributions about our own actions as well. Although we tend to explain other people's behaviors in terms of their dispositions ("Jack failed the test because he isn't very smart."), we often explain our own behaviors in terms of the situation ("I failed the test because it was too hard."). Jones and Nisbett called *the tendency to make dispositional attributions of others' behaviors and situational attributions of our own* the **actor-observer effect**. Today, social psychologists acknowledge that this phenomenon occurs because we're far more aware of our own conditions but often unaware of other people's situations. In other words, we see our own behavior within context but see other people's actions as context free, hence we assume it derives from dispositions.

Jones summed up the research he'd devoted his career to in his 1990 book *Interpersonal Perception*, published just a few years before he died (Gilbert & Lindzey, 1994). His contributions to attribution theory, including both the correspondence bias and the actor-observer effect, have stood the test of time and are now standard fare in both introductory and social psychology classes. Also important is the degree to which he collaborated with his colleagues in the development of attribution theory, which superseded dissonance theory as the focal point of social psychology in the 1970s and 1980s. The career of Edward Jones is a prime example of how psychological science is a social enterprise that requires the collaboration of many great minds working toward the common goal of understanding human nature.

Social Relations

When Kurt Lewin died in 1947, MIT was no longer interested in hosting his Research Center for Group Dynamics, but his successor Leon Festinger convinced the University of Michigan to house them. Around this same time, Michigan decided to establish the Institute for Social Research, which merged sociology and social psychology as a single program specializing in the training of social scientists at the doctoral level only. Soon, Michigan became a powerhouse for social psychology, attracting stellar researchers and training many of the next generation of leaders in the field. Among these, we'll consider two. The first is Theodore Newcomb, who became famous for his large-scale studies of social interactions in everyday life. And the second is Robert Zajonc (pronounced *ZYE-unts*), whose research interests ranged widely over his fifty-year career.

Theodore Newcomb

The son of a country pastor, **Theodore Newcomb** (1903–1984) was studying for the ministry at Union Theological Seminary in New York City when he crossed Broadway and took a psychology class at Columbia University (Newcomb, 1974). Finding his true calling, he gave up a religious career to earn a Ph.D. in psychology in 1929. At that time, most social psychology studies involved simple experiments in the lab. But Theodore Newcomb wanted to study social life as it's really lived, and today he's known as the *American social psychologist who studied attitude formation and the acquaintance process through longitudinal field studies.*

As a young faculty member at Western Reserve University (now Case Western Reserve University) in Cleveland, Ohio, Newcomb compared the attitudes of several hundred young adults with those of their parents (Newcomb, 1974). He was testing the Freudian prediction that their attitudes would pattern along the lines of their same-sex parent, but this wasn't what he found. Instead, all members of a family tended to have similar attitudes, and what predicted these were ethnicity, religion, and social class. This was his first indication that attitudes are shaped by social forces at a larger level than the individual's immediate environment.

Photo 12.6
Theodore Newcomb

Newcomb was an advocate of progressive education. When he was offered a position at newly established Bennington College in rural Vermont, he gladly accepted it (Converse, 1994). Bennington was an all-women's school with small classes and a pedagogical philosophy he admired. Ordinarily, leaving a large university for a small college spells the end of a research career, but Newcomb turned Bennington College into a "natural experiment" that made him famous. It's commonly observed that college students tend to become more politically liberal as they progress through their college years, and it's often assumed that this occurs because of the ideas they encounter in their classes. However, Newcomb suspected larger social forces were at work.

In what became known as the Bennington study, Newcomb surveyed the entire incoming freshman class and assessed them regularly until graduation, asking them questions about their social relations and their attitudes to current political issues (Douvan, 1986). First, he found that almost all of the young women came from wealthy, politically conservative families and that they tended to share the attitudes of their parents, just as he'd found in the Cleveland study. Over the next four years, though, most of them became much more liberal in their attitudes. However, Newcomb found that this change in attitudes came not from classroom experiences but rather the social influences of their classmates. Those who remained relatively aloof tended to maintain their conservative views, whereas those who were socially active became more liberal. Apparently, it was interactions with people from different backgrounds that led to more progressive attitude formation. Newcomb published the results of the Bennington study in his 1943 book *Personality and Social Change*. The study was unprecedented in size and scope, and it made Newcomb famous. Soon the University of Michigan offered him a faculty position, and he remained there for the rest of his career.

Newcomb assumed that the progressive young women graduating from Bennington College would return to their hometowns and revert to their original conservative views (Newcomb, 1974). So twenty-five years later, he conducted a follow-up study in which he sent out his graduate students to interview the participants in the original study. Although his assumption held up in a few cases, the vast majority of the women—now middle-aged—had found husbands who shared their liberal views and had moved into politically progressive social circles, meaning that their attitude formation in college had remained permanent.

At Michigan, Newcomb interacted with Leon Festinger and the other members of the Research Center for Group Dynamics, which had moved there from MIT after Kurt Lewin's death (Converse, 1994). Although Newcomb had never collaborated with Lewin, he was familiar with his approach to collecting real-world data over extended timeframes and thought of him as his "principal social-psychological hero" (p. 326). This was the approach he'd taken at Bennington, and he did it again at Michigan.

Newcomb convinced the university administration to provide free room and board in a special dormitory to incoming freshmen who agreed to be part of a longitudinal study (Douvan, 1986). Before the young men arrived on campus, they filled out a survey of their attitudes on a variety of issues. Then for the next two years, they completed weekly surveys that tracked their social relationships and their changing attitudes on a variety of topics, much like the Bennington study. Newcomb published the data from this study in his 1961 book *The Acquaintance Process*.

In this work, Newcomb described several processes involved in interpersonal attraction (Douvan, 1986). First, he noted that those who lived close to each other tended to become friends. He called this the **proximity principle**, which is *the observation that people tend to like others who share the same environment with them*. Second, he found that those with similar interests were also likely to become friends. He named this the **similarity principle**, which is *the observation that people tend to be attracted to those who have interests in common with them*. Finally, he observed how social networks form from dyads, or groups of two. This involves *the process in which members of the core group invite additional persons to join in, forming a larger social network*. Newcomb called this the **elaboration principle**. By the end of the study, the participants had organized themselves into two large groups based on common interests.

During the time that Newcomb was working on the Michigan study, he became familiar with Fritz Heider's work on balance theory (Newcomb, 1974). Recall that Heider (Chapter 6) had proposed the POX model, which described the relationship between a person P, another person O, and some object X that they both had an attitude about. Heider argued that when the relationship isn't in balance, P will change her attitude toward either O or X to bring it back in balance. Newcomb agreed with Heider, but he also argued that both persons, which he called A and B, were striving for balance at the same time (Figure 12.7). This approach to balance theory has become known as the **ABX model**, referring to *Newcomb's description of the forces that come into play as two people attempt to align their attitudes toward a third entity*. In other words, Heider looked at balance within the person, whereas Newcomb examined balance between persons.

Figure 12.7 ABX Model

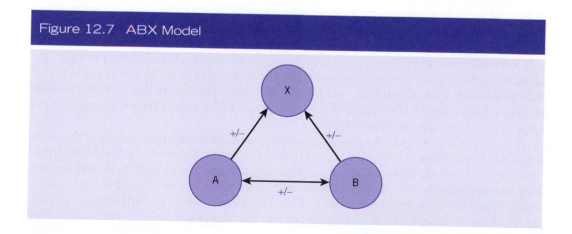

Newcomb's legacy to social psychology is the demonstration that longitudinal field experiments can be conducted in a rigorous manner to generate results with real-world applications (McGrath, 1978). His Bennington study was a landmark in social psychology not only because of the data it produced but also because it demonstrated that such large-scale studies were feasible. Even more impressive is the fact that it was conducted in the days before computers, meaning that all the data processing had to be done by hand. At least for his Michigan study he had computer punch cards at his disposal, but his skill at data management was still remarkable. In the end, Theodore Newcomb showed that social psychology doesn't have to be restricted to artificial social worlds created in the laboratory. Instead, he demonstrated by example that social psychologists can make important contributions when they go out into the real world and study social processes as they are playing out.

Robert Zajonc

"My name rhymes with science," **Robert Zajonc** (1923–2008) would tell people when he met them for the first time ("Memories," 2009). During a career lasting half a century, Zajonc pursued a wide range of research interests, always with the keen eye of a natural scientist seeking underlying simplicity to explain the apparent complexity of human social life. Although he's made many contributions to psychology, Robert Zajonc is best known today as the *Polish-American social psychologist who explained social facilitation and discovered the mere exposure effect.*

Zajonc was born in Poland (Burnstein, 2009). When he was fifteen, his home was bombed by invading Nazi forces—his parents were killed, and he woke up in a hospital badly injured. Later, he was sent to a Nazi prison camp in France, from which he escaped. Zajonc then joined the Resistance before fleeing to England to serve as a French and German translator for the American forces. After the war, he immigrated to the United States and enrolled at the University of Michigan. There, he completed undergraduate and graduate degrees before joining its faculty, remaining at Michigan in total for forty-five years. He had a significant impact on the field both in terms of the innovative research projects he pursued as well as the many graduate students he nurtured. Many of Zajonc's research endeavors have become standard fare in introductory psychology textbooks, and some have even caught the eye of the public media.

One of Zajonc's early research interests was **social facilitation** (Burnstein, 2009). This term refers to *the effect that the presence of others has on an individual's ability to perform a task.* At that time, there was much interest in the phenomenon, but the data were conflicting. Sometimes, psychologists found that the presence of others led to improvements in performance, but in other cases people performed worse when others were around. Zajonc found that the difference depended on whether the task was well practiced or not. The mere presence of other people is arousing, he argued. When engaging in an act that we do well, this social arousal enhances our performance. But if the task isn't well practiced, our performance suffers in the presence of others. Just think about professional musicians or athletes in front of an audience versus their novice counterparts. What's more, Zajonc demonstrated that social facilitation isn't a uniquely human phenomenon. In one of his most notorious experiments, he demonstrated that individual cockroaches run an alleyway faster but navigate a maze slower when there's a cockroach audience watching them! Demonstrating that supposedly uniquely human phenomena were also observable in other animals was one of the hallmarks of Zajonc's research. Incidentally, you should recognize that social facilitation is conceptually related to the Yerkes-Dodson law proposed by Robert Yerkes (Chapter 4) and his student in the early twentieth century.

Another of Zajonc's well-known research programs involved his discovery of the **mere exposure effect** (Fox, 2008). In contrast to more complex theories of preference formation, Zajonc made *the observation that people tend to like familiar items more than unfamiliar ones.* In particular, he found this occurred even when the participants in his experiments didn't know which items they'd seen before. In a classic series of experiments, Zajonc rapidly flashed images one after another, so fast that the participants never noticed that some of the items were repeated. Nevertheless, in a subsequent preference test, the participants consistently chose the familiar items over those that were less familiar. Similar results were obtained whether the items were geometric shapes, colored patterns, or even Chinese ideograms. Although this finding contradicts the old saw that "familiarity breeds contempt," advertisers have long understood the power of the mere exposure effect.

A more controversial study was Zajonc's investigation into birth order effects on intelligence (Swanbrow, 2008). It had long been thought that intelligence was a product of genetics, but Zajonc argued that the social environment in which a child is raised also has an impact on ultimate intellectual attainment. In examining a very large data set of IQ scores among family members, he found that first-born children tended to have the highest IQs, and that each subsequent child in the family had an IQ that was about 3 points lower than then next older sibling. Zajonc argued that this was because first-borns spend the earliest part of their life in an all-adult environment, whereas younger children share their parents' attention with their other siblings. In other words, the average IQ of the home environment is higher for the first-born child than it is for later-born children.

One more noteworthy research topic was Zajonc's investigation into the relationship between facial expressions and the experience of emotion (Burnstein, 2009). We're often encouraged to put on a happy face to make ourselves feel better, but does this really work? The data suggest that it could very well be true. Zajonc made *the observation that facial expressions and emotions may be linked through blood flow to the brain*, a phenomenon he called **facial efference**. Smiling relaxes facial muscles, he argued, and so there's more blood flow to the areas of the brain controlling emotion. As a result, we feel happy because we smile. In contrast, frowning tenses muscles, drawing blood toward the face and away from the brain. And so the result is that we feel worse when we frown.

Throughout his career, which spanned the last half of the twentieth century, Zajonc argued for the primacy of emotions at a time when psychologists were emphasizing the cognitive basis of behavior (Burnstein, 2009). Social facilitation worked because it affected our emotions, not our cognitions. The mere exposure effect demonstrated that we can like or dislike things without even being aware of them. And finally, facial efference showed that expressions of the face can elicit emotions without any underlying cognitions. Zajonc's claims were often considered controversial at the time—and some still are today. Although his research interests were eclectic, there was a common theme running through all of his work. Namely, this was the belief in an underlying simplicity below the surface confusion, meaning that complex social life can be explained if only we can find the rules that govern it. This was also the belief that Robert Zajonc instilled in his many students who are now among the leaders of social psychology.

Looking Ahead

Social psychology blossomed as an experimental science in the postwar years, growing into one of the main disciplines of the field. Although cognitive psychology dominated in the last half of the twentieth century, social psychologists often worked in parallel with their cognitive counterparts. Thus, while cognitive psychologists studied attention, perception, judgment, and decision making with regard to the physical world, social psychologists turned these concepts toward the social world that guides our lives. Social psychology also got a boost from the fact that many of its findings have obvious real-world applications, from combatting racism and sexism to promoting healthy and productive lifestyles. It seems the issues that matter most in modern life can only be understood by taking into account the social situations in which they play out. As we move deeper into the twenty-first century, one important question is whether social psychology can successfully integrate with neuroscience in the way that cognitive psychology has done. Can there be a brain science of social life? Can we someday understand how neural processes guide social interactions? These are the questions just now being posed by the first generation of social neuroscientists.

CHAPTER SUMMARY

Social psychology emerged as an important field of study after World War II. In the 1930s, Muzafer Sherif studied the spread of social norms using a simple laboratory setup, and later in his career he conducted field studies on intergroup conflict. Influenced by Gestalt psychologist Max Wertheimer, Solomon Asch turned his attention to conformity in groups, while Asch's student Stanley Milgram conducted his infamous study of obedience to authority. Modern social psychology has largely evolved from the group dynamics approach developed by Gestalt psychologist Kurt Lewin. Many of the first postwar generation of social psychologists were trained by Lewin, or by his student Leon Festinger after his death. Festinger developed the study of social cognition, which was continued by his students Stanley Schachter and Elliot Aronson, among others. Harold Kelley and John Thibaut were also students of Lewin, and they first turned their attention to the study of interpersonal relationships before expanding their research to include attempts to experimentally verify Fritz Heider's attribution theory. Around the same time, Edward Jones also took an interest in the predictable errors people make as they infer the causes of other people's behaviors. When Lewin's Research Center for Group Dynamics moved to the University of Michigan after his death, that school became a powerhouse for training and research in social science. Both Theodore Newcomb and Robert Zajonc were instrumental in building that program, but they're also noted for their important research contributions. Newcomb is recognized for his longitudinal field studies, in particular his Bennington study on attitude formation and his Michigan study on the acquaintance process. Zajonc was an eclectic researcher, mostly noted for his studies of social facilitation, the mere exposure effect, the effect of birth order on intelligence, and the relationship between facial expressions and the experience of emotion.

DISCUSSION QUESTIONS

1. Although Sherif's work on the psychology of social norms was highly praised, his Robbers Cave experiment continues to be controversial. Can you think of some potential confounds or ethical issues with this study? You may want to do some additional research.

2. Both Sherif and Asch were interested in how group members adjust their perceptions to create an agreed-upon social reality. Contrast their experimental approaches and the results they obtained.

3. Milgram's obedience experiment was intended to shed light on the reason for the Holocaust. In your opinion, does it provide any clarification of this tragic historical event? Defend your position.

4. According to Festinger's social comparison theory, we determine our abilities, opinions, and other personal characteristics by comparing them with what we observe in others. Do you agree, or do you think it's possible to accurately judge our own characteristics without comparing ourselves to others? Defend your position.

5. Schachter and Singer's two-factor theory of emotion proposes that all emotions can be broken down into physiological arousal and psychological evaluation. One implication is that any emotional state can be plotted on a plane where one axis ranges from high to low arousal and the other axis ranges from positive to negative evaluation. Come up with a list of common emotions and try plotting them on this plane. Are there any emotions that don't seem to fit? Why?

6. Although Leon Festinger first came up with the idea of cognitive dissonance, it was his student Elliot Aronson who developed the theory and proposed practical applications for it. Can you think of some examples of how you could induce cognitive dissonance in people to promote positive social change? Describe the procedure you would use and how you would test its effectiveness.

7. Kelley and Thibaut propose in their interdependence theory that partners assess the costs and benefits of the relationship as they decide whether to stay or leave. From your own experience and observations, do you think interdependence theory accurately describes the dynamics of close relationships? Defend your position.

8. Kelley's covariation model and Jones's correspondent inference theory are both examples of normative models. Since people rarely behave as predicted by these models, why bother formulating them in the first place? Do you think that normative models have a place in psychology, or should psychologists restrict their studies to behavior as it actually occurs? Defend your position.

9. Senator William Proxmire awarded Ellen Berscheid the "Golden Fleece" award for wasting taxpayer dollars on a "pointless" study of romantic love. How do you respond to this?

10. With Newcomb's principles of interpersonal attraction (proximity and similarity) in mind, consider how

you formed some of your important personal relationships. Give some examples of how these principles work in everyday life.

11. According to the mere exposure effect, people prefer familiar items even when they have no recollection of having seen them before. How can something be familiar if we have no memory of it? What are the implications of the mere exposure effect on our understanding of the nature of conscious experience?

12. Give some real-life examples of how social facilitation either helps or hinders performance. Apply Zajonc's explanation of the effect in terms of arousal to each of your examples.

ON THE WEB

On YouTube, you can find a short documentary on the **Muzafer Sherif Robbers Cave experiment** that includes original footage from the study. You can also find a short documentary on the **Solomon Asch conformity experiment** that includes a replication of the original study. While there are several short documentaries online about the **Stanley Milgram obedience experiment**, you might also want to watch the movie *Experimenter* (Abeckaser & Almereyda, 2015), which goes into more depth about Milgram's personal life and his relationship with his mentor Solomon Asch. YouTube hosts original footage from the **Leon Festinger cognitive dissonance experiment**. Meanwhile, **Elliot Aronson** has a significant presence on YouTube, including both lectures and interviews. You can also find interviews with **Richard Nisbett** as well as a TED Talk by **Lee Ross**.

iStock.com/FatCamera

Developmental Psychology

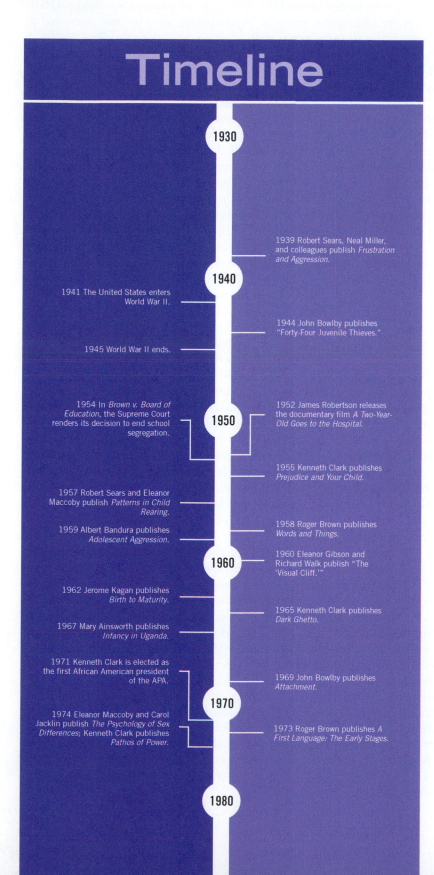

Timeline

1930

1939 Robert Sears, Neal Miller, and colleagues publish *Frustration and Aggression*.

1940

1941 The United States enters World War II.

1944 John Bowlby publishes "Forty-Four Juvenile Thieves."

1945 World War II ends.

1954 In *Brown v. Board of Education*, the Supreme Court renders its decision to end school segregation.

1952 James Robertson releases the documentary film *A Two-Year-Old Goes to the Hospital.*

1950

1955 Kenneth Clark publishes *Prejudice and Your Child*.

1957 Robert Sears and Eleanor Maccoby publish *Patterns in Child Rearing*.

1958 Roger Brown publishes *Words and Things*.

1959 Albert Bandura publishes *Adolescent Aggression*.

1960 Eleanor Gibson and Richard Walk publish "The 'Visual Cliff.'"

1960

1962 Jerome Kagan publishes *Birth to Maturity*.

1965 Kenneth Clark publishes *Dark Ghetto*.

1967 Mary Ainsworth publishes *Infancy in Uganda*.

1971 Kenneth Clark is elected as the first African American president of the APA.

1969 John Bowlby publishes *Attachment*.

1970

1974 Eleanor Maccoby and Carol Jacklin publish *The Psychology of Sex Differences*; Kenneth Clark publishes *Pathos of Power*.

1973 Roger Brown publishes *A First Language: The Early Stages*.

1980

Learning Objectives

After reading this chapter, you should be able to:

- Evaluate the contributions made by John Bowlby and Mary Ainsworth toward the development of attachment theory.

- Assess the evolution and application of social learning theory from Robert Sears to Eleanor Maccoby and Albert Bandura.

- Examine the shift in focus from learning to innate abilities in the work of Eleanor Gibson and Jerome Kagan.

- Discuss the contributions to the study of social development made by Roger Brown, Kenneth and Mamie Clark, and Martha Bernal.

Looking Back

Until the nineteenth century, children were often thought of as little adults, to the extent that their psychology was considered at all. However, as the twentieth century approached, psychologists began taking an interest in childhood development. The industrialized countries were just starting to institute universal education, and it soon became clear that not all children were benefitting from formal instruction. Although the impetus for child psychology was the need for better educational research, psychologists soon became interested in the process of development for its own sake as well.

Early twentieth-century developmental psychologists mainly focused their attention on problems in education. Wilhelm Wundt's student Lightner Witmer (Chapter 3) established the world's first psychology clinic in 1886 in Philadelphia for the purpose of helping children with learning or behavioral problems. Ten years later, John Dewey (Chapter 4) opened his Laboratory School at the University of Chicago. Around this same time, G. Stanley Hall (Chapter 4) established Clark University as a center for child research. Among his most notable students were Lewis Terman (Chapter 4), who studied gifted children, and Arnold Gesell (Chapter 4), who mapped out the maturational milestones of infancy and early childhood.

In the middle decades of the twentieth century, three schools dominated psychology in the United States: namely behaviorism, Gestalt psychology, and psychoanalysis. None of these schools focused on children, but a few practitioners in each made empirical or theoretical contributions to early childhood development. The behaviorist John Watson (Chapter 5) did some research on conditioned emotional responses in infants, and he wrote a controversial book on childrearing. Among the Gestalt psychologists, Kurt Koffka (Chapter 6) published *The Growth of the Mind*, which situated development within a Gestalt framework. Furthermore, Kurt Lewin (Chapter 6) spent the war years at the Iowa Child Welfare Research Station. Finally, Sigmund Freud (Chapter 7) developed what was probably the first theory of personality development in infancy and childhood. His psychosexual stage theory had considerable influence on thinking about development well into the 1950s.

The two dominant theories of cognitive development that frame research on that subject today were fleshed out during the decades before World War II. In France, Alfred Binet (Chapter 8) developed the first reliable intelligence test for children, with the aim of tailoring instruction to the children's ability. His test inspired Lewis Terman and his study of gifted children in the United States. Meanwhile in Europe, young Jean Piaget (Chapter 8) was administering intelligence tests at the model school that Binet had founded. However, Piaget was more interested in understanding why children gave incorrect solutions to problems that seemed quite easy. This curiosity led to a long career in the study of cognitive development, resulting in his influential stage model. At the same time, Lev Vygotsky (Chapter 9) in Russia was developing his theory of cognitive development through social interaction between the child and a caregiver. Today, Piaget and Vygotsky are the two guideposts for research on cognitive development.

In this chapter, we'll begin with an exploration of attachment theory, as propounded by John Bowlby, Mary Ainsworth, and others. Attachment theory had its roots in Freud's psychosexual theory of personality development, and it was also influenced by Harry Harlow's (Chapter 10) research on monkeys raised in isolation. Next, we'll turn to the social learning theory of Robert Sears, who tried to reconcile Freudian and behaviorist concepts in order to provide a more robust model of social and personality development in childhood. With the rise of the Cognitive Revolution, his colleagues Eleanor Maccoby and Albert Bandura developed cognitive versions of this theory, viewing children as active processors of information rather than as passive recipients of stimuli. Third, we'll look at the work of two psychologists who tested the relative contributions of nature and nurture to early development. Specifically, we'll consider Eleanor Gibson's studies on perceptual learning and the visual cliff as well as Jerome Kagan's investigations into the role of temperament in the developing personality. Finally, we consider the developing child within the social environment. We start with Roger Brown's studies of language development, and we then conclude with the work of minority researchers such as Martha Bernal and the husband-and-wife team of Kenneth and Mamie Clark, who studied the pernicious effects of racism on the developing sense of self.

Attachment

Psychologists have long recognized that the relationship between an infant and its primary caregiver is of key importance in social and personality development, and that it also has considerable impact even into adulthood. Psychoanalytic theorists traced the origins of psychological disorders in adulthood to early traumatic experiences, and Sigmund Freud's (Chapter 7) theory of psychosexual stages represents an attempt to understand the dynamics of the mother-child relationship and how they shape the developing personality. Freud also believed that the deep emotional bond between infant and mother arose through nursing—that is, through the provision of nutrition. However, Harry Harlow's (Chapter 10) studies of primate infants raised in isolation arose through contact comfort instead. Furthermore, many children were orphaned during World War II, providing psychologists with the opportunity to observe firsthand the devastating effects of severing the mother-infant bond. These were the circumstances that gave rise to attachment theory, a cornerstone of modern developmental psychology.

John Bowlby

John Bowlby grew up in a well-to-do family in Victorian England (van der Horst & van der Veer, 2010). Although his parents were distant and reserved, young John grew deeply attached to his nanny, and her departure when he was four years old left emotional scars. This painful experience also drove him toward a career in child psychiatry. Today, **John Bowlby** (1907–1990) is known as the *British psychologist who studied the impact of mother-child separation and proposed attachment theory to explain its effects.*

In 1944, Bowlby published the article "Forty-Four Juvenile Thieves" (van Rosmalen, van der Horst, & van der Veer, 2016). In this article, he compared case studies of youths at the London Child Guidance Clinic who were prone to stealing with an equal number of teens at the clinic who had no such criminal history. Almost all of the thieves had suffered extended separations from their mothers in early childhood. They were emotionally withdrawn, showed no concern for others, and did whatever they pleased. In contrast, few children in the control group had ever suffered any kind of maternal absence. At the time, it was generally assumed that as long as children's physical needs were met, they'd grow into healthy adults. But Bowlby suspected the mother-infant relationship was somehow a key aspect of social and personality development. The findings from the "Thieves" study supported his **maternal deprivation hypothesis**, which was *the proposal that prolonged separation from the mother in early childhood leads to pathological personality development in adolescence.*

At the end of World War II, Bowlby was hired as director of the children's department at the Tavistock Clinic, a noted mental health institution in London (Bretherton, 1992). At that time, the clinic was dominated by the Kleinian approach to psychoanalysis. Since Bowlby had trained under Melanie Klein (Chapter 7), he seemed the logical choice for the position. But even during his training, he'd fostered deep doubts about Klein's object-relations theory, which focused on children's internal conflicts between libidinal and aggressive drives instead of on their actual interactions with family members. Believing that social interactions played a far more significant role in the development of the child than did psychodynamic processes, he reoriented the clinic's therapeutic style from one that dealt only with children to one that also included family therapy as part of the treatment process.

In 1948, Bowlby initiated an extensive study with James Robertson (1911–1988) on the effects of maternal deprivation (Bretherton, 1992). Robertson was a social worker and psychoanalyst who'd worked at the Hampstead Nursery with Anna Freud (Chapter 7) during World War II, so he already had experience conducting detailed observations of children in institutions. This time, the project involved a study of children who'd experienced long periods of hospitalization during the first four years of their life. In those days, visitations were strictly limited, so these children spent most of their time isolated from their family members.

The researchers took a two-pronged approach (Ainsworth & Bowlby, 1991). First, they conducted a retrospective study in which they observed children who'd returned home after an extended stay in the hospital. They looked for signs of emotional or behavioral problems that could be attributed to the maternal separation, but this study yielded inconclusive data. Next, they ran a prospective study in which they observed children as they were admitted to the hospital, following them during their stay and subsequent return home. Robertson found that these children went through three stages after being separated from their mothers. First, they protested strongly and were clearly distressed, and this initial reaction then turned to a period of despair. If the separation lasted more than a week, the children became detached from their mother and showed no sign of affection upon her return. After they were reunited, many of the children rebuilt their relationship with their mother, albeit one tinged with a shade of distrust. Others remained emotionally aloof for years afterward.

Robertson was also skilled with the movie camera, and he filmed many of his encounters with these children during their hospitalization and after their return home (van Rosmalen et al., 2016). In 1952, he assembled these recordings into the documentary film *A Two-Year-Old Goes to the Hospital*. The heart-wrenching images of children crying in despair for their mothers moved both the general public and members of the medical profession alike, leading to reforms in hospital practices that allowed and even encouraged extended family visits for hospitalized children.

After Robertson left the Tavistock Clinic to advocate for hospital reform, Mary Ainsworth was hired to analyze the data from his study and write up the results (Bretherton & Main, 2000). Ainsworth had investigated mother-infant interactions at the University of Toronto, and she was deeply impressed by Robertson's findings. Both were already thinking about the mother-infant relationship in similar ways, and their interactions during this time helped Bowlby develop his mature version of attachment theory. Although Ainsworth only stayed three years at the clinic, she and Bowlby maintained a lifelong working relationship. Each was already thinking about the mother-infant bond in similar ways when they met, and although they worked independently for most of their careers, they provided each other with support and feedback on their projects. We'll consider Ainsworth's contributions in the next section, but for now let's focus on the theory of attachment that Bowlby constructed.

Attachment Theory

Trained in the psychoanalytic tradition, Bowlby had initially accepted the Freudian explanation for infant dependence on its mother (Ainsworth, 1992). According to Freud, a baby comes to love its mother because of the oral gratification it receives from breastfeeding. In fact, this is why Freud considered weaning to be such a traumatic event for the infant. Behaviorists also saw dependence as deriving from breastfeeding, although they viewed it as a reinforced habit instead. Furthermore, they saw dependence as an unhealthy habit that needed to be broken as the child matured.

As he delved into the ethological literature, Bowlby came to realize that the data did not support either explanation (Bretherton, 1992). One source of inspiration came from Harry Harlow's (Chapter 10) experiments raising monkeys with surrogate mothers. As you recall, infant monkeys clung to the warm, cloth-covered mechanical mother that provided comfort but no milk rather than to the cold, wire-mesh surrogate that provided milk but no comfort. Another source of inspiration came from a reading of Konrad Lorenz's (Chapter 10) studies of imprinting in geese. It seemed that imprinting created a special bond between goslings and their mother, such that they could keep safe by staying close to her. Both psychoanalytic and behaviorist theories pinpointed the origins of dependence in breastfeeding, but Lorenz had observed mother-infant bonds in bird species, which don't nurse their young. Bowlby wondered whether dependence grew not out of the infant's need for nutrition but rather its need for protection.

At this point, Bowlby read the literature on evolution (van der Horst & van der Veer, 2010). Human-like species such as *Homo erectus* arose from primate ancestors around 2 million years ago. Modern humans, or *Homo sapiens*, had arrived on the scene by 200,000 years ago. Until about 10,000 years ago, modern humans and their ancestors survived by hunting animals and gathering fruits and vegetables from the land around them. Bowlby referred to *the stable period of about 200,000 years during which humans lived as hunter-gatherers* as the **environment of evolutionary adaptedness**. That is to say, any innate behaviors that are uniquely human must have evolved during this time period, since the last 10,000 years of civilized life have been too short for natural selection to have had much effect.

When Bowlby imagined what life must have been like in the environment of evolutionary adaptedness, he understood that it had to have been very different from life in twentieth-century London (van der Horst & van der Veer, 2010). Early humans lived in the wild and had to face predators on a regular basis, so the only way for the prehistoric mother to keep her children safe was to keep them with her at all times, just as the mother goose does with her goslings. To survive, infants needed a strong fear of being separated their mothers, who provided security in a dangerous world.

In 1969, Bowlby published *Attachment*, the first of a three-volume series in which he laid out his mature theory of attachment (Ainsworth, 1992). In this work, he defines **attachment** as *the deep emotional bond that develops between an infant and its mother*. Importantly, he distinguished the concept of attachment from that of dependence. According to either psychoanalytic or behaviorist theory, dependence may be important in infancy and early childhood, but it has to be severed for healthy maturity into adulthood. In contrast, Bowlby saw attachment as forming the basis for all later relationships.

According to Bowlby, infants develop an **internal working model** through their interactions with their mother (Pallini & Barcaccia, 2014). This is *an infant's mental framework for understanding how relationships work based on interactions with caregivers*. If the mother reliably meets the needs of the child, it learns that people in general can be trusted. But if the mother is absent or inattentive, the child learns instead that people are unreliable relationship partners. Thus, Bowlby distinguished two attachment styles, secure and insecure.

In sum, **attachment theory** is the proposal that the kind of caregiver-infant bond that develops in the first year has significant consequences for later social, emotional, and personality development (van Rosmalen et al., 2016). Infants who bond securely with their mothers grow up to lead happy lives with fulfilling relationships. But infants who cannot do

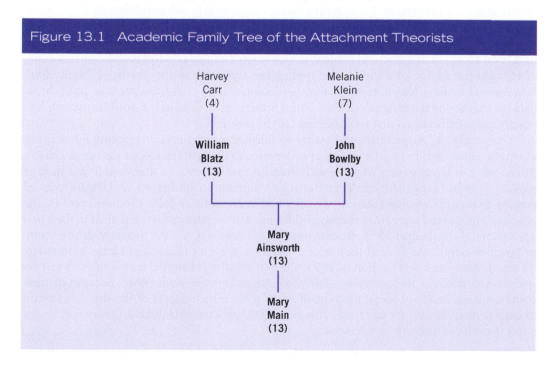

Figure 13.1   Academic Family Tree of the Attachment Theorists

so—for whatever reason—will likely end up as maladjusted adults. Attachment theory has had a significant impact on developmental psychology since the last half of the twentieth century. It also has ramifications for clinical psychology. Grounded in evolutionary theory and supported by a large number of observational studies, attachment theory makes predictable hypotheses that have inspired research in personality development for over fifty years. In the career-long collaboration between John Bowlby and Mary Ainsworth, it was he who provided the theoretical framework and she who conducted the first tests of attachment (Figure 13.1). This is the story we turn to next.

Mary Ainsworth

Attachment theory was the joint product of John Bowlby and Mary Ainsworth. Although they lived on opposite sides of the Atlantic, their career-long collaboration was remarkably fruitful, leading to one of the most important and well-supported theories of social development. Today, **Mary Ainsworth** (1913–1999) is noted as the *Canadian-American psychologist who developed the Strange Situation, a laboratory procedure for testing attachment style.*

Ainsworth was born in Ohio but grew up in Toronto (van Rosmalen et al., 2016). During the 1930s, she earned her bachelor's, master's, and doctorate degrees at the University of Toronto. There, she worked closely with her mentor **William Blatz** (1895–1964), a *Canadian developmental psychologist noted for his security theory, which was a precursor to attachment theory.* She then joined the Toronto faculty, where she stayed until 1950. Thus, Ainsworth collaborated with Blatz for two decades, conducting studies to test security theory.

In a nutshell, **security theory** is the proposal that infants need to develop a secure dependence upon their caregivers in order to develop the coping skills necessary for navigating a complex adult world (Ainsworth & Bowlby, 1991). At first, according to the theory, children develop an immature dependence on their parents, but they become more independent, or self-reliant, as they grow. However, healthy adult relationships also require a mature dependence, that is, a sense that others can be trusted while maintaining confidence in one's own ability to cope. These skills are developed in childhood during interactions with parents and other family members.

An important concept in security theory is the notion of a **secure base** (Bretherton & Main, 2000). This is *the conceptualization of the caregiver's role as providing a safe zone from which the child can explore the world and to which it can retreat when frightened.* If mothers serve as a secure base, then their children will grow into maturely dependent adults. However, if they're absent or inattentive, their children will become overly independent and aloof or else remain immaturely dependent on others as adults.

In 1950, Mary Ainsworth followed her husband Leonard to London, England, where he'd been accepted as a doctoral student at University College London (van Rosmalen et al., 2016). On the advice of a friend, she applied for a position at the Tavistock Clinic. John Bowlby was looking for an experimental psychologist who could analyze and publish the data on mother-infant separations that James Robertson had collected, and Ainsworth had exactly the qualifications that were needed for the position.

From early on, Ainsworth and Bowlby established a collaborative working relationship as equals, since each brought a wealth of experience to the task (van Rosmalen et al., 2016). Ainsworth had already been working with Blatz for two decades on studies of infant-mother relationships and how these affect emotional development in adulthood, and she introduced Bowlby to security theory. Likewise, Bowlby had been working for a similar period on the problem of maternal separation in early childhood. Ainsworth's influence is clear in their first joint paper, published in 1954. At that time, *attachment* was not yet a clearly defined term in Bowlby's mind, and instead they refer to Blatz's concept of *secure dependency relationship.* Although Ainsworth left London in 1953, she and Bowlby continued their collaboration via correspondence and frequent trans-Atlantic voyages to meet each other. Because of their continuous exchange of ideas, it's difficult to pinpoint which aspect of the theory to credit to each person. Rather, it's safe to say that from 1950 onward, attachment theory was a joint effort between Ainsworth and Bowlby.

Attachment Styles

Ainsworth's husband was offered a research position in Uganda when he finished his doctorate, and once again she gave up her job to follow him (Ainsworth & Bowlby, 1991). However, she was already determined to undertake an observational study to explore the formation of mother-infant bonds and what happens when they're disrupted. With funding from a research grant, Ainsworth located twenty-eight young mothers living in villages near Kampala, the capital, who were willing to take part. Accompanied by an interpreter, she visited these mother-infant pairs in their own homes every two weeks over a nine-month period. Her observations failed to support the Freudian view of oral-phase infants as passive and narcissistic. Instead, these babies were active participants in the relationship, using the mother as a secure base for exploring their environment and returning to her when they were hurt or frightened. They also actively sought out the breast and negotiated their feeding with their mother.

Ainsworth thought she discerned two types of attachment style in these infants, secure and insecure (Ainsworth & Bowlby, 1991). On the one hand, the securely attached babies were distressed when their mother left them alone, but they cheerfully greeted her upon her return. On the other hand, the insecurely attached babies fussed a lot, whether their mother was present or absent. She also noticed that the mothers of insecurely attached infants were less attentive to their babies' needs. It was clear to Ainsworth that her Uganda data fit well with both Blatz's security theory and Bowlby's attachment theory, but she didn't publish these findings until her 1967 book, *Infancy in Uganda*.

After two years in Uganda, Ainsworth followed her husband once again to a new job, this time in Baltimore (van Rosmalen et al., 2016). In 1955, she was offered a position as a clinical psychologist at Johns Hopkins. Because of her heavy clinical duties, she set aside her Uganda data for several years. During the same trip to the United States when Bowlby visited Harry Harlow in Wisconsin, he also met with Ainsworth in Baltimore. She showed him the Uganda data, and he was pleased to see how well her observations of secure and insecure attachment meshed with his theory. He invited her to attend the next meeting of the Tavistock Study Group, where she presented these data to a group of eminent developmental psychologists, including Harlow. This was followed by a jointly authored article by Ainsworth and Bowlby, which included the first use of the term *attachment* in its currently understood sense.

In the early 1960s, Ainsworth secured funding for another project exploring the development of attachment during the infant's first year (Bretherton & Main, 2000). The so-called Baltimore Study was perhaps the most ambitious project ever undertaken in developmental psychology at that point. Using pediatrician referrals, Ainsworth located twenty-six expectant mothers who agreed to participate in the year-long study. Every three weeks, a research assistant would make a four-hour visit to the home of the mother and infant, paying particular attention to the infants' attachment behaviors and their mother's responses. Thus, Ainsworth and her team could observe the development of attachment over the course of a year.

These in-home observations led Ainsworth (1979) to discern two different types of insecure attachment in addition to the secure attachment that had been observed in the Uganda study. Specifically, these three attachment styles had the following characteristics:

- **Secure attachment** is *a mother-infant bond in which the baby is distressed by its mother's departure but soothed by her return.* In fact, securely attached infants rarely showed signs of distress at home when their mothers left them briefly. However, if there was anything unusual about the situation, they usually fussed at such separations. Most of the infants in the Uganda and Baltimore studies displayed secure attachment.

- **Avoidant attachment** is *a mother-infant bond in which the baby isn't distressed by its mother's departure and shows little interest in her return.* A striking feature of this attachment style was that all of these mothers displayed an aversion to bodily contact, and so they rarely held their babies. Apparently, these infants had to find ways to soothe themselves since they couldn't rely on their mothers for comfort. This attachment style is sometimes called *anxious-avoidant* in the literature.

- **Anxious attachment** is a *mother-infant bond in which the baby is distressed by its mother's departure but isn't soothed by her return.* In general, these mothers were unreliable in meeting their baby's needs. Apparently, these infants learned that they had to be insistent to get their mother's attention. This attachment style is sometimes called *anxious-ambivalent* in the literature.

Strange Situation

The longitudinal in-home portion of the study was remarkable for the amount and detail of the data it produced (Bretherton, 1992). However, Ainsworth followed this up with a laboratory study to corroborate the observations made in the children's homes. At one of the Tavistock meetings, Harry Harlow reminded her that the home is usually a low-stress environment. To really test attachment styles, Ainsworth would have to observe infant reactions in high-stress settings. This led her to create the **Strange Situation** paradigm, which is a *laboratory procedure designed to test an infant's attachment style in which the mother briefly leaves her child alone in an unfamiliar room.*

The Strange Situation proved to be an effective method of assessing attachment styles (Ainsworth, 1979). That is to say, infants who'd been labeled secure, avoidant, or anxious during the in-home observations behaved similarly in the laboratory. Secure infants fussed at their mother's departure but were soothed by her return. Avoidant infants showed little response to either their mother's departure or her return. And the anxious infants fussed when their mother left and continued to fuss when she came back. Thus, the Strange Situation became a useful diagnostic for determining an infant's attachment style in the laboratory without the need for long-term observations at home.

Based on her observations of mother-infant interactions, Ainsworth (1979) believed that the different attachment styles develop due to differences in **maternal sensitivity**, or *the degree to which the mother is attentive and responsive to her infant's needs.* Infants whose mothers pick them up when they cry and feed them on demand grow into securely attached children who demonstrate self-confidence and effective social skills. In terms of Bowlby's internal working model, these children learn to trust their mothers, and as a result they're trusting in other relationships as well. However, when mothers are inattentive or unresponsive, their infants develop insecure attachments. That is, they learn that mother isn't to be relied on to meet their needs. Some of these children learn to self-soothe, in which case they develop avoidant attachment, and others learn that they have to constantly fuss to get their mother's attention, in which case they develop anxious attachment. It's important to note, however, that Ainsworth wasn't blaming the mother for insecure attachment, as she recognized that situational factors like postpartum depression, poverty, and family strife can lead to low maternal sensitivity even though the mother would like to do more for her child.

An important aspect of Bowlby's attachment theory is that the infant-mother bond serves as the model for all future relationships, even into adulthood (Ainsworth & Bowlby, 1991). Much of the research on the effects of attachment style in later life has been conducted by Ainsworth's student **Mary Main** (born 1943). She is an *American developmental psychologist who has constructed methods for assessing attachment style during the early school years, adolescence, and in adulthood.* Her Adult Attachment Interview (AAI) has proven useful in clinical studies, and she's found a greater incidence of psychological and relationship problems in insecurely attached adults. Furthermore, she's used the AAI to test cross-generational transmission of attachment styles, demonstrating that parents tend to pass their own attachment style on to their children.

Table 13.1 Attachment Styles

Attachment Style	Description	Explanation
Secure attachment	Baby is distressed by mother's departure but soothed by her return	Healthy attachment; baby has learned to use mother as a secure base from which to explore the world
Avoidant attachment	Baby isn't distressed by mother's departure and shows little interest in her return	Suggests lack of maternal sensitivity; baby has learned to self-soothe
Anxious attachment	Baby is distressed by mother's departure but isn't soothed by her return	Suggests lack of maternal sensitivity; baby has learned that mother's attention can only be garnered through extreme demands
Disorganized attachment	Baby shows inconsistent pattern of seeking out and retreating from mother	Suggests abuse; baby is dependent on mother but has learned it cannot use her as a secure base

Main (1996) is also known for discovering a fourth attachment style, which she calls *disorganized*. Working with diverse samples of mother-infant pairs, she found that some babies displayed behaviors that couldn't be accounted for by the other three attachment styles. For example, they first approached their mother on her return but then turned away. Others assumed a trance-like posture, rocked on their hands and knees, or stood with their face pressed against the wall. Main has speculated that a disorganized attachment style is a sign of abuse. When children learn to fear their parents, she maintains, they can no longer use them as a secure base, and so they experience a collapse of attachment behaviors. That is to say, they're dependent on their parents, but they're also afraid of them.

Mary Ainsworth has left an important legacy for developmental psychology. Through her meticulous observations of mother-infant interactions in Uganda and in Baltimore, she was able to discern three different attachment styles. Furthermore, she observed the dynamics of attachment formation in real time, leading her to the conclusion that maternal sensitivity was the driving force behind attachment style. In addition, her observations of securely attached infants led her to conclusions that contradicted the received wisdom of the behaviorist era. She found that babies grow into confident, self-reliant children and young adults if their mothers pick them up when they cry and feed them on demand. Such coddling didn't lead to clinginess or neediness, as the behaviorists had predicted. On the contrary, it was when mothers were insensitive to their infants' needs or forced them into a rigid schedule that the children became overly demanding. Although Ainsworth is best known for the development of the Strange Situation, it was in fact her decades of careful observations in naturalistic settings that provided the bulk of evidence supporting attachment theory (Table 13.1).

Social Learning

Behavioral learning theories were fairly robust at explaining the actions of rats and pigeons in the laboratory, and it was taken on faith that these principles would apply just as well to humans. However, child psychologists soon understood that more powerful mechanisms than reinforcement were needed to explain the rapid socialization of children during their first years. Thus, there were many attempts to expand behavioral learning theories to incorporate interpersonal and cultural processes. Many versions of social learning theory were proposed during the years following World War II, but in this section we'll focus on three pioneers: Robert Sears, Eleanor Maccoby, and Albert Bandura.

Photo 13.1
Robert Sears

Robert Sears

Robert Sears did his undergraduate work at Stanford, where his father was on the faculty ("American Psychological Foundation," 1981). There, he studied with Lewis Terman (Chapter 4), who suggested he pursue his doctorate degree with Clark Hull (Chapter 5) at Yale. Sears was drawn to Hull's form of neo-behaviorism, and he did his dissertation on conditioned reflexes in goldfish. But through a long and varied career, **Robert Sears** (1908–1989) became known as an *American developmental psychologist who was a pioneer in social learning theory.*

Sears's first academic position was at the University of Illinois, where he was asked to teach a course on personality, a subject quite unfamiliar to him ("American Psychological Foundation," 1981). As he delved into Freudian psychodynamics, he was struck by the parallels with Hullian learning theory. For example, both theories explained behavior in terms of drives, and Freud's pleasure principle was consistent with the concept of reinforcement. Psychoanalytic theory was often criticized for being untestable, but if its ideas could be recast in behaviorist terms, it could be tested after all. This was the idea Sears brought with him when he was invited back to Yale as a member of its faculty.

At Yale, Sears joined a group of interdisciplinary scholars, including both Hull and his student Neal Miller (Chapter 5), who sought a behaviorist reinterpretation of Freudian concepts (Grusec, 1992). Their first project looked at the relationship between frustration and aggression. According to Freudian theory, aggression arises as a way of dealing with frustration, such that by committing violent acts we achieve a catharsis or release from our pent-up emotions. The team reasoned that young children must experience a great deal of frustration as they learn to curb their impulses or else redirect them into socially approved channels. In particular, the researchers were interested in studying the ways in which children learn to deal with frustration by observing the actions of their parents.

This was the birth of **social learning theory**, which was the proposal that children learn strategies for dealing with the world by copying the behaviors of their parents (Grusec, 1992). The 1939 book *Frustration and Aggression*, coauthored by Sears, Miller, and others, outlined the social learning approach to development. Extending beyond frustration and aggression, Sears and his colleagues at Yale proposed that social behaviors and personality traits are also acquired through social learning.

In 1942, Sears accepted the directorship of the Iowa Child Welfare Research Station (Cronbach, Hastorf, Hilgard, & Maccoby, 1990). Kurt Lewin (Chapter 6) was there at that time. Although the men differed significantly in their theoretical outlooks—Sears the neo-behaviorist and Lewin the Gestalt psychologist—Lewin nevertheless had an influence on Sears, particularly in terms of the execution of large-scale observational studies. Until that time, Sears had had little experience working with children, but once again he soon came up to speed on the literature and made important new contributions.

In particular, Sears was interested in the ways that family dynamics socialize children, molding their social skills and shaping their personality (Grusec, 1992). Sears applied social learning theory to study three areas of development that were key aspects of psychodynamic theory: namely aggression, dependency, and identification. The studies on aggression, of course, were an extension of his work at Yale. And by dependency he was referring to the emotional bonds between mother and infant, which would later be known as attachment. Finally, identification was a Freudian concept that referred to the development of personality features such as morality and sex roles, which were presumed to be patterned on the behaviors of the same-sex parent. Sears believed that this socialization process was driven forward by parents exerting pressures on their children to conform to their models of behavior.

Trained in the techniques of Lewinian large-scale observational studies, Sears brought these skills with him when he was called to Harvard in 1949 (Grusec, 1992). There, Sears organized a series of studies aimed at assessing how parenting practices influence children's social development. Among those who collaborated with Sears on this massive research project was Eleanor Maccoby, whom we'll meet shortly. Sears led the team that used projective techniques such as guided doll play to assess children's learning of parental models, while Maccoby was in charge of the parental interviews. In the end, the data from the child studies yielded few useful results, but the interviews with the parents were more productive. The culmination of this project was the 1957 book *Patterns of Child Rearing*, which Sears coauthored with Maccoby. However, even before the data collection was complete, Sears had returned home to Stanford, and the two collaborated on the manuscript via mail.

When Lewis Terman died in 1956, Sears took over his longitudinal study of gifted children, who by that time were adults (Sears, 1977). One of the participants in this study was **Lee Cronbach** (1916–2001), who went on to become a well-known *American educational psychologist noted for his contributions to psychological testing and measurement*. In your statistics classes, you may have come across the term **Cronbach's alpha**, which is *a statistical technique for estimating the reliability of a psychometric test*. Most of his work is highly mathematical and beyond the scope of this book. In 1964, Cronbach joined the faculty at Stanford, and he collaborated with Sears on follow-up studies of Terman's gifted group as they matured into middle age.

Although Robert Sears was one of the leaders of developmental psychology during the height of his career, his influence waned in the last decades of the twentieth century (Grusec, 1992). In particular, his behaviorist version of social learning theory didn't fare well as the Cognitive Revolution swept through psychology. Nevertheless, his influence can still be felt in the work of those in the next generation, whom he mentored and inspired. In the following sections, we'll meet two of his Stanford colleagues who built on Sears's social learning theory—Eleanor Maccoby, most noted for her work on gender development in childhood, and Albert Bandura, whose famous Bobo doll experiments are standard fare in every introductory psychology course.

Eleanor Maccoby

After World War II, Robert Sears's social learning theory dominated child psychology in the United States. However, the field saw a shift from a behaviorist to a cognitive perspective over the next few decades. One of the leaders of the Cognitive Revolution within the field of developmental psychology was his protégée **Eleanor Maccoby** (1917–2018), the *American developmental psychologist best known for her work on sex differences, gender identity, and parent-child relationships*.

Eleanor Maccoby completed her undergraduate degree at the University of Washington in Seattle with Edwin Guthrie (Chapter 5; "Eleanor Emmons Maccoby," 1996). She married Nathan Maccoby, a fellow psychology student, and after graduation the couple went to work for the government in Washington, DC. They found jobs doing public opinion research with **Rensis Likert** (1903–1981; pronounced *LICK-urt*), the *American social psychologist best known for inventing the five-point rating scale that now bears his name*. At the Division of Program Surveys, the Maccobys worked mainly with colleagues who'd been influenced by Kurt Lewin (Chapter 6), and they learned that psychology entailed far more than Guthrie's contiguity theory.

After World War II was over, Likert moved his operation to the University of Michigan, and the Maccobys followed him there ("Eleanor E. Maccoby," 1989). While continuing their work with Likert, they also began their doctoral studies. Nathan graduated a year before Eleanor, and she followed him to his first academic position at Boston University. She had only the experiments for her dissertation left to complete, and B. F. Skinner at Harvard University graciously offered the use of his lab. While Maccoby was working in the Skinner lab, she got to know Jerome Bruner, who offered her a teaching position in the Department of Social Relations. Thus, a planned year at Harvard turned into nine.

Robert Sears arrived at Harvard the same year as Maccoby. After she'd completed her Ph.D., he offered her a position in his laboratory (Maccoby, 1989). This was when Sears was conducting his large-scale study on socialization processes in children. Because of his familiarity with psychodynamic theory, Sears led the portion of the study that used projective tests during doll play to assess children's identification with their parents. But he also needed someone to lead the interviews with the parents. Because of her extensive work in survey research with Likert, Maccoby had excellent credentials for the position. Although the child portion of the study yielded few useful data, the parental interviews provided much richer content, which Sears and Maccoby eventually developed into their jointly authored 1957 book *Patterns in Child Rearing*. After its publication, Sears invited the Maccobys to spend a year at Stanford as visiting professors. At the end of that visiting year, they were both offered full-time positions, Eleanor in the psychology department and Nathan in communications.

When she first arrived at Stanford, Eleanor Maccoby still thought of development in terms of social learning theory (Maccoby, 1989). But after Jean Piaget's works became available in English during the 1960s, she experienced a gradual shift in her thinking toward a more cognitive approach. Furthermore, by this time the Cognitive Revolution was in full swing, and psychologists now viewed people—including young children—as active processors of information rather than as passive receivers of stimuli.

During the early 1970s, Maccoby collaborated with Carol Jacklin (1939–2011) on a series of gender-related studies (Marecek & Thorne, 2012). In the 1974 book *The Psychology of Sex Differences*, Maccoby and Jacklin surveyed the existing literature on sex differences, including a large number of studies that had remained unpublished because they'd found no differences. Maccoby and Jacklin came to the conclusion that most of the widely believed differences between the sexes had little empirical support. That is to say, men and women are largely the same when it comes to psychological variables such as personality traits and cognitive abilities. This view fit well with emerging feminist attitudes of the time, and as such it was praised by advocates of gender equality in the political and economic realms.

At the same time, *The Psychology of Sex Differences* generated considerable controversy within psychology because it challenged widely held assumptions (Maccoby, 1990). First, Maccoby and Jacklin disputed the behaviorist-oriented assumptions of social learning theory. They argued that gender identity isn't simply the result of socialization processes that shape children's behaviors according to societal expectations. Instead, they argued, children play an important role in selecting the models they integrate into themselves. Second, they criticized both empiricist and nativist models of development, insisting instead on an interactionist perspective that sees innate factors working together with social influences in the environment to shape the personality and gender identity of the individual.

Eleanor Maccoby's shift in thinking from a behaviorist to a cognitive approach to studying development reflects the larger spirit of the times in which she worked. Although she was steeped in the contiguity theory of Edwin Guthrie and the social learning theory of Robert Sears, her mature works reflect modern thinking in the field, which views development as emerging from the interaction of innate characteristics and social influences. Eleanor Maccoby changed our view of children as passive organisms shaped by the actions of their parents to one that sees them as active participants in the processes of personality formation and gender identity.

Albert Bandura

Albert Bandura (born 1925) was born on a pioneer farm in rural Alberta, Canada (Bandura, 2007). During the summer before college, he joined a motley work crew maintaining the Alaska Highway, many of whom were fleeing creditors, ex-wives, or the law. Life in this gambling and drinking culture of the Canadian frontier gave him unique insights into the psychopathologies that afflict ordinary people. Although he's spent much of his later career in clinical psychology, early on Bandura developed a reputation as the *Canadian-American psychologist best known for his Bobo doll experiments exploring the social learning of aggression in young children*.

Bandura did his doctoral degree at the University of Iowa, attracted there by the work of Kenneth Spence (Bandura, 2007). As a student of Clark Hull, Spence believed that drive reduction was the most important motivator of learning. However, it was another one of Hull's students who had a greater impact on the thinking of young Dr. Bandura. Robert

Sears, then the chair of the psychology department at Stanford, hired the recent graduate in 1953, and there Bandura has remained to the present day.

Bandura's early research fit within the tradition of Sears's social learning theory (Grusec, 1992). Working with his first graduate student, Richard Walters, Bandura embarked on an extensive research program that led to several publications, including the book *Adolescent Aggression* in 1959. He understood that impoverished environments can be breeding grounds for hostile behavior, so to eliminate that factor he sought out hyper-aggressive boys from upper-middle-class neighborhoods where violence was rare. Bandura and Walters interviewed these boys and found out that they'd internalized aggressive acts they'd observed in their parents. Furthermore, the results of projective tests suggested that the boys engaged in violent behaviors in response to parental rejection or neglect.

Sears viewed social learning as an identification process whereby the child internalizes behavioral patterns of the parent (Grusec, 1992). By the early 1960s, however, Bandura was thinking of social learning instead as a process of modeling. In other words, the adult demonstrates—or models—behaviors that the child observes, remembers, and can choose to re-enact. Challenging the behaviorist establishment, he argued that modeling was a kind of learning that needed no reinforcement. Furthermore, he maintained that modeling was a far more important learning mechanism than reinforcement, at least in humans.

With this view of social learning as modeling, Bandura conducted the Bobo doll experiments he's famous for today (Bandura, Ross, & Ross, 1961). He recruited four-year-olds and brought them one at a time into a specially devised playroom furnished with various toys, including a Bobo doll. The child and an adult experimenter played for a while with Tinkertoys, but then the adult got up and acted aggressively toward the Bobo doll. He punched the doll in the nose, struck it with a mallet, pushed it to the floor and sat on it, and then tossed it in the air and kicked it about the room. Afterward, the researchers monitored the children for any aggressive behavior toward the doll. As expected, those who'd seen the adult's violent display engaged in more hostile acts than did those who hadn't witnessed the adult's aggression.

In a follow-up study, children saw the adult aggress against the Bobo doll and then get either praised or scolded for that aggression (Bandura, Ross, & Ross, 1963). As expected, many of those who saw the adult get praised imitated the aggression afterward. In contrast, few of those who saw the adult get scolded did so. This result contradicted a tenet of operant conditioning, which held that the organism itself had to experience the consequences to learn the outcomes of its behaviors. But in this case, the children had learned whether to repeat a behavior or not by observing the consequences the adult experienced. At least for humans, modeling clearly was a more powerful mechanism for learning than reinforcement.

Based on the results of these and other studies, Bandura became concerned with the effect that increasing levels of violence in the media might have on young people (Bandura, 2007). He was invited to join a government commission to look into the matter. But he soon learned that the membership was stacked in favor of the broadcast industry, which also engaged in a public slur campaign against him. After this unpleasant experience, Bandura explored other topics for research.

From the late 1960s, Bandura turned his attention to clinical psychology (Bandura, 2007). Working with a group of adults who suffered from severe snake phobia, he developed a technique called guided mastery to help them cope with their anxiety. These people had suffered from recurring nightmares of snakes for years, but with the help of guided mastery they were able to overcome their fear of snakes and in some cases even develop a positive attitude toward them. One woman even reported a dream in which a friendly snake helped her wash the dishes! He then conducted follow-up studies with patients suffering from agoraphobia, which is *the fear of leaving home or going into public places*. Although other forms of psychotherapy had had little success with this condition, guided mastery helped these people overcome their fears. Guided mastery, then, can be viewed as an early version of modern cognitive therapy.

Photo 13.2
Albert Bandura

In addition, patients who'd gone through guided mastery for phobia reported that their lives had changed in other ways too (Bandura, 2007). Having successfully overcome their worst fears, they felt more confident in other aspects of their lives as well. Bandura saw that the core of the guided mastery technique was the building of what he called **self-efficacy**, which is *a set of beliefs about one's ability to cope with particular challenges*. Self-efficacy then guides people's behavior, in that they tend to do well when self-efficacy is high, but they perform poorly or avoid the task altogether when it's low. Bandura even linked the concept of self-efficacy with attachment. Securely attached children have high self-efficacy, he said, and as they go through life they face challenges with confidence and generally succeed at the tasks they set for themselves. Conversely, insecurely attached children grow into adults with low levels of self-efficacy and suffer from their lack of confidence and anxiety when they feel when challenged.

Originally, Bandura referred to modeling as a form of social learning (Bandura, 1989). By the 1980s, however, it became clear to him that the modeling he'd demonstrated in the Bobo doll experiments and employed in guided mastery therapy was significantly different from traditional social learning theory. Sears's version of social learning was an amalgam of Freudian psychodynamics and Hullian neo-behaviorism, with the child viewed as the passive recipient of parental influences. But in Bandura's view, people—including children—are active participants in the learning experience. They also seek to actively influence their social environments rather than being passively shaped by them. Thus, he rejected social learning theory and proposed **social cognitive theory** in its place. This is *the proposal that people construct their own lives by choosing for themselves which models to emulate and which to reject.* Cognitive processes such as attention, memory, and decision making are at the core of the theory, and its cornerstone is self-efficacy. Those who are high in self-efficacy wisely choose the models that will benefit them, whereas those who are low in self-efficacy may get stuck in suboptimal patterns of behavior or select inappropriate models.

By focusing on the cognitive aspects of social learning, Bandura broke free of the behaviorist constraints that bound American psychology during the middle decades of the twentieth century (Grusec, 1992). In some respects, Bandura's social cognitive theory is a product of the Cognitive Revolution. Yet Bandura talked about people as agents who actively constructed their lives, an idea outside the comfort zone of many cognitive psychologists. In some respects, Bandura's ideas align with those of Jean Piaget, who saw children as "little scientists" trying to make sense of their world. However, there are no stages in social cognitive theory. Rather, the theory views modeling as a general learning mechanism applicable to all stages of life (Figure 13.2). It remains to be seen whether future generations of psychologists can successfully integrate Bandura's social cognitive theory with the learning theories of other greats in developmental psychology such as Piaget and Vygotsky.

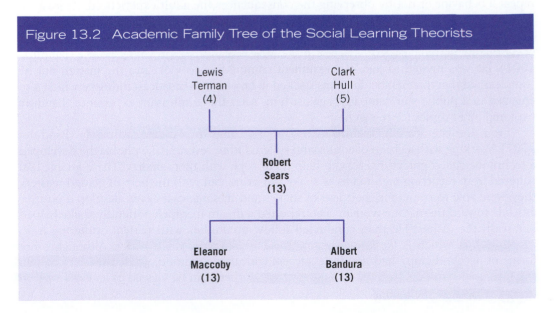

Figure 13.2 Academic Family Tree of the Social Learning Theorists

Nature and Nurture

Both attachment theory and social learning theory view early childhood experiences as the key drivers of social and personality development, and they give little consideration to the possibility that innate characteristics of the infant might also play a role. To a large extent, this bias toward nurture over nature was due to the long tradition of empiricism in British philosophy in general and to the dominance of behaviorism in North American in particular. This section introduces two developmental psychologists whose research careers spanned the Cognitive Revolution. Eleanor Gibson and Jerome Kagan were interested in quite different aspects of development. However, what they have in common is a transition from an emphasis on learning early in their careers to one on innate abilities or characteristics in their later research. Thus, the research programs of these two developmental psychologists reflect the greater willingness of American psychologists to consider innate factors in development during the last decades of the twentieth century.

Eleanor Gibson

Eleanor Jack was an undergraduate at Smith College when she met James Gibson (Gibson, 1980). Caught in a downpour after a garden party, he offered her a ride home. The next day, she enrolled in his experimental psychology course. By the end of the semester, she was in love with experimental psychology—and with the instructor. Remaining at Smith for her master's degree, she worked as James Gibson's research assistant. She also married him during that time, and after graduation she stayed on as an instructor.

Photo 13.3
Eleanor Gibson

Eleanor and James Gibson collaborated only occasionally, but there are clear parallels in their thinking. Both were interested in perception, but whereas James's research was highly theoretical, Eleanor turned her attention to perceptual learning, and particularly the question of which processes are innate and which are acquired through experience. Today, **Eleanor Gibson** (1910–2002) is known as the *American developmental psychologist who used the visual cliff procedure to test depth perception in human infants.*

In 1935, Gibson entered Yale University to do her Ph.D. (Gibson, 1980). She wanted to work on primates with Robert Yerkes, but he told her: "I have no women in my laboratory" (p. 246). So she sought out Clark Hull instead, to whom she proposed a set of experiments on verbal learning that fit within his theoretical system. By asking participants to learn arbitrary labels for random visual shapes, she explored the processes of generalization and discrimination. These studies then formed the basis for her career-long interest in perceptual learning.

After earning her Ph.D. in 1938, Gibson returned to Smith as an assistant professor (Caudle, 2003). When the United States entered World War II, she gave up that position to follow her husband to California, where he did research for the military. After the war, they returned to Smith, but James Gibson had found his calling in visual perception and yearned to work at a major research university. When he was offered a position at Cornell, Eleanor Gibson once again gave up her job to follow her husband. Cornell had nepotism rules that prohibited the hiring of spouses, but the university did allow her to use its research facilities. For the next sixteen years, she worked as an unpaid research assistant. Instead of protesting the injustice, she made the best of the situation and pursued a research program that eventually made her one of the most respected developmental psychologists of her time.

Because she wasn't a member of the faculty, Eleanor Gibson had to collaborate with other Cornell researchers (Gibson, 1980). She first worked with Howard Liddell at his "Behavior Farm," where he did research on sheep and goats. Liddell was trying to develop an animal model of neurosis by giving sheep electric shocks. According to Gibson, the animals were obviously perturbed by the shocks, but she saw no signs of neurosis in them. Meanwhile, she availed herself of the Behavior Farm's breeding population of goats to study mother-infant bonding. One day, she was attending to the birth of a baby goat when she discovered the mother was having twins. Because baby goats can walk from birth and Gibson didn't want the kid to get away, she set it on a small pedestal so she could deliver its sibling. The kid froze on the spot, and this incident later got Gibson thinking that depth perception in these animals had to be innate rather than learned. Eventually, this train of thought led to her famous experiments with the visual cliff.

Meanwhile, Eleanor Gibson also collaborated with her husband on a series of Air Force–funded experiments involving the perceptual learning of distance judgments (Caudle, 2003). In this case, husband and wife were a true research team, with each bringing his or her strengths to the project. On the one hand, James Gibson had a dynamic theory of visual perception that worked well in natural environments such as the open field in which they did their tests. On the other hand, Eleanor Gibson's thinking on perceptual learning was rapidly evolving, and by the end of the three-year project, she had a clear conception of what perceptual learning entailed. The behaviorists explained visual discrimination in terms of making new associations among stimuli, and the Gestalt psychologists viewed perception as the construction of a meaningful visual configuration from an impoverished sensory input. However, James Gibson had insisted that in the real world the sensory input was rich in information so there was no need for reconstruction.

Nevertheless, Eleanor Gibson maintained, we need to learn which details in the input are important and which can be ignored (Caudle, 2003). Thus, she redefined **perceptual learning** as *the process of becoming more sensitive to the meaningful aspects of a visual scene.* Take for example an X-ray photograph. You have no idea how to interpret the image, but the radiologist immediately spots the hairline bone fracture because of her years reading these images. In simple terms, we have to learn what to look for.

Eleanor Gibson also believed that perceptual learning was unique in that it required no reinforcement for it to occur (Gibson & Gibson, 1955; Pick, 1992). In one of the few papers she published with her husband, she tested children and adults on what became known as the scribble task. First, participants saw a spiral image and then were asked to pick out similar items from a series. They were never rewarded for correct responses or punished for incorrect answers. In fact, they were given no feedback at all. At first, performance was poor, but with practice the participants became quite skilled at identifying similar scribbles. These findings simply couldn't be explained in terms of standard behaviorist theories. In the scribble task, learning had occurred without drive reduction, in contrast with Hull's theory. Nor had there been any reinforcement through feedback, according to the learning theories of Thorndike or Skinner. And Guthrie's contiguity theory was irrelevant in this case. Only Tolman's idea of latent learning seemed close to Eleanor Gibson's concept of perceptual learning, as all that was needed was experience for a change in behavior to occur.

Returning to the baby goat on the pedestal at the Behavior Farm, Eleanor Gibson (1980) began speculating on the nature-nurture aspect of depth perception. She reasoned that since these goats live on steep mountainsides in the wild and because kids walk from birth, it made evolutionary sense for depth perception to be innate in goats. But what about species that aren't mobile from birth? She approached Cornell colleague Richard Walk, who had a rat lab, with an idea for an experiment. To start, they built what came to be known as a **visual cliff**. This was *an apparatus for testing depth perception consisting of a glass surface spanning a drop of several feet.* A high-contrast checkerboard pattern beneath the glass made the simulated cliff especially salient. As expected, newborn goats refused to venture onto the glass above the apparent drop. Less expected, however, was the fact that dark-reared rats avoided the cliff just like the rats that had been raised in the light. This finding suggested that depth perception in rats must be innate as well.

Studies with human infants on the visual cliff brought Eleanor Gibson national attention (Caudle, 2003). Just like goat kids, human kids avoid the visual cliff from the time they're able to crawl. Of course, human infants are six to nine months old before they become mobile, so they have plenty of time to learn to perceive depth cues. But given that depth perception was demonstrated to be innate in other species, Gibson speculated that it's likely to be so in humans as well. The visual cliff studies caught the attention of not only other psychologists but also the general public. Gibson and Walk (1960) published the article "The 'Visual Cliff'" in *Scientific American*, and *Life* magazine ran a feature on it as well. After Eleanor Gibson achieved such fame, Cornell found a way around its nepotism rules and offered her a position as full professor—although with only a half-time salary!

Eleanor Gibson had an especially long and productive career (Caudle, 2003). Perceptual learning remained the theme of her research as she explored a number of topics. For example, she studied how infants and toddlers judge support in their environment using a waterbed. The infants fearlessly crawled across the undulating surface, while the toddlers dared not walk out onto it, although some got on their hands and knees to cross over. In another important line of research, she studied the processes involved in learning how to read. She remained active throughout her life, publishing her last book the year before she died at the age of 92. But her legacy continues through the many graduate students she mentored over her long career.

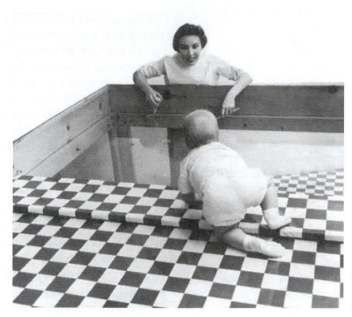

Photo 13.4
Visual cliff

Jerome Kagan

Harvard psychologist Jerome Kagan started his career as a student of Frank Beach at Yale, studying the sexual behavior of rats and dogs (Kagan, 2003). By the end of his student years, however, he understood that his real passion lay in the study of child psychology. Over the years, **Jerome Kagan** (born 1929) has built a reputation as an *American developmental psychologist who has argued for the role of temperament in the formation of attachment style in infancy and personality in adulthood.*

After a tour of military duty, Kagan was invited to the Fels Institute in Yellow Springs, Ohio, to take over the leadership of a longitudinal study of personality development from infancy to early adulthood (Kagan, 2003). Twenty years of data had already been collected, but the task of Kagan's team was to interview the adult participants and compare their current personality profile with earlier measurements. The result was the 1962 book *Birth to Maturity*.

The findings indicated that personality was quite fluid until the early grade-school years but became more consistent after that (Kagan, 2007). However, a small set of toddlers who habitually avoided strangers and withdrew from unfamiliar situations became inhibited, introverted adults who were constantly fearful before challenges and had great difficulty forming friendships and romantic relationships. Kagan wondered at the time whether this inhibition may be due to a genetic factor, but it would be decades before he'd amassed evidence to support this conjecture. The publication of *Birth to Maturity* gave Kagan a certain amount of celebrity, and in 1964 he was offered a position at Harvard, where he's remained ever since.

One of Kagan's first projects at Harvard was a longitudinal study of attentional abilities during the first year of life (Kagan, 2007). Kagan and his students measured how long infants of various ages paid attention to unusual events, and they found a shift toward longer attention spans between eight and twelve months of age. Kagan then related this finding to two other established facts. First, object permanence in Piagetian theory develops during this period. Second, **separation fear**, which is *an infant's distress at its caregiver's departure*, also emerges during this time. Kagan speculated that all three of these phenomena are related by brain maturation that expands working memory. Simply put, infants now search for the hidden object because they remember where it was placed, and likewise they cry when their mother is gone because they know she was just there.

This line of reasoning also led Kagan (2003) to question some of the assumptions of attachment theory. In the Strange Situation paradigm, a high degree of separation fear was interpreted as a sign of insecure attachment. Furthermore, Ainsworth attributed insecure attachment to a lack of maternal sensitivity. However, Kagan remembered that small group of infants in the Fels study who seemed to be genetically predisposed to fearfulness, and he questioned whether characteristics of the infant may also play a role in the formation of attachment styles.

During the late 1970s, Kagan challenged another tenet of attachment theory (Kagan, 2009). Bowlby had argued that any significant separation of the infant from its mother would lead to insecure attachment and anxiety. This claim had considerable political and economic ramifications. During World War II, many women had entered the work force as the men went off to fight. But after the war, women were asked to give up their jobs for the returning soldiers. Bowlby's early work on attachment was used as evidence that it was better for women to stay home with their children. But by the 1970s, liberalized social views were leading more women to seek employment, and these working women needed daycare for their children.

The initial purpose of Kagan's daycare studies was to determine if there were any behavioral differences in children staying at home and those attending a high-quality daycare center (Kagan, 2009). The researchers found that the daycare attendees were just as well adjusted as those who stayed home with their mothers. Clearly, attachment was more than just a bond between mother and infant. Rather, these children were able to form secondary bonds with multiple caregivers, and these had no impact on the quality of the primary attachment with the mother. This finding, of course, was good news for working women.

One of the daycare studies also yielded a surprising result (Kagan, 2007). This investigation was conducted at a daycare center in Boston's Chinatown, where about half of the children were ethnic Chinese and the other half were of European origin. Kagan and his students found that the Chinese American infants smiled and vocalized less frequently, were more fearful of unfamiliar events, and cried more intensely when their mothers left them. He also found similar patterns when he examined infants of Chinese ethnicity who stayed at home with their mothers. Kagan recalled the small group of inhibited children in the Fels study and his speculation that this was due to genetic factors. The fact that he now found an ethnic difference in infants' avoidance of the unfamiliar provided further evidence that this characteristic is innate and not due simply to maternal sensitivity.

While Ainsworth argued that attachment style is mostly shaped by the mother's sensitivity to her infant's needs, Kagan has argued that innate characteristics of the infant also play a role in the formation of attachment (Kagan & Snidman, 1991). In other words, attachment style is sculpted through an interaction of environmental factors, specifically maternal sensitivity combining with a set of genetic factors that Kagan calls **temperament**. By this term, he's referring to *the behavioral profile that is present in the infant at birth*. Although it doesn't determine the adult personality, temperament does set the initial conditions for personality development, making some outcomes more likely than others.

Among the many ways that infants can vary at birth, Kagan has found that their reaction to unfamiliar experiences is a good predictor of later adult personality (Kagan & Snidman, 1991). While infant reactivity ranges along a continuum, it tends to cluster at the two extremes. On the one extreme are low-reactive infants. They show little fear of strangers or novel stimuli, and they confidently explore new environments using their mother as a secure base. Longitudinal studies show that these uninhibited infants are likely to grow into extraverted adults who skillfully build relationships and gladly take on new challenges. On the other extreme are high-reactive infants. They're fearful of strangers and novel stimuli, and they cling to their mothers rather than using them as a secure base for exploration. These children tend to grow into highly introverted adults who have difficulty making friends, and they experience high levels of anxiety when challenged.

In a biographical essay, Kagan (2003) remarked that when he started his career he was certain that people's personalities were shaped almost entirely by the ways their parents had acted toward them as infants. Later in his career, however, his thinking became completely turned around. He now believes that infants are born with an innate temperament that biases their personality development in particular directions. Additionally, he sees the larger culture—especially social categories like gender, class, and ethnicity—as major contributors to the formation of adult personality. Thus, he favors neither nature nor nurture as an explanation for psychological traits. Rather, Jerome Kagan is one of the modern thinkers who view nature and nurture as two forces that interact within the organism to guide its development.

Social Development

Children grow up in a social and cultural environment that strongly influences their modes of thinking and behaving as adults. Although children learn aspects of their culture through modeling, language also plays a very important role in acculturation. Noam Chomsky (Chapter 11) proposed that innate knowledge of universal grammar drove the development of language in young children, but the first psychologist to provide strong empirical support for this assertion was Roger Brown, whose detailed studies of three young children clearly showed an unfolding of language according to a set of developmental milestones. Once acquired, language then becomes the primary channel for the transmission of culture. Furthermore, a key aspect of acculturation is developing a sense of self and an understanding of one's position in society. No society is completely egalitarian, and we all learn to play our expected roles. Along these lines, a number of minority psychologists, who experienced discrimination firsthand, have explored the pernicious effects that racism has on the development of self-identity. Specifically, we'll look at the research of the African American husband-and-wife team of Kenneth and Mamie Clark as well as that of Hispanic psychologist Martha Bernal, giving consideration to the impact they've had on the shaping of twentieth-first-century society.

Roger Brown

Roger Brown served in the Navy during World War II (Brown, 1989). His ship saw little action, but it did sail into the harbor of Nagasaki after its atomic destruction. He spent his days on board reading Watson and Freud, so by the time the war ended, he knew he wanted to be a psychologist. Benefitting from the G.I. Bill, he completed his bachelor's and doctorate degrees in psychology at the University of Michigan. And even though he always claimed his first love was social psychology, **Roger Brown** (1925–1997) is best known as the *American developmental psychologist who studied language acquisition in the early years of childhood.*

On graduation in 1952, Brown was hired by Harvard, where he collaborated with Jerome Bruner, and this experience led him to an interest in the psychology of language (Kagan, 1999). As is the tradition at Harvard, Brown was let go after his fifth year, but during his time there he gathered enough material for *Words and Things*, which he published in 1958. This was the first book on the psychology of language written in the spirit of the Cognitive Revolution that was just taking off at Harvard and other universities in the northeast. Brown spent the next five years at the Massachusetts Institute of Technology, where he interacted with Noam Chomsky and learned transformational-generative grammar. In 1962, he was called back to Harvard, where he remained until his retirement in 1994.

One of Brown's most noted studies in language was on the so-called **tip-of-the-tongue phenomenon** (Brown & McNeill, 1966). This is *the experience of knowing that you know a word without being able to name it.* You've no doubt had the experience of forgetting the name of a familiar object or even of someone you know. Eventually it comes to you, but in the meantime you have that frustrating experience of feeling that the word is almost there but just won't come out. Brown induced tip-of-the-tongue states in the laboratory by reading definitions from the dictionary to participants. About one in ten times, the participant would have a tip-of-the-tongue experience, in which the participant could tell things about the word, such as first letter or number of syllables, without being able to name the word itself. Incidentally, Brown's assistant on this project was his student David McNeill (born 1933), who later became one of the leading researchers in the field of psycholinguistics.

When Brown returned to Harvard, he began his project on early language acquisition, but it took more than a decade to complete the study and publish the results (Kagan, 1999). For the project, Brown recorded and transcribed the natural conversations of three children—whom he called Adam, Eve, and Sarah. He then shifted through this vast amount of data looking for patterns. What he found challenged many of the assumptions about language acquisition at that time. Of course it was already recognized that some children develop language faster than others, but Brown showed that they reach specific milestones in a predictable manner. For instance, all three children learned the s plural suffix for nouns long before they learned to use the s suffix on verbs correctly. He also developed a standard measure of language development that's still used today. This was the **mean length of utterance**, or MLU, which refers to *the average number of meaningful units per sentence, used as a measure of language development*. If you know the current MLU of a child, you can predict with fairly good accuracy which grammatical structures he or she has already acquired.

A First Language: The Early Stages, which Brown published in 1973, can be viewed as a full-on attack against Skinner's *Verbal Behavior* (Kagan, 1999). Skinner had argued that children learn syntactic structures through reinforcement. Chomsky had already made a convincing argument based on theoretical points. But Brown provided actual data clearly showing that parents simply don't correct the grammatical errors of their young children. Instead, they respond to the truthfulness of their children's utterances. If little Suzie says "Doggie running" and there is in fact a dog that is running, her parents will praise her instead of correcting her grammar. But if the running animal is actually a cat, they'll correct her for using the wrong word. Since children don't get feedback on their grammatically incorrect utterances, they must learn syntax by some other means than operant conditioning. Brown's entire corpus has been available in an online database for about two decades now, and many developmental psycholinguists have mined these data for their own research projects.

Brown's interests were eclectic, and during his career he followed many different research paths. However, his work on first-language acquisition inspired a whole generation of developmental psycholinguists who followed his approach of recording and transcribing natural language production. The work of Roger Brown and his many students has provided us with a much deeper understanding of how children learn language.

Kenneth and Mamie Clark

Inspired by Francis Cecil Sumner to pursue a career in psychology, **Kenneth Clark** (1914–2005) completed both his bachelor's and his master's degrees with him at Howard University in Washington (Jones & Pettigrew, 2005). Then he went on to Columbia, where he worked with Otto Klineberg (1899–1992), one of the few psychologists at the time who argued that racial differences were due to social factors and not genetics. From there, Clark joined the faculty at City College in New York, where he remained for the rest of his career. Kenneth Clark became famous as the *African American psychologist whose research was cited in the Supreme Court decision that declared segregation unconstitutional*.

During his last year at Howard, Kenneth Clark met Mamie Phipps, a math student (Jones & Pettigrew, 2005). His enthusiasm for psychology led her to change her major, and the project she completed for her master's thesis at Howard served as the starting point for the doll experiments that would make them both famous. When she earned her Ph.D. at Columbia three years after her husband, she searched for a counseling position in the private sector. At the time, few women were hired as professors, and her race made it virtually impossible to obtain a teaching position. Nevertheless, Kenneth and Mamie Clark collaborated as equals in research as well as in various social projects. Thus, it's best to remember **Mamie Clark** (1917–1983) as the *African American psychologist who developed the doll studies that were cited by the Supreme Court regarding the need for school desegregation*.

The legendary doll studies that Mamie and Kenneth Clark conducted over a number of years eventually made them famous not only among psychologists but among the general public as well (Keppel, 2002). They used white and brown

Photo 13.5
Kenneth Clark

dolls to explore racial identification and attitudes in African American children. First, they would ask children which doll looked like them. The overwhelming majority pointed to the brown doll. But when they were asked which one they wanted to play with, two-thirds chose the white doll. When asked why, typical responses were that the brown doll was ugly or dirty. And when the researchers reminded them that they'd already said they looked like the brown doll, many of the children became emotionally distraught. In follow-up experiments, the Clarks compared the reactions of African American youngsters growing up in the North and in the South. They found that the Northern children had more hostile responses to the discrepancy between their racial identity and their racial attitudes, whereas the Southern children were more likely to simply accept their inferior social status as a fact of life. These studies poignantly showed the harmful effects of segregation and racial discrimination, even among young children.

In an effort to help African American youth overcome the negative impact of discrimination, the Clarks founded the Northside Center for Child Development in Harlem in 1946 (Lal, 2002). Mamie was the director of the center and designed the interventions that the clinic provided, but Kenneth helped out by working with clients and recruiting financial donors. The Northside Center provided clinical consultations for behavioral problems, vocational guidance, training sessions for parents, and aptitude testing. By the end of its first decade, its clientele had more than doubled, its staff of volunteer counselors had sizably increased, and the center had developed deep connections with other community agencies such as local schools and churches.

In the early 1950s, the National Association for the Advancement of Colored People approached Kenneth Clark (Benjamin & Crouse, 2002). The NAACP was attempting to dismantle segregation on a state-by-state basis, and Clark agreed to testify at a hearing in South Carolina. He brought his brown and white dolls into the courtroom to graphically demonstrate the reactions of the children in the doll studies. As the question went before the Supreme Court, Clark wrote a report on the psychological effects of segregation that included the results of the doll studies. It was this document that the Supreme Court cited in the 1954 case of *Brown v. Board of Education* to support its decision that segregation was harmful and therefore unconstitutional.

Shortly after this, Kenneth Clark emerged as a public figure in the discussion on race relations and the pernicious effects of racism, and he wrote several books aimed at the general public (Keppel, 2002). In his 1955 book *Prejudice and Your Child*, he pointed out that racist attitudes are so entrenched in American society that people—both Black and White—see racial inequality as the natural order. His next book, *Dark Ghetto*, came out in 1965 at the height of the Civil Rights Movement. He interacted with other leaders of the movement such as Malcolm X, James Baldwin, and Martin Luther King Jr., and he was much sought out as a public speaker. In these two books, Clark expounded his vision of an America of racial integration, but by the time he published *Pathos of Power* in 1974, he'd turned pessimistic about ever accomplishing that dream. He lamented that American racism ran too deep for it to be eradicated in his lifetime. However, his unflagging efforts to enhance American social awareness of the ills of racism and inequality were recognized by the APA, which elected him president in 1971. To date, he's the only African American to have served in this capacity.

Although Kenneth Clark became a nationally recognized figure during and after the Civil Rights Movement, he always gave credit to Mamie as his partner and equal collaborator. Indeed, it was her early work in racial identity which led to the research that made Kenneth famous. It's only in recent years that Mamie's role in the famous doll experiments has been recognized, and she's finally getting the credit she deserves. Although racism is far from eradicated in the United States, the nation has nevertheless made important strides toward Mamie and Kenneth Clark's dream of a racially integrated society in which people are no longer judged by the color of their skin but by the worth of their character.

Martha Bernal

Martha Bernal was born in San Antonio, and she experienced racism at an early age when she was told she wasn't allowed to speak Spanish in school (Vasquez & Lopez, 2002).

As the *first Hispanic-American woman to earn a Ph.D. in psychology*, **Martha Bernal** (1931–2001) spent her career pursuing two goals. One was to fight the racism that was rampant within her field. And the other was to find effective treatments for children of color with behavior issues stemming from their unequal status in society.

Bernal completed her clinical Ph.D. at Indiana University, where she got solid training in the learning theories that dominated the early 1960s (Vasquez & Lopez, 2002). She was also appalled by the common use of methods in the clinic that were justified by theory but had no empirical support. In her treatment of childhood psychopathology, she employed rigorous tests to determine which methods were effective. During a career that included tenures at UCLA, the University of Denver, and Arizona State University, Bernal gained national attention for the development of behavioral interventions that were empirically supported. In her research, she particularly focused on the needs of children from ethnic minorities.

Although she'd experienced discrimination all her life, Bernal said she was never fully aware of its effects until she talked with fellow minority psychologists at conferences ("Martha Bernal," 2001). She came to understand that her experiences—being denied access to laboratories or resources in graduate school and rejections on job applications due to her gender and ethnicity—weren't unique. Rather, other women and minorities also had to overcome these obstacles. During her career, she strove to raise levels of awareness about the dangers of racism in academia. She pointed out that the systemic racism of American society was paralleled within the field of psychology. Thus, she insisted, psychology needed to find ways to help society become more equitable by advocating for a multicultural psychology that recognized the importance of diversity in training and research.

Looking Ahead

Traditionally, developmental psychology has focused on infancy, childhood, and, to a lesser extent, on adolescence. This is still true even in the twenty-first century. However, there's growing recognition that development isn't limited to the preadult years. Rather, as humanistic psychologist Erik Erikson (Chapter 15) argued in the middle of the twentieth century, development doesn't stop at adulthood but rather is a continuous process extending "from womb to tomb." Although psychologists have long paid lip service to Erikson's idea of lifespan development, we're beginning to see more developmental psychologists working outside of the traditional age ranges. In particular, we're seeing a lot of growth in recent years on development and aging. This is becoming a burgeoning area of research as people are now living much longer than ever before.

Nevertheless, the study of infancy and childhood still defines the scope of developmental psychology for most researchers. Furthermore, much of the research in recent decades has focused on cognitive development. In part, this is a reflection of the fact that cognitive psychology has dominated the field since the 1970s, making the study of cognitive development once again acceptable. Another important factor is the introduction to North America of the grand theories of cognitive development proposed much earlier by Jean Piaget and Lev Vygotsky. These theories have provided frameworks for investigations into the development of language, mathematics, and reasoning skills, among others. Finally, as the use of brain-imaging technology becomes more prevalent, these techniques are now being used to study development at the neural level, launching the new field of developmental neuroscience.

CHAPTER SUMMARY

An immediate concern after World War II was the fate of the many children who'd been separated from or lost their parents during the war. John Bowlby saw that maternal separation had long-term consequences for social and personality development and, drawing on support from comparative psychology, he proposed attachment theory to account for the importance of the mother-infant bond. His colleague Mary Ainsworth then provided the empirical support for this theory, arguing that maternal sensitivity was the key to secure attachment. Jerome Kagan challenged this view, maintaining that the infant is born with a behavioral profile he called temperament, which also influences the style of attachment that develops. In an effort to reconcile behavioral and psychoanalytic viewpoints, Robert Sears proposed social learning to explain how children's development is shaped through socialization processes. Influenced by the Cognitive Revolution, his colleagues Eleanor Maccoby and Albert Bandura viewed children as taking an active role in their development by choosing which models to emulate. Meanwhile, Eleanor Gibson's work on perceptual learning helped to push forward the view that development unfolds through an interaction of genetic and environmental factors. Other contributors to the field include Roger Brown, known as the father of developmental psycholinguistics, as well as Mamie and Kenneth Clark, who showed the pernicious effects of racial discrimination on a child's developing sense of self.

DISCUSSION QUESTIONS

1. Attachment theory is a classic example of how a grand theory is developed over time as ideas pass through a complex network of social relationships. Trace the roots of attachment, indicating the key persons and the ideas they contributed. You may find it helpful to organize this information in a flow chart or family-tree diagram.

2. Early theories of social development posited that young children identify with one of their parents. Two such conceptualizations are Freud's Oedipus complex and Bowlby's internal working model. Compare and contrast these two models of identification.

3. Starting with Freud, the mother-infant bond was viewed as a dependency that needed to be overcome, but from Bowlby it's been interpreted instead as an attachment with lifelong consequences. Trace the development of thinking from dependency to attachment.

4. According to attachment theory, the attachment style you develop in infancy carries into your adult relationships. Speculate on how a person with secure, avoidant, or anxious attachment will likely behave in friendships and romantic relationships, particularly during times of stress when attachment behaviors are activated.

5. Jerome Kagan proposed that temperament interacts with maternal sensitivity to shape attachment style. Consider the four possible interactions of high versus low reactivity (temperament) and high versus low maternal sensitivity, speculating on the likely attachment style that will develop in each case.

6. In his early work, Robert Sears accepted the Freudian proposal that aggression arises as a way of dealing with frustration. In your opinion, does frustration necessarily lead to aggression? Are there other causes of aggression? Back up your assertions with evidence.

7. Consider the ways in which social learning theory extends beyond the standard learning theories presented in Chapter 5.

8. Kersting (2004) quotes Eleanor Maccoby as stating: "Parenting isn't something you do to children or for children; it's something you do with children" (p. 39). What do you think she means by this? Construct some hypothetical situations to illustrate this assertion.

9. Contrast Albert Bandura's social cognitive theory with Robert Sears's social learning theory.

10. Albert Bandura's two main contributions to psychology are modeling and self-efficacy. Explain each concept, and then consider ways in which the two are related.

11. The question of whether perception is learned or innate has a long history in psychology. Trace the discussion from the British empiricists to the behaviorists and Gestalt psychologists. How do Eleanor Gibson's contributions add to this discussion?

12. Brown argued that all young children learn grammatical structures in the same order regardless of the forms they hear from their parents. Speculate on why this might be the case.

ON THE WEB

On YouTube, you can find videos of **John Bowlby**, **attachment theory**, **Mary Ainsworth**, and the **Strange Situation**. You can also find videos of **Jerome Kagan** discussing **temperament**. There are also videos of **Eleanor Maccoby** and **Albert Bandura** discussing their work, including film clips from the **Bobo doll experiment**. You can also find original footage of **Eleanor Gibson's visual cliff experiment**. YouTube also has film of interviews with **Kenneth Clark** as well as reenactments of his **doll experiments**.

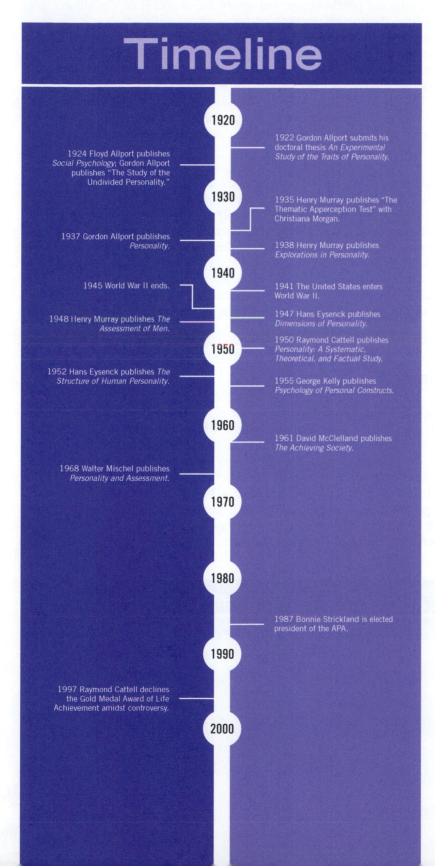

Timeline

1922 Gordon Allport submits his doctoral thesis *An Experimental Study of the Traits of Personality.*

1924 Floyd Allport publishes *Social Psychology*; Gordon Allport publishes "The Study of the Undivided Personality."

1930

1935 Henry Murray publishes "The Thematic Apperception Test" with Christiana Morgan.

1937 Gordon Allport publishes *Personality.*

1938 Henry Murray publishes *Explorations in Personality.*

1940

1945 World War II ends.

1941 The United States enters World War II.

1947 Hans Eysenck publishes *Dimensions of Personality.*

1948 Henry Murray publishes *The Assessment of Men.*

1950

1950 Raymond Cattell publishes *Personality: A Systematic, Theoretical, and Factual Study.*

1952 Hans Eysenck publishes *The Structure of Human Personality.*

1955 George Kelly publishes *Psychology of Personal Constructs.*

1960

1961 David McClelland publishes *The Achieving Society.*

1968 Walter Mischel publishes *Personality and Assessment.*

1970

1980

1987 Bonnie Strickland is elected president of the APA.

1990

1997 Raymond Cattell declines the Gold Medal Award of Life Achievement amidst controversy.

2000

Learning Objectives

After reading this chapter, you should be able to:

- Assess the trait approach and the contributions of Floyd and Gordon Allport to the foundation of a scientific approach to personality.

- Critique the dynamic approach of Henry Murray and David McClelland and its impact on personality research.

- Construct a timeline for the evolution of the five-factor model of personality from the London School through the work of Cattell and Eysenck to the current Big Five.

- Evaluate the social cognitive approach to personality as undertaken by Julian Rotter and Walter Mischel.

Looking Back

As the science of human affect, behavior, and cognition, psychology has mostly focused on those aspects that are common to all people. At the same time, it's undeniable that each of us is unique, and psychologists also need to take individual differences into account. The study of **personality**, or *an individual's characteristic ways of feeling, acting, and thinking*, was already of interest to the first experimental psychologists, but systematic thinking on the subject goes back as far as the Ancient Greeks.

Hippocrates (about 460–370 BCE) was a *Greek physician who proposed a theory of personality based on four "humors" or bodily fluids* (Merenda, 1987). This four-factor model was the dominant view of personality into the twentieth century, and his personality terms, such as *sanguine* and *melancholic*, are still used colloquially today (Table 14.1). Although Wilhelm Wundt insisted that experimental psychology should seek the general laws of human mental processes, he did propose a two-dimensional model of personality that arranged Hippocrates's four humors into two pairs of polar opposites.

In the early twentieth century, psychoanalysts also proposed theories of personality that had lasting influence on the field. These models were typically dynamic in nature, with opposing forces interacting to shape personality. Freud's interactive model of the id, ego, and superego is one example, and Jung's personality typology is another.

A final early influence on the field of personality research was Francis Galton's anthropometric approach to measuring all sorts of individual differences. His intellectual descendants developed a set of mathematical techniques collectively known as factor analysis that could help them explore the structure of individual differences. The factor approach has come to dominate thinking on personality in the twenty-first century. However, the Big Five model, which is now the consensus approach to personality, took a good century to develop. This is the story we tell in this chapter.

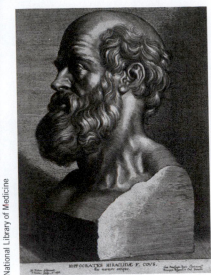

Photo 14.1
Bust of Hippocrates

Trait Approach

Our history of personality psychology starts with a tale of two brothers—Floyd and Gordon Allport—each with a personality quite distinct from the other (Nicholson, 2000). The elder Floyd was flamboyant. He was a snappy dresser, and he viewed himself as a real go-getter in the modern world. The younger Gordon, though, was more reserved and introspective, and he had a deep concern for the social welfare of others. Both rejected the exuberant, evangelical Methodism of their youth, but again in different ways. Floyd was the atheist scientist who put his faith in the power of experimental psychology to improve the lives of people. Gordon also professed faith in the scientific method, but he retained an inner spirituality that drew him to the sacrament and ritual of the Anglican Church.

Table 14.1   Four-Factor Theory of Hippocrates

Body Humor	Temperament	Characteristics
Blood	Sanguine	Optimistic, hopeful
Black bile	Melancholic	Sad, depressed
Yellow bile	Choleric	Angry, irritable
Phlegm	Phlegmatic	Apathetic, unexcitable

Floyd and Gordon Allport

As a graduate student at Harvard, **Floyd Allport** (1890–1978) was attracted to social psychology, and his mentor Hugo Münsterberg encouraged him to do a dissertation on social facilitation (Parkovnick, 2000). He was also greatly influenced by Edwin Holt (Chapter 11), who introduced him to the new doctrine of behaviorism. At the time, social psychology was largely a philosophical discipline, and its two main concepts were the group mind and instinct. A leader of this approach was William McDougall (Chapter 11), the British psychologist who came to Harvard in 1920. McDougall believed that individual behavior is determined by two factors, group norms and biological predispositions. Floyd Allport challenged both of these premises, by rejecting both the idea of groups as entities and the existence of instincts. Instead, he argued, groups are nothing but collections of individuals responding to environmental stimuli. He advocated this position throughout his career, building his reputation as an *American psychologist who pioneered the experimental approach to social psychology*.

In 1924, Floyd Allport published *Social Psychology*, which defined the field for decades (Katz, 1979). While rejecting the traditional approach of group mind and instinct, he also attempted to integrate the two ascendant frameworks of psychology at the time, namely behaviorism and psychoanalysis. In particular, behaviorism provided scientific rigor, while psychoanalysis described important social dynamics. Floyd Allport was the first psychologist to seek a synthesis of these two approaches, but in the following decades others would try their hand at it as well. The book was also important because of its description of personality. Floyd Allport knew that not all people react the same way in a given situation, and that personality as well as immediate environmental factors drive behavior. Here, Floyd Allport took his cue from John Watson, who'd defined personality as the sum of all learned responses of that individual. Since we all have different life histories, we all have different personalities. In a nutshell, personality is shaped by experience.

Floyd Allport had considerable impact on the growth of experimental social psychology during the middle decades of the twentieth century (Katz, 1979). Muzafer Sherif's (Chapter 12) study of social norms and Solomon Asch's (Chapter 12) experiments on group conformity were both extensions of his earlier research on these topics. And although research on social facilitation lay dormant for decades after his dissertation, it was picked up again by Robert Zajonc (Chapter 12) in the 1960s. Floyd Allport also had a great influence on the early thinking of his younger brother Gordon, whose story we turn to next.

Floyd was just starting graduate school at Harvard when he invited Gordon to come join him as an undergraduate (Nicholson, 2000). Like his brother, Gordon studied with Münsterberg, and later he took classes with McDougall, but by far Floyd was the greatest influence on his academic development during this time. This was when Floyd was formulating his thoughts on personality as the sum of an individual's learned responses. Gordon bought into this behaviorist approach, and it was reflected in his doctoral dissertation, one of the first to deal with the measurement of personality traits. He also coauthored a paper on the nature of personality with his brother. At this time, Gordon's views were essentially identical to those of his older brother, but within a few years his thinking diverged as he came under new influences. While Floyd later turned his attention toward other areas of social psychology, Gordon devoted much of his career to formulating a theory of personality. Thus, **Gordon Allport** (1897–1967) is the *American psychologist who is recognized as the founder of modern personality psychology*.

During his undergraduate years, Gordon Allport had been torn between social work and experimental psychology (Nicholson, 1998). No doubt Floyd nudged him toward psychology for graduate study, but Gordon retained an interest in social causes all his life (Figure 14.1). This dual focus was also indicated in his 1922 dissertation, titled *An Experimental Study of the Traits of Personality*. Among experimental psychologists, personality was considered a fringe topic, but the idea of developing tools for measuring personality had some currency among psychiatrists and social workers. After all, interventions had to

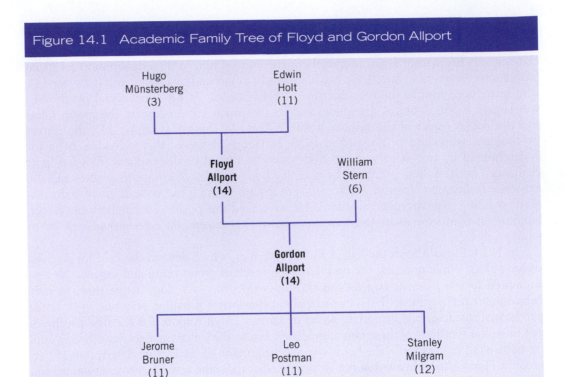

Figure 14.1 Academic Family Tree of Floyd and Gordon Allport

Hugo Münsterberg (3)

Edwin Holt (11)

Floyd Allport (14)

William Stern (6)

Gordon Allport (14)

Jerome Bruner (11)

Leo Postman (11)

Stanley Milgram (12)

be tailored to the particular characteristics of the individual, and a scientific approach to assessing personality would be extremely useful. That Allport was thinking of the practical applications of his dissertation research was indicated by its subtitle: *With Special Reference to the Problem of Social Diagnosis.*

After Gordon Allport earned his Ph.D., he was awarded a two-year fellowship to do postdoctoral research in Europe (Nicholson, 2000). Much of the first year was spent with the German psychologist William Stern (Chapter 6), who was developing a Gestalt-like theory of personality which viewed the self as the immutable core of an individual, in contrast to the behaviorist view of personality as the sum of an individual's particular behaviors. Allport was quickly won over to Stern's point of view, and soon Stern had replaced Floyd as his new mentor. Gordon Allport spent the next year at Cambridge, mainly pondering the implications of Stern's idea. By the end of that year, he'd completed a paper titled "The Study of the Undivided Personality," which he sent to the *Journal of Abnormal and Social Psychology,* the editor of which was none other than Floyd Allport. It's unclear whether this was an act of defiance on Gordon's part, but Floyd was nonplussed and made a snide remark about "pretzel" psychology. Nevertheless, Floyd agreed to publish the paper, but still a rift had split open between the two brothers that would never mend. At the end of his two-year fellowship, Gordon was offered an instructorship at Harvard. But by the time he returned, Floyd had moved on.

With the exception of a four-year sojourn at Dartmouth, Gordon Allport spent the rest of his career at Harvard (Nicholson, 1997). During his first year as an instructor there, he offered a course on personality, believed to be the first of its kind ever taught in an American university. He spent the following years developing his theory of personality.

Trait Theory

Rejecting the behaviorist view of personality as a set of learned responses, Gordon Allport envisioned it instead as a bundle of traits (Nicholson, 1998). The concept of trait as the variable of personality already had some currency, and as a student he'd collaborated with Floyd on a personality test to measure a trait they called "ascendance." This referred to the degree to which individuals are dominant in social interactions as opposed to being submissive. As his theory matured, Gordon Allport came to view a **trait** as *a stable internal characteristic of an individual that is a determinant of behavior.* While accepting the possibility that traits could be acquired through experience, Allport believed that they could also be biologically based.

Given that a personality is composed of traits, Allport next asked how many traits there are (John, Angleitner, & Ostendorf, 1988). He thought he could arrive at a tentative answer by looking at the words people use to describe personalities. Francis Galton, the nineteenth-century scientist who was interested in measuring individual differences, first considered the **lexical hypothesis**, which is *the proposal that words for personality traits should be common in any language because they serve an important role in social interactions.* Galton scanned a dictionary for words describing personality traits and came up with a list of around 1,000 words. Psychologists in Germany had undertaken a similar project for their language. Allport followed their lead, and he worked with a student to survey an unabridged English dictionary. The result was a list of over 4,500 words describing personality traits. While many of the items were synonyms and thus interchangeable, this still meant many hundreds of distinct traits. These then were the raw materials from which personalities were built, and each personality was unique because it was composed of a different combination of traits.

As we'll see, this isn't the way that modern personality theorists view the concept of trait (Zuroff, 1986). Nevertheless, Gordon Allport is still considered the founder of **trait theory**, which is *the proposal that personalities can be analyzed into a finite number of measurable traits.* Modern theories of personality are almost all versions of trait theory, differing mainly in the number and type of traits they propose as well as the way they're structured.

Allport drew together his ideas in his 1937 work *Personality* (Pettigrew, 1969). In this book, he chastised the behaviorists for their shallow view of personality, calling instead for a "full-bodied" approach to understanding the rich diversity of the human experience. Considered an instant classic, the book established personality research as a legitimate field of study by offering both a fully articulated theory of personality as well as a reasoned discussion of the proper methods for studying it.

With regard to methodology, Allport laid out the difference between nomothetic and idiographic approaches, a distinction he'd learned from William Stern (Chapter 6; Rosenzweig & Fisher, 1997). A **nomothetic approach** is *a research style of examining many examples to derive generalizations.* The natural sciences are nomothetic, as exemplified by their many general laws. American psychology, in its quest to become accepted as a legitimate experimental science, had assumed the nomothetic approach from the days of Wilhelm Wundt. However, Allport had absorbed the attitudes of his mentor William Stern, who'd argued that humans were too variable to be adequately described in terms of general laws. Instead, psychologists needed to adopt *a research style of examining individual persons in great depth.* He called this the **idiographic approach**. While Allport recognized the value of each approach, he encouraged personality psychologists to engage in more idiographic studies.

The brothers Floyd and Gordon Allport were both important pioneers in the development of the field during the 1920s and 1930s in that they each offered a fundamentally different conception of personality and how to study it (Barenbaum, 2000). Gordon Allport's view of personality as a bundle of enduring traits that motivate behavior served as the foundation for mainstream thinking on personality. At the same time, current theorists conceptualize traits much differently, thinking of them instead as the dimensions of personality. From this perspective, every individual has the same small set of traits, but what makes people different from each other is the values they have on each of these trait dimensions. Gordon Allport's view of traits as internal to the person and highly stable over time is still advocated by many trait theorists today.

Floyd Allport's view of personality was in line with the behaviorist theory that he subscribed to (Barenbaum, 2000). According to this view, personality amounts to little more than the sum total of learned responses to environmental stimuli. Thus, personality is shaped by external rather than internal forces. The implication of this view is that personality tends to be stable simply because it's difficult—but not impossible—to change well-learned habits. This way of thinking about personality is probably the minority position today, but it's certainly not without its promoters. As we'll see, one of the major debates in personality psychology later in the twentieth century was exactly the question that split the Allport brothers: Does personality arise from internal, probably biological, factors? Or is it shaped by experience, particularly from early childhood?

Dynamic Approach

Floyd Allport's view of personality was shaped by behaviorist doctrine, and Gordon Allport's mostly by Gestalt thinking. The third major school in the middle of the twentieth century was psychoanalysis, and many of the practitioners in this field offered their thoughts on personality development. In this section, we'll consider the work of two psychologists—Henry Murray and David McClelland—whose approach to personality was based on psychodynamic models.

Henry Murray

Born to a wealthy family in New York City, **Henry Murray** (1893–1988) grew up in a life of privilege and attended the most exclusive private schools (Murray, 1967). As an undergraduate at Harvard, he hoped for nothing more than to earn a "gentleman's C" in his classes, but he excelled at sports and was the captain of the rowing team. He became a more serious student when he enrolled at Columbia Medical School. After Murray earned an M.D. degree, he went to Cambridge University in England to earn a Ph.D. in biochemistry. But when he was thirty years old, he happened upon Carl Jung's *Psychological Types* in a bookstore, and reading the book changed his life. He became a scholar of Jung and Freud, and through connections he managed to get a position as a psychotherapist at the Harvard Psychological Clinic, where he remained for the rest of his career. During this time, Murray built a reputation as the *American personality psychologist mostly known for his development of the Thematic Apperception Test.*

Murray had become acquainted with Jung's work before leaving for Cambridge (Triplet, 1992). After reading all of Jung's books, he worked through Freud's as well. He also began a correspondence with Jung, and while at Cambridge he arranged to take a vacation to Zurich to meet Jung. The two became quick friends, and after three intense weeks of conversation, Murray felt he was a changed man. He now knew that psychology was where his passion lay, and particularly that of a psychoanalytic approach. Nevertheless, he returned to Cambridge and completed his Ph.D. in biochemistry, publishing several important papers in that field.

On his return to the United States, Murray got to know Morton Prince, a noted psychiatrist who subscribed to the theories of French psychologist Pierre Janet (Chapter 8; Smith & Anderson, 1989). Prince was the director of the Harvard Psychological Clinic, and he hired Murray as his assistant. During this time, Murray also undertook psychoanalytic training and began practicing psychoanalysis part-time. About a year after bringing Murray on board, Prince's health declined, and he named Murray as his successor. With the directorship came a faculty position, and thus Murray—who had no credentials as a psychologist—found himself a member of the Harvard psychology department, much to the chagrin of Edwin Boring, Karl Lashley, and Gordon Allport. For his part, Murray did little to ingratiate himself with his new colleagues. He was a vocal critic of experimental psychology for its pursuit of obscure topics with little practical application. While he freely admitted that psychoanalytic theory went far beyond what the data could support, at least the psychoanalysts were asking important questions about the human experience. What was needed, Murray insisted, was an experimental investigation of these issues.

When Murray went up for tenure, a controversy erupted (Smith & Anderson, 1989). Karl Lashley (Chapter 10) threatened to quit if Murray wasn't fired, and Allport—who feared he would be next on the chopping block—threatened to quit if Murray *was* fired. Boring suggested a compromise to the president—Murray was retained as director of the clinic but on contract instead of with tenure. Murray (1967) notes that he could accept this arrangement because he was financially independent and didn't have to rely on the meager salary Harvard offered him. No doubt his financial independence also gave him the courage to speak his mind without fear of offending his colleagues.

In 1935, Murray published the article that made him famous (Triplet, 1992). This piece described the **Thematic Apperception Test**, or TAT, which is a *projective personality test consisting of a series of ambiguous pictures that the subject is asked to describe*. Projective tests are based on the Freudian notion of projection, in which a person attributes his or her own thoughts and feelings to another person. As the subject describes each picture, the evaluator listens for evidence of projection that can provide insight into the subject's own motives. The Rorschach inkblot test was an earlier example of a projective technique for assessing personality, but the TAT was considered more reliable because it featured pictures of social situations that lent themselves to multiple interpretations.

Murray's collaborator on the project was Christiana Morgan (1897–1967), an artist and amateur Jung scholar (Schneidman, 2001). Both were already married, but Murray and Morgan were lovers for over forty years, a relationship that was tolerated by their spouses and was an open secret among the Harvard faculty and Boston high society. Carl Jung, who knew them both, is said to have encouraged the affair, seeing Morgan as the muse who would inspire Murray to greatness.

With a team of colleagues, Murray published *Explorations in Personality* in 1938 (Anderson, 2017). This book presents *Henry Murray's theory of personality formation throughout the lifespan by psychodynamic processes*, which he called **personology**. Although the theory isn't given much consideration today, it was quite influential from the 1950s to the 1970s. This book was published just a year after Gordon Allport's *Personality* appeared, and the two books together are often viewed as the launch of the experimental approach to the study of personality. And like Allport's work, this book presented both a theory of personality and a method for studying it.

The cornerstone of Murray's personology was his **need-press theory** (Triplet, 1992). This is *the view that personality is shaped by psychodynamic processes as the individual is driven by internal motivations and constrained by situational factors*. The name of the theory comes from the special terms he used for the internal and external forces acting on the individual. Murray called the emotions, impulses, and motivations that drive behaviors *needs*, and he labeled the situational factors that constrain behavior, such as physical limitations or social norms, as *presses*. Thus, Murray's model of personality is an interactionist model that incorporates both internal and external influences on behavior. Furthermore, he viewed personality as being shaped dynamically across the lifespan of the individual.

Another important concept in personology is the notion of **regnancy** (Epstein, 1979). Although Murray accepted the idea of unconscious drives, he gave much more weight to conscious motives, and in particular to *the central motivation in an individual's life that subordinates all other motives and brings unity to the personality*. The desire for fame or money is an example of regnancy, in that one driving force shapes the personality beyond any other factor. Like psychodynamic approaches, Murray recognized that the past has a great effect on personality, but he also saw the future as highly influential in that the individual's long-term goals also shape behavior in the present. Other personality psychologists have noted the similarities between Murray's notion of regnancy and Adler's idea of lifestyle.

The data for *Explorations in Personality* were gathered through a technique that Murray called the **multiform method** (Triplet, 1992). This is *a procedure for diagnosing a personality by subjecting the participant to a battery of tests conducted by a group of examiners who then discuss the case to reach a consensus*. Murray based this method on the practice he experienced in medical school known as the "grand rounds," in which doctors and students examined a patient together and then conferred to make a diagnosis. For *Explorations*, fifty college students were enlisted to undergo the many hours of testing required for the multiform method. He also recruited a group of psychotherapists to serve as the "Diagnostic Council," whose duty it was to come to a consensus on the personality description of each participant.

Henry Murray was a colorful character whose passions seemed to shift every few years (Smith & Anderson, 1989). During World War II, Murray worked for the Office of Strategic Services, the forerunner of the Central Intelligence Agency, administering personality tests to help select secret agents. Right after the war, Murray was deployed to China to provide military training. In 1948, he published a report of his wartime experiences in the book *The Assessment of Men*. Murray was finally granted tenure at Harvard in 1954, but by that time his creativity seems to have largely been spent. He started a number of grand projects only to drop them for other interests. Also, he was plagued by depression after the death of his wife and then of Christiana Morgan a few years later. His spirits recovered when he remarried in his early 70s, and those who knew him said his mind remained sharp until his death in his early 90s. However, he never again published anything of significance in the field.

Today, Henry Murray is recognized as one of the founders of modern personality theory, along with his Harvard colleague Gordon Allport. Furthermore, Murray was one of the first of the experimental personality psychologists to extend the field into the realm of abnormal psychology. Although his personology has been largely superseded by trait theories of personality, he nonetheless helped shape the field in the middle decades of the twentieth century.

David McClelland

**Photo 14.2
David McClelland**

As a graduate student at Yale in the early 1940s, **David McClelland** (1917–1998) learned the neo-behaviorist approach of Clark Hull, which focused on explaining an organism's motivation to engage in a behavior (Winter, 1998a). If his professors mentioned Henry Murray at all, it was to dismiss his personology as a form of pseudoscience. McClelland graduated in 1941 just as the United States was entering World War II. He was soon called on as a junior faculty member to teach a course in personality in place of the regular instructor, who'd joined the war effort. Immersing himself in the literature of personality, he soon became an expert in the field. Within a decade he'd published a textbook on the subject as well as a scholarly work outlining an experimental approach to personality assessment. Thus, David McClelland established his reputation as the *American psychologist best known for his "three needs" theory of personality*.

Influenced by Hull, McClelland came to think of personality in terms of motivations to act in particular ways (Winter, 1998b). He also thought that Murray's list of needs was a good place to start an exploration of human motivation. The late 1940s was the time of the New Look in psychology, and his student John Atkinson was investigating the effect of hunger on perception. The results were significant but not particularly interesting, and at some point they struck on the idea of using TAT pictures as stimuli. In their experiment, participants had gone one, four, or sixteen hours since their last meal, and they were asked to write brief stories in response to pictures of ambiguous social interactions. The stories of the hungry participants contained more food-related themes, particularly about the search for food rather than about the act of eating itself. McClelland and Atkinson had shown that the biological motivation of hunger could be detected in the TAT stories their participants produced, so they wondered if they could get similar results if they induced psychological motivations such as Murray's needs.

McClelland and Atkinson first turned their attention to Murray's need for achievement (Winter, 2000). Following Murray's thinking on the subject, McClelland believed that we all have a drive to accomplish things and to improve ourselves, but that this drive is stronger in some people than others. And as a student of Hull, he believed not only that motivations can be strengthened or weakened through experience but also that they can be aroused by specific aspects of the current situation. To arouse the need for achievement, McClelland and Atkinson first asked subjects to solve anagrams and other word puzzles under the guise of an intelligence test. The participants were then given false feedback, in which they were told after the first set of problems that they'd performed much better than others and after the second set that they'd performance much worse than others. The intention was to first set up the expectation that they were capable and then provide a motivation to improve themselves. The TAT stories of these participants contained more themes of striving to achieve a goal than did those in other conditions.

Having demonstrated a way to elicit and measure the need for achievement, McClelland next turned his attention to developing training programs to increase and direct this need, with the aim of improving entrepreneurship (Winter, 1998a). He and his student David Winter traveled to India to conduct workshops for small businessmen, and in follow-up assessments they found that participants afterward devoted more effort to expanding their businesses and developing new ones. McClelland also conducted sociological and historical investigations that led him to believe that the need for achievement was the driving force behind economic development. Furthermore, he asserted that the best way to help a country improve economically is by training a cohort of entrepreneurs with high need for achievement. He laid out these ideas in his best-known book, *The Achieving Society*, which he published in 1961.

Next, McClelland turned his attention to the related need for power (Harrell & Stahl, 1981). He found that people whose dominant motivation is the need for power can be divided into two types. On the one hand, those who seek social power want to influence others for the sake of achieving organizational goals. These are the inspirational leaders who encourage others to work for the good of the group. On the other hand, those who seek personal power do so only to attain their own selfish goals. They tend to be domineering and aggressive, and they're prone to fighting, sexual conquest, and excessive drinking. As national leaders, they have a tendency to draw their countries into war and conflict.

Because of the stress they bring upon themselves, those with a high need for power tend to have poor health outcomes in the long term (Winter, 1998a). McClelland identified a number of physiological correlates of the need for power, including higher levels of sympathetic nervous system arousal and lower immune functioning, resulting in greater susceptibility to infectious diseases. Moreover, the excessive drinking and substance abuse typical of those with a high need for personal power often lead to additional health issues. Encouraged by his success with training programs for increasing the need for achievement, McClelland developed programs to help people decrease their need for personal power and to increase what he believed to be the third basic motivator of humans (Table 14.2). Specifically, this is the need for affiliation, or the building of supportive social relationships, which buffer against the stressors that negatively impact health and well-being.

In sum, David McClelland's **three needs theory** was *the proposal that an individual's personality is shaped by the three basic needs of achievement, power, and affiliation, one of which will dominate.* His unusual approach to personality was built on Henry Murray's

Table 14.2 McClelland's Three Needs Theory		
Need	**Abbreviation**	**Characteristics**
Achievement	*n* Ach	Drive to succeed; compete against established goals; work best alone or with other high achievers
Power	*n* Pow	Drive to control others; compete against other people; may seek power either for personal gain or for the benefit of the group
Affiliation	*n* Aff	Drive to create and sustain harmonious relationships with others; desire to feel accepted; strive to conform to group norms

personology. Yet it failed to have a major impact on personality psychology, which at the time was converging on the view of personality as a set of dimensions, as we'll see in the following section. However, McClelland's work has enjoyed considerable currency in the field of industrial and organizational psychology, where it has served as a useful framework for studying managerial styles and group dynamics. His interdisciplinary approach extended from historical and sociological investigations into the social effects of individual personalities to physiological studies of the correlates between personality and health outcomes. In this way, McClelland demonstrated that the study of personality had practical applications in a wide range of fields.

Factor Approach

In the early twentieth century, a group of scholars tracing their academic lineage to Francis Galton formed an approach to psychology that came to be known as the London School. The members of the London School measured individual differences and searched for the laws governing those differences. At first they focused on mental testing and the nature of intelligence. But soon they found that the same tools could be used to measure individual differences in personality. The work of the London School prepared the field for the five-factor model of personality, the most widely accepted theory of personality today.

London School

The son of an aristocratic family, **Charles Spearman** (1863–1945) decided on a military career (Spearman, 1930). Wherever he was stationed, he brought along a small library of philosophy and psychology books. Learning of Wundt's laboratory of experimental psychology in Leipzig, the 34-year-old resigned his commission and went to Germany, completing his Ph.D. there in 1906. His experience in the lab taught him that experimental psychologists focused on narrow questions that had little real-world relevance. Instead, Spearman decided to devote his career to a kind of psychology that had practical value, and today he's best known as the *British psychologist who developed the theory of general intelligence*.

In 1907, William McDougall (Chapter 11) was leaving University College London to accept a position at Oxford, and Spearman was hired in his place (Spearman, 1930). McDougall was fascinated by the work that Francis Galton and Karl Pearson had done on mental tests as well as by the research of Alfred Binet in Paris, and he suggested Spearman pursue this topic. Spearman followed up on this advice, but he had a greater purpose in mind. Instead of administering mental tests to sort people into categories, he used the tests as a means of exploring the nature of intelligence. At the time, many psychologists subscribed to the idea of mental faculties, which were thought of as compartmentalized cognitive abilities. However, Spearman suspected that there may be some component in common among the different faculties. To test this idea, he looked at correlations among an individual's performance on a variety of tasks. If the mind were composed of faculties, then the correlations should be low. But instead he found them to be quite high, suggesting a singular intelligence rather than a collection of faculties.

This discovery led to the **two-factor theory of intelligence**, which was *Spearman's proposal that any cognitive ability consists of both general intelligence common to all tasks and the specific intelligence required for that particular task* (Spearman, 1930). Spearman labeled general intelligence g and specific intelligence s. Furthermore, he argued that g is due to the biological structuring of the nervous system, so it must be inherited. Although Spearman's idea of general intelligence had its adherents, it also had many detractors. For instance, you may recall from Chapter 4 that L. L. Thurstone challenged Spearman, claiming instead

Photo 14.3
Charles Spearman

Eugène Pirou, Bibliothèque nationale de France

to have found evidence for seven primary mental abilities. Until the middle of the twentieth century, a contentious debate raged on both sides of the Atlantic about whether intelligence was singular or multiple in its structure, and to some extent the argument continues to the present day.

As a skilled statistician, Spearman devised mathematical methods for demonstrating general intelligence, which came to be recognized as the first application of what became known as factor analysis (Lovie & Lovie, 1996). On the western side of the Atlantic, Thurstone refined Spearman's approach, using this new method of factor analysis to detect his proposed primary mental abilities. On the eastern side of the Atlantic, Spearman's many students remained loyal to their mentor's theory of general intelligence, and furthermore they devised their own factor-analytic techniques that were somewhat different from those used in North America.

During his career at University College London, Spearman built the first psychology department in Great Britain (Lovie & Lovie, 1996). He attracted a large number of students, who collectively became known as the London School. Based on the anthropometric tradition of Francis Galton and Karl Pearson, the London School focused on psychometrics, which is the field involved in the measurement of an individual's psychological characteristics. Although Spearman's interest was in studying the structure of intelligence, his students soon understood that psychometric techniques such as testing and factor analysis could also be used to explore other facets of psychology that involved individual differences, particularly personality.

Spearman's successor at University College London was **Cyril Burt** (1883–1971), an educational psychologist for the London school system (MacKay, 2013). Burt had been collecting data on children for nearly two decades when he assumed his position as the new leader of the London School. Burt was from an aristocratic family, and he firmly believed that the social inequalities existed because the political and economic system favored the rise of those with high intelligence to positions of wealth and power while leaving those of less intelligence in poverty. Furthermore, he believed that intelligence was strongly inherited and that the environment played little or no role in its development. In his quest to find evidence to support these beliefs, Burt became known as the *British psychologist who pioneered the use of twin studies to test the heritability of intelligence.*

Through connections in the London school system, Burt was able to locate a number of identical twins who'd been raised apart (Butler & Petrulis, 1999). He administered intelligence tests to these twins, and he also did assessments of their biological and adopted parents. The goal of this research program was to determine the heritability of intelligence. The term **heritability** has special meaning here, specifically referring to *a statistic indicating the degree to which genetic factors account for the observed variation in a population.* Heritability values range from zero, meaning no influence of genetics, to one, meaning no influence from the environment. It's important to note that the concept of heritability can only be used in reference to groups, not to individuals.

Burt was a prolific writer who published influential books on a range of topics in educational psychology, including adolescent delinquency and mental retardation in children (Jensen, 1991). Hailed as Britain's greatest psychologist, he was even knighted in 1949, the first psychologist to receive such an honor. Even after his retirement, he continued to publish frequently.

A series of articles Burt published after his retirement stirred up a controversy that rocked British psychology (MacKay, 2013). In these papers, Burt cited data from his twin studies. These data were accepted at face value while Burt was alive, but psychologists began noting inconsistencies in them shortly after his death. It's unclear why Burt reported false data in these papers. Of course, the numbers he gave strongly supported his thesis that intelligence is genetically based. And yet, by the time he published these reports, other researchers had already accumulated considerable evidence supporting the heritability of intelligence. Burt's supporters speculated that he may have been trying to reconstruct early data that had been lost during World War II. Nevertheless, both friends and foes had to admit that Burt had committed scientific fraud.

University of Liverpool

Photo 14.4
Cyril Burt

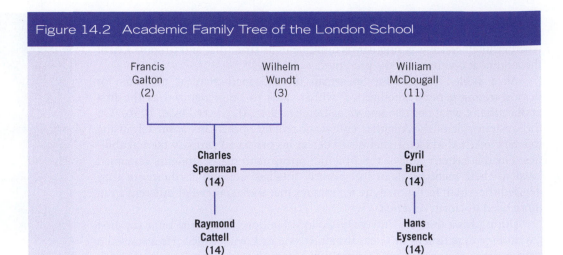

Figure 14.2 Academic Family Tree of the London School

After Burt's death, the London School became very influential in the development of modern personality theory, and yet it continued to be plagued by controversy (MacKay, 2013). This was because its members were often associated with the eugenics movement, both before and after World War II (Figure 14.2). As we've already seen, many members of the intellectual elite on both sides of the Atlantic advocated for eugenic measures in the early twentieth century, but after World War II more egalitarian attitudes toward social reform became the norm. In particular, the London School's emphasis on the heritability of intelligence and its rejection of environmental factors has been interpreted by many as racist. In the following sections, we'll meet two members of the London School who laid the groundwork for the Big Five model, now the most widely accepted theory of personality structure. And yet it was almost as if the ghost of Cyril Burt had come back to haunt these two men late in their careers.

Raymond Cattell

As an undergraduate at the University College London, **Raymond Cattell** (1905–1998) studied chemistry (Cattell, 1974). But he also had a strong desire to help solve the world's political and economic problems, and he felt he could do more if he studied psychology instead. Spearman taught him the methods of factor analysis, and Cattell earned his Ph.D. in 1929. Although he started in the field of intelligence testing, after he immigrated to the United States he spent most of his career using psychometric techniques to study the structure of personality. Thus, Cattell developed a reputation as the *British-American psychologist who proposed an influential sixteen-factor model of personality.*

For nearly a decade, Cattell lived hand-to-mouth on the paltry salaries he earned as a social worker and educational psychologist (Cattell, 1974). However, he also managed to publish some papers on intelligence that attracted the attention of Edward Thorndike, who invited him to a one-year visiting professorship at Columbia. After that, he was offered a position at Clark, and he decided to make the United States his new home.

During these years, Cattell developed his well-known theory of fluid versus crystallized intelligence (Horn, 2001). According to Cattell, **fluid intelligence** is *the ability to solve novel problems quickly,* whereas **crystallized intelligence** is *the accumulation of knowledge over a lifetime.* He also claimed that the intelligence tests then in use mainly measured crystallized intelligence, meaning that they were biased in favor of the educated American middle class.

Minorities and immigrants who were tested with these instruments necessarily performed poorly because their life experiences were different. To remedy this problem, he developed a **culture-free intelligence test**, which is *an instrument that measures fluid intelligence*. Using this kind of test, he claimed, people of all languages and cultures could be measured on an equal footing.

At the invitation of Edwin Boring (Chapter 5), Cattell joined the Harvard faculty in 1941 (Cattell, 1974). There, he interacted with Gordon Allport and Henry Murray, learning about their theories of personality. Cattell thought the factor-analytic methods that had been used to study the nature of intelligence could also be applied to an exploration of the structure of personality. Starting with Allport's list of 4,500 trait adjectives, he worked to condense these into thirty-five bipolar variables, with clusters of words at one end being rough synonyms and those at the other end rough antonyms of these. He then drew lists of words from these variables and asked participants to select which of these described either their own personality or that of someone they knew well. Afterward, he analyzed these data in an attempt to extract their factor structure.

Photo 14.5
Raymond Cattell

Cattell Family, via Wikimedia Commons, CC BY-SA 3.0, https://creativecommons.org/licenses/by-sa/3.0/deed.en

Shortly after the end of World War II, Cattell accepted a position at the University of Illinois (Revelle, 2009). Ordinarily, a shift from Harvard to Illinois would be seen as a large step downward in an academic's career, but Illinois had something Harvard didn't—the world's most powerful computer. Factor analysis is computationally intensive, and performing one by hand can take weeks to complete. But the new computer could reduce computation time to hours, and furthermore it could perform factor analyses on data sets far more extensive than were viable by hand. His goal was to map out the structure of human personality, just as the periodic table maps out the organization of the elements in chemistry. To this end, Cattell established a laboratory at Illinois that attracted a large number of graduate students and postdocs.

At Illinois, Cattell and his students were very productive, publishing dozens of articles and several books over the following decade (Horn, 2001). These analyses concluded that personality was composed of at least a dozen and up to sixteen first-order factors. However, these could be further condensed into five second-order factors. While the first-order factors described specific attributes of personality, the second-order factors described general tendencies to behave in ways that are expressed by the first-order factors. In other words, personality had a hierarchical structure, with broad second-order factors above and two or three narrow first-order factors clustered underneath each of these. He laid out this theory in his 1950 book *Personality: A Systematic, Theoretical, and Factual Study*.

Cattell also expanded his research repertoire beyond the lexical methods he'd adopted from Allport to include the use of questionnaires (Digman, 1990). To this end, he devised the Sixteen Personality Factor Questionnaire (16PF) to measure each of the first-order factors he'd found in his analyses. However, other researchers challenged such a complex structure of personality. When they administered the 16PF and performed factor analyses on the resulting data, they came up with far fewer factors. In most cases, what emerged from the analysis was a set of five factors resembling Cattell's second-order factors, with few or none of the first-order factors detected. As a result, other psychologists have named Cattell the father of the modern five-factor model of personality, a title he vigorously rejected. For the rest of his life, he insisted on the correctness of his sixteen-factor hierarchical model.

Having conquered intelligence and personality, Cattell sought to create a unified theory of human behavior (Ackerman, 2009). He saw the range of individual differences as extending across three interrelated domains—intelligence, personality, and motivation. If you could measure an individual's characteristics in each of these domains, you could make accurate predictions about behavior. For instance, a person high in intelligence but low in motivation may not learn to perform a task as well as a person of average intelligence but high motivation, who persists at the task until it's mastered.

Cattell received many honors during his lifetime (Horn, 2001). However, this impeccable reputation began to unravel during the last year of his life. When Cattell was forced to retire at 65, he moved to Hawaii, where he could pursue his hobby of sailing. He also kept busy writing, often on subjects far removed from his research. In a series of articles and a book, Cattell proposed a new religion he called "Beyondism" that was supposedly based on evolutionary theory. According to this view, natural selection should be allowed to take its course without human interference. In this way, superior individuals and groups would prosper while those who were inferior would go extinct. As a result, the human species would be much improved.

Cattell insisted he wasn't racist, as it was up to natural selection to decide who would flourish and who would fail (Tucker, 2005). But it also came out that Cattell had been very active in the eugenics movement back in England, and he'd even published on the subject. That in itself may have been forgivable, since many psychologists before World War II held similar views. However, many readers interpreted Beyondism as little more than eugenics in new garb. Such attitudes were simply unpalatable to most academics by the late twentieth century.

In 1997, the APA selected Cattell for their Gold Medal Award of Life Achievement in Psychological Science (Tucker, 2005). Frail with cancer, Cattell traveled from Hawaii to Chicago to accept the award. However, in the days before the presentation, several psychologists lodged protests, pointing not only to his earlier work in eugenics and his racially provocative ideas of Beyondism, but also claiming they had evidence of his involvement in the White supremacist movement. Cattell strongly denied the charge of racism, but he withdrew his name and returned to Hawaii without the award. A few months later, with the accusations against him never resolved, he died.

Raymond Cattell was one of the most influential psychologists of the last half of the twentieth century (Horn, 2001). He nurtured dozens of graduate students, many of whom become leaders in their field. Collaborating with students and colleagues, he produced more than forty books and 500 articles over a long career. The accusations of racism that blemished the end of his life, whether reasonable or not, certainly didn't represent the vast body of work he'd accomplished during his lifetime.

Hans Eysenck

Born in Berlin, **Hans Eysenck** (1916–1997; pronounced *EYE-sink*) grew up in a theatrical family (Eysenck, 1980). His parents were actors, and their stormy marriage was as melodramatic as the roles they played on stage. He was raised by his grandmother, an aspiring actor whose career was cut short when a dislocated hip left her with a heavy limp. As a college student, he fled Hitler's Germany for England, where he spent the rest of his life. But even when he'd developed a reputation as the *German-British psychologist who advanced a three-factor theory of personality*, he still showed a flair for the theatrical, with drama and controversy as distinguishing features in his colorful career.

Eysenck wanted to study physics, but the registrar at University College London wouldn't recognize the coursework he'd already done in Germany, so he declared psychology as his major instead (Eysenck, 1980). By this time, Charles Spearman had retired, and Cyril Burt was chair of the psychology department. Burt put Eysenck to work reanalyzing the data that Thurstone had used to challenge Spearman's concept of general intelligence. To Burt's satisfaction, Eysenck demonstrated the data could indeed be accounted for by Spearman's two-factor model. This was Eysenck's introduction to factor analysis, a technique he would frequently use during the rest of his career.

When Eysenck completed his Ph.D. in 1940, England was at war, he was declared an "enemy alien," and he was blocked from any further work in psychology (Eysenck, 1980). Burt suffered from paranoid tendencies,

Photo 14.6
Hans Eysenck

and fearing that his bright young student sought to usurp him as the leader of the London School, he denied Eysenck's application for a position at the college. There was only one other psychology department in the country, that of Frederic Bartlett at Cambridge. While the Cambridge School engaged in experimental psychology, the London School focused on psychometrics, and neither school recognized the other as legitimate. Eysenck spent the war years as a social worker in the slums of London, where this "enemy alien" endeared himself to the locals with his skills at soccer and cricket.

After the war, the Institute of Psychiatry was established in London as a training and research facility (Buchanan, 2011). Through connections he'd made during the war years, Eysenck was offered a research position at the institute, and there he remained for the rest of his career. In this position, he developed the first training program in clinical psychology in England that was separate from the psychiatric and psychoanalytic traditions, both of which he criticized for being unscientific. Instead, he advocated for the use of behavioral techniques, as validated through empirical research, to treat psychological disorders.

Eysenck (1980) was a strong proponent of the **scientist-practitioner model**, which is *an approach to training clinical psychologists both as researchers and as therapists*. He also believed that clinical psychologists should be permitted to practice therapy without the oversight of a psychiatrist. Over the years, Eysenck built the Institute of Psychiatry into one of the nation's premier research facilities, and he trained hundreds of graduate students, many of whom went on to illustrious careers in personality and clinical psychology. Through collaborations with his students and colleagues, Eysenck published eighty books and a thousand scholarly papers. He was also a popular writer, publishing bestselling books with catchy titles like *Know Your Own IQ* (1962) and *Fact and Fiction in Psychology* (1965).

When Eysenck joined the Institute of Psychiatry, the field was dominated by psychoanalytic theory (Wilson, 1998). An important task for the practitioners at the institute was the drawing up of a detailed personality profile for each patient. But Eysenck was skeptical of the projective tests in common use at the time, and he doubted the reliability of the psychiatrists' subjective assessments of their patients. Instead, he believed that more objective measures were needed, and to that end he developed the Eysenck Personality Questionnaire (EPQ), which underwent a number of revisions during his lifetime.

As data were obtained from patients, Eysenck subjected them to factor analysis to explore the structure of personality (Farley, 2000). The results suggested that the data could be accounted for by two distinct factors. One factor seemed to be related to the degree of sociability, and he called this "Extraversion," borrowing the term from Carl Jung. The second factor seemed to involve susceptibility to anxiety and emotional instability, and he called this "Neuroticism." Although Eysenck was influenced by Jung's ideas, there was also an important difference between the two men's approach to personality. Whereas Jung thought in terms of categories—you're either extraverted or introverted—Eysenck envisioned personality factors as dimensions. That is, you can range anywhere from extreme extraversion to extreme introversion, with most people clustering in the midrange.

At the time, the two main psychological diagnoses were hysteria and neurosis, and Eysenck (1980) believed the extraversion dimension is what distinguished the two. Both sets of patients were high on the neuroticism scale, but the hysterics were extraverted and expressed their symptoms outwardly as bizarre behaviors, whereas the neurotics were introverted and turned their symptoms inward as anxiety and depression. Eysenck described this two-factor theory of personality in his first book, *Dimensions of Personality* (1947). The extraversion and neuroticism factors have remained common to all subsequent factor theories of personality.

After collecting more data and conducting further analyses, Eysenck believed he'd detected a third factor of personality structure (Farley, 2000). This factor involved a person's ability to cooperate with others as opposed to being aggressive and hostile. At moderately high levels, this trait seemed to describe people who were ambitious and domineering. But Eysenck believed that extremely high levels led to a tendency toward schizophrenia, and for this reason he labeled the factor "Psychoticism." He published his modified three-factor theory in his 1952 book *The Structure of Human Personality*. This personality dimension remains contentious, with other personality theorists either denying its existence or else arguing that it was a conflation of other personality factors. Nevertheless, Eysenck remained committed to his PEN model (Psychoticism-Extraversion-Neuroticism) for the rest of his life.

In his theory, Eysenck went beyond a mere description of the structure of personality and tried to explain that structure by linking it to biological conditions of the nervous system (Rose, 2010). For instance, he explained extraversion in terms of resting levels of cortical activity. He believed that extraverted people had low levels of arousal, and so they sought out stimulating activities such as social interactions to bring their arousal up to the optimum, in accord with the Yerkes-Dodson law. In contrast, introverted people already have high levels of arousal, and they withdraw from social interactions because they find them overly stimulating. As evidence for this theory, he pointed to the known effects of certain commonly used drugs. On the one hand, stimulants like caffeine and amphetamines increase attention and decrease distractions—key characteristics of introverts. On the other hand, depressants such as alcohol tend to make people less inhibited and more easily distractible—key characteristics of extraverts.

Eysenck seemed to revel in the limelight of controversy, but two incidents in particular brought him scathing criticism from professional colleagues and the popular press alike. The first incident involved a major research project on the link between smoking and cancer (Buchanan, 2011). This epidemiological study was funded with generous research grants from the American tobacco industry totaling over a million dollars. Eysenck insisted he could remain unbiased despite the source of his funding, but others questioned his neutrality, especially after he came to the conclusion that smoking didn't cause cancer after all. Instead, he insisted, a cancer-prone personality type leads some people to both substance abuse and a higher incidence of cancer because of poor lifestyle choices. As usual, Eysenck remained steadfast in his conclusions despite vicious attacks against him.

The second incident occurred when one of his former students, Arthur Jensen (1923–2012), published an article that touched on the question of race and intelligence (Farley, 2000). In a nutshell, Jensen argued that centuries of systematic oppression and discrimination against African Americans had had a cumulative detrimental effect. As a result, simple equality of educational opportunities would not be enough to raise them to parity with European Americans, at least not within a single generation. This idea struck a raw nerve among academics beholden to the behaviorist attitude that intelligence is a product of experience alone. Eysenck rushed to Jensen's defense. The intention was to clarify the issue, but instead it only fanned the flames and made him a target of attack as well. If scholars disagreed with Jensen's arguments about the causes of group differences, Eysenck insisted, they should respond with facts to support their position rather than making personal attacks. This is sound advice, but of course Eysenck often failed to follow it in his own dealings with his competitors.

In the last half of the twentieth century, Hans Eysenck was one of the world's most famous psychologists, ranking in name recognition with B. F. Skinner and Sigmund Freud. Indeed, he did much to educate the general public on the most recent findings in scientific psychology. Professionally, he was a pioneer in at least two fields, personality research and clinical psychology. His PEN model has served as a foundation on which many other factor theories of personality are based. He was also responsible in large part for shaping clinical psychology into the form it has today, namely as a research-based therapeutic approach that is independent of psychiatry and psychoanalysis. Although his later career was mired in controversy, Eysenck would no doubt have seen this as inevitable—after all, a penchant for the theatrical was in his genes.

Big Five

The factor approaches pioneered by Raymond Cattell and Hans Eysenck set the benchmark for personality research in the last half of the twentieth century (John, Naumann, & Soto, 2008). As other researchers attempted to replicate these studies, they often came up with results that contradicted the original models. However, by the 1980s the work of various research groups began to converge on *a model of personality consisting of five factors* that has come to be known as the **Big Five**.

On the one hand, Cattell had used the lexical approach first developed by Gordon Allport, in which participants were asked to select from word lists those trait descriptors that applied either to themselves or to someone they knew well (John et al., 2008). In his factor analyses, Cattell reported sixteen primary factors that could be grouped into five secondary factors. Other researchers who took the lexical approach often failed to find Cattell's sixteen primary factors. However, their analyses frequently revealed five factors that seemed to be getting at the same broad set of traits as Cattell's secondary factors.

On the other hand, Eysenck employed a questionnaire approach in which respondents indicated which behavior they'd perform in a given situation (John et al., 2008). His analyses led him to the three-factor PEN model (Psychoticism, Extraversion, and Neuroticism). Other researchers using the questionnaire approach typically replicated the extraversion and neuroticism factors but not psychoticism. Instead, it appears that psychoticism was a mixture of two or three other factors. Most commonly, researchers using either approach found that five factors best fit their data.

Lewis Goldberg, who followed the lexical approach, argued that these various analyses converging on five factors were in fact homing in on the same five sets of broad personality traits, which he called the "Big Five" (John et al., 2008). By this term, he didn't mean that all of personality can be reduced to five simple traits. Rather, each of the Big Five factors stood for a broad category of interrelated facets of personality. For example, talkativeness, sociability, and outgoingness are all aspects of extraversion. According to Goldberg's Big Five model, the personality factors were:

- *Extraversion*, the same as in Eysenck's model.

- *Agreeableness*, a measure of how well an individual gets along with others.

- *Conscientiousness*, a measure of how reliable an individual is.

- *Emotional Stability*, the same as Eysenck's *neuroticism* dimension but labeled by its opposite pole.

- *Culture*, a global measure of an individual's intelligence and curiosity.

Meanwhile, the team of Robert McCrae and Paul Costa were converging on a five-factor model of personality using the questionnaire approach (John et al., 2008). Their original model had three factors, with two—neuroticism and extraversion—being the same as in the Eysenck model. But when they examined the characteristics of their third dimension, it didn't look at all like psychoticism. Instead, it seemed to involve something along the lines of curiosity, adventurousness, and worldliness. They called the factor *openness to new experiences*, or just openness for short. They'd also developed a reliable instrument for measuring these three traits, which they called the NEO-PI (Neuroticism-Extraversion-Openness Personality Inventory).

Seeing a similarity between their openness factor and Goldberg's culture factor, McCrae and Costa expanded the NEO-PI to also include questions about agreeableness and conscientiousness (John et al., 2008). The Five-Factor Model they proposed was arranged as follows (using the conventional OCEAN acronym):

- *Openness* to new experiences, corresponding to Goldberg's *culture*.

- *Conscientiousness*, as in Goldberg's model.

- *Extraversion*, as in Eysenck's and Goldberg's models.

- *Agreeableness*, as in Goldberg's model.

- *Neuroticism*, using Eysenck's term and the same as Goldberg's *emotional stability* but scored in reverse.

Table 14.3 Five-Factor Model of Personality

Factor	High	Low
Openness to experience	Imaginative, adventurous, and curious	Pragmatic, predictable, and conventional
Conscientiousness	Self-disciplined, orderly, and dependable	Impulsive, disorganized, and unreliable
Extraversion	Enthusiastic, action-oriented, and assertive	Quiet, deliberate, and reserved
Agreeableness	Friendly, trusting, and cooperative	Unfriendly, suspicious, and uncooperative
Neuroticism	Easily upset, emotionally unstable, and vulnerable to stress	Generally calm, emotionally stable, and less vulnerable to stress

Although there are many similarities between Goldberg's Big Five model and McCrae and Costa's Five-Factor Model, there's also an important difference (John et al., 2008). Goldberg views the Big Five only as a descriptive model of personality that likely reflects an interaction of universal and culturally specific traits. For instance, the lexical approach has now been attempted in over a dozen languages, typically with four or five of the original factors replicating but often with one or two culturally specific factors emerging from the analysis as well. In contrast, McCrae and Costa believe the Five-Factor Model to be a universal description of human behavior based on genetically determined biological structures and processes, just as Eysenck had argued. At any rate, the Big Five—or the Five-Factor Model, whichever name you prefer—has become the most widely accepted framework for thinking about personality in the twenty-first century (Table 14.3).

Social Cognitive Approach

There's a tendency among trait and factor theorists to assume that personality is largely innate and quite stable in adulthood. And yet social psychologists have amply demonstrated the power of social situations to shape behavior. In the last half of the twentieth century, a group of psychologists taking what became known as the social cognitive approach asked how the discrepancy between apparently enduring personality traits and the behavioral demands of social situations could be reconciled. What unfolded was an extended and often fierce debate between personality and social psychologists that eventually led to the synthesis that now unites the two fields today.

Julian Rotter

While growing up in Brooklyn, **Julian Rotter** (1916–2014, pronounced like *rotor*) enrolled at Brooklyn College, where Solomon Asch (Chapter 12) piqued his curiosity about psychology (Strickland, 2014). He also attended lectures by Alfred Adler (Chapter 7), who was then teaching at the Long Island College of Medicine, and he even joined the Society of Individual Psychology, which held its meetings at Adler's apartment. Adler passed away shortly after that, but Rotter followed Asch's recommendation to do graduate work at Iowa with Kurt Lewin (Chapter 6). Rotter's focus lay in clinical psychology, although he also studied individual differences throughout his career. Today he's best known as the *American psychologist who developed the social learning theory of personality and the concept of locus of control.*

During the year Rotter spent at Iowa, he took an interest in Lewin's **levels of aspiration theory** (Strickland, 2014). This is *the proposal that successful completion of a task depends not only on ability but also the motivation to complete it.* After Iowa, Rotter undertook an internship at Worcester State Hospital, where he developed an instrument for measuring level of aspiration, and he continued his research on individual differences in reaction to success or failure using this instrument for his dissertation research, earning his Ph.D. at the University of Indiana in 1941.

After graduation, Rotter enlisted in the Army, where he served as a clinical psychologist assessing the psychological fitness of hospitalized soldiers for a return to active duty (Ames & Riggio, 1995). To aid in this task, Rotter developed a projective test in which he asked his patients to complete sentence stems such as "I like . . ." or "My greatest worry is. . . ." The responses were then analyzed for signs of maladjustment. This instrument became known as the Rotter Incomplete Sentences Blank (RISB), which consisted of forty such sentence stems. The RISB became one of the most widely used projective tests in both research and clinical diagnosis during the last half of the twentieth century.

In 1946, Rotter was offered a faculty position at The Ohio State University, which was developing a program in clinical psychology ("Julian B. Rotter," 1989). It was during this time that he began forming his ideas on personality. He believed that at least some aspects of personality were due to life histories, and even in the Army he'd been trying to find a way to integrate current learning theories with the study of individual differences.

According to reinforcement theory, behaviors that lead to positive outcomes tend to be repeated (Rotter, 1975). While this may be true for nonhuman animals, Rotter insisted that people respond instead to their interpretation of the meaning of the reinforcement, and he explored this idea in a series of learning experiments. In one condition participants were consistently reinforced for their successes, but in the other condition reinforcement was random, sometimes occurring after successes and other times after failures. Most of the participants in the first condition soon learned that they had control over the reinforcement, that is, it consistently followed their successful performances. Likewise, most of the participants in the second condition learned that they had no control over the reinforcement, in that it occurred randomly. However, a few people in the first condition maintained the belief that the reinforcement remained outside of their control, while a few in the second condition maintained the belief that they controlled reinforcement outcomes.

Around this same time, Rotter also noticed in his clinical practice that some patients maintained the belief that events in their life were beyond their control (Rotter, 1990). That is, they often felt themselves to be the victims of bad luck or under the manipulation of powerful others, and furthermore they interpreted positive outcomes as chance occurrences rather than as something that had been brought about through their own efforts. These two observations—one in the laboratory and the other in the clinic—led him to propose the construct of **internal versus external control of reinforcement**. This refers to *the belief that life events are the outcome either of personal effort or of outside forces.*

People with internal beliefs see events in their lives as natural consequences of their behaviors, whereas those with external beliefs see the world as under the control of arbitrary forces (Rotter, 1975). The implication of this is that people with internal orientations should more readily adapt to reinforcements, which they see as meaningful because they view them as contingent on their behavior. In contrast, those with external orientations don't see reinforcements as meaningful because they don't perceive a relationship between their behaviors and reinforcements, and so they fail to learn from them. *Another term for internal versus external control of reinforcement* is **locus of control**. Although this term is more commonly used, it wasn't the expression Rotter preferred.

Locus of control may be the construct he's most famous for, but Rotter (1975) insisted it was but one part of his much larger **social learning theory of personality**. This was *Rotter's account of individual differences as developing through divergent life histories.* Rotter summed up the basic premises of his social learning in a simple equation, $BP = f(E\&RV)$. Here, BP stands for behavior potential, or the likelihood that a given person will engage in a particular behavior, and it depends on two variables. The first is the expectancy (E) that a reinforcement will follow the behavior, or in other words, locus of control. The second is the significance the person attaches to that reinforcement, which he called the reinforcement value (RV). In this equation, we can see the clear influence of Kurt Lewin, who had proposed that behavior is a function of both the person and the environment, or B = f(P,E). Rotter expanded Lewin's equation by taking into account the person's cognitions about the situation.

Rotter (1990) also lamented that many of his fellow psychologists had misconstrued locus of control as a personality trait without reference to social learning theory. First, he insisted that an internal or external locus of control was learned through a lifetime of experience. Second, he maintained that internal versus external orientations are endpoints on a continuous dimension rather than distinct categories. Third, he argued that internal and external orientations are dependent on the situation rather than being enduring characteristics of personality. And fourth, he objected to the widespread assumption that an internal locus of control was "good" while an external locus of control was "bad." Which orientation a person should take depends on the situation, and it's a sign of maladjustment to maintain a consistently internal or external locus of control despite evidence to the contrary.

Julian Rotter pursued studies of individual differences to provide insights into the minds of his clinical patients and to help him develop more effective approaches to therapy (Strickland, 2014). He also impacted the field of clinical psychology in other ways, first as mentor to over a hundred graduate students and second as an important advocate for the scientist-practitioner model, which became the standard for the field during the last half of the twentieth century. Finally, his social learning theory challenged many of the assumptions of personality psychology by presenting an interactionist interpretation of individual differences while emphasizing the cognitive and social factors that influence behavior. This social cognitive approach to personality was also adopted by many of his students, two of whom we'll meet in the following sections.

Walter Mischel

For his first eight years, **Walter Mischel** (1930–2018) enjoyed an affluent family life in Vienna (Mischel, 2007). His father was a prosperous and cheerful businessman, while his mother had little to do each day but look pretty and complain about her nerves. When the Nazis invaded Austria, the Mischels fled. They eventually settled in a poor immigrant neighborhood in Brooklyn, and his parents ran a five-and-dime store. Grieving the loss of his former life, his father turned solemn and depressed, while his mother became optimistic and confident as she managed the store and several other part-time businesses. The changes in personalities that Mischel witnessed in his parents turned into a theme for his career, and he developed a reputation as an *Austrian-American psychologist who advocated for a social cognitive approach to personality*.

Mischel initially studied art at New York University, but his interest soon turned to psychology (Mischel, 2007). He completed a master's degree in clinical psychology at the City College of New York, taking classes at night and serving as a social worker during the day. Although Mischel was fascinated by the psychoanalytic theory and clinical methods he learned, he also found them difficult to apply in his dealings with his clients living in the slums of the Lower East Side. Desiring to learn a scientifically supported approach to therapy and social work, he did his Ph.D. in the clinical psychology program at The Ohio State University, then considered one of the best in the nation.

There were two star professors in the Ohio State clinical program (Mischel, 2007). The first was Julian Rotter, who was developing his social learning theory of personality. The second was **George Kelly** (1905–1967), the *American psychologist who proposed personal construct theory*. During the years Mischel was at Ohio State, Kelly published his 1955 book *Psychology of Personal Constructs*, in which he laid out his **personal construct theory**. This was *Kelly's proposal that people actively interpret the situations they encounter in order to control and predict the events in their lives*. In other words, social situations have no intrinsic meaning that is objectively accessible to everyone. Rather, each individual interprets a given situation in a way that's meaningful to him or her. For instance, most people think clowns are entertaining, but some find them frightening. Kelly also had faith that people could act rationally—as amateur scientists testing hypotheses against experience as they interpret the events of their lives. Thus, he had a unique approach to psychotherapy that involved helping clients reinterpret problematic situations. For example, he would guide the person with a clown phobia to an understanding that a previous unpleasant experience doesn't mean that all clowns are bad.

Mischel (2007) noted that Rotter and Kelly had offices as far apart from each other as possible, and that they had little personal interaction and no cross-references in their publications. Each gathered a loyal group of graduate students who emulated their mentor and disparaged his rival. However, Mischel felt attracted to both men's theories, and he saw his own work as an attempt to integrate social learning and personal construct theories into a comprehensive framework for understanding personality.

After graduation, Mischel spent several summers on the Caribbean island of Trinidad studying members of a religious group called Shango that practiced spirit possession ("Walter Mischel," 1983). The plan was to use projective tests to explore the inner psyche of these cult members. Although they were eager to help him with his project, most of the stories they told in response to TAT pictures were related to the plots of recent American movies. He also did some testing in the local schools, in the process stumbling upon the research program that he's most famous for today.

The village where Mischel was staying was inhabited by two ethnic groups, who referred to themselves as Africans and East Indians (Mischel, 2007). In conversations with the villagers, he soon learned the local attitudes. According to the Africans, all the East Indians ever did was work hard and stuff their money under their mattress and they never had any fun. And the East Indian perspective was that all the Africans ever did was enjoy themselves in the moment with no thought for the future. Mischel wondered if there was any truth to this, so he conducted an informal test. After working with the schoolchildren, he offered them a choice of either a small treat today or a larger treat when he returned the following week. Indeed, the children tended to respond according to their ethnic stereotype, with the African children more likely to take the smaller treat now and the East Indian children more likely to wait for the larger treat.

It wasn't until Mischel joined the faculty of Stanford in 1966 that he began to formally investigate the delay of gratification in young children (Mischel, Shoda, & Rodriguez, 1989). Availing himself of the same nursery school on the Stanford campus that his colleague Albert Bandura (Chapter 13) had used in his famous Bobo doll studies, he tested the ability of young children to forego a smaller-but-sooner treat for a larger-but-later one. In the standard procedure, which has become known as the "marshmallow test," the child is seated at a table in front of a small treat, such as a marshmallow or pretzel. She's told that she can eat the treat whenever she wants, but if she waits until the experimenter returns in fifteen minutes, she can have two treats instead. The child is then left alone in the room, but her actions are recorded by a hidden video camera.

There was a clear difference in personality profiles between those children who waited for the later-but-larger treat and those who didn't (Mischel et al., 1989). Those who couldn't wait tended to focus their attention on the small treat in front of them, whereas those who waited were successful because they found ways to distract their attention away from the temptation. These differences in behavioral patterns were still evident in a follow-up study conducted ten years later. According to parental reports, those who'd delayed gratification at age four were doing better at school, exhibited fewer behavioral problems, and had better social skills. Furthermore, those who passed the marshmallow test scored higher on the Scholastic Aptitude Test (SAT). Not only does the ability to delay gratification develop at an early age, it also seems to be a persistent personality trait.

Person Versus Situation Debate

The marshmallow test caught the attention of the press and sparked the public's imagination. Among psychologists, however, Mischel is best known for his devastating criticism of personality theory in the mid-twentieth century, as well as for his framework for rethinking the nature of personality.

In 1968, Mischel published *Personality and Assessment* (Mischel, 2004). In that book, he proposed that personality research for more than half a century had been guided by untenable assumptions that had led the field astray. Specifically, he argued that the idea of personality traits as being consistent across all situations was simply not supported by the evidence. For instance, people who are extraverted in some situations may act introverted in others. As a result, personality assessments of enduring traits tend to have low predictive value when those people are observed in real-life circumstances. He was especially critical of projective tests, but he claimed that even questionnaires, which forced people to choose from a set of alternatives, were hardly any better at predicting behavior. The book created an uproar. Personality psychologists accused Mischel of trying to destroy the field, while social psychologists interpreted it as support for their position that situations were the major determinants of behavior. He became infamous as the psychologist who supposedly claimed we have no personalities, which of course was a complete misrepresentation of his position.

Personality and Assessment centered on a problem he called the **personality paradox** (Mischel, 2004). This is *the observation that people's behaviors are inconsistent across a wide range of situations even though our intuitions tell us that individuals display enduring personality traits.* Personality researchers already recognized this problem, but they attributed it to measurement error. If only they could come up with more precise measures of personality, they claimed, the paradox would disappear. But Mischel argued against this position, maintaining instead that the reason for the personality paradox is that situations are also important forces in shaping behavior.

The uproar caused by *Personality and Assessment* became known as the **person versus situation debate** (Mischel, 2004). This was *an argument among psychologists during the 1970s about whether personalities or situations were the main determinant of behavior.* There was much heat but little light in this protracted controversy, as personality psychologists contended that situations weren't important, and social psychologists maintained that personality wasn't important. In fact, both sides had missed the point. Mischel's thesis was that people's behavior was guided by an interaction between their personality and the current situation. Such a contention was hardly new, since Kurt Lewin (Chapter 6) had expressed the same idea in the 1930s. But it took a decade for the debate to calm down, and it still simmers to this day.

Mischel's solution to the personality paradox involved a blending of Rotter's social learning theory and Kelly's personal construct theory, which he called the **social cognitive approach** to personality (Mischel, 2004). This is *a model of personality proposing that behavior is driven by the individual's unique interpretation of a given situation.* People construe the same situation in different ways because they have different expectancies about how the situation will unfold and different goals they hope to accomplish. Mischel laid out these ideas and supported them with data in a series of articles he published in the 1970s and 1980s. In brief, he argued that our intuitions about enduring personality traits have some validity, in that people tend to act in consistent ways in similar situations. In other words, people don't behave consistently across a wide variety of situations, but their behavior is predictable across situations that the person perceives as having features in common. Thus, it's meaningless to say something like "Bill is very outgoing" unless you also specify the type of situation in which this trait is expressed, as in: "Bill is very outgoing at parties." Likewise, Marie may be level headed on most occasions, but she panics when she takes tests.

Walter Mischel was one of the most influential psychologists of the last half of the twentieth century. In his later years, he became well known to lay audiences for his 2014 popular press book *The Marshmallow Test*, followed by a number of television appearances. Although the marshmallow test captured the public's imagination, Mischel's most important contribution to psychology was his challenge to accepted personality theory, laying bare its fatal flaws and pointing in the direction psychologists needed to go if they truly sought a science of personality (Figure 14.3).

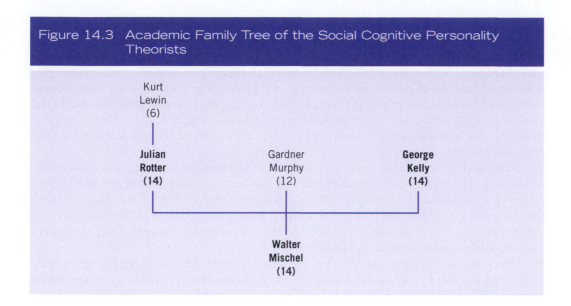

Figure 14.3 Academic Family Tree of the Social Cognitive Personality Theorists

Kurt Lewin (6)

Julian Rotter (14)

Gardner Murphy (12)

George Kelly (14)

Walter Mischel (14)

Bonnie Strickland

Bonnie Strickland (born 1936) grew up in Birmingham, Alabama, during the Great Depression, and she was determined to escape the oppressing poverty that plagued her family ("Gold Medal Award," 2014). Two childhood habits worked in her favor. First, she was a voracious reader, spending many hours in the local library, and as a result she also got good grades in school. Second, she learned to play tennis, and she got so good at it that she was even allowed to play on the all-male high school tennis team. Good grades and tennis skill earned her an athletic scholarship to Alabama College, which she never could have afforded otherwise. Going north to Ohio State for her graduate training was like traveling to a foreign country, Strickland says, as she often felt like an outsider among the Yankees. But this experience also set the tone for her career, and she became known as an *American psychologist who studied the mental health of persons and groups who are marginalized from mainstream society*.

Julian Rotter, who himself had experienced discrimination for being Jewish, was known for recruiting minority and underprivileged students, and he gave this poor young woman from the rural South a chance (Strickland, 2000). She soon got involved in his research on locus of control, and she used his Internal-External Locus of Control (IE) Scale in her doctoral research. Although she'd published several papers in prestigious journals, she was shut out from academic jobs because of her gender. But Rotter used his connections to get her a job at Emory University in Atlanta, which was just starting a clinical psychology program. She was the only woman in the department and one of just a few on the entire faculty.

Strickland arrived at Emory around the time of the Civil Rights Movement ("Bonnie R. Strickland," 1999). She was asked to assess the mental health of some civil rights activists who'd been arrested and hospitalized—under the assumption that the protesters must have psychological issues. Instead, she found them to be mentally well adjusted, and she found herself defending activists in court and even pleading for clemency in the governor's office. As she looked deeper into the civil rights movement, she found that Black activists had a strong internal locus of control compared with nonactivists, meaning that they believed their actions could bring about social change.

Strickland developed an IE scale for children and assessed the career aspirations of Black children, which she found to be lower than those of White children ("Gold Medal Award," 2014). In other words, the Black children felt they had few economic opportunities and so they kept their hopes for the future low. But she also found that Black children's ability to delay gratification was much greater in the presence of a Black experimenter compared with when the experimenter was White.

Throughout her career, Strickland frequently broached research topics that were considered taboo at the time ("Gold Medal Award," 2014). For instance, she assessed the mental health of gay men and lesbians and found that, contrary to professional opinion, they were just as psychologically well adjusted as their heterosexual counterparts. She conducted studies of gender diversity, and she probed the reasons why women were twice as likely to suffer from depression as men. Her daring research program caught the attention of the University of Massachusetts at Amherst, which, with its long history of diversity, saw her as a valuable addition to its faculty, and there she has remained for the rest of her career.

Strickland was also active in the governance of the American Psychological Association, advocating for greater inclusion of ethnic and gender minorities among its membership ("Bonnie R. Strickland," 1999). In 1987, she was elected president of the APA, signaling that her message of diversity had struck a chord among its members. Still, she remained a strident critic of American psychology because of its White-male dominance and its rampant discrimination against women and minorities.

However, she remained hopeful for the future (Strickland, 2000). In her acceptance speech for the 2014 Gold Medal Award for Life Achievement in Psychology in the Public Interest, Strickland cited her mentor Julian Rotter, who'd told her to learn from her students. She was confident that the rising generation of women and minority psychologists would overturn the patriarchal worldview, replacing it with a psychology that was open and applicable to all people.

Looking Ahead

By the last decades of the twentieth century, psychologists drew toward a consensus that the five-factor model provided a reasonably accurate depiction of the structure of psychology (Ashton & Lee, 2007). The lexical approach used by Goldberg and others had been corroborated by the questionnaire approach of McCrae and Costa. However, the model was built on English vocabulary and the responses of English-speaking participants. While the five-factor model was believed to be universal, that assumption needed to be tested through cross-cultural studies. When the lexical hypothesis was tested in other languages, however, the data were often best explained by a six-factor model instead. This has become known as the HEXACO model. Proponents argue that even English personality vocabulary fit the HEXACO model better than the Big Five. The six factors are as follows:

- H: Honesty-Humility. Sincere and modest versus greedy and pretentious.

- E: Emotionality. Similar to neuroticism in the Big Five.

- X: Extraversion. As in every other factor model.

- A: Agreeableness. As in the Big Five.

- C: Conscientiousness. As in the Big Five.

- O: Openness to Experience. As in the Big Five.

Although many of the factor names are similar, the details of their descriptions are somewhat different. In addition to fitting the cross-linguistic data better than the Big Five, HEXACO can supposedly also account for personality disorders. There's an active debate in the literature on the respective merits of the five-factor and six-factor models, and it remains to be seen which will win out in the end.

CHAPTER SUMMARY

Philosophers and psychologists have pondered the nature of individual differences at least since the time of the Ancient Greeks, but the scientific study of personality didn't begin until the twentieth century. The brothers Floyd and Gordon Allport both viewed personality in terms of traits, but Floyd viewed these from a behaviorist perspective as a set of well-learned habits, whereas Gordon took a Gestalt approach and saw them at least in part as innate tendencies. In the mid-twentieth century, Henry Murray took a psychodynamic approach to personality, which he argued was shaped by the interaction between internal needs and external presses. David McClelland further developed Murray's approach with his three needs theory of achievement, power, and affiliation. Psychometricians mainly associated with the London School began applying the method of factor analysis to the study of personality after World War II. The early work of

Raymond Cattell and Hans Eysenck laid the groundwork for the Big Five model, which is the most widely accepted framework for thinking about personality today. In the last half of the twentieth century, some psychologists argued for the need to integrate personality research with the other leading disciplines in psychology. Julian Rotter developed his social learning theory of personality, of which the best-known component is locus of control. Walter Mischel then attempted to synthesize Rotter's approach with George Kelly's personal construct theory in his social cognitive approach. Mischel's critique of personality research led to the person versus situation debate, which challenged long-held assumptions about the nature of psychology. Finally, Bonnie Strickland applied Rotter's social learning theory to the study of psychological adjustment among groups that have been marginalized by mainstream society.

DISCUSSION QUESTIONS

1. Outline the key assumptions of the lexical hypothesis. Do you think this is a reasonable approach to studying personality? Support your position with evidence and arguments.

2. Evaluate the strengths and weaknesses of projective tests versus personality inventories (questionnaires). In your opinion, which is the better approach to assessing an individual's personality? Defend your response.

3. McClelland's three needs theory didn't have much influence on the field of personality psychology, but it is widely used in industrial and organizational psychology. Consider the typical positions in companies, such as management, sales, customer service, and accounting, among others. Which need (achievement, power, or affiliation) should dominate in each of these positions?

4. The debate about general intelligence versus multiple intelligences continues to this day. What sort of evidence would you like to see to convince you to accept one position or the other?

5. Explain how twin studies are set up to test for the heritability of intelligence and personality.

6. Raymond Cattell received many honors during his lifetime, but he was disgraced by accusations of racism just before his death. How do you evaluate the

merits of a person's contributions in light of behaviors that are considered socially unacceptable?

7. Eysenck was a strong proponent of the scientist-practitioner model, which trains clinical psychologists both as researchers and as therapists. The alternate approach is the practitioner-scholar model, which de-emphasizes research and provides more training in the clinic. What are the advantages and disadvantages of each approach? Consider which approach you believe to be more effective, and defend it with evidence or arguments.

8. Eysenck was criticized for receiving research funds from the tobacco industry. Under what conditions do you think it is appropriate to accept corporate funding for research?

9. Explain Rotter's concept of locus of control. Give some examples of when it would be adaptive to view events as being under internal control, and other examples of when an external orientation would be better.

10. Explain how Mischel's marshmallow test works. Why is delay of gratification such an important ability for success in our society? Can you also think of some examples of when delaying gratification is not in your best interests?

11. What was the person versus situation controversy? Consider the implications of Mischel's social cognitive

approach on a factor theory of personality such as the Big Five. Can we still have personality traits if behavior is influenced by situations? Defend your position.

12. Theories of personality development can be grouped into three categories: (a) personality is innate from birth and changes very little over the lifespan; (b) personality develops during childhood and then becomes stable in adulthood; and (c) personality is changeable throughout the lifespan. Which perspective do you think is correct? Provide evidence to support your position.

ON THE WEB

On YouTube, you can find a short film clip of **Gordon Allport** humorously relating his one encounter with Sigmund Freud as a young man. You can also find an hour-long interview with **David McClelland** discussing the research behind his three needs theory. Several interviews with **Hans Eysenck** as well as some of his lectures are also available online. Finally, YouTube hosts a number of interviews with **Walter Mischel** as well as humorous clips of children undergoing the **marshmallow test**.

Humanistic Psychology

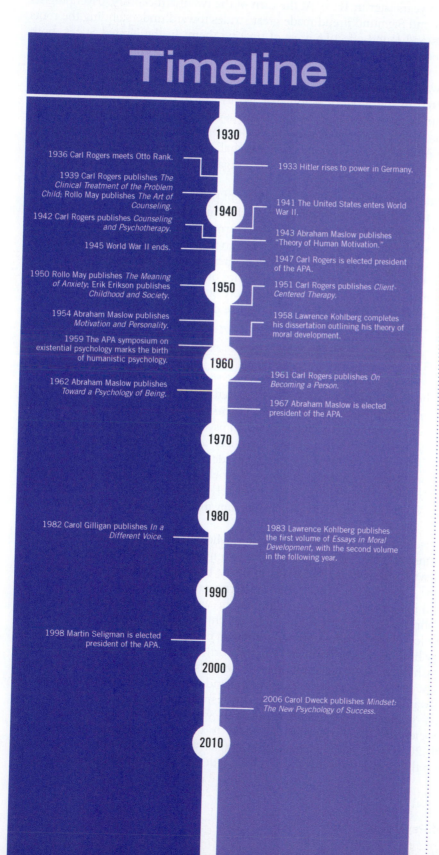

Timeline

1936 Carl Rogers meets Otto Rank.

1939 Carl Rogers publishes *The Clinical Treatment of the Problem Child*; Rollo May publishes *The Art of Counseling*.

1942 Carl Rogers publishes *Counseling and Psychotherapy*.

1945 World War II ends.

1950 Rollo May publishes *The Meaning of Anxiety*; Erik Erikson publishes *Childhood and Society*.

1954 Abraham Maslow publishes *Motivation and Personality*.

1959 The APA symposium on existential psychology marks the birth of humanistic psychology.

1962 Abraham Maslow publishes *Toward a Psychology of Being*.

1982 Carol Gilligan publishes *In a Different Voice*.

1998 Martin Seligman is elected president of the APA.

1930

1933 Hitler rises to power in Germany.

1941 The United States enters World War II.

1940

1943 Abraham Maslow publishes "Theory of Human Motivation."

1947 Carl Rogers is elected president of the APA.

1950

1951 Carl Rogers publishes *Client-Centered Therapy*.

1958 Lawrence Kohlberg completes his dissertation outlining his theory of moral development.

1960

1961 Carl Rogers publishes *On Becoming a Person*.

1967 Abraham Maslow is elected president of the APA.

1970

1980

1983 Lawrence Kohlberg publishes the first volume of *Essays in Moral Development*, with the second volume in the following year.

1990

2000

2006 Carol Dweck publishes *Mindset: The New Psychology of Success*.

2010

Learning Objectives

After reading this chapter, you should be able to:

- Critique the client-centered approach to psychotherapy as proposed by Carl Rogers and others.

- Appraise the hierarchy of needs proposed by Abraham Maslow.

- Evaluate Erik Erikson's stages of psychosocial development and Lawrence Kohlberg's stages of moral development.

- Assess the major concepts of positive psychology, including flow and eudaimonia.

Looking Back

Psychology was originally conceived as the scientific study of the human mind. Yet from the very beginning, psychologists have understood that their science would yield knowledge that could help improve the human condition. Wilhelm Wundt established the first psychology laboratory in 1879, and his student Lightner Witmer opened the first psychology clinic just seventeen years later in 1896. At the turn of the twentieth century, psychologists such as Pierre Janet and Sigmund Freud made great strides toward understanding the roots of mental disorders and found effective ways of treating them. In the United States, both functionalists and behaviorists saw the practical application of their work as contributing to the betterment of society.

World War II was a watershed event in human history. It changed the geopolitical world order, and it ushered in the modern world that we live in today. As we've seen, it also reshaped the discipline of psychology. As European psychologists fled to North America to escape the Nazis, they brought with them both Gestalt psychology and psychoanalysis, which took root in American soil. These new schools challenged the dominance of behaviorism over American psychology, which after the war reorganized itself into a set of disciplines defined by research topic.

The war also had a great influence on the practice of psychotherapy. The influx of many refugees and the return of millions of soldiers placed great stress on the facilities that provided mental health services. What was needed was a form of psychotherapy that was easy to learn and yielded fast results. This is the story we turn to first with the career of Carl Rogers. Additionally, the horrors of World War II led philosophers to question the very meaning of human existence, and these ideas influenced the practice of psychotherapy as well. The great question then became: How do we deal with the anxiety of the atomic age? It was the search for an answer to this vexing problem that led to the rise of humanistic psychology.

Carl Rogers

In his autobiography, **Carl Rogers** (1902–1987) claimed he "was fortunate in never having a mentor," which gave him the freedom to think for himself (Rogers, 1967, p. 376). This doesn't mean that Rogers invented his radical views on psychotherapy out of thin air. In fact, he was quite attuned to the frontline thinking of his day, and his contributions to psychology were mainly in the form of a creative synthesis of ideas current at the time. Thus, while no one person shaped Rogers's thinking, he was nevertheless influenced by many important psychologists. Through his writing and teaching, Carl Rogers became recognized as the *American psychologist who proposed client-centered therapy and founded the humanistic psychology movement.*

Rogers was raised in a fundamentalist household where even swearing and card playing were considered unspeakable sins (Rogers, 1967). He entered Union Theological Seminary in New York City with plans for a career in the ministry, but after a crisis of faith he decided on psychology and counseling instead. After transferring to Columbia University Teacher's College, he earned his Ph.D. in 1928. At Columbia, he was most impressed by the educational theory of John Dewey, who advocated for giving children the freedom to learn through their own exploration of the world. Rogers's thinking on clinical and educational psychology was influenced by his interactions with Leta Hollingworth (Chapter 4) as well as by lectures of Alfred Adler (Chapter 7). At the same time, Rogers also showed an interest in experimental psychology, particularly in the area of testing and measurement, and he was greatly influenced by Edward Thorndike (Chapter 4) in this respect.

When Rogers graduated, no academic positions were available, so he accepted an offer from the Society for the Prevention of Cruelty to Children in Rochester, New York (Barrett-Lennard, 2012). His teachers advised him against taking the position, viewing it as a dead-end job that would isolate him from the academic community, but Rogers had a family to support. Nevertheless, he spent the next twelve years at Rochester, immersing himself in the latest thinking on psychotherapy. Especially influential were the neo-Freudians, who rejected the idea that neuroses stem from childhood trauma and focused instead on helping their patients in the present. Two persons who were particularly important in shaping Rogers's thinking during this time were the Austrian psychoanalyst Otto Rank and the American social worker Jessie Taft.

Photo 15.1
Portrait of Carl Rogers

Otto Rank and Jessie Taft

For twenty years, **Otto Rank** (1884–1939) had been a close associate of Sigmund Freud (DeCarvalho, 1999). But as he grew in confidence, Rank expressed views that were heretical to psychoanalytic dogma, and he was cast out of Freud's inner circle. Rank left Vienna and resettled in Paris, where he practiced his own form of psychotherapy. Through his writings, he developed a reputation as an *Austrian psychoanalyst who argued that the normal course of a human life is a process of growth.*

To Rank, the purpose of psychotherapy wasn't to uncover the past, but rather to restore that natural growth process (DeCarvalho, 1999). This was achieved by building the patient's self-confidence and freedom from dependency relationships. There was no need, then, to explore the patient's childhood. Rather, the therapist needed to create a safe environment that would encourage patients to explore and express their innermost thoughts and feelings. Rank also criticized Freud for his emotional detachment from his patients and for treating them as patients to be operated on rather than as people to be related to. Instead, Rank insisted that healing could only take place when the therapist showed genuine empathy for the patient's perspective. And to do that, the therapist had to be completely present in the moment and interacting with the patient on a personal rather than professional level. Rank called his counseling approach "will therapy" because he saw it as helping people to recover their will or sense of self.

After Rank broke with Freud, he made a series of trips to the United States to connect with American psychoanalysts, believing they'd be more receptive to his ideas (DeCarvalho, 1999). The most important of these connections was with **Jessie Taft** (1882–1960), an *American social worker who developed an early form of client-centered psychotherapy known as relationship therapy.* Taft was especially interested in mental health issues surrounding the adoption process, and she devised therapeutic practices for helping adoptive parents and children adjust to their new family circumstances that are still in use today. It was clear that traditional psychoanalysis was inappropriate for her purposes, but she saw promise in Rank's approach to psychotherapy. As they got to know each other better, Taft undertook the translation of Rank's works, making them available to English readers for the first time. She also published a series of articles and a book describing relationship therapy, a clinical approach that put the therapist and patient on an equal footing and placed its emphasis on personal growth. In 1934, Taft helped Rank immigrate to the United States to escape the Nazis, and they remained friends until his death in 1939.

When Rogers arrived at Rochester, he was already disillusioned with the psychiatric and psychoanalytic methods he'd learned at Columbia, and he was open to new ideas (Kirschenbaum, 2004). Some of his colleagues at Rochester had trained with Jessie Taft, and they introduced him to her work. It was through her writings that Rogers was introduced to the ideas of Otto Rank. In 1936, Rogers invited Rank to give a three-day seminar in Rochester, and he was greatly impressed by the patient-centered approach that both Rank and Taft were proposing. Later in life, Rogers credited Rank as one of the most important influences in the development of his own client-centered approach to psychotherapy.

Photo 15.2
Jessie Taft

Rogers published his first book, *The Clinical Treatment of the Problem Child* in 1939 (Barrett-Lennard, 2012). At this point, Rogers had not yet formulated his own version of client-centered therapy. Instead, the book presented a review and evaluation of the available techniques for working with troubled youth. In particular, he was critical of traditional psychoanalytic approaches, but he was favorable to the ideas of Otto Rank and especially to the methods of Jessie Taft's relationship therapy. This book was widely praised and made Rogers famous among clinical psychologists. The following year, he was offered a full professorship at Ohio State University, which he gladly accepted.

Client-Centered Therapy

Working as a full-time therapist in Rochester, Rogers had gotten into the habit of trying out new approaches and noting whether they seemed to work or not (Kirschenbaum, 2004). But with the faculty position that Ohio State provided, Rogers for the first time could systematically test various techniques for their effectiveness. As a supervisor of graduate students training to be clinicians, Rogers came up with an idea that challenged accepted norms—he would record therapy sessions and study them. Others protested that this practice would violate therapist-patient confidentiality, but Rogers only recorded sessions when the patient consented. Afterward, his students transcribed the conversations, and therapist-patient interactions were analyzed. In particular, they classified therapist comments in terms of how directive they were—ranging from giving advice or instructions at one end to expressing empathy and understanding for the patient's perspective at the other end. They then evaluated the patient's responses to each type of therapist comment. This analysis led Rogers to the conclusion that a nondirective approach was more effective than directive styles of therapy. In other words, the patients needed to be heard and understood more than they needed to be told what their problem was or what to do about it.

Rogers published these findings in his 1942 book *Counseling and Psychotherapy* (Barrett-Lennard, 2012). In this work, we can see the first articulation of Rogers's unique approach to clinical practice, which at this point he called "nondirective therapy." According to Rogers, healthy personal growth can only take place when the therapist creates a supportive environment in which patients feel safe to express their thoughts and feelings. To accomplish this, the therapist had to be nonjudgmental and to refrain from coercing or pressuring the patient in any way. The goal of the counseling relationship was to help the patient develop self-understanding and self-acceptance, which would in turn lead toward a healthier personality. Furthermore, Rogers made no claims of priority, instead describing nondirective therapy as a current trend in clinical psychology. However, his contribution was that he had empirical support for its effectiveness. Also in this book, Rogers abandoned the word "patient" in favor of the term "client," suggesting a working relationship on an equal footing.

In 1945, Rogers accepted an invitation from the University of Chicago to establish a counseling center for students, where he remained for the next twelve years (Kirschenbaum, 2004). During this time, he continued his research by recording and analyzing therapy sessions, and he even experimented with filming therapist-client interactions. These were the years when Rogers defined his clinical approach, which he outlined in his 1951 book *Client-Centered Therapy*. Rogers

Table 15.1 Three Conditions for Rogers's Client-Centered Therapy

Condition	Definition
Unconditional positive regard	Complete acceptance and nonjudgment of the client
Empathy	The ability to take the client's point of view
Congruence	Genuine and authentic relationship between the therapist and the client

saw client-centered therapy as a method for facilitating personal growth. This was accomplished when three conditions were met (Table 15.1). First, the therapist had to demonstrate *complete acceptance and nonjudgment of another person*, which Rogers called **unconditional positive regard**. Second, the therapist had to have empathy, that is, an ability to take the client's point of view in order to understand the thoughts, feelings, and difficulties the client experienced. Third, there had to be what Rogers called **congruence**, referring to *a genuine and authentic relationship between the therapist and the client*. In other words, for real growth to occur, the therapist couldn't simply act out a role but had to establish a real personal relationship with the client.

From Chicago, Rogers moved to the University of Wisconsin, where he held joint appointments in the departments of psychology and psychiatry (Kirschenbaum, 2004). During this time, he conducted a massive research project testing the effectiveness of several treatment approaches for patients diagnosed with schizophrenia, including his own client-centered approach. The results showed that client-centered therapy led to no better patient outcomes than did the other approaches. However, he did find that patient outcomes were best when therapists displayed high levels of unconditional positive regard, empathy, and congruence, no matter which orientation they took. For Rogers, these findings vindicated his belief that the key to success in the clinical session was the creation of a genuine personal relationship between the therapist and the client.

In 1961, Rogers published his best-known work, *On Becoming a Person* (Kirschenbaum, 2004). This collection of essays was aimed at both professionals and the general public, and it was highly acclaimed by both audiences. In this book, Rogers contends that the process of socialization distorts people's sense of self by presenting them with norms and role models that are inconsistent with their true natures. This distortion of self-concept leads to distress and psychological disorders, and the role of psychotherapy is to help persons restructure their individual sense of self by making them aware of the ways in which society has led them astray. This new awareness that they don't need to live up to societal expectations then leads to a reduction of stress and a new openness to experiencing life in genuine manner.

Humanistic Psychology

Carl Rogers's meteoric rise to fame was due in large part to the conditions of the times in which he lived and worked (Barrett-Lennard, 2012). At mid-century, American psychology was dominated by two schools, psychoanalysis and behaviorism, each of which offered a contrasting approach to psychotherapy. On the one hand, psychoanalytic theory viewed humans as driven by unconscious and often destructive forces that needed to be tamed for the individual to lead a productive life. In a sense, then, psychoanalysis as a therapeutic technique could be viewed as a completion of the socialization process, in which patients reach adult maturity through the proper channelization of their animal instincts. On the other hand, behavioral psychotherapy was unconcerned with the inner thoughts and feelings of the patient and focused instead on changing outward behaviors. The assumption was that feelings of depression and anxiety would simply dissipate if only the person could learn to act as a normally functioning adult. But Rogers's view of human life as a process of growth offered a third alternative that had great appeal because it rejected both the pessimistic view of humanity offered by Freud and the deterministic view of humans as nothing more than biological machines.

The end of World War II also drove the popularization of Rogers's client-centered therapy (DeCarvalho, 1999). With large numbers of soldiers returning from war and struggling with their adjustment to civilian life, counseling services were in greater demand than ever. What was needed was a form of psychotherapy that was easy for new therapists to learn and inexpensive to administer. Psychoanalysis could hardly fit the bill, since the Freudian model required that psychoanalysts first earn their medical degrees. Furthermore, psychoanalytic therapy was time-consuming, typically involving daily sessions for months or years, making this approach too expensive to implement on a large scale. The various forms of behavioral therapy usually offered much shorter treatment regimens, but their practitioners were typically academics with doctorate degrees. However, Rogers's client-centered approach was easy to learn, and in fact he encouraged pastoral and school counselors to learn the method and employ it in their own practice. And like behavioral approaches, client-centered therapy focused on the person's present situation without delving deep into the past, thus requiring far fewer sessions than psychoanalysis to achieve satisfactory results.

The view that humans have an innate drive to grow toward fulfilling their potential in life became known as **humanistic psychology** (Kirschenbaum, 2004). This approach differed from both psychoanalysis and behaviorism in three important ways. First, it validated the individual's subjective experience as legitimate and worthy of respect, as opposed to evaluating the person according to some external criteria. Second, it shifted the focus of psychotherapy from the remediation of problems to the engendering of psychological health. And third, it emphasized those aspects of human beings, such as freedom, values, feelings, and goals, which distinguished them from all other species. In sum, Rogers and his followers believed that humans were by nature good, and that they only fall into destructive tendencies because they're led astray by societal forces. Thus, by rediscovering their true nature, they can learn to lead lives that enable them to reach their full potential.

However, Rogers was not without his critics (Kirschenbaum, 2004). Since his life and career paralleled that of B. F. Skinner, the two men and their approaches to psychology were often contrasted. They were brought together on several occasions to argue their points of view, the most notable of which was a six-hour dialogue-debate in 1962. Skinner dismissed Rogers's view that people's actions arise from their internal thoughts and feelings, insisting instead that behaviors are driven solely by environmental factors. In other words, Rogers wanted to change things inside the person, whereas Skinner wanted to change things on the outside.

Another critic of Rogers was **Albert Ellis** (1913–2007), an *American psychologist best known as the founder of rational emotive behavior therapy* (Holden, 1977). REBT is an approach that combines behavioral and cognitive methods, and it's one of the most commonly used forms of psychotherapy today. Ellis rejected Rogers's nondirective approach, contending that clients cannot find out for themselves what is wrong with them or what they need to do to get better. Instead, he insisted that therapy has to be directive, that is, clients need to be shown the way to psychological health rather than letting them flounder. Mockingly comparing client-centered therapy with the Boy Scouts, Ellis claimed Rogers's approach made people feel better while letting them get sicker. Despite his rejection of client-centered therapy, Ellis is often counted among the humanistic psychologists because in his writings he emphasized the notions of personal growth and acceptance of one's true nature. He's also considered to be the second most influential psychotherapist of the twentieth century, after Rogers (Smith, 1982).

Carl Rogers lived his life as an example of personal growth and striving toward his full potential. In his autobiography, Rogers (1967) stated that early in his career he wanted nothing more than a faculty position at a university. The Ohio State offer seemed to him like a dream come true, and his growing fame led to even more distinguished appointments at Chicago and Wisconsin. During these years, he established his reputation as a clinical psychologist who dared to test the effectiveness of various psychotherapeutic approaches, including his own client-centered therapy. Despite Rogers's challenge of traditional methods of psychotherapy, his client-centered approach resonated with the postwar Zeitgeist, as evidenced by the fact that he was elected president of the APA in 1947. Eventually, though, he grew tired of the petty politics of academia, and in 1964 he resigned from his professorship. He moved to southern California, where he opened a private practice and founded a nonprofit organization for advancing the cause of humanistic psychology. In the end, the great counselor returned to his original calling, with his two and a half decades in academia as a colorful side trip along his journey through life.

Abraham Maslow

As a graduate student, **Abraham Maslow** (1908–1970) studied primate behavior with Harry Harlow (Nicholson, 2001). He saw the monkeys as a mirror on humanity, and yet he grew disillusioned with the sterility of behaviorism and laboratory psychology. He reasoned that if he wanted to understand human behavior, he would have to study people, not primates. And to get deep into their inner thoughts and feelings, he developed an extended interview technique that became his hallmark research method. Along with Carl Rogers, Maslow is recognized as one of the founders of humanistic psychology, and during his lifetime he became famous as the *American psychologist who proposed an influential theory of motivation that included a hierarchy of needs and the concept of self-actualization*.

For his dissertation, Maslow studied patterns of sexual dominance in female rhesus monkeys (Nicholson, 2001). He found they fought each other for rank in the social hierarchy, with those at the top mating with the most virile males. And yet, while these "alpha females" dominated other females, they also became submissive in the presence of males they wanted to mate with. He suspected that human sexuality, at least in its natural state, was no different from that of other primates, and he undertook a research project to test this hypothesis during a postdoctoral fellowship with Edward Thorndike at Columbia (Figure 15.1). He recruited young women who were willing to discuss their sexual experiences during extended interview sessions in which he asked questions about sexual preferences and fantasies. Maslow interpreted the results as supporting his hypothesis. However, he also found that these women's sexuality had largely been driven underground—in the form of dreams and fantasies—by cultural taboos. The idea that Western culture had perverted human nature with unrealistic expectations, causing unhappiness and psychological problems, became an important theme in Maslow's career.

Hierarchy of Needs

In 1943, Maslow published his "Theory of Human Motivation" (Maslow, 1943). This paper established Maslow's reputation as a theorist. He chastised the behaviorists for ignoring motivation as a driving force in behavior, treating organisms—including humans—as simple stimulus-response devices. The product of conditioning was what he called *coping behaviors*, in which the animal learned to respond to the contingencies of the environment. Furthermore, when reinforcement stopped, so did the behaviors. However, the organism didn't simply wait for the environment to act on it. Rather, he insisted, it engaged in behaviors for its own purposes, and he cited Edward Tolman's (Chapter 5) work in support. He called these self-initiated actions *expressive behaviors*, and he maintained that they were responses to internal needs that the organism was experiencing. In this regard, he was influenced by Henry Murray's (Chapter 14) theory of needs. However, whereas Murray has simply grouped needs into categories based on similarity, Maslow believed that some needs were more basic than others.

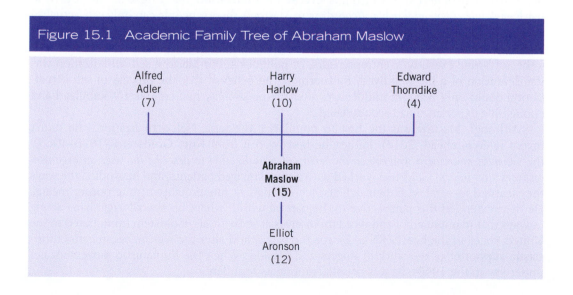

Figure 15.1   Academic Family Tree of Abraham Maslow

Thus was born the **hierarchy of needs**, which was *Maslow's contention that the more basic needs will dominate a person's thoughts and feelings until they are met, at which point higher-order needs will emerge* (Maslow, 1943). As Maslow put it, "man is a perpetually wanting animal" (p. 395), in that the satisfaction of needs at one level only serves to bring on a new set of needs at the next level up. Think about it: Can you study when you're hungry? Hunger is a basic biological need that must be met before you can even think about pursuing personal-growth needs such as passing this course.

Maslow (1943) proposed five levels of needs. At the lowest level are the *physiological needs*, such as food and water, which you must fulfill simply to stay alive. As long as any of these needs are unmet, nothing else matters in life. Once these needs are satisfied, *safety needs* emerge. We all have a need for order and stability in our environment, the lack of which causes distress. If you feel threatened, this dominates your thinking to the exclusion of all else. Imagine, for instance, the difficulties of a schoolchild trying to do homework in a family that's constantly bickering.

The next level is what Maslow (1943) called the *love needs*, by which he was referring to the need for affectionate social relationships with friends and family members, as well as sexual relationships in adults. When physiological and safety needs go unmet, people's thoughts are completely egocentric, but if their life is in no danger they desire interactions with others for their own sake. Maslow lamented that while few Americans struggle with physiological or safety needs, many experience loneliness, meaning that their love needs are going unmet. Once people have established satisfying social relationships for themselves, they then yearn for their *esteem needs* to be met. In other words, we not only want to be part of social groups, we also want other people to think highly of us. For example, shame is a powerful motivator that drives us to conform to social norms so that others will give us their approval.

In his later writings, Maslow referred to these first four needs as *deficiency needs*, or D-needs. This was because these needs derived from a lack of something necessary for life. In fact, Maslow insisted that even the safety, love, and esteem needs were just as basic—and instinctual—as physiological needs. For instance, persons with a deficiency of love and affection become sick just as they would from a lack of vitamin C. But once their deficiency needs are met, they then feel a drive toward improving themselves and reaching their fullest potential. Maslow called these B-needs, or *being needs*, which we turn to next.

Self-Actualization

Maslow's D-needs more or less encompass the list of needs that Murray proposed (D'Souza & Gurin, 2016). However, his proposal of B-needs was new, and these composed the fifth level of his hierarchy of needs. He called this level **self-actualization**, referring to *the innate drive to reach one's fullest potential in life*. According to Maslow's theory, people can only self-actualize after their deficiency needs have been met. Furthermore, the goal of self-actualization is different for each person. Some of us strive to be poets, artists, or musicians, while others seek to be corporate executives, entrepreneurs, or politicians. For Maslow, self-actualization was the definition of a life well lived. Furthermore, he believed that the process of self-actualization could only begin in middle age, after the personality had completely stabilized and enough life experience had accumulated.

Although Maslow was the first to popularize the term "self-actualization," he didn't invent it (Whitehead, 2017). Rather, he borrowed it from **Kurt Goldstein** (1878–1965), the *German neurologist who coined the term self-actualization to describe the way an organism recovers after injury*. Goldstein worked with brain-damaged patients, and he studied the ways they learned to cope with their deficits, recovering lost functionality through other means. He then extended this perspective to the natural world, where he saw all organisms acting in ways that maintained or enhanced themselves as individuals. Goldstein immigrated to the United States in the late 1930s to escape the Nazis, and after the war he became an enthusiastic supporter of the work of Rogers and Maslow. When the humanistic movement got underway in the 1960s, he was counted among its founders.

It's important to note how the meaning of the term "self-actualization" has changed from its original usage. Maslow (1943) admitted that he was using Goldstein's term in a more restricted meaning, and furthermore he insisted that self-actualization in his sense was a uniquely human need. That is, we share our D-needs with other animals, but only people have B-needs. Soon, Carl Rogers picked up the term "self-actualization" from Maslow's writings and began using it in his own work (Rennie, 2008). However, he separated it from the hierarchy of needs, insisting instead that self-actualization was the only motivator driving human behavior.

Maslow's conception of self-actualization has been criticized by various scholars (Winston, Maher, & Easvaradoss, 2017). First, some argued that the concept was nothing more than a product of individualistic Western culture. In collectivistic cultures, they contended, people strive for the good of the group rather than themselves, and so for them self-actualization is a meaningless concept. It's true that Maslow never traveled outside the United States, but he was well read in anthropology. He firmly believed that culture did little more than brush a veneer on people that made members of one group look different from another even though the core of human nature was universal. Second, critics tried to come up with examples of well-known persons who managed to achieve self-actualization even though they lived in poverty. Maslow responded that people can grow accustomed to an austere lifestyle, and as long as their D-needs are mostly met, they'll feel the drive to self-actualize.

Disdaining the laboratory as sterile and artificial, Maslow preferred studying people in their everyday environments and getting to know them on a personal level, rather than observing them at a distance (Guest, 2014). This led to two strands in his research. In the first strand, he visited workplaces, observing patterns of work practices with the goal of finding ways to organize the company so that employees would be motivated to work more effectively. The second strand involved the study of persons he saw as self-actualizers. Here the goal was to examine the underlying drives that motivate some people to self-actualize but not others. To this end, he conducted extensive interviews with corporate executives, even becoming friends with some of them. He published the results of these initial studies in his 1954 book, *Motivation and Personality*.

In that book, Maslow also expressed his opinion that Western culture had a corrupting influence on personality (Nicholson, 2001). Much like Carl Rogers, he believed that human nature was essentially good. However, our society presents us with norms and role models that turn us away from our true nature. Our relentless pursuit of wealth, our insecurities about our looks, and our inhibitions about sex are all products of the distorting forces of our culture. Because we no longer live according to our nature, we become sick—we live in gilt cages but wonder why we're unhappy. Maslow even applauded those who understood they needed counseling, because they were fighting against the perversions of the modern world. Likewise, self-actualizers have risen above the demands of society to pursue goals that are meaningful to them. These ideas had great appeal to those who were struggling to free themselves from the strictures of 1950s American society, and Maslow became an icon for the counter-culture and feminist movements of the 1960s.

Third Force

Gordon Allport (Chapter 14) first used the term "humanistic psychology" in a 1930 essay, and he repeated it in a number of other works after that (DeCarvalho, 1990). However, it wasn't until the 1960s that it was adopted as the name for a new movement in psychology. By the 1950s, there was growing discontent about what was viewed as the sterility of both behaviorism and psychoanalysis. In 1959, the APA sponsored a symposium on what they called "existential psychology." This was inspired by **existentialism**, which was *a mid-twentieth-century school of philosophy claiming the central problem that humans face is coming to terms with the anxiety of living in a meaningless world.* The solution to this problem, the existentialists said, was to live life authentically. This philosophy resonated with a number of psychologists we've already met, including Gordon Allport, George Kelly, and Henry Murray from Chapter 14, as

Photo 15.3
Rollo May

well as Carl Rogers and Abraham Maslow. This symposium marked the beginning of the humanistic movement in psychology, which was formalized the following year with the establishment of its own journal.

Another important founder of the humanistic movement in psychology was **Rollo May** (1909–1994), an *American psychologist who developed a form of counseling known as existential psychotherapy* (Bugental, 1996). As a young adult, May had studied individual psychology with Alfred Adler in Vienna, but fearing the rise of Nazism, he returned to the United States. May enrolled as an undergraduate at Union Theological Seminary in New York City, where he befriended the famous existential philosopher Paul Tillich, who'd just escaped Nazi Germany. May counted Tillich as his most important mentor. On graduation, May accepted a position as a student counselor at a small mid-Western college, during which time he published his first book, *The Art of Counseling*, in 1939.

In the early 1940s, May enrolled in the doctoral program in psychology at Teachers' College Columbia University, but he contracted tuberculosis and spent two years recovering in a sanatorium (Rabinowitz, Good, & Cozad, 1989). This was a time of great worry for May, and the problem of anxiety became a major theme in his career. He finally earned his Ph.D. in 1949 and published his dissertation the following year as *The Meaning of Anxiety*. At the time, anxiety was believed to always be an indicator of poor mental health. But May argued it was a useful emotion because it let us know there was something wrong. The key was to listen to that anxiety and make the necessary changes. May never held a full-time academic position, supporting himself instead through part-time teaching and private practice. Nevertheless, his many books helped spread the humanistic movement among both professional psychologists and the lay public alike.

Followers of humanistic psychology soon viewed themselves as the **third force** (DeCarvalho, 1991). This was *a catchphrase indicating that humanistic psychology stood in opposition to both behaviorism and psychoanalysis*. Members of the third force hoped that humanistic psychology would rise to the status of being the dominant school in psychology. It's probably true that humanistic psychology did much to release the stranglehold that behaviorism and psychoanalysis had on the field. And it's also the case that its founders rank among the most influential psychologists of the twentieth century. However, as we've already seen, American psychology reorganized itself after World War II into a set of collaborative disciplines based on topic as opposed to a group of competing schools based on philosophy. The humanistic movement helped shape psychology in the last half of the twentieth century, but it never defined the field.

In 1962, Maslow published his most popular book, *Toward a Psychology of Being* (Koltko-Rivera, 2006). In this work, he expressed doubts about self-actualization as the capstone of the hierarchy of needs. He'd became interested in what he called a **peak experience**, as reported to him by some of the self-actualizers he'd interviewed. This was *a deeply emotional experience in which the person comes to see the world in a new way*. He wondered whether peak experiences were a feature of self-actualization or a sign of yet another stage beyond. In a paper published shortly before his death, he reworked his theory of motivation to include a sixth level, which he called **self-transcendence** (Table 15.2). This was *the highest level in the hierarchy of needs in which self-actualized persons seek to become part of something greater than themselves*. This paper was published in an obscure journal, and it was largely forgotten until the twenty-first century, when a number of scholars revived the idea.

Abraham Maslow had a difficult childhood (Nicholson, 2001). He grew up in relative poverty in a New York City slum. And because he was frequently teased for his big nose and scrawny frame, he'd internalized the idea that he was ugly and undesirable, an insecurity he carried with him for the rest of his life. In his later years, he was a best-selling author and a speaker in high demand, and this popularity was no doubt reaffirming. At the same time, some of his colleagues ridiculed his work for what they perceived as a lack of rigor. This must have stung, especially for a man who'd been thoroughly trained in the scientific method. In hindsight, the problem wasn't so much Maslow's lack of rigor as it

Table 15.2 Maslow's Hierarchy of Needs

Category	Level	Need	Description
Being needs ("B-needs")	6	Self-transcendence	Need to become part of something greater than ourselves
	5	Self-actualization	Need to reach our fullest potential in life
Deficiency needs ("D-needs")	4	Esteem	Need to have others think highly of us
	3	Love	Need to have meaningful relationships with other people
	2	Safety	Need for order and stability in our environment
	1	Physiological	Basic needs, such as food, water, and shelter, which are necessary for staying alive

was the rigid inability of some psychologists to accept a kind of research approach that was so up close and personal.

Still, Maslow made an impact on psychology, and in 1967 he was elected president of the APA (Koltko-Rivera, 2006). But before he could give his acceptance speech, he suffered a near-fatal heart attack and was incapacitated for months. As he recovered his health, a group of corporation executives in San Francisco whom he'd befriended during his research on self-actualization offered him a fellowship that included a house with a swimming pool. Resigning his professorship at Brandeis University in Boston, where he'd spent most of his career, he settled into his new home in sunny California. For a short time he was very productive, but a year later a second heart attack took his life. In the end, the scrawny kid from Brooklyn achieved the accolades he'd long desired, leaving a lasting impression not only on the field of psychology but on the popular culture as well.

Charlotte Bühler

Strictly speaking, Maslow's hierarchy of needs applies only to adults (DeRobertis, 2006). However, even children have a drive toward improving themselves. An early advocate of the lifespan approach toward personal growth was **Charlotte Bühler** (1893–1974), a *German developmental psychologist and one of the founders of the humanistic psychology movement.*

After completing her Ph.D. at the University of Munich in 1918, Charlotte married her thesis advisor Karl Bühler (Korosoliev & Tsering, 2010). The couple worked at the Vienna Psychological Institute for fifteen years, where she conducted research on both infants and adolescents. She was convinced that even young infants were intentional agents who sought to accomplish goals, a radical view for the time. In addition, she used diary studies with teenagers to gain insights into their thought processes. Building on this research, she articulated her theory of life goals, in which she proposed that persons at each stage of development, from infancy to adulthood, strive to balance conflicting needs in order to achieve personal fulfillment.

Charlotte Bühler was internationally recognized as a leading developmental psychologist, and in the 1920s she was a visiting scholar in the United States, where she made connections that would save her life a decade later (Korosoliev & Tsering, 2010). When the Nazis invaded Austria in 1938, the Bühlers first sought refuge in several European countries before settling in the United States with help from her American friends. Her work was seen as dovetailing with that of Rogers and Maslow, and she rose to several prominent positions within the humanistic psychology movement. As an early champion of the view that development is a lifelong process, she laid the groundwork for many of the important theories in humanistic psychology that we are reading about in this chapter.

Photo 15.4
Charlotte Bühler

Human Development

Other psychologists working after World War II were also interested in the topic of personal growth. Even though they didn't consider themselves to be humanistic psychologists, they're often counted as such because of the themes they pursued in their research. Here we consider three such persons: Erik Erikson, with his theory of psychosocial development; Lawrence Kohlberg, with his theory of moral development; and Carol Gilligan, with her research on real-life moral decision making.

Erik Erikson

The psychologist we now know as **Erik Erikson** (1902–1994) was given the name Erik Homburger at birth (Whitfield, 2000). When he was a teenager, he learned that his mother's husband wasn't his biological father. This discovery set off a crisis of identity in the young man, and he wandered aimlessly about Europe for several years before meeting Anna Freud (Chapter 7), who trained him as a child psychoanalyst. This was the beginning of a colorful career in psychology, and today we know Erik Erikson as the *German-American psychologist who maintained that development is a lifelong process and proposed the eight stages of psychosocial development*.

As a young man, Erik Homburger had studied art in several European cities when he was offered a position as an art instructor at an international school in Vienna (Weiland, 1993). This school had been established by Dorothy Burlingham, the life partner of Anna Freud (Chapter 7). Homburger had a natural talent for working with children, and he soon caught the attention of Anna Freud, who offered him a scholarship to train as a child psychoanalyst. His work so impressed Freud and her colleagues that he was offered full membership in the International Psychoanalytical Association, which gave him license to practice anywhere in the world.

During his years in Vienna, Homburger got to know the Canadian dancer Joan Serson, who was undergoing analysis with one of Sigmund Freud's students (Hopkins, 1995). They soon married, and they remained intellectual partners for the rest of their lives. With the rise of Hitler in 1933, the newlyweds understood it was time to leave Europe, and they immigrated to the United States. With the start of a new life, Homburger also gave himself a new identity. Rejecting the name of the man who adopted him and not knowing the identity of his biological father, he named himself after himself—Erik Erikson.

Arriving in Boston, Erikson soon made the acquaintance of Henry Murray (Chapter 14), who offered him a position at the Harvard Psychological Clinic (Hopkins, 1995). Erikson also enrolled as a graduate student in psychology at Harvard, but he soon gave up on that. However, Erikson was good at networking and soon befriended many of the leading social scientists of his time. He embarked on excursions with anthropologists to study Native American tribes in the western United States, during which he observed child-rearing practices. Furthermore, his work with teenagers at the Harvard Psychological Clinic gave him deep insights into the issues that young people face. These experiences eventually formed the basis for his most important book—which launched him to international fame—but that project was temporarily put aside as the United States was pulled into the conflict in Europe.

During World War II, Henry Murray (Chapter 14) joined the Office of Strategic Services, the forerunner to today's CIA (Pietikainen & Ihanus, 2003). By this time, Erikson had become a naturalized U.S. citizen, and Murray recruited him as one of his assistants. Their task was to write up psychological assessments of the Nazi leadership, including Hitler. It's unclear whether this work made any real contribution to the war effort, but this assignment did give Erikson the opportunity to network with various government officials, and after the war Erikson was remarkably successful at securing grants from funding agencies for his research projects.

Photo 15.5
Erik Erikson

Erikson's magnum opus, *Childhood and Society*, was published in 1950 to much acclaim (Douvan, 1997). Standard Freudian theory posited that personality developed in early childhood through a series of psychosexual stages. Erikson didn't challenge the existence of these stages, but he insisted that personality development doesn't stop there. Instead, he maintained, it continues throughout the lifespan. He also minimized the notion of childhood sexuality—especially the Oedipus complex—as well as the idea that early events shape us for life. Rather, he contended that turning points later in life can have an even greater impact on the developing personality.

Downplaying Freud's emphasis on the pathological, Erikson focused instead on the developmental trajectory of the psychologically well-adjusted person (Massey, 1986). He also placed far more emphasis on the role of social interactions and cultural institutions in the shaping of the individual's personality. It was his emphasis on lifelong personal growth that led Maslow and other humanistic psychologists to claim Erikson as one of their own.

Erikson's **theory of psychosocial development** is *the proposal that all people pass through eight distinct stages that shape their sense of identity as they go through life* (Knight, 2017). On the one hand, the theory describes what a typical human life looks like over its time course (Table 15.3). On the other hand, it explains patterns of personality in terms of decisions people make at key milestones in their life. Each of these represents a **crisis**, or *a turning point in life that will set the direction for future personality development*. During the first year of life, for example, the infant needs to decide whether other people are trustworthy or not. During the process of secure attachment, infants learn that significant others are dependable, and they develop a trusting attitude toward relationships in general. But infants with an insecure attachment to their caregivers tend to be mistrusting of others throughout their lives.

Perhaps the most important of all the developmental milestones in Erikson's theory is the **identity crisis** (Knight, 2017). This is *the time during adolescence when emerging adults consolidate their sense of who they are as individuals*. For psychologically healthy teens, identity cohesion occurs during this time, as they experience growing self-esteem and the ability to engage in significant interpersonal relationships. For others, though, this is a time of role confusion, in which they're wracked with self-doubt and insecurities. This was a crisis that Erikson had personally struggled with when he learned he wasn't Homburger's son, and he wandered for several years before finding a path that would give meaning to his life. Modern society gives us unprecedented freedom to choose careers and social identities, but at the cost of an extended and often painful identity crisis for many emerging adults.

Erikson believed that these eight stages were universal, experienced by all persons in all cultures (Pietikainen & Ihanus, 2003). Critics questioned this assertion, however, arguing instead that the milestones marking these stages were products of Western culture and so

Table 15.3 Erikson's Stages of Psychosocial Development

Level	Stage	Crisis	Key Question
8	Old age	Integrity vs. Despair	Was my life successful?
7	Adulthood	Generativity vs. Stagnation	Am I making an important contribution to society?
6	Young adulthood	Intimacy vs. Isolation	Am I capable of bonding with an intimate life partner?
5	Adolescence	Identity vs. Confusion	Do I have a clear sense of who I am as an individual?
4	School age	Industriousness vs. Inferiority	Am I learning what I need to be a productive adult?
3	Play age	Initiative vs. Guilt	Do I have confidence to interact successfully with others?
2	Early childhood	Autonomy vs. Shame	Am I capable of taking care of my basic needs?
1	Infancy	Trust vs. Mistrust	Can I trust the other people in my life?

weren't necessarily applicable to non-Western societies. Erikson responded that he'd observed these same stages among the Native American populations he'd studied in the 1930s.

At the time he published *Childhood and Society*, Erikson was working at Berkeley (Mintz, 1996). But shortly after the book came out, he was faced with a crisis. These were the years of McCarthyism and its ungrounded fear that Communist agents had infiltrated government, education, and entertainment. When the Berkeley faculty was asked to sign a loyalty oath, Erikson joined Edward Tolman and others by resigning in protest. While Tolman and his colleagues sued to win back their jobs, Erikson had plenty of offers and returned to the East coast. After working a few years in a clinical position, Harvard University appointed Erikson as professor of human development, a title invented just for him. They also had to bend the rules so that they could allow a man with only a high school diploma to fill the position. There, he continued to publish books that made a lasting mark on the field.

Without doubt, Erik Erikson was one of the most influential psychologists of the twentieth century, both within the field and among the general public (Whitfield, 2000). No one has done more than Erikson to shift the focus of developmental psychology from a concentration on childhood to a consideration of the entire lifespan. While his training was in traditional psychoanalysis, he was never bound by dogma in his research, which no doubt explains why his ideas had so much currency among psychologists of all stripes. Furthermore, his emphasis on psychological health rather than disorder aligned him with the humanistic psychologists, even though he never counted himself among their numbers. In his youth, Erikson struggled with his own identity crisis as he learned he wasn't Homburger's son. Yet in his mature adulthood, he developed a theory that has shown us the pathway to creating a meaningful identity in our own lives.

Lawrence Kohlberg

Although he'd grown up in wealth and prestige, young **Lawrence Kohlberg** (1927–1987) had no interest in such a lifestyle (Rest, Power, & Brabeck, 1988). He'd just finished high school as World War II came to an end, and he was passionate about the Zionist movement, which had the goal of building a Jewish state in Palestine. At the time, however, Palestine was ruled by the British, who banned Jews from settling there. Kohlberg joined the crew of a ship that smuggled Jewish refugees to Palestine, and he even spent some time in British prison for this. Kohlberg struggled with the moral dilemma of acting toward a cause he deeply believed in while defying the laws of legitimate authorities, and this experience was reflected in his research career. Today, Lawrence Kohlberg is known as the *American psychologist who proposed an influential theory of moral development.*

When he returned to the United States, Kohlberg enrolled as an undergraduate student at the University of Chicago (Walsh, 2000). He took exams for course credit and graduated in just one year, so he decided to stay for his Ph.D. Initially he wanted to become a clinical psychologist, but then he discovered the works of Jean Piaget (Chapter 8), which had just been translated into English. He was impressed with Piaget's model of cognitive development as a progression of stages, each with its own set of mental structures. However, it was Piaget's work on moral reasoning in schoolboys that excited Kohlberg. Piaget had found that these children oriented their thinking on morality either toward rewards and punishments from adults or else toward acceptance and rejection from their peers. Kohlberg wondered whether children's moral reasoning would become more complex as they progressed into their teenage years, and this is what he tested in his dissertation research.

For his dissertation, which he completed in 1958, Kohlberg employed Piaget's clinical method (Krebs & Denton, 2005). Using a sample of eighty-four boys, he presented each with a series of vignettes containing moral dilemmas, and he asked them whether the actions portrayed were right or wrong. He then used probing questions to get at the underlying reasoning for these responses. The most famous of these moral dilemmas is the story of Heinz, whose wife is dying of cancer. Only one drug can save her life, but the chemist who manufactures the drug charges too much and Heinz can't afford it, so he steals it instead. Whether the subject judged Heinz's behavior as right or wrong was unimportant. Rather, Kohlberg wanted to know why each boy thought that way.

On the basis of his subjects' responses, Kohlberg devised a theory of cognitive moral development that posited six stages arranged on three levels (Krebs & Denton, 2005). The first level is known as the preconventional level, in which morality is viewed in terms of rewards and punishments. Stage 1 moral reasoning is oriented toward punishment and obedience. Typical responses include "Heinz was wrong because stealing is against the law" or "It's okay if Heinz doesn't get caught." Stage 2 is oriented toward self-interest, with typical responses such as "Heinz was wrong because he'll just go to jail and won't be able to spend time with his wife" or "It's okay if his wife is nice and pretty." This type of thinking dominates childhood, but it can be observed in some adults as well.

The second level is called the conventional level because this represents the kind of moral reasoning exhibited by most adolescents and adults (Krebs & Denton, 2005). Moral thinking at this level goes beyond self-centered interests such as rewards and punishments or gains and losses to consider social and institutional rules that people must follow even when it's not in their own best interest to do so. Stage 3 involves conformity to social expectations, what's sometimes called the "good boy, nice girl" attitude. Typical responses to the Heinz problem include "It's wrong because people will think badly of him for stealing" or "It's okay because he did it for his wife." Stage 4 orients moral thinking toward law and order. Responses at this stage could be "It's wrong because you can't just let people go around taking other people's property" or "It's okay because saving a human life is more important than protecting property." Kohlberg found that the moral development of most adults stopped at one of these two stages. However, some advanced to the next level.

The third level is named the postconventional level (Krebs & Denton, 2005). For those who reach this level, moral thinking becomes far more complex and is generally based on philosophical theories of morality. Stage 5 is oriented toward social contract theory as proposed by Thomas Hobbes (Chapter 1) and other Enlightenment philosophers, with the idea that we all have rights and responsibilities as members of society. At this stage, reasoning about the Heinz dilemma would have the following features: "The chemist has a right to profit from his invention, but he also has the responsibility to make the drug available to those who need it, especially in life-and-death cases. Heinz's wife has a right to life, and so it's wrong for the chemist not to sell it to her. Under the circumstances, Heinz has a moral obligation to steal the drug to save his wife's life, but he'll also have to accept the consequences for his actions, including possible incarceration." By stage 5, morality is no longer viewed as a black-and-white issue but rather is considered from the perspectives of all persons involved.

Kohlberg believed that some historical personages attained an even higher stage of moral thinking based on universal ethical principles (Pritchard, 1999). In his mind, leaders of civil rights movements in the mid-twentieth century, such as Mahatma Gandhi in India or Dr. Martin Luther King, Jr. in the United States, were examples of persons who had attained the pinnacle of moral reasoning. Kohlberg modeled this stage on the categorical imperative of Enlightenment philosopher Immanuel Kant (Chapter 1), who argued that the guiding principle of moral behavior was to treat every human being with dignity in all situations.

Over the next two decades, Kohlberg re-interviewed the participants of his dissertation research as they grew into adolescence and adulthood (Krebs & Denton, 2005). The results of this longitudinal study generally supported his assertion that people progress through these stages in order. Furthermore, Kohlberg asserted that there was no regression from a higher to lower stage because the transition from one stage to the next was driven by a reorganization of mental structures, just as Piaget had posited for his cognitive stages. However, he did revise his theory in one respect as a result of this longitudinal study. Since he found evidence of some of his participants reaching stage 5 but not stage 6, he decided it was unnecessary to separate these. In later versions of his theory, for example as expressed in his *Essays in Moral Development* (published as two volumes in 1983 and 1984), he combined both social contract and universal ethical principle orientations as a single stage 5 of the postconventional level (Table 15.4).

Table 15.4 Kohlberg's Stages of Moral Development

Level	Stage	Orientation	Description
Postconventional	6	Universal ethic principles	Moral judgments are made in terms of higher philosophical arguments.
	5	Social contract	Morality judgments are made in terms of rights and responsibilities of individuals cooperating within a society.
Conventional	4	Law and order	Morality judgments are made in terms of legality.
	3	Social norms	Morality judgments are made in terms of social expectations: "good boy, nice girl."
Preconventional	2	Self-interest	Morality judgments are made in terms of costs and benefits to one's self.
	1	Punishment and obedience	Morality judgments are made in terms of rewards and punishments meted out by authority figures.

Kohlberg enjoyed a remarkably fast rise through the ranks of academia (Rest et al., 1988). At first, his study of moral development was ignored by many psychologists as uninteresting or unoriginal. However, the 1960s were a tumultuous time in the United States, with the Civil Rights Movement and violent protests against the war in Vietnam. Suddenly, Kohlberg's ideas seemed to have immediate importance, and he became something of a celebrity both within the field and among the general public. In 1968, he was hired at Harvard, where he was active in establishing programs for moral education. While working on a cross-cultural project in Belize, however, Kohlberg contracted an abdominal infection that ruined his health. For years afterward, he was wracked with pain, constantly feeling dizzy and nauseous. There were times when he was bedridden for days, and he frequently slumped into depression. Although he tried pushing through the pain, he was simply unable to keep up his previous pace. As the years passed with no sign of the disease abating, Kohlberg became despondent. In January 1987, he drove to the edge of Boston harbor and threw himself into the icy water. His body was recovered a few days later. He was only fifty-nine years old.

Lawrence Kohlberg introduced his theory of cognitive moral development at a time when a discussion of thinking and reasoning was still anathema to many psychologists (Pritchard, 1999). To the extent that morality was even considered at that time, it was viewed as a product of either psychodynamic processes or social learning. But with the Cognitive Revolution of the 1960s, Kohlberg's theory became not only acceptable but also regaled for its social relevance during trying times. Yet Kohlberg also had his critics. Some maintained that his theory ignored the role of emotions in moral decision making, while others remarked that he'd never shown a connection between moral reasoning and moral behavior. Since his participants had only responded to hypothetical situations and not real-life circumstances, there was no way of knowing whether people really did act according to their beliefs. Still others challenged the universality of the theory, especially arguing that the postconventional level was a product of Western philosophy and individualism, and that it wasn't relevant to collectivistic societies. Finally, there was his Harvard colleague Carol Gilligan, who pointed out the Achilles heel in Kohlberg's research—no females were included in the study.

Carol Gilligan

Kohlberg wasn't the only psychologist at the time who'd built a supposedly universal theory of human development from the sampling of a few American *males*—Maslow and Erikson had done the same (Goldberg, 2000). In response, **Carol Gilligan** (born 1936) has been an important critic of male-centric psychology for four decades. With the publication of her 1982 book *In a Different Voice*, Gilligan became famous as the *American psychologist* who challenged Kohlberg's theory of moral development for its neglect of the kinds of moral decisions that women face. Particularly notable was her study of women considering abortions shortly after the *Roe v. Wade* decision of 1973. In making their decision, these women rarely grappled with the kinds of questions that defined Kohlberg's stages. Instead, they tended to think in terms of the implications their actions would have on their relationships. For instance, a woman may choose to have an abortion to keep her boyfriend from leaving her or to save her family from disgrace.

Photo 15.6
Carol Gilligan with her husband James

Gilligan's argument isn't that men and women are simply different when it comes to moral reasoning (Hayes, 1994). Rather, Kohlberg and Gilligan got different results not only because their participants were of different genders but also because they asked different kinds of questions. Kohlberg asked his boys to respond to hypothetical moral dilemmas, whereas Gilligan interviewed women who'd actually made difficult moral decisions in their lives. Plenty of studies have replicated Kohlberg's results, suggesting that people do engage in abstract moral reasoning in ways that the theory predicts. However, Gilligan believes that when men and women make real-life moral decisions, they tend to do so in ways that negotiate the needs of all the parties involved.

It's often reported that Gilligan was a student of Kohlberg, but this wasn't the case (Walsh, 2000). Gilligan graduated from Harvard in 1964, and she was teaching part-time there when Kohlberg was hired in 1968. Because of their similar interests, they collaborated on a research project, and she also taught a section of a course on moral and political choice that Kohlberg had designed. However, Gilligan maintained her intellectual independence from Kohlberg. For instance, when the "Kohlberg-Gilligan debate" gained notoriety she withdrew from the discussion, seeing it as benefitting Kohlberg more than herself. Nevertheless, *In a Different Voice* has had a major impact on the field, and in 1988 she was granted tenure at Harvard.

In the end, Gilligan's work wasn't a direct attack on Kohlberg's theory. Rather, her contribution has been to show her fellow psychologists that there's far more to moral decision making than reasoning based on abstract principles. This is a sentiment that many researchers in the field concur with today.

Positive Psychology

In his 1998 presidential address to the annual convention of the APA, **Martin Seligman** (born 1942) criticized the field of psychology for its focus on the negative aspects of human existence (Titova, Werner, & Sheldon, 2018). Especially since the end of World War II, psychologists have concentrated their efforts on finding effective therapies for psychological disorders. Certainly this is a noble cause, and much suffering has been alleviated as a result. However, the large majority of people don't suffer from poor mental health. Instead, they lead normal, reasonably happy lives. It was time, he said, for a "positive" psychology that would study the characteristics of a fulfilling life as well as the causes and consequences of happiness. Thus, Seligman established his reputation as an *American psychologist who is one of the founders of positive psychology and is best known for his research on learned helplessness.*

Martin Seligman

As a graduate student at the University of Pennsylvania, Seligman worked in the lab of **Richard Solomon** (1918–1995), an *American comparative psychologist noted for his work on avoidance learning* (LoLordo & Seligman, 1997). In an avoidance learning task, dogs are trained to jump a barrier when a light comes on to avoid an electric shock. At the time, avoidance learning was

Photo 15.7
Martin Seligman

a challenge to behaviorist theory because the jumping behavior seemed to be reinforced by a nonevent. Building on the two-factor theory of Hobart Mowrer, Solomon proposed that both classical and operant conditioning processes were involved. First, the dog associates the light with the shock in Pavlovian fashion, developing a fear response. Its jumping behavior is then reinforced by a reduction of fear. Solomon also understood that avoidance learning provided a good model of phobia. Because people avoid what they fear, they never get the opportunity to learn that their fear is irrational.

At the time Seligman was a student in the lab, Solomon was testing extensions of his two-factor theory of avoidance learning (Maier & Seligman, 2016). It was found that dogs who'd previously experienced shocks with no opportunity of escape failed to learn the jumping task later, passively waiting out the painful experience instead. To Seligman, these dogs looked depressed or "helpless." In a series of experiments, Seligman and fellow graduate student Steven Maier tested the hypothesis that these dogs had learned there was nothing they could do to avoid the shock. First, they tied the dogs to a harness and administered a series of electric jolts. A light was shone just before each shock. In early trials, the dogs would struggle in the harness each time the light came on, but in later trials they became passive. Then, when they were released from the harness, they continued to stay put, enduring each shock even though they now had the ability to escape. Thus, Seligman and Maier discovered **learned helplessness**, the term they used to refer to *a phenomenon in which an organism fails to escape a painful situation even when it is capable of doing so*.

Seligman next tested whether he could induce learned helplessness in college undergraduates (Maier & Seligman, 2016). Research participants were exposed to bursts of loud noise with no way to stop it. Later, when a switch for turning it off became available, many of them continued to endure the noise. In another approach, Seligman asked participants to try to solve anagrams that in fact had no solutions. Afterward, they were given simpler problems to work on, but many quit without much effort, often making comments like "What's the use?" or "There's no way I can do this." The *Diagnostic and Statistical Manual* (DSM) listed nine symptoms of depression, five of which were necessary for a diagnosis. In both his canine and human subjects, Seligman observed eight of the nine symptoms. (The only undetected symptom was suicidal ideation.) This led him to believe that learned helplessness could be used as a model of depression. Over the next few decades, Seligman, Maier, and many others induced learned helplessness in rats to study the neural circuitry of depression.

Mihaly Csikszentmihalyi

Positive psychology was the brainchild of Martin Seligman and his friend **Mihaly Csikszentmihalyi** (born 1934; pronounced *ME-high CHEEK-sent-me-high*; Seligman & Csikszentmihalyi, 2000). The son of a Hungarian diplomat, Csikszentmihalyi grew up in Italy. The family suffered little during World War II because of their protected diplomatic status. But after the Soviets installed a Communist government in Hungary, his father lost his post, and furthermore the family couldn't return to their home country. His family opened a restaurant in Rome, and teenaged Mihaly dropped out of school to wait tables. On a vacation in Switzerland, he attended a lecture by Carl Jung and became enthralled with psychology. Because there were no psychology programs in Italy, he traveled to the University of Chicago to study the subject there. What he found was a great disappointment—all his teachers talked about was rats and mazes, and they dismissed Jung as a crank. This wasn't the kind of psychology he wanted to study, but he persisted and eventually earned his Ph.D. Today, he is known as the *Hungarian-American psychologist who is one of the founders of positive psychology and who discovered a kind of peak experience known as "flow."*

Early in his research career, Csikszentmihalyi studied the creative process in artists (Beard, 2015). As he observed them at work, he noticed something that couldn't be explained by current theories of motivation. Although the artists were completely engrossed in the production of a painting, once they'd completed one, they just set it aside and started working on another piece. According to behaviorist theory, the finished product should have been the reward for the hard work of producing it. Yet the artists placed little value in it. Instead, they seemed to most enjoy the process of painting itself. When he interviewed the artists, they described painting as an almost ecstatic experience in which they lost track of time and their sense of self seemed to disappear. He then interviewed composers and poets, who gave similar descriptions of their creative experiences. Next he talked with other people, such as chess-players and athletes, who also seemed to become totally engrossed in their activities. Again, they gave similar descriptions of ecstasy, selflessness, and loss of time.

One word that frequently came up in these interviews was "flow" (Csikszentmihalyi, 1999). Artists claimed that the paint just flowed from the brush, and poets that the words just flowed from the pen, as if they had no conscious control over it. Also, they commented on how quickly time flowed when they were engaged in their activity. Because of this, Csikszentmihalyi gave the name **flow** to this kind of *a peak experience in which skilled practitioners report a sense of ecstasy and a loss of time and self*. In his work on self-actualization, Maslow had reported that many of his interviewees had described such peak experiences, and Csikszentmihalyi believed that the flow experience he'd discovered was the same sort of thing. He also found that people were quite happy after experiencing flow, even though it was rarely described as a happy experience in itself. In fact, interviewees reported that they were so absorbed in their work that they had little awareness of any feelings at all, even of basic bodily needs such as hunger or a full bladder. Only after coming out of flow were they aware of these urgent needs. But since a warm afterglow always followed, he wondered if the key to a happy life was frequent flow experiences.

Csikszentmihalyi found there are several requirements for a flow experience to occur (Beard, 2015). First, there needs to be a good balance between the challenge of the task and the skill of the practitioner. If the task is too difficult the result is frustration, and if the task is too easy the result is boredom. Second, there need to be clear goals for the task and unambiguous feedback during the process. For instance, the artist can look at the canvas and immediately tell whether that last stroke was just right or needs to be repaired. Third, the practitioner needs to completely concentrate on the task. This leads to the paradoxical situation in which the person is in total control and yet loses any sense of control. Finally, a task that elicits flow must be rewarding in itself, performed for no other reason than the sheer joy of doing it. In fact, the same task performed solely for monetary or other gain doesn't produce flow, and may even be perceived as drudgery.

Photo 15.8
Mihaly Csikszentmihalyi

Ehirsh, via Wikimedia Commons

Science of Happiness

Maslow coined the term "positive psychology" in his 1954 book *Motivation and Personality* (Kristjánsson, 2010). However, researchers in the twenty-first century define **positive psychology** as *the scientific study of happiness and the features of a life well lived*. Seligman, the leading spokesperson for the movement, claims there are three directions of research in the field: (1) the study of positive emotions, such as happiness, flow, and a sense of well-being; (2) the study of positive traits, and in particular strengths and virtues, that lead to a happy life; and (3) positive institutions, in particular how to arrange our social organizations, such as homes, schools, and workplaces, so that its members frequently experience flow.

Seligman and Csikszentmihalyi (2000) note a number of precursors to positive psychology. In the first half of the twentieth century, Lewis Terman (Chapter 4) studied the characteristics of giftedness in children and adults as well as the features of marital happiness. Likewise, John Watson (Chapter 5) proposed a behavioral approach to psychology that would yield practical benefits for society. In addition, both Alfred Alder and Carl Jung (Chapter 7) emphasized the importance of finding meaning in life. Even though the focus shifted from mental health to mental illness after World War II, the authors point to Alfred Bandura's (Chapter 13) work on self-efficacy as one important precursor to positive psychology. Finally, there were the humanistic psychologists, to whom the new movement owed a great debt.

However, the relationship between humanistic and positive psychologists has been marred with petty bickering (Waterman, 2013). Positive psychologists define their field by their empirical approach and their use of quantitative methods, as opposed to the experiential approach and qualitative methods of the humanistic psychologists. The implication has clearly been that positive psychology is superior because it's more scientific, and yet the humanistic psychologists rejected the sterile laboratory experiment as a way of understanding the human experience. Other philosophical differences also separate the two schools. As the field's first new movement of the twenty-first century, positive psychology has had to establish itself by pointing out the deficits of current approaches, which has inevitably created backlash from other psychologists with vested interests in preserving the status of their favored disciplines. Whether positive psychology will eventually be accepted into the fold remains to be seen.

Positive psychology may be the science of happiness, but positive psychologists haven't come to an agreement on what happiness is (Kristjánsson, 2010). There are three factions within the movement, divided by the answer they give to this question (Table 15.5). In brief, the three definitions of happiness are as follows:

- **Hedonism.** This is *the view that happiness is the product of pleasurable experiences.* Thus, hedonists try to maximize pleasure and minimize pain in their lives. The Ancient Greek philosopher Epicurus (342–270 BCE) first proposed a form a measured hedonism as the key to the good life, and British Empiricists such as John Locke, David Hume, and John Stuart Mill generally agreed that the good life was one that maximized pleasure and minimized pain. In the twenty-first century, cognitive psychologist Daniel Kahneman (Chapter 11) has become an important advocate of the hedonic view of happiness.

- **Subjective well-being.** The pursuit of pleasure certainly leads to happiness in the short term, but we soon habituate to pleasant experiences and become bored with them. This leads to a never-ending cycle of seeking out other pleasant experiences that are new or better than what we've had before. Since happiness from pleasures is fleeting, some psychologists have argued for *the view that happiness is a person's overall assessment of life satisfaction.* Subjective well-being, or SWB, is generally measured by questionnaires, and it can be assessed at an individual, group, or even national level. Ed Diener is the major proponent of this approach.

- **Eudaimonia.** Pronounced *you-die-muh-NEE-uh,* this is an idea that can be traced all the way back to Aristotle (Chapter 1). Traditionally translated as "happiness," in modern times it's often rendered instead as "flourishing." While Aristotle agreed that pleasurable experiences were an essential component of the good life, he also believed that truly happy or flourishing persons lived a virtuous life in which they fulfilled their physical and psychological potential. This concept comes close to Maslow's idea of self-actualization. In the twenty-first century, eudaimonia has become *the view of happiness as resulting from a life in which persons pursue self-actualization and the fulfillment of their potential.* A eudaimonic life is not necessarily an easy one, as is the hedonic lifestyle filled with fleeting pleasures. Rather, it can be replete with struggles and hardships. However, as people gain mastery of their lives, they experience flow frequently, and this provides sustained happiness. Seligman has been the major proponent of the eudaimonic approach to happiness. (By the way, this word is sometimes spelled *eudaemonia* or *eudemonia* and pronounced with the stress on the third syllable instead of the fourth. The spelling and pronunciation used here is closest to the original Ancient Greek.)

Table 15.5	Three Definitions of Happiness
Term	**Description**
Hedonism	Happiness is a product of pleasurable experiences.
Subjective well-being	Happiness is a person's overall assessment of life satisfaction.
Eudaimonia	Happiness is the pursuit of self-actualization and the fulfillment of one's potential.

Born at the turn of the twenty-first century, positive psychology is still in its childhood, and it remains to be seen whether it will mature into an established discipline of psychology. Its detractors dismiss it as little more than self-help with a veneer of experimental methodology. Nevertheless, by proposing that the ultimate goal of psychological research is to improve the quality of human life, positive psychologists have called on their field to return to its earlier purpose.

Carol Dweck

Inspired by Seligman's work on learned helplessness, **Carol Dweck** (born 1946) has devoted her career to studying the underlying mental processes that lead people to either give up or persevere when faced with difficult tasks (Aldhous, 2008). She was trained in traditional animal learning theory, but the Cognitive Revolution was in full swing when she earned her Ph.D. from Yale in 1972, and it was once again acceptable to talk about how people's thought processes influence behavior. Her reputation today is as an *American psychologist who maintains that people's attitudes about the nature of intelligence or willpower influence the amount of effort they put into difficult tasks.*

Photo 15.9
Carol Dweck

In her early research, Dweck looked at how students respond to failure ("Carol S. Dweck," 2011). Rather than approaching this phenomenon from a narrow perspective, she drew on various disciplines in psychology. In particular, she found that by combining the theory of learned helplessness from the clinical literature and attribution theory from social psychology, she could explain how students cope with failure. Some students hold *the belief that a person's intelligence is a fixed quantity that cannot change*, which she calls a **fixed mindset**. Tasks that come easily reaffirm students' beliefs about their academic abilities, but difficult tasks challenge their self-concept, so they avoid them. And if they can't avoid them, they sometimes even resort to cheating to maintain appearances. Other students hold *the belief that intelligence is a mutable quantity that can increase over time*, which she calls a **growth mindset**. When these students fail at a task, they see it as a challenge to work harder to overcome this deficiency in their knowledge.

In later research, Dweck found that she could influence students' mindsets about their academic abilities (Gupta, 2013). For instance, the participants who were praised for being intelligent were reluctant to attempt a challenging task afterward. However, those who were praised for their efforts were willing to try more difficult problems. According to Dweck, praising students for their intelligence instills a fixed mindset, and they interpret challenging tasks as a threat to their self-concept. In contrast, praising students for their diligence instills a growth mindset, whereby they view challenging tasks as opportunities to increase their intelligence. Her ideas on the underlying thought processes behind academic success and failure became widely known to lay audiences as well after the 2006 publication of her popular book, *Mindset: The New Psychology of Success.*

Looking Ahead

Twentieth-century psychologists took a rather bleak perspective on human nature. On the one hand, psychoanalysts viewed humans as essentially vile creatures, wracked by unconscious and conflicting desires, who could only become decent people through the overwhelming force of socialization. On the other hand, behaviorists saw people as nothing more than biological machines whose actions were totally under the control of environmental influences. Yet the humanistic psychologists offered a third view of human nature. To them, humans are essentially good, but they've been led astray by the perverted social norms of modern society. By rediscovering their true self, people can once again be happy and fulfill their potential in life. In the twenty-first century, positive psychologists have pushed the agenda of personal growth forward by claiming that they can study the causes and consequences of happiness in a scientific manner. Such a claim, if true, is certainly cause for optimism in the decades to come.

CHAPTER SUMMARY

The humanistic psychologists viewed themselves as a "Third Force" that challenged the dominance of psychoanalysis and behaviorism in American psychology after World War II. Carl Rogers developed client-centered psychotherapy based on the three conditions of unconditional positive regard, empathy, and congruence. This therapeutic approach had personal growth as its goal, and it was based on the earlier work of Otto Rank and Jessie Taft. Abraham Maslow arranged the needs that Henry Murray had listed into a hierarchy, with personal growth occurring as the individual progressed upward through the ranks. Once the deficiency needs were satisfied, according to the theory, the person would experience a drive to fulfill the being needs of self-actualization and self-transcendence. Students of human development during this time period are often counted among the humanistic psychologists. These include Erik Erikson with his theory of psychosocial development and Lawrence Kohlberg with his theory of moral development. Around the turn of the twenty-first century, a new discipline calling itself positive psychology was established. Also concerned with personal growth, positive psychologists have shifted from the disease model of humanistic psychology to a wellness model, with an emphasis on the causes and consequences of happiness.

DISCUSSION QUESTIONS

1. Contrast the methodologies and grounding assumptions of psychoanalytic, behavioral, and client-centered psychotherapy. What are the advantages and disadvantages of each approach?

2. Among humanistic thinkers, some argue that "essence precedes existence," meaning that the goal of psychotherapy is to help clients discover their true self that was already there but hidden by blind adherence to social norms. Others maintain that "existence precedes essence," meaning that the purpose of psychotherapy is to help clients build an authentic identity. Take a position on this issue, defending it with arguments and evidence.

3. Carl Rogers argued that clients can find out for themselves what's wrong with them and what they need to do to get better if they get support from an empathetic and nonjudgmental counselor. But Albert Ellis rejected this view, maintaining that clients need guidance to improve their lives. Take a position on this issue, defending it with arguments and evidence.

4. Maslow maintained that people's deficiency needs must be met before they feel a drive toward fulfilling their being needs. However, critics have offered examples of people who strove for self-actualization and self-transcendence even though they live in poverty. Can you think of any examples like this? Is there some way to argue that their deficiency needs are met despite their poverty?

5. Consider how the meaning of the term "self-actualization" has changed from its original usage by Kurt Goldstein, its borrowing by Carl Rogers, and its most well-known definition by Abraham Maslow.

6. A common theme in humanistic psychology is that psychological disorders are the product of distorting influences in society. According to this view, humans were happy in their original environment, but modern life has made them sick. If you know anything about the hunter-gatherer lifestyle, compare it with life in the twenty-first century. What differences in these two ways of living might account for the high degree of mental illness in modern life?

7. Evaluate Erikson's theory of psychosocial development by giving examples of each stage from your own life or from the lives of others you are familiar with. Do you have doubts about the universality of any of the stages? Can you think of other life crises that Erikson doesn't mention?

8. Come up with an example of a real-world moral dilemma and consider the types of responses you'd expect from persons at each of Kohlberg's six stages.

9. Consider a moral dilemma that you have had to face. Do you think your moral reasoning was more along the lines of Lawrence Kohlberg's or Carol Gilligan's theory? Explain.

10. The theory of learned helplessness attributes the cause of depression mainly to environmental influences. However, there's also strong evidence for a genetic component to the disorder. Pick one of these positions or describe a third alternative and defend it with arguments and evidence.

11. Do you ever experience flow in your life? If so, discuss the kinds of activities that tend to elicit flow. Also, describe what the flow experience is like, as well as your emotional state afterward.

12. Compare and contrast the three definitions of happiness proposed by positive psychologists. What do you think of Seligman's idea that authentic happiness includes a measured combination of all three?

ON THE WEB

YouTube hosts videos of **Carl Rogers** discussing client-centered therapy and **Abraham Maslow** talking about self-actualization. You can find an interview with **Erik Erikson** on the development of his theory of psychosocial stages as well. **Carol Gilligan** also presents an informal lecture on the development of moral principles. **Martin Seligman** has several lectures on YouTube as well as a TED Talk, as do **Mihaly Csikszentmihalyi** and **Carol Dweck.**

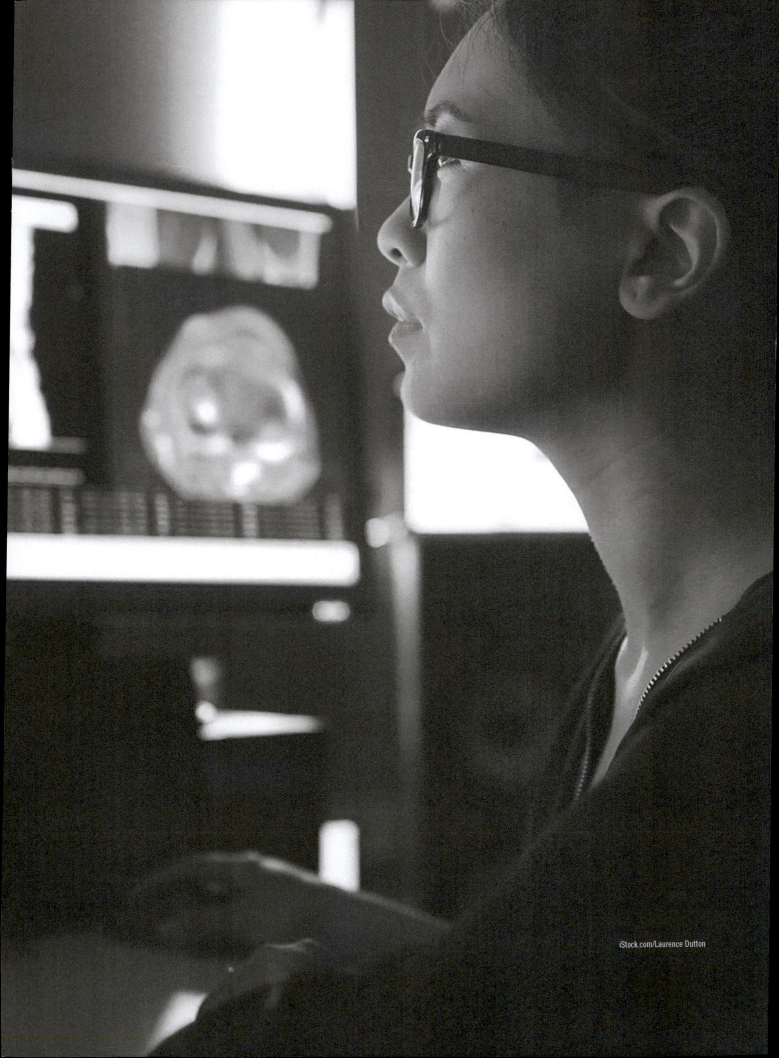

iStock.com/Laurence Dutton

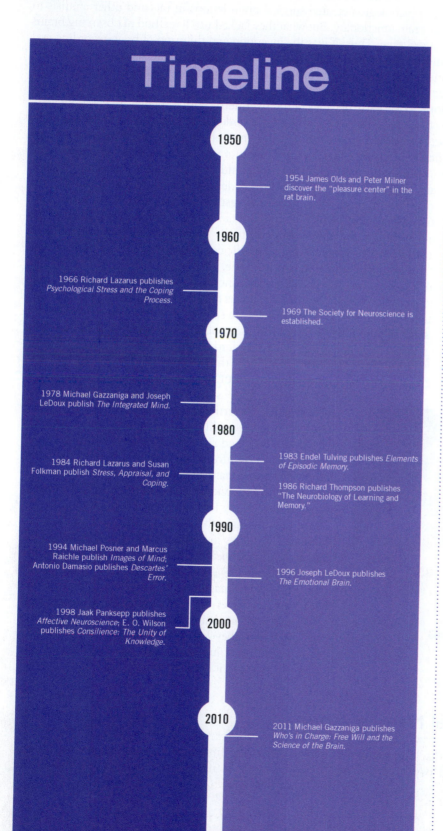

Timeline

1950

1954 James Olds and Peter Milner discover the "pleasure center" in the rat brain.

1960

1966 Richard Lazarus publishes *Psychological Stress and the Coping Process*.

1969 The Society for Neuroscience is established.

1970

1978 Michael Gazzaniga and Joseph LeDoux publish *The Integrated Mind*.

1980

1984 Richard Lazarus and Susan Folkman publish *Stress, Appraisal, and Coping*.

1983 Endel Tulving publishes *Elements of Episodic Memory*.

1986 Richard Thompson publishes "The Neurobiology of Learning and Memory."

1990

1994 Michael Posner and Marcus Raichle publish *Images of Mind*; Antonio Damasio publishes *Descartes' Error*.

1996 Joseph LeDoux publishes *The Emotional Brain*.

1998 Jaak Panksepp publishes *Affective Neuroscience*; E. O. Wilson publishes *Consilience: The Unity of Knowledge*.

2000

2010

2011 Michael Gazzaniga publishes *Who's in Charge: Free Will and the Science of the Brain*.

Learning Objectives

After reading this chapter, you should be able to:

- Evaluate the contributions of behavioral neuroscience to our understanding of the brain processes that underlie motivation and learning.

- Appraise the merits of cognitive neuroscience in revealing associations between localized brain activity and cognitive processes such as memory and attention.

- Assess the potential for affective neuroscience to contribute to the fields of clinical and health psychology.

- Critique the various scenarios that philosophers of science have envisioned for the future of neuroscience and psychology.

Looking Back

The scientific study of brain functioning goes back at least to the middle of the nineteenth century (Borck, 2016). As medical knowledge advanced, patients who suffered traumatic brain injuries often survived for years afterward, and changes in their cognitive or behavioral abilities were associated with the location and extent of their lesions. In the middle decades of the twentieth century, physiological psychologists created surgical brain lesions in rats and other animals to test hypotheses about brain functioning. But what they lacked was a method of observing brains as they functioned in real time. Thus, it was the invention and diffusion of brain recording and brain imaging techniques after World War II that led to the birth of modern-day neuroscience.

Many historians credit the German psychiatrist Hans Berger (1873–1941) as the first researcher to directly observe activity in a normally functioning human brain (Sannita, 2017). Working alone in the early decades of the twentieth century, Berger invented **electroencephalography**, or EEG. This is *a technique for recording electrical activity produced in the brain by placing a set of electrodes on the scalp.* At the time, physiologists were already making recordings by surgically inserting electrodes into the brains of animals, but the general consensus was that no meaningful patterns of activity could by observed at the scalp. In fact, Berger did find meaningful patterns, even with the crude instruments he had available. For instance, he found one rhythm of activity in brains at rest (which he called *alpha waves*) and a different pattern in brains at work (which he called *beta waves*). When Berger published his findings in 1929, they were ignored at first, but eventually physiologists replicated his findings, and this generated great excitement in the scientific community. At this point, however, World War II broke out, and EEG research was set aside.

After the war, researchers turned their attention once again to the EEG, making some important discoveries (Borck, 2005). For instance, it was found that the brain cycles through a series of distinct stages during sleep, each marked by a specific rhythm of electrical activity, including a special stage in which we dream. Moreover, the EEG proved useful in detecting anomalies in brain functioning, and today it's a standard diagnostic tool in cases of brain trauma. However, as an instrument for exploring how the brain worked, EEG left much to be desired. Although it produced a continuous readout of brain activity as it occurred, it was virtually impossible to tease out specific processes or locations. Nevertheless, it held out hope that more effective brain recording and brain imaging techniques could be developed as technology advanced.

The term "neuroscience" was first used in the name of an interdisciplinary research program started at MIT in the 1960s (Borck, 2016). The idea quickly caught on, and the Society for Neuroscience was established in 1969, thus marking the establishment of the new discipline. Early studies in neuroscience mainly relied on the standard physiological techniques of making lesions and inserting electrodes into the brains of animals, but by the 1980s brain imaging technologies such as PET and MRI were being developed that enabled neuroscientists to observe human brains in action. As these techniques were perfected, they led to what can only be called the Neuroscience Revolution, raising the discipline to the dominant position it holds in psychology today.

Wikimedia Commons

**Photo 16.1
Hans Berger**

Behavioral Neuroscience

When the interdisciplinary field of neuroscience was first created, behaviorism still dominated American psychology. Thus, it should come as no surprise that the early work in this field focused on *the study of the brain processes underlying motivation and learning*. This approach became known as **behavioral neuroscience**. Relying mostly on lesions to disrupt brain tissue and electrodes to stimulate it, the early behavioral neuroscientists demonstrated that a science of brain and behavior was feasible.

Richard Thompson

Karl Lashley was the scientific hero of **Richard Thompson** (1930–2014) ever since he first learned about his work in an introductory psychology class (Shors, 2015). Lashley (Chapter 10) had devoted much of his career in search of the engram—the hypothetical location in the brain where a memory is stored. In the end, Lashley failed to find the engram and came to the conclusion that it didn't exist. With the benefit of better technology, however, Thompson picked up the search for the engram, and after decades of dedicated research he and his students finally isolated the complete neural path for a conditioned response. Furthermore, he found it in a part of the brain Lashley would never have suspected. For this, Richard Thompson is remembered as the *American behavioral neuroscientist who isolated the engram and demonstrated the role of the cerebellum in learning and memory*.

Thompson earned his Ph.D. at the University of Wisconsin in 1956, working with a number of notable physiological psychologists, including Harry Harlow (Patterson, 2011). From the beginning, his research interests focused on how the structure of the nervous system changes as a result of learning. For more than a decade, he studied the processes of habituation and sensitization in spinal reflexes. Although they're innate responses, reflexes can either decrease in strength (habituation) or increase in strength (sensitization) due to repeated stimulation. While these studies were important contributions, even more important was that they gave Thompson the experience he needed to embark on a search for the engram, which dominated the middle decades of his career. This shift in research direction occurred when one of the postdoctoral fellows in his lab introduced him to a new technique for studying classical conditioning.

In 1986, Thompson published the research article "The Neurobiology of Learning and Memory" in the prestigious journal *Science* (Knowlton, 2016). He made two bold claims in this article. The first claim was that he'd traced the neural pathway of a conditioned response from sensory inputs to motor output, including the exact location that linked the stimulus with the response. In other words, he'd located an engram. The second claim was that this engram was situated in a most unexpected location, namely the cerebellum. Until that time, it was believed that the cerebellum played a role in maintaining balance and locomotion, and no one suspected that it was also involved in the higher processes of learning and memory. However, Thompson provided overwhelming evidence for his claims, and his critics were soon convinced. The story of this discovery is fascinating in its own right, and furthermore it illustrates how research was conducted in the early days of behavioral neuroscience.

In Search of the Engram

As we learned in Chapter 5, a common technique for studying learning in both human and nonhuman animals is eyelid conditioning (Foy & Foy, 2016). This is a classical conditioning procedure that pairs an auditory tone with a puff of air that makes the subject blink. In 1962, Isidore Gormezano, a former classmate of Thompson's at Wisconsin, constructed a device for conditioning the blink response in rabbits. It consisted of a narrow cage that held the rabbit so it couldn't move. A tube to deliver puffs of air was adjacent to one of the rabbit's eyes, and a loudspeaker above the cage played the tone. A sensor was also attached next to the rabbit's eye to measure blinks. This device could automatically condition the rabbit to blink to the tone by repeatedly pairing it with air puffs.

A few years later, a postdoc named Michael Patterson worked with Gormezano using the device (Patterson, 2011). Sometime later, Gormezano introduced Patterson to Thompson, who offered him a fellowship in his lab. After he joined Thompson's lab, Patterson told him about the eyelid conditioning device and offered to construct one for him. Once Thompson saw how efficiently it worked, he understood this could be the tool he needed to search for the engram—that is, the exact location in the brain where the memory of the eyeblink response was stored.

Thompson's approach was quite straightforward (Foy & Foy, 2016). He assigned a different part of the brain to each research assistant in his lab, who trained rabbits on the eyeblink response and then used various techniques to see which parts of the brain became active during the task. This was largely accomplished with electrodes inserted into the brain that measured electrical activity at the target area.

When a region of interest was identified, it was further tested with a **lesion study** (Foy & Foy, 2016). This is *a research technique that involves damaging a specific portion of the brain and observing any subsequent deficits.* In addition to brain surgery, lesions could be created by passing a strong electric current through the target area, injecting a poisonous chemical, or even through a blast of air passed through a narrow tube inserted into the brain. The disadvantage of creating lesions was that the animal was permanently damaged. However, by the 1970s neuroscientists had several methods for producing "temporary" lesions. One technique involved surgically introducing a small tube into the target area of the brain. When chilled water was run through the tube, the target area shut down, but warm water brought it back to working temperature. Another technique used a chemical that temporarily numbed the brain. Either technique provided the researcher with a "switch" to turn a specific portion of the brain on and off at will. Electrodes inserted into the site could also be used to stimulate the region of interest, and any resulting behavior was noted.

A brain region that originally looked promising was the hippocampus ("Gold Medal," 2010). Neuroscientists already knew from the work of Brenda Milner (Chapter 10) with the patient H.M. that the hippocampus was involved in the formation of long-term memories. Thompson's lab found that the hippocampus was quite active during eyeblink conditioning. However, even rabbits whose hippocampus had been removed were still able to learn the response without problems. Only in the case of long delays between the conditioned stimulus (the tone) and the unconditioned stimulus (the air puff) was the hippocampus necessary for learning the response. Eventually, this promising lead turned into a dead end.

Other members of Thompson's team found activity in the cerebellum during eyelid conditioning, and it soon became the focus of research in the lab (Foy & Foy, 2016). During the early 1980s, Thompson published a number of articles reporting on his lab's findings that the engram for the blink response seemed to be in the cerebellum. However, it took several years—and many rabbits—to pinpoint the exact location. Eventually, they found the engram was located in the interpositus nucleus of the ipsilateral cerebellum—that is, the same side as the conditioned eye. In addition, Thompson's team traced the neural pathway of both the conditioned tone stimulus and the unconditioned air puff stimulus from sensory input to the interpositus nucleus, as well as the neural pathway from the interpositus nucleus to the motor centers that generate the blink response.

In follow-up studies, Thompson's team found that they could create a conditioned eyeblink response without learning (Shors, 2015). Using electrodes, they repeatedly stimulated the neural pathways of the conditioned and unconditioned stimuli. Afterward, the rabbit blinked when it heard the tone, without having the prior experience of a subsequent air puff. This result provided further evidence that the interpositus nucleus was indeed the engram of the conditioned eyeblink response.

Thompson's research on the conditioned eyeblink response breathed life into the nascent field of behavioral neuroscience (Baudry & Swanson, 2011). He demonstrated that it was possible through painstaking and methodological testing to discover the biological links between brain and behavior. As a result, he inspired a generation of fledgling neuroscientists to commit to research careers with the goal of unraveling the mysterious connection between learning and the nervous system. Finally, Thompson gave psychologists hope that the age-old mind-body problem could be solved at last.

James Olds and Peter Milner

As a graduate student at Harvard, **James Olds** (1922–1976) studied motivation with Richard Solomon (Thompson, 1999). When he read Donald Hebb's *The Organization of Behavior*, he asked to do a postdoctoral fellowship with him at McGill University in Montreal. Hebb gave him free rein, but the person who most influenced Olds was Peter Milner, a graduate student in the lab. Working together, they made a chance discovery that helped define the field of behavioral neuroscience for decades. Today, James Olds is known as the *American psychologist who discovered the reward center in the brain along with Peter Milner*.

When Olds arrived at McGill, Milner showed him a device he'd constructed for administering mild electric currents to the brains of freely moving rats (de Haan, 2010). For several decades, physiological psychologists had electrically stimulated the outer surface of the brain to map its functional areas. More recently, some researchers had also been experimenting with surgically implanting needle-thin electrodes deep into the brains of rats. Using sensitive equipment to guide the electrode into place, the rat was left with a small piece of metal protruding from its skull, to which a wire could be attached for delivering the current. Prior research using this method had established the hypothalamus as a drive center for hunger, thirst, and sex. Olds and Milner thought they would explore a brainstem region known as the reticular formation, which was believed to be involved in arousal.

The skill with electrical devices that **Peter Milner** (1919–2018) displayed had come from his previous career as an electrical engineer (White, 2018). Born in England, he served during World War II on a project developing radar, and his assistant was a young psychologist from Cambridge named Brenda. The two fell in love, and when Peter was offered a position in Canada, they got married so she could accompany him. As you already know from Chapter 10, Brenda Milner did her Ph.D. with Donald Hebb and gained fame as the neuroscientist who studied the patient H.M. After learning about the fascinating work his wife was doing, Milner decided that he'd rather spend his career studying the brain than designing electrical components. Hebb accepted Peter Milner as a graduate student after he'd completed a year of undergraduate psychology, and he was in his third or fourth year when James Olds arrived. Today, Peter Milner is known as the *British-Canadian psychologist who discovered the reward center in the brain along with James Olds*.

As Olds (1956) tells the story, he and Milner had surgically implanted the electrode into their first rat early in the week, and they planned to begin testing the following Monday. On Sunday morning, Olds stopped by the lab to make that sure the rat had fully recuperated and that the equipment was working properly. He hooked the rat up to the wire and placed it in the test box, which had four corners labeled A through D. When the rat wandered into corner A, Olds pressed the button to release a brief electric current. The rat stayed put for a moment, wandered away from the corner, and then quickly returned. Olds zapped it again each time it approached corner A. Soon, it was staying put in that corner, but Olds coaxed it over to corner B by electrical stimulation each time it moved in that direction. It was almost as if he had a remote control for the rat. When the electricity was turned off, the rat lay down and went to sleep.

The next day, Olds (1956) showed Milner what he'd discovered. After that, they ran the rat through a series of tests. For instance, they found they could train the rat to navigate a maze simply by giving it a jolt each time it turned correctly. They also trained it to run down an alleyway to get a piece of food. But as the rat was running, they zapped it at the halfway point. The rat stopped there and never went for the food.

After that, they put the rat into an operant conditioning chamber so that the rat could press a lever to stimulate itself (Olds, 1956). Once the rat learned what the lever did, it self-stimulated at a rate of around 2,000 presses per hour, greatly exceeding typical rates when the lever press dispensed food. When the researchers turned off the electricity, the rat pressed the lever six or seven times, then curled up in a corner and went to sleep. Later when the rat awoke, they gave it one free jolt, after which it returned to its previous lever pressing rate. Finally, they found they could get the rat to run across a painful electrified grid to get to the lever to self-stimulate. Clearly, these mild electric currents applied deep inside its brain were strongly rewarding. Olds and Milner first published these results in 1954, and they reported a number of follow-up studies over the next few years.

As it turns out, the electrode bent during insertion, and it didn't go into the reticular formation as intended (Baumeister, 2006). Instead, it had landed in the hypothalamus. Olds and Milner tested a number of sites in this region, and they found that stimulating the nucleus accumbens led to the highest rates of self-stimulation. And in brazen defiance of behaviorist dogma, Olds even referred to this site as the brain's "pleasure center."

Neuroscientists now recognize the identification of the reward center in the brain by Olds and Milner as perhaps the single most important discovery in the field (Baumeister, 2006). Certainly we can argue that it marked the point where traditional physiological psychology transitioned into the newly conceived field of behavioral neuroscience. Olds and Milner had demonstrated that the technique of deep-brain electrical stimulation was a useful tool for studying the relationship between brain and behavior. Their work also inspired a whole generation of young researchers who built the field of behavioral neuroscience. Furthermore, the discovery led to a much greater understanding of important psychological issues such as drug addiction. Finally, this incident demonstrates the powerful role of serendipity in science. Had the electrode made it to its intended target, Olds and Milner may never have discovered the brain's reward center. No doubt someone else would have eventually found it, but the take-home lesson is the importance of keeping an open mind to unexpected possibilities when doing research—sometimes mistakes lead to the most important discoveries.

Mark Rosenzweig

As an undergraduate, **Mark Rosenzweig** (1922–2009) developed a lifelong passion for physiological psychology (Pawlik & Breedlove, 2010). He then entered Harvard, where he worked under the supervision of Edwin Boring (Chapter 3) studying the auditory system of cats. The electrophysiological techniques he used involved placing electrodes on the scalps of cats to detect patterns of brain activity. Although he made important advances in the application of this technology, he gave it up after accepting a position at Berkeley. There, he took up the question of how learning and memory are instantiated in the brain. Today, he's best known as the *American psychologist who discovered that neural plasticity continues even in adulthood.*

Edward Tolman (Chapter 5) spent the 1948–1949 academic year at Harvard while his challenge of Berkeley requirement that all faculty members sign loyalty oaths worked its way through the courts (Pawlik & Breedlove, 2010). Rosenzweig was just finishing his dissertation, and Tolman recommended him for a position at Berkeley, where he remained for the rest of his career. At Berkeley, Rosenzweig befriended David Krech (1909–1977), who pointed him in the direction that would define his research career. A Berkeley colleague had developed two strains of rats, known as "maze-bright" and "maze-dull," by interbreeding the best performers together and the worst performers together for several generations.

Krech suggested that there might be structural differences in the brains of these two strains of rats, and this proved to be a fruitful line of research ("Mark R. Rosenzweig," 1983). First, Rosenzweig and Krech found chemical differences in the brains of these two strains of rat. Specifically, the maze-bright rats had more of an enzyme known as acetylcholinesterase. However, follow-up studies showed that this difference wasn't just due to genetics. They found that rats raised in enriched environments with plenty of toys and other rats to interact with also had more of this enzyme in their brains than did those raised under impoverished circumstances. Furthermore, they found that the "enriched" rats had larger brain masses as well, suggesting that the brain actually changes its structure as a result of experience. The idea that the brain was plastic even in adulthood was met with criticism at first, since it was generally believed that brain structure was set after childhood. Nevertheless, the evidence that Rosenzweig, Krech, and their colleagues presented was overwhelmingly convincing, and today the notion of neural plasticity throughout the lifespan is generally accepted among neuroscientists.

Rosenzweig and his colleagues continued with an investigation of the neurochemistry of learning and memory ("Mark R. Rosenzweig," 1998). They discovered a cascade of chemicals involved in the formation of both short-term and long-term memories. Furthermore, they found that enriched environments can help even adult organisms overcome deficits due to brain lesions.

In addition to his research, Mark Rosenzweig was an international traveler ("Mark R. Rosenzweig," 1998). He spent several sabbaticals in France, and he visited a number of foreign countries as guest speaker. During one semester in France, he met Alexander Luria (Chapter 9) and accepted an invitation to Moscow to give a series of lectures. As a result, he was widely recognized for his efforts to help psychologists around the world connect and exchange ideas.

The notion that the brain's structure was fixed in adulthood has been dispelled thanks to the work of Mark Rosenzweig (Carey, 2009). We now understand that the brain continues to change and grow throughout the lifespan, and this knowledge has inspired a generation of researchers to further understand the principles of neural plasticity and the promise that idea holds for humanity.

Cognitive Neuroscience

With the rise of the Cognitive Revolution in the 1960s, neuroscientists turned their attention to *the study of the brain processes underlying memory and attention*. This approach was given the name **cognitive neuroscience**. Early studies examined the cognitive deficits of humans with brain damage and animals with induced lesions, but the advent of neuroimaging technologies has been a great boon to this field.

Endel Tulving

Growing up in Estonia, **Endel Tulving** (born 1927) suffered from the horrors of World War II, including time in a German prisoner-of-war camp (Habib, 2009). After the war, he immigrated to Canada, where he finished a bachelor's degree in psychology at the University of Toronto before enrolling in the doctoral program at Harvard. There, he interacted with many of the most important experimental psychologists of the twentieth century, including Edwin Boring (Chapter 3) and B. F. Skinner (Chapter 5), as well as George Miller and S. S. Stevens (Chapter 11), his thesis adviser. Earning his Ph.D. in 1956, Tulving returned to Toronto as a faculty member and remained there for the rest of his career. During his long career, he developed a reputation as an *Estonian-Canadian psychologist who advocated for episodic memory as a separate memory system*.

At the time, most psychologists viewed memory as a singular construct (Tulving, 2002). They recognized that it was often useful to distinguish different types of learned information, but they still maintained that all memories were stored in the same way and likely used the same brain processes. One common distinction was between **procedural memory**, which is *knowledge of how to do something*, and semantic memory, which is knowledge of facts and concepts about the world in general. In a nutshell, this is the difference between "knowing how" and "knowing what." In his 1983 book *Elements of Episodic Memory*, Tulving proposed a third distinction. As the title of the book implies, he called it **episodic memory**, by which he meant *the recollection of personal experiences*. According to Tulving, episodic memory wasn't just "knowing what" happened, but also "when" and "where." Psychologists saw this as a useful philosophical distinction while insisting on the underlying unity of all memory as a single system in the brain or mind.

Tulving (1985b) challenged the received wisdom by proposing that the three-way division of procedural, semantic, and episodic memory was more than just a convenient philosophical distinction (Table 16.1). Rather, he contended, these were three semi-independent memory systems that stored information in different ways and likely involved separate brain networks.

Table 16.1	Tulving's Three Memory Systems and Associated Levels of Consciousness	
Memory System	**Description**	**Associated Level of Consciousness**
Procedural memory	Ability to learn new responses to environmental or internal stimuli	"Non-knowing" consciousness as the organism interacts with the environment in the moment
Semantic memory	Ability to learn facts about the world	"Knowing" consciousness in which the organism recognizes familiar situations and responds accordingly
Episodic memory	Ability to perceive oneself as separate from the environment	"Self-knowing" consciousness in which the organism has a sense of self, enabling it to engage in mental "time travel" into the past or future

His reasoning was based on both evolutionary and clinical evidence. Furthermore, he maintained that each type of memory was associated with a different sort of consciousness:

- *Procedural memory* is associated with a "non-knowing" consciousness in which the organism can sense and respond to stimuli in the environment or even internal stimulation. Tulving acknowledged that simple animals such as insects have procedural memory and "non-knowing" consciousness. For instance, a honeybee can learn how to navigate to a new source of nectar. But it doesn't know any facts about the world, and doesn't have any sense of self.

- *Semantic memory* is associated with a "knowing" consciousness in which the organism has knowledge of facts about the world that it can use to guide its behavior. For example, your dog knows she'll get punished if she pees on the carpet. She also knows you'll open the door if she scratches at it. Tulving believed that at least birds and mammals have semantic memory and "knowing" consciousness, but he also insisted it was unlikely they had a clear sense of self as separate from the rest of the world.

- *Episodic memory* is associated with a "self-knowing" consciousness. To experience personal recollections, you need to first have a sense of self. This is because your episodic memories are inherently about you. After all, you can know about another person's life experiences, but you can't experience them as your own personal memories. Thus, Tulving reserves the term "remembering" for episodic memory and "knowing" for semantic memory. Tulving also insisted that only humans have episodic memories.

According to Tulving (1985b), episodic memory emerged fairly recently in the evolutionary history of humans. It also develops late, around three or four years of age. Furthermore, it's the memory system that's most easily disrupted, as in cases of brain trauma or dementia. Although Tulving cited a number of case studies reporting a loss of episodic memory while other forms of memory remained intact, most of his evidence came from a patient known by his initials K.C., who Tulving worked extensively with.

K.C. was born in 1951 and suffered a severe head injury due to a motorcycle accident (Tulving, 2002). As a result, K.C. suffered both retrograde and anterograde amnesia. **Retrograde amnesia** refers to *the loss of memories that have already been stored*, while the term **anterograde amnesia** indicates *the inability to form new memories*. K.C. suffered anterograde amnesia for both semantic and episode memories, meaning that he could learn no new facts and that he had no recollection of any events in his life after the crash. But the symptoms were different when it came to retrograde amnesia. K.C. still knew all the facts he'd accumulated up to the time of the accident, but he had no personal memories of his life at all. For instance, he knew the address of the house where he grew up, but he had no recollection of ever being there. Here was a clear-cut case in which semantic memory had been spared but episode memory was lost, implying that these were two separate systems.

Tulving (2002) found that K.C. also had an unexpected impairment. He clearly understood the concept of time, but if you asked him what he was doing later that day or the day after that, he had no idea. Apparently, he'd also lost the ability to imagine himself in a future scenario. Tulving's insight was to see that this was related to K.C.'s loss of recollections for past events. In other words, episodic memory wasn't a record of the personal past, which was already known to be quite unreliable. Rather, it was about the ability to subjectively travel in time, whether it's into the past or into the future. But to do either one, you have to have a self that gets projected in time, and this sense of self as separate from his conscious experience of the world appeared to be what K.C. had lost.

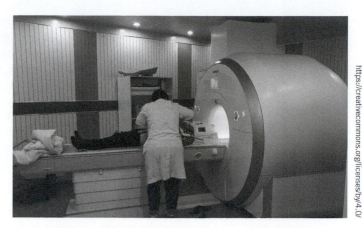

Photo 16.2
Magnetic resonance imaging scanner

As functional neuroimaging became available toward the end of the twentieth century, Tulving was one of the first psychologists to make use of this new technology for observing the brain in action (Habib, 2009). In a series of experiments, he demonstrated that the learning and recall of semantic and episodic memories take place in different brain networks. These studies have provided even more compelling biological evidence for his contention that these are two separate memory systems.

Although Tulving's argument for three separate memory systems was controversial when it was first proposed, the theory is now widely accepted among cognitive neuroscientists (Habib, 2009). For more than six decades, Tulving has been at the cutting edge of memory research, contributing many ideas that are now standard fair in introductory psychology textbooks. Perhaps more than any other psychologist, Endel Tulving has shaped our understanding of the nature of memory in the twenty-first century.

Michael Posner

As an undergraduate, **Michael Posner** (born 1936) majored in physics (Keele & Mayr, 2005). His first job was as a research engineer at Boeing, studying ways to reduce aircraft noise to levels tolerable by humans. This work in human-machine interactions led to an interest in psychology, and he pursued his Ph.D. at the University of Michigan. After accepting a position at the University of Oregon, he studied the process of reading, which piqued his interest in attention, and this became the dominant theme of his career. Today, Posner is recognized as a leading *American cognitive neuroscientist who studies the biological basis of attention.*

Along with other colleagues and graduate students, Posner set up what was perhaps the first computerized psychology laboratory in the world ("Michael I. Posner," 1981). Computers allow for the precise timing of stimuli presentation and response measurement, and they're ubiquitous in cognitive psychology laboratories today, but Posner and his associates were pioneers in this approach. One of the first projects in this computerized lab involved the study of the reading process. Posner broke down the reading task into what seemed to be its component parts and investigated how long on average it took participants to execute each task. *The measurement of the time course of cognitive events* is known as **mental chronometry**, and it was first pursued in the lab of Wilhelm Wundt in the late nineteenth century. But with the help of computers, Posner could make far more accurate measurements. For instance, in one experiment he asked participants to indicate whether two figures on the screen represented the same or different letters. He found that the reaction time was longer for upper and lower case pairs that were dissimilar, such as "A" and "a," compared with pairs that were similar, such as "C" and "c." The results of studies such as these convinced Posner that the time course of basic mental processes could be measured accurately.

Mental chronometry studies led to the development of the **Posner cueing task** (Keele & Mayr, 2005). This is *a laboratory procedure that is used to measure people's abilities to make* *rapid shifts of attention.* At the beginning of each trial, the participant stares at a fixation point marked by a cross at the center of the screen, with a box on each side (Figure 16.1). A cue such as an arrow briefly appears, either above the fixation point or in the periphery of the visual field. A target stimulus such as a star then appears in one of the two boxes, and the participant's task is to press a button as soon as it does so. In half of the tasks, the cue is invalid, meaning that it points away from, rather than toward, the target location. In these trials, the participant needs to make an attentional shift to perceive the target, so reaction time is delayed. This simple procedure has been used to test a number of hypotheses regarding the mechanics of attention in both healthy and patient populations.

Two counterintuitive findings came out of Posner's work with the cueing task (Keele & Mayr, 2005). The first was the observation that adults can shift attention within their visual field even though their eyes are fixated on a point. The second was the discovery of a phenomenon known as **inhibition of return**, which is *a delay in an attentional shift back to a previously attended location.* It's believed that this is an evolved feature of visual systems. In the real world, organisms need to constantly scan their visual fields for sudden changes in the environment, and this inhibition keeps them from repeatedly looking at the same location. It was the ability of computers to accurately control the presentation of stimuli and measure the timing of responses that enabled Posner and his team to make these discoveries.

Behavioral approaches to mental chronometry have an inherent weakness that was recognized even in the Wundt laboratory ("Michael I. Posner," 1981). Namely, this was that the measured reaction time includes the time course of both the mental processing of the stimulus and the motor programming of the response. In the late 1960s, Posner spent a yearlong postdoctoral fellowship at the Applied Psychology Unit of Cambridge to learn *a technique for measuring the time course of mental events based on EEG recordings.* This new method measured what was called an **event-related potential**, or ERP for short. The EEG, or electroencephalogram, measures electrical activity diffusing from the brain to the scalp,

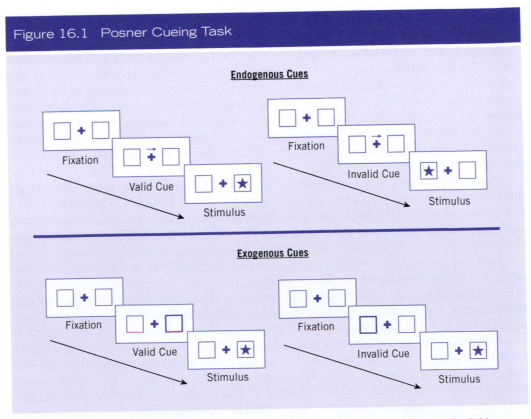

Figure 16.1   Posner Cueing Task

Endogenous Cues

Fixation
Valid Cue
Stimulus

Fixation
Invalid Cue
Stimulus

Exogenous Cues

Fixation
Valid Cue
Stimulus

Fixation
Invalid Cue
Stimulus

Source: Local870, via Wikimedia Commons, CC BY 3.0, https://creativecommons.org/licenses/by/3.0/.

and it can be thought of as the summation of all of the brain's electrical processes. However, the brain activity of a specific activity can be extracted through the averaging of EEG waveforms over many trials. Although the first ERP studies were conducted before World War II, the advent of computers made the complex calculations necessary to average waveforms much easier. Posner now had a noninvasive technique for accurately measuring the processing of mental events in the brain without having to take motor responses into account. In fact, ERP research doesn't require the participant to do anything at all. This technique became an important tool in Posner's lab after he established his lab at Oregon.

The strength of the ERP technique is that it yields a precise measure of the time course of brain activity ("Michael I. Posner," 1981). However, its weakness is that it gives little indication of the region where that activity is occurring. In an attempt to identify brain structures responsible for regulating attention, Posner spent six months with George Miller testing patients with brain damage. There was already a long history of lesion studies with the following rationale: If a patient with a lesion in area X has a deficiency performing cognitive task Y, then area X must somehow be involved in the production of task Y. By identifying patients who had difficulties in executing specific attentional processes, Posner could then correlate those processes with the damaged brain regions of those patients. Lesion studies in humans tend to yield only tentative results, since naturally occurring brain damage, such as from head injuries or stroke, is often diffuse and can involve multiple brain areas. Nevertheless, lesion studies can provide clues at least to the general brain regions that are involved.

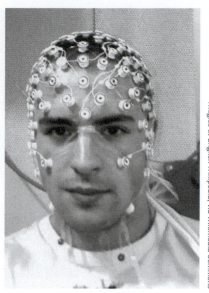

Photo 16.3
Electrode cap used in ERP research

In the 1980s, neuroimaging techniques became available, and Posner was one of the first neuroscientists to make use of them (Denis, 2008). Neuroimaging has complementary strengths and weaknesses compared with ERP. Although it doesn't provide a good measure of time course, it does pinpoint exact regions where brain activity occurs. The first technique to become available was PET, which measured blood flow as an indicator of brain activity. The disadvantage of this approach is that it requires the injection of mildly radioactive substances into the participant. Posner first conducted studies searching for attention areas in the brain using PET, but he switched to functional MRI (fMRI) when it became available. This technique uses the magnetic properties of water to track blood flow, and hence brain activity. But unlike PET, fMRI has no known health risks to the participant. When these brain imaging techniques first became available, many psychologists were skeptical that specific cognitive processes could be linked to specific brain regions. Yet Posner and his colleagues demonstrated that this was indeed possible, laying out the case in the 1994 book *Images of Mind*, which he coauthored with Marcus Raichle. Thus, Posner blazed the trail for neuroimaging research in the twenty-first century.

Posner next turned his research focus to the development of attentional processes in infants, considering both genetic and environmental influences (Denis, 2008). He found that newborns had limited control over attentional processes, which came online in a piecemeal fashion over the first few months of life. Although he was able to outline a typical developmental timeline, he also identified cultural and parenting influences as well as specific genetic factors that could speed up or slow down the development of attentional control.

For more than three decades, Posner's lab at the University of Oregon has been at the forefront of cognitive neuroscience research (Keele & Mayr, 2005). As a result, he's attracted a large number of graduate students, not just from across the United States but also from around the world. In fact, Posner has been a major proponent for the internationalization of psychology in the twenty-first century. He's trained many of the next generation of psychologists, who've gone on to positions in universities and research institutions around the globe. He was a pioneer in the use of many of the techniques that are now staples in the toolkit of scientists studying the interface between brain and mind, such as ERP and fMRI. For these reasons, he's rightfully called the father of cognitive neuroscience.

Photo 16.4
Patricia Goldman-Rakic

Patricia Goldman-Rakic

When she graduated from Vassar College, **Patricia Goldman-Rakic** (1937–2003; pronounced *rah-KEESH*) found there were few opportunities for women in academia (Aghajanian, Bunney, & Holzman, 2003). Nevertheless, she defied expectations and earned her Ph.D. in experimental psychology from the University of California, Los Angeles (UCLA) in 1963. Offered a position as a research scientist at the National Institute of Mental Health (NIMH), she began the program that would occupy her for the rest of her life. In 1974, she met the neuroscientist Pasko Rakic, who became her research partner and eventually her husband. The couple accepted positions at Yale, where they built a noted program in neurobiology. During this time, Patricia Goldman-Rakic earned a reputation as an *American cognitive neuroscientist whose research on the prefrontal cortex in primates led to a better understanding of the neural substrates of working memory.*

Throughout her career, Goldman-Rakic had a passion for the prefrontal cortex, the part of the forebrain that's most pronounced in humans and other primates (Levitt, 2003). It was believed to be the part of the brain responsible for complex thought processes, and many psychologists at the time thought there was no way it could be studied in a scientific fashion. But Goldman-Rakic was undeterred. She knew that a thorough investigation of the anatomy and physiology of the prefrontal cortex would require the use of invasive techniques such as surgical lesions and the insertion of electrodes, so human-subject research was out of the question. Instead, she chose to work with the rhesus monkey as a close proxy to humans.

Contrary to the received wisdom of the time, Goldman-Rakic demonstrated that the prefrontal cortex was anatomically and functionally similar to other areas of the brain that were better understood. To study the structure the prefrontal cortex, Goldman-Rakic used a method known as **autoradiography** (Fuster, 2004). This is *a method of producing an X-ray image by injecting a radioactive substance into the body.* This technique allowed her to trace the neural circuitry of the prefrontal cortex. She found that its neurons were arranged in columns, just as they were in the well-studied sensory and motor areas of the cerebral cortex. And since each column in those areas had a specific task to perform, she reasoned the same must be true of the prefrontal cortex. Goldman-Rakic then used lesion studies to test hypotheses about the functions of specific portions of the prefrontal cortex (Aghajanian et al., 2003). At the same time, she also discovered the remarkable plasticity of this area, especially early in development. She found that adult monkeys with lesions rarely regained lost functions, but young ones often did. It seemed that those lost functions could be taken on by other areas of the prefrontal cortex while the brain was still developing.

Evidence from human patients suggested that the prefrontal cortex played a role in **working memory** (Selemon, 2015). This is *the ability to hold on to information while it is being used to complete a task.* Working memory is usually tested in humans by giving them a list of words or digits to repeat back after a short delay. But since monkeys don't have language, Goldman-Rakic had to find a different approach. She decided on the **delayed-response task** as an operational definition of working memory. This is *a laboratory procedure in which the subject observes a desired object being hidden in one of two containers and is then distracted for a brief time, after which it is allowed to retrieve it.* This task is often used to measure working memory in both primates and young human children. She found that healthy monkeys completed this task easily, while those with lesions to the prefrontal cortex performed at chance. However, the monkeys with lesions could successfully retrieve the desired object as long as they could keep the container in sight the whole time.

Around this time, Goldman-Rakic was also investigating the neurochemistry of the prefrontal cortex (Aghajanian et al., 2003). She found that the predominant neurotransmitter in this area was dopamine. Furthermore, when she injected drugs that depleted dopamine into the brains of healthy monkeys, they lost their ability to complete the delayed-response task, just like those whose prefrontal cortex had been removed. It was already known at the time that dopamine was implicated in a number of psychological disorders, such as Parkinson's disease, schizophrenia, and Alzheimer's disease. Goldman-Rakic's investigations provided new insights into the underlying brain abnormalities involved in these conditions.

Late in the twentieth century, Goldman-Rakic made use of a new technology known as **microelectrode recording** (Fuster, 2004). This is *a brain recording technique in which an ultrathin electrode is inserted to a position where it can measure the activity of a single neuron*. Using this method, Goldman-Rakic found that certain neurons are only active during the delay portion of the delayed-response task in which the container holding the desired object isn't in view. She proposed that this activity represented the memory for the target that was being kept alive until the desired object could be obtained. This finding was also controversial because at the time many psychologists believed memory to be a singular process not generally associated with the frontal lobe. Thus, she challenged the received wisdom by demonstrating that working memory was situated in a separate structure of the brain from long-term memory.

Goldman-Rakic was at the height of her career when she was struck by a car while crossing a street on a summer afternoon (Selemon, 2015). She died two days later of her injuries. She and her team of researchers had so many ongoing projects at the time that papers including her name as an author were still being published five years after her death. By defying the rampant sexism of her time and establishing a career as one of the most influential neuroscientists of the twentieth century, Patricia Goldman-Rakic has become a role model for a new generation of scientists, both male and female, who are now working in a field that is just beginning to shed its tainted past of gender discrimination.

Michael Gazzaniga

When the first split-brain patient arrived at Roger Sperry's (Chapter 10) lab in 1961, he assigned the task of examining him to his newest graduate student, **Michael Gazzaniga** (born 1939; "Interview," 2011). The split-brain surgical technique, in which the corpus callosum connecting the two halves of the forebrain was severed, showed promise as a means of controlling severe epilepsy. It was also believed that the procedure had no negative effect on the patient's cognitive abilities, and in everyday interactions it was impossible to distinguish a split-brain patient from a person with an intact brain. However, Gazzaniga devised a number of tests that demonstrated the existence of two separate streams of consciousness within these patients. Continuing this line of research, Michael Gazzaniga built a reputation as the *American neuroscientist whose work with split-brain patients has led to our understanding of hemispheric specialization in the brain*.

Gazzaniga's first split-brain patient was known as W.J., who he tested both before and after surgery ("Interview," 2011). The key test involved the flashing of images onto either the left or the right visual field. Because the brain is organized contralaterally, images on the left are processed in the right hemisphere, and vice versa. The participant's job was simply to name the object. Before the operation, W.J. performed this task without difficulty. After the operation, though, he could only name objects viewed in the right visual field. In the case of objects projected to the left, he could still point to a copy of it on a sheet of paper in front of him, thus indicating that he was aware of which image he'd seen. This pattern of results confirmed evidence from brain-damaged patients that language processing takes place in the left hemisphere, yet it also suggested a kind of language-less consciousness on the right side of the brain.

Split-brain research showed that each hemisphere has a separate stream of consciousness, and yet our experience is of a unified self ("Michael S. Gazzaniga," 2008). Gazzaniga puzzled over this mystery for years, but some clues to an answer came when he was working with his graduate student Joseph LeDoux, whom we'll meet in the next section. Rather than relying on the behavioral data alone to understand what was going on in the minds of split-brain patients, Gazzaniga and LeDoux decided to ask the patients why they'd responded the way they did. They soon discovered that the patients made up plausible stories to account for their bizarre behaviors. In other words, their language-based left hemisphere was trying to interpret what the silent right hemisphere was doing. In healthy brains, Gazzaniga and LeDoux surmised, the left side has access to the right and thus can report on what its other half is doing, thus giving rise to a unified sense of self. The two researchers laid out their view of the left brain as "interpreter" in their 1978 book *The Integrated Mind*.

It's said that Michael Gazzaniga and George Miller (Chapter 11) were sharing a taxicab in New York City when they coined the term "cognitive neuroscience" to describe the newly emerging field relating mental functions to brain processes ("Interview," 2011). Whether this story is true or not, there's no doubt that Gazzaniga has been a major proponent of the field. In addition to building cognitive science programs at Dartmouth College and the University of California, Davis, he founded the *Journal of Cognitive Neuroscience* and the Cognitive Neuroscience Society. He's also written a number of popular books on topics in cognitive neuroscience, thus spreading knowledge of this exciting field to the general public. He also served on the Bioethics Committee convened by President George W. Bush to discuss important issues such as cloning and cognitive enhancement. In addition, he served on a national committee considering the relevance of neuroscience research to the law, grappling with questions such as whether brain scans should be admissible as evidence in criminal trials.

In his 2011 book *Who's in Charge: Free Will and the Science of the Brain*, Gazzaniga tackled the question of free will (Nair, 2012). In this work, he argues—much like his mentor Roger Sperry—that the apparent contradiction between a mechanistic brain and the existence of free will can be resolved. Whereas Sperry conjectured that free will arose as the brain gave rise to mind, Gazzaniga argues that, for centuries, philosophers and psychologists have been looking in the wrong place. The key issue in free will, he contends, is personal responsibility, and yet that is a social issue, not a characteristic of any individual. Even though we're biological machines, the social contract we share with others holds us responsible for our actions, and this is where free will arises.

Michael Gazzaniga is rightly viewed as one of the founders of cognitive neuroscience. Both in his compelling research exploring the specializations of the left and right hemispheres of the brain and in his service to the field, he remains one of the shakers and movers of this burgeoning enterprise exploring the interface between brain and mind.

Affective Neuroscience

The Cognitive Revolution broke the behaviorist stranglehold on American psychology, but it also imposed new restrictions on what was considered an acceptable topic for research. For instance, the computer metaphor of cognition gave little room for a discussion of emotion. But by the end of the twentieth century, more and more psychologists were recognizing the central role that affect, or emotion, plays in human lives. Building on the success of behavioral and cognitive neuroscience, these researchers have created the new field of **affective neuroscience**, which is *the study of the brain processes underlying emotion*. This endeavor holds promise to provide answers to important questions regarding mental health and disease.

Richard Lazarus

During World War II, **Richard Lazarus** (1922–2002) served as a military psychologist, evaluating inductees to see which ones were emotionally unfit for service (Whatmore, 1999). He also devised methods for detecting malingerers who feigned psychological disorders to avoid the draft. After the war, he earned his Ph.D. in 1948 from the University of Pittsburgh. Although behaviorism still dominated psychology, the New Look movement gave him the courage to pursue a cognitive-based research program in stress and emotions. Today Richard Lazarus is known as the *American psychologist who developed the transactional model of stress*.

Early in his career, he studied the unconscious nature of emotional responses (Hyman, 2002). He found that a visual stimulus previously associated with an electric shock would elicit a negative response even when it was presented for such a short interval of time that the participant had no conscious awareness of having seen it. Lazarus referred to the unconscious perception of an emotional stimulus as *subception*. The idea that perception could take place without conscious awareness was a novel—and controversial—idea at the time. However, subception is now a well-documented phenomenon.

As a military psychologist, Lazarus had studied the effects of stress on soldiers (Robinson, 2018). At the time, stress was viewed as a purely physiological response, but Lazarus believed it also contained a psychological component akin to emotions. Moreover, he noticed that people responded differently to similar stressors. In a series of classic experiments, he tested the hypothesis that the level of stress experienced depended on the way in which the individual appraised the stressful situation. Participants viewed a movie of an emotionally charged event such as a painful circumcision rite. The film was narrated in a calm, manner-of-fact manner in one condition, but the soundtrack emotionally emphasized the painful experience of the suffering person in the other. Those who watched the movie with the calm narration showed reduced stress indicators compared with those who heard the emotional soundtrack.

These findings led Lazarus to posit the **transactional model of stress**, which is *the proposal that stress is moderated by cognitive appraisal of the situation* (Robinson, 2018). In other words, it's not just the degree of stress that's important. Rather, the way in which the person thinks about the stress also matters. Lazarus presented this model and the evidence for it in his 1966 work *Psychological Stress and the Coping Process*. In this book, he proposes that appraisal takes place in two stages. On the one hand, primary appraisal involves an assessment of the potential effect of the stressful situation on the individual. Is this a challenging but potentially beneficial stressor? Or is this stressor likely to lead to physical or psychological harm? Our assessment of the stressor as potentially beneficial or harmful greatly influences our perception of its effect. On the other hand, secondary appraisal involves an assessment of our ability to cope with the stressful event. Even a potentially beneficial stressor can be perceived negatively if we feel we don't have the means to cope with it, while a potentially harmful stressor will have little impact if we believe we have the resources to handle it.

With a move to the University of California, Berkeley, Lazarus established the UC Berkeley Stress and Coping Project, which used both laboratory and field studies to investigate the ways in which people deal with stress (Robinson, 2018). The findings of this project were presented in the 1984 book *Stress, Appraisal, and Coping*, which he coauthored with his graduate student Susan Folkman. In this work, Lazarus and Folkman distinguished two types of coping. When people believe they have control over the situation, they engage in *problem-focused coping*, which is a direct attempt to solve the problem. For example, spouses who talk about their problems and find mutually agreeable solutions are engaging in problem-focused coping. However, when people believe they have no control over the situation, they use *emotion-focused coping*. Accepting the loss of a loved one as God's will would be an example of this second approach. Since there's no way to change the situation, we change our attitudes toward the situation instead as a means of reducing stress.

Richard Lazarus was a pioneer in the study of stress and emotions, challenging his colleagues to open up their field to research on this vital aspect of human psychology (Ekman & Campos, 2003). His experiments provided fresh insights for researchers in the areas of clinical and health psychology. But more importantly for us in this chapter, he also gave inspiration to a third wave of neuroscience that would attempt to find the underlying brain processes that give rise to conscious emotions.

Jaak Panksepp

At the height of his career, **Jaak Panksepp** (1943–2017) became famous as "The Rat-Tickler," doing the rounds of talk shows and interviews on popular media (Cromwell, 2018). In a career spanning nearly five decades, Panksepp explored the evolutionarily deep roots of emotions. By chance, he discovered that rats laugh when tickled just like humans, hence the nickname. It's just that no one had noticed this before because rat laughter consists of a series

**Photo 16.5
Jaak Panksepp (seated
on right)**

of chirps at a frequency above the range of human hearing. As the man who dared to challenge the standard view that emotional experience couldn't be studied scientifically, Jaak Panksepp is remembered today as the *Estonian-American psychologist who founded the field of affective neuroscience.*

Panksepp was born in Estonia in 1943, but the following year his family fled the country to escape the invading Russian Army (Eberle, 2017). They spent the next five years in refugee camps until they finally immigrated to the United States in 1949. While the adults of the camp struggled to survive, the children were left alone, and this experience of unsupervised rough-and-tumble play with same-aged children made a lasting impression on him, eventually becoming one of his key research interests.

Panksepp started his graduate studies in clinical psychology, but working in a mental hospital led him to the insight that emotional disturbances lay at the root of all psychological disorders (Davis & Montag, 2019). He was also convinced that emotions arose from deep within the mammalian brain. To study the neural substrates of emotion, he used the brain-stimulating technique pioneered by James Olds and Peter Milner. For his dissertation research, Panksepp found that he could elicit two types of attack in rats, depending on the deep brain region he stimulated. Moreover, he demonstrated that the rats experienced these two attack modes differently, in that they could be conditioned to turn on the stimulation for one mode and turn it off for the other. Further research showed that the "unpleasant" attack mode was related to predation, while the "pleasant" one was a key element in rough-and-tumble play.

In 1972, Panksepp accepted a faculty position at Bowling Green State University in Ohio (Eberle, 2017). This was a time when emotion research was generally off limits, especially at the prestigious universities, but at BGSU he had the freedom to pursue his research interests. Through a series of nearly 300 journal articles, he established himself as one of the leaders in the field of neuroscience.

Much of Panksepp's early work looked at the role of neurochemicals in mediating social emotions (Cromwell, 2018; Davis & Montag, 2019). During his student years working at a mental hospital, he noticed that many of the drug addicts he dealt with came from dysfunctional families, and he wondered if they took drugs as a substitute for the social bonding they lacked at home. Rat pups are distressed when they're separated from their mothers, emitting ultrasonic cries. But Panksepp found they were soothed when they were given small doses of morphine. This finding led to the **opioid hypothesis**, which was *the conjecture that the formation of social attachment and contact comfort is mediated by endogenous opioids.* Later, he also established the role of the neuropeptides oxytocin and vasopressin in mother-infant attachment formation as well as in sexual attraction among adults.

Using a three-pronged research approach of electrical stimulations, chemical injections, and brain lesions, Panksepp mapped out what he believed were the seven primary emotional systems in the mammalian brain (Davis & Montag, 2019). Each of these had a specific location deep within the brain, not on the cerebral cortex as had previously been assumed. Furthermore, each system had a specific repertoire of behaviors, and through operant conditioning studies they could be assessed as either a pleasant or an unpleasant experience for the animal. Panksepp cast the names of the seven primary emotion systems in all capital letters to distinguish them from the common meanings we associate with emotional words:

- SEEKING, which pushes animals to search for resources.

- RAGE, which drives them to compete for and defend those resources.

- FEAR, which impels them to escape bodily danger.

- LUST, which prods them to seek out mates and reproduce.

- CARE, which provides the desire to nurture offspring.

- PANIC, which is a feeling of distress at loss of social contact.

- PLAY, which helps the young to learn the rules of social interaction.

By demonstrating that neural processes could be linked not only to emotional expressions but also to their subjective experiences, Panksepp paved the way for a neuroscience of emotion (Cromwell, 2018). He presented his view of this new field in his aptly named book, *Affective Neuroscience*, which he published in 1998. While his arguments are cogent, they've also challenged the human-centric biases of many psychologists. In placing the seat of emotions deep within the brainstem, he makes the case that emotional experience is evolutionarily old and shared by a wide range of species. This position is simply a reiteration of Charles Darwin's continuity thesis, in which he contends that humans are no different from any other animals. It seems however that even neuroscientists in the twenty-first century are still influenced by the "mindless" behaviorism that dominated the twentieth as well as by a lingering Cartesian belief in the uniqueness of humans. Nevertheless, a younger generation has been convinced by Panksepp's contention that a science of emotion is the pathway to understanding human experience, both in its mundane and in its disordered states. These are the pioneers in the brave new field of affective neuroscience.

Joseph LeDoux

Some have called him "Dr. Fear" (Behar, 2008). **Joseph LeDoux** (born 1949) is an *American neuroscientist who studies the brain mechanisms that are responsible for fearful memories*. He also believes he can find a way to erase painful memories as a potential cure for post-traumatic stress disorder.

LeDoux earned his Ph.D. in 1977, working with Michael Gazzaniga at New York Stony Brook ("Joseph E. LeDoux," 2010). His dissertation research explored questions of cognition, emotion, and consciousness in split-brain patients. The findings from this project led to the book *The Integrated Mind*, which he coauthored with Gazzaniga. While his mentor's interests were clearly on the cognitive side of neuroscience, LeDoux found himself drawn to the interactions between cognition and emotion, and especially how they're processed in the brain. To get at these issues, he knew that human research was out of the question, so he turned to animal models instead.

During twelve years at Cornell, LeDoux investigated the brain mechanisms of emotion and memory using fear conditioning in rats ("Joseph E. LeDoux," 2010). In this method, the rats first heard a tone and then received a painful shock to the foot. Sometimes even after a single pairing of the tone with the shock, the rats became fearful whenever they heard the tone. Once the association was learned, LeDoux traced the neural connections that constituted the learned fear response. Not surprisingly, he found they converged on the amygdala, long thought to be the fear center of the brain. He later moved to New York University, where he has continued this line of research. There he discovered that drugs blocking the growth of new synapses prevented the rat from learning the fear response.

Ledoux published the book *The Emotional Brain* in 1996 (Almada, Pereira, & Carrara-Augustenborg, 2013). In that work, he laid out his dual-route theory of emotional processing in the brain. The "low road" constitutes a rapid emotional appraisal of the situation by subcortical structures such as the amygdala. This processing occurs outside of consciousness, and even the behavioral responses they evoke can occur before we're aware of what's going on. That feeling of chills running down your spine as you walk alone on a dark street would be an example of this. In contrast, the "high road" involves processing in the cerebral cortex as well as subcortical structures. This processing is slower and is to some degree accessible to consciousness. The disappointment you feel at failing a test would involve the high road, since there's no threat of bodily danger at the moment.

LeDoux had already found that some drugs block the formation of emotional memories ("Joseph E. LeDoux," 2010). However, an even more surprising discovery was that certain of these drugs could also erase specific memories. After conditioning rats on the learned fear response, he injected them with one of these drugs and then repeatedly played the tone, but this time without the electric shock. The next day, these rats showed no fear when they heard the tone. This finding suggests that long-term memories are unstable not only during formation but also during recall. LeDoux believes this research could eventually lead to a cure for post-traumatic stress disorder. Such a treatment is still a long way off, however, and LeDoux concedes that there are considerable ethical issues to work out with regard to memory erasure in humans.

"Dr. Fear" also has a life outside the laboratory ("Joseph E. LeDoux," 2010). LeDoux is a rock musician who plays with a band called the Amygdaloids. The band performs at various venues in New York City and has already produced a couple of albums. Just as you would expect, the band sings songs about adventures in neuroscience.

Antonio Damasio

The patient had damage to his ventromedial frontal lobe, and he showed no signs of feeling any emotions, even though he performed well on standard reasoning tasks (Pontin, 2014). It seemed a clear-cut case of losing emotion but sparing reason. That is, until it came time for the patient to make his next appointment, when he pondered the advantages and disadvantages of two possible dates for half an hour until someone else made the choice for him. This observation led **Antonio Damasio** (born 1944) to suspect that everyday decision making involves both reason and emotion, a topic he's studied now for decades, building a reputation as the *Portuguese-American neuroscientist who proposed the somatic marker hypothesis.*

Born in Portugal, Damasio earned a medical degree at the University of Lisbon before immigrating to the United States in 1976 to pursue a career as a neuroscientist ("Virtue in Mind," 2003). He's spent much of his career at the University of Iowa, with joint appointments at several other leading institutions. His research mainly involves working with stroke patients, mostly through the administration of behavioral tests early in his career but with more emphasis on neuroimaging techniques as these became available.

Damasio noticed that when a stroke occurred in certain areas of the brain, such as the ventromedial frontal lobe or the amygdala, the patient seemed to lose the ability to feel emotions (Johnson, 2004). They also exhibited alterations in their personalities, making poor decisions that wrecked their marriages and cost them their jobs. Although they could perform well on abstract reasoning tasks, their ability to make good decisions in everyday life was compromised.

Working with his colleagues, Damasio developed the **Iowa gambling task** as *a laboratory procedure for assessing decision-making abilities in brain-damaged patients* (Schmitt, Brinkley, & Newman, 1999). The task centers on four decks of cards (marked A, B, C, and D), each of which indicates a monetary win or loss. Patients select one card at a time from any deck, and they're instructed to try to maximize their winnings. Unknown to them, the game is rigged. Decks A and B offer large rewards but even larger punishments, while the gains and losses in Decks C and D are moderate. Normally functioning participants soon learn they'll maximize their earnings if they stick to Decks C and D. In contrast, patients with damage to emotional areas of their brains are attracted to the big gains of Decks A and B and discount the even bigger losses. The Iowa gambling task has now become a standard test of decision-making abilities in brain-damaged patients.

In the seventeenth-century, René Descartes had proposed a clear distinction between rational and emotional faculties, and this dichotomy has persisted into modern times (Brinkmann, 2006). But by the last decade of the twentieth century, Damasio began wondering if the French philosopher may have been

Photo 16.6
Antonio Damasio

wrong. These musings led to the publication of his 1994 book *Descartes' Error*, in which he lays out *the proposal that emotions play an essential role in everyday decision making*, which he calls the **somatic marker hypothesis**. According to Damasio, emotions are body states that arise in response to particular situations—hence the term "somatic," meaning "bodily." These emotions are perceived as either positive or negative, and they "mark" the situation as either beneficial or dangerous. Somatic marking occurs not only in real time, as we encounter potential opportunities and threats in our environment, but also when we generate possible future scenarios. Thus, whether you'll study for tomorrow's test or party with your friends depends on which scenario—the bad feeling of failing a test or the good feeling of having fun—produces the stronger somatic marking.

In addition to his numerous scholarly works, Antonio Damasio has also published a series of popular press books on topics in affective neuroscience for the general public. His somatic marker hypothesis has created a lot of excitement among professional and lay readers alike, but it has likewise generated considerable controversy in the fields of philosophy, psychology, and neuroscience. At present, the jury is still out on whether the error lies with Descartes or Damasio.

Neuroscience: The Future or the End of Psychology?

In the early twenty-first century, neuroscience has become the dominant field in psychology. From the start of experimental psychology, there was always the assumption that mind and behavior were products of brain activity, although how that occurred was anybody's guess. Now neuroscience holds the promise of finally solving the mind-body problem.

A strong bias toward neuroscience is clear in both hiring and funding practices (Schwartz, Lilienfeld, Meca, & Sauvigné, 2016). A recent survey found that between one-third and one-half of advertised positions for psychologists at top research universities were for neuroscientists. Likewise, funding agencies are allocating more and more of their resources to projects involving a neuroscience component. Indeed, the rising generation of experimental psychologists will find it difficult to obtain a job or grant if they don't include neuroimaging techniques as part of their research toolkit.

This state of affairs has led philosophers of science to speculate on the future of psychology in the coming decades (Sharp & Miller, 2019). Some believe that neuroscience will eventually become a grand unifying framework for a science that has been plagued with disunity from its inception. In other words, the future of psychology is neuroscience. Still others believe that neuroscience will finally provide answers about the ultimate causes of mind and behavior, making all other disciplines of psychology unnecessary. That is to say, neuroscience will spell the end of psychology.

Unifying Theory

The natural sciences all have unifying theories that give them cohesion and guide them toward new discoveries (Green, 2015). Newton's laws unified physics three centuries ago, giving it a framework for exploring the physical world. This led to rapid progress in the field, the fruits of which include the many technological wonders of the modern era, such as cars, airplanes, and even robotic missions to Mars. Likewise, Mendeleev's periodic table brought order to chemistry. And finally, the synthesis of Darwinian evolution with Mendelian genetics in the early twentieth century transformed biology from a descriptive to a predictive science.

Psychology has no such unifying theory, no doubt in part because it's such a new science (Henriques, 2013). It's often said that psychology is a science unified not by a theory but rather by its commitment to the scientific method. Yet even this view of unity is flawed. First, psychology is far from the only discipline studying human behavior that employs the scientific method, as sociologists, anthropologists, economists, and even political scientists do so as well. Furthermore, there are fields of psychology where commitment to the scientific method is weak. For instance, counseling psychologists trained under the practitioner-scholar model and holding doctor of psychology (Psy.D.) degrees have limited use for the scientific method in their profession, and yet we still count them as psychologists.

Philosophers of science also warn of what they call the unification trap (Schwartz et al., 2016). This happens when one school or discipline dominates the field to the extent that research outside a circumscribed area is discouraged or even thwarted altogether. The unification trap often comes in the guise of the "one true" approach to the field. In the early twentieth century, advocates of both psychoanalysis and behaviorism maintained that their schools represented the "true" psychology, predicting that their approach would eventually win out over all others. Of course, in neither case did this come to pass. In the early twenty-first century, proponents of neuroscience view their field as finally bringing order to psychology, but there are still plenty of skeptics who see it as yet another fad that will eventually pass, just like psychoanalysis and behaviorism.

Psychology suffers from an identity crisis of sorts (Zilio, 2016). One identity is that of a natural science, with a strong pull toward biology. This is especially true for those who study lower-level processes such as sensation, perception, and attention. But it's also the case for clinical psychologists who seek an understanding of disorders in terms of structural anomalies in the brain or imbalances of neurochemicals. The other identity is that of a social science. Those who study higher-level processes, such as decision making or interpersonal attraction, often collaborate with social scientists in related disciplines. It should come as no surprise that the two cognitive psychologists who won the Nobel Prize (Herbert Simon and Daniel Kahneman, Chapter 10) did so for their work in bridging psychology and economics.

Because of its dual identity, psychology may never find a single framework that can unify the field (Green, 2015). Instead, the tension between the social-science side and the natural-science side may eventually fracture psychology in two. According to this scenario, the gravitational pull of neuroscience will attract the natural-science side of psychology into its orbit, leaving the social-science side to either coalesce into a unified whole of its own or perhaps to be absorbed in the other social sciences. This is just one way that neuroscience could spell the end of psychology.

Reductionism

It could also be the case that neuroscience replaces psychology altogether (Zilio, 2016). In fact, some neuroscientists, such as Michael Gazzaniga, have already declared that psychology is dead. Such a stance is based on a belief in **eliminative reductionism**, which is *the notion that higher levels of explanation become unnecessary once lower levels of explanation have been fully developed.* After neuroscience has come up with a complete description of how brain activity produces mental states, these proponents claim, higher levels of explanation will become superfluous. In other words, we'll no longer need disciplines such as cognitive, social, developmental, or personality—or even clinical, for that matter—because neuroscience will explain the entire range of psychology from the bottom up. Thus, all of psychology will reduce to neuroscience, and so psychology itself will be eliminated.

Eliminative reductionism is certainly a seductive point of view, especially if you're a neuroscientist, since it's your field that wins out in the end (Schwartz et al., 2016). Sympathy toward this attitude is also revealed by the current bias in funding and hiring toward neuroscience. Skeptics, however, point to the natural sciences to confirm their doubts. We know that biological processes are built on chemical interactions, and that these in turn are determined by the laws of physics. Nevertheless, it simply isn't the case that explanations at the biological or chemical level are unnecessary, just because at bottom it's all physics. Rather, the biological and chemical levels provide additional explanatory power not found at the physical level. Another tack is to grant eliminative reductionism in principle but not in practice. If only we knew the position and velocity of every particle in the universe, we certainly could predict behavior even at the macroscopic level. But we don't have this information, and we never will, so the question of eliminative reductionism is moot.

This doesn't mean that psychologists should never resort to explanations at a lower level when studying a particular phenomenon (Sharp & Miller, 2019). For instance, a complete understanding of vision necessitates an investigation down to the level of the neurochemicals that interact with light from the environment during visual sensation. In contrast, if we want to make good predictions about consumer behavior, we probably only need to examine the issue at the social and cognitive levels. Going any deeper than that, say to the neurochemical level, is unlikely to yield any additional useful information. Certainly, neurochemical reactions are occurring inside the brain of the consumer, but for current purposes they're irrelevant.

Even if neuroscience can someday eliminate the need for psychology, it's still too early to sound its death knell (Schwartz et al., 2016). At present, all neuroscience can do is find correlations between brain activity and mental or behavioral processes, and we need to guard against the premature conclusion that the first causes the second. Nevertheless, since brain activity is objectively observable while mental processes are not, it's easy to slide into the assumption that data from neuroimaging are more real or more reliable than those from traditional psychology experiments.

This attitude percolates down even to the general public, who are enchanted with the promises of neuroscience (Schwartz et al., 2016). For instance, researchers have found that just adding the words "brain scans show" to a science report leads people to judge it as convincing, even though it contains logical errors and circular reasoning. Although neuroscientists know better than to fall for such fallacious reasoning, those who control the funding and hiring for psychology may not. Such a state of affairs could lead to a premature elimination of the rest of field, not because neuroscience has conclusively answered all the questions of psychology but rather because it's no longer supported with financial or human resources.

Levels of Analysis

Some philosophers of science maintain that the basic premise of eliminative reductionism is flawed (Sharp & Miller, 2019). They argue that even complete knowledge of the processes and interactions at the bottom level is insufficient to explain phenomena at the next higher level. Specifically, they take a **levels-of-analysis approach**, which is *the position that explanations at one level are unrelated to explanations at a higher or lower level*. Those with the levels-of-analysis viewpoint believe that the current hierarchy of sciences—ranging from physics to chemistry, and from biology to psychology—exist because the world itself is ordered in such a hierarchy. Since lower-level phenomena cannot explain higher-level phenomena, the idea of eliminative reductionism is unsound.

Evidence in support of the levels-of-analysis approach comes from observations of what is called an **emergent property** (Schwartz et al., 2016). This is *a phenomenon that arises from processes at a lower level but is not fully explicable in terms of those processes*. The classic example of an emergent property is that of liquid water as a product of the chemical combination of two gases, hydrogen and oxygen. According to this view, emergent properties delineate the levels of analysis, separating each of them and breaking the causal chain that supposedly links them. Thus, neuroscience can never eliminate other disciplines in psychology because it only provides explanations at its own level. This doesn't mean that we can't have recourse to explanations at other levels—water certainly is composed of hydrogen and oxygen, but it's more than just a combination of these two elements. In other words, phenomena at a higher level can never be fully explained by processes at a lower level.

The levels-of-analysis approach doesn't preclude the possibility that neuroscience will come to play a central organizing role in psychology (Schwartz et al., 2016). In fact, it's already assuming that position. In this chapter, we've seen how the study of behavior, cognition, and emotion have become well integrated into neuroscience. Hybrid fields such as developmental, social, and even clinical neuroscience are on the rise as well. But we need to be clear what these terms mean. For instance, "behavioral neuroscience" doesn't mean behavior explained solely in terms of brain activity. Rather, the term refers to an interdisciplinary approach in which a phenomenon is studied at two different levels simultaneously. In this sense, neuroscience wouldn't be a unifying theory for psychology, but it could serve as a backbone that connects with all of the disciplines.

Consilience

Finally, we need to consider the position of psychology in relation to the other social and natural sciences (Wilson, 1998). In his 1998 book *Consilience: The Unity of Knowledge*, biologist E. O. Wilson contends that the divisions we currently have in the sciences are getting blurred as our range of knowledge expands. The boundaries between physics and chemistry, between chemistry and biology, and between biology and psychology have all become fuzzy, and often the most exciting work in the twenty-first century is in the borderlands between the established sciences. Eventually, Wilson argues, there will be *a convergence of all knowledge into a single scientific structure*, a phenomenon he called consilience. It's important to note that consilience is not at all the same thing as eliminative reductionism. The higher levels don't get explained away by the lower levels. Rather, the gaps between the levels get filled in, so that scientists can move smoothly from one level to another. In Wilson's view, all intellectual endeavors, whether the natural or social sciences, philosophy or history, art or literature, have the same goal—a greater understanding of ourselves and of the world in which we live. As our knowledge expands, then, it's inevitable that the disparate pathways of knowledge we follow now will eventually converge.

In recent years, the psychologist Gregg Henriques (2013) has proposed a framework for situating psychology within the sciences that takes the entire history of the universe into account. According to his Tree of Knowledge System, the universe has undergone four great transitions since the beginning of time, each leading to a greater level of complexity. At the Big Bang 14 billion years ago, the first level of complexity was attained when Matter was created. Somewhat less than 4 billion years ago saw the emergence of Life, thus bringing on the second level of complexity. But this consisted only of single-celled organisms, and it wasn't until the Cambrian explosion 600 million years ago that multicellular organisms emerged. And among these, of course, were animals that moved about and so needed nervous systems, thus giving rise to the third level of complexity, Mind. Only in the last hundred thousand years did the fourth level of complexity arise, namely Culture, driven by the human ability to use language.

In Henriques's (2013) view, each of these levels of complexity is the purview of a particular type of science. Matter, the first level of complexity, is studied by the physical sciences. Life, the second level of complexity, is the realm of biology, while the third level, Mind, is the subject of psychology. Finally, Culture as the fourth level of complexity is the scope of the social sciences. Thus, the Tree of Knowledge System explains why the sciences divided up the way they did, in that the four levels of complexity provided natural boundaries for these different approaches to knowledge (Figure 16.2). At the same time, the framework also exhibits consilience, in that it shows how the various intellectual endeavors relate to one another. On this view, psychology is in no danger of becoming eliminated by neuroscience. Instead, the two will become more interconnected as time goes by, just like all the other sciences.

So much for gazing into the crystal ball. Predictions of the future are notorious for their failures to foresee even a few years ahead. Likewise, a new invention or discovery can quickly turn the trajectory of a science in an unexpected direction. But what we can say for sure is that psychology in the middle of the twenty-first century will be built by the current cohort of students. And that means you, the reader of this book, will be part of that exciting endeavor.

Figure 16.2 Tree of Knowledge System

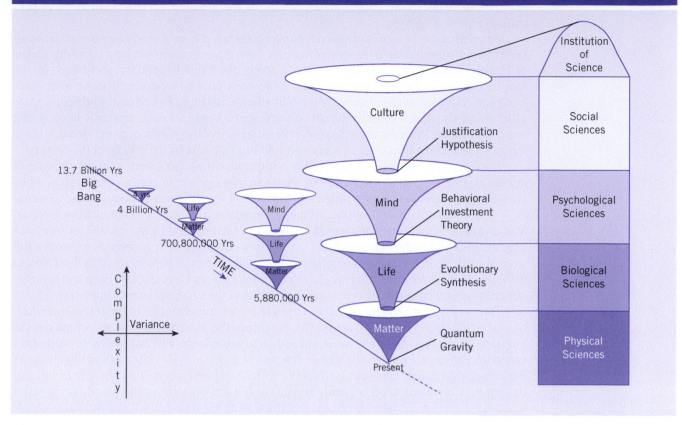

Source: Henriques, G. (2013). Evolving from methodological to conceptual unification. *Review of General Psychology, 17,* 168–173.

Looking Ahead

At the beginning of the twentieth century, experimental psychology was an international endeavor. Arising in Germany in the late nineteenth century, it attracted students from around the world, who learned the methods of this new science of the mind and took them back to their own countries. Within a couple of decades, a second center of psychology had emerged in the United States, where it was widely accepted because it gave the promise of finding solutions to pressing social problems.

The world of 1900 was highly interconnected, thanks to great strides in long-distance communication and transportation. But there were also significant geopolitical stresses that endangered this new world order, such as great powers jockeying for preeminence and growing unrest in the underdeveloped regions of the world. These stresses led to a world war, the rise of nationalism and fascism, a second world war, a cold war, and numerous wars of independence. By the middle of the twentieth century, Europe lay in ruins, divided into American and Soviet spheres of influence. Likewise, Japan was struggling to rebuild, and China was recovering from decades of foreign invasion and civil war. Meanwhile, political instability plagued much of the southern hemisphere. As the only world power to have been spared the destruction of World War II, it's no surprise that the center of the scientific enterprise, including psychology, shifted to the United States. This rise to global dominance was also bolstered by the mass immigration of European scientists in the 1930s.

During the middle decades of the twentieth century, very little psychological research was being conducted anywhere in the world outside of North America (Adair & Huynh, 2012). However, by the 1980s the rest of the developed world was well on the road to economic recovery, and we see a renewed international interest in experimental psychology around this time. In the last decades of the twentieth century, there was a large influx of graduate students to the United States, hinting at the growing internationalization of psychology that was to come.

When measured in terms of research publications, we first see a steady increase in the number of paper submissions to American journals from other English-speaking countries (Adair & Huynh, 2012). These include Australia, Canada, the United Kingdom, and Israel. By the turn of the twenty-first century, more and more contributions were also coming from other European countries, such as Germany, the Netherlands, Belgium, Switzerland, and Spain. Since 2010, we've also seen a considerable growth in research from East Asia, especially Japan, Hong Kong, and China. With the tremendous economic growth of this region in recent decades, some scholars predict that the center of science will shift to East Asia by the middle of the century.

The internationalization of psychology is imperative if we truly want to build a science of human experience (van de Vijver, 2013). There's an inherent bias in psychology constructed by Euro-American psychologists testing their theories on Euro-American populations. Centered as it is on Western individualistic culture, it's unrealistic to expect findings from a lab in Massachusetts to necessarily apply in Madagascar or Malaysia. And it's not enough for American psychologists to conduct cross-cultural studies to see whether their homegrown theories still work abroad. Rather, a truly universal psychology will have to be built by scholars from around the world representing the full array of diversity on the planet. Only through deep and continuous cultural exchange can we ever hope to understand the universal core of humanity.

The twenty-first century offers both opportunities and obstacles to the internationalization of psychology (van de Vijver, 2013). No doubt the most important opportunity is the internet, which has vastly increased our access to knowledge and our ability to communicate with colleagues around the globe. The rise of English as the international language of business, government, and science presents both an opportunity and an obstacle to full globalization. Communication is greatly enhanced, but the benefits accrue mainly to those for whom English is their native language, and those working with English as a second language will be disadvantaged as they interact on the global stage. Another obstacle to internationalization is the lack of scholarly mentorship in developing countries. Established researchers in the West will have to do their part to help guide young psychologists into mature scholars, in many cases through multinational collaborations. Finally, the greatest obstacle to internationalization is the same as it was at the turn of the previous century, namely geopolitical tensions that threaten once again to tear the global order asunder. We can only hope that our world leaders will act with more prudence than their predecessors did.

The same processes of integration are underway in the United States as well. Women are now taking leadership roles in psychology, and the barriers to entry by minorities are breaking down. These people will bring with them fresh perspectives that will enrich our understanding of the human experience. Perhaps as psychologists, we can even lead the way by example, showing how to build a diverse society where all are welcomed as equals and appreciated for the contributions they make. Despite the dangers we must all face together, there's certainly good reason to hope for a bright future.

CHAPTER SUMMARY

Neuroscience is built on previous work of the physiological psychologists in the middle of the twentieth century, but with support from new technologies that enabled scientists to record brain activity and create images of brain processes. The field got its name in the 1960s, but early work in what became known as behavioral neuroscience started a decade before that. Some of the key discoveries of behavioral neuroscience included the role of the cerebellum in learning, the reward center in the brain, and neuroplasticity, namely the ability of the brain to reorganize and even regenerate after injury. The Cognitive Revolution of the 1960s led researchers in the following decades to investigate relationships between cognitive functions and the brain processes that underlie them. Around the turn of the twenty-first century, researchers extended the reach of neuroscience to include the study of the brain processes that underlie emotion, in a field they called affective neuroscience. In the first decades of the twenty-first century, neuroscience has come to dominate psychology. Some philosophers of science speculate that neuroscience will become a unifying theory or framework that draws together the fractured disciplines of psychology. Others, however, believe that advances in neuroscience will eventually make standard approaches to psychological experimentation obsolete. With the growth of interdisciplinary research, it's also important to consider psychology's relationship to the other sciences as traditional boundaries become blurred.

DISCUSSION QUESTIONS

1. Outline the steps Richard Thompson took to locate the engram for the eyeblink response. Consider how this project serves as a model for brain research.

2. Describe the manner in which James Olds and Peter Milner discovered the reward center in the brain. Consider how this project illustrates the role of serendipity in research and the need for scientists to be open to unexpected findings.

3. Mark Rosenzweig demonstrated the brain's ability to reorganize and even regenerate after injury. If we could learn how to control neural plasticity, what sorts of applications might this technology have? Consider also any ethical issues regarding neural regeneration.

4. Endel Tulving proposed that there are three types of memory, each with an associated level of consciousness. As you review this theory, consider what it implies about the relationship between memory and consciousness. Can you come up with examples or counterexamples to the model?

5. Michael Posner was one of the pioneers in the use of both ERP and fMRI. Compare the strengths and weaknesses of each technique, explaining how the two serve as complementary methodologies.

6. Patricia Goldman-Rakic studied the biological basis of working memory by experimenting on rhesus monkeys. How confident are you that her findings can be extended to humans? Defend your position with evidence and arguments.

7. Michael Gazzaniga has lamented that his work on hemispheric specialization has led to many popular misconceptions about how the brain works. What are some of the left-brain/right-brain myths you've heard, and how would you counter them?

8. After describing Richard Lazarus's transactional model of stress, consider some of the stress-coping strategies it suggests. Illustrate these with real-life examples.

9. Outline Panksepp's seven primary emotion systems, evaluating how each maps onto our experience of emotion in daily life. Try to think of common emotions that aren't included in this list, and consider whether these might be complex emotions that can be broken down into a combination of basic emotional systems.

10. Joseph LeDoux thinks it may one day be possible to erase traumatic memories that lead to psychological disorders such as PTSD. What are the ethical implications of memory removal?

11. In the *Star Trek* universe, Captain Kirk is the emotional human and Mister Spock is the rational Vulcan. According to Damasio's somatic marker hypothesis, which would likely be the better decision maker? Explain.

12. How do you see the relationship between psychology and neuroscience progressing during your lifetime? Consider the various scenarios presented in this chapter, evaluating the likelihood of each.

ON THE WEB

Search **Richard Thompson eyeblink conditioning** for a short video of him demonstrating how this research was done. You can also search **James Olds and Peter Milner rat experiment** for a video showing the discovery of the reward center in the brain and self-stimulation by rats. YouTube hosts a brief documentary on the work of **Endel Tulving**, including snippets of an interview with him. Search **Michael Posner psychology** to find a twenty-minute interview with this neuroscientist. The work of **Michael Gazzaniga**, and especially that of **split-brain patients**, is portrayed in a number of YouTube videos. You can also find a TED Talk by **Jaak Panksepp** as well as several interviews with him. Finally, both **Joseph LeDoux** and **Antonio Damasio** have a number of videos posted on YouTube. While you're surfing the web, don't forget to check out the official website of the **Amygdaloids**.

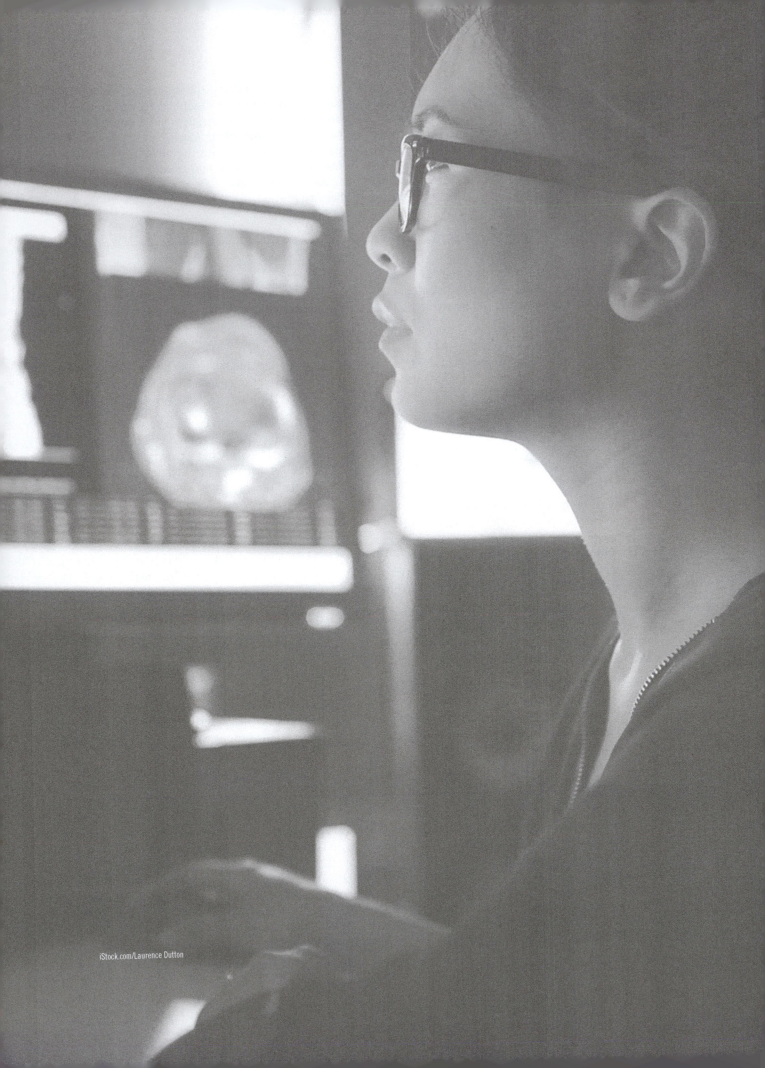

Concept Glossary

ABX model. Newcomb's description of the forces that come into play as two people attempt to align their attitudes toward a third entity. (12)

Accommodation. The process whereby new information leads to the construction of novel cognitive structures. (8)

Act psychology. An early school of psychology which held that mental phenomena are active rather than passive processes. (6)

Action research. Experimental investigations aimed at finding effective methods for social change. (6)

Activity theory. The theoretical position that physical activity during social interactions is the basis for cognitive development. (9)

Actor-observer effect. The tendency to make dispositional attributions of others' behaviors and situational attributions of our own. (12)

Affective neuroscience. The study of the brain processes underlying emotion. (16)

Affordance. What the environment offers to an organism. (11)

Age of Enlightenment. A period during the eighteenth century when religious dogma was questioned and reason was held as the ultimate authority. (1)

Agentic shift. A process in which individuals transfer responsibility for their own actions to an authority figure. (12)

Agoraphobia. The fear of leaving home or going into public places. (13)

Allegory of Meno's slave. A story in which Plato shows how Socrates draws out knowledge of geometry from an uneducated boy. (1)

Allegory of the cave. A story in which Plato argues that knowledge can only come from reason because the senses can deceive us. (1)

Anal stage. A time in psychosexual development when a child derives pleasure from the anus and buttocks. (7)

Analytical psychology. Jung's approach to depth psychology emphasizing the role of the collective unconscious and archetypes. (7)

Anchoring and adjustment. A way of estimating a value by moving away from a potentially arbitrary starting point. (11)

Anima. The ideal feminine image. (7)

Animus. The ideal masculine image. (7)

Anterograde amnesia. The inability to form new memories. (16)

Anxious attachment. A mother-infant bond in which the baby is distressed by its mother's departure but isn't soothed by her return. (13)

Aphasia. Loss of language functions due to brain damage. (9)

Apperception. The ability to reflect on one's own perceptions. (1)

Applied psychology. A field that uses psychological research to solve practical problems in daily life. (3)

Approach-avoidance conflict. A situation in which an organism simultaneously experiences a drive to obtain a desired object and a fear compelling it to flee the object. (5)

Archetypes. The primitive ideas contained in the collective unconscious. (7)

Artificial conditioned reflex. The association of an innate reflex with a novel stimulus. (9)

Artificial selection. The intentional breeding of desired characteristics in domestic animals and plants. (2)

Assimilation. The process whereby new information is incorporated into existing cognitive structures. (8)

Associated motor reflex. A muscle movement in response to a signal that a pain stimulus is about to occur. (9)

Associationism. The theory that knowledge develops as simple ideas combine to form complex ideas. (1)

Attachment. The deep emotional bond that develops between an infant and its mother. (13)

Attachment theory. The proposal that the kind of caregiver-infant bond that develops in the first year has significant consequences for later social, emotional, and personality development. (13)

Attenuation model. Treisman's proposal that attention increases the intensity of a wanted stimulus and decreases the intensity of an unwanted stimulus. (11)

Attribution. An inference about the cause of a behavior. (6)

Attribution theory. A framework for explaining the types of inferences people make about the causes of behavior. (6)

Autokinetic effect. A perceptual phenomenon in which a stationary point of light on a dark background appears to move. (12)

Automatism. A behavior that is performed without conscious awareness. (8)

Autoradiography. A method of producing an X-ray image by injecting a radioactive substance into the body. (16)

Availability heuristic. A way of judging the probability of an event by how easily examples come to mind. (11)

Avoidant attachment. A mother-infant bond in which the baby isn't distressed by its mother's departure and shows little interest in her return. (13)

Balance theory. A description of how people adjust their sentiments toward others to achieve a stable cognitive state. (6)

Baldwin effect. The observation that even though learned behaviors of parents cannot be inherited by offspring, the ability to quickly learn adaptive behaviors can be. (3)

Basic anxiety. Horney's term for a profound feeling of isolation and helplessness in an uncaring world. (7)

Behavioral neuroscience. The study of the brain processes underlying motivation and learning. (16)

Big Five. A model of personality consisting of five factors. (14)

Biofeedback. The process of gaining insights into physiological functions with the assistance of instruments that monitor them. (5)

Bit. The basic unit of information in communication and computing. (11)

Bounded rationality. The notion that humans make logical decisions within the limitations of their cognitive capacities and the availability of information. (11)

Brass instrument psychology. An early period in experimental psychology when stimuli were presented and responses were recorded by mechanical means. (3)

Cannon-Bard theory. The theory that stimulation of the thalamus leads to both physiological arousal and the psychological experience of emotion. (10)

Cartesian dualism. The proposal that the mind and the body are separate but interact with each other. (1)

Catastrophism. The idea that the Earth's geological features were formed during a small number of major cataclysms during the last few thousand years. (2)

Categorical imperative. Kant's fundamental moral law that we must always act in such a way as to respect the humanity of other people. (1)

Catharsis. The release of pent-up emotions that cause psychological distress. (7)

Cell assembly. A group of neurons that tend to fire together. (10)

Chemoaffinity hypothesis. The idea that developing nerve tracts find their destinations by following chemical trails. (10)

Child Study Movement. A late nineteenth-century campaign to reform educational practices based on the scientific study of child development. (4)

Chunk. A meaningful unit of information held in short-term memory. (11)

Clinical method. The investigative technique of asking probing questions and recording responses without judgment. (8)

Cocktail party effect. The ability to focus on one environmental stimulus while ignoring others. (11)

Cognitive dissonance. The mental discomfort that occurs when a person holds contradictory beliefs or when there is a mismatch between attitudes and behaviors. (12)

Cognitive map. A mental model of the spatial layout of a location. (5)

Cognitive neuroscience. The study of the brain processes underlying memory and attention. (16)

Cognitive science. An interdisciplinary approach to studying the mind and how it works. (1)

Collective unconscious. In Jungian theory, a storehouse of innate ideas that have been passed down through human evolutionary history. (7)

Combined motor method. An experimental procedure in which participants squeeze a rubber bulb as they give word-association responses. (9)

Common fate. The Gestalt principle that items moving together are perceived as a single object. (6)

Commonsense psychology. The set of beliefs about human behavior that people use to guide their interactions with others. (6)

Comparative psychology. The study of the origin, control, and consequences of behavior across a wide range of species. (10)

Comparison level. A consideration of the quality of the relationship in the current interaction as compared with past interactions. (12)

Comparison level of alternatives. A consideration of the other relationship options available to each partner. (12)

Compatibilism. The argument that human free will can still exist even in a fully deterministic world. (1)

Complex. Interrelated set of unconscious memories and emotions on a common theme. (7)

Computer metaphor. The notion that the mind is an information-processing device much like an electronic computer. (11)

Concrete operational stage. A period in which grade schoolers have the ability to think logically with the aid of manipulated objects. (8)

Conditioned emotional response. A process in which a person develops an emotional reaction to a previously neutral stimulus. (5)

Conditioned taste aversion. Learned avoidance of a food associated with illness. (10)

Confederate. A collaborator with the experimenter whose job it is to create a specific social situation in which to observe the participant's behavior. (12)

Congruence. A genuine and authentic relationship between the therapist and the client. (15)

Connectionism. The view that learning is fundamentally about forming new associations or connections. (4)

Conservation. The understanding that the mass of a substance remains the same even when its shape changes. (8)

Consilience. A convergence of all knowledge into a single scientific structure. (16)

Contiguity theory. The proposal that stimulus-response associations are created in a single instance when the stimulus and response co-occur at about the same time. (5)

Controversial Discussions. A series of meetings of the British Psychoanalytic Society in the early 1940s that pitted supporters of Anna Freud and Melanie Klein against each other. (7)

Corpus callosum. The band of nerve fibers connecting the left and right hemispheres of the cerebrum. (10)

Correspondence bias. The tendency to assume that behaviors reflect the true intentions of the people who perform them. (12)

Counter-attitudinal advocacy. A self-persuasion technique in which people are asked to take a public position on an issue that differs from their privately held beliefs. (12)

Covariation model. The proposal that people make attributions by considering which potential cause best predicts the behavior. (12)

Creationism. The idea that the various species existing today were created in their present form. (2)

Crisis. A turning point in life that will set the direction for future personality development. (15)

Cronbach's alpha. A statistical technique for estimating the reliability of a psychometric test. (13)

Crystallized intelligence. The accumulation of knowledge over a lifetime. (14)

Cultural-historical psychology. Vygotsky's theoretical approach emphasizing the role of social interaction in cognitive development. (9)

Culture-free intelligence test. An instrument that measures fluid intelligence. (14)

Curiosity and manipulation drives. Motivation to seek out novel experiences and explore new things. (10)

Deduction. A method of reasoning that applies general rules to specific cases. (1)

Defense mechanisms. Unconscious responses to anxiety-provoking situations. (7)

Delayed-response task. A laboratory procedure in which the subject observes a desired object being hidden in one of two containers and is then distracted for a brief time, after which it is allowed to retrieve it. (16)

Dichotic listening. A laboratory task in which the participant hears two different streams of speech through left and right headphones and is asked to only attend to one of them. (11)

Direct perception. The argument that we perceive the world as it is without having to process the sensory stimulus. (11)

Discrimination learning. The process of learning to respond differently to stimuli that differ in some particular aspect. (5)

Dissociation. A phenomenon in which persons become detached from their perceptions, memories, or behaviors. (8)

Doctrine of the idols. Bacon's assertion that the human mind is beset with biases that lead it to predictable errors. (1)

Double dissociation. The demonstration that two independent variables have different effects on two dependent variables. (10)

Double-aspect monism. The view that mind and body are two facets of the same universal substance. (1)

Drive reduction theory. The proposal that learning occurs when a behavior is impelled by an unpleasant state that is reduced after that the behavior is performed. (5)

Dualism. The philosophical stance that mind and body consist of distinct substances and are subject to different laws. (1)

Dynamic psychology. The position that behavior can only be explained if the motivations of the organism are first understood. (4)

Ego. The sense of self or agency. (7)

Egocentrism. A lack of awareness that other people have points of view different from one's own. (8)

Elaboration principle. The process in which members of the core group invite additional persons to join in, forming a larger social network. (12)

Electroencephalography. A technique for recording electrical activity produced in the brain by placing a set of electrodes on the scalp. (16)

Eliminative reductionism. The notion that higher levels of explanation become unnecessary once lower levels of explanation have been fully developed. (16)

Emergent property. A phenomenon that arises from processes at a lower level but is not fully explicable in terms of those processes. (16)

Empiricism. The philosophical stance that knowledge can only be obtained through experience. (1)

Engram. The hypothetical location in the brain where a memory is stored. (10)

Environment of evolutionary adaptedness. The stable period of about 200,000 years during which humans lived as hunter-gatherers. (13)

Epiphenomenalism. The position that consciousness is nothing more than a byproduct of brain activity. (3)

Episodic memory. The recollection of personal experiences. (16)

Epistemology. The study of knowledge, which asks questions such as what it means to know something and how knowledge can be acquired. (1)

Equilibration. The process of aligning cognitive structures with current environmental conditions. (8)

Equipotentiality. The observation that any part of a functional area of the brain is able to carry out the function of the whole area. (10)

Ethology. The study of animal behavior in natural settings. (10)

Eudaimonia. The view of happiness as resulting from a life in which persons pursue self-actualization and the fulfillment of their potential. (15)

Eugenics. The idea that the human race can be rapidly improved through artificial selection techniques. (2)

Event-related potential. A technique for measuring the time course of mental events based on EEG recordings. (16)

Evolution. The idea that species change over time as they adapt to new environments and challenges. (2)

Existentialism. A mid-twentieth-century school of philosophy claiming the central problem that humans face is coming to terms with the anxiety of living in a meaningless world. (15)

Expected utility theory. The standard mathematical model of decision making under risk. (11)

Eyelid conditioning. A classical conditioning procedure in which a light or tone is paired with a puff of air to the eye, causing the subject to blink. (5)

Facial efference. The observation that facial expressions and emotions may be linked through blood flow to the brain. (12)

Factor analysis. A statistical technique for reducing a large number of observed variables to a small number of underlying variables. (4)

Feature integration theory. Treisman's proposal that the role of attention is to bind features of objects, such as color or shape, into coherent wholes. (11)

Fechner's law. The proposal that the intensity of the sensation is related by a logarithmic function to the intensity of the stimulus. (2)

Field theory. Lewin's idea that an individual's behavior is determined by personal and situational forces. (6)

Fight-or-flight response. The body's arousal reaction to a dangerous situation. (10)

Figure-ground organization. The distinction between foreground and background. (6)

Filter model. Broadbent's description of attention as a bottleneck that limits the amount of information coming into the organism. (11)

First signal system. Pavlov's conceptualization of conditioned reflexes as adjustments to a changing environment. (9)

Fistula. A surgical opening that provides access for inserting tubes into internal organs. (9)

Fixed idea. A subconscious memory of a traumatic event. (8)

Fixed mindset. The belief that a person's intelligence is a fixed quantity that cannot change. (15)

Flashbulb memory. A vivid and detailed recollection of events after an emotionally charged experience. (11)

Flow. A peak experience in which skilled practitioners report a sense of ecstasy and a loss of time and self. (15)

Fluid intelligence. The ability to solve novel problems quickly. (14)

Flying man argument. A thought experiment intended to demonstrate the existence of self-awareness outside of the body. (1)

Forensic psychology. The application of psychological principles to the legal system. (3)

Formal operational stage. A period when adolescents acquire the ability to think logically about abstract or hypothetical situations. (8)

Framing effect. The observation that the way a problem is presented influences the decision that is made. (11)

Free association. A psychotherapy technique in which patients are encouraged to say whatever comes to mind without attempting to censor their thoughts. (7)

Freudian slip. A lapse of memory or an error in speech due to interference from a repressed memory. (7)

Frustration-aggression hypothesis. The proposal that people turn to aggression when they are frustrated in reaching their goals. (5)

Functionalism. An early American school of psychology that studied mental processes in terms of their adaptive value. (4)

Fundamental attribution error. The tendency to discount situational factors and to assume that behavior is driven by personal dispositions. (12)

Game theory. A framework for analyzing the costs and benefits of a social exchange to predict whether the partners will cooperate with each other or defect from the relationship. (12)

Genetic epistemology. In Piaget's terms, the study of the origin of knowledge. (8)

Genital stage. The period of mature psychosexual development in adulthood. (7)

Gestalt. German word for "configuration." (6)

Gestalt quality. An aspect of a configuration as a whole that none of its parts possesses. (6)

Group dynamics. The ways in which social organizations respond to changing circumstances. (6)

Growth mindset. The belief that intelligence is a mutable quantity that can increase over time. (15)

Habit. A behavioral pattern that develops as the nervous system reorganizes through repeated action. (4)

Hebbian learning. The proposal that when two adjacent neurons are repeatedly activated at the same time, the connection between them is strengthened. (10)

Hedonism. The view that happiness is the product of pleasurable experiences. (15)

Heritability. A statistic indicating the degree to which genetic factors account for the observed variation in a population. (14)

Heuristics. Intuitive decision-making processes that are fast and easy but prone to error. (11)

Hierarchy of needs. Maslow's contention that the more basic needs will dominate a person's thoughts and feelings until they are met, at which point higher-order needs will emerge. (15)

Higher nervous activity. Pavlov's term for the nervous system functions that coordinate the organism's interactions with its environment. (9)

Homeostasis. The processes by which the body maintains stable internal conditions. (10)

Humanistic psychology. The view that humans have an innate drive to grow toward fulfilling their potential in life. (15)

Hypothetico-deductive method. The scientific approach of generating falsifiable hypotheses that are then tested in experiments. (5)

Hysteria. An antiquated diagnosis for patients suffering from symptoms such as numbness and paralysis even though there's no damage to the nervous system. (7)

Id. The repository of innate drives or instincts. (7)

Idealism. The philosophical stance that the world consists solely of minds and the ideas they produce. (1)

Identity crisis. The time during adolescence when emerging adults consolidate their sense of who they are as individuals. (15)

Idiographic approach. A research style of examining individual persons in great depth. (14)

Imageless thought controversy. An extended debate between Titchener and his rivals about the nature of consciousness. (3)

Imprinting. A behavioral phenomenon in which a newly hatched chick identifies the first moving object as its mother. (10)

Inattentional blindness. A phenomenon in which persons fail to see something directly in front of them because their attention is focused elsewhere. (11)

Individual psychology. Adler's version of psychotherapy that emphasized the centrality of social functioning in mental health. (7) Binet's term for the study of individual differences in personality and intelligence. (8)

Individuation. A process in which unconscious complexes are brought into consciousness and integrated with the ego. (7)

Induction. A method of reasoning that examines specific cases in order to discover general rules. (1)

Industrial and organizational psychology. The application of psychological principles to business, manufacturing, and other large-group settings. (3)

Inferiority complex. A lifestyle dominated by a sense of helplessness and unworthiness. (7)

Ingratiation. The kinds of behaviors people engage in to get others to like them. (12)

Inhibition of return. A delay in an attentional shift back to a previously attended location. (16)

Instinct. A complex behavioral response to a specific stimulus or situation that doesn't require learning. (4)

Intelligence quotient. The ratio between the mental age and the chronological age of the test taker. (4)

Intentionality. The quality of being about something. (6)

Interdependence theory. A description of how the costs and benefits of particular interactions lead to decisions about whether to cooperate or compete and whether to continue or leave the relationship. (12)

Internal versus external control of reinforcement. The belief that life events are the outcome either of personal effort or of outside forces. (14)

Internal working model. An infant's mental framework for understanding how relationships work based on interactions with caregivers. (13)

Intervening variables. The internal states of the organism mediating between stimulus and response. (5)

Introspection. The careful observation of one's own mental states. (3)

Iowa gambling task. A laboratory procedure for assessing decision-making abilities in brain-damaged patients. (16)

Isomorphism. The idea that the structure of conscious experience is mirrored by similarly structured physical events in the brain. (6)

James-Lange theory. The idea that emotional experience is an interpretation of bodily arousal within a given situation. (4)

Jigsaw classroom. A pedagogical technique in which each member of a group has a different piece of information needed to complete the assignment. (12)

Judgment. The estimation of the likelihood of an event. (11)

Just-noticeable difference. The amount a stimulus has to be increased or decreased before a change in the stimulus can be detected. (2)

Lamarckism. A theory of evolution proposing that characteristics acquired during an organism's lifetime can be passed on to its descendants. (2)

Latency stage. A time in psychosexual development when a child's sexual feelings remain dormant. (7)

Latent content. The unconscious meaning of the dream. (7)

Latent learning. A type of learning that occurs without reward or drive reduction and without any overt expression of behavior. (5)

Law of effect. The observation that learning is strengthened when it is accompanied by a pleasant feeling and weakened when it is accompanied by an unpleasant feeling. (4)

Law of exercise. The observation that learning increases with the number of repetitions. (4)

Law of Prägnanz. The assertion that perceptual organization will be as good as the prevailing conditions allow. (6)

Law of readiness. The observation that individuals learn best when they are motivated and prepared to do so. (4)

Laws of association. Hume's description of how simple ideas adhere to each other to form complex ideas. (1)

Learned helplessness. A phenomenon in which an organism fails to escape a painful situation even when it is capable of doing so. (15)

Learning set. Understanding of how to approach a solution to a particular type of problem. (10)

Lesion study. A research technique that involves damaging a specific portion of the brain and observing any subsequent deficits. (16)

Levels of aspiration theory. The proposal that successful completion of a task depends not only on ability but also the motivation to complete it. (14)

Levels-of-analysis approach. The position that explanations at one level are unrelated to explanations at a higher or lower level. (16)

Lewin's equation. B=f(P,E), meaning that behavior (B) is a function (f) of both personal (P) and environmental (E) variables. (6)

Lexical hypothesis. The proposal that words for personality traits should be common in any language because they serve an important role in social interactions. (14)

Life space. Lewin's term referring to the totality of forces acting on an individual, including personality and motivation as well as social and environmental influences. (6)

Lifestyle. Adler's term for an individual's typical approach to dealing with the world. (7)

Little Albert experiment. A case study in which John Watson demonstrated a conditioned fear in a young boy. (5)

Locus of control. Another term for internal versus external control of reinforcement. (14)

Lost-in-the-mall technique. A laboratory procedure for implanting false memories. (11)

Lower nervous activity. Pavlov's term for the nervous system functions that regulate the internal organs. (9)

Manifest content. The narrative of a dream as recalled by the dreamer on awakening. (7)

Mass action. The observation that an impairment in functioning depended on the amount of brain tissue destroyed. (10)

Materialism. The view that there is only matter and that no separate substance is needed to explain the mind. (1)

Maternal deprivation hypothesis. The proposal that prolonged separation from the mother in early childhood leads to pathological personality development in adolescence. (13)

Maternal sensitivity. The degree to which the mother is attentive and responsive to her infant's needs. (13)

Maturationism. The belief that development unfolds according to a set schedule of milestones. (4)

Mean length of utterance (MLU). The average number of meaningful units per sentence, used as a measure of language development. (13)

Means-ends analysis. The problem-solving method of searching for ways to close the distance between the current state and the goal state. (11)

Mental chemistry. Mill's argument that complex ideas can have features not found in any of its components. (1)

Mental chronometry. The measurement of the time course of cognitive events. (16)

Mental test. An indirect assessment of intelligence based on simple measurements such as reaction time and memory span. (3)

Mere exposure effect. The observation that people tend to like familiar items more than unfamiliar ones. (12)

Metaphysics. The philosophical inquiry into the nature of the universe. (1)

Method of doubt. Descartes's way of avoiding unwarranted assumptions by questioning everything that cannot be logically verified. (1)

Method of dual stimulation. An experimental technique in which a child is first asked to solve a problem alone and then with the help of an adult. (9)

Methodological behaviorism. The position that psychology should ignore questions of consciousness and focus on behavior instead. (5)

Microelectrode recording. A brain-recording technique in which an ultrathin electrode is inserted to a position where it can measure the activity of a single neuron. (16)

Mill argument. Leibniz's thought experiment demonstrating that mental processes cannot be produced by mechanical means. (1)

Millisecond. A thousandth of a second. (3)

Mind-body problem. The question of how psychological experience is related to the physical world. (1)

Misinformation effect. The distortion of memory due to exposure to false or misleading information after the event. (11)

Modern synthesis. An explanation of Darwinian evolution in terms of Mendelian genetics. (2)

Molar behavior. The behavior of the organism as a whole, especially as directed toward a particular purpose. (5)

Molecular behavior. The movements of the individual muscles that make up a behavior. (5)

Monism. The philosophical stance that mind and body consist of the same substance and are subject to the same laws. (1)

Multiform method. A procedure for diagnosing a personality by subjecting the participant to a battery of tests conducted by a group of examiners who then discuss the case to reach a consensus. (14)

Natural selection. A theory of evolution proposing that individuals which are better suited to current circumstances are more likely to survive and reproduce. (2)

Nature and nurture. A catchphrase to describe the respective impact of biological inheritance and environmental upbringing on human development. (2)

Need-press theory. The view that personality is shaped by psychodynamic processes as the individual is driven by internal motivations and constrained by situational factors. (14)

Neo-behaviorism. An approach that sought to explain behaviors that could not be described as conditioned responses. (5)

Neurasthenia. An antiquated diagnosis for patients suffering from symptoms such as fatigue, headache, heart palpitations, anxiety, and depressed mood. (7)

Neurology. The branch of medicine that treats disorders of the nervous system. (7)

Neuropsychology. A field of study that seeks to find connections between brain locations and behavioral or cognitive functioning. (9)

Neurosis. A relatively minor psychological disorder that interferes with the patient's ability to lead a happy and productive life but without a loss of contact with reality. (7)

Nomothetic approach. A research style of examining many examples to derive generalizations. (14)

Normative model. A description of how people should act rather than how they really behave. (12)

Object permanence. The understanding that objects continue to exist even when out of sight. (8)

Object-relations theory. The proposal that relationships with significant others in infancy shape patterns of relating in adulthood. (7)

Oedipus complex. The proposal that all young children develop a sexual longing for their opposite-sex parent and a sexual jealousy toward their same-sex parent. (7)

Operant behavior. An action that is performed by an organism without being elicited by a stimulus in the environment. (5)

Operant conditioning. The process of an organism learning about the consequences of its behavior. (5)

Operation. Piaget's term for a logical thought process. (8)

Operationalization. The practice of defining variables in terms of the way in which they will be measured. (3)

Opioid hypothesis. The conjecture that the formation of social attachment and contact comfort is mediated by endogenous opioids. (16)

Optic flow. The observation that the visual scene appears to expand from a central point in front of a moving observer. (11)

Oral fixation. A behavior involving the mouth that is engaged in to relieve anxiety. (7)

Oral stage. A time in psychosexual development when an infant derives pleasure from nursing at the breast or bottle. (7)

Outcome matrix. A diagram that lays out the costs and benefits of an interaction for each participant. (12)

Paired-associates task. A test of learning in which the participant memorizes pairs of unrelated words. (4)

Panpsychism. The belief that all things in the universe, whether animate or inanimate, have consciousness. (2)

Peak experience. A deeply emotional experience in which the person comes to see the world in a new way. (15)

Penis envy. Freud's contention that women naturally feel inferior to men because they know they lack a penis. (7)

Perceptual learning. The process of becoming more sensitive to the meaningful aspects of a visual scene. (13)

Person versus situation debate. An argument among psychologists during the 1970s about whether personalities or situations were the main determinant of behavior. (14)

Persona. Jung's term for the self that each person presents to others. (7)

Personal conscious. The part of the mind that a person is aware of. (7)

Personal construct theory. Kelly's proposal that people actively interpret the situations they encounter in order to control and predict the events in their lives. (14)

Personal unconscious. A repository of repressed memories accumulated over a lifetime. (7)

Personality. An individual's characteristic ways of feeling, acting, and thinking. (14)

Personality paradox. The observation that people's behaviors are inconsistent across a wide range of situations even though our intuitions tell us that individuals display enduring personality traits. (14)

Personology. Henry Murray's theory of personality formation throughout the lifespan by psychodynamic processes. (14)

Phallic stage. A time in psychosexual development when a child derives pleasure from rubbing the genitals. (7)

Phi phenomenon. The apparent motion of stationary but rapidly changing objects. (6)

Physiological psychology. The study of how behavior is generated and guided by the nervous system. (10)

Physiology. A subfield of biology that studies the processes and functions of living organisms. (2)

Polymath. A scholar who makes important contributions to several different fields. (2)

Positive psychology. The scientific study of happiness and the features of a life well lived. (15)

Positivism. The philosophical stance that scientists can only know what they can directly observe through their senses or instruments. (5)

Posner cueing task. A laboratory procedure that is used to measure people's abilities to make rapid shifts of attention. (16)

Pragmatism. The philosophical stance that the truth of an idea should be judged according to its practical consequences. (4)

Preoperational stage. A period in which the reasoning of preschoolers is dominated by magical thinking rather than rational thought. (8)

Primary mental abilities. The seven basic forms of intelligence proposed by Thurstone. (4)

Principles of perceptual grouping. Descriptions of how features such as similarity and proximity guide the organization of sensory elements into Gestalten. (6)

Procedural memory. Knowledge of how to do something. (16)

Prospect theory. A model of human decision making under risk that is based on evidence from experimental psychology. (11)

Proximity principle. The observation that people tend to like others who share the same environment with them. (12)

Psychic secretion. Salivation at the expectation of food. (9)

Psychoanalysis. Freud's theory of the origin of psychological disorders and his method for curing them. (7)

Psychological analysis. Janet's approach to treating psychological disorders by identifying and eliminating fixed ideas. (8)

Psychometrics. The field involved in the measurement of an individual's psychological characteristics. (4)

Psychophysical parallelism. The idea that mind and body act in harmony even though they do not interact. (1)

Psychophysics. The study of the relationship between physical stimuli and the sensations associated with them. (2)

Psychosexual development. The proposal that infants progress through a series of stages, each centered on a body part that is a source of sensual pleasure. (7)

Psychosis. A severe psychological disorder involving hallucinations, delusions, and a general loss of contact with reality. (7)

Purposive behaviorism. The position that organisms engage in behaviors to achieve particular goals. (5)

Puzzle box. An enclosure from which a test animal can escape if it performs the correct behavior. (4)

Radical behaviorism. The philosophical stance that internal experiences of the organism are behaviors just like outwardly observable actions. (5)

Radical empiricism. The philosophical stance that we don't just perceive sensations but rather objects in relations with other objects. (4)

Rationalism. The philosophical stance that knowledge can only be obtained through reason. (1)

Recapitulation theory. The idea that a developing organism repeats all the stages of the evolution of its species. (4)

Recency principle. The proposal that a familiar stimulus will evoke the most recent response to it. (5)

Reflexology. Bekhterev's approach of using associated motor reflexes to make inferences about the nature of mental processes in the brain. (9)

Regnancy. The central motivation in an individual's life that subordinates all other motives and brings unity to the personality. (14)

Reinforcement. A consequence of a behavior that increases the likelihood it will be repeated. (5)

Reinforcement history. An organism's past experience with a behavior and its consequence. (5)

Representativeness heuristic. A way of judging the probability of an event by how typical it appears. (11)

Repression. The exclusion of an unwanted or traumatic memory from consciousness. (7)

Respondent behavior. An action that is performed by an organism in response to a stimulus. (5)

Retrograde amnesia. The loss of memories that have already been stored. (16)

Reversibility. The mental undoing of a process to demonstrate conservation. (8)

Satisficing. The practice of making choices that are good enough for current needs. (11)

Savings during relearning. A process that occurs when a person learns something, forgets it, but then learns it again at a faster rate. (2)

Scientist-practitioner model. An approach to training clinical psychologists both as researchers and as therapists. (14)

Second signal system. Pavlov's conceptualization of language as a means for adjusting each other's behavior. (9)

Secure attachment. A mother-infant bond in which the baby is distressed by its mother's departure but soothed by her return. (13)

Secure base. The conceptualization of the caregiver's role as providing a safe zone from which the child can explore the world and to which it can retreat when frightened. (13)

Security theory. The proposal that infants need to develop a secure dependence upon their caregivers in order to develop the coping skills necessary for navigating a complex adult world. (13)

Seduction theory. The proposal that psychological disorders in adulthood are caused by sexual abuse in childhood. (7)

Self-actualization. The innate drive to reach one's fullest potential in life. (15)

Self-efficacy. A set of beliefs about one's ability to cope with particular challenges. (13)

Self-psychology. The position that the proper subject of psychology is the study of conscious selves as they interact with their social and physical environments. (4)

Self-transcendence. The highest level in the hierarchy of needs in which self-actualized persons seek to become part of something greater than themselves. (15)

Semantic memory. Knowledge of facts and concepts about the world in general. (11)

Sensorimotor stage. A period in which babies learn how the world works by experiencing it through their own bodily sensations and muscle movements. (8)

Separation fear. An infant's distress at its caregiver's departure. (13)

Sexual selection. A theory of evolution proposing that traits can be selected through competition for mates and the preferences of mating partners. (2)

Shadow. An unconscious entity in Jungian theory that contains those aspects of the self which the person doesn't like and so represses. (7)

Sham feeding. A process in which a fistula is cut into the throat and a tube inserted so that everything eaten is diverted from the stomach. (9)

Shaping. Arranging the consequences so that desired behaviors are reinforced. (5)

Similarity principle. The observation that people tend to be attracted to those who have interests in common with them. (12)

Social cognition. The typical thought patterns that people engage in as they interact with others. (6)

Social cognitive approach. A model of personality proposing that behavior is driven by the individual's unique interpretation of a given situation. (14)

Social cognitive theory. The proposal that people construct their own lives by choosing for themselves which models to emulate and which to reject. (13)

Social comparison theory. The proposal that people evaluate their own opinions and abilities by comparing themselves to other people who are similar to them. (12)

Social exchange theory. The view that people enter into relationships in order to trade goods and services for mutual advantage. (12)

Social facilitation. The effect that the presence of others has on an individual's ability to perform a task. (12)

Social influence. The ways in which the social situation shapes a person's behavior. (12)

Social interest. Active engagement in meaningful relationships with others and a desire to make positive contributions to society. (7)

Social learning theory. The proposal that children learn strategies for dealing with the world by copying the behaviors of their parents. (13)

Social learning theory of personality. Rotter's account of individual differences as developing through divergent life histories. (14)

Social perception. The ways we make inferences about the motivations and intentions of those we interact with. (12)

Socratic ignorance. The argument that true wisdom comes from knowing the limits of one's knowledge. (1)

Socratic Method. The instructional technique of asking questions to guide students in a self-exploration of their own thoughts. (1)

Somatic marker hypothesis. The proposal that emotions play an essential role in everyday decision making. (16)

Somatosensory homunculus. A diagram illustrating how specific areas of the brain map onto specific body parts. (10)

Stage model of cognitive development. Piaget's theory that children's understanding of the world goes through a series of transformations as they reorganize their mental structures to adapt to new experiences. (8)

Stanford-Binet. The first successful English-language test of intelligence. (4)

Stevens' law. The observation that a power function best describes the relationship between physical stimuli and psychological sensation. (11)

Stimulus error. The error of describing the object of perception instead of the conscious experience of that object. (3)

Stimulus sampling theory. The proposal that stimulus-response associations are learned in a statistical, not absolute, manner. (5)

Strange Situation. A laboratory procedure designed to test an infant's attachment style in which the mother briefly leaves her child alone in an unfamiliar room. (13)

Stream of consciousness. A conception of the mind as a continuous, dynamic process. (4)

Striving for superiority. Adler's term for people's natural desire to improve themselves. (7)

Structuralism. An early school of psychology that sought to decompose consciousness into its component parts. (3)

Structure-of-intellect theory. The proposal that mental abilities could be organized in three dimensions, depending on the kinds of operations, contents, and products involved. (3)

Subconscious. A level of consciousness in which perceptions are experienced and behaviors are performed without being aware of them. (8)

Subjective well-being. The view that happiness is a person's overall assessment of life satisfaction. (15)

Subliminal consciousness. Cognitive processes occurring below the threshold of awareness. (4)

Superego. An internalization of social and moral rules. (7)

Superiority complex. A lifestyle dominated by a sense of being better than other people. (7)

Syllogism. A logical argument that uses deductive reasoning to reach a conclusion. (9)

Synchronicity. The idea that shared archetypes in the collective unconscious enable the occurrence of meaningful coincidences. (7)

Syndrome analysis. The process of breaking down higher cognitive functions into their component parts. (9)

Synesthesia. A perceptual phenomenon in which sensations from different modalities become automatically associated. (8)

Systematic introspection. A method of accurately reporting sensory experiences under carefully controlled experimental conditions. (3)

Tachistoscope. An instrument that displays images for precise durations of time. (6)

Teleology. An emphasis on the final result in a process as opposed to its initial conditions. (1)

Temperament. The behavioral profile that is present in the infant at birth. (13)

Texture gradient. A repeating pattern in the environment that conveys information about distance and relative size. (11)

Thematic Apperception Test. A projective personality test consisting of a series of ambiguous pictures that the subject is asked to describe. (14)

Theory of correspondent inferences. A normative description of the circumstances in which we should make personal rather than situational attributions about another's behavior. (12)

Theory of Forms. Plato's idea that the world as we experience it is but a poor reflection of the world as it truly is. (1)

Theory of psychosocial development. The proposal that all people pass through eight distinct stages that shape their sense of identity as they go through life. (15)

Theory of scales. The argument that scales of measurement should be categorized by the types of mathematical operations that can be performed on them. (11)

Think-aloud protocol. A laboratory procedure in which participants verbally reported their thought processes as they solved puzzles. (11)

Third force. A catchphrase indicating that humanistic psychology stood in opposition to both behaviorism and psychoanalysis. (15)

Three needs theory. The proposal that an individual's personality is shaped by the three basic needs of achievement, power, and affiliation, one of which will dominate. (14)

Three-step model of change. Lewin's process for reshaping the culture of a group by changing the attitudes and behaviors of its members. (6)

Tinbergen's four questions. A set of guidelines for interpreting observations of animal behavior. (10)

Tip-of-the-tongue phenomenon. The experience of knowing that you know a word without being able to name it. (13)

Trait. A stable internal characteristic of an individual that is a determinant of behavior. (14)

Trait theory. The proposal that personalities can be analyzed into a finite number of measurable traits. (14)

Transactional model of stress. The proposal that stress is moderated by cognitive appraisal of the situation. (16)

Transcendental idealism. Kant's contention that human experience consists solely of appearances and not of things in themselves. (1)

Transfer of training. The idea that learning in one subject will aid learning in a different subject. (4)

Transference. The placing of feelings for one person or object onto another. (5)

Transformational-generative grammar. A theory of sentence structure based on phrase-structure and transformational rules. (11)

Two-factor theory of emotion. The proposal that emotions consist of general physiological arousal and a cognitive evaluation based on the situation. (12)

Two-factor theory of intelligence. Spearman's proposal that any cognitive ability consists of both general intelligence common to all tasks and the specific intelligence required for that particular task. (14)

Two-point threshold. A measure of skin sensitivity in which two points are gradually brought closer together until they are experienced as a single point. (2)

Tyranny of the shoulds. Horney's term for the tension between the real and the ideal self. (7)

Unconditional positive regard. Complete acceptance and non-judgment of another person. (15)

Unconscious inference. Helmholtz's position that perception is a rational process of finding the best interpretation of the sensory input. (2)

Uniformitarianism. The idea that the Earth's geological features were formed gradually over hundreds of millions of years through uniform processes still occurring today. (2)

Variability hypothesis. The notion that men display more extremes in high and low intelligence, whereas women tend to cluster around average abilities. (4)

Verbal learning. A behavioral field of study that investigated the retention and recall of language-based materials such as word lists and word pairs. (5)

Vicarious trial and error. The hesitation that occurs when an organism is uncertain which choice to make. (5)

Visual cliff. An apparatus for testing depth perception consisting of a glass surface spanning a drop of several feet. (13)

Vivisection. The cutting open of a live animal to study the functioning of its internal organs. (9)

Vygotsky boom. A period in the 1980s and 1990s when both Western and Russian psychologists took a renewed interest in Vygotsky's theory of cognitive development. (9)

Weber's law. The finding that the just-noticeable difference is always a proportion of the original stimulus. (2)

Working memory. The ability to hold on to information while it is being used to complete a task. (16)

Yerkes-Dodson law. The observation that there is an optimal level of arousal, neither too high nor too low, for best performance on a complex task. (4)

Zeigarnik effect. The observation that the details of uncompleted tasks are better remembered than are those of completed tasks. (6)

Zeitgeist. German expression for "spirit of the times," referring to the currency of ideas in a given time period. (3)

Zone of proximal development. The difference between a child's actual and potential development. (9)

Person Glossary

Abraham, Karl. (1877–1925). German psychoanalyst who laid the groundwork for object-relations theory. (7)

Adler, Alfred. (1870–1937). Austrian psychologist who emphasized overcoming feelings of inferiority and maintaining active social interest as the keys to mental health. (7)

Ainsworth, Mary. (1913–1999). Canadian-American psychologist who developed the Strange Situation, a laboratory procedure for testing attachment style. (13)

Al-Kindi. (801–873). Islamic philosopher who tried to integrate Greek philosophy with Islamic theology. (1)

Allport, Floyd. (1890–1978). American psychologist who pioneered the experimental approach to social psychology. (14)

Allport, Gordon. (1897–1967). American psychologist who is recognized as the founder of modern personality psychology. (14)

Angell, James Rowland. (1869–1949). Early American psychologist who, with John Dewey, was one of the founders of the Chicago school of functionalism. (4)

Aristotle. (384–322 BCE). Ancient Greek philosopher who argued that all knowledge comes from experience. (1)

Aronson, Elliot. (Born 1932). American social psychologist who has used cognitive dissonance theory for the purpose of effecting positive social change. (12)

Asch, Solomon. (1907–1996). Polish-American social psychologist who studied conformity in a series of famous experiments. (12)

Averroes (1126–1198). Islamic philosopher who reintroduced Aristotelian philosophy to Europe. (1)

Avicenna (980–1037). Islamic philosopher who provided an influential thought experiment regarding the nature of self-awareness known as the "flying man" argument. (1)

Bacon, Francis. (1561–1626). English philosopher and the father of British empiricism who introduced the method of induction. (1)

Baldwin, James Mark. (1861–1934). Early American psychologist who was a pioneer in the fields of developmental and comparative psychology. (3)

Bandura, Albert. (Born 1925). Canadian-American psychologist best known for his Bobo doll experiments exploring the social learning of aggression in young children. (13)

Bartlett, Frederic. (1886–1969). Early twentieth-century British psychologist who argued for the reconstructive nature of memory. (11)

Beach, Frank. (1911–1988). American comparative psychologist who was instrumental in helping the European ethologists gain acceptance in North America. (10)

Bekhterev, Vladimir. (1857–1927). Russian neurologist who founded an approach to psychology known as reflexology based on the associated motor reflex. (9)

Berkeley, George. (1685–1753). Irish philosopher who did groundbreaking research on depth perception and promoted the philosophy of idealism. (1)

Bernal, Martha. (1931–2001). First Hispanic-American woman to earn a Ph.D. in psychology. (13)

Berscheid, Ellen. (Born 1936). American social psychologist who studies the dynamics of close interpersonal relationships. (12)

Binet, Alfred. (1857–1911). French psychologist who collaborated with Théodore Simon to produce the first reliable intelligence test. (8)

Blatz, William. (1895–1964). Canadian developmental psychologist noted for his security theory, which was a precursor to attachment theory. (13)

Boring, Edwin. (1886–1968). Early American psychologist who was a noted historian of psychology. (3)

Bower, Gordon. (Born 1932). American psychologist who developed influential mathematical and computational models of human learning and memory. (5)

Bowlby, John. (1907–1990). British psychologist who studied the impact of mother-child separation and proposed attachment theory to explain its effects. (13)

Brentano, Franz. (1838–1917). Austrian philosopher who advocated for a scientific approach to studying the mind that he called act psychology. (6)

Breuer, Josef. (1842–1925). Austrian neurologist who pioneered the use of the cathartic method to treat hysteria. (7)

Broadbent, Donald. (1926–1993). British psychologist who developed the filter model of attention. (11)

Brown, Roger. (1925–1997). American developmental psychologist who studied language acquisition in the early years of childhood. (13)

Bruner, Jerome. (1915–2016). American developmental psychologist who was one of the founders of the Cognitive Revolution. (11)

Bühler, Charlotte. (1893–1974). German developmental psychologist and one of the founders of the humanistic psychology movement. (15)

Burlingham, Dorothy. (1891–1979). American psychoanalyst and partner of Anna Freud who studied early childhood development. (7)

Burt, Cyril. (1883–1971). British psychologist who pioneered the use of twin studies to test the heritability of intelligence. (14)

Calkins, Mary. (1863–1930). Early American psychologist who is best known as the first female president of the APA. (4)

Cannon, Walter. (1871–1945). American physiological psychologist best known for his concepts of flight-or-flight and homeostasis. (10)

Carr, Harvey. (1873–1954). Early American psychologist who led the functionalist movement during its transition into behaviorism. (4)

Cattell, James McKeen. (1860–1944). Early American psychologist who brought experimental methods from Germany and pioneered the field of mental testing. (3)

Cattell, Raymond. (1905–1998). British-American psychologist who proposed an influential sixteen-factor model of personality. (14)

Charcot, Jean-Martin. (1825–1893). French neurologist who first described the symptoms and possible causes of hysteria. (8)

Chomsky, Noam. (Born 1928). American linguist who helped start the Cognitive Revolution by demonstrating that language cannot be learned through operant conditioning alone. (11)

Claparède, Édouard. (1873–1940). Swiss developmental psychologist who nurtured Piaget's career. (8)

Clark, Kenneth. (1914–2005). African American psychologist whose research was cited in the Supreme Court decision that declared segregation unconstitutional. (13)

Clark, Mamie. (1917–1983). African American psychologist who developed the doll studies that were cited by the Supreme Court regarding the need for school desegregation. (13)

Cronbach, Lee. (1916–2001). American educational psychologist noted for his contributions to psychological testing and measurement. (13)

Csikszentmihalyi, Mihaly. (Born 1934). Hungarian-American psychologist who is one of the founders of positive psychology and who discovered a kind of peak experience known as "flow." (15)

Damasio, Antonio. (Born 1944). Portuguese-American neuroscientist who proposed the somatic marker hypothesis. (16)

Darwin, Charles. (1809–1882). Nineteenth-century English scientist who proposed the theory of evolution by natural selection. (2)

Dembo, Tamara. (1902–1993). Russian-American psychologist who was a pioneer in the field of rehabilitation psychology. (6)

Descartes, René. (1596–1650). French philosopher who was one of the first thinkers of the early Modern Period to provide a detailed model of how the mind and body interact. (1)

Dewey, John. (1859–1952). Early American psychologist who, with James Rowland Angell, was one of the founders of the Chicago school of functionalism. (4)

Downey, June Etta. (1875–1932). American psychologist who was the first woman chair of a psychology department at a major university. (3)

Dweck, Carol. (Born 1946). American psychologist who maintains that people's attitudes about the nature of intelligence or willpower influence the amount of effort they put into difficult tasks. (15)

Ebbinghaus, Hermann. (1850–1909). Nineteenth-century German psychologist whose memory research demonstrated that higher mental processes could be studied using rigorous experimental methods. (2)

Ehrenfels, Christian v. (1859–1932). Austrian philosopher who introduced the concept of Gestalt quality. (6)

Ellis, Albert. (1913–2007). American psychologist best known as the founder of rational emotive behavior therapy. (15)

Erikson, Erik. (1902–1994). German-American psychologist who maintained that development is a lifelong process and proposed the eight stages of psychosocial development. (15)

Estes, William. (1919–2011). American psychologist who developed influential mathematical models of learning and memory. (5)

Eysenck, Hans. (1916–1997). German-British psychologist who advanced a three-factor theory of personality. (14)

Fechner, Gustav. (1801–1887). Nineteenth-century German scientist who founded the field of psychophysics. (2)

Festinger, Leon. (1919–1989). American social psychologist who developed social comparison theory and cognitive dissonance theory. (12)

Freud, Anna. (1895–1982). Austrian-British psychoanalyst who conducted pioneering research on early childhood development. (7)

Freud, Sigmund. (1856–1939). Austrian neurologist who developed the theory and therapy known as psychoanalysis. (7)

Frisch, Karl von. (1886–1982). Austrian ethologist noted for his work on perception and communication in bees. (10)

Galton, Francis. (1822–1911). Nineteenth-century English scientist who developed data gathering and analysis methods and who coined the term "nature and nurture." (2)

Gantt, Horsley. (1892–1980). American medical doctor who studied conditioned reflexes with Pavlov in Russia. (9)

Garcia, John. (1917–2012). First Hispanic-American psychologist and discoverer of conditioned taste aversion. (10)

Gazzaniga, Michael. (Born 1939). American neuroscientist whose work with split-brain patients has led to our understanding of hemispheric specialization in the brain. (16)

Gesell, Arnold. (1880–1961). Early American psychologist who measured developmental norms in infants and young children. (4)

Gibson, Eleanor. (1910–2002). American developmental psychologist who used the visual cliff procedure to test depth perception in human infants. (13)

Gibson, James. (1904–1979). American cognitive psychologist who developed the theory of direct perception. (11)

Gilligan, Carol. (Born 1936). American psychologist who challenged Kohlberg's theory of moral development for its neglect of the kinds of moral decisions that women face. (15)

Goldman-Rakic, Patricia. (1937–2003). American cognitive neuroscientist whose research on the prefrontal cortex in primates led to a better understanding of the neural substrates of working memory. (16)

Goldstein, Kurt. (1878–1965). German neurologist who coined the term self-actualization to describe the way an organism recovers after injury. (15)

Goodenough, Florence. (1886–1959). Early American developmental psychologist who pioneered field methods for studying children's behavior over time. (4)

Guilford, Joy Paul. (1897–1987). American psychologist who proposed the structure-of-intellect theory. (3)

Guthrie, Edwin. (1886–1959). American behaviorist who explained learning in terms of contiguity theory and the recency principle. (5)

Hall, G. Stanley. (1846–1924). Early American psychologist who pioneered developmental psychology. (4)

Harlow, Harry. (1905–1981). American comparative psychologist best known for his studies on the effects of social isolation in monkeys. (10)

Harrower, Molly. (1906–1999). British-American clinical psychologist best known for her study of Nazi personality. (6)

Hebb, Donald. (1904–1985). Canadian physiological psychologist who developed a highly influential theory of how learning takes place in the brain. (10)

Heider, Fritz. (1896–1988). German-American Gestalt psychologist who pioneered the field of social cognition with his attribution theory and balance theory. (6)

Helmholtz, Hermann von. (1821–1894). Nineteenth-century German scientist who made important contributions to the physiology of the nervous system and the senses. (2)

Hippocrates. (About 460–370 BCE). Greek physician who proposed a theory of personality based on four "humors" or bodily fluids. (14)

Hobbes, Thomas. (1583–1679). British philosopher who argued that the mind is nothing more than the product of a mechanical brain. (1)

Hollingworth, Leta. (1886–1939). Early American psychologist known for studies on the psychology of women and gifted children. (4)

Holt, Edwin. (1873–1946). Early twentieth-century American psychologist who proposed the motor theory of consciousness. (11)

Homskaya, Evgenia. (1929–2004). Russian neuropsychologist known for her studies on the role of the frontal lobes in regulating behavior. (9)

Horney, Karen. (1885–1952). German-American psychoanalyst who was a pioneer in feminist psychology. (7)

Howard, Ruth. (1900–1997). Second African-American woman to receive a Ph.D. in psychology. (4)

Hull, Clark. (1884–1952). American neo-behaviorist who emphasized the role of drives and motivation in learning. (5)

Hume, David. (1711–1776). Scottish philosopher who developed laws of mental association. (1)

Hypatia. (355–415 CE). Woman Greco-Roman philosopher who has become a symbol for the struggle between science and religion. (1)

Inhelder, Bärbel. (1913–1997). Swiss psychologist who discovered the formal operational stage in cognitive development. (8)

James, William. (1842–1910). Harvard philosopher who inspired the first generation of American psychologists. (4)

Janet, Pierre. (1859–1947). Clinical psychologist who became recognized as the father of French psychology. (8)

Jones, Edward. (1926–1993). American social psychologist who developed correspondent inference theory and discovered the correspondence bias. (12)

Jones, Mary Cover. (1896–1987). American developmental psychologist who pioneered behavior modification therapy. (5)

Jung, Carl. (1875–1961). Swiss psychologist noted for his theory of personality types and his idea of the collective unconscious. (7)

Kagan, Jerome. (Born 1929). American developmental psychologist who has argued for the role of temperament in the formation of attachment style in infancy and personality in adulthood. (13)

Kahneman, Daniel. (Born 1934). Israeli psychologist who won the Nobel Prize for his work on the heuristics and biases approach to judgment and decision making. (11)

Kant, Immanuel. (1724–1804). German philosopher who sought to reconcile the rationalist and empiricist approaches by arguing that knowledge is acquired through experience but ordered by innate rational processes. (1)

Kelley, Harold. (1921–2003). American social psychologist who played important roles in developing interdependence theory and attribution theory. (12)

Kelly, George. (1905–1967). American psychologist who proposed personal construct theory. (14)

Klein, Melanie. (1882–1960). Austrian-British psychoanalyst known for her development of object-relations theory. (7)

Koffka, Kurt. (1886–1941). German-American psychologist who introduced Gestalt theory to English-speaking psychologists. (6)

Kohlberg, Lawrence. (1927–1987). American psychologist who proposed an influential theory of moral development. (15)

Köhler, Wolfgang. (1887–1967). German-American Gestalt psychologist who studied intelligence and problem solving in chimpanzees. (6)

Külpe, Oswald. (1862–1915). Early student of Wundt who was one of the founders of experimental psychology in Germany. (3)

Kuo, Zing-Yang. (1898–1970). Chinese behaviorist who rejected the concept of instinct and maintained that development occurs through an interaction of nature and nurture. (5)

Ladd-Franklin, Christine. (1847–1930). Early American psychologist who developed the modern evolutionary theory of color vision. (2)

Lashley, Karl. (1890–1958). American physiological psychologist whose studies on how memories are formed in the brain led to his laws of equipotentiality and mass action. (10)

Lazarus, Richard. (1922–2002). American psychologist who developed the transactional model of stress. (16)

LeDoux, Joseph. (Born 1949). American neuroscientist who studies the brain mechanisms that are responsible for fearful memories. (16)

Leibniz, Gottfried. (1646–1716). German philosopher who argued for psychophysical parallelism as an alternative to Cartesian dualism. (1)

Leontiev, Alexei. (1903–1979). Russian developmental psychologist who revised Vygotsky's cultural-historical psychology into activity theory. (9)

Lewin, Kurt. (1890–1947). German-American Gestalt psychologist who was one of the founders of experimental social psychology. (6)

Likert, Rensis. (1903–1981). American social psychologist best known for inventing the five-point rating scale that now bears his name. (13)

Locke, John. (1632–1704). British empiricist philosopher who developed a mental philosophy known as associationism. (1)

Loftus, Elizabeth. (Born 1944). American psychologist who studies the unreliability of eyewitness testimony and personal memories. (11)

Lorenz, Konrad. (1903–1989). Austrian ethologist best known for his studies of imprinting in birds. (10)

Luria, Alexander. (1902–1977). Russian psychologist who was one of the pioneers in neuropsychology. (9)

Lyell, Charles. (1797–1875). Early nineteenth-century geologist who argued that the Earth was very old. (2)

Maccoby, Eleanor. (1917–2018). American developmental psychologist best known for her work on sex differences, gender identity, and parent-child relationships. (13)

Main, Mary. (Born 1943). American developmental psychologist who has constructed methods for assessing attachment style during the early school years, adolescence, and in adulthood. (13)

Maslow, Abraham. (1908–1970). American psychologist who proposed an influential theory of motivation that included a hierarchy of needs and the concept of self-actualization. (15)

May, Rollo. (1909–1994). American psychologist who developed a form of counseling known as existential psychotherapy. (15)

McClelland, David. (1917–1998). American psychologist best known for his "three needs" theory of personality. (14)

McDougall, William. (1871–1938). Early twentieth-century British psychologist and pioneer in social psychology. (11)

Meinong, Alexius. (1853–1920). Austrian philosopher who founded the Graz school of Gestalt psychology. (6)

Milgram, Stanley. (1933–1984). American social psychologist who conducted controversial experiments on obedience to authority. (12)

Mill, John Stuart. (1806–1873). British empiricist philosopher who declared that psychology was ready to become a natural science that could be used to improve individual lives and society as a whole. (1)

Miller, George. (1920–2012). American psychologist who led the Cognitive Revolution with his description of the mind as a limited-capacity information processor. (11)

Miller, Neal. (1909–2002). American learning theorist who sought to redefine Freudian concepts in behavioral terms. (5)

Milner, Brenda. (Born 1918). British-Canadian psychologist who studied memory in patients with brain damage. (10)

Milner, Peter. (1919–2018). British-Canadian psychologist who discovered the reward center in the brain along with James Olds. (16)

Mischel, Walter. (1930–2018). Austrian-American psychologist who advocated for a social cognitive approach to personality. (14)

Motora, Yujiro. (1858–1913). First Japanese psychologist to earn his doctorate at an American university. (4)

Münsterberg, Hugo. (1863–1916). Early German-American psychologist who was a pioneer in applied branches of psychology. (3)

Murphy, Gardner. (1895–1979). American social psychologist who advocated for a biosocial approach to personality. (12)

Murray, Henry. (1893–1988). American personality psychologist mostly known for his development of the Thematic Apperception Test. (14)

Neisser, Ulric. (1928–2012). German-born American cognitive psychologist who investigated the unreliability of flashbulb memories. (11)

Newcomb, Theodore. (1903–1984). American social psychologist who studied attitude formation and the acquaintance process through longitudinal field studies. (12)

Newell, Allen. (1927–1992). American psychologist who used computer simulations to study human problem solving. (11)

Nisbett, Richard. (Born 1941). American social psychologist known for his studies of cognition across cultures. (12)

Olds, James. (1922–1976). American psychologist who discovered the reward center in the brain along with Peter Milner. (16)

Panksepp, Jaak. (1943–2017). Estonian-American psychologist who founded the field of affective neuroscience. (16)

Pavlov, Ivan. (1849–1936). Russian physiologist who discovered the conditioned reflex. (9)

Pearson, Karl. (1857–1936). British statistician who developed the methods of correlation and regression. (2)

Penfield, Wilder. (1891–1976). Canadian neurosurgeon who mapped the somatosensory cortex. (10)

Piaget, Jean. (1896–1980). Swiss psychologist who developed a very influential theory of cognitive development. (8)

Plato. (427–347 BCE). Ancient Greek philosopher who argued that all knowledge comes from reason. (1)

Posner, Michael. (Born 1936). American cognitive neuroscientist who studies the biological basis of attention. (16)

Postman, Leo. (1918–2004). American cognitive psychologist who developed the interference theory of forgetting. (11)

Prosser, Inez. (1895–1934). First African American woman to earn a doctorate in psychology. (4)

Rank, Otto. (1884–1939). Austrian psychoanalyst who argued that the normal course of a human life is a process of growth. (15)

Rogers, Carl. (1902–1987). American psychologist who proposed client-centered therapy and founded the humanistic psychology movement. (15)

Rosenzweig, Mark. (1922–2009). American psychologist who discovered that neural plasticity continues even in adulthood. (16)

Ross, Lee. (Born 1942). American social psychologist who discovered the fundamental attribution error. (12)

Rotter, Julian. (1916–2014). American psychologist who developed the social learning theory of personality and the concept of locus of control. (14)

Rumelhart, David. (1942–2011). American psychologist who developed the parallel distributed processing model of perception. (11)

Schachter, Stanley. (1922–1997). American social psychologist who developed the two-factor theory of emotion. (12)

Sears, Robert. (1908–1989). American developmental psychologist who was a pioneer in social learning theory. (13)

Sechenov, Ivan. (1829–1905). Russian physiologist who argued that all behavior, no matter how complex, can be broken down into simple reflexes. (9)

Seligman, Martin. (Born 1942). American psychologist who is one of the founders of positive psychology and is best known for his research on learned helplessness. (15)

Sherif, Muzafer. (1906–1988). Turkish psychologist who studied the spread of social norms and the dynamics of intergroup conflict. (12)

Simon, Herbert. (1916–2001). American psychologist who studied decision making in humans and modeled those processes on computers. (11)

Simon, Théodore. (1872–1961). French psychologist who collaborated with Alfred Binet to produce the first reliable intelligence test. (8)

Skinner, Burrhus Frederic. (1904–1990). Prominent American psychologist who is best known for developing the methods of operant conditioning and for promoting radical behaviorism. (5)

Socrates. (469–399 BCE). Ancient Greek philosopher who was one of the first to turn philosophy toward questions about the nature of the mind. (1)

Solomon, Richard. (1918–1995). American comparative psychologist noted for his work on avoidance learning. (15)

Spearman, Charles. (1863–1945). British psychologist who developed the theory of general intelligence. (14)

Spence, Janet Taylor. (1923–2015). American clinical psychologist who was a leader in gender studies during the last half of the twentieth century. (5)

Spence, Kenneth. (1907–1967). American neo-behaviorist who was the major proponent of Hull's drive reduction theory. (5)

Sperry, Roger. (1913–1994). American psychologist who won the Nobel Prize for his research on split-brain patients. (10)

Spielrein, Sabina. (1885–1942). Russian psychoanalyst who made important contributions to the study of childhood development. (9)

Spinoza, Baruch. (1632–1677). Dutch philosopher who argued that mind and matter are but two aspects of the same underlying nature. (1)

Stern, William. (1871–1938). German psychologist who developed the concept of intelligence quotient, or IQ. (6)

Stevens, Stanley Smith. (1906–1973). American psychologist who developed the power law in psychophysics and an influential theory of scales of measurement. (11)

Strickland, Bonnie. (Born 1936). American psychologist who studied the mental health of persons and groups who are marginalized from mainstream society. (14)

Stumpf, Carl. (1848–1936). German philosopher who trained the first generation of Gestalt psychologists. (6)

Sumner, Francis Cecil. (1895–1954). First African American to earn a Ph.D. in psychology. (4)

Szemińska, Alina. (1907–1986). Polish psychologist who investigated the development of mathematical knowledge in children with Piaget. (8)

Taft, Jessie. (1882–1960). American social worker who developed an early form of client-centered psychotherapy known as relationship therapy. (15)

Terman, Lewis. (1877–1956). Early American psychologist who popularized the use of intelligence tests and performed landmark studies on gifted children. (4)

Thibaut, John. (1917–1986). American social psychologist who collaborated with Harold Kelley on interdependence theory and with Edward Jones on attribution theory. (12)

Thompson, Richard. (1930–2014). American behavioral neuroscientist who isolated the engram and demonstrated the role of the cerebellum in learning and memory. (16)

Thorndike, Edward. (1874–1949). Early American psychologist who pioneered learning theory and educational psychology. (4)

Thurstone, Louis Leon. (1887–1955). Early American psychologist who proposed that intelligence can be broken down into seven primary mental abilities. (4)

Tinbergen, Nikolaas. (1907–1988). Dutch ethologist best known for his field studies on the nature and function of instinctive behaviors. (10)

Titchener, Edward. (1867–1927). Early British-American psychologist who developed a school of experimental psychology known as structuralism. (3)

Tolman, Edward. (1886–1959). American neo-behaviorist who studied latent learning and cognitive maps in rats. (5)

Treisman, Anne. (1935–2018). British psychologist who proposed the attenuation model and the feature integration theory of attention. (11)

Tulving, Endel. (Born 1927). Estonian-Canadian psychologist who advocated for episodic memory as a separate memory system. (16)

Tversky, Amos. (1937–1996). Israeli psychologist who collaborated with Daniel Kahneman on the heuristics and biases approach. (11)

Vinh Bang. (1922–2008). Vietnamese psychologist who collaborated with Piaget and Inhelder for nearly half a century. (8)

Vygotsky, Lev. (1896–1934). Russian psychologist who emphasized the role of social interaction in cognitive development. (9)

Wallace, Alfred Russel. (1823–1913). Nineteenth-century British naturalist who was working on the problem of natural selection around the same time as Darwin. (2)

Washburn, Margaret. (1871–1939). Early American psychologist who was the first woman to earn a Ph.D. in psychology and a pioneer in animal research. (3)

Watson, John. (1878–1958). American psychologist best known as the founder of the behaviorist movement. (5)

Weber, Ernst. (1795–1878). German physiologist best known for his discovery that human sensory systems are limited in their ability to detect differences. (2)

Wertheimer, Max. (1880–1943). German-American psychologist who was the founder of Gestalt psychology. (6)

Witmer, Lightner. (1867–1956). Early American psychologist who pioneered the field of clinical psychology. (3)

Woodworth, Robert. (1869–1962). Early American psychologist whose dynamic psychology emphasized the role of motivation in behavior. (4)

Woolley, Helen Thompson. (1874–1947). Early American psychologist who made important contributions to the psychology of women and child development. (4)

Wundt, Wilhelm. (1832–1920). German physiologist who established the world's first psychology laboratory in 1879. (3)

Yerkes, Robert. (1876–1956). Early American psychologist who was a pioneer in the fields of comparative psychology and intelligence testing. (4)

Zajonc, Robert. (1923–2008). Polish-American social psychologist who explained social facilitation and discovered the mere exposure effect. (12)

Zeigarnik, Bluma. (1901–1988). Russian psychologist who studied memory for completed and uncompleted tasks. (6)

References

Abeckaser, D. A. (Producer), & Almereyda, M. (Director). (2015). *Experimenter* [Motion picture].

Abel, T. M. (1978). An experience during the last year of the life of E. B. Titchener. *American Psychologist, 33,* 767–777.

Ackerman, P. L. (2009). On weaving personality into a tapestry of traits. *British Journal of Psychology, 100,* 249–252.

Adair, J. G., & Huynh, C.-L. (2012). Internationalization of psychological research: Publications and collaborators of the United States and other leading countries. *International Perspectives in Psychology: Research, Practice, Consultation, 1,* 252–267.

Adler, H. E. (1993). William James and Gustav Fechner: From rejection to elective affinity. In M. E. Donnelly (Ed.), *Re-interpreting the legacy of William James* (pp. 253–261). Washington, DC: American Psychological Association.

Aghajanian, G., Bunney, B. S., & Holzman, P. S. (2003). Patricia Goldman-Rakic, 1937–2003. *Neuropsychopharmacology, 28,* 2218–2220.

Ainsworth, M. D. S. (1979). Infant-mother attachment. *American Psychologist, 34,* 932–937.

Ainsworth, M. D. S. (1992). John Bowlby (1907–1990). *American Psychologist, 47,* 668.

Ainsworth, M. D. S., & Bowlby, J. (1991). An ethological approach to personality development. *American Psychologist, 46,* 333–341.

Akhutina, T. V. (2003). L. S. Vygotsky and A. R. Luria: Foundations of neuropsychology. *Journal of Russian and East European Psychology, 41,* 159–190.

Aldhous, P. (2008). Free your mind and watch it grow. *New Scientist, 199*(2670), 44–45.

Alexander, I. E. (1982). The Freud-Jung relationship—the other side of Oedipus and countertransference: Some implications for psychoanalytic theory and psychotherapy. *American Psychologist, 37,* 1009–1018.

Alina Szeminska (1907–1986). (2011, December 14). *University of Geneva.* Retrieved from http://www.unige.ch/fapse/centenaire/personnes.html

Alina Szeminska. (n.d.). *University of Warsaw.* Retrieved from http://psych.uw.edu.pl/o-nas/historia/slawni-profesorowiezasluzeni-pracownicy/alina-szeminska/

Allen Newell. (1986). *American Psychologist, 41,* 347–353.

Almada, L. F., Pereira, A., Jr., & Carrara-Augustenborg, C. (2013). What affective neuroscience means for science of consciousness. *Mens Sana Monographs, 11,* 253–273.

Amann-Gainotti, M. (1992). Jean Piaget, student of Pierre Janet (Paris 1919–1921). *Perceptual and Motor Skills, 74,* 1011–1015.

American Psychological Foundation awards for 1980. (1981). *American Psychologist, 36,* 88–95.

Ames, P. C., & Riggio, R. E. (1995). Use of the Rotter incomplete sentences blank with adolescent populations: Implications for determining maladjustment. *Journal of Personality Assessment, 64,* 159–167.

Amsel, A. (1995). Kenneth Wartinbee Spence: 1907–1967. *Biographical Memoirs of the National Academy of Sciences, 66,* 334–351.

Anderson, J. R. (2001). Herbert A. Simon (1916–2001). *American Psychologist, 56,* 516–518.

Anderson, J. W. (2017). An interview with Henry A. Murray on his meeting with Sigmund Freud. *Psychoanalytic Psychology, 34,* 322–331.

Angell, J. R. (1936). James Rowland Angell. In C. Murchison (Ed.), *A history of psychology in autobiography* (Vol. III, pp. 1–38). Worcester, MA: Clark University Press.

Anne Treisman. (1991). *American Psychologist, 46,* 295–297.

Ansbacher, H. L. (2004). Adler—psychotherapy and Freud. *Journal of Individual Psychology, 60,* 333–337.

Araujo, S. de F. (2012). Why did Wundt abandon his early theory of the unconscious? Towards a new interpretation of Wundt's psychological project. *History of Psychology, 15,* 33–49.

Araujo, S. de F. (2014). The emergence and development of Bekhterev's psychoreflexology in relation to Wundt's experimental psychology. *Journal of the History of the Behavioral Sciences, 50,* 189–210.

Araujo, S. de F., & Marcellos, C. F. (2017). From classicism and idealism to scientific naturalism: Titchener's Oxford years and their impact upon his early intellectual development. *History of Psychology, 20,* 148–171.

Arievitch, I. M., & van der Veer, R. (2004). The role of nonautomatic processes in activity regulation: From Lipps to Galperin. *History of Psychology, 2,* 154–182.

Aristotle. *De anima (On the soul)* (J. A. Smith, Trans.). Retrieved from http://classics.mit.edu/Aristotle/soul.3.iii.html

Aristotle. (1999). *Nicomachean ethics* (W. D. Ross, Trans.). Kitchener, Ontario, Canada: Batoche Books.

Arnett, J. J., & Cravens, H. (2006). G. Stanley Hall's *Adolescence*: A centennial reappraisal: Introduction. *History of Psychology, 9,* 165–171.

Arnheim, R. (1985). The other Gustav Theodor Fechner. In S. Koch and D. E. Leary (Eds.), *A century of psychology as science* (pp. 856–865). Washington, DC: American Psychological Association.

Aronson, E. (1991). Leon Festinger and the art of audacity. *Psychological Science, 2,* 213–217.

Aronson, E. (1999). The power of self-persuasion. *American Psychologist, 54,* 875–883.

Aronson, E. (2007). Elliot Aronson. In G. Lindzey & W. M. Runyan (Eds.), *A history of psychology in autobiography* (Vol. IX, pp. 3–41). Washington, DC: American Psychological Association.

Aronson, E., Fried, C, & Stone, J. (1991). Overcoming denial and increasing the intention to use condoms through the induction of hypocrisy. *American Journal of Public Health, 81,* 1636–1638.

Aronson, E., & Linder, D. (1965). Gain and loss of esteem as determinants of interpersonal attractiveness. *Journal of Experimental Social Psychology, 1,* 156–171.

Aronson, E., & Mills, J. (1959). The effect of severity of initiation on liking for a group. *Journal of Abnormal and Social Psychology, 59,* 177–181.

Asch, S. E. (1968). Wolfgang Köhler: 1887–1967. *The American Journal of Psychology, 81,* 110–119.

Ash, M. G. (1992). Cultural contexts and scientific change in psychology: Kurt Lewin in Iowa. *American Psychologist, 47,* 198–207.

Ashton, M. C., & Lee, K. (2007). Empirical, theoretical, and practical advantages of the HEXACO model of personality structure. *Personality and Social Psychology Review, 11,* 150–166.

Astor, J. (2003). [Review of the book *Complete Correspondence of Sigmund Freud and Karl Abraham* by E. Falzeder]. *Journal of Analytical Psychology, 48,* 513–521.

Averill, J. R. (1993). William James's other theory of emotion. In M. E. Donnelly (Ed.), *Reinterpreting the legacy of William James* (pp. 221–229). Washington, DC: American Psychological Association.

Awards for distinguished scientific contributions: John Garcia. (1980). *American Psychologist, 35,* 37–43.

Backe, A. (2001). John Dewey and early Chicago functionalism. *History of Psychology, 4,* 323–340.

Bacon, F. (1620/2007). *The new organon: Or true directions concerning the interpretation of nature* (J. Bennett, Trans.). Retrieved from http://www.earlymoderntexts.com/assets/pdfs/bacon1620.pdf

Bacopoulos-Viau, A. (2012). Automatism, surrealism and the making of French psychopathology: The case of Pierre Janet. *History of Psychology, 23,* 259–276.

Bahrick, H. P. (1985). Associationism and the Ebbinghaus legacy. *Journal of Experimental Psychology: Learning, Memory, and Cognition, 11,* 439–443.

Baker, D. B. (1988). The psychology of Lightner Witmer. *Professional School Psychology, 3,* 109–121.

Balance, D. G., & Bringmann, W. G. (1987). Fechner's mysterious malady. *History of Psychology Newsletter, 19* (1–2), 36–47.

Baldwin, J. M. (1921). In memory of Wilhelm Wundt by his American students. *Psychological Review, 28*(3), 153–188.

Bandura, A. (1989). Human agency in social cognitive theory. *American Psychologist, 44,* 1175–1184.

Bandura, A. (2007). Albert Bandura. In G. Lindzey & W. M. Runyan (Eds.), *A history of psychology in autobiography* (Vol. IX, pp. 43–75). Washington, DC: American Psychological Association.

Bandura, A., Ross, D., & Ross, S. A. (1961). Transmission of aggression through imitation of aggressive models. *Journal of Abnormal and Social Psychology, 63,* 575–582.

Bandura, A., Ross, D., & Ross, S. A. (1963). Vicarious reinforcement and imitative learning. *Journal of Abnormal and Social Psychology, 67,* 601–607.

Barenbaum, N. B. (2000). How social was personality? The Allports' "connection" of social and personality psychology. *Journal of the History of the Behavioral Sciences, 36,* 471–487.

Bargal, D. (1998). Kurt Lewin and the first attempts to establish a department of psychology at the Hebrew University. *Minerva, 36,* 49–68.

Barone, D. F. (1994). Pioneers in psychology: John Dewey resurrected. *The General Psychologist, 30,* 58–66.

Barrett-Lennard, G. (2012). The Roosevelt years: Crucial milieu for Carl Rogers' innovation. *History of Psychology, 15,* 19–32.

Bartlett, F. C. (1960). Karl Spencer Lashley: 1890–1958. *Biographical Memoirs of Fellows of the Royal Society, 5,* 107–118.

Barton-Bellessa, S. M., Lee, J., & Shon, P. (2015). Correcting misconceptions about Alfred Adler's psychological theory of crime in introductory criminology textbooks: Moving Alder's theory of crime forward. *Journal of Individual Psychology, 71,* 34–57.

Bateson, P. (1990). Konrad Lorenz (1903–1989). *American Psychologist, 45,* 65–66.

Baudry, M., & Swanson, L. W. (2011). RF Thompson: A bridge between 20th and 21st century neuroscience. *Neurobiology of Learning and Memory, 95,* 103–104.

Baumeister, A. A. (2006). Serendipity and the cerebral localization of pleasure. *Journal of the History of the Neurosciences, 15,* 92–98.

Beach, F. A. (1959). Clark Leonard Hull, 1884–1952. *Biographical Memoirs of the National Academy of Sciences, 33,* 125–141.

Beach, F. A. (1961). Karl Spencer Lashley (1890–1958). *Biographical Memoirs of the National Academy of Sciences, 35,* 163–204.

Beach, F. A. (1987). Donald Olding Hebb (1904–1985). *American Psychologist, 42,* 186–187.

Beard, K. S. (2015). Theoretically speaking: Csikszentmihalyi on flow theory development and its usefulness in addressing contemporary challenges in education. *Educational Psychology Review, 27,* 353–364.

Beatty, B. (1998). From laws of learning to a science of values. *American Psychologist, 53,* 1145–1152.

Beauvais, C. (2016). Ages and ages: The multiplication of children's 'ages' in early twentieth-century child psychology. *History of Education, 45,* 304–318.

Beck, H. P., Levinson, S., & Irons, G. (2009). Finding Little Albert: A journey to John B. Watson's infant laboratory. *American Psychologist, 64,* 604–614.

Behar, M. (2008, January). Paging Dr. Fear. *Popular Science,* 50–55, 82.

Beilin, H. (1992). Piaget's enduring contribution to developmental psychology. *Developmental Psychology, 28,* 191–204.

Belardinelli, M. O. (2012). The debt of cognitive science to Ulric Neisser. *Cognitive Processes, 13,* 189–191.

Benjamin, L. T., Jr., & Crouse, E. M. (2002). The American Psychological Association's response to *Brown v. Board of Education:* The case of Kenneth B. Clark. *American Psychologist, 57,* 38–50.

Benjamin, L. T., Jr. (2006). Hugo Münsterberg's attack on the application of scientific psychology. *Journal of Applied Psychology, 91,* 414–425.

Benjamin, L. T., Jr. (2008, November). America's first black female psychologist. *Monitor on Psychology*, 20–21.

Benjamin, L. T., Jr., Durkin, M., Link, M., Vestal, M., & Acord, J. (1992). Wundt's American doctoral students. *American Psychologist*, 47, 123–131.

Benjamin, L. T., Jr., & Nielsen-Gammon, E. (1999). B. F. Skinner and psychotechnology: The case of the heir conditioner. *Review of General Psychology*, 3, 155–167.

Benjamin, L. T., Jr., Whitaker, J. L., Ramsey, R. M., & Zeve, D. R. (2007). John B. Watson's alleged sex research: An appraisal of the evidence. *American Psychologist*, 62, 131–139.

Benzaquén, S. A. (2001). Kamala of Midnapore and Arnold Gesell's *Wolf Child and Human Child*: Reconciling the extraordinary with the normal. *History of Psychology*, 4, 59–78.

Berkeley, G. (1709/2002). *An essay towards a new theory of vision.* [Annotated by D. R. Wilkins.] Retrieved from: http://www.maths.tcd.ie/~dwilkins/Berkeley/Vision/1709A/Vision.pdf

Berkeley, G. (1710/2002). *A treatise concerning the principles of human knowledge.* [Annotated by D. R. Wilkins.] Retrieved from http://www.maths.tcd.ie/~dwilkins/Berkeley/HumanKnowledge/1734/HumKno.pdf

Berlucchi, G. (2006). Revisiting the 1981 Nobel Prize to Roger Sperry, David Hubel, and Torsten Wiesel on the occasion of the centennial of the prize to Golgi and Cajal. *Journal of the History of the Neurosciences, 15*, 369–375.

Berscheid, E. (2003). Lessons in "greatness" from Kurt Lewin's life and works. In R. J. Sternberg (Ed.), *The anatomy of impact: What makes the great works of psychology great* (pp. 109–123). Washington, DC: American Psychological Association.

Berscheid, E. (2003). On stepping on land mines. In R. J. Sternberg (Ed.), *Psychologists defying the crowd: Stories of those who battled the establishment and won* (pp. 33–44). Washington, DC: American Psychological Association.

Bigelow, K. M., & Morris, E. K. (2001). John B. Watson's advice on child rearing: Some historical context. *Behavioral Development Bulletin, 1*, 26–30.

Billig, M. (2015). Kurt Lewin's leadership studies and his legacy to social psychology: Is there nothing as practical as a good theory? *Journal for the Theory of Social Behaviour, 45*, 440–460.

Birchard, K. (2011, November 1). "Nosy" and observant, a neuroscientist continues her memorable career at 93. *Chronicle of Higher Education*, p. A26.

Blowers, G. H. (2001). "To be a big shot or to be shot": Zing-Yang Kuo's other career. *History of Psychology, 4*, 367–387.

Bodrova, E., Leong, D. J., & Akhutina, T. V. (2011). When everything new is well-forgotten old: Vygotsky/Luria insights in the development of executive functions. In R. M. Lerner, J. V. Lerner, E. P. Bowers, S. Lewin-Bizan, S. Gestsdottir, & J. B. Urban (Eds.), Thriving in childhood and adolescence: The role of self-regulation processes. *New Directions for Child and Adolescent Development, 133*, 11–28.

Bogousslavsky, J., Walusinkski, O., & Veyrunes, D. (2009). Crime, hysteria and *belle époque* hypnotism: The path traced by Jean-Martin Charcot and Georges Gilles de la Tourette. *European Neurology, 62*, 193–199.

Bonnie R. Strickland: Award for distinguished contributions to the public interest. (1999). *American Psychologist, 54*, 950–952.

Booth, C. (2013, December). The myth of Hypatia. *Ancient Egypt*, 43–47.

Borck, C. (2005). Writing brains: Tracing the psyche with the graphical method. *History of Psychology, 8*, 79–94.

Borck, C. (2016). How we may think: Imaging and writing technologies across the history of the neurosciences. *Studies in History and Philosophy of Biological and Biomedical Sciences, 57*, 112–120.

Boring, E. G. (1952). Edwin Garrigues Boring. In E. G. Boring, H. Werner, H. S. Langfeld, & R. M. Yerkes (Eds.), *A history of psychology in autobiography* (Vol. IV, pp. 27–52). Worcester, MA: Clark University Press.

Bovaira, F., & Augustin, A. (Producers), & Amenábar, A. (Director). (2009). *Agora* [Motion picture]. Spain: Focus Features.

Bower, G. H. (2007). Gordon H. Bower. In G. Lindzey & W. M. Runyan (Eds.), *A history of psychology in autobiography* (Vol. IX, pp. 77–113). Washington, DC: American Psychological Association.

Bower, G. H. (2008). The evolution of a cognitive psychologist: A journey from simple behaviors to complex mental acts. *Annual Review of Psychology, 59*, 1–27.

Bower, G. H. (2011). Neal E. Miller. *Proceedings of the American Philosophical Society, 155*, 356–365.

Brainerd, C. J. (1996). Piaget: A centennial celebration. *Psychological Science, 7*, 191–195.

Brannigan, A. (2013). Stanley Milgram's obedience experiments: A report card 50 years later. *Society, 50*, 623–628.

Bretherton, I., & Main, M. (2000). Mary Dinsmore Salter Ainsworth (1913–1999). *American Psychologist, 55*, 1148–1149.

Bretherton, I. (1992). The origins of attachment theory: John Bowlby and Mary Ainsworth. *Developmental Psychology, 28*, 759–775.

Brigandt, I. (2005). The instinct concept of the early Konrad Lorenz. *Journal of the History of Biology, 38*, 571–608.

Bringmann, W. G., & Early, C. E. (2000). Ebbinghaus, Hermann. In A. E. Kazdin (Ed.), *Encyclopedia of psychology* (Vol. 3, pp. 124–128). Washington, DC: American Psychological Association.

Bringmann, W. G., Bringmann, M. W., & Early, C. E. (1992). G. Stanley Hall and the history of psychology. *American Psychologist, 47*, 281–289.

Brinkmann, S. (2006). Damasio on mind and emotions: A conceptual critique. *Nordic Psychology, 58*, 366–380.

Broadbent, D. E. (1980). Donald E. Broadbent. In G. Lindzey (Ed.), *A history of psychology in autobiography* (pp. 38–73). San Francisco, CA: W. H. Freeman & Co.

Brooks-Gunn, J., & Johnson, A. D. (2006). G. Stanley Hall's contribution to science, practice and policy: The child study, parent education, and child welfare movements. *History of Psychology, 9*, 247–258.

Brown, D. R. (2005). Leo Joseph Postman (1918–2005). *American Psychologist, 60*, 191–192.

Brown, E. M. (2003). Pierre Janet and *Félida Artificielle*: Multiple personality in a nineteenth-century guise. *Journal of History of the Behavioral Sciences, 39*, 279–288.

Brown, R. (1989). Roger Brown. In G. Lindzey (Ed.), *A history of psychology in autobiography* (Vol. VIII, pp. 36–60). Palo Alto, CA: Stanford University Press.

Brown, R., & McNeill, D. (1966). The "tip of the tongue" phenomenon. *Journal of Verbal Learning and Verbal Behavior, 5*, 325–337.

Bruce, D. (2001). Fifty years since Lashley's "In search of the engram": Refutations and conjectures. *Journal of the History of the Neurosciences, 10*, 308–318.

Bruner, J. (1992). Another look at New Look 1. *American Psychologist, 47*, 780–783.

Bruner, J. S. (1980). Jerome S. Bruner. In G. Lindzey (Ed.), *A history of psychology in autobiography* (Vol. VII, pp. 75–151). San Francisco, CA: W. H. Freeman & Co.

Bruner, J. S., & Goodman, C. S. (1947). Value and need as organizing factors in perception. *Journal of Abnormal and Social Psychology, 42*, 33–44.

Bruner, J. S., & Postman, L. (1949). On the perception of incongruity: A paradigm. *Journal of Personality, 18*, 206–223.

Buchanan, R. D. (2011). The controversial Hans Eysenck. *The Psychologist, 24*, 318–319.

Bugental, J. F. T. (1996). Rollo May (1909–1994). *American Psychologist, 51*, 418–419.

Bühler, K.-E., & Heim, G. (2011). Etiology, pathogenesis, and therapy according to Pierre Janet concerning conversion disorders and dissociative disorders. *American Journal of Psychotherapy, 65*, 281–309.

Burghardt, G. M. (2009). Darwin's legacy to comparative psychology and ethology. *American Psychologist, 64*, 102–110.

Burkholder, E. O., & Peláez, M. (2000, Spring). A behavioral interpretation of Vygotsky's theory of thought, language, and culture. *Behavioral Development Bulletin, 9*, 7–9.

Burman, J. T. (2012). Jean Piaget: Images of a life and his factory. *History of Psychology, 15*, 283–288.

Burman, J. T., Guida, A., & Nicolas, S. (2015). Hearing the inaudible experimental subject: Echoes of Inaudi, Binet's calculating prodigy. *History of Psychology, 18*, 47–68.

Burnes, B. (2004). Kurt Lewin and complexity theories: Back to the future? *Journal of Change Management, 4*, 309–325.

Burnstein, E. (2009). Robert B. Zajonc (1923–2008). *American Psychologist, 64*, 558–559.

Buss, D. M. (2009). The great struggles of life: Darwin and the emergence of evolutionary psychology. *American Psychologist, 64*, 140–148.

Butler, B. E., & Petrulis, J. (1999). Some further observations concerning Sir Cyril Burt. *British Journal of Psychology, 90*, 155–160.

Byford, A. (2016). V. M. Bekhterev in Russian child science, 1900s–1920s: "Objective psychology"/"reflexology" as a scientific movement. *Journal of the History of the Behavioral Sciences, 52*, 99–123.

Cahan, E. D. (1984). The genetic psychologies of James Mark Baldwin and Jean Piaget. *Developmental Psychology, 20*, 128–135.

Cahan, E. D. (1992). John Dewey and human development. *Developmental Psychology, 28*, 205–214.

Cairns, R. B. (1994). The making of a developmental science: The contributions and intellectual heritage of James Mark Baldwin. In R. D. Parke, P. A. Ornstein, J. J. Rieser, & C. Zahn-Waxler (Eds.), *A century of developmental psychology* (pp. 127–143). Washington, DC: American Psychological Association.

Calkins, M. W. (1930). Mary Whiton Calkins. In C. Murchison (Ed.), *A history of psychology in autobiography* (Vol. 1, pp. 31–62). Worcester, MA: Clark University Press.

Carey, B. (2009, August 12). Mark Rosenzweig, 86, brain researcher. *New York Times*, A22.

Carey, B. (2017, May 15). Brenda Milner, eminent brain scientist, is "still nosy" at 98. *New York Times*. Retrieved from https://www.nytimes.com/2017/05/15/science/brenda-milner-brain-cognitive-neuroscience.html

Carmichael, L. (1957). Robert Mearns Yerkes: 1876–1956. *Psychological Review, 64*, 1–7.

Carol S. Dweck: Award for distinguished scientific contributions. (2011). *American Psychologist, 66*, 658–660.

Carr, H., & Watson, J. B. (1908). Orientation in the white rat. *Journal of Neurology and Psychology, 18*, 27–44.

Carroy, J., & Plas, R. (2000). How Pierre Janet used pathological psychology to save the philosophical self. *Journal of the History of the Behavioral Sciences, 36*, 231–240.

Carson, J. (2014). Mental testing in the early twentieth century: Internationalizing the mental testing story. *History of Psychology, 17*, 249–255.

Carter, D. (2011). Carl Jung in the twenty-first century. *Contemporary Review, 293*, 441–451.

Catania, A. C. (1992). B. F. Skinner, organism. *American Psychologist, 11*, 1521–1530.

Cattell, R. B. (1974). Raymond B. Cattell. In G. Lindzey (Ed.), *A history of psychology in autobiography* (Vol. VI, pp. 61–100). Englewood Cliffs, NJ: Prentice-Hall.

Caudle, F. (2003). Eleanor Jack Gibson (1910–2002). *American Psychologist, 58*, 1090–1091.

Cerami, C. (2012). [Review of the book *Al-Kindi* by P. Adamson]. *Aestimatio, 9*, 294–299.

Chalmers, D. (2014). How do you explain consciousness? *TED*. Retrieved from https://www.ted.com/talks/david_chalmers_how_do_you_explain_consciousness

Chaplin, J. P. (2000). Functionalism. In A. E. Kazdin (Ed.), *Encyclopedia of psychology* (Vol. 3, pp. 416–419). Washington, DC: American Psychological Association.

Chavoushi, S. H., Ghabili, K., Kazemi, A., Aslanabadi, A., Babapour, S., Ahmedli, R., & Golzari, S. E. (2012). Surgery for gynecomastia in the Islamic Golden Age: Al-Tasrif of Al-Zahrawi (936–1013 AD). *International Scholarly Research Network: Surgery, 2012,* 934965.

Cherry, F., Unger, R., & Winston, A. S. (2010). Gender, ethnicity, and career trajectories: A comment on Woodward. *History of Psychology, 15,* 181–187.

Chiesa, M. (1992). Radical behaviorism and scientific frameworks: From mechanistic to relational accounts. *American Psychologist, 47,* 1287–1299.

Chomsky, N. (1957). *Syntactic structures.* The Hague, Netherlands: Mouton.

Chomsky, N. (1959). A review of B. F. Skinner's *Verbal Behavior. Language, 35,* 26–58.

Christensen, A.-L., & Caetano, C. (1996). Alexander Romanovich Luria (1902–1977): Contributions to neuropsychological rehabilitation. *Neuropsychological Rehabilitation, 6,* 279–303.

Cicciola, E., Foschi, R., & Lombardo, G. P. (2014). Making up intelligence scales: De Sanctis's and Binet's tests, 1905 and after. *History of Psychology, 17,* 223–236.

Clark, A. J., & Butler, C. M. (2012). Degree of activity: Relationship to early recollections and safeguarding tendencies. *Journal of Individual Psychology, 68,* 136–147.

Clark, D. O. (2005). From philosopher to psychologist: The early career of Edwin Ray Guthrie, Jr. *History of Psychology, 8,* 235–254.

Coghlan, D., & Brannick, T. (2003). Kurt Lewin: The "practical theorist" for the 21st century. *Irish Journal of Management, 24*(2), 31–37.

Cohler, B. J., & Galatzer-Levy, R. M. (2008). Freud, Anna, and the problem of female sexuality. *Psychoanalytical Inquiry, 28,* 3–26.

Colangelo, N. (1997). The "Termites" grow up and grow old. *PsycCRITIQUES, 42,* 208–209.

Cole, M. (1978). Alexander Romanovich Luria: 1902–1977. *The American Journal of Psychology, 91,* 349–352.

Cole, M. (1979). Introduction. In A. Luria, *The making of mind: A personal account of Soviet psychology.* Cambridge, MA: Harvard University Press.

Cole, M. (2002). Alexander Luria, cultural psychology, and the resolution of the crisis in psychology. *Journal of Russian and East European Psychology, 40,* 4–16.

Coleman, S. R. (2010). Edwin Ray Guthrie. *American National Biography.* doi:10.1093/anb/9780198606697.article.1400249

Collins, A. (2006). The embodiment of reconciliation: Order and change in the work of Frederick Bartlett. *History of Psychology, 9,* 290–312.

Comrey, A. L. (1993). Joy Paul Guilford: 1897–1987. *Biographical Memoirs of the National Academy of Sciences, 62,* 199–209.

Converse, P. E. (1994). Theodore Mead Newcomb, 1903–1984. *Biographical Memoirs of the National Academy of Sciences, 64,* 320–339.

Coons, E. E. (2002). Neal Elgar Miller (1909–2002). *American Psychologist, 57,* 784–786.

Coons, E. E. (2014). Neal E. Miller: 1909–2002. *Biographical Memoirs of the National Academy of Sciences,* 1–25.

Cooper-White, P. (2015). "The power that beautifies and destroys": Sabina Spielrein and "Destruction as a cause of coming into being." *Pastoral Psychology, 64,* 259–278.

Corbett, M. (2015). From law to folklore: Work stress and the Yerkes-Dodson law. *Journal of Managerial Psychology, 30,* 741–752.

Corrington, R. S. (1987). Hermeneutics and psychopathology: Jaspers and Hillman. *Theoretical and Philosophical Psychology, 7,* 70–80.

Costall, A. (1992). Why British psychology is not social: Frederic Bartlett's promotion of the new academic discipline. *Canadian Psychology/Psychologie Canadienne, 33,* 633–639.

Craik, F., & Baddeley, A. (1995). Donald E. Broadbent (1926–1993). *American Psychologist, 50,* 302–303.

Crandall, C. S., Silvia, P. J., N'Gbala, A. N., Tsang, J., & Dawson, K. (2007). Balance theory, unit relations, and attribution: The underlying integrity of Heiderian theory. *Review of General Psychology, 11,* 12–30.

Croce, P. J. (2010). Reaching beyond Uncle William: A century of William James in theory and in life. *History of Psychology, 13,* 351–377.

Cromwell, H. C. (2018). In memoriam: Jaak Panksepp (1943–2017). *American Psychologist, 73,* 202.

Cronbach, L. J., Hastorf, A. H., Hilgard, E. R., & Maccoby, E. E. (1990). Robert R. Sears (1908–1990). *American Psychologist, 45,* 663–664.

Crosby, D. A., & Viney, W. (1993). Toward a psychology that is radically empirical: Recapturing the vision of William James. In M. E. Donnelly (Ed.), *Reinterpreting the legacy of William James* (pp. 101–117). Washington, DC: American Psychological Association.

Crowther-Heyck, H. (1999). George A. Miller, language, and the computer metaphor of mind. *History of Psychology, 2,* 37–64.

Csikszentmihalyi, M. (1999). If we are so rich, why aren't we happy? *American Psychologist, 54,* 821–827.

Cutting, J. E. (2012). Ulric Neisser (1928–2012). *American Psychologist, 67,* 492.

D'Souza, J., & Gurin, M. (2016). The universal significance of Maslow's concept of self-actualization. *The Humanistic Psychologist, 44,* 210–214.

Daly, J. C., & Canetto, S. S. (2006, Summer). Bärbel Inhelder: A distinguished developmental psychologist (1913–1997). *The Feminist Psychologist, 7.*

Damianova, M. K., & Sullivan, G. B. (2011). Rereading Vygotsky's theses on types of internalization and verbal mediation. *Review of General Psychology, 15,* 344–350.

Damjanovic, A., Milovanovic, S. D., & Trajanovic, N. N. (2015). Descartes and his peculiar sleep pattern. *Journal of the History of the Neurosciences, 24,* 396–407.

Darwin, C. (1859/2002). *On the origin of species by means of natural selection.* London, England: John Murray. Retrieved from http://darwin-online.org.uk/converted/pdf/1859_Origin_F373.pdf

Davidson, T. L., & Riley, A. L. (2015). Taste, sickness, and learning. *American Scientist, 103,* 204–211.

Davis, H. B. (2006). [Review of *Sabina Spielrein: Forgotten Pioneer of Psychoanalysis* by C. Covington & B. Wharton (Eds.)]. *Psychologist-Psychoanalyst*, *26*, 49–52.

Davis, K. L., & Montag, C. (2019). Selected principles of Pankseppian affective neuroscience. *Frontiers in Neuroscience*, *12*, 1025.

Davis, M. F., & Mattoon, M. A. (2006). Reliability and validity of the Gray-Wheelwrights Jungian type survey. *European Journal of Psychological Assessment*, *22*, 233–239.

De Haan, H. J. (2010). Origins and import of reinforcing self-stimulation of the brain. *Journal of the History of the Neurosciences*, *19*, 24–32.

De Kock, L. (2014). Voluntarism in early psychology: The case of Hermann von Helmholtz. *History of Psychology*, *17*, 105–128.

De Rivera, J. (1995). Tamara Dembo (1902–1993). *American Psychologist*, *50*, 386.

De Vecchi, N. (2003). The place of Gestalt psychology in the making of Hayek's thought. *History of Political Economy*, *35*, 135–162.

Deaux, K. (2016). Janet Taylor Spence (1923–2015). *American Psychologist*, *71*, 73–74.

DeCarvalho, R. J. (1990). Who coined the term humanistic psychology? *The Humanistic Psychologist*, *18*, 350–351.

DeCarvalho, R. J. (1991). The humanistic paradigm in education. *The Humanistic Psychologist*, *19*, 88–104.

DeCarvalho, R. J. (1999). Otto Rank, the Rankian circle in Philadelphia, and the origins of Carl Rogers' person-centered psychotherapy. *History of Psychology*, *2*, 132–148.

DeGree, C. E., & Snyder, C. R. (1985). Alder's psychology (of use) today: Personal history of traumatic life events as a self-handicapping strategy. *Journal of Personality and Social Psychology*, *48*, 1512–1519.

Delgado, F. (2012). The neurosciences in Averroes' "Principles of Medicine." *Annals of Saudi Medicine*, *32*, 327–331.

Delprato, D. J., & Midgley, B. D. (1992). Some fundamentals of B. F. Skinner's behaviorism. *American Psychologist*, *47*, 1507–1520.

Denis, M. (2008). Prof. Michael I. Posner, first recipient of the Mattei Doan Foundation Prize in Psychological Science. *International Journal of Psychology*, *43*, 997–1002.

DeRobertis, E. M. (2006). Charlotte Bühler's existential-humanistic contributions to child and adolescent psychology. *Journal of Humanistic Psychology*, *46*, 48–76.

Descartes, R. (1641/1911). *Meditations on first philosophy*. Retrieved from http://selfpace.uconn.edu/class/percep/DescartesMeditations.pdf

Descartes, R. (1664/1972). *Treatise on man* (T. S. Hall, Trans.). New York, NY: Prometheus.

Dewsbury, D. A. (1990). Nikolaas Tinbergen (1907–1988). *American Psychologist*, *45*, 67–68.

Dewsbury, D. A. (1993). William James and instinct theory revisited. In M. E. Donnelly (Ed.), *Reinterpreting the legacy of William James* (pp. 263–291). Washington, DC: American Psychological Association.

Dewsbury, D. A. (1997). In celebration of the centennial of Ivan P. Pavlov's (1897/1902) *The Work of the Digestion Glands*. *American Psychologist*, *52*, 933–935.

Dewsbury, D. A. (1999, Summer). Molly Harrower (1906–1999). *Psychology of Women*, 24–27.

Dewsbury, D. A. (2000). Molly Harrower (1906–1999). *American Psychologist*, *55*, 1058.

Dewsbury, D. A. (2002). Constructing representations of Karl Spencer Lashley. *Journal of the History of the Behavioral Sciences*, *38*, 225–245.

Dewsbury, D. A. (2009). Charles Darwin and psychology at the bicentennial and sesquicentennial. *American Psychologist*, *64*, 67–74.

Diamond, S. (1998). Francis Galton and American psychology. In R. W. Rieber & K. Salzinger (Eds.), *Psychology: Theoretical-historical perspectives* (2nd ed., pp. 88–99). Washington, DC: American Psychological Association.

Dickerson, C, Thibodeau, R., Aronson, E., & Miller, D. (1992). Using cognitive dissonance to encourage water conservation. *Journal of Applied Social Psychology*, *22*, 841–854.

Diehl, L. A. (1986). The paradox of G. Stanley Hall: Foe of coeducation and educator of women. *American Psychologist*, *41*, 868–878.

Digdon, N. (2017, January 26). The Little Albert controversy: Intuition, confirmation bias, and logic. *History of Psychology*. doi:10.1037/hop0000055

Digman, J. M. (1990). Personality structure: Emergence of the five-factor model. *Annual Review of Psychology*, *41*, 417–440.

Dinsmoor, J. A. (1992). Setting the record straight: The social views of B. F. Skinner. *American Psychologist*, *11*, 1454–1463.

Dionnet, S. (2009, February 14). Vinh Bang (1922–2008). *Jean Piaget Society*. Retrieved from http://www.piaget.org/news/bang-obit.html

Doherty, B. (2015). Cyril and Hypatia: Tracing the contours of an anti-Christian myth. *Phronema*, *30*, 63–90.

Donaldson, G. (1998). Between practice and theory: Melanie Klein, Anna Freud and the development of child analysis. *Journal of the History of the Behavioral Sciences*, *32*, 160–176.

Donaldson, G. (2000). Klein, Melanie. In A. E. Kazdin (Ed.), *Encyclopedia of psychology* (Vol. 4, pp. 446–447). Washington, DC: American Psychological Association.

Dorahy, M. J., & van der Hart, O. (2006). Fact or fable? Did Janet really come to repudiate his dissociation theory? *Journal of Trauma & Dissociation*, *7*, 29–37.

Douvan, E. (1986). Theodore M. Newcomb (1903–1984). *American Psychologist*, *41*, 1380–1381.

Douvan, E. (1997). Erik Erikson: Critical times, critical theory. *Child Psychiatry and Human Development*, *28*, 15–20.

Duarte, S. (2009). Ideas and confusion in Leibniz. *British Journal for the History of Philosophy*, *17*, 705–733.

Dunn, D. S. (2011). Situations matter: Teaching the Lewinian link between social psychology and rehabilitation psychology. *History of Psychology*, *14*, 405–411.

Eberle, S. G. (2017). In memoriam: Jaak Panksepp. *American Journal of Play*, *9*, 406–409;

Eckhardt, M. H. (2005). Karen Horney: A portrait. *The American Journal of Psychoanalysis*, *65*, 95–101.

Ekman, P., & Campos, J. (2003). Richard Stanley Lazarus (1922–2002). *American Psychologist, 58*, 756–757.

Eleanor E. Maccoby. (1989). *American Psychologist, 44*, 621–623.

Eleanor Emmons Maccoby. (1996). *American Psychologist, 51*, 757–759.

Elizabeth F. Loftus. (2003). *American Psychologist, 58*, 864–873.

Emde, R. N. (1992). Individual meaning and increasing complexity: Contributions of Sigmund Freud and René Spitz to developmental psychology. *Developmental Psychology, 28*, 347–359.

Epstein, S. (1979). Explorations in personality today and tomorrow: A tribute to Henry A. Murray. *American Psychologist, 34*, 649–653.

Epstein, W. (1991). Helmholtz: The original cognitive scientist. *Contemporary Psychology, 36*, 669–670.

Erneling, C. E. (2014). The importance of Jean Piaget. *Philosophy of the Social Sciences, 44*, 522–535.

Estes, W. K. (1989). William K. Estes. In G. Lindzey (Ed.), *A history of psychology in autobiography* (Vol. VIII, pp. 94–124). Palo Alto, CA: Stanford University Press.

Eysenck, H. J. (1980). Hans Jürgen Eysenck. In G. Lindzey (Ed.). *A history of psychology in autobiography* (Vol. VII, pp. 153–187). San Francisco, CA: W. H. Freeman & Co.

Faber, D. P. (1997). Jean-Martin Charcot and the epilepsy/hysteria relationship. *Journal of the History of the Neurosciences, 6*, 275–290.

Fagan, T. K. (1996). Witmer's contributions to school psychological services. *American Psychologist, 51*, 241–243.

Fallon, D. (1992). An existential look at B. F. Skinner. *American Psychologist, 47*, 1433–1440.

Fancher, R. E. (2000). Leibniz, Gottfried Wilhelm. In A. E. Kazdin (Ed.), *Encyclopedia of psychology* (Vol. 5, pp. 42–44). Washington, DC: American Psychological Association.

Fancher, R. E. (2004). The concept of race in the life and thought of Francis Galton. In A. S. Winston (Ed.), *Defining difference: Race and racism in the history of psychology* (pp. 49–75). Washington, DC: American Psychological Association.

Fancher, R. E. (2009). Scientific cousins: The relationship between Charles Darwin and Francis Galton. *American Psychologist, 64*, 84–92.

Farley, F. (2000). Hans J. Eysenck (1916–1997). *American Psychologist, 55*, 674–675.

Festinger, L. (1950). Informal social communication. *Psychological Review, 57*, 271–282.

Festinger, L. (1954). A theory of social comparison processes. *Human Relations, 7*, 117–140.

Festinger, L. (1957). *A theory of cognitive dissonance*. Stanford, CA: Stanford University Press.

Festinger, L., & Carlsmith, J. M. (1959). Cognitive consequences of forced compliance. *Journal of Abnormal and Social Psychology, 58*, 203–210.

Festinger, L., Riecken, H., & Schachter, S. (1956). *When prophecy fails*. London, England: Pinter & Martin.

Fischer, K. W., & Hencke, R. W. (1996). Infants' construction of actions in context: Piaget's contribution to research on early development. *Psychological Science, 7*, 204–210.

Fitzgerald, M. (2017). Why did Sigmund Freud refuse to see Pierre Janet? Origins of psychoanalysis: Janet, Freud, or both? *History of Psychiatry, 28*, 358–364.

Flavell, J. H. (1996). Piaget's legacy. *Psychological Science, 7*, 200–203.

Fowler, R. D. (1990). In memoriam: Burrhus Frederic Skinner, 1904–1990. *American Psychologist, 45*, 1203–1204.

Fox, M. (2008, December 6). Robert Zajonc, who looked at mind's ties to actions, is dead at 85. *New York Times*. Retrieved from http://www.nytimes.com/2008/12/07/education/07zajonc.html?_r=0

Foy, M. R., & Foy, J. G. (2016). The search for the engram in eyeblink conditioning: A synopsis of past and present perspectives on the role of the cerebellum. *Behavioral Neuroscience, 130*, 547–552.

Frauenglass, M. H., & Diaz, R. M. (1985). Self-regulatory functions of children's private speech: A critical analysis of recent challenges to Vygotsky's theory. *Developmental Psychology, 21*, 357–364.

Freud, S. (1900). *The interpretation of dreams*. Retrieved from https://www.sigmundfreud.net

Freud, S. (1905). *Three essays on the theory of sexuality*. Retrieved from https://www.sigmundfreud.net

Freud, S. (1923). *The ego and the id*. Retrieved from https://www.sigmundfreud.net

Fuchs, A. H. (2012). William Kaye Estes (1919–2011). *The American Journal of Psychology, 125*, 233–235.

Furumoto, L. (1992). Joining separate spheres—Christine Ladd-Franklin, woman scientist (1847–1930). *American Psychologist, 47*, 175–182.

Furumoto, L. (1995). Christine Ladd-Franklin's color theory: Strategy for claiming scientific authority. In H. E. Adler & R. W. Rieber (Eds.), *Aspects of the history of psychology in America: 1892–1992* (pp. 91–100). Washington, DC: American Psychological Association.

Furumoto, L. (1998). Lucy May Boring (1886–1996). *American Psychologist, 53*, 59.

Fuster, J. M. (2004). Patricia Shoer Goldman-Rakic (1937–2003). *American Psychologist, 59*, 559–560.

Galef, B. G., Jr. (1998). Edward Thorndike: Revolutionary psychologist, ambiguous biologist. *American Psychologist, 10*, 1128–1134.

Garcia, J. (1981). Tilting at the paper mills of academe. *American Psychologist, 36*, 149–158.

Garcia, J. (1997). Tolman: Creative surges and dubious second thoughts. *PsycCRITIQUES, 42*, 285–291.

Garcia, J. (2003). Psychology is not an enclave. In R. J. Sternberg (Ed.), *Psychologists defying the crowd: Stories of those who battled the establishment and won* (pp. 67–77). Washington, DC: American Psychological Association.

García, L. N. (2016). Before the "boom": Readings and uses of Vygotsky in Argentina (1935–1974). *History of Psychology, 19*, 298–313.

Gardner, H. (2017). Jerome Seymour Bruner. *Proceedings of the American Philosophical Society, 161*, 354–361.

Garrison, D. (1981). Karen Horney and feminism. *Signs, 6*, 672–691.

Gazzaniga, M. (2006). Leon Festinger: Lunch with Leon. *Perspectives on Psychological Science, 1*, 88–94.

Gelfand, T. (2000). Neurologist or psychiatrist? The public and private domains of Jean-Martin Charcot. *Journal of the History of the Behavioral Sciences, 36*, 215–229.

Gewirtz, J. L. (2001). J. B. Watson's approach to learning: Why Pavlov? Why not Thorndike? *Behavioral Development Bulletin, 1*, 23–25.

Ghassemzadeh, H., Posner, M. I., & Rothbart, M. K. (2013). Contributions of Hebb and Vygotsky to an integrated science of the mind. *Journal of the History of the Neurosciences, 22*, 292–306.

Gibby, R. E., & Zickar, M. J. (2008). A history of the early days of personality testing in American industry: An obsession with adjustment. *History of Psychology, 11*, 164–184.

Gibson, E. J. (1980). Eleanor J. Gibson. In G. Lindzey (Ed.), *A history of psychology in autobiography* (Vol. VII, pp. 239–271). San Francisco, CA: W. H. Freeman & Co.

Gibson, E. J., & Walk, R. D. (1960, April). The "visual cliff." *Scientific American, 202*, 64–71.

Gibson, J. J. (1950). *The perception of the visual world.* Boston, MA: Houghton Mifflin.

Gibson, J. J. (1966). *The senses considered as perceptual systems.* Boston, MA: Houghton Mifflin.

Gibson, J. J. (1967). James J. Gibson. In E. G. Boring & G. Lindzey (Eds.), *A history of psychology in autobiography* (Vol. V, pp. 125–143). East Norwalk, CT: Appleton–Century-Crofts.

Gibson, J. J. (1979). *The ecological approach to visual perception.* Boston, MA: Houghton Mifflin.

Gibson, J. J., & Gibson, E. J. (1955). Perceptual learning: Differentiation or enrichment? *Psychological Review, 62*, 32–41.

Gilbert, D. (1998). Speeding with Ned: A personal view of the correspondence bias. In J. Darley & J. Cooper (Eds.), *Attribution and social interaction: The legacy of Edward E. Jones* (pp. 5–66). Washington, DC: American Psychological Association.

Gilbert, D., & Lindzey, G. (1994). Edward E. Jones (1926–1993). *American Psychologist, 49*, 756–757.

Gildersleeve, M. (2014). Unconcealing Jung's transcendent function with Heidegger. *The Humanistic Psychologist, 43*, 297–309.

Gleitman, H., Rozin, P., & Sabini, J. (1997). Solomon E. Asch (1907–1996). *American Psychologist, 52*, 984–985.

Glickman, S. E., & Zucker, I. (1989). Frank A. Beach (1911–1988). *American Psychologist, 44*, 1234–1235.

Glozman, J. M., & Tupper, D. E. (2006). Obituary—Evgenia Davydovna Homskaya. *Neuropsychology Review, 16*, 95–98.

Gluck, J. P. (1997). Harry F. Harlow and animal research: Reflection on the ethical paradox. *Ethics & Behavior, 7*, 149–161.

Gluck, M. (2011). Remembering William K. Estes. *APS Observer.* Retrieved from https://www.psychologicalscience.org/observer/remembering-william-k-estes

Gold Medal Award for Life Achievement in Psychology in the Public Interest. (2014). *American Psychologist, 69*, 474–476.

Gold Medal Award for Life Achievement in the Science of Psychology. (2010). *American Psychologist, 65*, 379–381.

Goldberg, M. F. (2000). An interview with Carol Gilligan: Restoring lost voices. *The Phi Delta Kappan, 81*(9), 701–74.

González Rey, F. L. (2014). Advancing further the history of Soviet psychology: Moving forward from dominant representations in Western and Soviet psychology. *History of Psychology, 17*, 60–78.

Goodman, E. (1979, December). Margaret Floy Washburn: 'A complete psychologist.' *APA Monitor*, 3–4.

Goodwin, C. J. (2005). Reorganizing the Experimentalists: The origins of the Society of Experimental Psychologists. *History of Psychology, 8*, 347–361.

Gordon H. Bower. (1980). *American Psychologist, 35*, 31–37.

Gottlieb, G. (1972). Zing-Yang Kuo: Radical scientific philosopher and innovative experimentalist (1898–1970). *Journal of Comparative and Physiological Psychology, 80*, 1–10.

Graebner, W. (2006). "Back-fire to lust": G. Stanley Hall, sex-segregated schooling, and the engine of sublimation. *History of Psychology, 9*, 236–246.

Graham, C. H. (1967). Robert Sessions Woodworth: 1869–1962. *Biographical Memoirs of the National Academy of Sciences, 39*, 541–572.

Grant, H. (2009). Who's Hypatia? Whose Hypatia do you mean? *Math Horizons, 16*(4), 11–15.

Green, C. D. (1998). The thoroughly modern Aristotle: Was he really a functionalist? *History of Psychology, 1*, 8–20.

Green, C. D. (2009). Darwinian theory, functionalism, and the first American psychological revolution. *American Psychologist, 64*, 75–83.

Green, C. D. (2015). Why psychology isn't unified, and probably never will be. *Review of General Psychology, 19*, 207–214.

Greenberg, G. (2016, September). Zing Yang Kuo (Part 1). *Behavioral Neuroscientist and Comparative Psychologist*, 5–13.

Greenwood, J. D. (2003). Wundt, *Völkerpsychologie*, and experimental social psychology. *History of Psychology, 6*, 70–88.

Gregory, R. L. (1982). Images of thought. *Contemporary Psychology, 27*, 760–763.

Gruber, H. E. (1998). Bärbel Inhelder (1913–1997). *American Psychologist, 53*, 1221–1222.

Grünbaum, A. (1992). Freud's theory: The perspective of a philosopher of science. In R. B. Miller (Ed.), *The restoration of dialogue: Readings in the philosophy of clinical psychology* (pp. 366–387). Washington, DC: American Psychological Association.

Grünbaum, A. (2006). Is Sigmund Freud's psychoanalytic edifice relevant to the 21st century? *Psychoanalytic Psychology, 23*, 257–284.

Grundlach, H. (2014). Max Wertheimer, *Habilitation* candidate at the Frankfurt psychological institute. *History of Psychology, 17*, 134–148.

Grusec, J. E. (1992). Social learning theory and developmental psychology: The legacies of Robert Sears and Albert Bandura. *Developmental Psychology, 28*, 776–786.

Gudan, E. (2008). Karen Horney and personal vocation. *The Catholic Social Science Review, 13*, 117–127.

Guest, H. S. (2014). Maslow's hierarchy of needs—the sixth level. *The Psychologist, 27*, 982–983.

Guilford, J. P. (1957). Louis Leon Thurstone: 1887–1955. *Biographical Memoirs of the National Academy of Sciences, 30*, 349–382.

Guilford, J. P. (1967). Joy Paul Guilford. In E. Boring & G. Lindzey (Eds.), *A history of psychology in autobiography* (Vol. V, pp. 167–191). East Norwalk, CT: Appleton-Century-Crofts.

Gupta, S. (2013). Q&As with Carol S. Dweck. *Proceedings of the National Academy of Sciences, 110*, 14818.

Guski-Leinwand, S. (2009). Becoming a science: The loss of the scientific approach of *Völkerpsychologie*. *Zeitschrift für Psychologie/Journal of Psychology, 217*, 79–84.

Guthrie, R. V. (2000). Sumner, Francis Cecil. In A. E. Kazdin (Ed.), *Encyclopedia of psychology* (Vol. 7, pp. 515–516). Washington, DC: American Psychological Association.

Habib, R. (2009). Introduction to the special issue on episodic memory and the brain. *Neuropsychologia, 47*, 2155–2157.

Hagen, M. A. (1985). James J. Gibson's ecological approach to visual perception. In S. Koch & D. E. Leary (Eds.), *A century of psychology as a science* (pp. 231–249). Washington, DC: American Psychological Association.

Haggbloom, S. J., Warnick, R., Warnick, J. E., Jones, V. K., Yarbrough, G. L., Russell, T. M., . . . & Monte, E. (2002). The 100 most eminent psychologists of the 20th century. *Review of General Psychology, 6*, 139–152.

Hakkarainen, P. (2013). The methodological crisis in Russian (and Western) psychology. *Journal of Russian and East European Psychology, 51*, 3–6.

Harlow, H. F. (1958). The nature of love. *American Psychologist, 13*, 673–685.

Harrell, A. M., & Stahl, M. J. (1981). A behavioral decision theory approach for measuring McClelland's trichotomy of needs. *Journal of Applied Psychology, 66*, 242–247.

Harris, B. (2011). Arnold Gesell's progressive vision: Child hygiene, socialism and eugenics. *History of Psychology, 14*, 311–334.

Harrower, M. (1978). A. R. Luria: A personal remembrance. *American Psychologist, 33*, 767.

Harrower-Erickson, M. R. (1942). Kurt Koffka: 1886–1941. *The American Journal of Psychology, 55*, 278–281.

Hart, M. J. (2017). A modest classical compatibilism. *Disputatio: International Journal of Philosophy, 9*, 265–285.

Hartley, E. L. (1980). Gardner Murphy (1895–1979). *American Psychologist, 35*, 383–385.

Harvey, A. M. (1995). W. Horsley Gantt—A legend in his time. *Integrative Physiological and Behavioral Science, 30*, 237–243.

Harvey, O. J. (1989). Muzafer Sherif (1906–1988). *American Psychologist, 44*, 1325–1326.

Harzem, P. (2001). The intellectual dismissal of John B. Watson: Notes on a dark cloud in the history of the psychological sciences. *Behavioral Development Bulletin, 1*, 15–16.

Haste, H., & Gardner, H. (2017). Jerome S. Bruner (1915–2016). *American Psychologist, 72*,707–708.

Hayes, R. L. (1994). The legacy of Lawrence Kohlberg: Implications for counseling and human development. *Journal of Counseling & Development, 72*, 261–267.

Hazin, I., & da Rocha Falcão, J. T. (2014). Luria's neuropsychology in the 21st century: Contributions, advancements, and challenges. *Psychology & Neuroscience, 7*, 433–434.

Healy, A. F., Gluck, M. A., Nosofsky, R. M., & Shiffrin, R. M. (2012). William K. Estes (1919–2011). *American Psychologist, 67*, 570–571.

Hebb, D. O. (1980). D. O. Hebb. In G. Lindzey (Ed.), *A history of psychology in autobiography* (Vol. VII, pp. 273–303). San Francisco, CA: W. H. Freeman & Co.

Hegarty, P. (2007). From genius to gendered intelligence: Lewis Terman and the power of the norm. *History of Psychology, 10*, 132–155.

Heider, F. (1967). On social cognition. *American Psychologist, 22*, 25–31.

Heider, F. (1989). Fritz Heider. In G. A. Lindzey (Ed.), *A history of psychology in autobiography* (Vol. VIII, pp. 126–155). Palo Alto, CA: Stanford University Press.

Hein, R. (2018). June Downey: Scientist, scholar and poet. *WyoHistory. org*. Retrieved from https://www.wyohistory.org/encyclopedia/june-downey-scientist-scholar-and-poet

Held, L. (2010). Ruth Howard. *Psychology's Feminist Voices.* Retrieved from https://www.feministvoices.com/ruth-howard/

Henle, M. (1978, October). One man against the Nazis—Wolfgang Köhler. *American Psychologist, 33*, 939–944.

Henriques, G. (2013). Evolving from methodological to conceptual unification. *Review of General Psychology, 17*, 168–173.

Hess, U., & Thibault, P. (2009). Darwin and emotion expression. *American Psychologist, 64*, 120–128.

Hewstone, M., & Jaspars, J. (1987). Covariation and causal attribution: A logical model of the intuitive analysis of variance. *Journal of Personality and Social Psychology, 53*, 663–672.

Hilgard, E. R. (1948). *Theories of learning.* East Norwalk, CT: Appleton-Century-Crofts.

Hilgard, E. R. (1965). Robert Mearns Yerkes, 1876–1956. *Biographical Memoirs of the National Academy of Sciences, 38*, 385–425.

Hilgard, E. R. (1967). Kenneth Wartinbee Spence: 1907–1967. *The American Journal of Psychology, 80*, 314–318.

Hilgard, E. R. (1986). Edwin Garrigues Boring (1886–1968): In memoriam. *APA Division 26, Society for the History of Psychology*, 93–96.

Hillier, H. C. (2017). Ibn Rushd (Averroes). *Internet Encyclopedia of Philosophy*. Retrieved from http://www.iep.utm.edu/ibnrushd/

Hirsch, P. (2005). Apostle of freedom: Alfred Adler and his British disciples. *History of Education, 34*, 473–481.

Hochberg, J. (1994). James Jerome Gibson: 1904–1979. *Biographical Memoirs of the National Academy of Sciences, 63*, 150–171.

Hodgson, S. (2004, Fall). Tamara Dembo (1902–1993): A life of science and service. *The Feminist Psychologist*, 14–16.

Hogan, J. D., & Broudy, M. S. (2000, Spring). June Etta Downey (1875–1932). *The Feminist Psychologist, 27*. Retrieved from https://www.apadivisions.org/division-35/about/heritage/june-downey-biography

Holden, C. (1977). Carl Rogers: Giving people permission to be themselves. *Science, 198*, 31–35.

Holland, J. G. (1992). B. F. Skinner (1904–1990). *American Psychologist, 47*, 665–667.

Honeycutt, H. (2011). The "enduring mission" of Zing-Yang Kuo to eliminate the nature-nurture dichotomy in psychology. *Developmental Psychobiology, 53*, 331–342.

Hopkins, J. R. (1995). Erik Homburger Erikson (1902–1994). *American Psychologist, 50*, 796–797.

Horn, J. (2001). Raymond Bernard Cattell (1905–1998). *American Psychologist, 56*, 71–72.

Horowitz, F. D. (1992). John B. Watson's legacy: Learning and environment. *Developmental Psychology, 28*, 360–367.

Horton, A. M., Jr. (1987). Luria's contributions to clinical and behavioral neuropsychology. *Neuropsychology, 1987*, 39–44.

Hovland, C. I. (1952). Clark Leonard Hull, 1884–1952. *Psychological Review, 59*, 347–350.

Howard, G. S. (1998). Aristotle, teleology, and modern psychology. *Theoretical & Philosophical Psychology, 10*, 31–38.

Hull, C. L. (1952). Clark L. Hull. In E. G. Boring, H. Werner, H. S. Langfeld, & R. M. Yerkes (Eds.), *A history of psychology in autobiography* (Vol. IV, pp. 143–162). Worcester, MA: Clark University Press.

Hume, D. (1739/1896). *A treatise of human nature*. Oxford, England: Clarendon Press. Retrieved from https://people.rit.edu/wlrgsh/Hume Treatise.pdf

Hume, D. (1748). *An enquiry concerning human understanding*. Retrieved from http://socserv2.socsci.mcmaster.ca/econ/ugcm/3ll3/hume/enquiry.pdf

Hunt, J. (2018). Psychological perspectives on the Garden of Eden and the fall in light of the work of Melanie Klein and Eric *Pastoral Psychology, 67*, 33–41.

Hunt, J. M. (1992). Joy Paul Guilford: 1897–1987. *The American Journal of Psychology, 105*, 115–118.

Hunter, W. S. (1951). James Rowland Angell, 1869–1949. *Biographical Memoirs of the National Academy of Sciences, 26*, 191–208.

Hyman, C. (2002, December 4). Richard Lazarus, UC Berkeley psychology faculty member and influential researcher, dies at 80. *Campus News*. Retrieved from https://www.berkeley.edu/news/media/releases/2002/12/04_lazarus.html

Inhelder, B. (1989). Bärbel Inhelder. In G. Lindzey (Ed.), *A history of psychology in autobiography* (Vol. VIII, pp. 208–243). Palo Alto, CA: Stanford University Press.

Innis, N. K. (2000). Tolman, Edward Chace. In A. E. Kazdin (Ed.), *Encyclopedia of psychology* (Vol. 8, pp. 92–94). Washington, DC: American Psychological Association.

Interview with Michael Gazzaniga. (2011). *Annals of the New York Academy of Sciences, 1224*, 1–8.

Ireland, M. E., & Pennebaker, J. W. (2010). Language style matching in writing: Synchrony in essays, correspondence, and poetry. *Journal of Personality and Social Research, 99*, 549–571.

Ivan Pavlov: Biographical. (1967). *Nobel Lectures, Physiology or Medicine 1901–1921*. Amsterdam, Netherlands: Elsevier. Retrieved from http://www.nobelprize.org/nobel_prizes/medicine/laureates/1904/pavlov-bio.html

Iversen, I. H. (1992). Skinner's early research: From reflexology to operant conditioning. *American Psychologist, 47*, 1318–1328.

Jahoda, G. (2000). Piaget and Lévy-Bruhl. *History of Psychology, 3*, 218–238.

Janet Taylor Spence, PhD: 1984 APA President. (2019). *American Psychological Association*. Retrieved from https://www.apa.org/about/governance/president/bio-janet-spence

Jensen, A. R. (1991, Fall). IQ and science: The mysterious Burt affair. *Public Interest, 105*, 93–106.

John, O. P., Angleitner, A., & Ostendorf, F. (1988). The lexical approach to personality: A historical review of the trait taxonomic research. *European Journal of Personality, 2*, 171–203.

John, O. P., Naumann, L. P., & Soto, C. J. (2008). Paradigm shift to the integrative Big-Five trait taxonomy: History, measurement, and conceptual issues. In O. P. John, R. W. Robins, & L. A. Pervin (Eds.), *Handbook of personality: Theory and research* (pp. 114–158). New York, NY: Guilford Press.

Johnson, A. (2015). Florence Goodenough and child study: The question of mothers as researchers. *History of Psychology, 18*, 183–195.

Johnson, D. F. (1997, Winter) Margaret Floy Washburn. *APA Division 35, Society for the Psychology of Women*, 17–18.

Johnson, S. (2004). Antonio Damasio's theory of thinking faster and faster. *Discover, 25*(5), 44–49.

Jones, E. E. (1979). The rocky road from acts to dispositions. *American Psychologist, 34*, 107–117.

Jones, E. E., & Harris, V. A. (1967). The attribution of attitudes. *Journal of Experimental Social Psychology, 3*, 1–24.

Jones, E., Kelley, H., & Schopler, J. (1987). John Walter Thibaut (1917–1986). *American Psychologist, 42*, 874–875.

Jones, J. M., & Pettigrew, T. F. (2005). Kenneth B. Clark (1914–2005). *American Psychologist, 60*, 649–651.

Jones, M. C. (1974). Albert, Peter, and John B. Watson. *American Psychologist, 29*, 581–583.

Jones, R. A. (1987). Psychology, history, and the press: The case of William McDougall and *The New York Times*. *American Psychologist, 42,* 931–940.

Jorati, J. (2019). Gottfried Leibniz: Philosophy of mind. *Internet Encyclopedia of Philosophy.* Retrieved from http://www.iep.utm.edu/lei-mind/

Joseph E. LeDoux: Award for distinguished scientific contributions. (2010). *American Psychologist, 65,* 707–709.

Josephs, L. (2015). How children learn about sex: A cross-species and cross-cultural analysis. *Archives of Sexual Behavior, 44,* 1059–1069.

Josephs, L., Katzander, N., & Goncharova, A. (2018). Imagining parental sexuality: The experimental study of Freud's primal scene. *Psychoanalytic Psychology, 35,* 106–114.

Joyce, N. (2009, March). In search of the Nazi personality. *Monitor on Psychology,* 18–19.

Julian B. Rotter. (1989, April). *American Psychologist,* 625–626.

Kagan, J. (1999). Roger William Brown, 1925–1997. *Biographical Memoirs of the National Academy of Sciences, 77,* 20–33.

Kagan, J. (2003). An unwilling rebel. In R. J. Sternberg (Ed.), *Psychologists defying the crowd: Stories of those who battled the establishment and won* (pp. 91–103). Washington, DC: American Psychological Association.

Kagan, J. (2007). Jerome Kagan. In G. Lindzey & W. M. Runyan (Eds.), *A history of psychology in autobiography* (Vol. XI, pp. 115–153). Washington, DC: American Psychological Association.

Kagan, J. (2009). Historical selection. *Review of General Psychology, 13,* 77–88.

Kagan, J., & Snidman, N. (1991). Temperamental factors in human development. *American Psychologist, 46,* 856–862.

Kahneman, D. (2002). Daniel Kahneman: Biographical. *The Nobel Prize.* Retrieved from https://www.nobelprize.org/prizes/economics/2002/kahneman/auto-biography

Kahneman, D. (2011). *Thinking, fast and slow.* New York, NY: Farrar, Straus and Giroux.

Kahneman, D., & Shafir, E. (1998). Amos Tversky (1937–1996). *American Psychologist, 53,* 793–794.

Kahneman, D., & Tversky, A. (1979). Prospect theory: An analysis of decision under risk. *Econometrica, 47,* 263–292.

Kant, I. (1781/2017). *Critique of pure reason* (J. Bennett, Trans.). Retrieved from https://www.earlymoderntexts.com/assets/pdfs/kant1781part1.pdf

Karpov, Y. (2007). Alexander R. Luria: His life and work. *The American Journal of Psychology, 120,* 153–159.

Karpov, Y. V., & Haywood, H. C. (1998). Two ways to elaborate Vygotsky's concept of mediation: Implications for instruction. *American Psychologist, 53,* 27–36.

Karrel, A., & Gill, J. (2002). A comparison of Alfred Adler's and Heinz Kohut's conceptions of psychopathology. *Journal of Individual Psychology, 58,* 160–168.

Katona, G. (2002). The evolution of the concept of psyche from Homer to Aristotle. *Journal of Theoretical and Philosophical Psychology, 22,* 28–44.

Katz, D. (1979). Floyd H. Allport (1890–1978). *American Psychologist, 34,* 351–353.

Keele, S. W., & Mayr, U. (2005). A tribute to Michael I. Posner. In U. Mayr, E. Awh, & S. W. Keele (Eds.), *Developing individuality in the human brain: A tribute to Michael I. Posner* (pp. 3–16). Washington, DC: American Psychological Association.

Kelcourse, F. (2015). Sabina Spielrein from Rostov to Zürich: The making of an analyst. *Pastoral Psychology, 64,* 241–258.

Kemp, S. (1998). Medieval theories of mental representation. *History of Psychology, 1,* 275–288.

Kendler, H. H. (1967). Kenneth W. Spence: 1907–1967. *Psychological Review, 74,* 335–341.

Keppel, B. (2002). Kenneth B. Clark in the patterns of American culture. *American Psychology, 57,* 29–37.

Kersting, K. (2004, January). Three decades at the top. *Monitor on Psychology,* 38–39.

Kincheloe, J. L., & Tobin, K. (2009). The much exaggerated death of positivism. *Cultural Studies of Science Education, 4,* 513–528.

King, D. B., Wertheimer, M., Keller, H., & Crochetière, K. (1994). The legacy of Max Wertheimer and Gestalt psychology. *Social Research, 61,* 907–935.

Kinlen, T. J., & Henley, T. B. (1997, Winter). Hugo Münsterberg and modern forensic psychology. *APA Division 26, Society for the History of Psychology,* 70–72.

Kirschenbaum, H. (2004). Carl Rogers's life and work: An assessment on the 100th anniversary of his birth. *Journal of Counseling & Development, 82,* 116–124.

Klein, R. M. (1999). The Hebb legacy. *Canadian Journal of Experimental Psychology, 53,* 1–3.

Klimenko, V. M., & Golikov, U. P. (2008). The Pavlov department of physiology: A scientific history. *Proceedings of the 11th International Multidisciplinary Neuroscience and Biopsychiatry Conference "Stress and Behavior."* St. Petersburg, Russia.

Knight, Z. G. (2017). A proposed model of psychodynamic psychotherapy linked to Erik Erikson's eight stages of psychosocial development. *Clinical Psychology & Psychotherapy, 24,* 1047–1058.

Knowlton, B. J. (2016). Introduction to the special section on new ideas about the cerebellar function. *Behavioral Neuroscience, 130,* 545–546.

Köhler, W. (1942). Kurt Koffka: 1886–1941. *Psychological Review, 49,* 97–101.

Kollock, P. (2000). Introduction of Harold H. Kelley: Recipient of the 1999 Cooley-Mead award. *Social Psychology Quarterly, 63,* 1–2.

Koltko-Rivera, M. E. (2006). Rediscovering the later version of Maslow's hierarchy of needs: Self-transcendence and opportunities for theory, research, and unification. *Review of General Psychology, 10,* 302–317.

Korosoliev, A., & Tsering, T. (2010). Charlotte Buhler. *Psychology's Feminist Voices*. Retrieved from http://www.feministvoices.com/charlotte-buhler

Kostyanaya, M. (2014, April–June). Bluma Wulfova Zeigarnik. *The Neuropsychotherapist*, 102–105.

Kotik-Friedgut, B., & Friedgut, T. H. (2008). A man of his country and his time: Jewish influences on Lev Semionovich Vygotsky's world view. *History of Psychology, 11*, 15–39.

Krebs, D. L., & Denton, K. (2005). Toward a more pragmatic approach to morality: A critical evaluation of Kohlberg's model. *Psychological Review, 112*, 629–649.

Kressley-Mba, R. A. (2006). On the failed institutionalization of German comparative psychology prior to 1940. *History of Psychology, 9*, 55–74.

Kristjánsson, K. (2010). Positive psychology, happiness, and virtue: The troublesome conceptual issues. *Review of General Psychology, 14*, 296–310.

Kumar, D. R., Aslinia, F., Yale, S. H., & Mazza, J. J. (2011). Jean-Martin Charcot: The father of neurology. *Clinical Medicine & Research, 9*, 46–49.

Kunstreich, T. (2014). [A review of the books *Karl Abraham: The Birth of Object Relations Theory* by I. Sanfeliu and *Karl Abraham: Eine Biographie im Kontext der psychoanalytischen Bewegung*]. *The German Quarterly, 87*, 527–528.

Kupfersmid, J. (1992). The "defense" of Sigmund Freud. *Psychotherapy, 29*, 297–309.

Lachapelle, S. (2008). From the stage to the laboratory: Magicians, psychologists, and the science of illusion. *Journal of the History of the Behavioral Sciences, 44*, 319–334.

Lacoursiere, R. B. (2008). Freud's death: Historical truth and biographical fictions. *American Imago, 65*, 107–128.

Lal, S. (2002). Giving children security: Mamie Phipps Clark and the racialization of child psychology. *American Psychologist, 57*, 20–28.

Lamiell, J. T. (2000). Stern, Louis William. In A. E. Kazdin (Ed.), *Encyclopedia of psychology* (Vol. 7, pp. 470–472). Washington, DC: American Psychological Association.

Landy, F. J. (1992). Hugo Münsterberg: Victim or visionary? *Journal of Applied Psychology, 77*, 787–802.

Lang, P. J. (1994). The varieties of emotional experience: A meditation on James-Lange theory. *Psychological Review, 2*, 211–221.

Langermann, Y. T. (2000). [Review of the book *Magic, Causality, and Intentionality: The Doctrine of Rays in Al-Kindi* by P. Travaglia]. *Speculum, 77*, 256–258.

Larson, C. A. (1979, May). Highlights of John B. Watson's career in advertising. *APA Division 14, Society for Industrial and Organizational Psychology*, 3–5.

Leahey, T. (2014). The decline and fall of introspection. *PsycCRITIQUES, 59*, 3, 8.

Leahey, T. H. (2003). Herbert A. Simon: Nobel Prize in Economic Sciences, 1978. *American Psychologist, 58*, 753–755.

Leão, M. de F. F. C., Laurenti, C., & Haydu, V. B. (2016). Darwinism, radical behaviorism, and the role of variation in Skinnerian explaining behavior. *Behavior Analysis: Research and Practice, 16*, 1–11.

LeBlanc, A. (2004). Thirteen days: Joseph Delboeuf versus Pierre Janet on the nature of hypnotic suggestion. *Journal of the History of the Behavioral Sciences, 40*, 123–147.

Levine, J. M. (1999). Solomon Asch's legacy for group research. *Personality and Social Psychology Review, 3*, 358–364.

Levitt, P. (2003). Patricia Goldman-Rakic: The quintessential multidisciplinary scientist. *PLoS Biology, 1*, 152–153.

Lewin, K. (1937). Carl Stumpf. *Psychological Review, 44*, 189–194.

Ley, R. (1997). Köhler and espionage on the island of Tenerife: A rejoinder to Teuber. *The American Journal of Psychology, 110*, 277–284.

Likierman, M. (2008). Melanie Klein and envy: A static totalitarian script or a sample of our protean theories? *Psychoanalytic Dialogues, 18*, 766–775.

Locke, J. (1690/2004). *An essay concerning humane understanding* [Project Gutenberg e-book]. Retrieved from http://www.gutenberg.org/ebooks/10616

Loftus, E. F. (1999). Lost in the mall: Misrepresentations and misunderstandings. *Ethics & Behavior, 9*, 51–60.

Loftus, E. F. (2007). Elizabeth F. Loftus. In G. Lindzey & W. M. Runyan (Eds.), *A history of psychology in autobiography* (Vol. IX, pp. 199–227). Washington, DC: American Psychological Association.

Loftus, E. F. (2008, May). Perils of provocative scholarship. *Observer, 21*, 13–15.

LoLordo, V. M., & Seligman, M. E. P. (1997). Richard Lester Solomon (1918–1995). *American Psychologist, 52*, 567–568.

Long, K. M., Clarkson, L., Rockwell, S., & Zeavin, L. (2015). Perspectives following Klein and Bion on the development of the internal world: Clinical implications. *Psychoanalytic Inquiry, 35*, 370–384.

Lovie, P., & Lovie, A. D. (1996). Charles Edward Spearman, F.R.S. (1863–1945). *Notes and Records of the Royal Society of London, 50*, 75–88.

Luria, A. R. (1974). A. R. Luria. In G. Lindzey (Ed.), *A history of psychology in autobiography, Vol. VI: Century Psychology Series* (pp. 253–292). Englewood Cliffs, NJ: Prentice Hall.

Maaske, J. (2002). Spirituality and mindfulness. *Psychoanalytic Psychology, 19*, 777–781.

Maccoby, E. E. (1989). Eleanor E. Maccoby. In G. Lindzey (Ed.), *A history of psychology in autobiography* (Vol. VIII, pp. 290–335). Palo Alto, CA: Stanford University Press.

Maccoby, E. E. (1990). Gender and relationships: A developmental account. *American Psychologist, 45*, 513–520.

MacKay, T. (2013). The foundations of educational psychology: The legacy of Cyril Burt. *Educational & Child Psychology, 30*, 37–45.

Madigan, S., & O'Hara, R. (1992). Short-term memory at the turn of the century: Mary Whiton Calkins's memory research. *American Psychologist, 47*, 170–174.

Maier, S. F., & Seligman, M. E. P. (2016). Learned helplessness at fifty: Insights from neuroscience. *Psychological Review, 123,* 349–367.

Main, M. (1996). Introduction to the special section on attachment and psychopathology: 2. Overview of the field of attachment. *Journal of Consulting and Clinical Psychology, 64,* 237–243.

Malle, B. F. (2008). Fritz Heider's legacy: Celebrated insights, many of them misunderstood. *Social Psychology, 39,* 163–173.

Malone, J. C. (2014). Did John B. Watson really "found" behaviorism? *Behavior Analyst, 37,* 1–12.

Marecek, J., & Thorne, B. (2012). Carol Nagy (Jacklin) (1939–2011). *American Psychologist, 67,* 802.

Mark R. Rosenzweig. (1983). *American Psychologist, 83,* 14–23.

Mark R. Rosenzweig. (1998). *American Psychologist, 53,* 413–415.

Marlo, H., & Kline, J. S. (1998). Synchronicity and psychotherapy: Unconscious communication in the psychotherapeutic relationship. *Psychotherapy, 35,* 13–22.

Marshall, M. (1987). G. T. Fechner: In memoriam. *History of Psychology Newsletter, 19*(1–2), 1–9.

Marshall, M. (1990). The theme of quantification and the hidden Weber in the early work of Gustav Theodor Fechner. *Canadian Psychology/Psychologie Canadienne, 31,* 45–53.

Martha Bernal: Award for distinguished senior career contributions to the public interest. (2001). *American Psychologist, 56,* 922–924.

Martin, J. (2016). Ernest Becker and Stanley Milgram: Twentieth-century students of evil. *History of Psychology, 19,* 3–21.

Maslov, K. S. (2016). "Enmity rather than a competition": The relationship between V.M. Bekherev and I.P. Pavlov. *Journal of Russian & East European Psychology, 53,* 1–24.

Maslow, A. H. (1943). A theory of human motivation. *Psychological Review, 50,* 370–396.

Massey, R. F. (1986). Erik Erikson: Neo-Adlerian. *Individual Psychology: The Journal of Adlerian Theory, Research & Practice, 42,* 65–91.

May, M. A. (1949). James McKeen Cattell: Man of science, 1860–1944. *Psychological Bulletin, 46,* 85–88.

Mayer, S. J. (2005). The early evolution of Jean Piaget's clinical method. *History of Psychology, 8,* 362–382.

McGrath, J. E. (1978). Theodore M. Newcomb and the acquaintance process: A commentary. *Journal of Personality and Social Psychology, 36,* 1084–1086.

McGuigan, F. J. (1981). W. Horsley Gantt (1892–1980). *American Psychologist, 36,* 417–419.

McNulty, J. (1999, May 3). A lifetime of curiosity about human motivation garners psychology's top prize for Elliot Aronson. *UC Santa Cruz Currents.* Retrieved from https://currents.ucsc.edu/archives/

McReynolds, P. (1987). Lightner Witmer: Little-known founder of clinical psychology. *American Psychologist, 42,* 849–858.

McReynolds, P. (1996). Lightner Witmer: A centennial tribute. *American Psychologist, 51,* 237–240.

Meehan, W. (2009). Partem totius naturae esse: Spinoza's alternative to the mutual incomprehension of physicalism and mentalism in psychology. *Journal of Theoretical and Philosophical Psychology, 29,* 47–59.

Meischner-Metge, A. (2010). Gustav Theodor Fechner: Life and work in the mirror of his diary. *History of Psychology, 13,* 411–423.

Memories of Robert B. Zajonc. (2009, April). *APS Observer.* Retrieved from https://www.psychologicalscience.org/observer/memories-of-robert-b-zajonc

Merenda, P. F. (1987). Toward a four-factor theory of temperament and/or personality. *Journal of Personality Assessment, 51,*367–374.

Messer, S. B., & McWilliams, N. (2003). The impact of Sigmund Freud and *The Interpretation of Dreams.* In R. J. Sternberg (Ed.), *The anatomy of impact: What makes the great works of psychology great.* Washington, DC: American Psychological Association.

Meyer, A., Hackert, B., & Weger, U. (2018). Franz Brentano and the beginning of experimental psychology: Implications for the study of psychological phenomena today. *Psychological Research, 82,* 245–254.

Michael I. Posner. (1981). *American Psychologist, 36,* 38–42.

Michael S. Gazzaniga: Award for distinguished scientific contributions. (2008). *American Psychologist, 63,* 636–638.

Midgley, N. (2007). Anna Freud: The Hampstead War Nurseries and the role of the direct observation of children for psychoanalysis. *International Journal of Psychoanalysis, 88,* 939–959.

Mikkelsen, J. M. (2000). Kant, Immanuel. In A. E. Kazdin (Ed.), *Encyclopedia of psychology* (Vol. 4, pp. 430–432). Washington, DC: American Psychological Association.

Milar, K. S. (1999). "A coarse and clumsy tool": Helen Thompson Woolley and the Cincinnati Vocation Bureau. *History of Psychology, 3,* 219–235.

Milar, K. S. (2010, February). Overcoming 'sentimental rot.' *Monitor on Psychology,* 26–27.

Milgram, S. (1963). Behavioral study of obedience. *Journal of Abnormal and Social Psychology, 67,* 371–378.

Mill, J. S. (1843/2009). *A system of logic, ratiocinative and inductive* [Project Gutenberg e-book]. Retrieved from https://www.gutenberg.org/files/27942/27942-pdf.pdf

Mill, J. S. (1873/2003). *Autobiography* [Project Gutenberg e-book]. Retrieved from http://www.gutenberg.org/cache/epub/10378/pg10378.txt

Miller, G. A. (1956). The magical number seven, plus or minus two: Some limits on our capacity for processing information. *Psychological Review, 63,* 81–97.

Miller, G. A. (1975). Stanley Smith Stevens, 1906–1973. *Biographical Memoirs of the National Academy of Sciences, 47,* 425–459.

Miller, G. A. (1989). George A. Miller. In G. A. Lindzey (Ed.), *A history of psychology in autobiography* (Vol. VIII, pp. 390–418). Palo Alto, CA: Stanford University Press.

Miller, N. E. (1982). John Dollard (1900–1980). *American Psychologist, 37,* 587–588.

Milner, P. M. (1993, January). The mind and Donald O. Hebb. *Scientific American, 268*, 124–129.

Milner, P. M., & Milner, B. (1996). Donald Olding Hebb. *Biographical Memoirs of the Fellows of the Royal Society, 42*, 193–204.

Minton, H. L. (2000a). Psychology and gender at the turn of the century. *American Psychologist, 55*, 613–615.

Minton, H. L. (2000b). Terman, Lewis Madison. In A. E. Kazdin (Ed.), *Encyclopedia of psychology* (Vol. 8, pp. 37–39). Washington, DC: American Psychological Association.

Mintz, N. L. (1996). On Erik Erikson's Berkeley resignation. *American Psychologist, 51*, 266.

Mironenko, I. A. (2014). Integrative and isolationist tendencies in contemporary Russian psychological science. *Psychology in Russia: State of the Art, 7*, 4–13.

Mischel, W. (2004). Toward an integrative science of the person. *Annual Review of Psychology, 55*, 1–22.

Mischel, W. (2007). Walter Mischel. In G. Lindzey & W. M. Runyan (Eds.), *A history of psychology in autobiography* (Vol. IX, pp. 229–267). Washington, DC: American Psychological Association.

Mischel, W., Shoda, Y., & Rodriguez, M. L. (1989). Delay of gratification in children. *Science, 244*, 933–938.

Moroz, O. (1989). The last diagnosis: A plausible account that needs further verification. *Soviet Review, 1989, 6*, 82–102.

Murray, D. J. (1990). Fechner's later psychophysics. *Canadian Psychology/Psychologie Canadienne, 31*, 54–60.

Murray, D. J. (2000). Weber, Ernst Heinrich. In A. E. Kazdin (Ed.), *Encyclopedia of psychology* (Vol. 8, pp. 236–238). Washington, DC: American Psychological Association.

Murray, H. A. (1967). Henry A. Murray. In E. G. Boring & G. Lindzey (Eds.), *A history of psychology in autobiography* (Vol. 5, pp. 285–310). New York, NY: Appleton-Century-Crofts.

Mussen, P., & Eichorn, D. (1988). Mary Cover Jones (1896–1987). *American Psychologist, 43*, 818.

Nair, P. (2012). Q&As with Michael S. Gazzaniga. *Proceedings of the National Academy of Sciences, 109*, 5137.

Nakayama, K. (1994). James J. Gibson—an appreciation. *Psychological Review, 101*, 329–335.

Neisser, U. (1981). James J. Gibson (1904–1979). *American Psychologist, 36*, 214–215.

Neisser, U. (2002). Wolfgang Köhler, 1887–1967. *Biographical Memoirs of the National Academy of Sciences, 81*, 186–197.

Neisser, U. (2007). Ulric Neisser. In G. Lindzey & W. M. Runyan (Eds.), *A history of psychology in autobiography* (Vol. IX, pp. 269–301). Washington, DC: American Psychological Association.

Nelson, T. O. (1985). Ebbinghaus's contribution to the measurement of retention: savings during relearning. *Journal of Experimental Psychology: Learning, Memory, and Cognition, 11*, 472–479.

Newcomb, T. M. (1974). Theodore M. Newcomb. In G. Lindzey (Ed.), *A history of psychology in autobiography* (Vol. VI, pp. 367–391). Englewood Cliffs, NJ: Prentice Hall.

Newman, E. B. (1944). Max Wertheimer: 1880–1943. *The American Journal of Psychology, 57*, 428–435.

Nicholson, I. A. M. (1997). To "correlate psychology and social ethics": Gordon Allport and the first course in American personality psychology. *Journal of Personality, 65*, 733–742.

Nicholson, I. A. M. (1998). Gordon Allport, character, and the "culture of personality," 1897–1937. *History of Psychology, 1*, 52–68.

Nicholson, I. A. M. (2000). "A coherent datum of perception": Gordon Allport, Floyd Allport, and the politics of "personality." *Journal of the History of the Behavioral Sciences, 36*, 463–470.

Nicholson, I. A. M. (2001). "Giving up maleness": Abraham Maslow, masculinity, and the boundaries of psychology. *History of Psychology, 4*, 79–91.

Nicolas, S., & Ferrand, L. (2002). Alfred Binet and higher education. *History of Psychology, 5*, 264–283.

Nicolas, S., & Gounden, Y. (2011). The memory of two great calculators: Charcot and Binet's neglected 1893 experiments. *The American Journal of Psychology, 124*, 235–242.

Nicolas, S., & Levine, Z. (2012). Beyond intelligence testing: Remembering Alfred Binet after a century. *European Psychologist, 17*, 320–325.

Nicolas, S., & Ludovic, F. (1999). Wundt's laboratory at Leipzig in 1891. *History of Psychology, 2*, 194–203.

Nicolas, S., & Sanitioso, R. B. (2012). Alfred Binet and experimental psychology at the Sorbonne laboratory. *History of Psychology, 15*, 328–363.

Nielsen, M., & Day, R. H. (1999). William James and the evolution of consciousness. *Journal of Theoretical and Philosophical Psychology, 19*, 90–113.

Nisbett, R. E. (2000). Stanley Schachter, 1922–1997. *Biographical Memoirs of the National Academy of Sciences, 78*, 1–15.

Novotney, A. (2011, December). The real secrets to a longer life. *APA Monitor*, 36–39.

Olds, J. (1956). Pleasure centers in the brain. *Scientific American, 195*(4), 105–117.

Overholser, J. C. (2010). Psychotherapy that strives to encourage social interest: A simulated interview with Alfred Adler. *Journal of Psychotherapy Integration, 20*, 347–363.

Overskeid, G. (2007). Looking for Skinner and finding Freud. *American Psychologist, 62*, 590–595.

Oyama, T., Sato, T., & Suzuki, Y. (2001). Shaping of scientific psychology in Japan. *International Journal of Psychology, 36*, 396–406.

Pallini, S., & Barcaccia, B. (2014). A meeting of the minds: John Bowlby encounters Jean Piaget. *Review of General Psychology, 4*, 287–292.

Palmer, L. (2008). Kant and the brain: A new empirical hypothesis. *Review of General Psychology, 12*, 105–117.

Parkovnick, S. (2000). Contextualizing Floyd Allport's *Social Psychology. Journal of the History of the Behavioral Sciences, 36*, 429–441.

Patterson, M. M. (2011). Two streams make a river: The rabbit in Richard F. Thompson's laboratory. *Neurobiology of Learning and Memory, 95*, 106–110.

Pawlik, K., & Breedlove, S. M. (2010). Mark R. Rosenzweig (1922–2009). *American Psychologist, 65*, 610–611.

Pearce, T. (2015). "Science organized": Positivism and the Metaphysical Club, 1865–1875. *Journal of the History of Ideas, 75*, 441–465.

Pettigrew, T. F. (1969). Gordon Willard Allport: 1897–1967. *Journal of Personality and Social Psychology, 12*, 1–5.

Pick, H. L., Jr. (1992). Eleanor J. Gibson: Learning to perceive and perceiving to learn. *Developmental Psychology, 28*, 787–794.

Pickering, A. D. (1997). The conceptual nervous system and personality: From Pavlov to neural networks. *European Psychologist, 2*, 139–163.

Pietikainen, P., & Ihanus, J. (2003). On the origins of psychoanalytic psychohistory. *History of Psychology, 6*, 171–194.

Pillsbury, W. B. (1947). James McKeen Cattell, 1860–1944. *Biographical Memoirs of the National Academy of Sciences, 25*, 1–16.

Pillsbury, W. B. (1957). John Dewey, 1859–1952. *Biographical Memoirs of the National Academy of Sciences, 30*, 105–124.

Pinker, S. (2013). George A. Miller (1920–2012). *American Psychologist, 68*, 467–468.

Plato. *Apology*. Retrieved from http://www.sjsu.edu/people/james.lindahl/courses/Phil70A/s3/apology.pdf

Plato. *Meno*. Retrieved from http://classics.mit.edu/Plato/meno.html

Plato. *Republic*, Book VII. Retrieved from http://classics.mit.edu/Plato/republic.8.vii.html

Polkinghorne, D. E. (2003). In R. J. Sternberg (Ed.), *The anatomy of impact: What makes the great works of psychology great* (pp. 43–70). Washington, DC: American Psychological Association.

Pontin, J. (2014). Q+A: Antonio Damasio. *MIT Technology Review, 117*(4), 48–51.

Posner, M. I., & Rothbart, M. K. (2004). Hebb's neural networks support the integration of psychological science. *Canadian Psychology, 45*, 265–278.

Prenzel-Guthrie, P. M. (2000). Guthrie, Edwin Ray. In A. E. Kazdin (Ed.), *Encyclopedia of psychology* (Vol. 4, pp. 43–44). Washington, DC: American Psychological Association.

Pritchard, M. S. (1999). Kohlbergian contributions to educational programs for the moral development of professionals. *Educational Psychology Review, 11*, 395–409.

Proctor, R. W., & Evans, R. (2014). E. B. Titchener, women psychologists, and the Experimentalists. *The American Journal of Psychology, 127*, 501–526.

Puente, A. E. (1995). Roger Wolcott Sperry (1913–1994). *American Psychologist, 50*, 940–941.

Quick, J. C. (1990, October). Walter B. Cannon: Research physiologist with a psychologist spirit. *APA Division 14, Society for Industrial and Organizational Psychology*, 35–36.

Quick, J. C., Quick, J. D., Nelson, D. L., & Hurrell, J. J., Jr. (1997). *Preventive stress management in organizations*. Washington, DC: American Psychological Association.

Rabinowitz, F. E., Good, G., & Cozad, L. (1989). Rollo May: A man of meaning and myth. *Journal of Counseling and Development, 67*, 436–441.

Rachlin, H. (1995). Burrhus Frederic Skinner, 1904–1990. *Biographical Memoirs of the National Academy of Sciences, 67*, 362–377.

Radick, G. (2016). The unmasking of a modern synthesis: Noam Chomsky, Charles Hockett, and the politics of behaviorism, 1955–1965. *Isis, 107*, 49–73.

Raven, B. H., Pepitone, A., & Holmes, J. (2003). Harold H. Kelley (1921–2003). *American Psychologist, 58*, 806–807.

Ravindran, S. (2012). Profile of Lee D. Ross. *Proceedings of the National Academy of Sciences, 109*, 7132–7133.

Reisenzein, R., & Rudolf, U. (2008). The discovery of common-sense psychology. *Social Psychology, 39*, 125–133.

Reisenzein, R., & Sprung, H. (2000). Stumpf, Carl. In A. E. Kazdin (Ed.), *Encyclopedia of psychology* (Vol. 7, pp. 495–497). Washington, DC: American Psychological Association.

Rennie, D. L. (2008). Two thoughts on Abraham Maslow. *Journal of Humanistic Psychology, 48*, 445–448.

Rest, J., Power, C., & Brabeck, M. (1988). Lawrence Kohlberg (1927–1987). *American Psychologist, 43*, 399–400.

Revelle, W. (2009). Personality structure and measurement: The contributions of Raymond Cattell. *British Journal of Psychology, 100*, 253–257.

Rilling, M. (2000). John Watson's paradoxical struggle to explain Freud. *American Psychologist, 55*, 301–312.

Rizvi, S. H. (2017). Avicenna (ibn Sina). *Internet Encyclopedia of Philosophy*. Retrieved from http://www.iep.utm.edu/avicenna/

Robinson, A. M. (2018). Let's talk about stress: History of stress research. *Review of General Psychology, 22*, 334–342.

Robinson, D. K. (2010). Fechner's "inner psychophysics." *History of Psychology, 13*, 424–433.

Robinson, D. N. (2000). Berkeley, George. In A. E. Kazdin (Ed.), *Encyclopedia of psychology* (Vol. 1, pp. 406–407). Washington, DC: American Psychological Association.

Robinson, K. (2015). Remembering, repeating and working through: The impact of the controversial discussions. *British Journal of Psychotherapy, 31*, 69–84.

Robinson, K. (2017). [Review of the book *Karl Abraham: Life and Work, a Biography* by A. B. van Schoonheten]. *British Journal of Psychotherapy, 33*, 264–275.

Rogers, C. R. (1967). Carl R. Rogers. In E. G. Boring & G. Lindzey (Eds.), *A history of psychology in autobiography* (Vol. V, pp. 341–384). East Norwalk, CT: Appleton-Century-Crofts.

Root-Bernstein, R. (2005). Roger Sperry: Ambicerebral man. *Leonardo, 38*, 224–225.

Rose, S. (2010) Hans Eysenck's controversial career. *The Lancet, 376*, 407–408.

Rosenzweig, S., & Fisher, S. L. (1997). "Idiographic" vis-à-vis "idiodynamic" in the historical perspective of personality theory:

Remembering Gordon Allport, 1897–1997. *Journal of the History of the Behavioral Sciences, 33*, 405–419.

Rotter, J. B. (1975). Some problems and misconceptions related to the construct of internal versus external control of reinforcement. *Journal of Consulting and Clinical Psychology, 43*, 56–67.

Rotter, J. B. (1990). Internal versus external control of reinforcement: A case history of a variable. *American Psychologist, 45*, 489–493.

Routh, D. K. (1996). Lightner Witmer and the first 100 years of clinical psychology. *American Psychologist, 51*, 244–247.

Ruckmick, C. A. (1937). Carl Stumpf. *The Psychological Bulletin, 34*, 187–190.

Rudolph, U., & Reisenzein, R. (2008). 50 years of attribution research. *Social Psychology, 39*, 123–124.

Russell, G. (2016). A variation on forced migration: Wilhelm Peters (Prussia via Britain to Turkey) and Muzafer Sherif (Turkey to the United States). *Journal of the History of the Neurosciences, 25*, 320–347.

Rustin, M. (2016). Young children and works of the imagination. *Infant Observation, 19*, 139–148.

Rustom, M. (2018). [Review of the book *Self-Awareness in Islamic Philosophy: Avicenna and Beyond* by J. Kaukua]. *Journal of the American Oriental Society, 138*, 206–209.

Rutherford, A. (2000). Radical behaviorism and psychology's public: B. F. Skinner in the popular press, 1934–1990. *History of Psychology, 3*, 371–395.

Rutherford, A. (2010). Mary Cover Jones. *Psychology's Feminist Voices.* Retrieved from http://www.feministvoices.com/mary-cover-jones/

Rutherford, A. (2017). B. F. Skinner and technology's nation: Technocracy, social engineering, and the good life in 20th-century America. *History of Psychology, 20*, 290–312.

Rychlak, J. F. (1997). *In defense of human consciousness.* Washington, DC: American Psychological Association.

Rychlak, J. F. (1998). Is there an unrecognized teleology in Hume's analysis of causation? *Journal of Theoretical and Philosophical Psychology, 18, 1*, 52–60.

Sabini, J. (1986). Stanley Milgram (1933–1984). *American Psychologist, 41*, 1378–1379.

Saltzman, A. L. (2001, Spring). Ruth Winifred Howard (1900–). *The Feminist Psychologist,* 28–30.

Sannita, W. G. (2017). Higher brain function and the laws of thermodynamics: Hans Berger and his time. *Journal of Psychophysiology, 31*, 1–5.

Sato, T., Mizoguchi, H., Arakawa, A., Hidaka, S., Takasuna, M., & Nishikawa, Y. (2016). History of "history of psychology" in Japan. *Japanese Psychological Research, 58*, 110–128.

Sato, T., & Sato, T. (2005). The early 20th century: Shaping the discipline of psychology in Japan. *Japanese Psychological Research, 47*, 52–62.

Sawyer, T. F. (2000). Francis Cecil Sumner: His views and influence on African American higher education. *History of Psychology, 3*, 122–141.

Scarborough, E. (1988). Christine Ladd-Franklin (1847–1930): In memoriam. *History of Psychology Newsletter, 20*, 55–56.

Scarborough, E. (2000). Washburn, Margaret Floy. In A. E. Kazdin (Ed.), *Encyclopedia of psychology* (Vol. 8, pp. 230–232). Washington, DC: American Psychological Association.

Schachter, S. (1951). Deviation, rejection, and communication. *Journal of Abnormal and Social Psychology, 46*, 190–207.

Schachter, S. (1959). *The psychology of affiliation.* Palo Alto, CA: Stanford University Press.

Schachter, S. (1968). Obesity and eating. *Science, 161*, 751–756.

Schachter, S. (1977). Nicotine regulation in heavy and light smokers. *Journal of Experimental Psychology: General, 106*, 5–12.

Schachter, S. (1989). Stanley Schachter. In G. Lindzey (Ed.), *A history of psychology in autobiography* (Vol. VIII, pp. 448–470). Palo Alto, CA: Stanford University Press.

Schachter, S. (1994). Leon Festinger, 1919–1989. *Biographical Memoirs of the National Academy of Sciences, 64*, 98–110.

Schachter, S., & Singer, J. E. (1962). Cognitive, social, and physiological determinants of emotional state. *Psychological Review, 69*, 379–399.

Schmidt, M. A. (2017). Planes of phenomenological experience: The psychology of deafness as an early example of American Gestalt psychology, 1928–1940. *History of Psychology, 20*, 347–364.

Schmitt, W. A., Brinkley, C. A., & Newman, J. P. (1999). Testing Damasio's somatic marker hypothesis with psychopathic individuals: Risk takers or risk averse? *Journal of Abnormal Psychology, 108*, 538–543.

Schneidman, E. S. (2001). My visit with Christiana Morgan. *History of Psychology, 4*, 289–296.

Schooler, J. W. (2011). Introspecting in the spirit of William James: Comment on Fox, Ericsson, and Best (2011). *Psychological Bulletin, 137*, 345–350.

Schwartz, S. J., Lilienfeld, S. O., Meca, A., & Sauvigné, K. C. (2016). The role of neuroscience within psychology: A call for inclusiveness over exclusiveness. *American Psychologist, 71*, 52–70.

Sears, R. R. (1977). Sources of life satisfactions of the Terman gifted men. *American Psychologist, 32*, 119–128.

Sears, R. R. (1982). Harry Frederick Harlow (1905–1981). *American Psychologist, 37*, 1280–1281.

Sejnowski, T. J. (2003). The once and future Hebb synapse. *Canadian Psychology, 44*, 17–20.

Selemon, L. D. (2015). Modular organization of the prefrontal cortex: The legacy of Patricia Goldman-Rakic. In M. F. Casanova & I. Opris (Eds.), *Recent advances in the modular organization of the cortex* (pp. 15–33). Dordrecht, Netherlands: Springer.

Seligman, M. E. P., & Csikszentmihalyi, M. (2000). Positive psychology: An introduction. *American Psychologist, 55*, 5–14.

Shapira, M. (2017). Interpersonal rivalries, gender and the intellectual and scientific making of psychoanalysis in 1940s Britain. *History of Psychology, 20*, 172–194.

Sharp, P. B., & Miller, G. A. (2019). Reduction and autonomy in psychology and neuroscience: A call for pragmatism. *Journal of Theoretical and Philosophical Psychology*, 39, 18–31.

Sharps, M. J., & Wertheimer, M. (2000). Gestalt perspectives on cognitive science and on experimental psychology. *Review of General Psychology*, 4, 315–336.

Sheffield, F. D. (1959). Edwin Ray Guthrie: 1886–1959. *The American Journal of Psychology*, 72, 642–650.

Shields, S. A. (2000). Hollingworth, Leta Stetter. In A. E. Kazdin (Ed.), *Encyclopedia of psychology* (Vol. 4, pp. 138–140). Washington, DC: American Psychological Association.

Shields, S. A., & Bhatia, S. (2009). Darwin on race, gender, and culture. *American Psychologist*, 64, 111–119.

Shors, T. J. (2015). Richard F. Thompson (1930–2014). *American Psychologist*, 70, 472.

Sidowski, J. B., & Lindsley, D. B. (1989). Harry Frederick Harlow: 1905–1981. *Biographical Memoirs of the National Academy of Sciences*, 58, 219–257.

Siegler, R. S. (1992). The other Alfred Binet. *Developmental Psychology*, 28, 179–190.

Silverman, L. K. (1992). Leta Stetter Hollingworth: Champion of the psychology of women and gifted children. *Journal of Educational Psychology*, 84, 20–27.

Simon, H. A. (1993). Allen Newell (1927–1992). *American Psychologist*, 48, 1148–1149.

Simonton, D. K. (2003). Francis Galton's *Hereditary Genius*: Its place in the history and psychology of science. In R. J. Sternberg (Ed.), *The anatomy of impact: What makes the great works of psychology great* (pp. 3–18). Washington, DC: American Psychological Association.

Simonton, D. K. (2018). Intellectual genius in the Islamic Golden Age: Cross-civilization replications, extensions, and modifications. *Psychology of Aesthetics, Creativity, and the Arts*, 12, 125–135.

Skinner, B. F. (1967). B. F. Skinner. In E. G. Boring & G. Lindzey (Eds.), *A history of psychology in autobiography, Vol. V: Century Psychology Series* (pp. 385–412). East Norwalk, CT: Appleton-Century-Crofts.

Slamecka, N. J. (1985). Ebbinghaus: Some associations. *Journal of Experimental Psychology: Learning, Memory, and Cognition*, 11, 414–435.

Smith, D. (1982). Trends in counseling and psychotherapy. *American Psychologist*, 37, 802–809.

Smith, L. D. (2000a). Bacon, Francis. In A. E. Kazdin (Ed.), *Encyclopedia of psychology* (Vol. 1, pp. 360–361). Washington, DC: American Psychological Association.

Smith, L. D. (2000b). Hull, Clark Leonard. In A. E. Kazdin (Ed.), *Encyclopedia of psychology* (Vol. 4, pp. 168–170). Washington, DC: American Psychological Association.

Smith, M. B., & Anderson, J. W. (1989). Henry A. Murray (1893–1988). *American Psychologist*, 44, 1153–1154.

Smith, W. B. (2007). Karen Horney and psychotherapy in the 21st century. *Clinical Social Work Journal*, 35, 57–66.

Snyder, P. J., & Whitaker, H. A. (2013). Neurologic heuristics and artistic whimsy: The cerebral cartography of Wilder Penfield. *Journal of the History of the Neurosciences*, 22, 277–291.

Sokal, M. M. (1984). The Gestalt psychologists in behaviorist America. *The American Historical Review*, 85, 1240–1263.

Sokal, M. M. (1995). James McKeen Cattell, the New York Academy of Sciences, and the American Psychological Association, 1891–1902. In H. E. Adler & R. W. Rieber (Eds.), *Aspects of the history of psychology in America: 1892–1992* (pp. 13–35). Washington, DC: American Psychological Association.

Sokal, M. M. (2009). James McKeen Cattell, Nicholas Murray Butler, and academic freedom at Columbia University, 1902–1923. *History of Psychology*, 12, 87–122.

Soloviev, E. Y. (2018). Immanuel Kant: The ethical response to the challenge of the secularization era. *Russian Studies in Philosophy*, 56, 277–295.

Spanos, N. P. (1996). *Multiple identities & false memories: A sociocognitive perspective*. Washington, DC: American Psychological Association.

Spearman, C. (1930). C. Spearman. In C. Murchison (Ed.), *A history of psychology in autobiography* (Vol. I, pp. 237–264). Worcester, MA: Clark University Press.

Sperry, R. W. (1995). The future of psychology. *American Psychologist*, 50, 505–506.

Spinoza, B. (1677/2009). *The ethics* [Project Gutenberg e-book]. Retrieved from https://www.gutenberg.org/files/3800/3800-h/3800-h.htm

Staley, K. (1989). Al-Kindi on creation: Aristotle's challenge to Islam. *Journal of the History of Ideas*, 50, 355–370.

Sternberg, R. J., & Jarvin, L. (2003). Alfred Binet's contributions as a paradigm for impact in psychology. In R. J. Sternberg (Ed.), *The anatomy of impact: What makes the great works of psychology great*. Washington, DC: American Psychological Association.

Stevens, S. S. (1973). Edwin Garrigues Boring, 1886–1968. *Biographical Memoirs of the National Academy of Sciences*, 43, 41–76.

Stevens, S. S. (1974). S. S. Stevens. In G. Lindzey (Ed.), *A history of psychology in autobiography* (Vol. VI, pp. 395–420). Englewood Cliffs, NJ: Prentice Hall.

Stock, A. (2014). Schumann's wheel tachistoscope: Its reconstruction and its operation. *History of Psychology*, 17, 149–158.

Strickland, B. R. (2000). Misassumptions, misadventures, and the misuse of psychology. *American Psychologist*, 55, 331–338.

Strickland, B. R. (2014). Julian B. Rotter (1916–2014). *American Psychologist*, 69, 545–546.

Strube, M. J., Yost, J. H., & Bailey, J. R. (1993). William James and contemporary research on the self: The influence of pragmatism, reality, and truth. In M. E. Donnelly (Ed.), *Reinterpreting the legacy of William James* (pp. 189–207). Washington, DC: American Psychological Association.

Swanbrow, D. (2008, December 8). Robert Zajonc. Retrieved from http://www.ur.umich.edu/0809/Dec08_08/obits.php?print

Takeda, T., Ando, M., & Kumagai, K. (2015). Attention deficit and attention training in early twentieth-century Japan. *ADHD: Attention Deficit and Hyperactivity Disorders, 7,* 101–111.

Taylor, E. (2000). Psychotherapeutics and the problematic origins of clinical psychology in America. *American Psychologist, 55,* 1029–1033.

Terman, L. M. (1932). Lewis M. Terman. In C. Murchison (Ed.), *A history of psychology in autobiography* (Vol. II, pp. 297–331). Worcester, MA: Clark University Press.

Teuber, M. L. (1994). The founding of the primate station, Tenerife, Canary Islands. *The American Journal of Psychology, 107,* 551–581.

Thelen, E., & Adolph, K. E. (1992). Arnold L. Gesell: The paradox of nature and nurture. *Developmental Psychology, 28,* 368–380.

Thibaut, J. W., & Kelley, H. H. (1959). *The social psychology of groups.* Oxford, England: John Wiley.

Thomas, J. (Producer), & Cronenberg, D. (Director). (2011). *A dangerous method* [Motion picture]. US: Sony Pictures Classics.

Thomas, R. K. (1994). Pavlov was "mugged." *History of Psychology Newsletter, 26,* 86–91.

Thompson, D. N. (2000). Goodenough, Florence Laura. In A. E. Kazdin (Ed.), *Encyclopedia of psychology* (Vol. 3, p. 507). Washington, DC: American Psychological Association.

Thompson, R. F. (1999). James Olds (1922–1976). *Biographical Memoirs of the National Academy of Sciences, 77,* 246–263.

Thorndike, E. L. (1936). Edward Lee Thorndike. In C. Murchison (Ed.), *A history of psychology in autobiography* (Vol. III, pp. 263–270). Worcester, MA: Clark University Press.

Thurstone, L. L. (1952). L. L. Thurstone. In E. G. Boring, H. Werner, H. S. Langfeld, & R. M. Yerkes (Eds.), *A history of psychology in autobiography* (Vol. IV, pp. 295–321). Worcester, MA: Clark University Press.

Titova, L., Werner, K. M., & Sheldon, K. M. (2018). Translating positive psychology. *Translational Issues in Psychological Science, 4,* 211–214.

Todes, D. P. (1997). From the machine to the ghost within: Pavlov's transition from digestive physiology to conditioned reflexes. *American Psychologist, 52,* 947–955.

Tolman, C. W. (2000a). Angell, James Rowland. In A. E. Kazdin (Ed.), *Encyclopedia of psychology* (Vol. 1, pp. 169–170). Washington, DC: American Psychological Association.

Tolman, C. W. (2000b). Carr, Harvey A. In A. E. Kazdin (Ed.), *Encyclopedia of psychology* (Vol. 2, pp. 42–43). Washington, DC: American Psychological Association.

Tolman, E. C. (1948). Cognitive maps in rats and men. *Psychological Review, 55,* 189–208.

Tolman, E. C. (1952). Edward Chace Tolman. In E. G. Boring, H. S. Langfeld, & R. M. Yerkes (Eds.), *A history of psychology in autobiography* (Vol. IV, pp. 323–339). Worcester, MA: Clark University Press.

Traxel, W. (1985). Hermann Ebbinghaus: In memoriam. *History of Psychology Newsletter, 17,* (2), 37–41.

Triplet, R. G. (1992). Henry A. Murray: The making of a psychologist? *American Psychologist, 47,* 299–307.

Tucker, W. H. (2005). The racist past of the American psychology establishment. *The Journal of Blacks in Higher Education, 48,* 108–112.

Tulving, E. (1985a). Ebbinghaus's memory: What did he learn and remember? *Journal of Experimental Psychology: Learning, Memory, and Cognition, 11,* 485–490.

Tulving, E. (1985b). How many memory systems are there? *American Psychologist, 40,* 385–398.

Tulving, E. (2002). Episodic memory: From mind to brain. *Annual Review of Psychology, 53,* 1–25.

Turner, R. S. (2000). Helmholtz, Hermann von. In A. E. Kazdin (Ed.), *Encyclopedia of psychology* (Vol. 4, pp. 109–111). Washington, DC: American Psychological Association.

Tversky, A., & Kahneman, D. (1974). Judgment under uncertainty: Heuristics and biases. *Science, 185,* 1124–1131.

Uhrbrock, R. S. (1932). June Etta Downey. *Science, 76,* 585–586.

Ushakova, T. N. (1997). Pavlov's theory and Russian psychology. *European Psychologist, 2,* 97–101.

Van de Vijver, F. J. R. (2013). Contributions of internationalization to psychology: Toward a global and inclusive discipline. *American Psychologist, 68,* 761–770.

Van der Horst, F. C. P., & van der Veer, R. (2010). The ontogeny of an idea: John Bowlby and contemporaries on mother-child separation. *History of Psychology, 13,* 25–45.

Van der Horst, F. C. P., LeRoy, H. A., & van der Veer, R. (2008). "When strangers meet": John Bowlby and Harry Harlow on attachment behavior. *Integrative Psychological and Behavioral Science, 42,* 370–388.

Van der Veer, R. (2000). Tamara Dembo's European years: Working with Lewin and Buytendijk. *Journal of the History of the Behavioral Sciences, 36,* 109–126.

Van Elteren, M. (1992). Kurt Lewin as filmmaker and methodologist. *Canadian Psychology/Psychologie Canadienne, 33,* 599–608.

Van Geert, P. (1998). A dynamic systems model of basic developmental mechanisms: Piaget, Vygotsky, and beyond. *Psychological Review, 105,* 634–677.

Van Lange, P. A. M., & Balliet, D. (2015). Interdependence theory. In M. Mikulincer & P. R. Shaver (Eds.), *APA handbook of personality and social psychology, Vol. 3: Interpersonal relations* (pp. 65–92). Washington, DC: American Psychological Association.

Van Raaij, W. F. (1998). The life and work of Amos Tversky. *Journal of Economic Psychology, 19,* 515–527.

Van Rosmalen, L., van der Horst, F. C. P., & van der Veer, R. (2016). From secure dependency to attachment: Mary Ainsworth's integration of Blatz's security theory into Bowlby's attachment theory. *History of Psychology, 19,* 22–39.

Vasquez, M. J. T., & Lopez, S. (2002). Martha E. Bernal (1931–2001). *American Psychologist, 57,* 362–363.

Vassilieva, J. (2010). Russian psychology at the turn of the 21st century and post-Soviet reforms in the humanities disciplines. *History of Psychology, 13,* 138–159.

Vicedo, M. (2009). The father of ethology and the foster mother of ducks: Konrad Lorenz as expert on motherhood. *Isis, 100,* 263–291.

Vidal, F. (2001). Sabina Spielrein, Jean Piaget—going their own ways. *Journal of Analytical Psychology, 46,* 139–153.

Vinh-Bang (1922–2008): Psychologue. (2018, June 4). *Foundation Jean Piaget.* Retrieved from http://www.fondationjeanpiaget.ch/fjp/site/presentation/index_auteur.php?PRESMODE=1&auteurID=10

Violino, B. (2011, May). David E. Rumelhart: 1942–2011. *Communications of the ACM,* 15.

Virtue in mind. (2003). *New Scientist, 180*(2420), 48–51.

Virues-Ortega, J., & Pear, J. J. (2015). A history of "behavior" and "mind": Use of behavioral and cognitive terms in the 20th century. *Psychological Record, 65,* 23–30.

Voneida, T. J. (1997). Roger Wolcott Sperry: 1913–1994. *Biographical Memoirs of the National Academy of Sciences, 71,* 315–332.

Wagemans, J., Elder, J. H., Kubovy, M., Palmer, S. E., Peterson, M. A., Singh, M., & von der Heydt, R. (2012). A century of Gestalt psychology in visual perception: I. Perceptual grouping and figure-ground organization. *Psychological Bulletin, 138,* 1172–1217.

Walsh, C. (2000). The life and legacy of Lawrence Kohlberg. *Society, 37*(2), 36–41.

Walter Mischel. (1983). *American Psychologist, 38,* 9–14.

Washburn, M. F. (1932). Margaret Floy Washburn. In C. Murchison, (Ed.), *A history of psychology in autobiography* (Vol. II, pp. 333–358). Worcester, MA: Clark University Press.

Waterman, A. S. (2013). The humanistic psychology-positive psychology divide: Contrasts in philosophical foundations. *American Psychologist, 68,* 124–133.

Watson, J. B. (1913/1994). Psychology as the behaviorist views it. *Psychological Review, 101,* 248–253.

Watson, J. B. (1936). John Broadus Watson. In C. Murchison (Ed.), *A history of psychology in autobiography* (Vol. III, pp. 271–281).

Watson, J. B., & Rayner, R. (1920/2000). Conditioned emotional reactions. *American Psychologist, 55,* 313–317.

Weiland, S. (1993). Erik Erikson: Ages, stages, and stories. *Generations, 17*(2), 17.

Wentworth, P. A. (1999). The moral of her story: Exploring the philosophical and religious commitments in Mary Whiton Calkins' self-psychology. *History of Psychology, 2,* 119–131.

Wertheimer, M. (2003). Music, thinking, perceived motion: The emergence of Gestalt theory. *History of Psychology, 2,* 131–133.

Wertheimer, M. (2014). Music, thinking, perceived motion: The emergence of Gestalt theory. *History of Psychology, 17,* 131–133.

Wertheimer, M., King, D. B., Peckler, M. A., Raney, S., & Schaef, R. W. (1992). Carl Jung and Max Wertheimer on a priority issue. *Journal of the History of the Behavioral Sciences, 28,* 45–56.

Wesselmann, E. D., Williams, K. D., Pryor, J. B., Eichler, F. A., Gill, D. M., & Hogue, J. D. (2014). Revisiting Schachter's research on rejection, deviance, and communication (1951). *Social Psychology, 45,* 164–169.

Whalen, R. W. (2005). A surprising pre-history of postmodernism: Franz Brentano, *Fin de siècle* Vienna, and contemporary European thought. *Modern Austrian Literature, 38,* 1–11.

Whatmore, L. (1999). Book review [*The Life and Work of an Eminent Psychologist: Autobiography of Richard S. Lazarus*]. *Stress Medicine, 15,* 135–136.

White, N. M. (2018). Peter M. Milner, 1919–2018. *Journal of Psychiatry & Neuroscience, 43,* 428–429.

White, S. H. (2002). G. Stanley Hall: From philosophy to developmental psychology. In W. E. Pickren & D. A. Dewsbury (Eds.), *Evolving perspectives on the history of psychology* (pp. 279–302). Washington, DC: American Psychological Association.

Whitehead, P. M. (2017). Goldstein's self-actualization: A biosemiotics view. *The Humanistic Psychologist, 45,* 71–83.

Whitfield, S. J. (2000). Becoming Erikson. *Reviews in American History, 28*(1), 134–141.

Wieser, M. (2014). Remembering the "lens": Visual transformations of a concept from Heider to Brunswik. *History of Psychology, 17,* 83–104.

Wilson, E. O. (1998). *Consilience: The unity of knowledge.* New York, NY: Knopf.

Wilson, G. (1998). Hans Jurgen Eysenck. *European Psychologist, 3,* 78–79.

Windholz, G. (1997). Ivan P. Pavlov: An overview of his life and psychological work. *American Psychologist, 52,* 941–946.

Winston, C. N., Maher, H., & Easvaradoss, V. (2017). Needs and values: An exploration. *The Humanistic Psychologist, 45,* 295–311.

Winter, D. G. (1998a). The contributions of David McClelland to personality assessment. *Journal of Personality Assessment, 71,* 129–145.

Winter, D. G. (1998b). "Toward a science of personality psychology": David McClelland's development of empirically derived TAT measures. *History of Psychology, 1,* 130–153.

Winter, D. G. (2000). David C. McClelland (1917–1998). *American Psychologist, 55,* 540–541.

Wiseman, D. B. (2000). Subjective science: Kenneth Spence's human learning research program. *History of Psychology, 3,* 262–283.

Witmer, L. (1907/1996). Clinical psychology. [Reprint.] *American Psychology, 51,* 248–251.

Wolf, T. H. (1961). An individual who made a difference. *American Psychologist, 16,* 245–248.

Wong, W. (2009). Explorations in the disciplinary frontiers of psychology and in *Völkerpsychologie. History of Psychology, 12,* 229–265.

Woodworth, R. S. (1932). Robert S. Woodworth. In C. Murchison (Ed.), *A history of psychology in autobiography* (Vol. II, pp. 359–380). Worcester, MA: Clark University Press.

Woodworth, R. S. (1948). Margaret Floy Washburn, 1871–1939. *Biographical Memoirs of the National Academy of Sciences, 25,* 273–295.

Woodworth, R. S. (1952). Edward Lee Thorndike, 1874–1949. *Biographical Memoirs of the National Academy of Sciences, 27,* 209–237.

Wozniak, R. H. (2009). Consciousness, social heredity, and development: The evolutionary thought of James Mark Baldwin. *American Psychologist, 64*, 93–101.

Wozniak, R. H., & Santiago-Blay, J. A. (2013). Trouble at Tyson Alley: James Mark Baldwin's arrest in a Baltimore bordello. *History of Psychology, 16*, 227–248.

Wright, B. (1989). Extension of Heider's ideas to rehabilitation psychology. *American Psychologist, 44*, 525–528.

Wright, B. A. (1993). Tribute to Tamara Dembo: May 28, 1902–October 17, 1993. *Rehabilitation Psychology, 38*, 285–286.

Wundt, W. (1873/1912). *Principles of physiological psychology* (E. Titchener, Trans.). Boston, MA: Houghton, Mifflin, and Co.

Yasnitsky, A. (2011). Vygotsky circle as a personal network of scholars: Restoring connections between people and ideas. *Integrative Psychological and Behavioral Science, 45*, 422–457.

Yasnitsky, A., & Ferrari, M. (2008). Rethinking the early history of post-Vygotskian psychology: The case of the Kharkov school. *History of Psychology, 11*, 101–121.

Yerkes, R. M. (1932). Robert Mearns Yerkes. In Murchison, C. (Ed.), *A history of psychology in autobiography, Vol. III: The International University Series in Psychology* (pp. 381–407) Worcester, MA: Clark University Press.

Yerkes, R. M. (1946). Walter Bradford Cannon: 1871–1945. *Psychological Review, 53*, 137–146.

Young, J. L. (2010). Mary Whiton Calkins. *Psychology's Feminist Voices*. Retrieved from http://www.feministvoices.com/mary-whiton-calkins/

Young-Bruehl, E. (2004). Anna Freud and Dorothy Burlingham at Hempstead: The origins of psychoanalytic parent-infant observation. *Annals of Psychoanalysis, 32*, 185–197.

Zagorski, N. (2005). Profile of Elizabeth F. Loftus. *Proceedings of the National Academy of Sciences, 102*, 13721–13723.

Zajonc, R. B. (1990). Leon Festinger (1919–1989). *American Psychologist, 45*, 661–662.

Zayed, R. S., & Mook, B. (1999). Jung's concept of the archetype: An existential phenomenological reflection. *The Humanistic Psychologist, 27*, 343–368.

Zeigarnik, A. V. (2007). Bluma Zeigarnik: A memoir. *Gestalt Theory, 29*, 256–268.

Zilio, D. (2016). On the autonomy of psychology from neuroscience: A case study of Skinner's radical behaviorism and behavior analysis. *Review of General Psychology, 20*, 155–170.

Zuroff, D. C. (1986). Was Gordon Allport a trait theorist? *Journal of Personality and Social Psychology, 51*, 993–1000.

Author Index

Huynh, C. L., 397, 398
Hyman, C., 388

Ihanus, J., 362, 363
Inhelder, B., 191, 192
Innis, N. K., 107
Ireland, M. E., 162
Irons, G., 101
Iversen, I. H., 113, 114

Jahoda, G., 187
Jarvin, L., 183, 184
Jaspars, J., 288, 289
Jensen, A. R., 333
John, O. P., 327, 338, 339, 340
Johnson, A., 92, 93
Johnson, A. D., 79, 80
Johnson, D. F., 65, 66
Johnson, S., 392
Jones, E., 287, 288
Jones, E. E., 290, 291
Jones, J. M., 318
Jones, M. C., 102
Jones, R. A., 248
Jones, V. K., 66, 82, 117
Jorati, J., 18
Josephs, L., 155
Joyce, N., 139

Kagan, J., 315, 316, 317, 318
Kahneman, D., 266, 267, 268
Kant, I., 19
Karpov, Y., 214
Karpov, Y. V., 210
Karrel, A., 160
Katona, G., 6, 7
Katz, D., 325
Katzander, N., 155
Kazemi, A., 14
Keele, S. W., 383, 384, 385
Kelcourse, F., 207
Keller, H., 133
Kelley, H., 133, 287, 288
Kelley, H. H., 287
Kemp, S., 12
Kendler. H. H., 109
Keppel, B., 318, 319
Kersting, K., 321
Kincheloe, J. L., 98
King, D. B., 133, 162
Kinlen, T. J., 60, 61
Kirschenbaum, H., 353, 354, 355, 356
Klein, R. M., 232, 233
Klimenko, V. M., 202, 204, 205
Kline, J. S., 163
Knight, Z G., 363
Knowlton, B. J., 377
Köhler, W., 137
Kollock, P., 289
Koltko-Rivera, M. E., 360, 361
Korosoliev, A., 361
Kostyanaya, <⁄, 143
Kotik-Friedgut, B., 208
Krebs, D. L., 364, 365
Kressley-Mba, R. A., 135

Kristjánsson, K., 369, 370
Kubovy, M., 132
Kumagai, K., 83
Kumar, D. R., 179
Kunstreich, T., 165
Kupfersmid, J., 154

Lachapelle, S., 184
Lacoursiere, R. B., 172
Lal, S., 319
Lamiell, J. T., 144
Landy, F. J., 61
Lang, P. J., 226
Langermann, Y. T., 11
Larson, C. A., 101
Laurenti, C., 113
Leahey, T., 64
Leahey, T. H., 256, 257
Leão, M. de F. F. C., 113
LeBlanc, A., 181
Lee, J., 159, 160, 161
Lee, K., 346
Leong, D. J., 215
LeRoy, H. A., 239, 240
Levine, J. M., 277
Levine, Z., 184
Levinson, S, 101
Levitt, P., 386
Lewin, K., 130
Ley, R., 134
Likierman, M., 167
Lilienfeld, S. O., 393, 394, 395
Linder, D., 285
Lindsley, D. B., 237, 238, 240
Lindzey, G., 290, 291
Link, M., 53
Locke, J., 21–22
Loftus, E. F., 264, 265
LoLordo, V. M., 367
Lombardo, G. P., 185, 186
Long, K. M., 167
Lopez, S., 319, 320
Lovie, A. D., 333
Lovie, P., 333
Ludovic, F., 53
Luria, A. R., 215, 216

Maaske. J., 163
Maccoby, E. E., 308, 309, 310
MacKay, T., 333, 334
Madigan, S., 77
Maher, H., 359
Maier, S. F., 368
Main, M., 302, 304, 305, 307
Malle, B. F., 145, 146
Malone, J. C., 98
Marcellos, C. F., 62, 63, 64
Marecek, J., 310
Marlo, H., 163
Marshall, M., 39
Martin, J., 278, 279
Maslov, K. S., 200, 207
Maslow, A. H., 357, 358, 359
Massey, R. F., 363
Mattoon, M. A., 162

Vasquez, M. J. T., 319, 320
Vassilieva, J., 209, 212
Vestal, M., 53
Veyrunes, D., 179
Vicedo, M., 241, 242, 243
Vidal, F., 188
Viney, W., 74, 75
Violino, B., 268
Virues-Ortega, J., 98
von der Heydt, R., 132
Voneida, T. J., 235, 236

Wagemans, J., 132
Walk, R. D., 315
Walsh, C., 364, 367
Walusinkski, O., 179
Warnick, J. E., 66, 82, 117
Warnick, R., 66, 82, 117
Washburn, M. F., 62, 65, 66
Waterman, A. S., 370
Watson, J., 99
Watson, J. B., 99, 100, 101
Weger, U., 127, 128
Weiland, S., 362
Wentworth, P. A., 77
Werner, K. M., 367
Wertheimer, M., 131, 133, 135, 162
Wesselmann, E. D., 283
Whalen, R. W., 127
Whatmore, L., 388
Whitaker, H. A., 231
Whitaker, J. L., 101
White, N. M., 379
White, S. H., 79
Whitehead, P. M., 358
Whitfield, S. J., 362, 364

Wieser, M., 144
Williams, K. D., 283
Wilson, E. O., 396
Wilson, G., 337
Windholz, G., 205
Winston, A. S., 142
Winston, C. N., 359
Winter, D. G., 330, 331
Wiseman, D. B., 110, 111
Witmer, L., 58
Wolf, T. H., 185
Wong, W., 54, 55
Woodworth, R. S., 65, 89, 90, 91
Wozniak, R. H., 59, 60
Wright, B., 146
Wright, B. A., 142
Wundt, W., 53

Yale, S. H., 179
Yarbrough, G. L., 66, 82, 117
Yasnitsky, A., 209, 211
Yerkes, R. M., 77, 78, 227
Yost, J. H., 75
Young, J. L., 77
Young-Bruehl, E., 171

Zagorski, N., 264
Zajonc, R. B., 282
Zayed, R. S., 163
Zeavin, L., 167
Zeigarnik, A. V., 143
Zeve, D. R., 101
Zickar, M. J., 91
Zilio, D., 394
Zucker, I., 242
Zuroff, D. C., 327

Subject Index

Minorities
    intelligence test bias and, 334–335
    in Soviet Union, 214–215, 217
    See also African Americans; Hispanics
Minsky, Marvin, 26
Mischel, Walter, 342–344
Misinformation effect, 264
MIT. *See* Massachusetts Institute of Technology
MLU. *See* Mean length of utterance
Modern period
    British empiricism, 12, 19–25, 63, 74–75, 77, 128, 370
    continental rationalism, 14–19
Modern synthesis, 35
Molar behavior, 107, 120
Molecular behavior, 107, 109, 120
Monism
    of Aristotle, 8
    of Averroes, 13–14
    of Charcot, 179
    defined, 4–5
    double-aspect, 17, 39, 40, 42
    of experimental psychologists, 230–231
    of functionalists, 70
    of Gestalt psychologists, 135
    Hobbesian materialism, 17
Monkeys. *See* Primates
Mood and anxiety disorders, 152, 153
    See also Anxiety
Moral development stages, 174, 188, 364–367,
        366 (table)
Moral reasoning, 364–365, 367
    See also Ethics
Morgan, Christiana, 329, 330
Moscow Institute of Psychology, 209
Mothers
    children separated from, 301–302, 304
    employment, 316
    as secure base, 239, 304, 305, 307
    sensitivity, 306, 307, 316
    See also Infant-mother bonding; Parents
Motivation
    curiosity and manipulation drives, 238
    Maslow's hierarchy of needs, 357–359, 361 (table)
    needs as, 330–331, 357
    regnant, 329
    Woodworth on, 91
    See also Drive reduction theory
Motor theory of consciousness, 259
Motora, Yujiro, 83, 83 (photo)
Mowrer, Hobart, 368
Muhammad, 10
Multiform method, 329–330
Multiple personality cases, 181
Münsterberg, Hugo, 60–61, 61 (photo)
    academic family tree, 62 (figure)
    on eyewitness testimony, 184
    functional approach, 74
    influence, 62
    students, 60–61, 77, 107, 325
Murphy, Gardner, 274–275, 275 (figure),
        275 (photo), 277
Murray, Henry, 328–330, 331–332, 335, 357, 362
Music, 41, 129, 131
Muslims. *See* Islamic Golden Age
Myers-Briggs Type Indicator, 164, 174
Mythology, 55

National Association for the Advancement of Colored People (NAACP), 319
National Institute of Mental Health (NIMH), 386
Nativism, 5, 8, 191
Natural selection
    behaviors shaped by, 35, 224
    Darwin on, 33–34, 35, 59
    functionalism and, 70, 75
    Galton on, 36, 56
    in humans, 35, 336
    operant conditioning and, 113
    See also Evolution
Nature and nurture
    birth order effects, 295
    ethologists on, 242
    Galton on, 37–38
    gender differences, 87
    innate characteristics, 313, 314–315, 316–317
    intelligence, 80, 92, 232
    interaction, 231, 275, 310, 317
    Kuo's experiments, 108–109
    maturationism, 82
    personality, 325, 328
    Piaget on, 214
    Sperry's research, 235–236
    structure-of-intellect theory, 69
    triplet studies, 93–94
    Vygotsky on, 214
Nazi Germany
    emigration from, 131, 133, 136, 140, 224, 358
    eugenics policies, 37
    Holocaust, 278
    leaders, 362
    military psychologists, 241
    Nuremberg trials, 278
    personalities of leaders, 139
    racial policies, 118, 133, 136, 140, 208, 242, 276, 278
    sympathizers in Austria, 117–118, 171
    takeover of Austria, 172, 241–242, 342, 361
    See also World War II
Need-press theory, 329
Neisser, Ulric, 262–263
Neo-behaviorism, 92, 105–112, 308, 330
Neo-Freudians, 353
Neo-Platonism, 9, 11
Nervous system
    autonomic, 118, 226
    chemoaffinity hypothesis, 235–236
    disorders, 179
    fight-or-flight response, 225–226
    higher nervous activity, 202–203, 204, 205
    lower nervous activity, 202
    personality and, 338
    physiology, 43
    sympathetic, 226, 284, 331
    See also Brain; Conditioned reflexes
Neural networks, 268, 269
Neural plasticity, 380, 381
Neurasthenia, 153, 166
Neurology, 153
Neuropsychology, 213, 215–217
Neuroscience
    affective, 388–393
    Avicenna and Averroes on, 11, 12, 13–14
    behavioral, 234, 376–381, 396
    cognitive, 235, 381–388
    Descartes on, 14–15

Proximity principle, 293
Proxmire, William, 289
Psyche, 6
Psychic secretion, 202–203
Psychoanalysis
  behaviorism and, 105
  of children, 165–166, 167, 171, 172, 301, 362
  defined, 152
  in England, 167, 172, 337
  goals, 355
  Kleinian approach, 166, 167, 301
  in Soviet Union, 207–208
  spread, 173
  transference, 100
  in United States, 169, 224, 248, 328, 355
  See also Freud, Sigmund
Psychodynamic theory, 308, 328–332
Psychological analysis, 182, 194
Psychological Corporation, 57, 90, 91
Psychological disorders
  classifications, 152, 152 (table)
  cultural context, 152–153
  outdated diagnoses, 153
  treatments, 152, 153
Psychology
  definitions, 248
  future of, 393–396, 398
  internationalization, 385, 397–398
  as science, 25
  transition from schools to disciplines, 243, 360
Psychometrics, 87, 333, 334
Psychophysical parallelism, 18
Psychophysics, 39–43, 45–46, 127–128
Psychoses, 152
Psychosexual development, 155–157, 156 (table), 166, 173–174, 300, 301,
  302, 308, 363
Psychosocial development stages, 174, 320, 363 (table), 363–364
Psychotherapy
  behavioral approach, 355
  client-centered, 353–356, 354 (table)
  free association, 154, 182
  guided mastery technique, 311–312
  Janet's approach, 182, 194
  Jungian, 164
  Münsterberg on, 61
  Rank's approach, 353
  rational emotive behavior therapy, 356
  relationship therapy, 353, 354
  See also Clinical psychology; Psychoanalysis
Psychoticism, 337–338, 339
Purposive behaviorism, 107
Puzzle box, 89, 104

Quetelet, Adolphe, 37

Racial groups. *See* African Americans; Minorities
Racial identity, 318–319
Racism, 286, 318–320, 336, 338, 345
Radiation research, 230
Radical behaviorism, 111–117
Radical empiricism, 75
Raichle, Marcus, 385
Rakic, Pasko, 386
RAND Corporation, 257
Rank, Otto, 353, 354
Rational emotive behavior therapy (REBT), 356

Rationalism, 4, 14–19
Rats
  approach-avoidance conflict, 118
  cognitive maps, 107, 252
  criticism of research focused on, 242–243
  electrical stimulation of brains, 379–380
  fear conditioning, 391, 392
  laughter, 389–390
  learning experiments, 107–108, 224, 238
  lesion studies, 227, 376
  Little Albert experiment, 100–101, 113
  memory experiments, 227
  navigation, 99, 227
  operant conditioning, 112–113, 116
  visual perception, 231
Rayner, Rosalie, 100, 101, 101 (photo), 102
Reaction formation, 118, 171
Reaction times
  individual differences, 54, 185
  measuring, 43, 53, 56, 384–385
Reading, 383
REBT. *See* Rational emotive behavior therapy
Recapitulation theory, 80
Recency principle, 103, 104
Reductionism, 394
Reflex arc, 15, 15 (figure), 84, 228
Reflexes. *See* Associated motor reflex; Conditioned reflexes
Reflexology, 207
Regnancy, 329
Regression, 140, 171
Regression, statistical, 38
Rehabilitation psychology, 142–143
Reinforcement
  defined, 113
  internal versus external control, 341, 342, 345
Reinforcement history, 113–114, 116
Reinforcement theory, 282, 285–286, 341
Relationship therapy, 353, 354
Religion
  Beyondism, 336
  Christianity, 9, 10, 15–16
  creation story, 31, 34
  Islamic Golden Age, 10–14
  millennial groups, 281
  science and, 9, 11, 13, 16, 18, 22–23, 31, 34, 42
  Shango, 343
Renaissance, 10, 12, 14
Representativeness heuristic, 266
Repression, 117, 154, 155, 161, 171, 181, 264–265
Research Center for Group Dynamics, 141–142, 281,
  282–283, 287, 290, 293
Respondent behavior, 113
Retrograde amnesia, 382
Reversibility, 192
Riecken, Henry, 281
RISB. *See* Rotter Incomplete Sentences Blank
Robbers Cave experiment, 276
Robertson, James, 301–302, 304
Roe v. Wade, 367
Rogers, Carl, 352–356, 353 (photo)
  client-centered therapy, 353–356, 354 (table)
  criticism of, 356
  influences on, 85, 92, 352, 353, 359
  self-actualization, 170
  Skinner and, 356
  students, 94

VTE. *See* Vicarious trial and error
Vygotsky, Lev, 208–213, 209 (photo)
    academic family tree, 143, 212 (figure)
    on child development, 209–210, 300
    cultural-historical approach, 55, 209, 211, 212, 214–215, 274
    influence, 210, 212–213, 216, 218
    influences on, 60, 188, 208, 209
    Luria and, 213–214
    zone of proximal development, 210, 211 (figure)
Vygotsky boom, 212

Walk, Richard, 314–315
Wallace, Alfred Russel, 34
Walters, Richard, 311
Washburn, Margaret, 62, 65 (photo), 65–66, 102, 224
Watergate scandal, 263
Watson, John, 99 (photo), 99–101
    academic family tree, 101 (figure)
    Baldwin and, 60
    conditioned emotional responses, 89, 100–101, 239, 300
    epiphenomenalism, 61
    influence, 102
    influences on, 89, 112–113, 207
    leadership of behaviorism, 94, 98, 99, 122
    Little Albert experiment, 100–101, 101 (photo), 102, 113
    on personality, 325
    students, 87, 227
    Yerkes and, 78
    See also Behaviorism
Weber, Ernst, 40, 41 (photo)
Weber's law, 41
Well-being, subjective, 370
    See also Happiness
Wertheimer, Max, 132 (photo), 132–134, 134 (figure), 137, 144, 147, 277
Wilson, E. O., 396
Winter, David, 331
Wisconsin General Test Apparatus, 237–238
Witmer, Lightner, 57–59, 58 (photo), 300
Wolfe, Harry Kirk, 103
Women
    abortion decisions, 367
    in academic positions, 69–70, 92, 93, 111, 313, 315, 345
    African American, 93–94, 318–319
    anima, 163
    APA presidents, 66, 76, 111, 346
    in clinical psychology, 59
    education, 80
    excluded from psychological research, 366–367
    in experimental psychology, 63, 65–66
    feminist psychology, 168–169, 170
    feminists, 9, 310, 359
    graduate students, 45, 63, 65, 66–67, 69, 77, 87, 93–94, 111, 313, 386
    housewives, 140–141
    hysteria diagnoses, 153, 179
    menstruation, 92
    oppression, 168, 179
    psychoanalysts, 164, 165–173, 174
    psychology of, 92
    rights, 159
    scientists, 44–45, 386
    sexism and, 63, 65, 66, 87, 160, 313, 320, 345
    See also Gender differences; Mothers
Wood, Carolyn, 276
Woodworth, Robert, 77, 90, 91 (photo), 91–92, 105
Woodworth Personal Data Sheet (WPDS), 91
Woolley, Helen Thompson, 87

Word associations, 162, 213
Working memory, 386, 387
World War I
    anti-German sentiment, 61
    intelligence testing, 67, 78, 81, 90
    opponents of U.S. entry, 57, 106
    reparations, 118
    Russia in, 200, 204
    shell shock, 91
World War II
    brain injuries, 143, 215
    British psychological research, 248–249
    German bombing of England, 119, 172
    influence on psychotherapy, 352, 355
    intelligence testing, 186, 234
    Jewish refugees, 266
    Lorenz in, 241
    meat shortage, 140–141
    military psychologists, 69, 241, 281, 282, 287, 388, 389
    in Netherlands, 242
    orphans, 240, 242
    Pearl Harbor attack, 262
    personality tests, 330, 362
    pilots, 234, 249, 259, 260
    Polish resistance, 193, 294
    refugees, 390
    in Soviet Union, 208, 215
    women in work force, 316
    See also Nazi Germany
WPDS. *See* Woodworth Personal Data Sheet
Wundt, Wilhelm, 52 (photo), 52–55
    academic family tree, 56 (figure)
    Brentano and, 127
    on emotions, 129
    as founder of experimental psychology, 49, 52, 53, 67, 127, 274
    influence, 55, 68, 70
    influences on, 42–43, 44, 52–53, 56
    personality model, 324
    physiological psychology, 52–53, 224
    students, 53–54, 55–65, 79, 83, 103, 206, 300, 332

Yale Clinic of Child Development, 82
Yale University
    faculty, 82, 278–279, 308
    Institute of Human Relations, 86, 117
    researchers, 105, 242, 386
    students, 109, 260, 282, 313, 315, 330
    See also Yerkes Laboratory of Primate Biology
Yerkes, Robert, 67, 68, 77–78, 78 (photo), 86
    influences on, 60–61
    intelligence testing, 67, 78, 81, 186
    Pavlov and, 78, 100
    primate research, 78, 86, 134, 224
    students, 78, 107, 313
Yerkes Laboratory of Primate Biology, 78, 86, 109, 228, 232, 233, 235, 244
Yerkes-Dodson law, 78, 294
Young, Thomas, 43, 45
Young-Helmholtz theory, 43

Zajonc, Robert, 292, 294–295, 325
Zeigarnik, Bluma, 139, 143, 143 (photo), 209
Zeigarnik effect, 139, 143
Zeitgeist, 67–68
Zionist movement, 364
Zone of proximal development (ZPD), 210, 211 (figure)